In American Samoa, where I live, South Pacific Handbook has scooped even the most inventive island travelers. The best guidebook this road junkie has seen anywhere.
—Robert Brock, THE CoEVOLUTION QUARTERLY, Sausalito, California

A must-buy guide for people interested in back-packing, and other lower-than-usual cost ways of visiting the Pacific Islands. A most-unusual book... the best, most current information which is at the same time the hardest to obtain.
—HAWAII GEOGRAPHIC SOCIETY

Stanley provides the reader with solid up-to-date information on the geography, traditional and modern history, and contemporary trends of every part of the Pacific islands in which even the most avid travel buff is likely to find himself.
—Norman Douglas, PACIFIC ISLANDS MONTHLY, Sydney, Australia

The South Pacific Handbook is difficult to review. Family members keep borrowing the review copy for leisure reading. It's that fascinating. Information is in narrative form and presented with good humor.
—Stuart Lillico, HAWAIIAN SHELL NEWS, Honolulu

...a remarkable travel guide... with Australian tourism increasing to short-haul destinations such as the Pacific, the author's advice is timely and necessary. The most positive test of a guide book is to compare its advice with personal experience and this one shapes up excellently on that basis—Vanuatu, Fiji, Noumea, and New Zealand being the sections scrutinised closely.
—John Kirby, THE NEWS, Adelaide, South Australia

...a gold mine of practical and interesting information about some 500 Pacific Islands. I can attest—having devoured the first book, verified it through firsthand travel and then read much of the 2nd edition...this is the book. The tips about people and customs are, in my mind, the highlight of the book...the way to preserve the good feelings and hospitality of Pacific islanders. My kind of travel. My kind of book.
—Fred Swegles, THE DAILY SUN—POST, San Clemente, California

...one of the best publications on the South Pacific I have yet come across... the South Pacific Handbook is both informative and entertaining and might just entice you off the beaten track in the author's footsteps. A word also to teachers. There is very little information available on the islands of the South Pacific. I cannot recommend this Handbook more highly for classroom use. Projects may cease to become just another tourist pamphlet eye-view.
—Mary Costello, EVENING STANDARD, Auckland, New Zealand

...the information source most often recommended by young budget travelers...the cheapest and most interesting means to visit over 500 South Sea islands... for the adventurous there are suggested mountain climbs, jungle walks, cave explorations, river trips, camping, bicycle routes, skin-diving and snorkeling locations. Among the most valuable points are ideas on how to get around the islands on your own, from money-saving freighter travel to island transportation systems. The South Pacific Handbook by David Stanley is well worth the investment.
—Lucy Izon, TORONTO STAR, Canada

The great thing in this world is not so much where we stand, as in what direction we are moving... We must sail sometimes with the wind and sometimes against it—but we must sail, and not drift, nor lie at anchor.

Oliver Wendell Holmes

SOUTH PACIFIC HANDBOOK

ILLUSTRATIONS AND PHOTOS

front cover: Western Samoa Visitors Bureau. *back cover:* Don Pitcher. *black and white photos:* Tahiti Tourist Development Board (Tini Colombel) — pages 14, 47, 85, 86, 98, 108; Office of Tourism, Government of American Samoa (Teva Sylvain) — pages 24, 233, 251, 270; Naval Historical Center, Washington, D.C. — pages 32, 80, 247; Hawaii State Archives, Honolulu — pages 36, 524, 525, 526, 548; Air New Zealand — pages 37, 52, 160, 161, 384, 535; David Stanley — pages 41, 62, 64, 71 (below), 72, 81 (right), 94, 95, 105, 110, 112, 114, 116, 162, 166, 167, 171 (above), 177, 179, 180, 189, 193, 201, 205, 208, 212, 214, 216, 219, 220, 225, 226, 238, 248, 256, 267, 268, 276, 278, 300, 303, 310, 324, 333, 341, 356, 359, 371, 372, 389, 395, 397, 400, 402, 403, 415, 422, 434, 436, 438, 440, 444, 459, 463, 468, 470, 478, 482, 485, 515, 545; Auckland Institute and Museum — pages 42, 45, 81 (left), 100, 174, 188, 258, 493, 497; Vanuatu Chamber of Commerce — pages 43, 426, 430, 441, 442; John Penisten — pages 65, 206; Ministry of Information, Fiji — pages 71 (above), 305; Ny Carlsberg Glyptotek, Copenhagen — page 89; Field Museum of Natural History, Chicago — pages 122, 125, 181, 184, 202, 361, 392, 414, 457, 458, 474, 476, 494, 509, 511, 547; Ocean Voyages — page 130; Smithsonian Institution, Washington. D.C. — page 135; Rautenstrauch-Joest-Museum, Cologne, West Germany — pages 136, 483, 486; Michael Jackson — page 191; *The Tonga Chronicle* (Sione Langi) — pages 198, 200, 213 (Paua Manu'atu); Jean P. Haydon Museum, Pago Pago — page 231; Richard Eastwood — pages 232, 349; National Archives, Washington, D.C. — pages 235, 433, 455, 542; Richard A. Goodman — page 250; Matthew McKee — pages 283, 308; Meriam Library, California State University, Chico — page 289; *The Fiji Times* (Balram) — page 326; Melanesian Tourist Services (Bob Halstead) — page 344; New Caledonia Tourist Office — pages 375 (Gilbert Thong), 380, 388, 393; Information and Public Relations Dept., Vanuatu Government — page 413; Solomon Islands Government Information Service (Ted Marriott) — pages 461, 475, 488; Survey and Mapping Division, Solomon Islands Government — page 495; Australian Tourist Commission — pages 503, 505; N.Z. Government Tourist Office — pages 510, 512, 516, 518, 519; Hawaii Visitors Bureau — page 542 (above). *illustrations:* Gordon Ohliger — pages 15, 48, 68, 77, 127, 133, 139, 157, 187, 195, 229, 245, 273, 281, 287, 293, 367, 405, 449, 499, 500, 507, 521; Diana Lasich — pages 16, 19, 35, 59, 88, 90, 99, 186, 194, 286, 340, 363, 417; Louise Foote — pages 17, 22, 23, 25, 31, 40, 44, 46, 101, 102, 103, 106, 117, 127, 131, 146, 152, 171 (below), 185, 206, 239, 262, 266, 272, 279, 291, 292, 304, 312, 315, 318, 330, 335, 348, 353, 365, 369, 374, 381, 385, 398, 401, 412, 420, 429, 437, 445, 448, 467, 479, 480, 490, 492, 501, 506, 537; Salvatore Casa — page 346.

an invitation: Readers are welcome to submit their own photos for consideration of publication in the next edition of the *South Pacific Handbook*. The publisher cannot undertake to return this material, so send only good quality duplicate color slides or black and white prints (color prints are of little use). This is a low-profit operation so we cannot afford to pay for photos, however photographers will be credited and receive a free copy of the edition in which their photo first appears. By the act of submitting photos, it's understood that the photographer is thereby granting Moon Publications the non-exclusive right to publish the photo(s) on the above terms. The scenes depicted in all photos must be specifically identified if they are to be useable.

SOUTH PACIFIC HANDBOOK

THIRD EDITION

DAVID STANLEY

PUBLICATIONS

Please send all comments,
corrections, additions, amendments
and critiques to:

**DAVID STANLEY
MOON PUBLICATIONS
722 WALL STREET
CHICO, CA 95928, USA**

SOUTH PACIFIC HANDBOOK (third edition)

Published by
Moon Publications
722 Wall Street
Chico, California, 95928, USA
tel. (916) 345-5473

FIRDT EDITION — 1979
SECOND EDITION — 1982
THIRD EDITION — 1986
reprinted — December 1987

Printed by
Colorcraft Ltd., Hong Kong

© David Stanley 1986

Library of Congress Cataloging in Publication Data

Stanley, David.
South Pacific Handbook

Bibliography: p. 551
Includes index.
1. Islands of the Pacific–Description and travel–
Guide-books. I. Title.
DU15.S76 1985   919'.04   85-13734
ISBN 0-918373-05-0

SUDSEE-HANDBUCH: A German translation of this book is published by Verlag Gisela E. Walther,
Verdunstrasse 28, D-2800 Bremen 1, West Germany.

CONTENTS

PREFACE

INTRODUCTION

POLYNESIA

MELANESIA

ANGLONESIA

LIST OF MAPS

LIST OF MAPS (CONT.)

LIST OF TABLES AND CHARTS

ABBREVIATIONS

a/c — air conditioned
BBQ — barbecue
C — Centigrade
C. — century
d — double
DMA — Defense Mapping Agency
E — east
ha — hectare
I. — island
Is. — islands

km — kilometer
kph — kilometers per hour
L — left
LDS — Latter-day Saints (Mormons)
LMS — London Missionary Society
LST — landing ship, tank
m — meter
min. — minutes
MV — motor vessel

N — north
no. — number
OW — one way
PNG — Papua New Guinea
pp — per person
P.W.D. — Public Works Dept.
R — right
Rep. — republic
RR — railroad

RT — round trip
s — single
S — south
SDA — Seventh-day Adventist
t — triple
tel. — telephone
W — west
WW II — World War Two
YHA — Youth Hostel Assoc.
YWCA — Young Women's Christian Association

PREFACE

PROBLEMS IN PARADISE

The standard image of the South Pacific is one of wide white beaches, turquoise lagoons, and deep green vegetation curving around as far as the eye can see. To this the travel brochures add smiling natives offering tropical drinks. Paradise seems timeless, and each perfect day adds to the illusion that here, at last, is the one corner of our world where the worries of modern man may be forgotten as we return to a simpler, more natural existence. But let's examine the stereotype. The media of the industrialized world provide little more than a carefully orchestrated stream of escapist literature from the travel industry, and perhaps an occasional piece on the sex life of young Polynesians. Even atomic explosions at Moruroa do little to shake the tranquility of those who'd rather not know or tell. During the past two decades, nine new Pacific nations emerged as Britain dismantled its colonial system. Only a short-lived rebellion in Vanuatu (1980) gave any indication that something was amiss, but the press laughed it off as the "Coconut War." Today, in New Caledonia, a more serious confrontation is shaping up as the French send hardened veterans from Algeria to deal with a Kanak revolution. The next decade will also see the creation of four new political entities in Micronesia (the area between Hawaii and the Philippines), as the United States restructures its colonial empire to remove the Trust Territory of the Pacific Islands from United Nations observation. New military bases are planned for these islands as America's military might further encroaches on Asia's doorstep. American MX missiles glide silently over the Pacific to the Kwajalein Missile Range, while nuclear submarines patrol quietly, their bellies bulging with atomic death. In Japan, barrel after barrel of murderous nuclear wastes are accumulating, and the planners gaze south

across the ocean, awaiting the chance to dump. Nuclear and neutron bombs explode unabated in a lonely corner of Eastern Polynesia for the glory of France, sending tremors of terror though the region. Against all appeals to logic and conscience, Japanese and Soviet whalers continue to hunt the great whales to extinction. The modern world is catching up with the Pacific. Outboards replace outriggers, Coca-Cola substitutes for coconuts. Consumerism has caught on. As money becomes more important, the islanders learn the full meaning of urban unemployment, inequality, and acculturation. These next few years will be years of struggle to rediscover traditional values, to win back captive islands, and establish a nuclear-free zone. This book is about *that* Pacific. It will guide you to all the perfect places and help you enjoy your visit in a simple island way. But it will also bring you closer to the people who've made this wide ocean their home. Too often publications about the South Seas avoid reality in their desire to paint a pretty picture. This book paints that picture too, but it tells you something more, something you may not hear anywhere else. It will make you less of a tourist and more of a friend.

PACIFIC ISSUES

decolonization: The South Pacific has been the last region on earth to undergo political decolonization, a process which began with the independence of Western Samoa in 1962 and continues today with the independence struggles of New Caledonia, Eastern Polynesia, and Micronesia. Despite lofty promises, French President Mitterand has failed to resolve his colonial dilemma. In Irian Jaya the native Papuans are waging a last-ditch struggle against Indonesian colonialists who were handed the territory in 1962 by the Dutch on pressure from the Soviets and Americans. Over 100,000 East Timorese have been killed since Indonesia invaded that country in 1975.

the arms race: The Pacific has been more directly affected by the nuclear arms race than any other area on earth. Since 6 Aug. 1945, not a year has passed without one super-power or another testing its weapons here. The U.S., Britain, and France have exploded some 250 nuclear bombs, an average of over six a year for forty years. The U.S. testing was only halted by the 1963 Partial Nuclear Test Ban Treaty with the Soviets, while the French continue testing today. In 1980, the United Nations International Commission on Radio-logical Protection reported that the combined effects of these tests will kill more than 15,000 people in the Southern Hemisphere. The Mar-shallese still suffer radiation sickness from U.S. testing in the '40s and '50s; the conse-quences of testing in Micronesia, Polynesia, and Australia are still ticking away in the genes of thousands of servicemen and civilians present in these areas at the time. To-day an estimated 10,000 nuclear warheads are stored or deployed on naval vessels or at various island bases around the Pacific. Microwave radiation from missile-tracking radar causes cataracts among islanders resi-dent in the vicinity of these facilities. The U.S. alone has 517 military bases in the Pacific, the French fifteen, the Soviets ten. The islanders, many of whom were caught in a crossfire dur-ing WW II, are becoming more vocal in their rejection of this military overkill.

mining and dumping: Australia, with twenty percent of the world's reserves of uranium, continues to allow mining. This devastates the environment and leaves tailings which will be radioactive for 80,000 years. Mine workers are exposed to lung cancer, and sooner or later wastes from commercial reactors are reprocessed into nuclear weapons or warship fuel. Many thousands of tons of radioactive wastes have been dumped into the ocean. The Soviets have been dumping in the

North Pacific for years, and the Japanese wish to follow their lead on a massive scale. Should Japan succeed, the U.S. plans to use the same dump site north of the Mariana Islands. Radioactivity enters the food chain and we have yet to reap the full harvest. The islanders are forced to share the hazards of nuclear energy without enjoying any benefits.

a nuclear-free Pacific: The concept of a nuclear-free Pacific is not just a dream. In 1967, twenty-two Latin American countries declared such a zone in the Tlatelolco Treaty. The city of Chico, California, among others, declared itself a nuclear-free zone in 1984. Also in 1984 the South Pacific Forum unanimously adopted a treaty which would ban nuclear testing and dumping from their territories, but have no effect on visits by nuclear warships. About the same time Prime Minister David Lange, following the example of Vanuatu and a few other Pacific countries, took the extra step of banning these ships from New Zealand's ports. It's worth noting that the U.S./Japan Mutual Defense Treaty also bans nuclear weapons from Japanese ter-ritory, but since it's U.S. policy to neither con-firm nor deny their presence they are able to violate the treaty with impunity. Barak Sope, Vanuatu's Ambassador-at-Large, explained his government's position thus: "In the past the colonialists wanted our labour, so they kidnapped us. Then they wanted our land, so they stole it for their plantations. Now they want our sea for the dumping of nuclear waste, testing of nuclear missiles, and passage of nuclear submarines. The Trident submarine may be a far cry from a blackbird-ing vessel, but to us they are both ships from the same old fleet. That is why Vanuatu is op-posing nuclear colonialism in the Pacific." The situation in Belau, where the U.S. is trying to force military installations on an unwilling populace, underlines the need for the nuclear-free principle to be enshrined in treaties and national constitutions to be effective.

tourism: Tourism is already a major source of income in the South Pacific, and for some countries, one of the only avenues open for economic development. To date much of it has been the hard, conventional tourism of transnational corporations centered on luxury resorts and elitist all-inclusive tours — the exotic rather than the authentic. (For more information on this see "Economy" in the main "Introduction.") Almost all the large hotels and resorts are owned and managed by outsiders, and most of the profits flow out of the country. To boot, nearly everything consumed in these enclaves has to be imported. All the locals get as compensation for the swarms of tourists invading their privacy and violating their customs are a few menial jobs. Through this book we've tried to encourage a softer, people-oriented tourism, more directly beneficial to the islanders themselves. Whenever possible we've featured smaller, family-operated, locally-owned businesses. By patronizing these you'll not only get to meet the inhabitants on a person-to-person basis, but you'll contribute to local development. As a visitor you can help by consciously attempting to consume products which originated in the country itself. Instead of duty-free goods buy local handicrafts. Help the locals capitalize on their beautiful natural environment (and save a lot of money) by staying at *real* native resorts. Guest house tourism offers excellent employment opportunities for island women as proprietors, *and* it's exactly what most visitors want. Budget travelers may spend less per day than jet-setters, but they invariably stay longer, and learn to appreciate and respect the cultures of the places they visit. Appropriate tourism requires little investment, there's less disruption, and full control remains with the people themselves.

ACKNOWLEDGEMENTS

special thanks: To Dr. John Connell of Sydney University who kindly agreed to share his Pacific-wide experience by correcting substantial portions of the manuscript. Intrepid Pacific explorer Robert Kennington sent letter after letter, packed with updating material on the remotest corners of Polynesia. David Harcombe forwarded nearly a hundred pages of fine notes on Melanesia. Michael Green filed a penetrating report on the Solomons; unfortunately Michael's notes on other Pacific countries were lost with his luggage by Air Nauru. Georgia Lee updated the Easter Island chapter; Jan and Lesley Geursen did a complete rewrite of Tuvalu. Bengt Danielsson of Tahiti corrected important sections of the Eastern Polynesia chapter. Tim Thorpe sent information on the hiking trails of Erromango, while Jeffrey Hanna supplied birdwatching tips. Roger A.C. Williams gave valuable descriptions of hikes and climbs in the Samoas and elsewhere (and personally escorted the author to the top of Matafao in heavy rain when he passed through Tutuila). Rod Buchko sent much new information on Micronesia. Paul Bohler checked data at Zurich University and supplied photos. Dr. Armand M. Kuris, University of California (Santa Barbara), read the section on corals, reefs, flora, and fauna, and offered a unique perspective. Thanks too to Elizabeth Quinlan on the big Pacific island of Vancouver for providing a temporary refuge, and Ingrid L. Hansen (the eyes and ears of Pan Am) for checking "Getting There" in the "Introduction" and updating hotel prices.

trail-blazers: Many thanks to the following trail-blazing travelers who provided feedback since publication of the second edition of *South Pacific Handbook* in 1982: Karen Addison (and Jordan), Charles Andera, Deborah J. Arness, Jane Belmare, Andrew Benkovich, C.R. Bennett, Sinclair Bennett, Yolanda Bernhauser, Mary Boyajean, Richard Brindle, Glenda Browne, Michael Brumby, David Bulbeck, Anne Calvert, Ric Cammick, Jausto Cepeda Proano, Brian L. Chamberlain, Carlos Coelho, Margaret Cunningham, Geraldine Davis, A. Michael Dekle, Cathie Diller, William Dixon, W. Donald Duckworth, Ellen Kay Duke, Richard Eastwood, Ellen Elliott, Phil Esmonde, Mauricio Espinar, Warren R. Evans, P.R. Feigen, Roger Forester, Finn Gaarden Jensen, V. Gavriloff, John A. Gibson, Melfen Gideon, Bob Gilmore, Werner and Maria Gisner, R. Givoni, Traugott Goll, Diane Goodwillie, Hans-Peter Gopel, Elizabeth

Gowans, Dieter Grabher, Michael Green, T. Grieg, Ben Grummels, Eva Guenther, Valentine Guinness, R. Gwoni, Mary Hall, Richard Hardegger, Simon Hayman, Bressin Hepworth, Tom Hepworth, Manfred Hermann, Wolfgang Herrmann, Barry Hill, Hammer Ishai, John Jackson, E.F. Johnsen, Giff Johnson, Sonya Kamana, Walter Kamm, R.D. Keall, George Kelsall, David Kendrick, D.K. Khalsa, Claire Kinwood, Art Kleiner, Dr. Heinz Kruparz, Ludo Kuipers, James Kuhns, Isabella Kuttel, Muven Kuve, Werner Lackner, Laura Lafferty, David T. Lotz, Gregory MacKenzie, Dee MacLeod, Roger Malcolm, John Mangun, Vreni Marbacher, James D. McEwan, Bill Modesitt, Peter Moree, David Moynahan, Forrest A. Nelson, H.J.V. Nielsen, Werner Nink, Gundi Norwig, Daniel Joseph O'Toole, D. Paton, Charlie S. Panakera, Karl Partridge, Susan Peacock, Rod Perren, Denise Pietershanski, M.H. Pryce, John Purse, Larry Rogers, Agustin Sanchez Vidal, Philip Sargent, David J. Scoble, Dr. J.B. Senilagakali, Elaine Shaw, Marilyn Sigman, Kevin Silva, Don Spencer, Robert Sperry, Peter Splinter, Gerhard Sporis, Denise Stevens, R. Steiger, Dieter Stoecker, Mike Stone, Rolf Stuttgen, Tahanga, Ron Tannock, Paula Tarmpul, Alan Taylor, Biteti Tentoa, Gerhard Tillmann, Bill Turner, Edward F. Twohill, Rob Wallace, David and Sheila Warth, William Weir, Ulrich Weissbach, John W. Wells, Pamela Whihock, Bill Whitacre, Steve Williams, Ann Wood-Dodt, and David Yost. All the varied information and insights contained in their letters has been worked into the book you have in your hands.

others: Thanks to the hundreds of Pacific islanders who assisted the author during his eleven-month field research trip, especially Gene Ashby (Ponape), Paula Baleilevuka (Koro, Fiji), Roman Bedor (Belau), Helentina Black (Majuro), Ben N. Devi (Solomon Islands), Jacqui Drollet (Papeete), Christophe Gargiulo (New Caledonia), A. Roy Horn (Honolulu), Carl Johansson (Saipan), Madison Nena (Kosrae), Nachima Orlando (Truk), Palisio Tuauli (Wallis), and Steve Yaqona (Suva). The cooperation of Air Caledonie, Air Melanesiae, Air Pacific, Fiji Air, Island Air (Fiji), Polynesian Airlines, and South Pacific Island Airways is also appreciated.

mixed emotions: Valentine Guinness sent a searing report on Micronesia, especially Majuro, which he termed "the most depressing and filthiest place I visited in the Pacific." Although Michael Garthwaite found the *Handbook* "a trendy, brainwashed, mind-bending caricature of scientific omniscience" he sent us a superb, blow-by-blow account of his trip through fourteen South Pacific island groups. Henry Thompson had the most poignant comment of all: "I have a lot of material on Belau but due to a moral stance concerning tourism I've only included a few things. You'll have some heavy decisions yourselves, no doubt. It's like the Zen situation: 'Those who know do not speak, those who speak do not know.' People who are bent on traveling are going to do it, not caring if there's a guidebook or not, and they'll probably get lost and have a ball more often than the book-bound masses on the classic routes. It's kind of disappointing to go somewhere and find that someone's got it in a guide. Exclusivity aside, it marks the beginning of the end." Finally, no thanks to the *Cook Islands News* which, instead of presenting a thoughtful examination of "controlled tourism," published an intriguing review of this *Handbook* which concluded: "...the tourist who takes this advice from this book is no economic asset, he is a parasite." Now don't you wish everyone was that frank!

meet the Moonies: A book of this complexity involves the efforts of many talented people. The first to see the manuscript was editor Deke Castleman. Long ago Deke gave up trying to bring the author back into the mainstream, concentrating instead on consistency and balance. If the book reads smoothly, thank Deke. Mark Morris contributed his expertise by checking the entire manuscript against the maps just prior to typesetting. Mark did such a fine job on the copy editing we expect to lose him to Park Ave. tomorrow. The maps were drawn from oversized blueprints, daubed in yellow and green, by Asha, Louise Foote, and Dave Hurst. Dave also designed the book, and helped

Asha with the camera work and mechanical paste-up—so if you find any blatant technical errors, write him a nasty letter; even call him up! Louise Shannon set the charts and checked the hyphenation. Michael D. Wilson helped with library research. The index was done by "Miss California," Kim Weir. Extra special thanks to bookkeeper Howard Sciligo and order clerk Rick Johnson who help keep the wolf away from the door. I'd also like to thank the following people who had nothing much to do with getting the book out, but by their daily presence contributed to the pandemonium at Moon Publications: Donna Galassi, Peter Harper, Linda Jones, Randy Smith (ask for Randy, our computer wiz, if you're a salesman), Helen the cat, and the ghost of Rasputin. Thanks too to the TRS-80 Model 4 Microcomputer, which proved an appropriate companion for the author. Finally there's publisher *extraordinaire* Bill Dalton, who provided the best facilities a writer ever had—virtually turning over his entire production staff for nine months. Bill also created the *Handbook* concept: the Aussies must loathe the day they kicked him out of Australia.

IS THIS BOOK OUT OF DATE?

Hello out there! Welcome to the South Pacific! Now that you're part of the family, can we ask a favor of you? We've done everything possible to provide the best information to help make your trip a success. But things change fast—you'll understand how hard it is for us to keep up. Since you're right there, how about letting us know if prices have skyrocketed, turning a place that was once a good deal into a rip-off. If you get off the beaten track and make discoveries, please share them with us. Although everything is eventually field-checked by the author himself, your lead may be invaluable, allowing him to zoom right in on some feature which might otherwise be overlooked. Did something in the *Handbook* lead you astray? Please tell us! If you're an island entrepreneur with a service or product to offer travelers, bring it to our attention—there's no charge. Female travelers often face different situations than a male travel writer. Share them with us and we'll share them with others. Maybe there's a map we could have included which would have saved you some trouble. If we know

about it we'll do our best to map that place next time. When writing always be as specific and accurate as you can. Please don't send us information you're not sure of, however, as it's often impossible to check. Notes made on the scene are far better than later recollections. Write your comments into your copy of *South Pacific Handbook* as you go along, then send us a synopsis when you get home. (Spanish and French-speaking readers may write in their own languages—*hablamos espanol y frances*—but no letters in German please!) Your contributions will eventually be shared with hundreds of others traveling through the area. This book speaks for you, the budget traveler, so help keep us in the *avant-garde* by giving us the facts. Address your letters to:

David Stanley
c/o MOON PUBLICATIONS
P.O. Box 1696
Chico, CA 95927 USA

Mount Otemanu, Bora Bora, Eastern Polynesia

INTRODUCTION

THE LAND

The Pacific, greatest of oceans, has an area exceeding all dry land on the planet. Covering more than a third of Earth's surface—as much as the Atlantic, Indian, and Arctic oceans combined—it's the largest geographical feature in the world. Its awesome 165,384,000 sq km (up to 16,000 km wide and 11,000 km long) have an average depth of 4,000 m. The greatest depths in any ocean are encountered in the western Pacific, reaching 11,524 m in the Philippine Trench, deepest point on earth. One theory claims the moon may have been flung from the Pacific while the world was still young. It's believed there are some 30,000 islands in the Pacific Basin—more than are found in all other oceans and seas combined.

plate tectonics: Much of the western Pacific is shaken by the clash of tectonic plates (a phenomenon once referred to as continental drift), where one section of the earth's drifting surface collides head-on with another. The northern and central Pacific rests on the Pacific Plate, while New Guinea, Australia, Fiji,

New Caledonia, and part of New Zealand sit on the Indo-Australian Plate. The W edge of the Pacific Plate runs NE from New Zealand up the E side of Tonga to Samoa where it swings W and continues up the SW side of Vanuatu and the Solomons to New Britain. North of New Guinea the Pacific Plate faces the Eurasian Plate, with a series of ocean

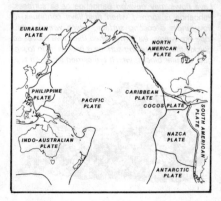

trenches defining the boundary. The dividing line between the Pacific Plate and the plates to the W is known as the Andesite Line, part of the circumpacific "Ring of Fire." In the South Pacific much of the land W of this line remains from the submerged Australasian continent of 100 million B.C. East of the line, only volcanic and coraline islands exist. As the Pacific Plate pushes under Tonga at the Tonga Trench, volcanoes erupt and atolls tilt. Farther W the Indo-Australian Plate dives below the Pacific Plate, causing New Caledonia to slowly sink as parts of Vanuatu and the Solomons belch, quake, and heave. Fiji, between these 2 active areas, is strangely stable.

THE BIRTH OF AN ATOLL

The great island chains of Oceania formed from "hot spots," fractures in the earth's crust through which volcanic lava was able to escape into the sea. A submarine volcano would build up slowly until it finally broke the surface, becoming a volcanic island. The Pacific Plate moves NW approximately 10 cm a year, so over geologic eons a volcano would become disconnected from the "hot spot" or crack from which it emerged. It then begins to sink under its own weight, perhaps only one cm a century, but erosion also cuts into the now-extinct volcano. In warm clear waters a living coral reef begins to grow along the

shore. As the island subsides, the reef continues to grow upwards. In this way a lagoon forms between the reef and the shoreline of the slowly sinking island. The barrier reef marks the old margin of the original island. The process is helped along by rising and falling ocean levels during the various ice ages, which could expose more than 50 m of volcanic and coral material to weathering. (According to the "greenhouse theory," sea levels will rise 56-345 cm over the next century, as the polar icecaps melt due to an increase of carbon dioxide in the atmosphere. Ports around the world will be flooded, and atolls and beaches submerged. There might be a terrible price yet to pay for the convenience of the motorcar.) Rainwater causes a chemical reaction which converts the limestone into dolomite, giving the reef a much denser base. Eventually, as the volcanic portion of the island sinks completely into the lagoon, only the atoll reef remains to tell how big the volcanic island once was.

island chains: As the "hot spot" moves SE, in an opposite direction to the sliding Pacific Plate (and shifting magnetic pole of the earth), the process is repeated, time and again, until whole chains of islands ride the blue Pacific. In every case, the islands at the SE end of the chains are the youngest. In Hawaii the 4,205-m-high Big Island is still actively volcanic, while many of the Northwest Hawaiian Islands between Kauai and Midway are low

Lava flows may develop pahoehoe or aa surfaces. Pahoehoe is formed when fluid lava continues to flow under a cooling surface, which wrinkles into rope-like waves. Aa forms when thick lava moves so quickly that the cooling surface is broken up in to jagged, angular blocks, which are carried along on top.

aa or block lava (left) and
pahoehoe or pancake lava
(above)

The theory of atoll formation according to Darwin: As the volcanic portion of the island subsides, the fringing reef is converted into a barrier reef. After the volcanic core has disappeared completely into the lagoon, the remaining reef island is called an atoll.

atolls. In the Society Islands, Tahiti is younger than Moorea, and Bora Bora is already halfway to becoming an atoll. In the Tuamotus, all now atolls, the Gambier Islands clearly originated out of the same "hot spot," and volcanic peaks remain inside a giant atoll reef. By drilling into the Tuamotu atolls, scientists proved their point conclusively: the coral formations are about 350 m thick at the SE end of the chain, 600 m thick at Hao near the center, and 1000 m thick at Rangiroa near the NW edge of the Tuamotu Group. Clearly Rangiroa, where the volcanic rock is now a km below the surface, is many millions of years older than the Gambiers, where a volcanic peak still stands 482 m above sea level. Equally fascinating is the way ancient atolls can be uplifted by adjacent volcanoes. The upper crust of Earth is an elastic envelope enclosing an incompressible fluid. When this envelope is stretched taut the tremendous weight of a volcano is spread over a great area, deforming the seabed. In the Cook Islands, for example, Atiu, Mauke, Mitiaro, and Mangaia were uplifted by the weight of Aitutaki and Rarotonga.

life of an atoll: A circular or horseshoe-shaped coral reef bearing sandy, slender islets *(motus)* of debris thrown up by storms, surf, and wind is known as an atoll. Atolls can be up to 100 km across, but the width of dry land is usually only 200-400 m from inner to outer beach. The central lagoon can measure anywhere from one to 50 km in diameter, although Kwajalein Atoll in the Marshall Islands has a width of 129 km. Entirely

landlocked lagoons are rare; passages through the barrier reef are usually found on the leeward side. Where the volcanic island remains there's often a deep channel between the barrier reef and shore; the reef forms a natural breakwater which shelters good anchorages. Australia's Great Barrier Reef is 1,600 km long and 25 to 44 km offshore. Most atolls are no higher that 4-6 m. A raised or elevated atoll is one that has been pushed up by some trauma of nature to become a platform of coral rock rising up to 60 m above sea level. Raised atolls are often known for their huge sea caves and steep oceanside cliffs. Soil derived from coral is extremely poor in nutrients, while volcanic soil is known for its fertility. Dark-colored beaches are formed from volcanic material; the white beaches of travel brochures are entirely coral-based.

CORAL REEFS

To understand how a basalt volcano becomes a limestone atoll, it's necessary to know a little about the growth of coral. Worldwide, coral reefs cover some 200,000 sq km between 35 degrees N and 32 degrees S latitude. A reef is created by the accumulation of millions of tiny calcareous skeletons left by long generations of tiny coral polyps. Though the skeleton is usually white, the living polyps are of many different colors. They thrive in clear, salty water where the temperature never drops below 20 degrees C. They must also have a base not over 25 m from the surface on which to form. The coral colony grows slowly up-

LARGEST ISLANDS IN THE SOUTH PACIFIC

New Guinea, P.N.G./Indonesia	820,033 sq km
South Island, New Zealand	149.861 sq km
North Island, New Zealand	114,682 sq km
New Britain, P.N.G.	37,736 sq km
Grande Terre, New Caledonia	16,192 sq km
Big Island, Hawaii	10,458 sq km
Viti Levu, Fiji Islands	10,429 sq km
Bougainville, P.N.G.	10,000 sq km
New Ireland, P.N.G.	8,650 sq km
Vanua Levu, Fiji Islands	5,556 sq km
Guadalcanal, Solomon Islands	5,336 sq km
Isabela, Galapagos Is.	4,588 sq km
Isabel, Solomon Is.	4,014 sq km
Espiritu Santo, Vanuatu	4,010 sq km
Malaita, Solomon Is.	3,885 sq km
New Georgia, Solomon Is.	3,365 sq km
Makira, Solomon Is.	3,188 sq km
Choiseul, Solomon Is.	2,538 sq km
Malakula, Vanuatu	2,053 sq km
Manus, P.N.G.	1,943 sq km
Maui, Hawaii	1,885 sq km
Stewart, New Zealand	1,746 sq km
Savai'i, Western Samoa	1,709 sq km
Oahu, Hawaii	1,572 sq km
New Hanover, P.N.G.	1,544 sq km
Kauai, Hawaii	1,432 sq km
Fergusson, P.N.G.	1,345 sq km
Lifou, New Caledonia	1,196 sq km
Upolu, Western Samoa	1,114 sq km
Tahiti, Society Is.	1,045 sq km

ward on the consolidated base of its ancestors until it reaches the low tide mark, after which development extends outward on the edges of the reef. Sunlight is critical for coral growth. Colonies grow quickly on the ocean side due to clearer water and greater abundance of food. A strong healthy reef can grow 4-5 cm a year. Fresh or cloudy water inhibits coral growth, so villages and ports all across the Pacific are located at the reef-free mouths of rivers. Polyps extract calcium carbonate from the water and deposit it in their skeletons. All reef-building corals contain limy encrustations of microscopic algae within their cells. The algae, like all green plants, obtain their energy from the sun and contribute this energy to the growth of the skeleton of the reef. As a result, corals behave (and look) more like plants than

animals. They compete for sunlight just as terrestrial plants do. Some polyps are also carnivores, and supplement their energy by capturing small planktonic animals at night with minute stinging tentacles. A piece of coral is a colony composed of large numbers of polyps.

coral types: Corals belong to the phylum *Cnidaria*, a broad group of stinging creatures which includes the hydroids (polyps), soft corals, sea anemones, sea fans, and jellyfish *(medusae)*. Only those types with hard skeletons are considered true corals. The order *Madreporia,* such as brain, honeycomb, or mushroom corals, have external skeletons and are important reef builders. The *octorallians,* such as fan corals, black corals, and sea whips, have internal skeletons. The fire corals belong to the order *Milleporina.* The stinging toxins of this last group can easily penetrate the human skin and cause swelling and painful burning lasting up to an hour. The many varieties of soft, colorful anemones gently waving in the current might seem inviting to touch, but beware! Many are also poisonous. The corals, like most other forms of life in the Pacific, colonized the ocean from the fertile seas of Southeast Asia. Thus the number of species declines as you move E: the Western Caroline Islands have 3 times as many varieties of coral as Hawaii. There are over 600 species of coral in Pacific, compared to only 48 in the Caribbean. The diversity of coral colors and forms is endlessly amazing. This is our most unspoiled environment, a world of almost indescribable beauty.

exploring a reef: Until you've explored a good coral reef you haven't experienced one of the greatest joys of nature. Be careful, however, for there are dangers. Practice in the shallow water; don't snorkel in deep water until you're sure you've got the hang of it. Breathe easily; don't hyperventilate. When snorkeling on a fringing reef, beware of deadly currents and undertows in channels which drain tidal flows. Observe the direction the water is flowing before you swim into it. If you feel yourself being dragged out to sea through a reef passage, try swimming across the current rather than against it. If you cannot resist the pull at all it may be better to let yourself be carried out. Wait till the current diminishes, then swim along the reef face until you find somewhere to come back in. Or use your energy to attract the attention of someone on shore. Most beach drownings occur in such situations, so be careful. Snorkeling on the outer edge or drop-off of a reef is thrilling for the variety of fish and corals, but it can only be done on a very calm day. Even then you must have someone on shore or standing on the edge of the reef (at low tide) to watch for occasional big waves which can smash you into the rocks if you're unprepared. Beware of unperceived currents outside the reef—you may not get a second chance. A far better idea is to limit your snorkeling to the protected inner reef and leave the open waters to the scuba diver. Many of the scuba operators listed in this book offer resort courses for beginning divers. They know their waters and will be able to show you the most amazing things in perfect safety. The main constraint is financial: snorkeling is free, while scuba diving becomes expensive. For information on hazardous marine animals see "Fauna" below.

conservation: Coral grows very slowly: by breaking off pieces you can destroy in a few minutes what took decades to form. We recommend that you not remove seashells, coral, plantlife, or marine animals from the sea. In a small way, you are upsetting the delicate balance of nature, and coral is much more beautiful underwater anyway! This is especially a problem along shorelines frequented by large numbers of tourists who can soon completely strip a reef. If you'd like a souvenir, content yourself with what you find on the beach. In many places coral reefs are protected by law. We also recommend you think twice about purchasing jewelry or souvenirs made from coral or seashells. Why pay someone to do something you wouldn't do yourself? Wisely, several countries have already banned the use of spearguns. Spearfishing with scuba equipment is a cowardly act no self-respecting diver would consider. It may seem hard to believe, but the fish soon learn to recognize man as an enemy in places where spearfishing is active. Isn't it enough just to look without having to kill? Spearfishing is also a sure way to attract sharks, so the tables could turn on you. Fishing with a handline or net is more sportsmanlike. It's perhaps rough justice that man's greatest marine adversary, the shark, is a factor discouraging even more widespread depredations against life in the sea. There's an urgent need for stricter government regulation of the marine environment. As consumerism and industrialism spread, once-remote areas become subject to the problems of pollution and overexploitation. As a visitor, don't hesitate to practice your conservationist attitudes.

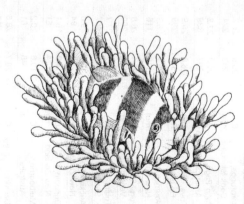

A clown or damselfish (Amphiprion clarkii) nestles among the venomous tentacles of an anemone. A mucous secretion protects the fish from the creature's stinging cells, providing it with a safe refuge. Anemones gather plankton from the water, but also feed on mussels, snails, or barnacles which fall their way.

PACIFIC CLIMATE CHART

LOCATION		JAN.	FEB.	MAR.	APRIL	MAY	JUNE	JULY	AUG.	SEPT.	OCT.	NOV.	DEC.	ALL YEAR
Honolulu, Hawaii	C	22.3	22.3	22.7	23.4	24.3	25.4	25.9	26.3	26.2	25.6	24.4	23.0	24.3
	mm	124	86	96	27	17	4	10	23	17	34	58	83	579
Papeete, Tahiti	C	26.1	26.2	26.5	26.3	25.6	24.8	24.3	24.0	24.4	24.9	25.6	26.0	25.4
	mm	364	272	164	147	121	66	66	50	75	84	175	289	1873
Easter Island	C	23.6	24.1	23.5	21.8	20.4	18.7	18.2	18.0	18.7	19.7	21.0	22.3	20.8
	mm	111	83	113	114	118	129	92	90	76	70	112	127	1235
Rarotonga, Cook Islands	C	25.9	26.2	25.9	25.1	23.6	22.5	21.9	21.7	22.2	23.1	24.0	24.9	23.9
	mm	249	224	267	185	169	106	97	128	106	124	144	229	2028
Pago Pago, American Samoa	C	27.3	27.2	27.1	27.1	26.7	26.3	25.9	25.8	26.2	26.4	26.9	26.9	26.7
	mm	297	339	332	350	271	230	200	201	146	331	253	377	3327
Suva, Fiji Islands	C	26.8	26.9	26.8	26.1	24.8	23.9	23.1	23.2	23.7	24.4	25.3	26.2	25.1
	mm	314	299	386	343	280	177	148	200	212	218	268	313	3158
Noumea, New Caledonia	C	25.7	26.3	25.4	23.8	21.3	21.0	19.8	19.9	20.6	22.1	23.7	25.0	22.9
	mm	110	116	152	116	93	95	97	72	49	46	44	76	1066
Port Vila, Vanuatu	C	26.4	26.8	26.1	25.2	24.0	23.2	22.4	22.7	23.2	23.9	25.0	25.9	24.6
	mm	272	260	312	239	148	129	103	93	104	103	161	183	2107
Tulagi, Solomon Islands	C	27.7	27.7	27.7	27.7	27.5	27.1	27.1	27.0	27.2	27.4	27.8	28.1	27.5
	mm	381	407	373	256	214	174	195	219	208	221	258	264	3170
Auckland, New Zealand	C	19.2	19.6	18.4	16.4	13.8	11.8	10.8	11.3	12.6	14.8	15.9	17.7	15.2
	mm	64	94	86	114	127	135	137	142	94	107	84	84	1268
Dunedin, New Zealand	C	14.9	15.1	13.6	11.6	8.9	6.9	6.4	7.3	9.4	11.2	12.8	13.9	11.0
	mm	74	61	76	74	71	66	56	46	48	58	71	71	772
Melbourne, Australia	C	19.6	20.2	18.4	15.2	12.5	10.2	9.7	10.7	12.6	14.6	16.4	18.5	14.9
	mm	48	51	56	58	49	52	49	51	56	67	59	60	656
Darwin, Australia	C	28.7	28.6	28.7	28.8	27.4	25.8	25.1	26.2	28.1	29.4	29.8	29.4	28.0
	mm	411	314	284	78	8	2	1	1	15	49	110	218	1491

CLIMATE

Tropical seas and skies are always electrifying. Rain falls abundantly and frequently in the islands during the southern summer months (Dec. to March). This is also the hurricane season S of the equator, a dangerous time for cruising yachts. However, New Zealand and southern Australia, outside the tropics, get their best weather at this time; many boats head S to sit it out. The SE tradewinds sweep the South Pacific from April to Nov., the cruising season. Cooler and drier, these are the best months for travel in insular Oceania. Temperatures range from warm to hot year-round, however the ever-present sea moderates the humidity by bringing continual cooling breezes. Windward slopes of the high islands catch the trades head-on and are usually wet, while the leeward side may be dry. There's almost no twilight in the tropics. When the sun begins to go down, you have less than half an hour before darkness.

FLORA AND FAUNA

The variety of species encountered in the Pacific islands declines as you move away from the Asian mainland. The Wallace Line between Indonesia's Bali and Lombok was once believed to separate the terristrial fauna of Southeast Asia from that of Australia. Although it's now apparent there's no such clear-cut division, it still provides a frame of reference. Many of the marsupials and monotremes of Australia are also native to Papua New Guinea. Sea cows *(dugongs)* are found in New Guinea, the Solomons, and Micronesia. The fauna to the E of New Guinea is much sparser, with flying foxes and insect-eating bats the only mammals which spread to all of Oceania (except Eastern Polynesia) without the aid of man. Ancient navigators introduced wild pigs, dogs, and chickens; they also brought along rats and mice (though a few species of mice are native to Australia and New Guinea). Island birdlife is far more abundant than land-based fauna, but still reflects the decline in variety from W to east. Bird-watching is a highly recommended pursuit for the serious Pacific traveler; you'll find it opens unexpected doors. Good field guides are few (ask at local bookstores, museums, and cultural centers), but a determined interest will bring you into contact with fascinating people and lead to great adventures. The best time to observe forest birds is in the very early morning—they move around a lot less in the heat of the day.

introduced fauna: The Indian mynah bird was introduced to many islands over 50 years ago to control insects which were damaging the citrus and coconut plantations. The birds have multiplied so profusely that they themselves are now a major pest, inflicting great harm on the very trees they were brought in to protect. The mynahs also compete with native birds for habitat, and many indigenous birds have become scarce. On Guam the introduction of a tree-climbing snake from the Philippines during or shortly after WW II has all but elimated Guam's native birds. The mongoose was introduced to many islands over a century ago to combat rats which were damaging the plantations. Unfortunately, no one realized at the time that the mongoose hunts by day while the rats are nocturnal, thus the two seldom meet. Today, the mongoose is the scourge of chickens, native birds, and other animals.

MARINE LIFE

Among the fishes and corals of the sea is found the richest store of life. It's believed that most Pacific marine organisms evolved in the triangular ocean area bounded by New Guinea, the Philippines, and the Malay Peninsula. This "Cradle of Indo-Pacific Marine Life" includes a wide variety of habitats and has remained stable through several geologic ages. From this "cradle" the rest of the Pacific was colonized.

sharks: The danger from sharks has been exaggerated. Of some 300 different species, only 28 are known to have attacked man. The most dangerous are the white, tiger, hammerhead, and blue sharks. Fortunately, all inhabit deep water, far from the coasts. Sometimes, however, attracted by wastes thrown overboard, they follow ships into port and create serious problems. There are an average of 50 shark attacks a year worldwide, so considering the number of people who swim in the sea, your chances of being in-

volved are pretty slim. Sharks are not dangerous where food is abundant, but they can be very nasty far offshore. You're always safer if you keep your head underwater (with a mask and snorkel) and don't panic if you see a shark—you might attract it. Usually they're only curious, so look them straight in the eye, and slowly back off. Shiny objects (a knife), bright colors, urinating, and splashing attract sharks. Divers should ease themselves into the water. Never swim alone if you suspect the presence of sharks. If you see a shark get out of the water quickly and calmly, and go elsewhere (unless you're with someone knowledgeable, such as a local divemaster). Sharks normally stay outside the reef, but ask local advice. White beaches are safer than dark. Avoid swimming in places where sewage or edible wastes enter the water. Recent studies indicate that sharks, like many other creatures, are territorial. Thus an attack could be a shark's way of telling man to get out of his back yard. Over half the victims of these incidents are not eaten, but merely wounded and left to tell about it. Perhaps we underestimate the shark. Let common sense be your guide, not blind fear or carelessness.

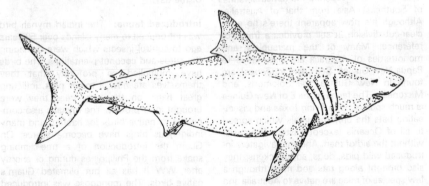

the great white shark (Carcharodon carcharias): This species, found throughout the Pacific, grows up to 12 m long and can weigh over 3,000 kilos. The interlocking serrated teeth are razor sharp and replace themselves regularly. Swimming constantly, the great white has evolved into a fearsome predator which will eat almost anything to obtain the needed energy. The stomach of one "white death" taken in Australia contained an entire horse! Sea lions, seals, sturgeons, and whole tunas have been found in the monster's stomach. Because the great white also eats man, some islanders catch this shark for food. Its color ranges from salty-brown, dull slate-blue, leaden grey, to almost black above, shading to dirty-white below.

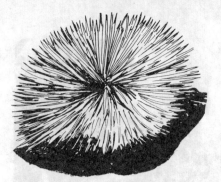

The sea urchin feeds on seaweed and uses tubular feet on its underside for locomotion. The long protective spines do not always protect it from hungry snails and fish.

sea urchins: Sea urchins—living pin-cushions—are common in tropical waters. The black variety is the most dangerous: their long, sharp quills can go right through a snorkeler's fins. Even the small white ones, which you can easily pick up in your hand, can pinch you if you're careless. Sea urchins are found on rocky shores and on reefs, but not on clear sandy beaches where the surf rolls in. Most are not poisonous, but quill punctures are painful and can become infected if not treated. The pain is caused by a protein which you can eliminate by holding the injured area in a pail of very hot water for about 15 minutes. This will coagulate the protein, eliminating the pain for good. Otherwise, soak the area in vinegar or urine for a quarter hour. Remove the quills if you can, but being made of calcium they'll decompose in a couple of weeks anyway—not much of a consolation as you limp along in the meantime. In some places sea urchins are a favorite delicacy: the orange or yellow innards are delicious with lemon and salt.

reptiles: Saltwater crocodiles, an endangered species, are present from the Western Caroline Islands down through Australia. Sea turtles are becoming rare due to overhunting and harvesting of eggs. For this reason the import of all turtle products is prohibited by most countries. Geckos and skinks are small lizards often seen in the islands. The skink hunts insects by day; its tail will break off if you catch it. The gecko is nocturnal and has no eyelids. Adhesive toe pads let it pass along vertical surfaces, and it's able to change color to avoid detection. There are few land snakes in Oceania. This, and the lack of leeches, poisonous plants, and dangerous wild animals make the South Pacific a paradise for hikers.

barracuda: Swimmers need not fear an attack by barracuda. In these lush tropical waters where marinelife abounds, barracudas can find a lot more tasty food than our salty, tobacco-tainted flesh. Most cases of barracuda attack are provoked: a spearfisherman shoots one in the tail, another is attracted by the spearfisherman's catch, or it's simply startled by chance. Still, if you see a barracuda, it's wise to swim away from it; it will usually swim away from you.

others: Although jellyfish, stonefish, crown-of-thorns starfish, cone shells, eels, and poisonous sea snakes are hazardous, injuries resulting from any of these are rare. Gently apply methylated spirit or alcohol (but not water, kerosene, or gasoline) to areas stung by jellyfish. Stonefish rest on the bottom and are hard to see due to camouflaging; their dorsal fins inject a painful, often lethal poison which burns like fire in the blood if you happen to step on one. Never pick up a live cone shell; some varieties have a deadly stinger which can reach any part of the shell's outer surface. Eels hide in reef crevices by day and most are dangerous only if you inadvertently poke your hand or foot in at them. Of course, never tempt fate by approaching them. The tiny blue-ring octopus is only 5 cm long, but packs a poison which can kill a human. The flesh of some types of fish is also poisonous, so ask local advice before eating your catch.

the jungles of Tutuila, American Samoa

FLORA

The flora of Oceania, like the fauna, originated in the Malaysian region. Here too one sees the same decline in the variety of genera as one moves E: even in distant Hawaii very few native plants have an American origin. Although some species may have spread by means of floating seeds or fruit, wind and birds were probably more important. The microscopic spores of ferns can be carried vast distances by the wind. Later, man became the vehicle: the Polynesians introduced taro, yams, breadfruit, plantains, coconuts, sugarcane, *kava,* paper mulberry, and perhaps much more, to the islands. Oceania's high volcanic islands are well wooded with many more species than on the low coral atolls, yet even large islands such as Fiji's Viti Levu are extremely limited when compared to Indonesia. One sees ecological niches filled by similar plants on the Malay Peninsula. Mangrove swamps, for example, are common in both Polynesia and Micronesia. Hillsides in the drier areas are covered with coarse grasses. Man has greatly altered the original vegetation by cutting the primary forests and introducing exotic species. For example, most of the plants now seen in the coastal areas of Tahiti are introduced. Short-sighted politicians in the Solomons and elsewhere have delivered their islands to transnational logging corporations for quick profit, and the virgin rainforests of the world continue to disappear at the rate of 20 ha a minute. Distance, drought, and poor soil have made atoll vegetation among the most unvaried on earth. Though a tropical atoll might seem "lush" to a superficial viewer, no more than 15 native species may be present! The vegetation of a raised atoll is apt to be far denser with many more species, yet it's likely less than half are native.

HISTORY

THE ERA OF DISCOVERY AND SETTLEMENT

prehistory: Oceania was the last area on earth to be settled by humans. Over 50,000 years ago migrants from Southeast Asia arrived in New Guinea and Australia, at a time when they formed a single land mass. During the Pleistocene (Ice Age), sea level was 100 m lower; people could cross the narrow channels from Indonesia on rafts without losing sight of land. Cut off by rising waters 10,000 years ago, the Australian Aboriginals maintained their Paleolithic (Old Stone Age) culture undisturbed until modern times. The Papuan peoples, characterized by convex noses and non-Austronesian languages, reached New Guinea next. Similar short, black peoples are found in various parts of Asia (the Philippine Negritos, for example). Some of the Dravidian peoples of southern India are also very short and dark, indicating the direction from which these migrations came. Next to arrive were the broad-nosed Melanesians (Austronesian speakers), perhaps about 3000 B.C. They settled in enclaves along the coast of New Guinea, and gradually populated the islands of Melanesia as far as Fiji. They mixed with the Papuans, and might have given them their Neolithic (New Stone Age) culture. The earliest confirmed date for agriculture in the Western Highlands of Papua New Guinea is 4000 B.C., suggesting that the shift away from hunting and gathering was even earlier. The Melanesians almost certainly introduced pottery and had more advanced outrigger canoes.

the *lapita* people: The Polynesians entered the Pacific from Indonesia or the Philippines. Distinctive *lapita* pottery, decorated in horizontal geometric bands and dated from 1500 to 500 B.C., has been found at sites ranging from New Britain to New Caledonia, Tonga, and Samoa—the greater abundance

to the E again implying the direction of migration. By A.D. 300 at the latest the Polynesians had ceased to make pottery. The *lapita* people were great traders: obsidian from Talasea on New Britain Island (P.N.G.) was exported to Santa Cruz in the Solomons—some 1,700 km away. It's interesting to note that the third millennium B.C. saw continuous movement of peoples from Southeast Asia and southern China into Indonesia. This proto-Malay migration brought the "Ancient Peoples" (Toraja, Dayak, Batak) into Indonesia about 3000 B.C. The deutero-Malay migrations followed around 2000 B.C., which continue in our time (contemporary Javanese colonization of West Papua). Could it be that the Polynesians were somehow part of these migrations, or perhaps pushed along by them? Archaeologists presently at work in Sulawesi and Maluku may eventually fill in the missing details. The colorful theory that Oceania was colonized from the Americas is no longer seriously entertained. The Austronesian languages are today spoken from Madagascar through In-

This lapita *pottery shard dated 500 B.C. was found on Watom I. off New Britain, Papua New Guinea.*

donesia all the way to Easter Island and Hawaii, half the circumference of the world! All of the introduced plants of old Polynesia, except the sweet potato, originated in Southeast Asia. The endemic diseases of Oceania, leprosy and the filaria parasite (elephantiasis), were unknown in the Americas. The amazing continuity of Polynesian culture is illustrated by motifs in contemporary tattooing and *tapa,* which are very similar to those on ancient *lapita* pottery.

the colonization of Polynesia: Archaeologists have constructed the following outline: sailing purposefully, against the prevailing winds and currents, Polynesians reached the Bismarck Archipelago by 1500 B.C., Tonga (via Fiji) by 1300 B.C., and Samoa by 1000 B.C. Perhaps due to overpopulation in Samoa, some Polynesians pressed on to the Society Islands and the Marquesas by A.D. 300. About this time a backtracking movement settled the outliers of the Solomons, probably originating in Tuvalu or Futuna.

Hawaii (A.D. 500), Easter Island (A.D. 500), and Mangareva (A.D. 900) were all reached by Polynesians from the Marquesas. Migrants to New Zealand (A.D. 850), the Tuamotus, and the Cook Islands (A.D. 900) were from the Society Islands. The shell fishhooks, stone food pounders, carved figures, and tanged adzes of Eastern Polynesia are not found in Samoa and Tonga, indicating that they were later, local developments of Polynesian culture. These were no chance landfalls but planned voyages of colonization: the Polynesians could (and often did) return the way they came. That one could deliberately sail such distances against tradewinds and currents, without the help of modern navigational equipment, was proved in 1976 and again in 1980 when the *Hokule'a,* a reconstructed ocean-going canoe, sailed 5,000 km S from Hawaii to Tahiti. The expedition's Micronesian navigator succeeded in setting a course by the ocean swells and relative positions of the stars alone, which guided them very precisely along their way. Other signs used to locate an island

In 1976 and again in 1980 the double-hulled sailing canoe Hokule'a sailed from Hawaii to Tahiti without modern navigational instruments.

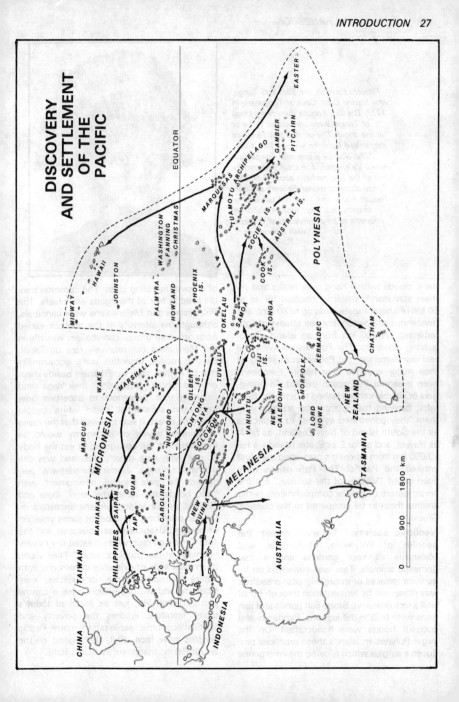

DISCOVERY AND SETTLEMENT OF THE PACIFIC

Fatafehi Paulaho, the 36th Tu'i Tonga, who hosted Capt. Cook at Tongatapu in 1777. The Tu'i Tongas (hereditary kings of Tonga) were considered to be of divine origin. The creator god Tangaloa descended from the sky and had a son, 'Aho'eitu, by a beautiful Tongan girl named Va'epopua. The child became the first of the line, perhaps about A.D. 950. These absolute monarchs were the only Tongan males who were not tattooed or circumcised; there was an elaborate etiquette to be observed in all contacts with their subjects.

were clouds (which hang over peaks and remain stationary), seabirds (boobies fly up to 50 km offshore, frigate birds up to 80 km), and mysterious *te lapa* (underwater streaks of light radiating 120-150 km from an island, disappearing closer in). The Polynesians were the real discoverers of the Pacific, completing all their major voyages long before Europeans even dreamed this ocean existed. In outriggers or double canoes lashed together to form rafts, carrying their plants and animals with them, they penetrated as close to Antarctica as the South Island of New Zealand, as far N as Hawaii, and as far E as Easter Island—a full 13,000 km from where it's presumed they first entered the Pacific! The Polynesians have been called "Vikings of the sunrise," but the heroic nature of their accomplishments better entitles them to be compared to the classical Greeks.

Neolithic society: To some extent, the peoples of Polynesia, Micronesia, and Melanesia all kept gardens and a few domestic animals. Taro was cultivated on ingenious terraces or in organic pits; breadfruit was preserved by fermentation through burial (still a rare delicacy). Stone fish ponds and fish traps were built in the lagoons. Pandanus and coconut fronds were handcrafted. On the larger Polynesian islands these practices produced a surplus which allowed the emergence

of a powerful ruling class. The common people lived in fear of their gods and chiefs. The Polynesians and Melanesians were cannibals, although the intensity of the practice varied from group to group: cannibalism was rife in the Marquesas but relatively rare on Tahiti. Early European explorers were occasionally met by natives who would kneel beside them on the shore, squeezing their legs and pinching their posteriors to ascertain how tasty and substantial these white people would be to eat. It was believed that the *mana* or spiritual power of an enemy would be transferred to the consumer; to eat the body of one who was greatly despised was the ultimate revenge. Some Melanesians perceived the pale-skinned newcomers with "odd heads and removable skin" (hats and clothes) as evil spirits, perhaps ancestors intent on punishing the tribe for some violation of custom. Jean-Jacques Rousseau and the 18th C. French rationalists created the romantic image of the "noble savage." Their vision of an ideal state of existence in harmony with nature disregarded the inequalities, cannibalism, and warfare which were a central part of island life, just as much of today's travel literature ignores the poverty and political/economic exploitation many Pacific peoples now face. Still, the legend of the South Pacific maintains its magic hold.

EUROPEAN CONTACT AND EXPLORATION

Hispanic exploration: The first Europeans on the scene were Spaniards and Portuguese. The former were interested in gold and silver, new territories and colonies, and conversion of the heathen, while the latter were concerned with finding passages from Europe to the Moluccas, fabled Spice Islands of the East. In 1565 a Spanish friar-seaman, Fray Andres de Urdaneta, succeeded in returning eastward to Mexico after a voyage deep into the Pacific Ocean. He did it by making a wide sweep to almost 40 degrees N latitude where he picked up the westerlies. This enabled a ship, if it left Manila in June, to sail to Acapulco in 5-6 months, a navigational discovery which turned the Pacific into a settled highway. Previously it had been easy to enter the Pacific, but another matter to return the same way. Quiros' voyage from what is now Tuvalu to the Philippines in the early 17th C., against contrary winds, in rotten ships with a starving, dying company, must rank as one of the greatest feats of Pacific journeying. The 16th C. Spaniards defined the bounds of the Pacific, and added whole clusters of islands to geographic knowledge.

terra australis incognita: The systematic European exploration of the Pacific was actually a search for *terra australis incognita,* a great southern continent believed to balance the continents of the north. There were many daring voyages during this period. The 17th C. was the age of the Dutch explorations. The first Dutch ships followed the routes pioneered by the Spanish and made few discoveries of significance. However, Van Diemen, the Dutch governor-general of Batavia (present-day Jakarta) and a man of vision and great purpose, provided the backing for Tasman's great voyage of 1642, which entered the Pacific from the W rather than the east. Tasman was instructed to find "the remaining unknown part of the terrestrial globe." Because of his meticulous and painstaking daily journals, Tasman is known as the historian of Pacific explorers. Negative though they were, his observations proved invaluable to geography. Roggeveen's voyage in 1722 also failed to discover the unknown continent, but narrowed down the area of conjecture considerably. The geographical success of the 18th C. English was due to this 17th C. scientific labor. And using 17th C. equipment, William Dampier explored with an 18th C. attitude. In 1745, the British Parliament passed an act promising 20,000 pounds to the British subject who, in a British ship, could first discover and sail through a strait between Hudson's Bay and the South Seas.

EUROPEAN CONTACT COUNTDOWN

1513	Balboa	Spanish	Pacific Ocean
1521	Magellan	Spanish	Mariana Is., Philippines
1526	Meneses	Portuguese	Irian Jaya
1527	Saavedra	Spanish	Marshall Is.
1543	Villalobos	Spanish	Caroline Is.
1545	Ortiz de Retes	Spanish	New Guinea
1568	Mendana	Spanish	Tuvalu, Solomon Is.
1595	Mendana	Spanish	Marquesas Is.
1606	Quiros	Spanish	Tuamotu Is., Vanuatu
1606	Torres	Spanish	Australia
1616	Schouten/ Le Maire	Dutch	Futuna
1642	Tasman	Dutch	Tasmania, New Zealand
1643	Tasman	Dutch	Tonga, Fiji
1722	Roggeveen	Dutch	Easter I. Samoa
1765	Byron	English	Tokelau Is.
1767	Wallis	English	Tahiti, Wallis
1767	Carteret	English	Pitcairn
1769	Cook	English	Leeward Society Is., Australs
1773	Cook	English	Cook Is.
1774	Cook	English	Niue, New Caledonia Norfolk
1777	Cook	English	Christmas I.
1778	Cook	English	Hawaiian Is.
1791	Vancouver	English	Chatham Is., Rapa
1798	Fearn	English	Nauru

Thus many explorers were spurred to investigate the region. This route would have proven infinitely shorter than the one around Cape Horn where the weather was often foul, and the ships in perpetual danger; on Wallis' voyage of 1766-67, his 2 ships took 4 months to round the chaotic Straits of Magellan. Byron ignored his orders to find a passage between Hudson's Bay and the South Seas and instead sought the Solomons, discovered initially by Mendana. His circumnavigation took only 2 years. The great ocean was becoming an explorer's lake.

Omai, a Polynesian from Huahine, Eastern Polynesia, accompanied Capt. Cook to England and returned. This 1774 drawing is by Sir Nathaniel Dance.

Captain Cook: The extraordinary achievements of James Cook on his 3 voyages in the ships *Endeavor, Resolution, Adventure,* and *Discovery* left his successors with little to do but marvel over them. Cook, a product of the Age of Enlightenment, was a mathematician, astronomer, practical physician, and master navigator. He was the first captain to eliminate scurvy from his crew (with sauerkraut). The scientists of his time needed accurate observations of the transit of Venus, for if the passage of Venus across the face of the sun were measured from points on opposite sides of the earth, then the size of the universe could be determined for the first time. In turn, this would make possible accurate predictions of the movements of the planets, vital for navigation at sea. Thus Cook was dispatched to Tahiti, and Father Hell to Vardo, Norway. Cook's first voyage (1768-71) was primarily to take these measurements. His second purpose was to further explore the region, in particular to find *terra australis incognita.* After 3 months on Tahiti, he sailed W and spent 6 months exploring and mapping New Zealand and the whole E coast of Australia, nearly tearing the bottom off his ship, the *Endeavor,* on the Great Barrier Reef in the process. Nine months after returning to England, Cook embarked on his second expedition (1772-75), resolving to settle the matter of *terra australis incognita* conclusively. The invention of the chronometer in the 1760s had made possible the determination of longitude for the first time; Cook took one on his second voyage. In the *Resolution* and *Adventure,* he sailed entirely around the bottom of the world, becoming the first to cross the Antarctic Circle and return to tell about it. In 1776 he set forth from England for a third voyage, this time to find a Northwest Passage from Pacific to Atlantic. He rounded Cape Horn and headed due north, discovering Kauai in what we know as the Hawaiian Islands on 18 Jan. 1778. After two weeks in Hawaii, Cook continued N, but was forced back by ice in the Bering Strait. With winter coming, he returned to Hawaiian waters, and located the two biggest islands of the group, Maui and Hawaii. On 14 Feb. 1779, in a short, unexpected, petty skirmish with the

Hawaiians, Cook was killed. Today he remains the giant of Pacific exploration. He'd dispelled the compelling, centuries-old hypothesis of an unknown continent, and his explorations ushered in the British era in the South Seas.

the fatal impact: Most early contacts with Europeans had a hugely disintegrating effect on native cultures. European sicknesses — mere discomforts to the white man — devastated whole populations when introduced into the South Pacific. Measles, influenza, tuberculosis, dysentery, smallpox, typhus, typhoid, and whooping cough were deadly, because the islanders had never developed resistance to them. The white man's alcohol, weapons, and venereal disease further accelerated the process.

CONVERSION, COLONIALISM, AND WAR

conversion: The systematic exploration of the South Pacific began in the 18th C. as the Industrial Revolution in Europe stimulated the need for raw materials and markets. After the American Revolution, much of Britain's colonizing energy was directed toward Africa, India, and the Pacific. This gave them an early lead, but France and the U.S. weren't far behind. As trade with China developed in the late 18th and early 19th centuries, Europeans combed the Pacific for products to sell to the Chinese. A very profitable triangular trade developed in which European ships traded the natives cheap whiskey, muskets, and glass beads, for sandalwood, *beche de mer,* pearls, and turtle shell, which were then sold to the Chinese for silk, tea, and porcelain. Ruffian American whalers flooded in. After the easily-exploited resources were depleted, white planters arrived to set up copra and cotton plantations on the best land. Missionaries preceded them to "civilize" the natives by teaching that all their customs — cannibalism, warring with their neighbors, having more than one wife, wearing leaves instead of clothes, dancing, drinking *kava,* chewing betelnut, etc. — were wrong. They taught hard work, shame, thrift, abstention, and obedience. Tribes now had to wear sweaty,

rain-soaked, germ-carrying garments of European design. Men dressed in singlets and trousers, and the women in Mother Hubbards, a one-piece smock trailing along the ground. To clothe themselves and build churches required money, obtained only by working as laborers on European plantations or producing a surplus of goods to sell to European traders. In many instances this austere, harsh Christianity was grafted onto the numerous taboo systems of the Pacific. Many islanders themselves became missionaries: some 1,200 of them left their homes to carry the word of God to other islands. After the 1840s, natives who resisted were kidnapped by "black-birders" who sold them as slaves to planters in Fiji and Queensland. Worst were the Peruvians, who left few survivors.

colonialism: Not wishing to be burdened with the expense of administering insignificant, far-flung colonies, Britain at first resisted pressure to officially annex the South Pacific islands. Then construction of the Panama Canal and the emergence of imperialist Germany led to a sudden rush of annexations by Britain, France, Germany, and the U.S. between 1870 and 1900. Australia and New Zealand were already British colonies, to

sea slug, sea cucumber, trepang, *or* beche-de-mer: *The 5 rows of feet along the length of this echinoderm show its close relationship to the sea urchin and starfish. Food particles caught on the long sticky tentacles are licked off in the mouth. These creatures, obtained in the South Pacific by early traders, are still eaten in China as an aphrodisiac.*

As a Korean scout-interpreter of the 2nd Marine Raider Battalion savors his rice-mash-and-tea breakfast, Solomon Islanders prepare to move.

The U.S. forces on Guadalacanal enjoyed the islanders' full cooperation during WW II.

which Britain transferred responsibility for many island groups around the time of WW I. The struggle for hegemony in capitalist Europe from 1914-18 prompted Germany's colonies (New Guinea, Samoa, and Micronesia) to be taken by the British and Japanese empires. By the late 19th C., the colonies' tropical produce (copra, sugar, vanilla, cacao, and fruits) had become more valuable and accessible; minerals such as nickel, phosphates, and guano were also exploited. Total control of these resources passed to large European trading companies which owned the plantations, ships, and retail stores. Many of these companies are still powerful today. This colonial interference stimulated immigration of large groups of Asian laborers (who now form a majority in Fiji and Hawaii), the loss of major tracts of native land, and a drop in the in-

digenous populations by a third, not to mention the destruction of their cultures. Between the world wars, Japan developed Micronesia militarily and economically by bringing in thousands of Koreans, Okinawans, and Japanese who supplanted the native populations. Although the U.S. had gained a toe-hold in the Pacific by taking Hawaii and the Spanish colonies (Guam and the Philippines) in 1898, further expansion was frustrated by the British and Japanese.

war: World War II provided the U.S. with unparalleled opportunities. Japan had hoped to become the dominant power in Asia and the Pacific by establishing a "Greater East Asia Co-Prosperity Sphere." After the Japanese occupation of French Indochina in July 1941, an embargo on iron from the U.S. and oil from the Dutch East Indies presented the Japanese with a choice: strangulation, retreat, or war. The history of the Pacific War can be found in many books. Half a million Japanese soldiers and civilians died far from their shores. The only area covered in this book actually occupied by Japanese troops was the Solomon Islands; a description of the fighting there is included in that chapter's introduction. At 0815 on 6 Aug. 1945 the world entered the atomic age as a Japanese city was obliterated by an American bomb. Heat from the blast slipped the skins off the victims and melted their eyeballs. Rescue workers found the river clogged with bodies of those who had tried to find relief from their burns. Thousands more died over the next few weeks. The final toll reached almost a quarter million. To this day the survivors, the *hibakusha,* lead broken, distorted lives with little aid or recognition, tormented by nuclear-related diseases. Two days after Hiroshima the Soviets, who had been neutral up to this point, launched an assault on Manchuria and Korea, and grabbed the Japanese Kurile Islands. World War II also gave the U.S. almost the entire North Pacific. Since 1945 they have used the area for nuclear testing and military operations, while instilling total dependency among the indigenous peoples. The South Pacific has been luckier and since 1962 nine South Pacific countries have re-established their independence. Only France's intransigent colonialism continues to destabilize the region.

GOVERNMENT

The South Pacific is the Third World region where democracy is strongest: virtually every country and territory operates on the basis of constitutional law and an independent judiciary. Elections are held on a regular basis, and almost everywhere (except Tonga and the French colonies) the head of government is chosen by the people. The 2-party system followed in many Pacific countries is a legacy of the last days of British, New Zealand, or Australian rule. Traditionally, Melanesians governed themselves by consensus: those involved would sit down and discuss an issue until a compromise was reached, which everyone then accepted. This grass-roots democracy still governs life all over Melanesia, although centralized bureaucracies are developing in the capitals (a form of neocolonialism). There were no regional leaders or powerful chiefs in Melanesia before the arrival of Europeans (the Fijian political system was influenced by Polynesians). The Polynesians have a tradition of powerful, hereditary chiefs and kings. The king of Tonga is still the most important figure in his country, and even elected officials such as Albert Henry in the Cook Islands and Hammer DeRoburt of Nauru sometimes try to establish a form of personal rule. Many islanders regret the divisions and inefficiencies of the 2-party system, and this is manifested in coalitions, one-party, and no-party systems.

regional organizations: The South Pacific Commission (headquartered in Noumea) was established in 1947 to promote regional economic and social development through annual conferences, research, and technical assistance and advice. Its main areas of interest are agriculture, fisheries, rural development, and community services. Almost all Oceania's countries and territories are represented, including the colonial powers. The South Pacific Conference is the annual meeting of delegates from the SPC countries who discuss their problems, pass resolutions, etc. Controversial political issues are avoided. Most of the money needed to run the SPC comes out of grants from Australia, France, New Zealand, the U.K., and the U.S. The island governments contribute only token amounts. The South Pacific Forum is the banner under which the heads of government of the region's independent countries meet each year for informal discussions. The Forum grew out of dissatisfaction with the SPC, which seemed dominated by Britain and France. The first meeting was held in 1971; in 1973 the Forum established the South Pacific Bureau for Economic Cooperation (SPEC), with of-

OCEANIA AT A GLANCE

COUNTRY	POPULATION	PERCENT URBAN	POPULATION DENSITY	LAND AREA	SEA AREA	CAPITAL	POLITICAL STATUS	CURRENCY
Eastern Polynesia	166,753	59	51	3,265	5,030	Papeete	France 1842	CFP
Pitcairn Islands	54	–	1	37	800	Adamstown	Britain 1838	NZ$
Easter Island	2,100	100	13	166	*355	Hanga Roa	Chile 1888	peso
Galapagos	4,410	*44	1	7,877	857	Baquerizo	Ecuador 1832	sucre
Cook Islands	17,669	27	74	240	1,830	Avarua	N.Z. 1901	NZ$
Niue	3,000	23	12	259	390	Alofi	N.Z. 1900	NZ$
Kingdom of Tonga	100,230	26	145	691	700	Nuku'alofa	ind. 1970	pa'anga
American Samoa	32,297	43	161	201	390	Utulei	U.S. 1900	US$
Western Samoa	157,349	21	55	2,842	120	Apia	ind. 1962	tala
Wallis and Futuna	14,000	*22	55	255	300	Mata Utu	France 1887	CFP
Tokelau	1,595	–	133	12	290	Fakaofo	N.Z. 1925	tala
Tuvalu	8,364	29	335	25	900	Funafuti	ind. 1978	A$
TOTAL POLYNESIA	507,821		32	15,870	11,962			
Fiji	645,000	37	35	18,272	1,290	Suva	ind. 1970	F$
New Caledonia	145,368	61	8	18,576	1,740	Noumea	France 1853	CFP
Vanuatu	128,000	18	11	12,189	680	Vila	ind. 1980	vatu
Solomon Islands	258,193	9	9	27,556	1,340	Honiara	ind. 1978	S$
Papua New Guinea	3,060,600	13	7	462,243	3,120	Moresby	ind. 1975	kina
Irian Jaya	1,173,875	21	3	421,981	*659	Jayapura	Indonesia 1962	rupiah
TOTAL MELANESIA	5,411,036		6	960,817	8,829			
Nauru	8,100	100	386	21	320	Yaren	ind. 1968	A$
Kiribati	59,957	36	68	822	3,550	Bairiki	ind. 1979	A$
Marshall Islands	30,873	60	276	112	2,131	Majuro	U.S. 1945	US$
Federated States	73,160	26	104	701	2,978	Ponape	U.S. 1945	US$
Belau	12,116	63	25	494	629	Koror	U.S. 1945	US$
Guam	105,000	91	194	541	218	Agana	U.S. 1898	US$
Northern Marianas	17,000	94	36	478	1,823	Saipan	U.S. 1945	US$
TOTAL MICRONESIA	302,206		95	3,169	11,649			
Australia	15,276,100	80	2	7,682,300	6,800	Canberra	ind. 1901	A$
Norfolk Island	1,800	100	51	35	430	Kingston	Australia 1913	A$
New Zealand	3,190,124	84	12	268,103	4,116	Wellington	ind. 1907	NZ$
Hawaii	1,023,200	86	61	16,641	2,158	Honolulu	U.S. 1898	US$
TOTAL ANGLONESIA	19,491,224		2	7,967,079	13,504			
TOTAL OCEANIA	25,712,287		3	8,946,935	45,944			

Notes on the Oceania Chart

*For geographical convenience, Galapagos is included with Polynesia, although it's in no way part of that cultural area. Similarly, New Zealand and Hawaii, which **are** part of Polynesia, are lumped together with Australia as "Anglonesia," a designation which more accurately reflects ethnic realities. Land areas are in square kilometers, and sea areas (the ocean area included within the 200-nautical-mile Exclusive Economic Zone of each country) are expressed in thousands of square kilometers. The population density (number of persons per square kilometer) of each country was obtained by dividing the population by the land area. The category "political status" gives the year in which the country became independent, or the territory/province/state fell under colonial rule by the power named. In cases where statistics were unavailable and the author forced to make a rough estimate, an asterisk (*) appears as a warning. The sea areas (and various other figures) were taken from **South Pacific Economics 1981: Statistical Summary**, published by the South Pacific Commission, Noumea.*

fices in Suva. SPEC is mostly involved in economic programs, while the SPC places more emphasis on social matters. SPEC has set up a regional shipping line (the Pacific Forum Line), a fisheries agency, trade commission, association of airlines, relief fund, and environmental program.

others: Other institutions fostering a feeling of regional unity include the University of the South Pacific, the South Pacific Festival of the Arts, the South Pacific Games, and the Nuclear Free Pacific Conference. The University of the South Pacific was organized at Suva in 1967. The main campus is still at Suva, where hundreds of islanders from across the Pacific study. USP extension centers are also found in most Pacific countries, and the USP has far more impact on the region than, say, the University of Papua New Guinea or the University of Hawaii. Nuclear Free Pacific Conferences are held periodically (Fiji 1975, Ponape 1978, Hawaii 1980, Vanuatu 1983) to allow activists from around the Pacific to get together and map out strategy and solidarity in the struggle against militarism and colonialism in the region. The Pacific Council of Churches includes the major denominations, both Protestant and Catholic. Many South Pacific countries are members of the British Commonwealth. The European Economic Community also has ties to the area through Britain and France; it offers soft loans, import quotas and subsidies, technical assistance, etc. The United Nations offers significant aid programs. The Asian Development Bank (founded 1966) helps stimulate economic growth by lending funds, promoting development, and providing technical help. Fiji, Tonga, Western Samoa, Cook Islands, Vanuatu, and Solomon Islands are members of the bank, which is headquartered in Manila. The least likely contributor to Pacific unity is an erratic little airline known as Air Nauru, an image-builder which absorbs a multimillion dollar subsidy from the phosphate-rich Central Pacific republic every year. By linking countries that could never sustain a purely commercial operation, Air Nauru has gone far to bring the islands and islanders together.

strand morning glory (Ipomoea pes-caprae)

ECONOMY

Many Pacific economies are based on subsistence agriculture: most of what is produced is consumed locally, often by the producers themselves. As yet consumerism is largely restricted to the towns where, instead of providing security, the modern infrastructure fosters dependence. There's a growing gap between the new middle class with government jobs and the majority still in the villages. The influx to the towns has strained social services to the breaking point, and created serious housing and employment problems, especially for the young. The main social problem facing the region is suicide by young men alienated from their traditional society. Crime is still petty but the example of increasing violence and disregard for the law in Papua New Guinea is frightening. The high birth rate (often over 3 percent a year) severely taxes the best efforts of governments with limited resources. Emigration to N. America and New Zealand relieves the pressure a little and provides income in the form of remittances sent back. However, absenteeism also creates the problem of idled land. In several cases, such as Wallis and Futuna, the Cook Islands, Niue, and American Samoa, more islanders now live outside their home islands than on them. Education has aroused expectations the island economies are unable to fulfill, and consumer values are replacing the traditional way of life. The monetary economy is often based on tourism or a few cash crops and, occasionally, mining. There is little industrialization. Most islands simply do not have a stable economic base upon which to effect development. Agricultural production is often limited to cash crops subject to fluctuating world prices. A quarter of the world's copra originates in the islands, but this market is declining due to increasing use of soybean oil, which is easily produced elsewhere. The ocean would seem a bountiful resource but on many islands the reef waters are already overharvested, and the inhabitants lack the ability to fish the open sea. Thus the bitter irony of tinned Japanese mackerel. Local politicians often pay lipservice to the concept of self-reliance, but the reality is invariably the opposite. Despite valiant efforts to encourage horse-drawn implements in Tonga, for example, there has been a steady increase in the number of tractors. These vehicles and all the fuel they consume must be imported.

business: The large Australian trading companies, Burns Philp and Carpenters, have what amounts to a stranglehold on the retail trade in the islands. They sell their goods at Australian prices but pay their island employees a fifth of Australian wages—their profits are profligate. The encroachment of

In 1888 trade flowed through Honolulu Harbor on sailing ships such as these.

The nickel smelter just N of Noumea, New Caledonia, is one of the largest industrial installations in the South Pacific.

transnational corporations increases dependence by making the island economies part of something over which they have no control. Foreign investment in tourism, commerce, banking, construction, transportation, and mining is heavy. Even a so-called progressive country like Vanuatu, which proudly beats its breast about its non-aligned status, has turned nearly its entire tourist industry over to Australian corporations. Exploitative foreign logging operations and local slash-and-burn agriculture threaten the rainforests of the high islands. Governments such as the Solomon Islands' are still in the Neanderthal Age in terms of conservation, eagerly granting timber concessions to greedy foreign companies set on quick profits. One hopeful sign as far as industrial employment goes is the Pacific Islands Industrial Development Scheme (PIIDS), which assists in establishing new factories and encouraging exports. The South Pacific Regional Trade and Economic Cooperation Agreement (SPARTECA) allows most products of 10 South Pacific countries duty-free entry into New Zealand and Australia on a non-reciprocal basis. So far, Japan and the U.S. have failed to offer anything like this to the islanders. Tonga has set up a reasonably good, small-industries center as a result of PIIDS and SPARTECA.

fishing: Tuna is the second most important fishery in the world (after shrimp and prawns), and 70 percent of the world's catch is taken in the Pacific. The western Pacific, where most of the islands are located, is twice as productive as the eastern. Although US$400 million in tuna was swept from the 200-nautical-mile exclusive economic zones of the island nations in 1981, only US$13 million was paid in licensing fees to local governments—far less than they'd expected from one of their only renewable resources. The economic zones are hard to enforce, and the U.S., in its own interest as the major consumer of tuna, maintains that the zones don't apply to migratory species. In 1984, when Solomon Islands seized an American purse seiner caught poaching well within their waters, the U.S. slapped an embargo on fish from the Solomons, a standard response. The U.S. has rejected the long-negotiated International Law of the Sea, largely because it would make them one among equals, unable to dictate policy (130 countries approved the treaty, 17 abstained, and only 4 refused to sign). Most local governments are incapable of creating and maintaining a deep-water fishing industry. A workable fishing fleet requires at least 10 boats, plus large amounts of fresh water and electricity for processing. Also, U.S. customs regulations tax tuna heavily unless it's processed in an American territory, which is why the canneries are at Pago Pago. Very little of the catch is unloaded in the countries where it's caught.

minerals: Mineral wealth is often more of a detriment than a blessing: the French are determined to hold New Caledonia for its rich nickel deposits, while the British only gave independence to Kiribati when the phosphates of Ocean Island were exhausted. Fiji has a gold mine (Australian-operated); mineral deposits in the Solomons will soon be handed over to foreign companies. More important are the undersea mineral nodules within the exclusive economic zones of Eastern Polynesia, the Cook Islands, and Kiribati. Three known nodule deposits sit in over 600 m of water in the Pacific: one stretches from Mexico to a point SE of Hawaii; another is between Hawaii and the Marshall Islands; a third is in Eastern Polynesia. The potato-sized nodules contain manganese, cobalt, nickel, and copper valued at US$3

trillion, enough to supply the world for thousands of years. This wealth was another major factor in convincing the U.S. not to sign the Law of the Sea (which would have required them to share the benefits with developing nations), and has made France unwilling to consider independence for Polynesia. There are potential oil basins around Tonga, Fiji, New Caledonia, Vanuatu, and the Solomons, but as yet no oil has been produced.

aid and advice: Not only are most Pacific countries heavily dependent on outside aid, but many rely on a single donor, making them highly susceptible to pressure. There is a growing imbalance between the cost of government in relation to locally generated revenues. France and the U.S. have increased aid to Fiji as a means of dampening their antinuclear spirit, and the ploy has been highly successful. Otherwise, the French and Americans mostly provide aid to their dependent territories. Japanese aid has been limited mostly to ensuring access to rich fishing waters. Too often, aid is spent in the capitals by expatriate officials, prompting unproductive migrations from the countryside. Much money is wasted on prestige projects, while those which benefit the island people themselves (such as the construction of village kitchens in Tonga's Ha'apai Group by

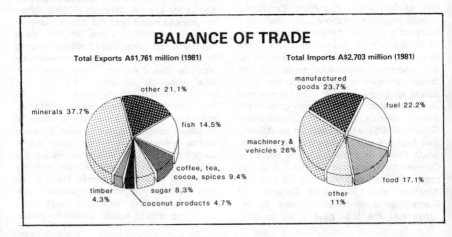

BALANCE OF TRADE

Total Exports A$1,761 million (1981)

other 21.1%
minerals 37.7%
fish 14.5%
coffee, tea, cocoa, spices 9.4%
timber 4.3%
sugar 8.3%
coconut products 4.7%

Total Imports A$2,703 million (1981)

manufactured goods 23.7%
fuel 22.2%
machinery & vehicles 26%
food 17.1%
other 11%

the South Pacific Peoples Foundation of Canada) are the exception rather than the rule. Aid is needed which increases the indigenous capacity to identify, understand, and resolve problems. Aid levels to countries like Pitcairn (about NZ$18,000 per capita) and Tokelau (A$1,063 pp) are extraordinary by global standards, an exceptional dependence. Dependency is also increased by outside advisers who teach the islanders to fulfill their expected roles in tourism, communications, and defense. United Nations tourism advisers display their backgrounds by recommending conventional tourism based on transnational corporations and bourgeois models—fine for affluent outsiders but of little use to local residents.

trade: Australia and New Zealand have huge trade surpluses with the Pacific islands. In 1981, for example, Australia sold them A$679 million in goods while only purchasing A$178 million worth. New Zealand sells nearly 4 times more than it buys. These deficits make the industrialized, exporting nations the main beneficiaries of island economies. For Australia and New Zealand the South Pacific market is not very important, but for every island nation this trade is vital to their interests. While the value of agricultural exports continues to decline, the cost of imported manufactured goods and fuel increases yearly. Most island products purchased by New Zealand are raw agricultural commodities, processed and marketed outside the islands by transnationals such as Nestle, Cadbury, Unilever, etc., which take the biggest profits. New Zealand purchases far more bananas from Ecuador than it does from its neighbors. In addition, products such as sugar, cacao, bananas, pineapples, copra, coffee, etc. are subject to great price fluctuations over which local governments have no control, plus low demand and severe competition from more reliable substitute producers. Efforts to increase the quantity of these commodities often reduce local food production, leading to expensive food imports. Most island land is split into micro-holdings which make efficient management difficult. The Lome Convention provides for the entry of set

TRADING PARTNERS

(1981 - A$ Million)	Imports from	Exports to
Australia	679	178
New Zealand	215	57
France	350	229
United Kingdom	94	115
Other Europe	135	253
U.S.A.	341	278
Japan	312	403
All others	577	248
	2703	1761

quotas of agricultural commodities from Commonwealth countries into the European Economic Community market at fixed prices. This arrangement is vital to countries like Fiji which rely on a single export such as sugar for most of their foreign exchange. Aid, investment, and tourism help offset the trade imbalance, but this also fosters dependence. The U.S. and France take advantage of this dependency by using their islands as nuclear test sites and military outposts. Trade between the various South Pacific countries is limited by a basic similarity of their products and shipping tariffs which encourage bulk trade with Australia and New Zealand rather than local interisland trade.

tourism: In 1979 tourism, the third largest industry in the South Pacific, employed only 4 percent of the working population. Most of the large hotels are owned by transnational corporations, which only promote travel to areas where they have sizable investments such as Tahiti, Bora Bora, and Viti Levu. Only about 25 percent of the net earnings from this kind of tourism actually stays in the host country. The rest flows out in repatriated profits, salaries for expatriates, commissions, imported goods, food, fuel, etc. To encourage hotel construction, local governments must commit themselves to crippling tax concessions and large infrastructure investments for the sole benefit of these companies. On several islands foreign corporations have gained such a death grip over the industry that they can shut off the flow of visitors overnight

TOURIST ARRIVALS

(1980)

American Samoa	43,283
Cook Islands	21,051
Fiji Islands	189,996
Guam	300,767
Micronesia	20,415
New Caledonia	78,040
Papua New Guinea	40,011
Solomon Islands	10,517
Tahiti	88,959
Tonga	13,585
Vanuatu	21,973
Western Samoa	37,535

simply by cancelling tours, bookings, and flights. This elitist tourism has perpetuated the colonial master-servant relationship as condescending foreigners instill a feeling of in-feriority in local workers. Tourism also plays a role in undermining the social fabric by establishing little enclaves of affluence which create local dissatisfaction and desires impossible to satisfy. Traditional ways of making a living are disrupted as agricultural land is converted to resort and recreational use. Major beauty spots are purchased and commercialized, often rendered inaccessible to the locals. Many island governments are publicly on record as favoring development based on local resources and island technology, yet inexplicably this concept is rarely applied to tourism. Island tourism officials are bundled off to Hawaii where their attitudes harden along conventional lines. In the "Preface" to this book we've proposed an alternative form of tourism the islanders themselves can run. The luxury hotels and tours are monotonously uniform around the world—the South Pacific's the place for something different.

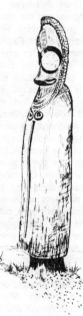

slit gongs: *Among the most imposing musical instruments of the Pacific are the slit gongs of Ambrym, Vanuatu, which stand up to 5 m tall. Topped by a stylized face, the gongs stood in clusters by the village dance grounds. At ceremonies marking sacrifices and initiations complex rhythms were beaten on the thick edges of the slit and the voice of the ancestors spoke to those present.*

THE PEOPLE AND THEIR ARTS

The notion that the Pacific islands and their peoples are all similar—if you've seen one you've seen 'em all—is a total fallacy. No other group of 5 million people on Earth comes from such varying cultures. Ninety percent of them live on high islands, the rest on low islands and atolls. Some 800,000 reside in urban areas. Oceania is divided into 3 great areas: Polynesia and Melanesia, lying mostly below the equator, and Micronesia lying above it. The name Polynesia comes from the Greek words *polus* (many) and *nesos* (islands). The Polynesian Triangle has Hawaii at its N apex, New Zealand 8,000 km to the SW, and Easter Island the same distance to the southeast. Melanesia gets its name from the Greek word *melas* (black), probably named for the dark appearance of its inhabitants as seen by the early European navigators. Micronesia comes from the Greek word *mikros* (small), thus, the "small islands." In towns and villages it's fun to sit outside the post office to watch people coming and going. The charming, gentle, graceful peoples of this region are one of the main reasons to visit.

THE POLYNESIANS

The Polynesians, whom Robert Louis Stevenson called "God's best, at least God's sweetest work," are a tall, golden-skinned people with straight or wavy, but rarely fuzzy, hair. They have fine features, almost intimidating physiques, and a soft-flowing language. They evolved their great bodily stature through a selective process on their long ocean voyages. The larger individuals with more body fat were better able to resist the chill of evaporating sea spray on their bodies. More than 150 years after conversion by early missionaries, most maintain their early Christian piety and fervid devotion. The ancient Polynesians developed a rigid social system with hereditary chiefs; descent was usually through the father. At the time of European arrival on Tahiti, there were 4 social classes: chiefs, landowners, commoners, and slaves. People lived in scattered dwellings rather than villages, although there were groupings around the major temples and chiefs' residences. Each caste had more or less *mana* (psychic power) than the other, and it was dangerous and *tabu* to defile oneself by contact with another.

gods: The Polynesians worshipped a pantheon of gods, who had more *mana* than any human. The most important was Tangaroa (the creator and god of the oceans), and Oro or Ku (the god of war), who demanded human sacrifices. The most fascinating figure in Polynesian mythology was Maui, a Krishna-or Prometheus-like figure who caught the sun with a cord to give its fire to the world. He lifted the firmament to prevent it from crushing mankind, fished the islands out of the ocean with a hook, and was killed trying to gain the prize of immortality for humanity. Also worth noting is Hina, the heroine who fled to the moon to avoid incest with her brother, and so the sound of her *tapa* beater wouldn't bother anyone. Tane (the god of light) and Rongo (the god of agriculture and peace) were other important gods. This polytheism, which may have disseminated from Raiatea in the Society Islands, was most important in Eastern Polynesia. The Arioi confraternity centered in Raiatea and thought to be possessed by the gods traveled about putting on dramatic representations of the myths.

The Eastern Polynesians were enthusiastic temple builders, evidenced today by widespread ruins. Known by the Polynesian names *marae* or *heiau,* these low walls or terraces of coral blocks are often surrounded by flat, erect slabs. Once temples for religious cults, they were used for seating the gods, and for presenting fruits and other foods to them at ritual feasts. Sometimes, but rarely, human sacrifices took place on the *marae.* Religion in Tonga and Samoa was very low key, with few priests or cult images. No temples have been found in Tonga and very few in Samoa. The gods of Eastern Polynesia were represented in human form. There was an undercurrent of ancestor worship, but this was nowhere as strong as in Melanesia. The ancestors were more important as a source of descent for social ranking, and genealogy was carefully preserved.

art: The Polynesians used no masks and few colors, usually leaving their works unpainted. Artforms were also very traditional, carried out by a defined class of artists. Their handicrafts display a remarkable delicacy and deftness. Three of the 5 great archaeological areas of Oceania are in Polynesia: Easter Island, Huahine, and Tongatapu (the other two are Ponape and Kosrae in Micronesia).

moai on the slopes of Rano Raraku, Easter Island

THE MELANESIANS

The Melanesians have negroid features and wear their hair in great halo-like afros. Their color ranges from chocolate-brown to deep blue-black. The inhabitants of the Western Solomons are known as the most heavily pigmented people in the world. Most Melanesians live on high, volcanic islands. Great differences exist between the bush people of the interiors and the saltwater people of the coasts. There's also great variety among the tribes of the interior because of the terrain; for centuries they waged wars with each other. Some clans were matrilineal, others patrilineal.

art and society: The Melanesians have developed a startling variety of customs, traditions, and cultures. The tremendous variety of art objects and styles however, is in no way due to any creative freedom or experimentation. Unlike the Western artist who must invent his own personal expressive form or style, art among the Melanesians was a rigidly traditional medium of expression. If an object didn't correspond precisely to an accepted form, it couldn't capture the magic and the spirits, thus would be meaningless and useless. The variety of styles is due to the vast number of microsocieties; there was little variation within a single clan. Melanesian society was based on consensus, gift giving, exchange, and obligation. Although there was a headman and some sorcerers in each village, these were either elected at village councils or they "bought" their way up in society by giving feasts and pigs. Unlike the Polynesians, there were no hereditary classes of rulers or priests, and no political unions outside the clan unit. Secret societies existed and needed objects for initiation ceremonies and feasts to mark a man's passage to a higher grade. Some objects ensured fertility for man and the soil, others celebrated the harvest. Totemic figures (animals believed to be related to the clan by blood) were common, especially among the Australian Aboriginals.

man blong Vanuatu

Everyday objects were artistically made, and almost everything was brightly painted. Many figures and masks were made specifically for a single ceremony, then discarded or destroyed. More important than the social function of art was the religious function, especially the cult of the dead. Ancestors were believed to remain in this world, and their advice and protection were often sought. The skull, considered the dwelling place of the soul, was often decorated and kept in the men's house. Sometimes carvings were made to provide a home for the spirits of the ancestors, or they were represented by posts or images. Masks were used to invoke the spirits in dance. The beauty of the objects was secondary; what the Melanesian artist sought to create was an embodied symbolism of the ancestors. In this rigid, ritual world the spirits of the dead possessed greater power than the living, and this power could be both harmful and beneficial. Today we know little about the precise meaning of many Melanesian art objects, largely due to the haphazard, unscientific way in which they were collected many years ago. Yet we can appreciate and enjoy their beauty and power nonetheless, just as we may enjoy a song sung in a language we don't know.

LANGUAGE

Some 1,200 languages, a quarter of the world's total, are spoken in the Pacific islands. Most have very few speakers. The Austronesian language family includes over 900 distinct languages spoken in an area stretching from Madagascar to Easter Island. Of all the Oceanic languages, only the Papuan do not belong to this group. Many islanders are trilingual, equally fluent in the national *lingua franca* (pidgin), a local tribal tongue (or 2), and a colonial or international language, of which English is the most common.

pidgin: There are 3 Pacific pidgins: Tok Pisin (P.N.G.), Pijin (Solomon Islands), and Bislama (Vanuatu). Solomons' pidgin is the more Anglicized; the other 2 are surprisingly similar. Because many separate local languages might be spoken on a single Melanesian island, often in villages only a few km apart, the need for a common language arose when it became possible for people to travel beyond tribal boundaries. Pidgin developed in Fiji and Queensland during the labor trade of the late 19th century. Pacific Pidgin, although less sophisticated than W. African or China Coast Pidgin, is quite ingenious within its scope. Its vocabulary is limited, however, and pronouns, adverbs, and prepositions are lacking, but it has a bona fide Melanesian syntax. A very roundabout speech method is used to express things: "mine" and "yours" are *blong mifela* and *blong yufela*, and "we" becomes *yumi tufela*. Frenchman is *man wewi* (oui-oui), *meri* is woman, while *bulamakau* (bull and cow) means beef or cattle.

Polynesian: The Polynesians speak one homogeneous language, subject to local variations and consonantal changes, but intelligible in all the different parts of Polynesia. The word for land varies between *whenua, fenua, fanua, fonua, honua, vanua,* and *henua.* In the Polynesian dialects the words are softened by the removal of certain consonants. Thus the Tagalog word for coconut, *niog,* became *niu, ni,* or *nu.* They're musical languages whose accent lies mostly on the vowels. Words borrowed from European languages are infused with vowels to make them more melodious to the Polynesian ear. Special vocabularies, used to refer to or address royalty or the aristocracy, also exist.

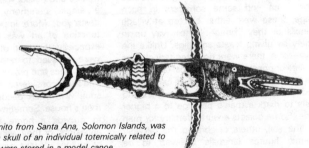

This carving of a bonito from Santa Ana, Solomon Islands, was used to preserve the skull of an individual totemically related to the fish. The bones were stored in a model canoe.

CRAFTS

When considering the arts and crafts of the South Pacific, it's important to remember that today's products usually have little in common with the older, pre-contact pieces now in museums and private collections. Today metal tools are used, the paint is imported, and the items are made for sale to outsiders. The meanings of the designs, the symbolism, and the socio-religious functions are often lost or forgotten. A craftsman might be forgiven if he doesn't put the same loving care into an item made for a tourist as he would into something intended for his ancestors, gods, or chief. A tourist will purchase whatever corresponds to his image of the producing community and is small enough to fit in his suitcase. A visitor to Fiji, for example, might be looking for masks, figures with big penises, or carvings of pigs, even though none of these has any place in Fijian tradition. The transformation of primitive art into airport art cannot be avoided. Sales are a source of income for many people and even sustain a semblance of an art which might otherwise disappear. Not surprisingly, it's the practical arts done by women (weaving, basketmaking, *tapa*) which have best survived. In the few cases where items still serve their original function (such as the astoundingly intricate fine mats of Samoa—not for sale to tourists), they remain as significant as ever.

buyer beware: When considering painting and sculpture, visitors should realize that they will rarely find authentic "primitive" pieces. Instead they should look for evolved arts based on the heritage of the island but made to the demands of today. These are the real arts and crafts of contemporary Oceania, not the cheap tourist pieces mass-produced and sold to the undiscerning. Beware of fake handicrafts such as the *tikis* of Samoa and Tonga which have absolutely no precedents in Samoan tradition. Often items like these are not even made in the country where they're sold. Also avoid crafts made from endangered species such as sea turtles (tortoise shell) and

marine mammals (whales' teeth, etc.). Prohibited entry into most countries, they will be seized by Customs if found. It's not well-known that the kangaroo is on the U.S. Threatened Species List, so souvenirs made from the bodies are also banned. Buy handicrafts from local women's committee shops, church groups, local markets, or from the craftspeople themselves. Items sold at the airports or in luxury hotels are the most likely to be fakes.

weaving: Woven articles are the most widespread handicrafts: examples are found in almost every South Seas district. Pandanus fiber is the most common, but coconut leaf and husk, vine tendril, banana stem, tree and shrub bark, the stems and leaves of water weeds, and the skin of the sago palm leaf are all used. On some islands the fibers are first

a Marquesan woodcarving

passed through a fire, boiled, then bleached in the sun. Vegetable dyes of very lovely mellow tones are sometimes used, but gaudier store dyes are much more prevalent. Shells are occasionally utilized to cut, curl, or make the fibers pliable. Polynesian woven arts are characterized by colorful, skillful patterns.

tapa: On many islands *tapa* making is still an integral part of the everyday lives of the people, as well as providing income from tourists. Tongans, for example, use *tapa* as clothing, bedding, room dividers, and as ceremonial "red carpets." To make *tapa,* the inner, water-soaked bark of the paper mulberry tree *(Broussonetia papyrifera)* is scraped with shells and pounded with wooden mallets, then the pieces are joined together with manioc juice. In Fiji, stencils with raised designs stitched to a bark or fiber base are used to decorate *tapa (masi).* The stain is rubbed on in the same manner one makes temple rubbings from a stone inscription. Sunlight deepens and sets the colors. Each island group had its characteristic colors and patterns, ranging from plant-like paintings to geometric designs. Sheets of *tapa* feel like felt when finished.

woodcarving: Though ground shells are sometimes used for polishing the finest artifacts, steel tools are employed for the most part. Designs are passed down from generation to generation. Melanesia is especially well-known for its infinite varieties of woodcarving. Melanesian woodcarvings often suggest the mystic feelings of their former religious beliefs, the somber spirits of the rainforests and swampy plains of Melanesia. Polynesia also produces fine woodcarvings, and those of the Marquesas Group are outstanding in detail.

other products: There's a great variety of other handicrafts such as polished shell, inlays of shell in ebony, spears with barbs of splintered bone, thorn spines or caudal spines, "bride money," shell necklaces, and anklets. Varieties of European-derived skills abound: the "patch-work quilts" *(tifaifai)* of Tahiti and the Cooks, hand-painted and silk-screened dress fabrics of Western Samoa and Tahiti, etc. **musical instruments:** The Eastern Polynesians had sharkskin drums in olden times, while the Western Polynesians used the slit gong. Pan pipes were also used in the western Pacific, and the flute was known everywhere.

A food bowl from the eastern Solomons carved in the form of a frigate bird holding a fish, used for ritual offerings to ancestral spirits.

EVENTS

The special events of each island group are described in the respective chapters. Their dates often vary from year to year, so it's best to contact the local tourist information office soon after your arrival to learn just what will be happening during your stay. Try to participate, rather than only watch like a tourist. Nuclear Free Pacific Day is 1 March, in commemoration of the 1954 atmospheric hydrogen bomb test on Bikini Atoll in the Marshall Islands which severely contaminated hundreds of islanders. Check locally to see if any demonstrations are planned. Hiroshima Day (6 Aug.) and Nagasaki Day (9 Aug.) are also widely observed, and present the opportunity for you to join the local people in expressing your abhorrence of war and all that goes with it.

major events: The most important event of the region is the South Pacific Festival of the Arts, held every 4 years (Suva, Fiji, 1972; Rotorua, N.Z., 1976; Port Moresby, P.N.G., 1980). The 1984 festival was to have been in New Caledonia but was cancelled due to French political disturbances. The festival gathers in one place the cultures and folklores of all the Pacific islands. The next Festival of the Arts will be in Townsville to coincide with Australia's 1988 bicentenary celebrations. The 10,000 Aboriginal and Torres Strait people resident in and around Townsville are expected to take a leading part—don't miss it. The South Pacific Games, the area's major sporting event, was created at the 1961 South Pacific Conference to promote friendship among the peoples of the Pacific and encourage the development of local amateur sports. Since that time there have been 7 games (every 3 years) with the larger Pacific countries (New Caledonia, Fiji, Papua New Guinea, and Eastern Polynesia) dominating. To give the smaller countries a better chance, Australia, Hawaii, and New Zealand don't participate in the games. The eighth South Pacific Games were scheduled to take place in New Caledonia in 1987. In 1985-87 the tradi-

tional sailing canoe *Hokule'a* will be navigating in South Sea waters—keep an eye out.

religion: The best thing to do on Sunday is to go to church. Of course, it could be a problem if your clothes are ragged, but at least try to look as clean as you can. Don't walk out halfway through the service—see it through. You'll be rewarded by the joyous singing and fellowship, and you'll encounter the islanders on a different level. After church, people gather for a family meal or picnic, and spend the rest of the day relaxing and socializing. If you're a guest in an island home you'll be invited to accompany them to church. Leave your materialistic attitudes at home and go native.

a Tahitian dancer at a Papeete hotel

GETTING THERE

preparations: First decide where you're going and how long you wish to stay. Some routes are more available or practical than others. If you're planning a really extensive trip to islands well off the beaten track, you'll have to do much of the preliminary work yourself. Any good library will have a copy of either the *ABC World Airways Guide* or the *Official Airline Guide* (OAG), monthly telephone book-size directories listing nearly every scheduled flight in the world. This will tell you what's possible. The major arrival points for visitors are Honolulu, Guam, Nandi, Noumea, Pago Pago, Papeete, and Port Moresby; you'll notice how "feeder" flights radiate from these hubs. Your plane ticket will be your greatest single expenditure, so no amount of time spent getting it right is wasted. Airline offices are only interested in selling tickets on their own services—they have neither the time nor the desire to help you work out something that's an exceptional deal. However, in N. America, most airlines have toll-free telephone numbers you can use to determine the current fare. These numbers are often answered evenings and weekends, and it'll be a lot easier to get through then than during peak business hours. To get the number of the different airlines, call toll-free information at 1-800-555-1212. Or ask an airline to suggest a travel agent. They won't *recommend* any, but they will give you the names of a few in your area that specialize in Pacific travel.

travel agents: A travel agent's commission is paid by the airline, so you've nothing to lose. Don't waste your agent's time; know where and when you're going before you go in. Pick your agent carefully, as most are pitifully ignorant about the South Pacific. Those belonging to ASTA (the American Society of Travel Agents) must conform to a strict code of ethics. Often travel agencies which deal in bulk can sell you a ticket for less than the airline itself charges. Most travel agencies, however, are geared to sell package tours. They often know little about discounts, cheap flights, or alternative routes. With alarming frequency they give wrong or misleading information in an offhand manner. Since most airline tickets are refundable only in the place of purchase, it's important to know with whom you're dealing. There can be tremendous variations in what different passengers on the same flight have paid for their tickets, so allow yourself time to shop around. A few hours spent telephoning, asking questions, could save you hundreds of dollars. A recommended travel agency in Canada is WestCan Treks Adventure Travel: in Vancouver, tel. 604-734-1066; in Calgary, tel. 403-283-6130; in Edmonton, tel. 404-439-0024; in Toronto, tel. 416-922-7584.

current trends: Soaring fuel costs have caused many airlines to switch to wide-bodied aircraft and long-haul routes with less frequent service and fewer stops. In the South Pacific this works to your disadvantage as many islands get bypassed. Some airlines now charge extra for stopovers that once were free, or simply refuse to grant any stopovers at all on the cheaper fares. Mileage tickets were once the best way to tour the South Pacific, but since Pan Am withdrew from many of its Pacific routes they've become harder to obtain. Companies like Continental Airlines and Air New Zealand only wish to sell tickets for their own "on line" services. Unrestricted "interline" tickets now cost more.

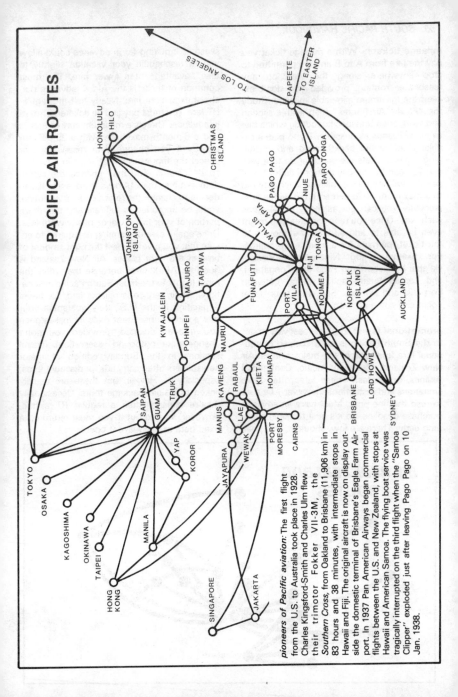

PACIFIC AIR ROUTES

TO LOS ANGELES

TO EASTER ISLAND

PAPEETE

HONOLULU • HILO

CHRISTMAS ISLAND

PAGO PAGO

NIUE

RAROTONGA

JOHNSTON ISLAND

WALLIS • APIA

TONGA

TARAWA

MAJURO

FUNAFUTI

FIJI

AUCKLAND

KWAJALEIN

POHNPEI

PORT VILA

NAURU

NOUMEA

NORFOLK ISLAND

SAIPAN

TRUK

GUAM

KAVIENG

RABAUL

KIETA

HONIARA

BRISBANE

LORD HOWE

YAP

KOROR

MANUS

LAE

WEWAK

PORT MORESBY

SYDNEY

TOKYO

OSAKA

KAGOSHIMA

OKINAWA

TAIPEI

JAYAPURA

MANILA

CAIRNS

HONG KONG

SINGAPORE

JAKARTA

pioneers of Pacific aviation: The first flight from the U.S. to Australia took place in 1928. Charles Kingsford-Smith and Charles Ulm flew their trimotor Fokker VII-3M, the *Southern Cross*, from Oakland to Brisbane (11,906 km) in 83 hours and 38 minutes, with intermediate stops in Hawaii and Fiji. The original aircraft is now on display outside the domestic terminal of Brisbane's Eagle Farm Airport. In 1937 Pan American Airways began commercial flights between the U.S. and New Zealand, with stops at Hawaii and American Samoa. The flying boat service was tragically interrupted on the third flight when the "Samoa Clipper" exploded just after leaving Pago Pago on 10 Jan. 1938.

mileage tickets: With a mileage ticket you pay the fare from A to B and are permitted to stop anywhere along the way on any reasonable routing, provided you don't exceed the maximum allowable mileage. Study the "Pacific Air Routes" map in this section and work out a transpacific routing which hits as many islands as possible. Try to plan a circular route; avoid backtracking and zigzagging. These tickets are good for up to a year and you can fly any day there's a flight. You'll pay the full fare plus a mileage surcharge (up to a maximum of 25 percent), but with a little creativity you can get as many as 14 stops each way. Once you're in the area you might even be able to add additional stopovers to the ticket, perhaps for a small extra charge. For example, add Niuatoputapu-Vava'u-Ha'apai between Pago Pago and Tongatapu, and Lamap-Norsup-Espiritu Santo between Port Vila and Honiara. See what your travel agent can come up with.

promotional fares: The cheapest way to get to the South Pacific is on a special, promotional fare from one of the major airlines (Air New Zealand, Canadian Pacific, Continental Airlines, or Qantas). These fares often have limitations and restrictions, however — be sure to read the fine print. Most have an advance purchase deadline, so it's best to begin shopping early. There are low, shoulder, and peak seasons: inquiring far in advance could allow you to reschedule your vacation slightly to take advantage of a lower fare. The most common of these is the APEX (advance purchase excursion) fare. Nearly half the regular RT fare, you must pay and be ticketed 21 days in advance. There's a minimum stay of 9 days and a 6-month maximum, with a 25 percent penalty if you change your reservations or cancel the trip less than 21 days in advance, so be careful. You may change the return date, not less than 14 days in advance. If you decide to change the return on shorter notice, you'll be upgraded to full fare and the return portion of your ticket will be nearly worthless. Once again, careful planning is required to ensure that you give yourself the right amount of time in the right places. Air New Zealand is good on APEX fares because they offer the most flights to the most South Pacific destinations. Their service is reliable and, for travel originating in the U.S., they guarantee your fare against subsequent price increases once you've been ticketed (provided you don't change your outbound reservation). Travel sections in the Sunday edition of major newspapers often carry ads for discount fares, especially to Hawaii, but these are usually linked to insipid package tours. Occasionally they're cheaper than a regular RT airfare, however, so find out if you must return on a fixed date or can leave it open.

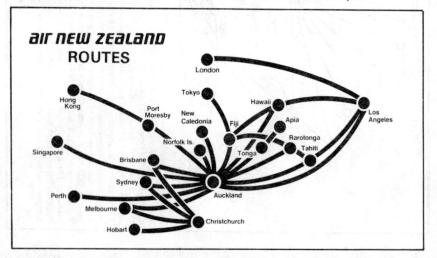

AIR SERVICES

from North America: Air New Zealand, Continental Airlines, and Qantas are the major carriers serving the South Pacific out of Los Angeles and San Francisco, while Canadian Pacific departs from Toronto and Vancouver. Qantas flies Tahiti-Auckland-Christchurch-Sydney-Brisbane-Cairns-Fiji-Honolulu (US$1,100 APEX low season). Continental serves only Honolulu-Auckland-Sydney-Melbourne-Fiji (US$1,100 APEX), but their tickets are refundable and carry fewer restrictions. Air New Zealand has more to offer with its "Super Pass" from Los Angeles or San Francisco to Tahiti-Rarotonga-Auckland-Wellington-Christchurch-Sydney-Fiji-Honolulu (US$1,100 APEX low season). Fares on Air New Zealand (and some other carriers) vary according to seasons: low (April to Aug.), shoulder (March, Sept. to Nov.), and peak (Dec. to Feb.). Note that a RT to Fiji costs about the same as a RT to Australia/New Zealand, so you might as well shoot the works. Hawaii is an important gateway to the South Pacific, and it's sometimes cheaper to fly to Honolulu on a special fare, then buy another ticket to Pago Pago. Ask about APEX fares from Honolulu to Pago Pago. Since flights to American Samoa charge U.S. domestic airfares, tickets from Honolulu are relatively cheap. You always get a free stopover in Honolulu on tickets to the South Pacific.

Circle-Pacific fares: Thanks to agreements between the carriers mentioned above and Asian or American companies such as Cathay Pacific, Japan Air Lines, Malaysian Airlines, Northwest Orient Airlines, Singapore Airlines, and United Airlines you can now get a Circle-Pacific fare which combines the South Pacific with Singapore, Bangkok, Hong Kong, Taipei, and Tokyo. These tickets must be purchased 30 days in advance, but they're valid up to a year and only the initial flight out of N. America has to be booked 30 days ahead. The rest of the ticket can be left open-dated. Prices run US$1,870 RT from Los Angeles,

CAN$2,100 from Vancouver, or CAN$2,566 from Toronto. You're allowed 4 free stopovers; additional stopovers are about US$50 apiece. Once again, Air New Zealand has the most to offer in the South Pacific, but the different carriers offer differing routes in Asia. Due to the determination of the Japanese government to continue commercial whaling despite a decision by the International Whaling Commission to end the practice in 1986, the Greenpeace Foundation is urging a boycott of Japan Air Lines (38 percent of which is owned by the government of Japan). If you care about whales, please observe this boycott and avoid Circle-Pacific fares which include any routing on Japan Air Lines. Ask your travel agent to explain the alternatives to you. The Circle-Pacific fares, also available in New Zealand and Australia, are excellent value.

TONGA
THE FRIENDLY ISLANDS

Protect the Whales

64s Postage

HUMPBACK WHALE
Megaptera novaeangliae

from Australia: To help subsidize the state-owned carrier, Qantas, the Australian government keeps airfares out of Australia as high as they can; they also require foreign carriers to set high fares. The APEX and Circle-Pacific fares described above are available, however. See a travel agent. Hideaway Holidays (1071 Victoria Rd., West Ryde, NSW 2114) specializes in tours to out-of-the-way destinations such as Savai'i, Vava'u, Niue, and the Solomons. Manager Val Gavriloff knows his stuff. For information on special fares available from Student Travel Australia, see "student fares" below.

from New Zealand: Despite such a good national carrier, unrestricted low airfares to the South Pacific are surprisingly hard to come by in New Zealand itself. Some of the best tickets have advance purchase requirements, so you have to start shopping well ahead. Ask around at a number of different travel agencies for special "under the counter" fares such as a cheap Auckland-Tahiti-Los Angeles ticket on UTA. Government regulations limit what Student Travel Services in Auckland and Wellington can offer, but they do have an Auckland-Fiji-Honolulu-Los Angeles student fare. Student discounts are more easily arranged in Australia, so buy a ticket there if it's on your way. Air New Zealand has 21-day advance purchase EPIC fares to Fiji and the Cook Islands. Again, see your travel agent. Fares to Tahiti allow a stop in the Cook Islands, but it's hard to get a reservation.

from Singapore: It's possible to get cut-rate tickets on UTA French Airlines flights across the South Pacific from Singapore. Singapore-Jakarta-Sydney-Noumea-Auckland-Papeete-Los Angeles costs US$780. Although UTA regularly sells their tickets at a big unofficial discount, you have to go through a travel agency (the main UTA office is required to charge full fare). Not all travel agents can arrange the discount, so ask around. Try Sunseekers Travel and Tours, 324 Orchard Towers, Singapore 9, or MAS Travel, Suite 544, Tanglin Shopping Center, Singapore 10. In Penang it's Silvergate Travel in the Mandarin Hotel Arcade, Northstar Travel, 282 Chulia St., or Muhibbah Travels, 22 Liegh Street. The UTA tickets are valid up to a year and have no restrictions, but book early — the flights are often full. Discount UTA tickets are not available in Australia, the U.S., or France. Americans can easily take advantage of these fares, however, by flying to Singapore or Bangkok on the cheapest OW flight, and buying a discount UTA ticket back to L.A. from there. Discount Air New Zealand tickets (Singapore-Auckland-Fiji-Rarotonga-Tahiti-Los Angeles) are also available in Singapore and Penang (about US$725 OW).

from South America: LAN Chile Airlines flies Santiago-Easter Island-Papeete twice a week, but it's not cheap. A OW ticket costs US$1,079. It may be cheaper to include Easter Island in a through-ticket from Australia or New Zealand to Madrid/Paris/Frankfurt, or vice versa. LAN Chile has a special 21-day "Visit Chile Pass" which allows unlimited travel on all their domestic flights (including Easter Island and Punta Arenas, but not Tahiti) for a flat fee of US$449. This ticket must be purchased outside Chile. Also, ask about their Circle-Pacific fare: Miami-Santiago-Easter Island-Papeete-Los Angeles for US$1,450 (valid one year — no restrictions). Fares to Easter Island can vary spectacularly: during a spot check one week, Air New Zealand in Vancouver quoted a fare almost double that given by LAN Chile over their U.S. toll-free number (tel. 800-225-5526)! The flights are heavily booked, so reserve far in advance.

from Europe: Since few European carriers reach the South Pacific, you may have to use a gateway city such as Singapore, Hong Kong, Tokyo, Honolulu, or Los Angeles. The Trans-Siberian Railway inexpensively connects Moscow to Hong Kong or Tokyo, and Tokyo-Saipan is relatively cheap (US$261). The Scandinavian Student Travel Service arranges 3-week tours from Helsinki to Yokohama over the Trans-Siberian for about US$900 all-inclusive. In Saipan or Guam you can connect with Air Nauru to the South Pacific. One place to look for discount tickets to the South Pacific is Globetrotter Travel Service, Rennweg 35, 8001 Zurich, Switzerland (branches in Bern and Basel). Manager Walter Kamm claims his company sells discount UTA tickets for less than you'd pay in Singapore; in fact, he sends almost a thousand people a year that way! Write for a copy of Kamm's newspaper, *Ticket-Info,* which lists about 500 cheap fares; "only the tip of the iceberg." In London get discount UTA tickets from Trail Finders Travel Center, 44-48 Earls Court Rd., Kensington, London W8 6EJ (tel. 01-937-9631).

Air Nauru: Air Nauru links North and South Pacific out of Nauru, a tiny, phosphate-rich island in the Central Pacific. They have flights to all the main South Pacific islands, plus Auckland and Melbourne, from Micronesia, Guam, and a series of Asian cities such as Kagoshima (Japan), Taipei, and Manila. There's also a weekly flight from Honolulu to Nauru (US$368 OW). They take you across the very heart of this great ocean, instead of skirting it as most other carriers do. In Micronesia they connect with Continental Air Micronesia, which flies Koror-Yap-Guam-Truk-Ponape-Majuro-Honolulu 3 times a week (US$646 OW with all the stops). Air Nauru's fares are reasonable. Though they have a reputation for cancelling flights on a moment's notice and bumping confirmed passengers to make room for local V.I.P.s, they fly modern jet aircraft and have a good safety record. One drawback is ground expenses on Nauru, which has only 2 higher-priced hotels (A$28 s). Another is the difficulty in obtaining reliable information — only the main offices are computerized. On many islands you'll end up going standby unless you book weeks ahead. Note too that Air Nauru tickets cannot be used or refunded more than a year after the date of purchase, unless they've been endorsed at an Air Nauru office. Also add to all fares the compulsory A$10 airport departure tax everyone (even through passengers continuing on the same aircraft) is charged at Nauru (they don't tell you about it). Here's a list of a few Air Nauru offices:

AIR NAURU OFFICES

Auckland: 283 Karangahape Rd., Newton (tel. 796-979)

Guam: Marine Drive, Agana (tel. 477-7106)

Hong Kong: Kai Tak, Commercial Building 317 Des Voeux Rd., (tel. 3-722-1036)

Honolulu: Suite 506, 841 Bishop Street, (tel. 531-9766)

Manila: Legaspi Towers 300, 2600 Roxas Blvd., (tel. 595-935)

Melbourne: 80 Collins St., (tel. 653-5709)

Sydney: Ground Floor, 72 Pitt Street, (tel. 221-3761)

Tokyo: Tokyo Club Building, 2-6 Kasumigaseki 3-Chome, Chiyoda-ku (tel. 0992-22-7575)

student fares: If you're a student or recent graduate, you're eligible for special student fares to the South Pacific on Air New Zealand. These must be purchased through a student travel office, and you'll probably have to pay a nominal fee for an official student card. The STA/STN "Associate Members Club," which entitles you to the fares, is open to almost anyone who ever studied at a university and can prove their travel is in some way related to their "professional development." One of the best organizations handling these tickets is Student Travel Australia and their N. American affiliate, the Student Travel Network. Basically, they will sell you the same APEX and Circle-Pacific tickets described above, but at a lower price and without any restrictions whatsoever (although there are still low, shoulder, and peak season fare variations). You can make your reservations over the phone a few days before, pick up your ticket at their Los Angeles office (tel. 213-380-2184) departure-day morning, and be on a flight to Hawaii or Tahiti that night. Reservations may be changed at will and the ticket is refundable. Here's a partial list of STA/STN offices and affiliates:

STUDENT TRAVEL OFFICES

NORTH AMERICA

STN, 1831 S. King St., #202, Honolulu
STN, 2500 Wilshire Blvd., #920, Los Angeles
STN, 8949 Reseda Blvd., #201 Northridge, CA
STN, 1551 Camino Del Rio South, #202, San Diego
STN, 166 Geary St., #702, San Francisco
CUTS, 44 St. George St., Toronto
CUTS, 1516 Duranleau St., Vancouver

AUSTRALIA / NEW ZEALAND

STA, 55A O'Connell St., North Adelaide
STS, 61 Shortland St., Auckland
STA, Shop 2, 40 Creek St., Brisbane
STA, Concessions Bldg., ANU, Canberra
CAMPUS TRAVEL, Canterbury U., Christchurch
STA, 220 Faraday St., Carlton, Melbourne
STA, 424 Hay St., Subiaco, Perth
STA, 1A Lee St., Railway Square, Sydney
STS, 15 Courtenay Place, Wellington

EUROPE / ASIA

NBBS, Dam 17, Dam Square, Amsterdam
ARTU, Hardenbergstrasse 9, Berlin 12
DIS, Skindergade 28, Copenhagen K
USIT, 7 Anglesea St., Dublin 2
SSR, 3 Rue Vignier, 1205 Geneva
HKSTB, 130-2 Des Voeux Rd., Hong Kong
STA, 74 Old Brompton Rd., South Kensington S.W.7, London
USIT, 6 Rue de Vaugirard, Paris
CTS, Via Genova 16, Rome
STA, Ming Hotel Court, Singapore
SFS-RESOR, Drottninggatan 89, Stockholm
NFUCA, Sanshin-Hokusei Bldg., 2-4-9-Yoyogi, Shibuya-ku, Tokyo
SSR, Leonhardstrasse 10, Zurich

Slightly different student fares are available from Council Travel Services, a division of the Council on International Educational Exchange. They're much stricter about making sure you're a "real" student: you must first obtain the widely recognized International Student Identity Card (US$8) to get a ticket at the student rate. Some fares are limited to students and youths under 26 years of age, but part-time students qualify. Get hold of a copy of their *CIEE Student Travel Catalog* which, although mostly oriented toward travel to Europe, outlines many exciting travel opportunities for students. In addition to offering the Air New Zealand student fares, Council Travel Services is one of the only companies in the U.S. selling the cheap UTA ticket described under "from Singapore" above. They also have special connecting student flights to Los Angeles from other U.S. points. Here are a few Council offices:

COUNCIL TRAVEL OFFICES

Austin, Texas: 1904 Guadalupe 6 (tel. 512-472-4931)
Berkeley: 2511 Channing Way (tel. 415-848-8604)
Boston: 729 Boylston St. (tel. 617-266-1926)

Long Beach: 5500 Atherton #210
(tel. 213-598-3338)

Los Angeles: 1093 Broxton Ave.
(tel. 213-208-3551)

Miami: 701 S.W. 27 Ave.
(tel. 305-642-1370)

New York: 205 E. 42nd St.
(tel. 212-661-1450)

Portland: 715 S.W. Morrison #1020
(tel. 503-228-1900)

San Diego: 4429 Cass St.
(tel. 619-270-6401)

San Francisco: 312 Sutter St. #407
(tel. 415-421-3473)

Seattle: 1314 N.E. 43rd St. #210
(tel. 206-632-2448)

important note: De-regulation of the U.S. airline industry has caused airfares, rules, and regulations to fluctuate daily like the stock market, so much of the above may already be out of date. This is only a guide; we've included precise fares to give you a rough idea how much things once cost, not so you can quote them authoritatively to travel agents. Your agent will know best what's available at the time you're ready to travel. If you're not satisfied with his/her advice, keep shopping around. The biggest step is to decide to go—once you're over that the rest is easy!

PROBLEMS

delays: It's an established practice among airlines to provide light refreshments to passengers delayed 2 hours after the scheduled departure time and a meal after 4 hours. Don't expect to get this on an outer island, but politely request it if you're at a gateway airport.

cancelled flights: If your flight is cancelled due to mechanical problems with the aircraft, the airline will cover your hotel bill and meals. If they reschedule the flight on short notice for reasons of their own, they should also pay. They may not feel obligated to pay, however, if the delay is due to weather conditions, a strike by another company, national emergen-

cies, etc., although the best airlines still pick up the tab in these cases. Again, don't expect much from small, local airlines on remote islands where such things are routine. International airlines, however, are a different matter. During the author's recent trip his flights were delayed 3 times: Air Pacific provided a hotel voucher without having to be asked, Air Nauru did so after a couple of courteous requests, and Air Caledonie International refused to accept any responsibility (due to a strike).

others: To compensate for "no shows," most airlines overbook their flights. To avoid being "bumped," check in early and go to the departure area well before flight time. Of course, if you *are* bumped by a reputable airline at a major airport you'll be regaled with free meals and lodging, and sometimes even free flight vouchers (don't expect anything like this on a remote Pacific island). Whenever you break your journey for more than 72 hours, always reconfirm your onward reservations. Failure to do so could result in the cancellation of your complete remaining itinerary. The most important attributes of an airline are safety and reliability; whether they serve you an extra cup of orange juice or have charming hostesses is secondary. If that huge piece of machinery is there, gets off the ground, and flies you right where you want to go on time, it's kind of amazing.

baggage: One reason for lost baggage is that people fail to remove used baggage tags after they claim their luggage. Get into the habit of tearing off old baggage tags, unless you want your luggage to travel in the opposite direction! As you're checking in, look to see if the 3-letter city code on your baggage tag and boarding pass are the same. Label your luggage inside and out with your name and home address. If your baggage is damaged or doesn't come out the other end on arrival at your destination, unless you inform the airline officials immediately and have them fill out a report, future claims for compensation will be compromised. Airlines will usually provide cash for out-of-pocket expenses if your baggage is lost or delayed over 24 hours. The amount varies from US$25-50. Your chances of getting it are better if you're polite but firm. Keep receipts for any money you're forced to spend to replace missing articles. Claims for lost luggage can take weeks to process. Keep in touch with the airline to show your concern; hang onto your baggage tag until the matter is resolved. If you feel you did not receive the attention you deserved, write the airline an objective letter outlining the case. Get the names of the employees you're dealing with so you can mention them in the letter. Don't threaten people, though. They don't want the problem any more than you do. Of course, don't expect pocket money or compensation on a remote, outer island. Report the loss, then wait till you get back to their main office.

AIRPORTS: U.S.A.

Los Angeles: Los Angeles International Airport (LAX) is 27 km SW of the city center. Take the free LAX shuttle bus C out of the airport, then transfer to RTD bus no. 42 into Los Angeles. Get off at 6th St. and walk a few blocks over to the Greyhound terminal, for buses and coin lockers at 75 cents a day. For information on Green Tortoise "magic buses" to Seattle and New York, tel. 213-392-1990. The Student Travel Network, 2500 Wilshire Blvd., Ste. 507 (walking distance from MacArthur Park) has the cheapest tickets to the South Pacific (tel. 213-380-2184). The Australian Consulate nearby issues visas promptly. The L.A. Visitor Information Center is on B level in the underground shopping mall at the Atlantic Richmond Plaza, 505 S. Flower St. and 6th St. If they're closed get a free map of the city from the concierge of the adjoining Bonaventure Hotel. The cheapest hotels, along Main St. near Greyhound, are depressing and potentially dangerous. The youth hostel is S of the airport and the city on the way to Long Beach. Get there from the airport by taking shuttle bus C to the transfer point, then board bus No. 232. Get off at Pacific Coast Highway and Normandie, then ask directions to the hostel at 1502 Palos Verdes Dr. North. Bus No. 232 continues to the Greyhound terminal at Long Beach (the closest to the hostel); tel. 831-8109 for hostel

information. The overnight charge is $5 for members, $7 for others, and you cannot check in before 1630:

San Francisco: San Francisco International Airport (SFO) is 24 km S of the city. The Samtrans bus (No. 7B or 7F) operates approximately every 15 minutes from the airport to the Transbay Terminal at First and Mission streets downtown (80 cents). For information on Green Tortoise "magic buses" to Seattle and New York, tel. 821-0803. The Student Travel Network (166 Geary St., Ste. 702) has the cheap airfares. Visitor Information is in the underground concourse at Market and 5th streets. The Greyhound terminal's a little farther down Market St. at Seventh. There are a lot of fairly liveable cheap hotels with low weekly rates along O'Farrell, Geary, and Post streets near Jones. Many advertise in the classified section of the daily newspapers. The youth hostel (tel. 771-7277) is in Fort Mason, not far from Fisherman's Wharf (bus No. 30 to Bay and Van Ness). Overnight charges are $8 (3-night maximum stay); check in after 1630.

Oakland: Oakland International Airport (OAK) is linked by shuttle bus (75 cents) to the Coliseum station of BART (commuter trains) which runs directly into San Francisco and Berkeley.

GETTING AROUND

BY AIR

Air Pacific: Although it costs a lot to get to the South Pacific, travel within the area is reasonable. Air Pacific has 2 different triangle tickets, a good way to get around around and experience the region's variety of cultures: Fiji-Noumea-Port Vila-Fiji for F$406, and Nandi-Suva-Samoa-Tonga-Fiji for F$397. Both are valid for one year, and can be purchased at any travel agency or direct from the airline. These circular tickets combine perfectly with discount fares on UTA and Air New Zealand, bringing the whole South Pacific within reach.

Polynesian Airlines: For Australians with a month to see the islands, Polynesian Airlines offers the Polypass (not available in New Zealand), which allows unlimited travel on their network (including one RT Sydney/Melbourne-Vanuatu) over the 30-day period for US$999. Since Polynesian flies to all the main South Pacific islands (and most of their flights are only weekly), it would take 2 Polypasses to exhaust all the possibilities. All

flights should be booked well ahead, so have your travel agent outline the various itineraries. There's a US$200 charge to refund an unused ticket (no refund after one year). More useful for N. Americans is their 21-day 7-Islander ticket (US$399) which allows flights from Pago Pago to Apia, Savai'i, Nandi, Nuku'alofa, Vava'u, and Niue within that period. Conditions of sale are similar to those mentioned above. While these tickets are great if your time is limited, they're far too rushed if it's not.

domestic air services: Nearly every Pacific country has its local airline servicing the outer islands. These flights, described in their respective chapters of this guide, can be booked on arrival. The most important local carriers are Air Caledonie (New Caledonia), Air Melanesiae (Vanuatu), Air Polynesie (Eastern Polynesia), Air Rarotonga (Cook Islands), Cook Islandair (Cook Islands), Fiji Air (Fiji), and Solair (Solomon Islands). Most fly small aircraft so only 10-kg free baggage may be allowed. Fiji Air offers an unlimited travel Discover Fiji ticket (F$199 for 14 days).

AIR PACIFIC
ROUTES

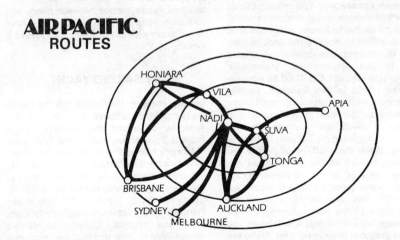

BY SEA

by ship: Much Pacific shipping was destroyed during WW II and many new air-fields were built around the same time, radically altering the transportation patterns of the Pacific. Ninety-eight percent of travel to the South Pacific is now by air, and with few exceptions, travel by freighter is a thing of the past. Most islands export similar products and there's little interregional trade; large container ships headed for Australia, New Zealand, and Japan don't accept passengers. However, local boats to the outer islands within a single country are available everywhere. They don't run according to any set schedule, so you'll have to take your chances. All major shipping possibilities are explored in the different chapters of this book. The only regular international service is Pago Pago to Apia. The Tonga-based Warner Pacific Line offers monthly service between Tonga-Apia-Pago Pago. Their freighters (no cabins—bring your own food) call occasionally at Suva, Tuvalu, Wallis and Futuna, Niue, etc., and passengers are accepted. Due to N.Z. government regulations they can't take passengers there.

work-a-way passages: You can sometimes arrange free passage on big container ships of the Columbus, Pacific Forum, or Sofrana lines if you're willing to work in the deck, engine room, or catering departments as unpaid crew. In Los Angeles call Transpacific Transportation Co. (tel. 629-4192) for information (also offices in San Francisco, Seattle, and Vancouver). In Australia contact Columbus Overseas Services in Melbourne and Sydney, or Seabridge Australia Pty. in Brisbane. In Auckland it's Columbus Maritime Services. While these offices might tell you something about it (if they've got time), the only real way to get on a ship is to see the captain. Arrival and departure times of vessels appear in the daily newspapers, or phone the harbormaster of the port concerned. Since these ships are only in port 4 or 5 hours you must be prepared to jump right on. Try to see

the captain as soon as they've cleared Customs. Most of the ships make regular trips around the Pacific on fixed schedules, so if you work hard and gain a captain's favor, you might be able to jump off, then rejoin the same ship when they return a few weeks later. All valuables will be held by the captain and you must work the same hours as the regular crew. You'll be asked to put up a cash bond of US$300 or more, and money will be deducted from the bond for days you don't work. Unless you're a citizen of the country of disembarkation, you'll have to present a return air ticket. West German passport holders are given preference on Columbus Line ships. This is an excellent opportunity to experience life on a freighter.

cruise ships: If you want an in-depth experience of the South Pacific, don't take a cruise. Tourists on these ships pay over US$100 a day to be shuttled between the most commercialized centers in the islands, where they're badgered by vendors and shopkeepers from the moment they arrive to the time they reboard the ship. All they see of the islands is a blurred image out the window of a bus as they're hustled from one tourist stop to the next. Fellow passengers will be little old ladies with blue hair and rhinestone eyeglasses spending insurance money, loud-mouthed Aussie yahoos between beers, and bourgeois American couples who will bore you to death with talk of their country. Give it a miss.

BY SAILING YACHT

getting aboard: Hitch rides into the Pacific on yachts from California, New Zealand, and Australia, or around the yachting triangle Papeete-Suva-Honolulu. At home, look in the "Mariner's Market Place" section of *Yachting* magazine for classified listings of yachts seeking crews, yachts to be delivered, etc.; you can even advertise yourself for about US$20. Check out the St. Francis Yacht Club in San Francisco or the Newport Beach Yacht Club, S of Los Angeles. Cruising yachts are recognizable by their foreign flags, wind-vane

steering gear, sturdy appearance, and laundry hung out to dry. Put up notices on yacht club and marine bulletin boards, and meet people in bars. When a boat is hauled out, you can find work scraping and repainting the bottom, varnishing, and doing minor repairs. It's easier, however, to crew on yachts already in the islands. In Tahiti, for example, after a month on the open sea, some of the original crew may have flown home or onward, opening a place for you. Pago Pago and Vava'u are other places to look for a boat. If you've never crewed before it's better to try for a short passage the first time. Once at sea on the way to Tahiti, there's no way they'll turn around to take a seasick crew member back to Hawaii. Good captains evaluate crew on personality and attitude more than experience, so don't lie. Be honest and open when interviewing with a skipper—a deception will soon become apparent. It's also good to know what a captain's *really* like before you commit yourself to an isolated month with her/him. Once you're on a boat and part of the yachtie community, things are easy. (P.S. from veteran yachtie Peter Moree: 'We do need more ladies out here—adventurous types naturally.")

time of year: The first thing to be aware of is hurricane season: Nov. to March in the South Pacific, July to Dec. in the NW Pacific (near Guam), and June to Oct. in the area between Mexico and Hawaii. Few yachts will be cruising at these times; around Aug. or Sept. start looking for a ride to Hawaii or New Zealand. Also, know which way the winds are blowing; the prevailing tradewinds in the tropics are from the NE north of the equator, from the SE south of the equator. North of the Tropic of Cancer and S of the Tropic of Capricorn the winds are out of the west. The best season for rides in the South Pacific is July to Sept.; sometimes you'll even have to turn one down.

yachting routes: The common yachting route across the Pacific utilizes the NE and SE trades: from California to Tahiti via the Marquesas or Hawaii, then Rarotonga, Vava'u, Suva, and New Zealand. In the other direction, you'll sail on the westerlies from New Zealand to a point S of the Australs, then N on the trades to Tahiti. Some 300 yachts leave the U.S. West Coast for Tahiti every year, almost always crewed by couples or men only. Most stay in the South Seas about a year before returning to N. America, while a few continue around the world. About 60-80 cross the Indian Ocean every year (look for rides from Sydney in May, Cairns or Darwin from June to Aug., Bali from Aug. to Oct., Singapore from Oct. to Dec., or Sri Lanka and Mauritius); around 700 sail from Europe to the Caribbean (from Gibraltar and Gran Canaria from Oct. to Dec.). Cruising yachts average about 150 km a day. When calculating time allow a month to get from the West Coast to Hawaii, then another month from Hawaii to Papeete. The South Pacific is good for sailing; there's not too much traffic, and no piracy like you'd find in the Mediterranean Sea or in Indonesian waters.

from Panama: Yacht traffic from the Caribbean to the U.S. West Coast via Panama (with an extension to the Galapagos and Eastern Polynesia) is fairly regular, and the yachties are often looking for crew (best from Jan. to March). Check out the Panama Canal Yacht Club at Cristobal or the Balboa Yacht Club near Panama City; both will have notice boards. Help yachts with lines in the canal locks. You could also take the daily ferry from Panama City to nearby Taboga Island, where many cruising yachts anchor. If nothing turns up (unlikely), the French Line (C.G.M. — offices at Cristobal) has about 3 passenger-carrying freighters a month from Panama to Papeete. The OW fare of US$800 is steep, but it's a great way to travel.

life aboard: To crew on a yacht you must be willing to wash and iron clothes, cook, steer, keep watch at night, and help with engine work. Other jobs might include changing and resetting sails, cleaning the boat, scraping the bottom, pulling up the anchor, climbing the main mast to watch for reefs, etc. Do more than is expected of you. A safety harness must be worn in rough weather. As a guest in someone else's home you'll want to wash your dishes promptly after use and put them, and all other gear, back where you found it. Tampons must not be thrown in the toilet bowl. Smoking is usually prohibited as a safe-

ty hazard. You'll be a lot more useful if you know how to use a sextant — the U.S. Coast Guard Auxiliary holds periodic courses to teach its use. Also learn how to tie knots like the clove hitch, rolling hitch, sheet bend, double sheet bend, reef knot, square knot, figure eight, and bowline. Anybody who wants to get on well under sail must be flexible and tolerant, both physically and emotionally. Expense-sharing crew members pay US$50 a week or more per person. After 30 days you'll be happy to hit land for a freshwater shower. Give adequate notice when you're ready to leave the boat, but *do* disembark when your journey's up. Boat people have few enough opportunities for privacy as it is. If you've had a good trip, ask the captain to write you a letter of recommendation; it'll help you hitch another ride.

food for thought: When you consider the big investment, depreciation, cost of maintenance, operating expenses, and considerable risk (most cruising yachts are not insured), travel by sailing yacht is quite a luxury. The huge cost can be surmised from charter fees (several hundred dollars a day for a 10-m yacht). International law makes a clear distinction between passenger and crew. Crew members paying only for their own food, cooking gas, and part of the diesel are very different from passengers who do nothing and pay full costs. The crew is there to help in operating the boat, adding safety, but like passengers, they're very much under the control of the captain. Crew has no say in where the yacht will go. The skipper is personally responsible for crew coming into foreign ports: he's entitled to hold their passports, to see that they have an onward ticket and sufficient funds for further traveling. Otherwise the skipper might have to pay their hotel bills and even a return airfare to the crew's country of origin. Crew may be asked to pay a share of third-party liability insurance. Possession of dope can result in seizure of the yacht. Because of such considerations, skippers often hesitate to accept crew. Crew members should remember that at no cost to themselves they can learn a bit of sailing and see places nearly inaccessible by other means.

OTHER TRAVEL OPTIONS

Ocean Voyages Inc.: For those who love sailing but have to plan their vacations for a set period, this Sausalito-based company offers a variety of trips on chartered sailing vessels to the remotest corners of the South Pacific. The voyages last anywhere from a week to 3 months, and the groups are limited to a maximum of 15 participants, often less. Prices average a little over US$100 a day but they're all-inclusive, covering everything but liquor. Ocean Voyages caters to a very select, professional clientele and their crews are carefully chosen. Over 35 percent of the participants are repeaters—the best recommendation there is. Write Ocean Voyages Inc., 1709 Bridgeway, Sausalito, CA 94965 USA for details.

a hot tip: Northern Lights Expeditions (5220 NE 180th, Seattle WA 98155, USA; tel. 206-362-4506) offers exciting beach-camping tours to the Galapagos and Fiji using inflatable ocean kayaks to get into the really remote areas (such as Taveuni's wild E coast). Brainchild of diver/photographer David Arcese, Northern Lights' full program is still being developed, so write for the latest offerings. The tour prices are unbeatable, and you'll be accompanied by expert guides every paddle of the way. If you're looking for an adventure, get in on this one now before too many people find out about it. Highly recommended.

other tours: Poseidon Ventures (359 San Miguel Dr., Newport Beach, CA 92660 USA) runs dive trips to Rangiroa for scuba nuts. It's preferable, however, to take a scuba diving tour to Fiji, the Galapagos, or elsewhere with See & Sea Travel, Inc. (680 Beach St., Suite 340, San Francisco, CA 94109 USA)—you sleep on the dive boat itself rather than in a hotel. Special Odysseys (Box 37, Medina WA 98039 USA) organizes tasteful, unescorted tours to Fiji, Samoa, Tonga, and the Cook Islands for those who'd like to have everything organized without having to join a group.

by bicycle: Bicycling in the South Pacific? Sure, why not? You'll be able to go where and when you please, stop easily and often to meet people and take photos, save money on truck fares—really see the countries. It's great fun, but it's best to have bicycle touring experience beforehand. Be careful on coral roads, especially inclines: if you slip and fall you could hurt yourself badly. Know how to fix your own bike. Take along a good repair kit; bicycle shops are poor to non-existent in the islands. Most airlines willingly accept bicycles as baggage, usually at no extra charge. Take off the pedals and panniers and clean off the dirt before checking in. Interisland boats sometimes charge a token amount to carry a bike; other times it's free. Have plenty of time if you're going this way.

ACCOMMODATIONS

hotels: This book lists every inexpensive place to stay that we know about, plus the best of the middle-and higher-priced establishments. The emphasis is on locally-owned or family-operated appropriate accommodations, rather than international tourist resorts run by transnationals. Often you get what you pay for, so don't bitch unless you've spent top dollar. Many budget places are low-profit operations, so do your part to help keep the place clean and avoid any temptation to walk off without paying, steal the towels, etc. If you're on a budget avoid prepaying hotel accommodations. On arrival you'll always be able to find a cheaper place than anything you could book from home.

homestays: In Hawaii and Eastern Polynesia there are active bed and breakfast (*logement chez l'habitant*) programs, where you pay a set fee to stay with a local family in their home. Meals may not be included in the price, but they're often available, tending toward your host family's fare of seafood and native vegetables. In Hawaii you must book ahead (see "Hawaii" chapter for details). Ask about homestays at tourist information offices once you're in the islands—Fiji and American Samoa have been considering getting programs going.

staying in villages: If you're in the islands long and get off the beaten track, you'll eventually be invited to spend the night with a local family. There's a certain etiquette to follow and you'll be a lot more welcome if you observe the customs. For example, in Fiji the guest is expected to present a bundle of *kava* roots to the host (see the "Fiji" chapter for details). Although payment is rarely the

Reece's Place on Ngaloa I. off Kandavu, Fiji, ranks among the ten best resorts in the South Pacific for budget travelers. It's rustic charm more than makes up for the lack of electricity and private bath.

THE SOUTH PACIFIC'S TOP TEN

Ask a group of people to give you a list of their ten favorite restaurants and no two lists will be the same. So at the risk of censure and objection, the author places his neck on the cutting board once more by naming not only his ten favorite restaurants, but also bars, beach resorts, and dormitories. These were his criteria: the restaurants had to serve good portions of tasty food in pleasant surroundings at reasonable prices; the bars were chosen for popularity with local residents and island atmosphere; all of the beach resorts are small to medium operations with a friendly, helpful management and low rates--those that allowed camping on the premises earned points; the dormitories were selected for offering safe, clean, inexpensive town accommodations. Facilities with a slick, international air didn't qualify. The listings are in alphabetical order and full information on each is in the text. Readers are cordially invited to submit their own pick of the top ten (give *reasons* for your choices)--we'll update the lists as often as we can. The reader who comes closest to the final selection each time will be listed too; this time it's David Stanley

TEN BEST RESTAURANTS

Akiko's Restaurant, Nuku'alofa, Tonga
Chung Kou Cafe, Lautoka, Fiji
Hare Krishna Restaurant, Suva, Fiji
Restaurant Hameau II, Noumea, New Caledonia
Shanghai Restaurant, Suva, Fiji
Singatoka Hotel, Singatoka, Fiji
Taporo Milk Bar, Port Vila, Vanuatu
Tasty Broiler, Honolulu, Hawaii
Te'o Bros. Kitchen, Fagatogo, American Samoa
Wong Kee Restaurant, Apia, Western Samoa

TEN BEST DORMITORIES

Chez Aime Mare, Bora Bora, Polynesia
Chez Fineau-Tautu, Papeete, Tahiti
Coconut Inn, Suva, Fiji
Dive Rarotonga Hostel, Rarotonga, Cook Islands
Kalfabun's Guest House, Port Vila, Vanuatu
Matareka Heights Guest House, Rarotonga, Cook Islands
Noumea Youth Hostel, Noumea, New Caledonia
Olivia's Accommodations, Apia, Western Samoa
Parker's Guest House, Apia, Western Samoa
Sela's and Atolo's Guest House, Nuku'alofa, Tonga

TEN BEST BEACH RESORTS

Albert's Plantation Hideaway, Kandavu, Fiji
Angermeyer Hostel, Puerto Ayora, Galapagos
Evaloni Beach Resort, Ha'apai, Tonga
Gite de Luecilla, Lifou, New Caledonia
Good Samaritan Inn, Tongatapu, Tonga
Ha'atafu Beach Motel, Tongatapu, Tonga
Kontiki Island Lodge, Nananu-i-ra, Fiji
Poasa's Rest House, Vanua Mbalavu, Fiji
Reece's Place, Kandavu, Fiji, San Gabriel Bungalows, Yate, New Caledonia

TEN BEST BARS

Banana Court, Rarotonga, Cook Islands
Chequers Nightclub, Suva, Fiji
Hotel Rossi, Port Vila, Vanuatu
La Terraza, Puerto Ayora, Galapagos
Le Hubert, Noumea, New Caledonia
Lucky Eddy's, Suva, Fiji
Mt. Vaea Club, Apia, Western Samoa
Seaside Garden Club, Pago Pago, American Samoa
Tumunu Bar, Rarotonga, Cook Islands
Vava'u Club, Vava'u, Tonga

islander's objective in inviting you, it's sort of expected that you'll somehow pay them back. The peoples of the Pacific are so naturally hospitable that it often works to their disadvantage (see the "Western Samoa" chapter for more on this). We recommend that you repay their kindness with either cash (US$5-10 pp a day is standard) or gifts. In places that obviously receive a regular flow of visitors, such as villages on hiking trails or surfing beaches, the villagers are probably used to receiving money. Explain to them how they could create a small business for themselves by setting up a basic rest house for travelers to use. If you come across something like this which we don't mention, please let us know; we'll include it in the next *Handbook* (but make sure it's *really* operating and not just talk). Things to take with you as gifts include sneakers and canvas shoes, T-shirts, blue jeans, sporting gear such as soccer or volleyballs, flashlights and batteries, animal ear markers, powdered pig wormer, relevant books such as *Small Scale Fish Processing* or *Careful Storage of Yams,* sheath knives, dog collars, fishing gear, a big jar of instant coffee, and marbles and balloons for the kids (not candy which rots their teeth and attracts ants). You might also be able to buy a few things at village trade stores to leave as gifts, but don't count on it. If you're headed to a really remote atoll for an extended stay, take with you all the food you'll eat, plus gifts. If you take any photos of your host family be sure to send them prints. From home you could also mail them good used clothes. We're not suggesting that hospitality is a commodity to be bought and sold, but it's easy to see how the unscrupulous can and have taken advantage of the situation. The offer of a little money to show your appreciation may not be accepted, but it won't cause offense when done proper-ly and with sincerity. If you're embarking on a trip which involves staying in villages, make sure everyone who's going agrees in advance on what you're going to do to compensate the islanders. If you meet travelers who argue that it's unnecessary to repay hospitality in any way, don't go with them but be sure to get their names and home addresses so we can list them in the next edition as a good free place to stay. If you really can't afford to contribute anything to your hosts, it's better to camp or sleep on the beach. Staying in villages is a way to meet and communicate with the people, an act of good will with great reward. It's *not* a cheap way to travel.

camping: Your best home away from home is a tent. There are now organized camp-grounds in Hawaii, Eastern Polynesia, Galapagos, Tonga, Fiji, New Caledonia, Australia, and New Zealand. Elsewhere you should request permission of the landowner. You'll rarely be refused in places off the beaten track, but set a good precedent by not leaving a mess or violating custom. If you pitch your tent in a village or on private property without asking permission, you're asking for problems. Otherwise, camp out in the bush away from gardens and trails. The only territory where camping is prohibited is the Cook Islands which operates under a "controlled tourism" system similar to that of the USSR (see the "Cook Islands" chapter for details). Make sure your tent is water and mosquito-proof, and try to find a spot swept by the trades. Never camp under a coconut tree as falling coconuts hurt (actually, coconuts have two eyes so they only strike the wicked). If you hear a hurricane warning, pack up your tent and take immediate cover with the locals.

FOOD AND DRINK

Root crops and fruit, plus lagoon fish and the occasional pig, comprise the diet of most Pacific islanders. Vegetables include taro, yams, cassava (manioc), breadfruit, and sweet potatoes. The sweet potato is something of an anomaly—it's the only Pacific food plant with a South American origin. How it got to the islands is not known, but it and tobacco seem to have been introduced into New Guinea about 1600, suggesting the possibility of an Hispanic connection. Breadfruit grows on trees (remember Captain Bligh?). Taro is an elephant-eared plant cultivated in freshwater swamps. Although yams are considered a prestige food, they're not as nutritious as breadfruit and taro. Yams can grow up to 3 m long and weigh hundreds of kilos. Atoll dwellers especially rely on the coconut for food. The tree reaches maturity in 8 years, then produces about 50 nuts a year for 60 years. Papaya (pawpaw) is nourishing: a third of a cup contains as much vitamin C as 18 apples. To ripen a green papaya overnight, puncture it a few times with a knife. Don't overeat papaya—it's an effective laxative. Many islanders eat raw shellfish and fish, but know what you're doing before you join

them—their stomachs may be stronger than yours. It's safer to eat well-cooked food and to peel your own fruit. Keep in mind that almost everything edible you see while you're out hiking was planted by and belongs to somebody. People working in their gardens will always be willing to sell you fresh fruit at market prices if they've got any (in fact, they'll usually just give it to you, but offer to pay). Islanders in the towns now eat mostly imported foods, just as many Americans opt for fast foods instead of meals made from basic ingredients. Seventh-day Adventists don't smoke, drink tea, coffee, or alcohol, eat pork or rabbit, dance, or chew betelnut. They're exceptional people! Whenever your travels start to get to you and it's time for a lift, splurge on a good meal then see how the world looks.

cooking: The ancient Polynesians, who stopped making pottery over a millennium ago, developed an ingenious way of cooking in an underground earth oven *(umu)*. First a stack of dry coconut husks is burned in a pit. Once the fire is going well, coral stones are heaped on top. When most of the husks have burnt away the food is wrapped in banana leaves and

Uncovering a Fijian lovo or umu (earth oven); the basket in the foreground contains cassava (manioc), while chunks of taro, breadfruit, and yams rest on the stones.

placed on the hot stones, fish and meat below, vegetables above. The whole is then covered with more leaves and stones, and left to cook for a couple of hours. Water can be boiled in a coconut shell placed on the hot stones of the *umu;* so long as it doesn't come into contact with a flame it won't catch fire. If you decide to give the *umu* a try, be sure to break open any sections of bamboo you plan to burn in the campfire. Otherwise get ready for a series of devastating explosions.

others: Betelchewing is a widespread practice among men, women, and children in the Western Pacific, as far S and E as Santa Cruz in the Solomons. First the unripe nut of the Areca palm is chewed, then the leaves of the fruit of the betel pepper. Lime from a gourd (made by burning coral or shells, or grinding limestone) is inserted into the mouth with a spatula, and the whole saliva turns bright red. It's said to relieve hunger and fatigue—give it a try and the locals will love you. *Kava* drinking is easier to get into (see the "Fiji" chapter for a full description). While *kava* is extremely popular in Fiji and Tonga, extremely potent in Vanuatu, and extremely elevated in Samoa, it's unknown in Tahiti, Hawaii, New Zealand.

MONEY AND MEASUREMENTS

money: All prices quoted here are in the local currency unless otherwise stated. The monthly Fiji-based magazine *Islands Business* lists the current rates in each issue. It's convenient to have about US$10 in the local currency on arrival. Where banks exist in South Pacific airports, this isn't necessary; find this information at the end of the introduction to each chapter. Try to avoid changing money at American banks and "foreign exchange dealers" which charge high commissions, give the worst rates, and *never* post them. Banks in the South Pacific seldom charge commission. Be aware that Western Samoa *tala* and Solomon Islands dollars are difficult to exchange outside those countries. If you're having money wired to a local bank, have an odd amount (such as $501.35) sent. If there's an error a figure like this would be easier to trace in bank ledgers or computer printouts than a round figure like $500, which might be one of dozens of similar transactions. Most of the businesses listed in this book don't accept credit cards. Americans will be pleased to hear that most Pacific countries don't have sales taxes. If you'll be visiting a U.S. territory, buy enough U.S. dollar travelers cheques at home to see you through. Bargaining is not common: the first price you're quoted is usually it. Note well that tipping is *not* the custom in the South Pacific, and generates more embarrassment than gratitude.

measurements: Since this book is used by people from all around the world, the metric system is employed throughout. Here are the equivalents:

1 inch	= 2.54 centimeters (cm)
1 foot	= .3048 meters (m)
1 mile	= 1.6093 kilometers (km)
1 km	= .6214 miles
1 nautical mile	= 1.852 km
1 fathom	= 1.8288 m
1 chain	= 20.1168 m
1 furlong	= 201.168 m
1 acre	= .4047 hectares (ha)
1 sq km	= 100 ha
1 sq mile	= 2.59 sq km
1 ounce	= 28.35 grams
1 pound	= .4536 kilograms (kg)
1 short ton	= .90718 metric ton
1 short ton	= 2000 pounds
1 long ton	= 1.016 metric tons
1 long ton	= 2240 pounds
1 metric ton	= 1000 kg
1 quart	= .94635 liters
1 U.S. gallon	= 3.7854 liters
1 Imperial gallon	= 4.5459 liters

To compute Centigrade temperatures, subtract 32 from Fahrenheit and divide by 1.8. To go the other way, multiply Centigrade by 1.8 and add 32. To avoid confusion, all clock times appear according to the 24-hour airline timetable system, i.e., 0100 is 1:00 AM, 1300 is 1:00 PM, 2330 is 11:30 PM. From noon to midnight, merely add 12 onto regular time to derive airline time. Islanders operate on "coconut time": the coconut will fall when it's ripe. Unless otherwise indicated, north is at the top of all maps. When using official topographic maps, determine the scale by taking the representative fraction (RF) and dividing by 100. This will give the number of meters represented by one centimeter. For example, a map with an RF of 1:10,000 would represent 100 m for every cm on the map. The maps in this book are not meant to be used for navigation.

electric currents: If you're taking along a plug-in razor, radio, or other electrical appliances, be aware that two different voltages are used in the South Pacific. The American territories—Hawaii, American Samoa, and Micronesia—use 110 AC, while most of the rest use 220 AC. Most appliances require a converter to change from one voltage to another. You'll also need an adapter to cope with varying socket types. Pick both items up before you leave home as they're hard to find in the islands. Keep voltages in mind if you buy duty-free appliances: dual voltage (110-220 V) items are best.

others: Always use airmail when posting letters from the South Pacific. Airmail takes 2 weeks to reach N. America and Europe, surface mail takes up to 5 months. When writing to South Pacific individuals or businesses, try to include the post office box number since mail delivery is rare. If it's a remote island or small village you're writing to, the person's name will be sufficient. When collecting mail at poste restante (general delivery), be sure to check for the initials of your first and second names, plus any initial which is similar. Have your correspondents print and underline your last name. Despite what you're told, airport X-ray machines *do* cloud film, so request a visual inspection. The old high-dose units are the worst, but even low-dose inspection units can ruin fast film (400 ASA and above).

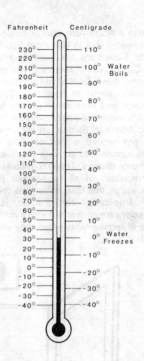

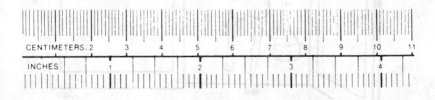

VISAS

If you're a North American or European you won't need a visa to visit most South Pacific islands. Exceptions are Australia and Papua New Guinea, which require a visa of almost everyone. New Zealand asks brown-skinned nationals such as Italians, Spaniards, Austrians, and American Samoans for visas. The U.S. requires a visa of everyone but Canadians; American Samoa, on the other hand, does not require a visa of most tourists. You're supposed to get your U.S. visa in your own home country. The U.S. refuses entry to "communists" of all nationalities (U.S. officials assign this label to anyone they don't like). Ironically, the Pacific islanders themselves are confronted with a complicated series of requirements when they attempt to travel.

other requirements: Everyone must have a passport, sufficient funds, and ticket to leave. Your passport should be valid 6 months beyond your departure date. Occasionally, Immigration officials will insist on a ticket back to your home country no matter how much money you show them. The easy way to get around this if you're on an open-ended holiday or are traveling by yacht or freighters is to purchase a regular OW ticket back to Hawaii or Los Angeles from Air New Zealand. This will be accepted without question; Air New Zealand offices throughout the Pacific will re-issue the ticket, so it's always a ticket to leave from the next country on your itinerary. When you finally get home you can turn in the unused coupons for a full refund.

Customs: Agricultural regulations in most Pacific countries prohibit the import of fresh fruit, flowers, meat (including sausage), live animals and plants, as well as any old artifacts that might harbor pests. If in doubt ask about having your souvenirs fumigated and a certificate issued prior to departure. Canned food, dried flowers, mounted insects, mats, baskets, *tapa* cloth, etc., are usually okay. If you've been on a farm, wash your clothes and shoes before going to the airport.

officials: When dealing with officials it's very important to remain calm, patient, and polite. Remember, if you think a situation is ridiculous or intolerable, you yourself will probably only be affected by it temporarily, but the official has to live with it all his working hours. A smile and a show of cooperation will help to smooth out almost any problem. If you're a yachtie about to clear Customs, however, it's a useful precaution to close all the hatches and windows just before they arrive. They won't want to hang around if it's stifling hot inside. Some officials object to tourists who like to camp or stay with friends, so if asked, name a likely hotel.

moving to the South Pacific: Telephoned inquiries are continually received at Moon Publications from North Americans wishing to emigrate to the South Pacific. Well, here's a little free advice: no country or territory in the South Pacific is accepting immigrants, unless you happen to be a Frenchman bound for Tahiti or Noumea. Population densities in the Pacific islands are among the highest in the world, and North Americans who do settle there take the best jobs away from the islanders. Local Immigration officials are wary of Europeans attempting to escape the dreary wastelands of the industrial world, hence the "ticket to leave" requirement. Marriage to a local woman is no passport for a European

PACIFIC TIME		
Standard Time		
	Hours from GMT	Time at 1200 GMT
Easter Island	- 6	0600
California	- 8	0400
Hawaii, Tahiti	- 10	0200
Cook Islands	- 10	0200
Niue, Samoa	- 11	0100
(International Dateline)		
yesterday		
today		
Tonga	+ 13	0100
Fiji Islands	+ 12	2400
Tuvalu, Tarawa	+ 12	2400
Majuro, Nauru	+ 12	2400
New Zealand	+ 12	2400
New Caledonia	+ 11	2300
Vanuatu	+ 11	2300
Solomon Islands	+ 11	2300
Ponape	+ 11	2300
Queensland	+ 10	2200
Papua New Guinea	+ 10	2200
Truk, Guam	+ 10	2200
Japan, Koror	+ 9	2100

note: Easter Island, Cook Islands, New Zealand, and Vanuatu adopt Daylight Saving Time from Oct. to Feb., while California does so from May to October. The others do not. GMT is Greenwich Mean Time, the time at London, England.

man to spend the rest of his days in the islands; in fact, in the Solomons a tourist who attempts to marry a local person is subject to immediate deportation. A foreign woman, on the other hand, *may* be allowed to stay if she's married to an islander. It's wise that island governments keep Americans out because they soon form alien enclaves which their government uses as a justification to intervene in local affairs (as happened in Texas, Hawaii, Grenada, etc.). If you'd like to live in a condo on a tropical island we'd recommend Maui, St. Thomas, or Guam.

HEALTH

The South Pacific's a healthy place. If you take a few precautions you'll never have a sick day. Avoid jetlag by setting your watch to local time at your destination as soon as you board the flight. If you start feeling seasick on board ship stare at the horizon, which is always steady, and stop thinking about it. The water is good and can usually be imbibed straight from the tap. If in doubt, boil it or use purification pills. Wash or peel fruit and vegetables if you can. To prevent infection from coral cuts, wash them immediately with soap and freshwater, then rub alcohol (whisky will do) into the wounds—painful but effective. All cuts turn septic quickly in the tropics so try to keep them clean and covered. Antibiotics should only be used to treat serious wounds on medical advice. Note that the sort of medications persons from industrialized countries are accustomed to are often unobtainable in the islands, so bring a supply of whatever you think you'll need. If you have to see a dentist or private doctor, ask a local pharmacist to recommend the best.

sunburn: Begin with short exposures to the sun, perhaps half an hour, followed by an equal time in the shade. Drink plenty of liquids to keep your pores open. Use a sunscreen lotion containing PABA rather than oil (don't forget your nose, lips, forehead, neck, hands, and feet). Sunscreens protect you from ultraviolet rays (a leading cause of skin cancer), while oils magnify the sun's effect. After sunbathing take a tepid shower rather than a hot one which would wash away your natural skin oils. Stay moist and use a vitamin E evening cream to preserve the youth of your skin. Lotion soothes skin already burnt, as does coconut oil. A vinegar solution reduces peeling. Take aspirin if your skin itches. The fairer your skin the more essential it is to take care. Avoid the sun from 1000 to 1400. Clouds and beach umbrellas will not protect you fully. Wear a T-shirt while snorkeling to protect your back. Sunbathing is the main cause of cataracts to the eyes, so wear sunglasses and a wide-brimmed hat. Remember, a sunburn will be funny to everyone but you.

ailments: Body lice are common in the South Pacific—you'll certainly pick them up if you spend many nights in local homes. Pharmacists and general stores usually have a remedy which will eliminate the problem in minutes (pack a bottle with you if you're uptight). You'll know you're lousy when you start to scatch: pick out the little varmints and snap them between your thumb nails for fun. The locals pluck the creatures out of each other's hair one by one, a way of confirming friendships and showing affection. Intestinal parasites (worms) are also widespread. If you go barefoot through gardens and plantations you're sure to pick up something. Use anti-diarrheal medications sparingly. Rather than take drugs to plug yourself up, drink plenty of unsweetened liquids like green coconuts to help flush yourself out. If the diarrhea is persistent or you experience high fever, drowsiness, jaundice, or blood in the stool, stop traveling, rest, and consider attending a clinic. For bites, burns, and cuts, an antiseptic spray such as Solarcaine speeds healing and helps prevent infection. Be aware of venereal disease.

malaria: Malaria is the most serious health hazard, but it's limited to Vanuatu, Solomon Islands, and Papua New Guinea. Read the relevant references in the "Vanuatu" and "Solomon Islands" chapters a couple of weeks before you embark for those islands. Guadalcanal now ranks as one of the most malarial areas in the world and chloroquine-resistent malaria is spreading. It can be avoided, however. People taking vitamin B-1 aren't bitten as often by mosquitoes for some reason. There's still no successful vaccination against malaria. It's something of a scandal in the medical profession that while hundreds of millions of dollars are spent annually on

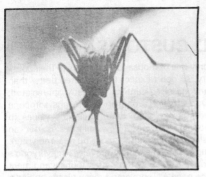

Solomon Island mosquitos are as big as pigeons.

research into the diseases of the affluent such as cancer, heart disease, etc., comparatively little is allocated to the tropical and parasitic diseases of the Third World.

other diseases: Infectious hepatitis can be a problem. You'll know you've got the hep, a liver ailment, when your eyeballs and urine turn yellow. Time and rest are the only cure. Dengue fever is a mosquito-transmitted disease: signs are headaches, sore throat, pain in the joints, fever, and nausea. It can last anywhere from 5-15 days; although you can relieve the symptoms somewhat, the only real cure is to stay in bed and wait it out. It's painful, but dengue fever usually only kills infants. Horrible disfiguring diseases such as leprosy and elephantiasis are hard to catch, so it's unlikely you'll be visited by one of these nightmares of the flesh. There have been sporadic outbreaks of cholera in the Gilbert and Caroline islands (in Micronesia).

vaccinations: Officially, most visitors are not required to get any vaccinations at all before coming to the South Pacific. In 1978 smallpox was eradicated worldwide by the World Health Organization, so forget it. The cholera shot is only 30 percent effective and is valid just 6 months, but get it if you know you're headed for an infected area (such as Truk or Kiribati). While yellow fever is confined to the jungles of S. America and Africa, this vaccination is listed as a requirement if you're coming from those areas. Since the vaccination is valid 10 years, get one if you're an inveterate globetrotter. Tetanus, typhoid fever (TABT), polio, diphtheria, and gamma globulin (for hepatitis) shots are not required, but they're a good idea if you're going off the beaten track.

It's unlikely you'll meet another tourist on this deserted beach N of Tua Tua, Koro I., Fiji.

CONDUCT AND CUSTOMS

Foreign travel is an exceptional experience enjoyed only by a privileged few. Too often, affluent visitors from the industrialized world behave like snails, unable to shed the familiar, protective shell. By transferring their lifestyles to tropical islands, they sacrifice whatever it is they came to seek. Travel can be a learning experience if approached openly and with a positive attitude. A wise traveler soon passes from hearing and seeing to listening and observing. Talking is good for the ego and listening is good for the heart. The path is primed with packaged pleasures, but pierce the environmental bubble of tourism and you'll encounter something far from the schedules and organized efficiency: time to learn how other people live. Walk gently, for human qualities are as fragile and responsive to abuse as the brilliant reefs. Don't underestimate the islanders, they understand far more than you think. Consider that you're

only one of thousands of visitors to their country, so don't expect to be treated better than anyone else. Humility is greatly appreciated. Don't try for a bargain if it means someone will be exploited. Keep your time values to yourself; saving a few minutes is not an islander's first concern. If you're alone you're lucky, for the single traveler is everyone's friend. Get away from other tourists and meet the people. There aren't many places on Earth where you can still do this meaningfully but the South Pacific is one. Try to see it their way. Take an interest in local customs, language, challenges, and successes. If things work differently than they do back home give thanks—that's why you've come. Reflect on what you've experienced and return home with a better understanding of how much we all have in common, outwardly different as we may seem. Do that and your trip won't have been wasted.

island-style dress at Ngao I., Fiji

the Pacific way: A smile costs nothing but is priceless. Islanders smile at one another; tourists look the other way. In Western societies wealth is based on the accumulation of goods; in Pacific societies it's based on how much you can give away. Obligations define an individual's position in society, while sharing provides the security that holds a community together. Tradition is the bottom line. It's an island custom that a gift must be reciprocated. This is why tipping has never caught on. questions: The islanders are eager to please, so phrase your questions carefully. They'll answer yes or no according to what they think you want to hear—don't suggest the answer in your question. Test this by asking your informant to confirm something you know to be incorrect. If you want to be sure of something, ask several people the same question in different ways.

dress: It's important to know that the dress code in the islands is strict. Short shorts, halter tops, and bathing costumes in public are considered offensive: a *sulu* wrapped around you solves this one. Women should wear dresses that adequately cover their legs while seated. Cruise ships are traveling freak shows whose bizarrely-attired aliens are tolerated only for the money they spend. Nothing will mark you so quickly as a tourist or make you more popular with street vendors than scanty dress. There *is* a place for it, of course: that's on the beach in front of a resort hotel. In a society where even bathing suits are considered extremely risque for local women, public nudity is unthinkable. Exceptions are Tahiti, Bora Bora, and Noumea where the French influence has led to beautiful topless beaches.

others: Request permission before taking pictures. You'll get a lot better photos if you spend a few minutes talking to your subjects before you stick a camera in their face. You'll seldom be asked, but for the record, don't pay for photos. Don't violate local taboos by entering sacred compounds such as archaeological sites or royal burials without permission. It may be hard to believe but you *will* be punished: the author was laid up 2 weeks with a terrible sunburn when he entered Ponape's Nan Madol without asking permission of the Nahnmwarki of Madolenihmw. Another time his camera jammed instantly when he took a photo of an ancient marker without asking permission of the present owner. Be careful! Whenever you leave a place always remember to say good-bye to the children as well as the adults.

children: Karen Addison of Sussex, England, sent us the following: "Traveling with children can have its ups and downs, but in the Pacific it's definitely an up. Pacific islanders are warm, friendly people but with children you see them at their best. Your children are automatically accepted, and you, as an extension of them, are as well. As the majority of the islands are free of any deadly bugs or diseases, acclimatizing to the water, food, and climate would be your paramount concern. Self-contained units, where you can do your own cooking, are easy to find and cheap, as well as giving children a sense of security, having set meals every day. Not having television as a distraction I've attempted to teach my son the rudiments of reading and writing. As a single mother with a little boy, traveling with him has opened my eyes to things I'd normally overlook, as well as being an education to us both."

WHAT TO TAKE

packing: Assemble everything you simply must take and cannot live without—then cut the pile in half. If you're still left with more than will fit into a medium-size backpack, continue eliminating. Now fit it into your pack. If the total (pack and contents) weighs over 16 kg, you'll sacrifice much of your mobility. If you can keep it down to 10 kg, you're traveling *light*. Categorize, separate, and pack all your things into plastic bags or stuff sacks for convenience and protection from moisture. Couples traveling together should each carry a few necessities that belong to the other. That way you'll still have the essentials if one bag is delayed or lost on a flight. Carry what can't be replaced in your hand luggage. **your pack:** A medium-size backpack with an internal frame is best. Big external-frame packs are fine for mountain climbing, but don't fit into public lockers and are very inconvenient on public transport. Look for a pack with double, 2-way zipper front and pockets, which you can lock with miniature padlocks. It might not stop a thief but it could be enough to make him look for another mark. A 60-cm length of lightweight chain and another padlock will allow you to fasten your pack to dormitory beds or bus luggage racks, again just enough of a deterrent for your peace of mind. Some packs have a zippered compartment in back where you can tuck in the straps and hip belt before turning your pack over to an airline or bus. Jansport's "Framesack," among others, is of this type.

camping equipment and clothing: In addition to your backpack you'll want a day pack or airline flight bag. A small nylon tent will guarantee you a place to sleep every night. For the islands all you'll need is the cheapest 2-person tent you can find. It *must* be mosquito and waterproof; get a tent fly, then waterproof both tent and fly with a can of waterproofing spray such as Thompson's Water Seal (available at any U.S. hardware store). You'll seldom need a sleeping bag in the tropics, but it will be essential in New

Zealand, Australia, and at higher altitudes on the islands. A youth hostel sleeping sheet is ideal—all Y.H.A. handbooks give instructions on how to make your own. For clothes take loose-fitting cotton washables, light in color and weight. Synthetic fabrics can be hot and sticky in the tropics. For an excellent color catalogue of stylish travel and safari clothing, send US$1 to: Banana Republic, Box 7737, San Francisco CA 94120 USA. Better yet, buy island clothes once you get there and give your old stuff away. Rubber thongs are very handy, especially in communal showers to avoid foot disease. Scuba divers' rubber booties are lightweight and perfect for both crossing rivers and reefwalking. If you're a serious scuba diver, write to the operators you'll be diving with and ask their equipment requirements. Scuba equipment can only be purchased in major centers such as Honolulu, Suva, Papeete, or Noumea. Below we've provided a few checklists to help you assemble your gear. Of course there's no way you'd be able to take all this and still stay under 16 kg, so pick out what suits you:

> pack with internal frame
> day pack or airline bag
> nylon tent and fly
> tent patching tape
> synthetic sleeping bag
> YH sleeping sheet
> hat
> essential clothing only
> bathing suit
> hiking boots
> rubber thongs
> rubber booties
> mask and snorkel

accessories: Look in the ads in photographic magazines for deals on mail-order miniature 35 mm cameras, or buy one at a discount shop in downtown Los Angeles (there are many). Register valuable cameras or electronic equipment with Customs before you leave home, so there won't be any argument about where you bought the items when you return home. If this is too much trouble, at least carry the original bill of sale. Keep your camera in a plastic bag during rain or while traveling in motorized canoes, etc. Take lots of film: only in American Samoa, Fiji, and Vanuatu is it cheap and readily available. Also take along postcards of your hometown, snapshots of your house, family, workplace, etc; islanders love to see these. Always keep a promise to mail the islanders photos you take of them. Think of some small souvenir of your country (such as a lapel pin bearing a kangaroo or maple leaf) which you can take along as gifts. Miniature compasses sold in camping stores also make good gifts. Take an extra pair of eyeglasses (if you have them). Keep the laundry soap inside a couple of layers of plastic bags. To cook at campsites you'll often need a small stove: trying to keep rainforest wood burning will drive you to tears from smoke and frustration. Camping fuel cannot by carried on commercial airliners, however, so choose a common fuel like kerosene or gasoline.

> camera and 5 rolls of film
> compass
> pocket flashlight
> candle
> pocket/alarm calculator
> pocket watch
> sunglasses
> padlock and lightweight chain
> collapsible umbrella
> twine for a clothes line
> powdered laundry soap
> sink plug (one that fits all)
> mini-towel
> sewing kit
> mini-scissors
> nail clippers
> fishing line for sewing gear
> plastic cup
> can and bottle opener
> cork screw
> pen knife
> spoon
> canteen
> matches
> tea bags
> hot sauce

> sardines
> dried fruits
> nuts
> crackers
> chewing gum
> plastic bags
> gifts

toiletries and medical kit: Everyone has their favorite medicines and brand names vary from country to country, so there's no point going into detail here. Note, however, that even the basics (such as aspirin) are unavailable on some outer islands, so be prepared. A pre-packaged medical kit may not fit your needs and will certainly cost more, so assemble your own. Use a medicated powder for prickly heat rash. Charcoal tablets are useful for diarrhea and poisoning (absorbs the irritants). Take an adequate supply of any personal medications required, plus your prescriptions (in generic terminology). See "Health" above for more ideas.

> soap in a plastic container
> soft toothbrush
> toothpaste
> stick deodorant
> shampoo
> white toilet paper
> multiple vitamins and minerals
> Cutter's insect repellent
> PABA sunscreen
> ChapStick
> a motion sickness remedy
> contraceptives
> iodine
> water purification pills
> delousing powder
> a diarrhea remedy
> Tiger Balm
> a cold remedy
> Alka Seltzer
> aspirin
> an antihistamine
> Calmitol ointment
> an antibiotic
> a pain killer
> disinfectant
> simple dressings
> BandAids

money and documents: Any post office will have a passport application. Traveler's cheques in U.S. dollars are recommended. In the South Pacific, American Express is by far the most efficient company as far as refunds for lost cheques go. Also have a few US$10 bills for last-minute expenditures. Carry your valuables in a money belt worn around your waist under your clothing. Most camping goods stores have these. Make several photocopies of the information page of your passport, personal identification, airline tickets, receipt for purchase of traveler's cheques, eyeglass and medical prescriptions, etc. — you should be able to get them all on one page. Put them inside a plastic bag to protect them from moisture. Carry them in different places and mail one home. If you're planning to remain in one place for long, you can store your valuables in safety deposit at the local bank for a nominal charge. Become a life member of the Youth Hostel Association if you feel the wanderlust in your veins. If you have a car at home bring along your insurance receipt so you don't have to pay insurance again every time you rent a car. Ask your agent about this. How much money you'll need depends on your lifestyle, but time is also a factor. The longer you stay, the cheaper it gets. Suppose you have to lay out US$1,000 on airfare, and have (for example) US$15 a day left over for expenses. If you stay 30 days, you'll average US$48 a day ($15 times 30 plus $1,000 divided by 30). If you stay 90 days, the per-day cost drops to US$26 ($15 times 90 plus $1,000, divided by 90). If you stay a year it'll cost only US$18 a day. Some countries are more expensive than others: while you'll certainly want to experience the spectacular scenery of Tahiti or Hawaii, spend those extra days lounging in the sun in Fiji, Tonga, or Western Samoa. Note that the binding of *South Pacific Handbook* tends to deteriorate with constant use, so tape up the spine securely before leaving home.

> passport
> vaccination certificates
> airline tickets
> student card
> youth hostel card
> drivers license
> scuba certification
> travelers cheques
> some U.S. cash
> photocopies of documents
> money belt
> address book
> notebook
> envelopes
> extra ballpoint
> *South Pacific Handbook*

further information: For a selection of standard travel brochures on the various Pacific countries, write to the respective tourist information offices;

TOURIST OFFICES

Australian Tourist Commission, 324 St. Kilda Rd., Melbourne, Victoria 3004, Australia

Broadcasting and Information Office, Vaiaku, Funafuti, Tuvalu

Cook Islands Tourist Authority, Box 14, Rarotonga, Cook Islands

Department of Economic Development, Box 862, Apia, Western Samoa

Economic Development/Tourism Office, Box 1147, Pago Pago, American Samoa 96799 USA

Fiji Visitors Bureau, GPO Box 92, Suva, Fiji Islands

Hawaii Visitors Bureau, 2270 Kalakaua Ave., Suite 801, Honolulu HI 96815 USA

Office Territorial du Tourisme, B.P. 688, Noumea, New Caledonia

New Zealand Government Tourist and Publicity Dept., Private Bag, Wellington, New Zealand

Niue Tourist Board, Box 67, Alofi, Niue

Servicio Parque Nacional Galapagos, Puerto Ayora, Isla Santa Cruz, Galapagos, Ecuador

Solomon Islands Tourist Authority, Box 321, Honiara, Solomon Islands

Tahiti Tourist Board, B.P. 65, Papeete, Tahiti, Polynesia

Tonga Visitors Bureau, Box 37, Nuku'alofa, Kingdom of Tonga

Vanuatu Visitors Bureau, Box 209, Port Vila, Vanuatu

EASTERN POLYNESIA

INTRODUCTION

Legendary Tahiti, island of love, has long been the vision of "La Nouvelle Cythere," the earthly paradise. Explorers Wallis, Bougainville, and Cook told of a land of spellbinding beauty and enchantment, where the climate was delightful, hazardous insects and diseases unknown, and the islanders, especially the women, among the handsomest ever seen. A few years later, Fletcher Christian and Capt. Bligh acted out their drama of sin and retribution. The list of famous authors who came and wrote about these islands reads like a high school literature course: Herman Melville, Robert Louis Stevenson, Pierre Loti, Rupert Brooke, Somerset Maugham, Charles Nordhoff and James Norman Hall (the Americans who wrote *Mutiny on the Bounty*), among others. The most unlikely P.R. man of them all was an obscure French painter named Paul Gauguin, who transformed the primitive color of Tahiti and the Marquesas into powerful visual images seen around the world. When WW II shook the Pacific from Pearl Harbor to Guadalcanal, rather than bloodcurdling banzais and saturation bombings, Polynesia got a U.S. serviceman named James Michener, who added Bora Bora to the legend. Marlon Brando arrived in 1961 on one of the first jets and, along with thousands of tourists and adventurers, has been coming back ever since.

trouble in paradise: Also in the early '60s, President Charles de Gaulle transferred France's atomic testing program from Algeria to Polynesia. Since then nearly 100 nuclear explosions, 41 of them in the atmosphere, have rocked the Tuamotus, spreading contamination as far as Peru and New Zealand. The official French attitude to its Pacific colonies has changed little since 1842 when Admiral Du Petit-Thouars sailed into Papeete harbor and informed the Tahitians that the islands had become a protectorate of France. In the mid-1980s, as independence blossoms across the South Pacific, France is tightening its

POLYNESIA AT A GLANCE

	POPULATION (1983)	AREA (ha)
SOCIETY ISLANDS	142,129	159,760
Tahiti	115,820	104,510
Moorea	7,059	12,520
Huahine	3,877	7,480
Raiatea	7,400	17,140
Bora Bora	3,238	1,830
TUAMOTU ISLANDS	11,211	72,646
Rangiroa	1,169	7,900
MARQUESAS ISLANDS	6,548	104,930
Nuku Hiva	1,797	33,950
Hiva Oa	1,522	31,550
GAMBIER ISLANDS	582	4,597
AUSTRAL ISLANDS	6,283	14,784
Rururu	1,971	3,235
Tubuai	1,741	4,500
EASTERN POLYNESIA	166,753	356,717

EASTERN POLYNESIA

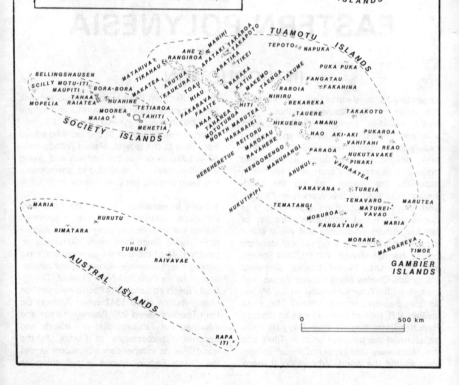

strategic grip on Eastern Polynesia. New wealth has been discovered on the seabed and the arms race is far from over. Deadly plutonium, with a radioactive half-life of 24,000 years, could now be entering the sea from dumps and cracks at the French facilities on Moruroa. The price of French security may yet be paid by all of us.

the land: Eastern Polynesia consists of 5 great archipelagos: the Society Islands (including Tahiti and Bora Bora), the Austral Islands, the Tuamotus, the Gambiers, and the Marquesas. The Society Is. are subdivided into the Windwards, *Iles du Vent* (Tahiti, Moorea, and others), and the Leewards, *Iles Sous Le Vent* (including Raiatea, Maupiti Bora Bora, and Huahine). Tahiti, just over 4,000 km from both Auckland and Honolulu, is not only the best known of the islands, but also the largest. Together the 118 islands of Eastern Polynesia total only 3,567 sq km, yet they're scattered over 4 million sq km of ocean, from the Cooks in the W to Pitcairn in the east. At its widest point, Eastern Polynesia would stretch between England and Yugoslavia, encompassing all of Europe. There is a wonderful geological diversity to these islands, from the dramatic, jagged outlines of the Society Is. and Marquesas, to the 400-m-high hills of the Australs and Gambiers, to the low coral atolls of the Tuamotus. Bora

Bora is noted for its combination of high volcanic peaks with a low coral ring. In the Marquesas, precipitous and sharply crenelated mountains rise hundreds of meters, with craggy peaks, razor-back ridges, plummeting waterfalls, deep fertile valleys, and dark broken coastlines pounded by surf. Compare them to the pencil-thin strips of green and white enclosing the turquoise Tuamotu lagoons. In all, Eastern Polynesia offers some of the most varied and spectacular scenery in the entire South Pacific.

climate: The hot, humid season runs from Nov. to April (best for fishing); the climate is somewhat cooler and drier the rest of the year. May to Aug. sees the SE tradewinds, varying to easterlies from Sept. to December. The NE trades blow from Jan. to April (hurricane season). Eastern Polynesia encompasses such a vast area that latitude is a factor: at 27 degrees S, Rapa is far cooler than Nuku Hiva (9 degrees S). Rainfall is greatest in the mountains and along the windward shores of the high islands. The NE coast of Tahiti gets almost twice as much rain as the W coast due to the prevailing winds. Statistics indicate that the Society Is. are far damper than the Marquesas (1,873 mm annual rainfall at Papeete versus only 1,156 mm at Atuona). In fact, the climate of the Marquesas is erratic: although some years the islands experience serious

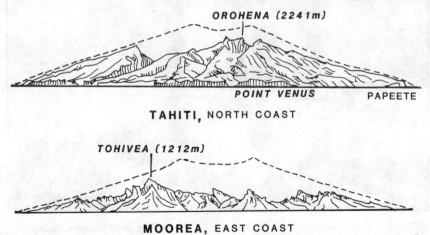

OROHENA (2241m)

POINT VENUS   PAPEETE

TAHITI, NORTH COAST

TOHIVEA (1212m)

MOOREA, EAST COAST

droughts, it could easily rain the whole time you're there. March to May are supposedly the rainiest months in the Marquesas. The low Tuamotu Is. get the least rainfall of all. In the evening the heat of Tahiti afternoons is replaced by a soft, fragrant mountain breeze which drifts down to the sea.

HISTORY

early contacts: The first migrants reached the Society Islands and the Marquesas about A.D. 300, probably from Samoa. From the Marquesas, groups of Polynesians sailed on to Hawaii and Easter I. somewhere around A.D. 500; from the Society Is., they arrived in the Cooks and New Zealand around A.D. 1000. Prior to European contact there were no paramount chiefs, but numerous local chieftains. Raiatea dominated the Society Is. through its priestly class. Captain Wallis on the *Dolphin* happened upon Tahiti on 18 June 1767. A landing party named the island "King George III," turned some sod, and hoisted the Union Jack. The islanders, wanting to trade for provisions, loaded down the Englishmen with pigs, fowl, and fruit. Nails were the most in de-

mand, and Tahitian women lured the sailors to exchange nails for love. Consequently, to prevent the ship's timbers from being torn asunder for the nails, no man was allowed on shore except in parties strictly for food and water. A year later Bougainville arrived, unaware of Wallis' discovery, and claimed Tahiti for the King of France. In 1769, the island group to which Tahiti belongs was named the Society Islands by Capt. James Cook, in honor of the Royal Society which had dispatched him to Tahiti to observe the transit of Venus. Tahiti was visited in 1788 by H.M.S. *Bounty*, then in 1791 by the *Pandora* which was searching for the *Bounty* mutineers, intending to take them back to England for trial. They captured 14 survivors of the 16 who had been so foolish as to stay behind when Fletcher Christian and the others moved on to Pitcairn.

kings and missionaries: By 1797, the year the *Duff* dropped off 18 missionaries from the London Missionary Society, the chief of the area adjoining Matavai Bay, where Cook and most of the others anchored, had become powerful enough through European firearms to establish the Pomare Dynasty. Pomare I

Then as now the French show off their military muscle in Polynesia. The cruiser Duquesne, *flagship of the French Pacific Squadron, and escorts were photographed in Papeete Harbor during the mid-1880's.*

tomb of King Pomare V, Tahiti: *Pomare V's mother died in 1877 after reigning for 50 troubled years during which she was exhorted to accept a French protectorate over her Polynesian kingdom. A less heroic figure than his mother, King Pomare V (above, left), the fifth and last of his name to hold the throne, took over a luckless dynasty and also took to drink. He was particularly fond of Benedictine and he even arranged that the distinctive symbol of his favorite alcohol be enshrined forever on his monument in Arue: a massive pylon-shaped tower on top of which sits a giant Benedictine bottle. He died in 1891, an unhappy man.*

died in 1803 and his son, Pomare II, fled from his enemies to Moorea in 1808. The missionaries went with him and by 1815 had managed to convert high priest Patii to Protestantism. The old heathen idols were burned at Papetoai, where the octagonal church is today. Although Pomare II himself was only a nominal Christian, the missionaries helped him regain Tahiti in 1815. When Pomare II died in 1821 the crown passed to his infant son, Pomare III, but he passed away in 1827. At this junction the most remarkable Tahitian of the 19th C., Aimata, sister of Pomare III, became Queen Pomare IV.

the rape of Polynesia: Queen Pomare ruled Tahiti, Moorea, and part of the Austral and Tuamotu groups for half a century until her death in 1877. She allied herself closely with the LMS missionaries. When French Catholic missionaries arrived in Tahiti in 1836 from their stronghold at Mangareva (Gambier Islands), the thoroughly Protestant Tahitians threw them off the island. This affront brought a French frigate to Papeete in 1838, demanding $2000 compensation and a salute to the French flag. Although the conditions were met, the Queen and her chiefs wrote to England appealing for help, but none came. A second French gunboat returned and threatened to bombard Tahiti unless its missionaries were given free entry. A French consul was appointed and in 1841, while the Queen and George Pritchard, the English consul, were away, he had a few local chiefs unwittingly sign a petition to be brought under French "protection." The French, peeved at having been beaten to New Zealand by the English in

1840, sent an admiral to Papeete with 500 troops in 1842, who hauled down the Queen's red and white flag, and declared Tahiti a French protectorate. Queen Pomare fled to Raiatea and Pritchard was deported to England in 1844, bringing Britain and France to the brink of war. The Tahitians resisted as best they could: old French forts and war memorials recall the struggle.

a French colony: By 1847 Queen Pomare realized that no British assistance was forthcoming, so she and her people reluctantly accepted the French protectorate. As a compromise the British extracted a promise from the French not to annex the Leeward Is., so Raiatea, Huahine, and Bora Bora remained independent until 1888. The French had seized the Marquesas in 1842, even before taking Tahiti. Queen Pomare tried to defend the interests of her people as best she could, but much of Polynesia was dying: between the 18th C. and 1916 the population of the Marquesas dropped from 50,000 to only 2,094. The royal family itself suffered from tuberculosis: the name *Pomare* means "night cough" from *po*, night, plus *mare*, cough. Pomare V, the final, degenerate member of the line, was more interested in earthly pleasures than the traditions upheld by his mother. In 1880, with French interests at work on the Panama Canal, he signed his kingdom away for a pension. Eastern Polynesia then became the full French colony it is today, the "Etablissements Francais de l'Oceanie." In 1957 the name was changed to "La Polynesie Francaise." The most earthshaking event between 1880 and 1961 was a visit by 2 German cruisers, the *Scharnhorst* and *Gneisenau,* which shelled Papeete in 1914.

recent history: The early 1960s were a momentous time for Polynesia. Within a few years the French began testing their atomic bombs, an international airport opened on Tahiti, and MGM filmed *Mutiny on the Bounty.* The spirit of the time is best summed up in the life of one man, Pouvanaa a Oopa, an outspoken WW I hero from Huahine. In 1949 he became the first Polynesian to occupy a seat in the French Chamber of Deputies. A

dedicated proponent of independence, Pouvanaa was arrested in 1958 on trumped up charges of insurrection, imprisoned, and exiled by the French government, which wanted him out of the way while they set up their nuclear testing program. He was banned from Polynesia until 1968; in 1971 he was elected to the French Senate, a post he held until his death in 1977. A large statue of the man now stands in front of Papeete's Territorial Assembly. Pouvanaa's successors, John Teariki (now deceased) and Francis Sanford, were also defenders of Polynesian automony. In 1963, when all political parties protested the invasion of Polynesia by thousands of French troops and technicians sent to establish a nuclear test center, President Charles de Gaulle, the same de Gaulle who had the audacity to campaign for separatism in Quebec in 1967, simply outlawed them.

independence: While the British have been voluntarily withdrawing from their Pacific colonies over the past 20 years, the French have been digging in. This has created the anachronism of a few highly visible bastions of white colonialism in the midst of a sea of English-speaking independent nations. France has made itself the pariah of the Pacific, and the U.S. has endangered its position as an ally and good neighbor by failing to condemn French colonialism and nuclear testing. New Zealand and several other countries are now backing away from their military alliances with the U.S. as a result. The road to independence in Polynesia is fraught with dangers. France has a huge air and seaport on Hao in the Tuamotus; they've hinted they intend to hang onto Hao, Moruroa, and Fangataufa for nuclear testing even if forced to grant independence to Tahiti. Within the last few years another giant airfield has been built on Nuku Hiva, raising the specter that they plan to slice off the Marquesas as well.

GOVERNMENT

An organic decree in 1885 created the system of government which remained in effect until the proclamation of a new statute in 1958, which made Eastern Polynesia an overseas territory. In 1977, when Francis Sanford, Polynesia's representative in the French Parliament, threatened to launch an independence campaign, the French granted the territory partial internal self-government: an elected 30-member Territorial Assembly, which in turn elects 6 of the 7 members of a Government Council. The vice-president is the highest locally-elected post; the high commissioner, appointed by the French government in Paris, is the president of the Government Council. The territory is represented in Paris by 2 elected deputies and a senator. French soldiers and civil servants have a vote in local elections virtually from the day they arrive in the territory, and there are thousands of them. The French government, through its high commissioner, assisted by a Secretary General of his choice, retains control over defense, foreign affairs, immigration, the police, the civil service, foreign trade, TV and radio broadcasting, and secondary education. Eastern Polynesia is divided into 48 communes, each with an elected Municipal Council which chooses a mayor from its ranks. These elected bodies, however, are controlled by appointed French civil servants who run 5 administrative subdivisions, one for each island group.

politics: Ia Mana Te Nunaa (Let the People Take the Power) is a grassroots political party founded in 1975 to campaign for land redistribution and an independent, socialist state. The movement is moderate, pragmatic, and growing—in the 1982 territorial election, Ia Mana Te Nunaa won 15 percent of the vote and 3 seats in the Territorial Assembly. Jacqui Drollet, secretary-general of the party and one of the members, is a man to watch. The Gaullist party, Tahoera'a Huira'atira, led by Gaston Flosse, scored only 29 percent of the votes in that election. The most radical of the pro-independence groups is the Te Taata Tahiti Tiama, led by the mercurial Charlie Ching. The French have made something of a martyr of Ching by repeatedly jailing him on dubious charges. The French government attempts to control what happens in the territory through the state-owned TV and radio. Also, all non-French printed matter entering the colony is censored by police, which explains why you will not see the *South Pacific Handbook* in Papeete bookstores.

ECONOMY

trade and taxation: Except for tourism, the economy of Eastern Polynesia is now totally dominated by French government spending. Prior to the start of the nuclear testing program in the early '60s, trade was fairly balanced. Only 20 years later imports stood at A$485,337,000, while exports amounted to only A$25,321,000, one of the highest disparities in the world, although much of it is consumed by the French administration itself. Half the imports come from France, which has imposed a series of self-favoring restrictions. The only significant exports are coconut oil (from the mill at Papeete) and cultured pearls (from farms in the Tuamotus). Vanilla, though still insignificant, is making a comeback. Imports include food, fuel, building material, consumer goods, and automobiles. There is no income tax. This is fine for businessmen and civil servants who earn high wages, but of no benefit to the common people. Most local revenues are obtained from custom duties on imported goods, leading to highly inflated prices which hurt the little guy most.

government spending: In 1983 the French government spent f.42,250 million in the territory, nearly half of it on the military. Much of the rest goes into inflated salaries for French civil servants, who hold the best jobs. Posts in the colonies are much sought after among French officials for the high salaries and benefits, exotic location, lack of taxation, short working hours, and position of superiority over the natives. This privileged class is a built-in lobby to perpetuate its own existence. Only a third of the population receive any direct benefit from French spending. The rest feel only the effects of soaring inflation, inequalities, and foreign interference in their lives. The nuclear testing program has provoked an influx of over 15,000 French residents, plus a massive infusion of capital which distorted the formerly self-supporting economy into one totally dependent on France. In the early '60s, many Polynesians left their homes for construction jobs for the *Centre d'Experimentation du Pacifique* (CEP), the government, and hotel chains. Now that this work is decreasing in volume, most of them subsist in precarious circumstances on Tahiti, dependent on continued colonial spending. Some 2,000 locals are presently employed by the testing program (compared to 10,000 in 1968). The CEP is headquartered at Pirae, just E of Papeete, with a major support base opposite the yacht club at Arue. Some 3,000 persons live and work on Moruroa (of whom 700 are Polynesian). Despite protests by almost every Pacific nation, the French tests continue. In fact, this program has become the major incentive for the French government to hold onto their colony, since underground nuclear testing on *their* continent would never be accepted by Europeans, regardless of French assurances that it is "safe." Polynesia is far away and the population small; it is expendable.

business: Business is concentrated in a few hands. The Martin family (French/Polynesian) owns the electric company (EDT), Hinano brewery, and Vaima, the huge commercial center. The French banker Breaud runs Total (Standard Oil of California), owns much real estate, and has an important interest in the Banque de Tahiti. The powerful Sing Tung Hing dynasty controls the local Mobil Oil of Australia, Gaz de Tahiti, the Banque de Polynesie, insurance companies, and auto imports. Aline (Chinese) dominates imports and merchandising. Virtually all shipping and docking, both local and international, is in the hands of the Cowan family (French/Polynesian). These ruling groups get the most out of French rule and are the strongest supporters of its continuation.

other activities: Tourism is almost totally in the hands of transnational corporations, either hotel chains (French, Australian, American), or airlines (Air Polynesie is owned by UTA). A casino is planned for Tahiti. Foreigners other than French are not usually permitted to purchase land in Polynesia. The vast distances between the islands themselves and the outside world are one reason for the slow development of the territory. Despite the potential, fisheries are almost totally undeveloped. It is known that vast mineral deposits are scattered across this seabed awaiting the technology to exploit them. The French government has adamantly refused to give the Territorial Assembly any jurisdiction over this tremendous resource, an important indicator as to why they are determined to hold onto their colony at any price.

THE PEOPLE

The indigenous people of Eastern Polynesia are all Polynesian. About 55 percent are Protestant, 30 percent Catholic. The Evangelical Church, founded by the early LMS missionaries, is the largest denomination. The first contingent of 329 Chinese laborers arrived in 1865 to work in a cotton plantation on the S side of Tahiti. Their descendants stayed on to dominate commerce throughout the territory, and today there's an unfor-

French colonies in Africa. French is spoken throughout the territory, and visitors will often have difficulty making themselves understood in English. Refer to the "Capsule French Vocabulary" at the end of the New Caledonia chapter. Say *"Ia Orana!"* to the Tahitians as a friendly greeting.

EVENTS

The big event of the year is the month-long Tiurai Festival, during which Bastille Day (14 July) occurs. This *fete* brings contestants and participants to Tahiti from all over Eastern Polynesia to take part in elaborate processions, competitive dancing and singing, feasting, and partying. There are bicycle and outrigger canoe races, spear-throwing contests, firewalkers from Raiatea, sidewalk bazaars, arts and crafts exhibitions, tattooing, games, and joyous carnivals. Bastille Day itself, which marks the fall of the Bastille in Paris on 14 July 1789, features a military parade. The July celebrations on Bora Bora are as good as those on Tahiti, and not as commercial. Note well that all ships, planes, and hotels are fully booked around 14 July, so be in the right place beforehand or get firm reservations, especially if you want to be on Bora Bora that day. Chinese New Year in Jan. or Feb.

tunate undercurrent of antagonism between Tahitians and Chinese. The current population breakdown is 68.5 percent Polynesian, 11.6 percent European, 9.5 percent Polynesian/European, 4.5 percent Chinese, 3.8 percent Polynesian/Chinese. About 70 percent of the total population live on Tahiti. Nearly 1,500 immigrants a year arrive from France and other French territories, such as former

a canoe race at Papeete

Big Bad Mama proves she can pull a paddle as well as the rest.

is celebrated with dances and fireworks. The anniversary of the first French atomic test in the Pacific in 1966 is 2 July. Public holidays in Eastern Polynesia include Labor Day (1 May), All Saints Day (1 Nov.), Armistice Day (11 Nov.), plus Good Friday and Easter Monday, Ascension Day, Whitsunday and Whitmonday, Assumption Day, Christmas, and New Year's Day. On All Saints Day the locals illuminate the cemeteries at Papeete, Arue, Punaauia, and elsewhere with candles. On New Year's Eve the waterfront at Papeete is beautifully illuminated and there's a 7-km foot race. One group, the *Te pupu arioi*, is a Polynesian cultural revival movement inspired by a pre-European sacred society. They travel throughout Eastern Polynesia presenting traditional music, theater, legends, and games to the island people. Ask at the "Departement Fetes et Manifestations" in Papeete's Cultural Center about special events.

PRACTICALITIES

getting there: Tahiti is serviced by Air New Zealand, LAN Chile Airlines, Polynesian Airlines, Qantas, SPIA, and UTA French Airlines. **getting around:** Air Polynesie, the domestic carrier, flies to all parts of Eastern Polynesia. They don't allow stopovers on their tickets, so if you're flying to Bora Bora RT from Tahiti and wish to stop at Raiatea on the way out and Huahine on the way back, you'll have to purchase 4 separate tickets (total US$150). Nor are there student discounts. Your reservations will be cancelled automatically unless you reconfirm your onward flight from an outer island. Flights to the Marquesas (US$250 OW) are heavily booked. Air Polynesie tickets are refundable at place of purchase, but you must cancel your reservations to avoid a penalty. The baggage allowance is 10 kilos. Flying is 4 times as expensive as cruising: interisland shipping services are outlined in the Papeete section below. On an outer island be wary when someone, even one of the crew, tells you the departure time of a ship: they're as apt to leave early as late.

accommodations: Hotels are expensive. There's a 7-percent tax, and many add a surcharge to the bill if you only stay one night. Wherever moderately-priced accommodations exist, we list them. There is also a well-organized homestay program, in which you stay with a local family. *Logement chez l'habitant* is available on all the outer islands, and even in Papeete itself; the tourist office supplies mimeographed lists. As in other expensive areas, your best home-away-from-home is a tent. The Polynesians don't usually mind if you camp, and quite a few French locals also do it. There are organized campgrounds on Moorea and Bora Bora, plus a free campsite in the center of Papeete. Elsewhere ask permission of the landowner, or camp well out of sight of the road. Make sure your tent is water and mosquito proof. Don't litter.

food: Restaurant meals in Papeete are even more expensive than in Noumea. Groceries are a good alternative and there are lots of nice places to picnic. As in France, the wine, cheese, and bread are good and cheap. There's also Martinique rum, and remember the f.60 deposit on Hinano beer bottles, which makes it cheap to buy. Coconut patties (f.100) are a local treat to watch for on grocery store check-out counters. Attend a *tamaaraa* (feast) and try some Polynesian dishes. There's pork wrapped in banana leaves roasted in an *ahimaa* (underground oven), baked taro, *umara* (sweet potato), and *fafa,* a spinach-like cooked vegetable. Also sample the gamey flavor of *fei,* the red cooking banana that grows wild in Tahiti's uninhabited interior. *Poisson cru,* raw fish marinated with lime juice and soaked in coconut milk, is enjoyable, as is *fafaru* ("smelly fish"), prepared by marinating pieces of fish in a little seawater in an airtight coconut-shell container. Like the durian, although the smell is repugnant, the first bite can be addicting. In 1983 French actress Brigitte Bardot launched a unique campaign to convince tourists not to visit Polynesia because the Tahitians eat dogs. You might like to try a bit—it's nice and lean like goat meat. *Poe* is a pudding made of arrowroot flour flavored with banana and pawpaw, and topped with salted coconut milk sauce. There are many varieties of this treat throughout Polynesia. The local coffee is flavored with vanilla bean, and served with sugar and coconut cream.

money: The currency is the French Pacific franc, or *Cour de Franc Pacifique* (CFP). Both Eastern Polynesia and New Caledonia use it, so there's no need to change back what you have left over if you are going on to the other. One French franc is worth 18.18 Pacific francs, so you can determine how many CFP you'll get for your dollar or pound by finding out how many French francs you get, then multiplying by 18.18. Since the French Socialists came to power in 1981 the franc has lost half its value, so it's pointless to quote exchange figures here. Travelers cheques bring a higher rate of exchange than cash. Banks charge a rip-off commission of f.300 for each transaction so estimate how much you'll need and change only once. Though banking hours vary slightly, they are usually 0800-1530 weekdays. The Socredo branch on the waterfront near Papeete Post Office is open weekdays 0800-1100/1400-1700, Sat. 0800-1030. Note that there is no tipping in Eastern Polynesia and they *mean* it.

visas: French citizens are admitted freely for an unlimited stay, and citizens of Common Market (EEC) countries get 3 months with no visa. Most others get 30 days without a visa, and 3 months with a visa. Extensions of stay up to 6 months are possible after you arrive. You must have an onward ticket. Anyone arriving by yacht (other than the owner) without an onward ticket must put down a deposit of US$1,800. If the individual doesn't have the money, the captain is responsible. After clearing Customs in Papeete, outbound yachts may spend the duration of their period of stay cruising the outer islands.

health: Although cancer is on the up-swing among Polynesians, short-term visitors are still unlikely to be affected by contamination from the nuclear testing program. Fallout from the French tests in the '60s is still ticking away in the tissues of local residents and the bitter

harvest may not be reaped until the mid-'80s onward. Unofficial reports of increasing cases of leukemia and thyroid tumors are confirmed by the refusal of the French military authorities to release complete public health statistics for the territory. (The Public Health Service of Polynesia is run by a French general.) French officials have attempted to hush up certain nuclear accidents (see "The Nuclear Test Zone" below) and keep tourists away from the sensitive areas. However, no checks are made to determine whether the fish sold at Papeete market are radioactive. Jean Rostard, a biologist at the French Academy, has warned: "Every increase of the radioactive dose, however slight it may be, enhances the possibility of a mutation."

airport: Faaa Airport (PPT) is 6 km SW of Papeete, f.90 by *le truck* (f.150 at night). The information desk at the airport is useless. A bank (f.300 commission) opens for the arrival and departure of all international flights. There's a row of broken coin lockers in the terminal, so you'll have to use the luggage storage counter which is open from 0700-1700 and just prior to international departures (you hope). There's a good bookstore in the terminal where you can spend those leftover francs. Many flights to Tahiti arrive in the middle of the night, but if you go up the stairs to the terrace, turn L, and stretch out, the security guard will wake you gently at dawn. All passengers arriving from Samoa or Fiji must have their baggage fumigated upon arrival, a process which takes about 2 hours. Be careful when dealing with Immigration officials in the airport; for example, don't complain if arriving French V.I.P.s cut in front of you in line. Immigration won't hesitate a minute to push you around. A servile attitude works best. There is no airport tax.

les trucks *line the streets adjoining Papeete market*

TAHITI

Tahiti, largest of the Society Islands, is an island of legend and song lying in the eye of Polynesia. Like Maui, Tahiti consists of 2 ancient volcanoes joined by a low isthmus. The rounded, verdant summits of Orohena (2,241 m) and Aorai (2,066 m) rise in the center and, contrary to the popular stereotype, brown/black beaches fringe the turtle-shaped island. To find the white/golden sands of the travel brochures you must cross over to Moorea. The NE coast is rugged and rocky, with an intense, pounding surf; villages lie on a strip between mountains and ocean. The S coast is broad and gentle with large gardens and coconut groves; a barrier reef shields it from the sea's fury. And the flowers! Fragrant frangipani, bursting bougainvillaea, delicate, heavy-scented gardenias (*tiare Tahiti*), many varieties of hibiscus, feathery casuarinas, pandanus, and palms. The mornings are softly, radiantly calm. Paul Gauguin (goh-GANN) arrived at Papeete in 1891 after a 63-day sea voyage from France. He discovered that Papeete "was Europe—the Europe which I had thought to shake off...it was the Tahiti of former times which I loved. That of the present filled me with horror." So Gauguin left the town and, with his adolescent mistress, established a studio at Punaauia: "The gold of Tehura's face flooded the interior of our hut and the landscape round about with joy and light." Somerset Maugham's *The Moon and Sixpence* is a fictional tale of Gauguin's life on the island. Today, Quinn's Tahitian Hut no longer graces Papeete's waterfront and the Lafayette Nightclub is gone from Arue, but Tahiti remains a delightful, enchanting place. In the late afternoon, while Tahitian crews practice canoe racing along Papeete's waterfront, and Moorea gains a pink hue, the romance lingers. But steer clear of the traffic jams and congestion in commercial Papeete and avoid the tourist ghettos W of the city to get a taste of the magic Gauguin encountered. In fact, it's on the outer islands of Polynesia, away from the tourists and military complexes, that the real flavor lives on.

PAPEETE

Papeete (pa-pay-EH-tay) has been the capital of Eastern Polynesia since the early 19th century. 64,193 persons live in this cosmopolitan city and its suburbs, Faaa, Pirae, and

Gauguin's "Girl with a Flower," now in the Carlsberg Glyptotek, Copenhagen. Gauguin was one of the first patrons of the French impressionists. Before he turned professional painter, Gauguin was a successful broker who worked at the Paris exchange. He went further than most of his contemporaries to search out the exotic, to paint in strong flat color, and to employ broad, bold, decorative patterns made popular in France by the widespread distribution of Japanese wood block prints. Whereas later painters borrowed from African masks and carvings, Gauguin himself traveled directly to the source of his inspiration, arriving in Tahiti on 28 June 1891.

Arue—over half the population of Tahiti. In addition, some 4,000 French soldiers are stationed here, mostly teenage conscripts who face prison unless they serve. The French navy maintains a large force of frigates and destroyers at Papeete to defend their interests. Since the opening of the airport in 1961 Papeete has blossomed with new hotels, expensive restaurants, bars with wild dancing, electric rock bands pulsing their jet-age beat, radio towers and skyscrapers. Noisy automobiles and motorbikes clog Papeete's downtown and roar along the boulevards buffeting pedestrians with pollution and noise. Crossing the street can literally be a matter of life and death. Along the waterfront yachts from many countries rock luxuriously in their Mediterranean moorings (anchor out and stern lines ashore). The city is definitely worth exploring, but make it only a gateway and not a final destination.

SIGHTS

Begin your visit in Bougainville Park beside the post office. There's a monument to Bougainville himself, who sailed around the world in 1766-69. It's flanked by 2 old naval guns; one, stamped "Fried Krupp 1899," is from a German raider sunk at Tahiti in WW I. Go through the park and cross the busy street to Place Tarahoi. Ahead to your R is the residence of the French high commissioner,

while on the L is the Territorial Assembly, surrounded by lovely gardens. Ask permission to visit the assembly. In front of the entrance gate is a monument to Pouvanaa a Oopa (1895-1977), the Tahitian war hero who struggled 80 years for the independence of his country. A plaque on the monument provides a few details. Continue NE on Rue du General de Gaulle to the Catholic cathedral, which houses a wonderful series of paintings of the crucifixion. The Polynesian faces, combined with a melange of Tahitian and Roman dress, are worth noting. Papeete market is only 1.5 blocks beyond the cathedral. The colorful throng of islanders and local produce is a visual delight anytime, but especially from 1600-1700 when the fishmongers come to life. The biggest market of the week begins about 0500 Sun. morning and is over by 0730. Using our map continue E about 2 blocks to the old Town Hall, which gives a taste of the Papeete Gauguin saw. A fuller taste is to be had at the Catholic Archbishop's Palace (1869), just E of downtown (ask for the *archeveche catholique*). Without doubt, this place is the best extant piece of colonial architecture in Eastern Polynesia. The relaxing grounds are planted in citrus trees and the modern open-air church nearby also merits a quick look. If you'd like to make a short trip out of the city, return to the market and take a MAMAO-TITIORO *truck* to the Bain Loti, 3 km up the Fautaua Valley from the new Mormon Temple. There's a bust of the writer Pierre Loti in the park, but the area has been spoiled by tasteless construction. Since the valley is part of a water catchment you're not permitted to walk farther up, the most beautiful part.

east of Papeete: Point Venus and the tomb of Pomare V can easily be done as a half-day sidetrip from Papeete by *truck*. Begin by taking a MAHINA *truck* from the market to Point Venus itself (11 km). Many early explorers anchored in Matavai Bay, and Capt. Cook made camp on the point during his visit to observe the transit of the planet Venus on 3 June 1769. On 5 March 1797, the first members of the London Missionary Society also landed here, as a monument recalls. It was from Tahiti that Protestantism spread throughout Polynesia and as far as Vanuatu. Today

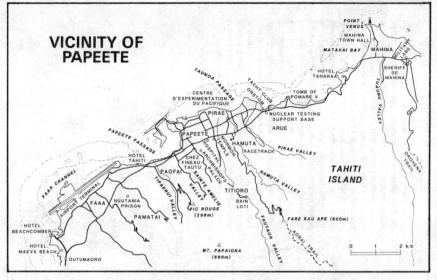

VICINITY OF PAPEETE

there's the small Museum of Discovery (open 0900-1200 daily, f.50) in the beautiful park, and an old lighthouse (1867). The view of Tahiti across Matavai Bay is superb, and Orohena is also in view (you can't see it from Papeete itself). Topless sunbathing on the wide dark sands along the bay is common. Weekdays, Point Venus is a peaceful place, the perfect choice if you'd like to get away from the rat race of Papeete. You could also camp in the park, but first get permission at the Mairie de Mahina nearby (open weekdays). Don't try camping on a weekend when the park is overrun by local picnickers. On your way back to Papeete stop to visit the tomb of Pomare V at Arue, 5 km outside the city. Pomare died of drink in 1891 and a marble Benedictine bottle was placed atop his mausoleum. A great *marae* (Polynesian temple) once stood on this spot, but nothing remains of it today.

AROUND THE ISLAND

A 117-km road runs right around Tahiti Nui, the larger of the 2 parts of this hourglass-shaped island. Go clockwise to get over the most difficult stretch first; also, you'll be riding on the inside lane of traffic and less likely to go off a cliff in case of an accident. The best surfing beaches are at Papara, Papenoo, and Puraauia, in about that order of preference. The Arahoho Blowhole is 22 km from Papeete. Just a little farther, a road to the R leads to the Faarumai Waterfalls. There are 3 separate falls; a path to the R leads to one, and another to the L leads to 2 more, the farthest of which has a pool deep enough for swimming. Bring insect repellent. The coast is very rugged all along this side of the island. At Taravao is an old French fort (1842) still in use. From here you can go east and visit Tautira on Tahiti Iti, one of Robert Louis Stevenson's old haunts. Rugged backpackers could hike S across the peninsula from the Vaitepiha Valley (near Tautira) to the Vaiarava Valley and Teahupoo. You'll have to find your own way through rough country, so be prepared. It's reported that *tikis* are hidden in there. An easier option would be to hike along the S coast from Teahupoo to Vaipoiri Grotto, where you could camp in perfect solitude.

the south coast: Port Phaeton on the SW side of the Taravao Isthmus is an excellent harbor. The Gauguin Museum (daily 0900-1700, f.250), in Papeari District, 51 km from

toxic fish: Over 400 species of tropical fish, including wrasses, snappers, groupers, barracudas, jacks, moray eels, and surgeonfish, are known to cause seafood poisoning *ciguatera*. There's no way to tell if a fish will cause *ciguatera*: a species can be poisonous on one side of the island but not on the other. Several years ago scientists on Tahiti determined that a micro-algae called *dinoflagellate* was the cause. Normally these algae are found only in the ocean depths, but when a reef is disturbed by natural or human causes they can multiply dramatically in a lagoon, and enter the food chain through the fish which feed on them. There's no treatment except to relieve the symptoms (vomiting, prickling, itching, tingling), which usually subside in a few days. Avoid *ciguatera* by cleaning fish as soon as they're caught, discarding the head and organs, and taking special care with oversized fish. Local residents often know from experience which species may be eaten.

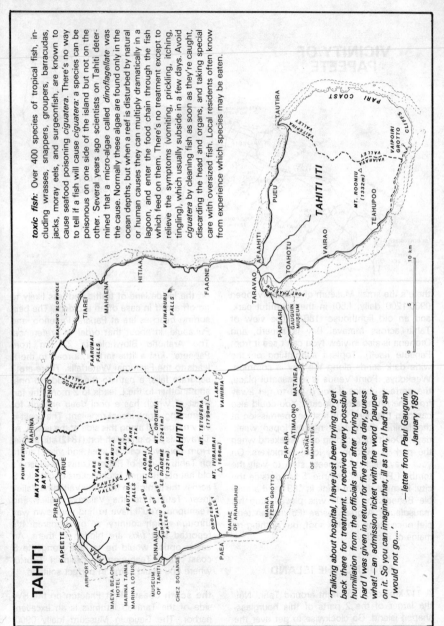

TAHITI

Papeete (measured now from the W), tells the painter's life story, and exhibits a couple of woodcarvings and prints by Gauguin, but no major artworks. Gauguin lived as a near outcast among his countrymen on the island in his own time, but now a Papeete street and school are named after him. The giant 2.74-m, 2-ton basalt *tiki* on the museum grounds is said to be imbued with a sacred *tapu* spell. Tahitians believe this *tiki*, carved on the island of Raivavae hundreds of years ago, still lives. When it was moved from Papeete in 1965, no Tahitian would lift it; 4 Marquesans had to do it. A botanical gardens is part of the museum complex. Visit the gardens first, before going to the museum; the grounds are open to the L as you enter. If you see the gardens second, you'll be charged f.200 extra admission. But none of the plants are labeled, so you could easily give it a miss. About 4 km W of the museum, a rough track leads 11 km up to Tahiti's only lake, Lake Vaihiria, located at 473 m altitude, well known for its eels. This area is undergoing hydroelectric development. It's possible to hike across Tahiti from Lake Vaihiria to the Papenoo Valley and out to the N coast, but again, you'll have to be experienced and able to find your own way. This is not easy, so don't try it if you're at all unsure, and not during the rainy season. The Marae of Mahaiatea, by the beach at Papara a km off the main road, was once the most important temple on Tahiti, but now it's only a crumbling mound of stones. Maraa Fern Grotto, 28 km from Papeete, is between Papara and Paea.

the west coast: The Marae of Arahurahu (Temple of Ashes) near Paea was completely restored in 1954. This temple, lying in a tranquil verdant spot under high cliffs, is perhaps Tahiti's only remaining pagan mystery. See ancient open altars built from thousands of black volcanic rocks. Admission to the park (open daily) is f.50. For some hiking, access to the Orofero Valley at Paea is unrestricted, and camping is possible up beyond the end of the road (6 km). At Punaauia is the Museum of Tahiti and the Islands (Tues. to Sun. 0830-1615, admission f.100, Sat. free). Located in a large, modern complex on the

ocean about a km down a narrow road, sections of the museum remain closed to the public for extended periods. When the waves are right you can sit on the seawall behind the museum and watch the Tahitian surfers bob and ride, with the outline of Moorea behind. On your way back to the main highway from the museum, look up to the top of the hill at an old French fort used to subjugate the Tahitians in the 1840s. Gauguin had his studio at Punaauia from 1897-1901, but nothing remains of it; his *Two Tahitian Women* was painted here. A route up the Punaruu Valley behind Punaauia past the city dump (good pickings!) leads to the fantastic Plateau of Oranges with the pinnacles of Le Diademe (1,321 m) towering above. Unfortunately, entry is arbitrarily forbidden. As you re-enter Papeete, on your R is Uranie Cemetery. The W coast of Tahiti can also be visited as a daytrip from Papeete; start by taking a *truck* to Paea and work your way back.

mountain climbing: Tahiti's finest climb is to the summit of Aorai (2,066 m), second highest peak on the island. An obvious beaten track all the way to the top makes a guide unnecessary. Food, water, flashlight, and long pants are required, plus a sleeping bag and sweater if you plan to spend the night on top. Some maps show "chalets" and "refuges" along the trail, but don't count on it—they're often blown away by hurricanes. At last report there was a small lean-to capable of sleeping 3 at Fare Mato (1,403 m), and a canvas tent for up to 10 at Fare Ata (1,836 m). Camping is more practical; there are good places to pitch a tent at Hamuta (750 m), Fare Mato, Fare Ata, and the summit itself, but try to keep your weight down as this climb is tough. You can ride to the trailhead at Far Rau Ape (600 m) to which an expensive restaurant, Le Belvedere (tel. 2-73-44), offers a free *truck* from Papeete at 1100 and 1700 for clients (f.2400 a meal), the easiest way to get there. Go for lunch to be able to reach a good campsite before dark. Taxis want f.3000 for the 8-km trip to the restaurant. Few people live up here, so hitching would be a matter of finding some tourists headed for the restaurant. Weekends are best. Just above the restaurant is the Cen-

The track to the top of Aorai runs along this razor-back ridge.

tre d'Instruction de Montagne of the French army where you must sign the register, but otherwise no problem. From Fare Rau Ape to the summit takes 7 hours: 1.5 hours to Hamuta, another 2 to Fare Mato (good view of Le Diademe, not visible from Papeete), then 2.5 to Fare Ata, where most hikers spend the first night in order to cover the last 40 min. to the summit the following morning. The view from Aorai is magnificent, with Papeete and many of the empty interior valleys in full view. To the N is Tetiaroa atoll, while Moorea's jagged outline fills the west. Even on a cloudy day the massive green hulk of neighboring Orohena (2,241 m) often towers above the clouds like Mt. Olympus. Orohena itself is seldom climbed, involving serious risks as you work your way along a crumbly ridge with a thousand-m drop on each side. Ropes would be required. The route up Orohena begins at the office of the Sheriff de Mahina opposite the military laboratories. You can drive about 5 km to the 500-m level, then walk. Leave this one to the experts, but Aorai can be done by anyone in reasonable physical shape. A bonus is the chance to see some of the original native vegetation of Tahiti, which survives better at the high altitudes and in isolated gulleys. In good weather Aorai is exhausting but superb; in the rain it would be a disaster.

offshore: Tetiaroa, 40 km N of Tahiti, is a low coral atoll with a lagoon and many small islets. Until 1904 it was a Tahitian royal retreat, but in that year the Pomare family gave it to a Canadian dentist to pay a bill. The dentist's daughter sold it to Marlon Brando in 1966, who uses it as a small tourist resort (US$200 pp daily, meals and air transfer included). Mehetia is an uninhabited high island (435 m) about 100 km E of Tahiti. Mehetia is just a km across and landing is difficult. Maiao, 70 km SW of Moorea, is a low coral island with a rounded 154-m hill at the center. On each side of this hill is a large turquoise lake. A few hundred people live on Maiao, all Polynesians.

ACCOMMODATIONS

in town: The Hotel Mahina Tea, Rue Sainte-Amelie, has 16 rooms with private bath at f.3500 s or d (f.2800 for twin beds) with discount if you stay 2 nights or more. There are also 6 small studios with cooking facilities at f.4000 s or d. At night, the rooster noise can be annoying. If the Mahina Tea is full, try Chez Nicole Sorgniard (no sign) just a little farther inland on the same street beyond Snack Chez Yvonne. Nicole has nice rooms overlooking a large terrace at f.2500 s, f.3500 d, f.4500 t. If you're alone, tell Nicole that you don't mind sharing a room, and the price may come down. It's clean, comfortable, and pleasant—recommended. To meet interesting people, try Chez Fineau-Tautu, 8 Rue du Pont Neuf (tel. 43-74-99). Shared accommodations with basic cooking facilities are f.1500 pp.

above, clockwise: Na Pali coastline, Kauai, Hawaii (D. Stanley); Tapuaetai (One Foot Island), Aitutaki, Cook Is. (D. Stanley); taro fields in the Hanalei Valley, Kauai, Hawaii (D. Stanley); Afareaitu Falls, Moorea, Eastern Polynesia (Don Pitcher); Oneroa, Mangaia, Cook Is. (D. Stanley)

above, clockwise: threadfin butterflyfish; leaffish; soft coral; acropora; damselfish (all photos this page taken at Rose I., American Samoa, by Gerald M. Ludwig, U.S. Fish and Wildlife Service)

English is spoken. You stay in a characterful old house in an attractive neighborhood just a short walk E of downtown near the Archbishop's Palace. A step down from these is the Lagon Hotel "Le Point" where rooms with private bath are f.2500 s or d, shared bath f.2000 s or d. This place is popular with cockroaches, as well as French sailors looking for easy women.

youth hostel: The Papeete Youth Hostel opposite the Cultural Center offers dormitory accommodations to those with a current YHA or student card. One night costs f.1000, 2 nights or more f.800 each; you can check in weekdays 0800-1200/1400-1800, Sat. 0800-1200/1500-1800, Sun. 1000-1200. The rooms are accessible all day (midnight curfew), but there are no cooking facilities. The hostel will store excess luggage for you. The management does not allow visitors in the rooms, nor is it permitted to store luggage for friends not staying there. If you arrive outside the check-in hours or would like to camp, there's a free camping area hidden among the banana trees just across the little stream from the hostel. Put a small contribution in the jar on the picnic table and do your part to help keep this place clean. The caretaker rents tents to those without for f.300 a day. Women can sometimes stay at the Foyer de Jeunes Filles de Paofai (f.600) run by the Evangelical Church.

out of town: If you can afford it, the efficient Hotel Tahiti between Papeete and the airport is the best of the higher-priced hotels. There are 111 rooms at f.6500 s, f.7000 twin, or bungalows at f.8500-9500. Some of the rooms are prone to traffic noise. The hotel has a pool, bar, restaurant, etc., plus a lovely setting on the lagoon and a gracious South Seas atmosphere. Snorkel along the reef off the end of their pier. If you're tired of the Hilton/Sheraton stereotype, the Hotel Tahiti is for you. The only inexpensive place near the beach is Chez Solange (tel. 8-21-07) opposite the Mobil station "Raumanu" (the second Mobil station S of Punaauia). Rooms (with cooking) are f.2500 s or d (breakfast included), but they're often full so call first. Single women are permitted to camp beside the guest house for f.300 pp—a good, safe place to stay. Couples are only permitted to camp when it's not crowded.

FOOD AND ENTERTAINMENT

food: The snack bar at the Cultural Center is good for breakfast. The Foyer de Jeunes Filles de Paofai has a good modern cafeteria (closed Sun.) with a fixed menu including a small salad, main plate, bread, and dessert for f.660 lunch or dinner. La Pizzeria (closed Sun.) near the Paofai cafeteria prepares real pizza in a brick oven and the price is surprisingly

The food trucks along the Papeete waterfront near the Moorea ferry wharf are about the best place in the city to eat.

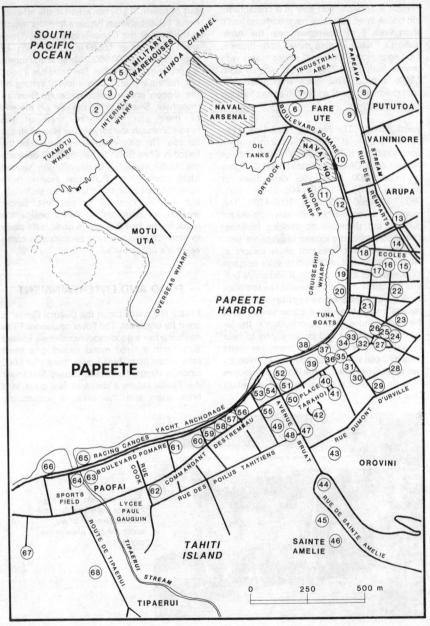

reasonable for the waterfront location—it's all spelled out in a big tabloid menu. For real homecooking try the Chez Melie Restaurant beside Compel Pacific. This place is so low-profile you'll probably have to ask directions the first time. Lunch specials are posted on a blackboard outside. Snack Mimiche, around the corner from Chez Fineau-Tautu, serves a cheap Chinese lunch weekdays 1030-1200. Snack Robert next to the cathedral offers good plate lunches, cheap salads, real espresso coffee, and ice cream. Locate this one early in your visit! The *plat du jour* at Big Burger beside Aline is often big value, and it's not fast food as the name implies. There are many Chinese restaurants in Papeete, but they're no special bargain. The most popular is the Waikiki Restaurant (open daily 1100-1300/1800-2100, closed Sun. lunch) near the market. Three Chinese restaurants are side by side on Rue Colette just W of the Town Hall—take your pick. More fun are *les brochettes,* a long row of food trucks which create a colorful night market at the Moorea ferry landing every evening after 1700. Steak with real *pommes frites* (f.600) is popular. Sailors strolling by with their *wahines,* as the city lights wink gently across the harbor, add a touch of romance to the scene. If you're catching an interisland ship, it's good to know about the Foyer des Dockers near the wharf where *Temehani* and *Taporo* dock. Lunch is

PAPEETE

1. Moorea Car Ferry
2. coconut oil mill
3. copra storage
4. Bureau *Temihani/Taporo IV*
5. Foyer des Dockers
6. Bureau *Taporo III* and *IV*
7. Marine Corail
8. Lagon Hotel "Le Point"
9. Service d'Higiene
10. Andre Rent-a-Car
11. Moorea passenger ferries
12. Evening food trucks
13. Bureau *Tamarii Tuamoto*
14. Bar Kikiriri
15. Town Hall
16. Chinese restaurants
17. Restaurant Waikiki
18. Piano Bar
19. House of Shells
20. tourist office
21. market
22. Bureau *Taporo II*
23. Chinese restaurants
24. La Boutique Klima
25. Manuia Curios
26. Snack Robert
27. Catholic cathedral
28. Clinique Cardella
29. Chez Melie Restaurant
30. Societe des Etudes Oceaniennes
31. Tiki d'Or Bar Americain
32. Air New Zealand
33. Vaima Center
34. Pince a Linge

35. Big Burger
36. Libre Service Aline
37. Socredo Bank
38. Tahiti Mer et Loisirs
39. post office
40. monument to Pouvanaa a Oopa
41. Territorial Assembly
42. High Commissioner's Residence
43. army barracks
44. Gendarmerie
45. Hotel Mahina Tea
46. Chez Nicole
47. War Memorial
48. police station
49. courthouse
50. Government Council
51. Compagnie Generale Maritime
52. Air Polynesie/UTA
53. Ping Pong Bookstore
54. Hachette Pacifique Bookstore
55. Section Topographie
56. Robert Rent-a-Car
57. La Pizzeria
58. Tahiti Pearl Center
59. Protestant Church
60. Foyer de Jeunes Filles de Paofai
61. Clinique Paofai
62. la Mana Te Nunaa
63. campsite
64. Papeete Youth Hostel
65. Cultural Center
66. Olympic Swimming Pool
67. Uranie Cemetery
68. Matavai Hotel

fire dancers at a Papeete resort

the evening show could be a problem—try hitching if you're stuck. The first Sun. of each month at 1200, this hotel puts on a full Tahitian feast, complete with earth oven (*ahima'a*) and 3-hour show (f.3150). Reservations (tel. 28042, ext. 0924) are recommended if you intend to dine. That, and the camera show in the hotel garden Sun. at 1300 (free), are easier to catch. Not as good but more convenient is the Tahitian dancing at the Matavai Hotel, a 5-min. walk from the Cultural Center (Fri. and Sat. at 2000, Sun. at 1200). You can see it for the price of a drink at the bar (no cover). To observe French justice in action attend a trial at the courthouse on Ave. Bruat weekday mornings 0800-1100. The public gallery is up the stairway and straight ahead.

PRACTICALITIES

shopping: Normal shopping hours in Papeete are weekdays 0730-1130/1400-1730, Sat. 0800-1130. There are 2 big supermarkets: downstairs in the Vaima Center, and at Libre-Service Aline. The Tahiti Pearl Center beside the Protestant church on the waterfront is well worth visiting. There's a pearl museum (free), aquarium, and showroom where you can purchase famous Gambier black pearls. A video presentation on the industry is shown on request. For reproductions of authentic Marquesan woodcarvings, have a look in Manuia Curios on the E side of the cathedral. Marie Ah You between the tourist office and the Vaima Center sells very chic island fashions with prices to match. You can pick up a T-shirt (f.600) bearing the double spiral emblem of the Polynesian independence movement at the office of la Mana Te Nunaa, corner *rues* Cook and Commandant Destremeau, 2 blocks from the Cultural Center. The Philatelic Bureau at the post office sells the stamps of all the French Pacific territories.

services: Place long-distance telephone calls at the post office. The post office will forward mail for f.200. If you need a doctor, the Clinique Paofai accepts outpatients weekdays and Sat. morning, emergencies anytime. The facilities and attention are excellent, but be

good and there are big bottles of cold beer. Indulge before you embark.

entertainment: All films shown at local cinemas are dubbed into French. The Piano Bar on Rue des Ecoles is a transvestite disco, right in the heart of Papeete's nightlife district. The show on the sidewalk outside is often amusing. Also check the Bounty Bar just up the street, but beware of inflated cover charges. The Pitate Bar, on the corner of Ave. Bruat beside the UTA office, picks up after 2200; sometimes you can hear Tahitian music here. Club 106 beside Ping Pong Bookstore is the disco for the "in" set. For more earthy interplay try the Bar Kikiriri near the Town Hall. The Tiki d'Or Bar Americain on the back street near the Vaima Center gets lively around happy hour. You'll locate it by the ukuleles and impromptu singing. Happy hour at Le Junk Bar on the waterfront opposite the end of Ave. Bruat is a yachtie institution. Recitals by well-known classical musicians take place at the Cultural Center Fri. and Sat. at 2000 (admission f.1000).

sideshows: There's Tahitian dancing at the Maeva Beach Hotel Wed. (island food) and Fri. (seafood buffet) at 2000. You can have the salad only (f.850), instead of the complete dinner (f.2500). Transport back to Papeete after

prepared for fees beginning at US$20. Dr. Sit-jar above Boutique Klima beside the cathedral also handles general consultations (f.1800). Get cholera and yellow fever vaccinations (f.400) from the Service d'Higiene, open weekdays 0800-0900. The Immigration office at the airport (open weekdays 0800-1200) will give two 3-month visa extensions (f.250 and one photo), provided you have a ticket to leave and enough money to support yourself. It's important to be patient and courteous with these officials if you want good service. For those uninitiated into the French administrative system, the police station opposite the War Memorial on Ave. Bruat deals with Papeete matters, while the gendarmerie at the head of Ave. Bruat is concerned with the rest of the island. The Olympic Swimming Pool (f.100) is open to the public Tues. to Sat. 0730-1630. Laundromat Pince a Linge (closed Sat.) in the Vaima Center extorts f.600 a load to wash, f.600 to dry. They take more than your clothes to the laundry.

information: The tourist office (open weekdays 0800-1700, Sat. 0800-1600) on the waterfront can answer basic questions, but they have no information on hiking and are none too friendly. The Institute Territorial de la Statistique, 2nd floor, Bloc Donald (behind Voyagence Tahiti, opposite the Vaima Center) sells a quarterly *Statistical Bulletin* (f.300). Researchers should contact the secretary of the Societe des Etudes Oceaniennes, 114 Rue Georges Lagarde. La Boutique Klima behind the cathedral sells old topographical maps, nautical charts, and many interesting books on Polynesia. Newer topographical maps (f.500) of some islands are available from the Section Topographie, 4th floor, Administrative Bldg., Rue du Commandant Destremeau. For the best selection of French navigational charts, visit O.C.I. (Ouverages Cartes et Instruments) in the white military-style building next to the UTA office on the waterfront. There's a public library in the Cultural Center. The biggest bookstore is Hachette Pacifique, 10 Ave. Bruat. The Ping Pong Bookstore on the waterfront nearby specializes in recycled books. There are 2 French morning papers, *La Depeche* and *Les Nouvelles;* the latter has a page of world news in English. The weekly *Tahiti Sun Press* (free), edited by Al Prince, is worth perusing. The best local guidebook is *Tahiti, Circle Island Tour Guide* by Bengt Danielsson.

TRANSPORT

a slow boat to Baltimore: The only regular international passenger service by sea is the monthly Compagnie Generale Maritime freighter from Papeete to Baltimore, Maryland, via the Panama Canal (US$775 OW). The ship carries a total of 2 passengers and it's usually booked 6 months ahead (any good travel agent can do it), but you can sometimes get a cancellation the week before sailing. Ask at the C.G.M. office on Rue du General de Gaulle.

ferries to Moorea: Four ships offer several departures daily to Moorea. Three of them, *Keke III* (f.750), *Maire,* and *Tamarii Moorea II* (both f.600), leave from the waterfront downtown, while the larger, car-carrying *Moorea Ferry* (f.600) leaves from the port at Motu Uta. All depart Papeete around 0900; there are also afternoon sailings listed on

Go native in a Tahitian pareu. Throw one corner over your right shoulder, then pass the other under your left arm and pull tight. Tie the ends and you're dressed.

*Early tourists ride in style in this 1910
photo taken at Punaauia.*

boards at the landing. The *Keke III* is a fast luxury cruiser; the *Maire* and *Tamarii Moorea II* are slower, but you can stroll around on deck and better enjoy the crossing (1.5 hours). The slower boats sometimes offer a free *truck* ride to anywhere on Moorea from the landing at Vaiare (ask), which would be reason enough to choose them. Don't visit Tahiti without making this excellent sidetrip (see "Moorea" below).

ships to the Leeward Islands: Two ships, the *Temehani* and the *Taporo IV*, depart Papeete every Mon. afternoon for Huahine, Raiatea, Tahaa, and Bora Bora. After calls at Huahine (at 0200), Raiatea (at 0600), and Tahaa (at 1200), they reach Bora Bora at 1700 Tuesday. Both depart for Papeete once again very early Wed. morning, call at Raiatea (at 1200) and Huahine (at 1600), reaching Papeete early Thurs. morning (you can stay on board till dawn). The *Temehani* sometimes visits Tahaa on the way up; the *Taporo IV* calls on the way back. The *Taporo IV* also makes a short trip to Huahine and Raiatea only Thurs. at 1900. All these schedules are approximate—ask at the company offices. The *Temehani* has a good covered sleeping area

for deck passengers, and they'll open the hold for you if there's not too much cargo. You won't get much sleep, however, due to noise and commotion during the early morning stops. Fares on the *Taporo IV* to Huahine are f.1100 deck, f.1540 dormitory; to Raiatea f.1300 deck, f.1820 dorm; to Bora Bora f.1500 deck, f.2100 dorm. The *Temehani* charges the same deck, but also has 3-bed cabins which are slightly more than *Taporo IV* dorm rates. Interisland deck fares between Huahine-Raiatea-Tahaa are f.600 each. No meals are included, although *Taporo IV* has a snack bar. Take food with you. Tickets for *Taporo IV* are sold at the Compagnie Francais Maritime in Fare Ute, or at the agency near the interisland wharf across the harbor from downtown Papeete. The Bureau Temehani is also near this wharf. Cabin or dormitory space is recommended—try to reserve it at least a week ahead. Deck passage is usually available right up to departure day (except holidays), but buy your ticket ahead as there can be problems for non-Tahitians trying to pay once the ship is underway. In the Leeward Is. buy a ticket from the agent on the wharf as soon as the boat arrives. If you've got some time to kill before your ship leaves Papeete, have a look around the coconut oil mill beside the wharf.

ships to other islands: The *Tuhaa Pae II* leaves twice a month for the Austral Is.: f.11,000 deck, f.20,000 cabin for the 15-day RT (no meals included). Their office is near the interisland wharf. Several ships head to the Tuamotu Is. (f.2800 to Rangiroa); ask around at the interisland wharf and beside the *Moorea Ferry* landing nearby. The *Taporo II* departs monthly for the Tuamotu and Gambier islands, f.5000 OW deck, f.8750 OW dorm, plus f.1500 daily for compulsory meals. Their office is near Papeete market. The *Taporo III* makes a grand tour of the Marquesas Is. twice a month, and may stop at some of the Tuamotus en route. The RT fare is f.30,000 deck, f.45,000 cabin, or f.12,000 deck and f.17,750 cabin OW. Food is included but it's marginal, so take extras like grapefruit and nuts. Bring your own bowl; also no pillow or towel are supplied in the cabins. The shower is open 3 hours a day. The agent is

Compagnie Francaise Maritime at Fare Ute. A few other ships, such as the *Tamarii Tuamotu II* and the *Aranui,* also sail to the Marquesas. The *Tamarii Tuamotu II* departs monthly, f.5000 OW deck (no cabins), plus f.1500 a day for basic meals. Check at their city office indicated on the map. The *Aranui* has been fixed up for tourists, making it far more expensive. Deck passage for an 18-day, 7-island cruise to the Tuamotus and Marquesas will cost f.118,000 RT; the cheapest cabin is f.210,600 RT, all meals included. Their office is at the interisland wharf adjacent to Bureau Temehani.

le truck: You can go almost anywhere on Tahiti by *le truck,* converted cargo vehicles with long benches and loudspeakers in back. The eastbound *trucks* park on one side of Papeete market, westbound on the other. Fares run f.90 to Punaauia, f.120 to Paea, f.140 to Papara, f.180 to Mataiea or Papeari, f.260 to Teahupoo. There are *trucks* to the airport and the Maeva Beach Hotel at Faaa every few minutes during the day, and sporadic service after dark till 2400. On Sun. *trucks* run only in the very early morning and again in the evening. Note that although a couple of *trucks* go as far as Tautira and Teahupoo on the peninsula, none goes right around the island and you could have difficulty getting a *truck* back to Papeete. To go around the island by *truck,* start early and go clockwise, as there's more traffic along the S coast and it will be easier to find a ride. Hitching back this way is usually no problem. Any *truck* to Mahina will get you started.

rentals: Due to insurance problems, it's not possible to rent a motorcycle or bicycle. Robert (tel. 2-97-20) and Andre (tel. 2-94-04) have the cheapest rental cars, beginning at about f.1000 a day, plus f.23 per km (50 km daily minimum). Public liability insurance is included, but collision waiver is f.400 extra per day. Gas is not included. **taxis:** Don't take a taxi in Papeete unless it has a rate card you can check. Taxi fares are doubled from 2200 to 0600.

scuba diving: Tahiti Mer et Loisirs in the houseboat tied up opposite the post office arranges scuba diving for f.1900 a dive. Diving is on the reef off the Marina Taina, S of the Maeva Beach Hotel. Tahiti Plongee (Box 3506, Papeete; tel. 3-62-51) offers scuba diving several times daily from its base at the Marina Lotus, Punaauia. The charge is f.3000 per dive all-inclusive, or f.13,000 for a 5-dive card. Mr. Henri Pouliquen, director of the center, was one of the first to teach scuba diving to children, some as young as 4 years old. Since 1979 Tahiti Plongee has arranged over 10,000 dives with children, certainly a unique accomplishment. If you only want to rent tanks (f.600 a day, f.900 a weekend), go to Marine Corail at Fare Ute. Favorite scuba locales include a scuttled Pan Am Catalina PBY seaplane near the airport, its upper wing 12 m down; a schooner wreck 10 m down about 45 m from the breakwater at the entrance to the harbor; and the Punaauia reef. Diving conditions are far superior in the Tuamotus, but there aren't any facilities.

The tiare Tahiti (Gardenia taitensis) *is a symbol of the island.*

MOOREA

This enticing, triangular island, only 16 km NW of Tahiti, is actually the surviving S rim of a volcano once 3,000 m high. Moorea is twice as old as Tahiti, and weathering is more advanced. The jagged grandeur of the crescent of peaks facing the 2 northern bays is scenically superb. One curiosity is a hole right through the summit of Mt. Mouaputa, said to have been made by the spear of the demigod Pai, who tossed it across from Tahiti to prevent Mt. Rotui (879 m) from being carried off to Raiatea. In most ways Moorea is quieter than Tahiti, but the area around Paopao is becoming built up and congested. There never was a good beach at Paopao, though the windsurfing in Cook's Bay is the best in

Eastern Polynesia. The finest beaches are at the NW tip of Moorea near Club Med. Tourism is concentrated along the N coast of the island; most of the locals live in the south.

sights: Afareaitu, the administrative center, has a hospital, police station, etc. Hike an hour up the Afareaitu Valley from the old Protestant church (1912) to a high waterfall which cascades down a sheer cliff into a pool. Keep straight on the main track till it becomes a footpath, and you're almost there. Tohivea (1,207 m) towers to one side. There's a good beach down the sideroad through the coconut grove across from the post office near the airport. The Catholic church at Paopao has an in-

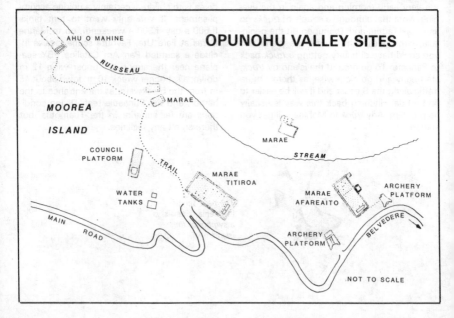

OPUNOHU VALLEY SITES

AHU O MAHINE

RUISSEAU

MOOREA ISLAND

MARAE

MARAE

MARAE TITIROA

COUNCIL PLATFORM

TRAIL

WATER TANKS

MAIN ROAD

STREAM

MARAE AFAREAITO

ARCHERY PLATFORM

ARCHERY PLATFORM

BELVEDERE

NOT TO SCALE

teresting mural (1946) by Peter Heyman. Shrimp are kept in large tanks at the head of Opunohu Bay. The octagonal Protestant church at Papetoai was built on the site of the temple of the war god Oro in 1822. Despite having been rebuilt in the original form in 1887-91, it's known as "the oldest European building still in use in the South Pacific." A paved road winds up the Opunohu Valley to the Belvedere, a viewpoint from which much of northern Moorea is visible. A group of Polynesian temples is near the top. The first one you see is also the largest, Marae Titiroa. Just 50 km NW near the water tanks is a long council platform, and 50 m farther in are 2 smaller *marae* surrounded by towering trees. The most evocative of the group is 4-tiered Marae Ahu O Mahine, some 250 m down a deteriorating trail. Try to find it. If you're keen, you'll see a number of other crumbling structures in the bush across the stream. Continue up the main road about 300 m from Marae Titiroa and look for an access trail to the L leading to some stone archery platforms, where men proved their skill in the old days. Less than 100 m farther up on the L is access to another archery platform and Marae Afareaito. The slabs you see sticking up in the middle of the *marae* were backrests for participants of honor.

hiking: An excellent 3-hour hike along a shaded trail takes you from Vaiare to Paopao. The way is clearly marked by red paint dabbed on tree and rock, but it's easier to follow from the Vaiare side. Take the road inland about 50 m S of the first bridge just S of the Vaiare ferry wharf. At the fork, cross a creek on the R and look for the first red marks. All the locals know the way. When you reach the divide, go a short distance S along the ridge to a super viewpoint over the pineapple plantations behind Paopao. On a clear day the rounded double peak of Orohena, Tahiti's highest, is visible, plus the whole interior of Moorea. If you're fresh off the ferry, no other introduction to the island could be more spectacular. The hike is also worth doing simply to see a good cross section of the vegetation. Don't miss it.

a basalt food pounder, Tahiti

PRACTICALITIES

accommodations and food: If you have a tent the best place to stay on Moorea is the private campground just S of Club Med. It's beautifully set in a coconut grove right on the beach; they charge f.300 pp, (f.1000 deposit), toilets and showers provided. It's possible to snorkel to one of the offshore *motus* from this beach. Across the street from Club Med is a grocery store. Watch for a blue combi van selling chocolate cake and noodle rolls in this vicinity. Club Med has been renovated and expanded, with a capacity for 700 pleasure-seekers. You can arrange to join them upon payment of f.12,000 pp per day (double occupancy) at the Club Med office in the Vaima Center, Papeete. The price includes all meals and a wide range of activities, but no transfers. Good for singles. If you only want to crash Club Med for food, water-skiing, or men/women, remove all watches and jewelry—that's how they identify outsiders. There's a smaller Club Med on Bora Bora. Surfers should know about Chez Nicole (tel. 6-15-66) on the S side of the island opposite Avarapa Pass. Rooms start at f.2500 (double bed) and there are cooking facilities, but bring groceries: the nearest stores are in Maatea (4 km) and Haapiti (7 km). Hotel Pauline (tel.

6-11-26) in Afareaitu village between the 2 stores has rooms with double beds from f.2000. There's a picturesque restaurant and the place would have great atmosphere were it not for the abrupt manner of the proprietress. Make sure you're clear about prices before you order a meal at Pauline's. There are 3 reasonable places to stay on the N coast. Mr. Pierre Cordier (tel. 6-10-35) of the Tiaia Village has 8 bungalows with cooking facilities on the beach near Maharepa. Each bungalow houses up to 3 persons and is f.4000 daily, f.60,000 monthly (4-night minimum stay). There's a store nearby. Chez Mama Loulou (tel. 6-10-71), not far from the Tiaia Village, offers 2 small cottages on the inland side of the road—no cooking, shared bath, f.2400 a day. Ask directions at Boutique Bahia. Finally, Motel Albert (tel. 6-12-76), on the hillside above Paopao overlooking Cook's Bay, includes 15 units at f.3000 s or d, f.4000 t (2-night minimum stay). Each has cooking facilities and there are several stores nearby.

No reservations are accepted. Don't ask Albert for permission to pitch your tent on the grounds—he doesn't care for campers. None of the restaurants on Moorea are worth listing.

transport: For details of the ferry service from Papeete see "Tahiti—Transport" above. Several of them include a *truck* ride to anywhere on Moorea—ask. The cruiser *Keke* does not offer this service; their passengers pay f.100 to Paopao, f.200 to Club Med. Car rental charges are exhorbitant and the 61-km road around Moorea is too far to walk. Arii Rent-A-Car at Vaiare Wharf has scooters for f.2500 half day, f.3500 whole day; cars at f.3800 a day plus f.1200 optional insurance. Other agencies are located at Paopao and opposite Club Med. Sadly, bicycles are hard to find, may be in poor shape, and often have miniature wheels. Ask for them at all the agencies, as they're sometimes kept in a back room out of sight.

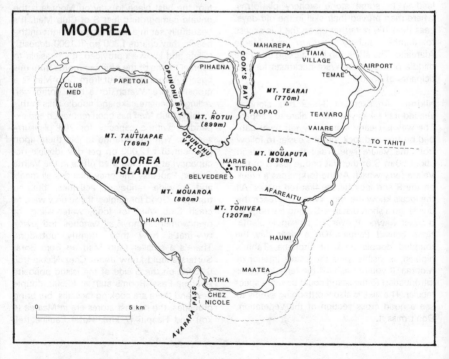

RAIATEA

Raiatea, second largest of the Society Is., was also the ancient religious, cultural, and political center of the group. Tradition holds that the great Polynesian voyages to Hawaii and New Zealand parted from these shores. The Leeward Is., of which Raiatea is today the administrative center, remained independent until 1888; armed resistance to French rule was only overcome in 1897. Today, 80 percent of the population of the Leewards is Protestant. There are no beaches on this big, hulking island, but the W coast S of Tevaitoa is old Polynesia through and through. Uturoa, the commercial and bureaucratic center, is a pleasant, unspoiled town, much like Papeete was long ago. It has many Chinese stores, a colorful market (Wed., Fri., and Sun. mornings), 4 banks (f.250 commission to change travelers cheques), but nowhere to stay. Tourism is looked upon as more of a nuisance than a salvation.

sights: For a view of 4 islands climb Tapioi Hill (294 m), the one with the TV antenna on top behind Uturoa. Take the road beside the Gendarmerie Nationale up past the locked gate and ignore any bad dogs you might encounter: visitors are allowed. A 60-km road runs right around Raiatea. The road down the E coast circles Faaroa Bay, associated with the legends of Polynesian migration. Just beyond Opoa, 35 km from Uturoa, is Marae Taputa-puatea, one of the largest and best preserved of its kind in Polynesia. Its mighty *ahu* is 50 m long, 10 m wide, and over 3 m high. Before it is a rectangular courtyard paved with black volcanic rocks. A small platform in the middle of the *ahu* once bore the image of Oro, the god of war. The high chiefs' backrests still mark the courtyard. Marae Taputapuatea is directly opposite Te Ava Moa Pass, and fires on the *maraes* may once have been a beacon to ancient navigators. The village of Fetuna has an attractive setting and there are 2 Chinese stores. Behind the church at Tevaitoa, on the W side of Raiatea, is Marae Tainuu.

hiking: Legend claims that the ferocious god Oro was born from the molten rage of Mt. Temehani (772 m), the cloud-covered plateau that dominates the N end of the island. Temehani is most easily climbed from Pufau, the second bay S of Apooiti Marina. Note the series of concrete benches by the road as you

*horseplay at Raiatea
as an interisland ship
arrives at Uturoa*

come around the N side of the bay. The jeep track inland is about 200 m S of the bridge. You climb straight up through pine reforestation till you have a clear view of Temehani Rahi and Temehani Ute, divided by a deep gorge. Descend to the R and continue up the track you see on the opposite hillside. It takes about 3 hours from the main road to the Temehani Rahi Plateau. Notice the small pink orchids on the way. *Tiare apetahi,* a sacred white flower which exists nowhere else on Earth and resists transplantation, grows on the slopes around the summit. The fragile blossom represents the 5 fingers of a beautiful Polynesian girl who fell in love with a handsome prince, but couldn't marry him due to her low birth.

accommodations: There are no budget hotels on Raiatea. The American-owned Bali Hai Hotel S of Uturoa is Hilton-priced. Camping in the interior or at villages on the S side of the island should be no problem. In a pinch you could camp at the Centre Nautique ("la piscine") on the waterfront just N of Uturoa, but be prepared for juveniles who will wake you at midnight with their cries—best just to befriend them. If you need a roof over your head, Pension Ariane Brotherson (tel. 6-33-70) near Avera School, 10 km S of Uturoa, is your best bet. The charge is f.4000 s, f.7000 d, but that includes breakfast and dinner, airport transfers, and sightseeing excursions. The Pension Yolande Roopinia (tel. 6-35-28) nearby is more expensive and doesn't offer the trips. Hotel Le Motu opposite the bank in Uturoa is f.6500 d. **food and entertainment:** Restaurant Remy, between Uturoa market and the wharf, has coffee and omelettes in the morning, meals on request. Restaurant "Te Orama" on the main street near the Banque de Tahiti serves unpretentious, filling meals. Restaurant "Au Motu" up the stairway opposite "Te Orama" is more expensive but good. Try the fried fish. Ask about firewalking shows at the exclusive Bali Hotel, just S of Uturoa.

transport: The airport is 3 km NW of Uturoa. Catch the *Temehani* or *Taporo IV* to Bora Bora or Huahine weekly. The *Taporo I,* a small cargo/passenger ship, shuttles regularly be-

tween the Leeward Islands. There are 2 departures a week from Raiatea for Bora Bora (f.600) and Maupiti (f.750), one to Huahine. The *Taporo I* departs Bora Bora 3 times a week for Maupiti (f.850), twice to Raiatea. You can sometimes find a boat to Maupiti from Tahaa. Exact times should be verified locally as they are constantly changing. Finding a boat to Tahaa is usually no problem. The *Rainui* leaves Uturoa for Tahaa weekdays at 1130 and 1600, Sat. at 1000. Several other boats run between Raiatea and Tahaa Tues., Wed., and Fri. (f.300). *Trucks* depart Uturoa for Fetuna (f.150) and Opoa every afternoon but never on Sunday. Mr. Charles Brotherson, the gentleman barber, rents mopeds (f.2500-4000 for 8 hours) out of his shop opposite the Banque de Tahiti. Charles is the most knowledgeable person on Raiatea and he speaks good English.

OTHER ISLANDS

Tahaa: Tahaa (90 sq km), like Raiatea, has few beaches. The administrative center is at Patio on the N coast, but the ship from Papeete ties up at the wharf at Tapuamu. There is a large covered area at the terminal where you could spread a sleeping bag in a pinch. Madame Mama Marae and Simeon Chu rent rooms at Patio for about f.2500 s or d. *Trucks* on the island are few, so you may have to hitch to wherever you want to go. A road cuts across the island from Tiva to Haamene, and farther across to Faaha. Notice the vanilla plantations.

Maupiti: Little Maupiti, 44 km W of Bora Bora, is the least known of the accessible Society Islands. Soaring cliffs and luxuriant vegetation on the 380-m-high main island contrast with magnificent beaches of the *motus* surrounding the lagoon. There is an archaeological site on Motu Pae'ao. It takes only 3 hours to walk right around the island, past crumbling *maraes,* freshwater springs, and a beach along the way. Several of the 794 inhabitants take paying guests at about f.3000 pp, all meals included. In Vai'ea village try Chez Papa Roro, Chez Tinorua Anua, or Chez Tavaearii Augusta. In Farauru it's Chez Teupoohuttua Teha. Pension "Le Motu" (f.4000 pp) is quiet and offers superb food. This may be the closest thing to experiencing the true atmosphere of Polynesia without any of the discomforts. **getting there:** Apart from the *Taporo I* from Raiatea and Bora Bora, Air Polynesie has flights to Maupiti from Raiatea (f.3425 OW) and Bora Bora (f.3080 OW). Like Bora Bora, you'll land on a small *motu* and take a launch to the main island.

BORA BORA

Bora Bora is everyone's idea of a South Pacific island. Dramatic basalt peaks soar 700 m above a gorgeous, multi-colored lagoon. Slopes and valleys blossom with hibiscus. Some of the most perfect beaches you will ever see are here, complete with topless sunbathers. Tiny Motu Tabu is the island depicted on travel brochures, a recent Tahitian stamp, etc. Bora Bora was once an isle of exile where Tahitians sent their outcasts. During WW II the Americans set up a refueling base on the island; you can still see the remains. The departing American soldiers left behind a generation of half-caste war babies. Today, packaged American tourists pour in and a new Hyatt Regency Hotel has popped up on a swampy shore at the far N end of the island opposite the airport. This is the best place for it: isolated from the local population at Vaitape and not congesting the far better beaches at the S end of the island where the more knowledgeable French tourists stay.

SIGHTS

south of Vaitape: The good, level 32-km road around the island makes it natural to see Bora Bora by bicycle. Start from Vaitape's wharf where there's a monument to Alain Gerbault, who sailed his yacht, the *Fire Crest,* around the world from 1923-29. On the N side of Pofai Bay a cluster of anomalous buildings by the road remains from the making of the movie *Hurricane.* Notice an odd assortment of looted artifacts in front of an abandoned A-frame museum at the head of Pofai Bay. The 7-inch American naval gun dragged here from Tereia Point is hard to miss. A total of 8 of these guns remain on Bora Bora: this one and 7 others still in place (locations given below). A track up over the saddle and across the island departs from opposite the forlorn, violated gun. The finest beach on the island stretches E from Hotel Bora Bora to Matira Point. Off the small point at Hotel Bora Bora is some of the best snorkeling in the world, for varied multitudes of colorful tropical fish. There are 2 naval guns on the ridge above the Hotel Matira. The trail behind the hotel leads right to them (10 min.), with good views of the lagoon and neighboring islands on the way.

the east coast: Continue up the E side of Bora Bora past Anau to Vairou Bay. An overgrown footpath crosses the mountains from behind Francois Temanua's house at the head of Vairou Bay to Faanui. Just a little farther along, the *ahus* of 3 *maraes* can be seen by the water. A short distance down a side track off the main road is the best of these, Marae Aehautai, from where there's a stupendous view of Otemanu. Two more American 7-inch guns sit atop Fitiiu Point. To get to them continue E along the shore from Marae Aehautai till the way becomes constricted and you are forced onto a black rocky outcrop. Go back just a little and look for a trail up to the ridge, where you'll find the guns. Once again, the view alone makes the visit worthwhile. Other than the Hyatt Regency, there is little of interest farther N on this side of the island.

north of Vaitape: One American naval gun remains on the hillside above the rectangular water tank at Tereia Point. The housing of a second gun, vandalized in 1982, is nearby. The remains of several American concrete wharfs can be seen along the N shore of Faanui Bay. Marae Fare Opu, just E of a small

boat harbor, is notable for petroglyphs of turtles carved into the stones of the *ahu.* Just E of the coconut husk-fueled electricity generating plant between Faanui and Farepiti wharf is Marae Taiahapa; its long *ahu* is clearly visible from the road. The most important *marae* on Bora Bora was Marae Marotetini on the point near Farepiti wharf. The great stone *ahu,* 50 m long and up to 3 m high, is visible from approaching ships. The last 2 American guns are on the ridge above Club Med, a 10-min. scramble from the main road. At the

one of 8 U.S. naval guns left behind in 1945

end of the ridge there's a good view of Te Ava Nui Pass, which the guns were meant to defend. Maupiti is farther out on the horizon.

hiking: If you're experienced, it's possible to climb Mt. Pahia in a couple of hours. Take the first road inland S of the large Protestant church at Vaitape and go up the depression past a series of mango trees, veering slightly left. Circle the cliffs near the top on the L side, and come up the back of Snoopy's head and along his toes. (These directions will take on meaning if you study Pahia from the end of Vaitape's wharf.) There's no set trail; you must bushwack. Avoid rainy weather when the way will be muddy and slippery. Note that Otemanu has *never* been climbed because clamps pull right out of the vertical, crumbly cliff face.

events: Stone fishing, a local curiosity, can be organized at Motu Ahuna by the chief of Vaitape for a mere US$7000. Eighty outrigger canoes and the whole population participate. The *Fetes de Juillet* are celebrated at Bora Bora with special fervor. There are canoe and bicycle races, javelin throwing, flower cars, singing and dancing competitions which run until 0300 nightly, and a public ball which goes till dawn on the Sat. closest to 14 July. Try to participate in the 10-km foot race to prove that all tourists aren't lazy, but don't take the prizes away from locals. Even if you

win, be sure to give the money back to them for partying. You will make good friends that way and have more fun dancing in the evening. The stands are beautiful because the best decorations win prizes too.

PRACTICALITIES

accommodations: Chez "Aime Mare," a km S of Vaitape pier, offers simple shared rooms at f.700 pp if you stay 3 nights. With good cooking facilities, and bicycles for rent at f.300 per half day, this place is recommended, but often full. A few hundred m down the road from "Aime Mare" is Fredo's (no sign) with a f.800 dorm and f.900 pp doubles. Cooking and bicycles are also available, and Fredo has a few small bungalows (f.4000 d) if you want privacy. At Chez Denis Tetuanui (no sign), near the Mormon church 300 m S of the Hotel Oa Oa, rooms are f.2000 s, f.3000 d, or f.3500 s, f.6000 d, breakfast and dinner included (no cooking facilities). If the rooms are full a bed in the corridor will run f.1000 pp, or they may let you camp in the yard. The Denise Fariua Hostel on the lagoon side between Hotel Oa Oa and Vaitape offers Tahitian-style accommodations with full cooking facilities. Rates are f.1200 pp for the first night, f.900 pp for the second, and f.800 pp for subsequent nights. For something better, consider Hotel Bloody Mary (tel. 6-70-66). There are 5 pleasant cottages, each with a small kitchen and bathroom, on a beach about a km N of Hotel Bora Bora. There's a spectacular view across Pofai Bay to the island's soaring peaks. The charge is f.5500 d, but if you stay a week the price drops to f.3300 daily. Snorkel off the hotel pier. Bloody Mary's Seafood Restaurant across the road is excellent, but watch the cost of wine and drinks. Hotel Bora Bora is only US$250 s for an over-water bungalow and meals. To stay longer, ask for Dick Sarcione. Dick knows all there is to know about Bora Bora and he or his family can help you find a house to rent by the week or month. Hotel Oa Oa provides free mooring and showers for yachties. Note that Bora Bora suffers from serious water shortages, so use it sparingly.

camping: Free camping on public land is prohibited. You may camp by the beach at Matira Tours on Matira Point for f.300 pp, but no showers, electricity, or stores are nearby. The best campground on the island is at Anau on the far side of the island. Look for the CLIMAT DE FRANCE *truck* at the wharf and ask for Chez Steleo—transfers are f.250 pp. There's a toilet and shower block for campers (f.300 pp). A shortcut trail straight across the island begins opposite the campground (follow the power lines). Steleo owns land on beautiful Motu Vaivahia: it shouldn't take much to persuade him to drop you off there for a few idyllic days (take food and water). Ask him about renting an outrigger canoe (*pirogue*), if you know how to swim. Recommended. Bora Bora is overrun by land crabs, funny little creatures which make camping exciting.

food and entertainment: Several well-stocked grocery stores are open Mon. to Sat., 0600-1730 in Vaitape. The only other place is the general store at Anau, half-way round the island. It closes from 1200-1330 and on Sunday. Cold beer is available at a shack across the street, a favorite local watering hole. The assorted snack bars in Vaitape need no introduction, but the restaurants are a little

pricey. The best bar (no sign) in Vaitape is opposite the Banque de Polynesie. Surprisingly, non-guests are welcome to indulge in the nightlife at Club Med, just N of Vaitape. Witness the evening dancing at Hotel Bora Bora for free by grabbing a beachside seat before it starts.

transport: Bora Bora's vast airfield, on a *motu* N of the main island, was built by the Americans during WW II. Until 1961 all international flights to Eastern Polynesia arrived here; passengers were then transfered to Papeete by seaplane. Today, arriving air passengers are transfered to Vaitape wharf by launch (included in the plane ticket). If you're flying to Bora Bora from Papeete go early in the morning and sit on the L side of the aircraft for spectacular views—it's only from the air that Bora Bora is the most beautiful island in the world. The Air Polynesie office is behind the Town Hall (*mairie*) adjoining the wharf. Ships from Raiatea and Papeete tie up at Farepiti wharf, 3 km N of Vaitape. The shipping companies have no representatives on Bora Bora, so for departure times just keep asking. Drivers of the *trucks* are most likely to know. You buy your ticket when the ship arrives. Most of the *trucks* you see around town are strictly for guests of the luxury hotels, although a few will deign to take you to Matira for f.200 OW. The trucks marked CLIMAT DE FRANCE are the most cooperative; the surly drivers of those operated by Hotel Bora Bora won't acknowledge your presence even if you ask them something. Many places at Vaitape rent bicycles (f.600 a day). Bora Rent-a-Car near Chez Aime has scooters from f.3500 a day and mini-mokes from f.5800, but dispense with motorized transport on little Bora Bora. Matira Tours (tel. 6-70-97) offers a round-the-island boat trip (f.5000 pp) departing Matira Point daily at 0900. The price includes a seafood picnic lunch on a *motu,* reefwalking, and snorkeling gear, plus a chance to see giant clams and sharks.

HUAHINE

Huahine is outstanding for its variety of scenery, splendid beaches, archaeological remains, and characterful main town. In many ways this lush, mountainous island has more to offer than even Bora Bora. A narrow channel crossed by a bridge divides Huahine into Huahine Nui and Huihine Iti (Great and Little Huahine, respectively). The land N of Lake Fauna, where the airstrip is located, is an elevated barrier reef, and there are white sandy beaches all along this N side. Huahine is known to cognoscenti as a surfing locale: there are good waves in the passes right off Fare. When the wind's coming out of the E, take the Maeva truck to Tiare Pass near Faie for surfing. The little town of Fare, with a tree-lined boulevard along the quay, is joyfully peaceful after the roar of Papeete. There are 7 other villages here with winding, picturesque roads between them. France finally annexed Huahine in 1897, and English missionaries who had been there 88 years were sent packing. Some of the greatest leaders of the struggle for the independence of Polynesia have come from this idyllic spot.

SIGHTS

Huahine Nui: To see a beautiful *mape* (chestnut) forest in the valley behind Fare, walk inland on the road which begins beside the building marked OLIVETA near the post office. The archaeological area at Maeva, at the end of Lake Fauna 6 km E of Fare, is one of the 5 most important in Oceania (the other 4 are on Easter I., Tongatapu, Ponape, and Kosrae). Numerous *maraes* are strewn along the lakeshore and in the nearby hills; each district chief on Huahine Nui had his own. The great numbers of small fish in the lake were able to support a large chiefly and priestly class. Under the bridge at the E end of the village ancient stone fish traps can be seen. A footpath leads up through foothills planted in vanilla, passing several restored *maraes* and superb panoramic viewpoints. Marae Mata'irea Rahi was the most sacred place on Huahine, dedicated to Tane, the god of light. The backrests of Huahine's 8 principal chiefs are still visible on the southernmost com-

Marae Fare Miro at Huahine's Maeva

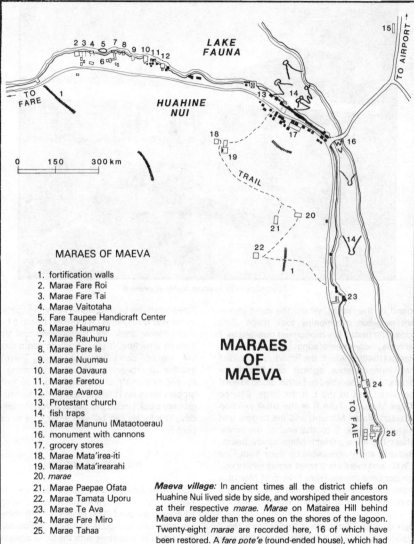

LAKE
FAUNA

HUAHINE
NUI

2 3 4 5 7 8 9 10 11 12
6

TO
FARE

1

0   150   300 km

15

TO AIRPORT

13   14

18
19

TRAIL

17

16

20

21

14

22

1

23

**MARAES
OF
MAEVA**

MARAES OF MAEVA

1. fortification walls
2. Marae Fare Roi
3. Marae Fare Tai
4. Marae Vaitotaha
5. Fare Taupee Handicraft Center
6. Marae Haumaru
7. Marae Rauhuru
8. Marae Fare Ie
9. Marae Nuumau
10. Marae Oavaura
11. Marae Faretou
12. Marae Avaroa
13. Protestant church
14. fish traps
15. Marae Manunu (Mataotoerau)
16. monument with cannons
17. grocery stores
18. Marae Mata'irea-iti
19. Marae Mata'irearahi
20. *marae*
21. Marae Paepae Ofata
22. Marae Tamata Uporu
23. Marae Te Ava
24. Marae Fare Miro
25. Marae Tahaa

24

TO
FAIE

25

Maeva village: In ancient times all the district chiefs on Huahine Nui lived side by side, and worshiped their ancestors at their respective *marae*. Marae on Matairea Hill behind Maeva are older than the ones on the shores of the lagoon. Twenty-eight *marae* are recorded here, 16 of which have been restored. A *fare pote'e* (round-ended house), which had been used as a meeting house for over 100 years, was finally judged beyond repair in 1972. A replica of this house — in size and the use of local materials — was built in 1974. The fish traps in the lagoon, recently repaired, are still being used. Fish enter the stone traps with the incoming and outgoing tides.

This bridge links Huahine Nui to Huahine Iti.

pound of the *marae,* where the most important religious ceremonies took place. Just across the bridge is a monument guarded by 7 cannons, commemorating the Battle of Maeva (1846) in which the islanders defended their independence against the French invaders. A few hundred m farther along toward the ocean and to the L is the large, 2-tiered Marae Manunu. Turn R at the small junction between Marae Manunu and the bridge, and follow the track S to the end of the *motu,* where there's a perfect white sandy beach. Maeva is easily accessible by *truck* from Fare (f.100), and there are 2 small stores where you can get cold drinks. From Faie, S of Maeva, a steep track crosses the mountain, making a complete circuit of Huahine Nui possible.

Huahine Iti: Although a bridge joins the 2 islands, Huahine Iti is far less accessible than Huahine Nui. *Trucks* to Parea (f.250) run only once a day, so you'll have to stay the night unless you rented a bicycle or scooter. Pension "Meme" in Parea offers rooms with shared bath at f.4000 with 3 meals. An exclusive American resort has been erected on

Parea's pristine beach. Marae Anini, dedicated to the war god Oro, is on a golden beach a km from Parea; look for petroglyphs on the 2-tiered structure. If you decide to camp near the *marae,* don't leave a mess. There's another nice beach with better swimming a couple of km W of Marae Anini. The only grocery store on Huahine Iti is at Haapu, but a grocery truck circles the island several times a day. The locals can tell you what time to expect it.

PRACTICALITIES

accommodations: There are several inexpensive hotels in Fare, none outstanding. Cheapest are the f.2000 rooms (s or d) above the post office. Inquire at Chez Ah Foussan, the large Chinese store with the Coke signs on the waterfront. Madame Marama Vaiho, opposite the Total service station "Fare Mati," offers similar rooms, but they're often full. Just up the waterfront is the gloomy, overpriced Hotel Lovina (f.2000 s, f.3000 d). There's no cooking and their meals are mediocre. The big 3-story Hotel Huahine at the end of the waterfront is not bad at f.1700 s, f.2500 d, but they have water problems. Don't order any meals here as the food is lousy and far too expensive. French-operated Pension "Enite" nearby insists you take all your meals there for f.4600 pp (2-day minimum stay). Given the lackluster competition, it might just be the best deal around. If all this sounds forbidding, camp free in the coconut plantation on the beach 300 m N of town near the Bali Hai Hotel. Find public showers on the Fare waterfront. Take care with your gear as there have been thefts from campers and sunbathers along the beach at Fare. The Hotel Bellevue (tel. 6-82-76), 6 km S of Fare, offers rooms in the main building at f.3000 s, f.3500 d, bungalows twice that. There's an expensive restaurant with a view of Maroe Bay. Considering the high price, isolation, and absence of a beach, the Bellevue has little going for it. Finally, if you're a multimillionaire, the Bali Hai will not disappoint you.

food and entertainment: All the restaurants in Fare are expensive enough to induce indigestion. The only reasonable places to get something to eat are the food trucks, which congregate at the wharf when a ship is due in. One truck is there every afternoon making *crepes breton.* Fortunately, there are numerous Chinese stores selling groceries and cold beer. What you would pay for the very cheapest item on the menu at the "snack bar" will get you the makings of the most exquisite sandwiches. Don't miss the half-price drinks during happy hour 1730-1900 Sun. at the Bali Hai Hotel (no shorts allowed). Tuesday at 2030 there's Polynesian dancing at the Bali Hai: see it all for the price of a Perrier.

transport: The airport is 4 km from Fare, f.300 by minibus. The Papeete ships tie up to

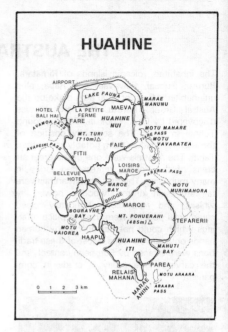

the wharf in the middle of town. Transportation on Huahine is not good. You'll find *trucks* to anywhere on Huahine when a ship arrives; otherwise they're irregular. Dede, beside the Town Hall (*mairie*), rents scooters at f.1500 half day, f.2500 whole day (0730-1800). But the fuel tanks are so small you'll run out of gas on the other side of the island and the only service station is in Fare. Kake Rent-A-Car beside the entrance to the Bali Hai Hotel also has scooters and cars (f.5000). Rent a bicycle at the Huahine Hotel (f.1000). Those nice shiny bicycles you see tourists riding around on are for Hotel Bali Hai guests only. Le Petite Ferme, between Fare and the airport, offers horseback riding.

THE AUSTRAL ISLANDS

The inhabited volcanic islands of Rimatara, Rurutu, Tubuai, Raivavae, and Rapa, plus uninhabited Maria (or Hull) atoll make up the Austral Group. Rurutu, the largest, was discovered by Capt. Cook in 1769; he found Tubuai in 1777. The southerly position of these islands makes them notably cooler than Tahiti. The Australs were one of the great art areas of the Pacific, represented today in many museums. The best-known artifacts are tall sharkskin drums, wooden bowls, fly whisks, and *tapa* cloth. Intricately-incised ceremonial paddles were used to place offerings which could not be touched by human hands onto sacred altars. Most of these traditions were effaced by European contact, and the carving done today is crude in comparison.

the famous tiki *from Raivavae, now at Tahiti's Gauguin Museum*

Raivavae: This appealing, 7-km-long island rises to 437 m at Mt. Hiro. A barrier reef surrounds Raivavae, and there are small coral *motus* off the E end of the island. Ships enter the lagoon through a pass on the N side and anchor off Rairua village where there is a stone pier. The tropical vegetation is rich: rosewood and sandalwood are used to make perfumes for local use. Thor Heyerdahl explored the ancient temples and terraces of Raivavae in 1956. There were once many oversized stone statues on the island, but most have been removed. One may be seen at the Gauguin Museum on Tahiti.

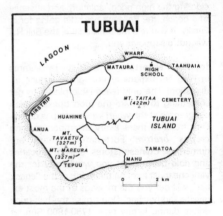

Tubuai: High hills on the E and W sides of Tubuai are joined by low land in the middle; when seen from the sea, Tubuai looks like 2 islands. In 1789 the *Bounty* mutineers attempted to establish a settlement at Taahuaia on Tubuai, but left after only 2 months following a misunderstanding and battle with the islanders. Oranges and European vegetables grow well on Tubuai, and the islanders weave fine hats. There's an airstrip with service from Tahiti. Ships enter the lagoon through a passage in the barrier reef on the NW side of the island and proceed to the wharf at Mataura, the administrative center. Several people rent rooms to visitors at about f.2000 pp, meals extra. At Mataura, try Chez Taro Tanepau or Chez Caroline Chung Thien. The Ermitage Sainte Helene (Madame Tehinarii Ilari) at Mahu is quieter.

Rururu: This island, 572 km S of Tahiti, is shaped like a miniature African continent. Excavations at Vitaria village on the NW coast uncovered 60 round-ended houses arrayed in parallel rows, with 14 *marae* scattered among them. Rurutuans still practice the ancient art of stone lifting. Men get 3 tries to hoist a 130-kg boulder up onto their shoulder, while women attempt a 60-kg stone. The people of Rurutu weave fine hats and mats. Madame Atai Aapae at Moerai rents rooms at f.1000 pp. There's an airstrip on Rurutu with regular service from Tahiti.

Rapa: Rapa, the southernmost point in Eastern Polynesia, is one of the most isolated and spectacular islands in the Pacific. It's sometimes called Rapa Iti (Little Rapa) to distinguish it from Rapa Nui (Easter Island). Rapa's crater harbor, the western portion of a drowned volcano, is magnificent. It is surrounded by soaring peaks reaching 650 m; the absence of reefs lets the sea cut into the island's outer coasts. The climate is foggy and temperate. The E slopes of the mountains are bare, while large fern forests are found on the west. A timeworn Polynesian fort with ter-

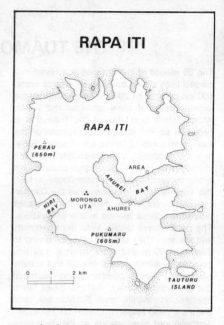

races is situated on the crest of a ridge at Morongo Uta, commanding a wide outlook over the steep rugged hills. Rapa was discovered in 1791 by George Vancouver. The present population of about 200 lives at Area and Ahurei villages on the N and S sides of Rapa's great open bay.

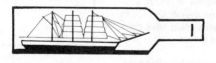

THE TUAMOTU ISLANDS

The 69 islands of the Tuamotus, arrayed in 2 parallel lines strung out over an area of ocean 600 km wide and 1,200 km long, comprise the largest group of coral atolls in the world. Although the land area of the Tuamotus is only 726 sq km, the interior lagoons of the atolls total some 12,000 sq km of water. Forty-one are inhabited. Variable currents, sudden storms, and poor charts make cruising this group by yacht extremely hazardous — in fact, the Tuamotus are also known as the Danger-ous Archipelago. A series of hurricanes devastated these islands in the early 1980s. The people have always lived from coconuts and the sea. They attained fame by diving to depths of 30 m and more wearing only tiny goggles to collect pearl shells but this activity has largely ceased: overharvesting has made the shells rare. Today, cultured pearl farms operate on Manihi and S. Marutea, and there's a pearl research station on Takapoto. The cultured black pearls of the Tuamotus and Gambiers are world famous. Tourism is concentrated on Rangiroa and Manihi.

history: On 2 June 1722, a landing was made on Makatea by Roggeveen's men. To clear the beach beforehand, the crew opened fire on a crowd of islanders. The survivors pretended to be pacified with gifts, but the next day the explorers were lured into an am-bush by women and stoned, leaving 10 Dutchmen dead and many wounded. Nearly 225 years later, a group of Scandinavian adventurers under the leadership of Thor Heyerdahl landed on Raroia in 1947, after drifting from S. America on the raft *Kon Tiki* to prove that Peruvian Indians could have done the same thing centuries before.

Rangiroa: Seventy-seven-km-long Rangiroa, Tuamotus' largest atoll, offers excellent swim-ming and snorkeling. Its great lagoon is 24 km across, and the strong tidal currents (*opape*) through Avatoru and Tiputa passes generate flows of 3-6 knots. It's exciting to shoot the passes on an incoming tide wearing a mask and snorkel, and the hotels offer this activity (f.750) using a small motorboat. The fishlife is fantastic and sharks may be seen, but they're *usually* harmless black-tip reef sharks. Air Polynesie flies Tahiti-Rangiroa daily except Tues. (f.11,460 OW). The airstrip is about 5 km from Avatoru village. There are also ships from Papeete (f.2800 OW). Several people at Avatoro rent rooms with all meals: Chez Jean and Temarama Ami (f.2500 pp); Chez Nanua and Marie Tamaehu (f.2500 pp); Chez Tahurai Bennett (f.3000 pp); Chez Teina and Marie Richmond (f.4000 pp). You could also camp beside the Kia Ora Hotel. In Tiputa, the other village, is Chez Josephine Mauri (f.3000 pp).

others: At Manihi stay at Chez Rei Estall (f.3000 pp) or Chez Marguerite Fareea (f.3500 pp); both include all meals. Makatea is an uplifted atoll 8 km long and 110 m high. The phosphate mine there was abandoned in 1966. The lagoon at Niau is enclosed by an un-broken circle of land. There was once a leper colony on Reao, now closed.

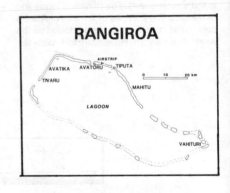

THE NUCLEAR TEST ZONE

French President de Gaulle decided in 1963 to use Moruroa and Fangataufa atolls for nuclear testing when the previous test sites in Algeria were lost to Algerian independence. More than 100 nuclear blasts have been made from 1966 to the present and the tests continue at the rate of 7-10 a year. France has not limited itself to testing atomic and hydrogen devices: the neutron bomb has also been exploded at Moruroa. Up to 1974, 41 bombs were tested in the atmosphere, but worldwide protests forced the French to switch to underground tests. On 23 June 1973, the World Court urged France to discontinue nuclear tests which would drop radioactive material on surrounding territories. When France refused to recognize the Court's jurisdiction in the matter, New Zealand Prime Minister Norman Kirk ordered the N.Z. frigate *Otago* to enter the danger zone off Moruroa. On 23 July Peru broke off diplomatic relations with France. On 15 Aug. French commandos boarded the protest vessels *Fri* and *Greenpeace III* and brutally attacked the crews. The forward base at Hao allows the French to fly nuclear materials directly into the area without passing through Faaa airport. Evidence of the testing is kept well away from the eyes of tourists on Tahiti—you'll find no mention of these tests in any of the official tourist brochures. The Polynesian name "Moruroa" means "place of the great secret."

the land: Underground testing is now carried out in Moruroa's basalt core. So many tests have taken place that Moruroa is now as punctured as a Swiss cheese and sinks 2 cm after every test, or a total of 1.5 m since 1975. The atoll has become so fractured that there are now 4 major cracks in the 60-km coral rim of the atoll. There's also a severely contaminated area to which access is forbidden. In 1981 the French switched to underwater testing in the lagoon, to be closer to the middle of the island's core. On 25 July 1979, a nuclear device became stuck 800 m down a 1,000-m shaft. When the scientists were unable to move the device, they exploded it where it was, causing a massive chunk of the atoll to collapse outwards. This generated a huge tidal wave which hit Moruroa 3 hours later, overturning cars and injuring 7 people. After the blast, a crack 40 cm wide and 2 km long appeared on the surface of the island. As a precaution, the French have now erected

towers every 700 m right around the atoll as a refuge for their employees stationed on Moruroa. For an hour before and after each test all personnel must wait in the towers. The reef at Moruroa has become impregnated with plutonium, the most deadly substance known to man, with a radioactive half-life of 24,000 years. The long half-life allows ample time for the contamination to spread throughout the Pacific. Nearby Fangataufa atoll is now being prepared as an alternative test site once Moruroa has to be abandoned.

accidents: On 6 July 1979, there was an explosion and fire in a laboratory bunker on the reef at Moruroa. Two were killed and 4 others returned to France for treatment. For 2 weeks after the incident, workers in protective suits tried to clean up the area contaminated with plutonium by the explosion. Up until 1981 wastes and contaminated debris were carelessly stored in plastic bags on the N side of Moruroa. On 11 March 1981, a violent storm tore away the asphalt covering the material

One of the 23 towers on Moruroa where workers involved in the testing program seek refuge from hurricanes and tidal waves.

and washed large quantities of nuclear waste into the lagoon and surrounding sea. That Aug., a second storm spread more nuclear wastes from the same dump Enough radioactive debris to fill 200,000 44-gallon drums is now lying on the atoll. Although the French stopped publishing comprehensive public health statistics for the islands in 1966, some 80 people suffered from ciguatera (fish poisoning) in the nearby Gambier Islands in 1981, out of a population of about 500. The official rate in Eastern Polynesia is 57 cases per 10,000 persons. The only explanation is a disturbance of the coral reefs by nuclear testing. A 1980 report prepared for the U.N. by the International Commission on Radiological Protection predicts that over 15,000 people in the Southern Hemisphere will eventually die as a result of radiation doses received from French, American, and British nuclear tests in the Pacific since 1946.

the issue: The French have maintained that their tests are safe, that every precaution has been taken, and that allegations such as those repeated above are lies. In 1983 a delegation

of scientists from Australia, New Zealand, and Papua New Guinea visited Moruroa for 4 days. Significantly, they were not permitted to take samples from the northern or western areas of the atoll, nor of lagoon sediments. The scientists reported that "if fracturing of the volcanics accompanied a test and allowed a vertical release of radioactivity to the limestones, specific contaminants would, in this worst case, enter the biosphere within five years." The radioactivity at Moruroa will remain for hundreds, perhaps thousands of years. The unknown future consequences of the program are the most frightening part of it. Certainly, the underground tests could be carried out much more effectively, safely, and cheaply in France itself. The claim that the tests are "safe" is disproved by the very choice of their test site, on the opposite side of the globe from France: yes, safe for natives, but politically untenable in Europe. As Albert Schweitzer put it: "Those who claim these tests are harmless are liars." With each successive blast the world moves closer to an irreversible nuclear catastrophe. It is an affront to the dignity of people everywhere.

THE MARQUESAS

THE MARQUESAS

The Marquesas Islands are the farthest N of the high islands of the South Pacific, on the same latitude as Honiara. These wild, rugged islands feature steep cliffs and valleys leading up to high central ridges, which section the islands off into a cartwheel of segments, creating major transportation difficulties. Ocean swells reach the shores, creating rough anchorages for yachties, but good conditions for surfers. The absence of protective reefs offshore has inhibited the creation of coastal plains, and most of the people live in the narrow, fertile river valleys. The remainder of the islands is empty. Of the 10 islands forming a line 300 km long, only 6 are inhabited: Nuku Hiva, Ua Pou, Ua Huka, Hiva Oa, Tahauta, and Fatu Hiva. Much of the original vegetation has been devastated by introduced domestic animals. There are many wild horses on the islands. Although known to the Polynesians as Te Fenua Enata (The Land of Men), depopulation during the 19th and 20th centuries has left many of the valleys empty. Since then, the Marquesas have been left behind by their remoteness.

pre-European society: The Marquesans lived in houses built on high platforms (*paepae*) scattered through the valleys. Each valley had a center (*tohua*) from which the chiefs exercised authority. Then as now, the valleys were isolated from one another by high ridges and turbulent seas, yet warfare was vicious with cannibalism an important incentive. An able warrior could attain great power. Archaeologists are still able to trace stone temples (*me'ae*), agricultural terraces, and earthen fortifications (*akua*) half hidden in the jungle, evocative reminders of a vanished civilization. The Marquesans' artistic style was one of the most powerful and refined in the Pacific. The ironwood war club (see illustration) was their most distinctive symbol, but there were also finely carved wooden bowls, fan handles, and *tikis* of stone and wood, both miniature and massive. The carvings are noted for the faces: the mouth with lips parted, and bespectacled eyes. The women wore carved ivory ear plugs. Men's entire bodies were covered by bold and striking tattoos, a practice banned by the French in 1884. Stilts were used by boys for stilt racing and mock fighting. There was a strong cult of the dead, and the mummies and skulls of ancestors were carefully preserved. The civil strife which eventually combined with introduced diseases to destroy the Marquesans may long have forced small groups to depart in search of new homes. Both Hawaii and Easter I. were colonized from here.

European contact: The existence of these islands was long concealed from the world by the Spanish, to prevent the English from set-

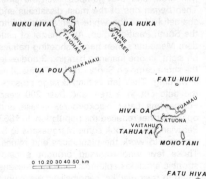

HATUTU
EIAO

MARQUESAS ISLANDS

NUKU HIVA
TAIPIVAI
TAIOHAE

UA HUKA
HANE
VAIPAEE

UA POU
HAKAHAU

FATU HUKU

HIVA OA
PUAMAU
ATUONA
VAITAHU
TAHUATA
MOHOTANI

0 10 20 30 40 50 km

FATU HIVA
HANAVAVE
OMOA

The Marquesans preserved the skulls of their ancestors.

tling there to "do much mischief in the (Pacific) area." The Marquesas were discovered by Mendana on 21 July 1595 during his second voyage from Peru. He named them Las Marquesas de Mendoza after his benefactor, the Spanish viceroy. The islands at first seemed uninhabited, but as the *San Jeronimo* sailed nearer the S coast of one, scores of outriggers appeared, paddled by about 400 robust, light-skinned natives. Their hair was long and loose, and they were naked and tattooed in blue patterns. The natives boarded the ship, but when they became overly curious and bold, Mendana ordered a gun fired, and they jumped over the side. Then began one of the most disastrous and shameful of all the white man's entries into the South Pacific region. As a matter of caution, Mendana's men began shooting natives on sight, in one instance hanging 3 bodies in the shore camp on Santa Cristina (Tahuata) as a warning. They left behind 3 large crosses, the date cut in a tree, and over 200 dead Polynesians. Later, blackbirders, disease, and opium further reduced the population. In 1863 Peruvian slavers took some Marquesans to S. America to work the plantations and mines. Those few who returned brought a catastrophic smallpox epidemic. The Marquesans clung to their warlike, cannibalistic ways until 95 percent of their number had died—the remainder adopted Catholicism. From 50,000 at

the beginning of the 19th C., the population fell to about 20,000 by 1842 when the French annexed the group, and to a devastated 2,000 by 1926. Today there are some 6,548 Marquesans on the islands.

transport: To visit the Marquesas requires either a lot of time or money. Air Polynesie flies from Tahiti to Nuku Hiva weekly (US$275 OW, 5 hours). There are also occasional flights to Nuku Hiva from Napuka and Rangiroa in the Tuamotus (US$225 OW). Interisland flights between Nuku Hiva, Ua Huka, Hiva Oa, and Ua Pou operate several times a week. All flights are heavily booked, and tourists must make way for traveling administrators and local residents. Tahuata and Fatu Hiva are without air service. For details of the supply ships from Papeete see "Tahiti—Transport."

NUKU HIVA

sights: Nuku Hiva, the largest and most populous of the Marquesas, culminates in Mt. Tekao (1,183 m). Herman Melville's *Typee,* written after a 1-month stay here in 1846, is still the classic narrative of Marquesan life during the 19th century. See the fine woodcarvings in the new Catholic cathedral at Taiohae, the main town; many stone and woodcarvers still live on Nuku Hiva. Climb up to Muake (864 m) for a good view of Taiohae Bay. Lifts are possible to the Toovii Plateau with market gardeners headed for the agricultural station there. About a dozen families live in Taipivai and Hatiheu, NE of Taiohae. The huge *tohua* of Vahangeku'a (Taipivai) is a whopping 170 by 25 meters. Great stone *tikis* watch over the *me'ae* of Paeke, also near Taipivai. At Hakaui, W of Taiohae, a river rushes down a fantastic, steep-sided valley, with a fantastic 350-m waterfall dropping from the plateau at the inland end, 4 km from the coast.

Taiohae: In 1813 Capt. David Porter of the American raider *Essex* annexed Nuku Hiva for the United States, though the act was never ratified. Porter built a fort near the present site of Taiohae, which he named Madisonville for the U.S. president of his day. Nothing remains of this or a fort erected by the French in 1842. Sandalwood traders followed Porter, then whalers. Today Taiohae is the administrative center of the group. The deep harbor offers excellent anchorage and cruising yachts are often seen here, although they can also clear Customs at Atuona. Yachties who figure they'll need fuel when they get to the Marquesas should write a letter to Magasin Maurice, Taiohae, and ask him to order an extra drum or 2 from Papeete. There's a Banque Indosuez branch at Taiohae. Nukuataha Airport (NHV) is at the NW corner of Nuku Hiva. To reach Taiohae (60 km), you take a bus from the terminal to Haahopu Bay (f.250, 15 min.), then a launch (f.700, 1.5 hours) to Taiohae.

accommodations and food: The Keikakanui Inn at Taiohae, run by American yachties Rose and Frank Corser, offers screened rooms at f.2500 s, f.4000 d, with continental breakfast. Meals in the dining room are f.1500 each. A bungalow at Chez "Becfin" (Marcel Bonnefin) is f.1600 pp, breakfast in-

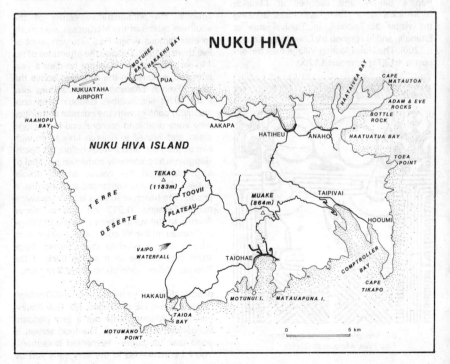

NUKU HIVA

MOTUHEE BAY · HAKAEHU BAY · MOTUNEE BAY · HAATAIVEA BAY · CAPE MATAUTOA · ADAM & EVE ROCKS · BOTTLE ROCK · HAATUATUA BAY · TOEA POINT · COMPTROLLER BAY · CAPE TIKAPO · HOOUMI · TAIPIVAI · ANAHO · HATIHEU · AAKAPA · PUA · NUKUATAHA AIRPORT · HAAHOPU BAY · **NUKU HIVA ISLAND** · TEKAO △ (1183m) · TERRE DESERTE · TOOVII PLATEAU · MUAKE (864m) · VAIPO WATERFALL · TAIOHAE · HAKAUI · MOTUNUI I. · MATAUAPUNA I. · TAIOA BAY · MOTUMANO POINT

0   5 km

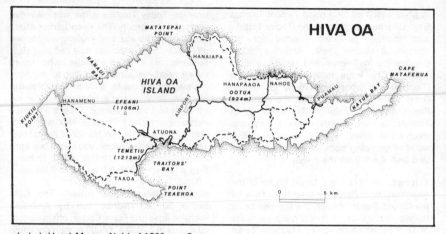

HIVA OA

cluded. Hotel Moana Nui is f.1300 pp. Or try Chez Fetu Peterano, f.1600 pp. There's also a room at Ika's Restaurant. Get bread from Ropa's Bakery and supplies at Maurice McKitrick's store. Take care about drinking the water at Taiohae. In Taipivai stay at Emma's, and in Hatiheu try Chez Matu Katupa (f.1200). The Hotel Moetai Village near the airport is f.1300 pp, meals f.1200.

a contemporary tapa *design from Fatu Hiva, Marquesas Islands*

HIVA OA

Atuona, the administrative center of the southern cluster of the Marquesas, was made forever famous when Paul Gauguin went to live there in 1902. Despite the attentions of his 14-year-old mistress, Vaeoho, he died a year later and is buried in the cemetery above the town. French *chanson* singer Jacques Brel (died 1978) lies nearby. Gauguin was constantly in conflict with the colonial authorities who were unable to comprehend his strange ideas, and wished to have as little to do with him as possible. Just a week before his death, Gauguin was summarily convicted of "libel of a *gendarme* in the course of his official duties," fined, and sentenced to 3 months in prison. The beach at Atuona is poor for swimming. Temetiu (1,213 m) towers above Atuona to the west. There's a second village at Puamau on the NE coast, about 30 km from Atuona over a winding road. Several huge stone *tikis* can be seen at the back of the Puamau Valley—one stands over 2 m high.

practicalities: The airstrip is on a 400-m-high plateau 12 km NE at Atuona. Mr. Guy Rauzy, mayor of Atuona, rents out a few pleasant bungalows at f.1100 pp. The food served is good (ask for *popoi*—fermented breadfruit). You'll be awakened in the very early AM by noisy roosters, dogs, people. In Puamau stay at Chez Bernard Teitaa (f.2500 pp including all meals).

OTHER ISLANDS

Fatu Hiva: Thor Heyerdahl spent most of 1936 on this southernmost island; a book of the same name describes his experiences. Fatu Hiva is far wetter than the northern islands. Hanavave's Bay of Virgins offers one of the most fantastic scenic spectacles in all of Polynesia. *Tapa* cloth is still made here. Many local families take paying guests at about f.2000 pp including all meals. In Omoa ask for Joseph Tetuanui, Kehu Kamia, Tehau Gilmore, or Francois Peters; in Hanavave try Veronique Kamia or Yvonne Tevenino.

Ua Huka: Archaeological excavations dated a coastal site on Ua Huka as one of the oldest in Eastern Polynesia, and it was probably a major dispersal point. You can visit *tikis* in the valley of Hane. The airstrip is on a hilltop between Hane and Vaipaee, closer to the latter. Ships tie up to a wharf at Vaipaee. There's a small museum of local artifacts in Vaipaee. Stay with Joseph Lichtle, Miriama Fournier, or Laura Raioha in Vaipaee. Meals are available. Joseph is reputedly the best cook in the Marquesas and his son, Leon, mayor of Ua Huka, is extremely helpful. Woodcarvers are active on the island.

Ua Pou: Several jagged volcanic plugs loom behind Hakahau, the main village on the N coast. There's a track right around the island. In Hakahau stay at Chez Rosalie, Chez Yvonne and Jules Hituputoka, or Chez Jules Aitotaa, all about f.1500 pp. Ask about horses for rent.

Eiao: Uninhabited Eiao and Hatutu islands, 85 km NW of Nuku Hiva, are mysteries of the Marquesas. Eiao is a large island, 10 km long and 576 m high, with landings on the NW and W sides. Wild cattle forage across Eiao, ravaging the vegetation, and suffering from droughts.

An ironwood Marquesas war club (u'u), *once carried as a mark of authority or rank. The object has an arresting surreal presence, forming a face with eyes and a nose which are other faces.*

THE GAMBIER ISLANDS

The whole archipelago of Little Gambier, 1700 km SE of Tahiti, appears as a solid mass rising from the sea, contrasting sharply with the low coral atolls of the Tuamotus. The cluster is enclosed on 3 sides by a gigantic semicircular barrier reef 65 km in circumference, with 4 inhabited islands and numerous islets in the lagoon. Mangareva, the main island and largest, means "floating mountain," named by the Polynesians who found and peopled it. The tomb of the last king of Mangareva, Gregorio Maputeoa (died 1868), is on a platform overlooking Rikitea, the main port, where you can stay at Chez Francois Labbeyi

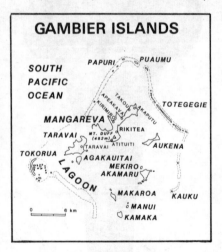

(f.1000 pp). Mr. Jean Anania offers speedboat charters and fishing trips. Black pearls are cultured at a farm at Takou. The airstrip is on Totegegie, 8 km NE of Rikitea. Small groups of people also live on Taravai and Kamaka. Makaroa is a barren, rugged 136-m-high island in the Gambier lagoon S of Mangareva.

history: Mangareva was possibly the jumping-off place for early Polynesians who, on their voyages of discovery, sailed over 1,600 km farther SE to Easter Island. Its European discoverer, Capt. James Wilson of the London Missionary Society's ship *Duff,* gave Mangareva's twin wedge-shaped peaks their name in 1797. Once a center of trade and Catholic missionary activity for the whole Eastern Pacific, Mangareva was the area of operations for a fanatical Belgian priest, Pere Laval, who, with his own hands, toppled the dreaded stone effigy of the god Tu on the island's sacred *marae* in 1836. He single-handedly imposed a ruthless and inflexible moral code on the islanders, recruiting them as virtual slaves to build his church and convents, with the result that he utterly destroyed this once vigorous native culture, and practically wiped out its people. You can still see his church standing to this day, the twin towers of white coral rock and the interior shining with mother-of-pearl—a monument to horror and yet another lost culture. This story inspired one of Michener's tales in his book *Return to Paradise.*

above, clockwise: a Samoan at Pago Pago, American Samoa (Paul Bohler); Tongan wedding party, Tongatapu, Kingdom of Tonga (Robert Kennington); coconut crabs, Suwarrow, Cook Is. (Roland E. Hopkins); removing coconut meat, Kingdom of Tonga (Phil Esmonde); girl at Atiu, Cook Is. (D. Stanley)

above, clockwise: making a *tuvaevae* quilt, Atiu, Cook Is. (D. Stanley); collecting toddy, Nukunonu, Tokelau (Robert Kennington); a Samoan *fale* (Traugott Goll); a pandanus hat, Mauke, Cook Is. (D. Stanley); church window, Palmerston, Cook Is. (Roland E. Hopkins)

PITCAIRN ISLANDS

Legendary Pitcairn Island, hideout of the mutinous crew of H.M.S. *Bounty,* is still the remotest populated place in the Pacific today. It's one of the ironies of history that Pitcairn, born out of treason to the British crown, was the first island in the Pacific to become a British colony (1838), and the last and only remnant of that empire to survive today.

the land: Pitcairn, more than 2,000 km SE of Tahiti, sits alone between Callao (Peru) and New Zealand. Its nearest inhabited neighbor is Mangareva, a small island in Eastern Polynesia 500 km to the northwest. Easter Island lies 1,900 km to the east. A high volcanic island, Pitcairn reaches 335 m, and is bounded by rocks and high cliffs on all sides. There is no coral reef, and the breakers roll right in to shore. The island is only 5 sq km, yet the interior depression contains a number of fertile plateaus, well suited for human habitation.

HISTORY

the lost civilization: Although Pitcairn was uninhabited when the 9 *Bounty* mutineers arrived in 1790, the remains of a vanished civilization were clearly evident. The sailors found 4 platforms with large stone statues similar to those on Easter I. on a hilltop overlooking Bounty Bay. Being good Christians, the Pitcairners destroyed these platforms and threw the images into the sea. Unfortunately, almost nothing remains of them today. The only surviving piece of sculpture resides at the Otago Museum (Dunedin, N.Z.). Sporadic visits by European archaeologists have uncovered traces of ancient burials and stone axes, and 22 petroglyphs have been noted below "The Rope" at the W end of the island. This evidence indicates that Pitcairn was occupied for a considerable period in the past, but where these ancient people came from or where they went is still a mystery.

European discovery: Pitcairn was discovered in 1767 by Carteret on the H.M.S. *Swallow*. The island was named for the son of Major Pitcairn of the marines, the first to sight it. **mutiny on the Bounty:** The H.M.S. *Bounty* sailed from England in 1787 to collect breadfruit plants to supplement the diet of slaves in the West Indies. Because the *Bounty* arrived at Tahiti at the wrong time of the year, it was necessary to spend a long 5 months there collecting samples. During this time, part of the crew became overly attached to the isle of pleasure. On 28 April 1789, under 24-year-old Lt. Fletcher Christian, they mutinied against Capt. Bligh in Tongan waters and set him adrift in an open boat with the 18 men who chose to go with him. Bligh accomplished the amazing feat of sailing 3,618 nautical miles in 41 days and reached Dutch Timor to give the story to the world. **the search for a refuge:** After the mutiny, the *Bounty* sailed back to Tahiti. An attempt to colonize Tubuai in the Austral Is. failed, and Fletcher Christian set out with 8 mutineers, 18 Polynesian men and women, and one small

girl, to find a new home where they would be safe from capture. The few mutineers who chose to remain on Tahiti were eventually picked up by the H.M.S. *Pandora* in 1791, and returned to England for trial. Three were executed. The *Bounty* sailed through the Cook Is., Tonga, and Fiji, until Christian remembered Carteret's discovery. They changed course for Pitcairn and arrived on 15 Jan. 1790.

colonizing Pitcairn: After removing everything of value, the mutineers burned the *Bounty* to avoid detection. Bounty Day, the anniversary, is still celebrated every 23 Jan. when a model of the *Bounty* is launched and burned. The Pitcairners are planning a big bicentennial celebration for 1990. For 18 years after the mutiny the world heard nothing of the final resting place of the *Bounty* until the American whaler *Topaz* called at Pitcairn for water and solved the mystery. The first years on Pitcairn were an orgy of jealousy, treachery, and murder, resulting from the lack of sufficient women after the accidental death

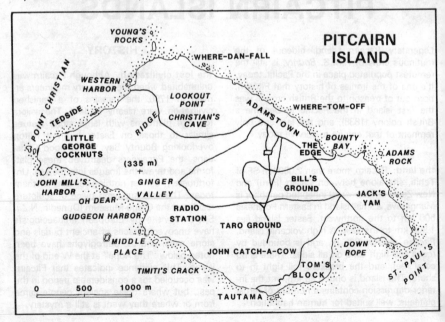

PITCAIRN ISLAND

YOUNG'S ROCKS

WHERE-DAN-FALL

WESTERN HARBOR

POINT CHRISTIAN

TEDSIDE

RIDGE

LOOKOUT POINT

CHRISTIAN'S CAVE

ADAMSTOWN

WHERE-TOM-OFF

LITTLE GEORGE COCKNUTS

(335 m)

GINGER VALLEY

THE EDGE

BOUNTY BAY

ADAMS ROCK

JOHN MILL'S HARBOR

OH DEAR

GUDGEON HARBOR

RADIO STATION

BILL'S GROUND

JACK'S YAM

TARO GROUND

MIDDLE PLACE

JOHN CATCH-A-COW

DOWN ROPE

TIMITI'S CRACK

TOM'S BLOCK

ST. PAUL'S POINT

TAUTAMA

0   500   1000 m

of one of them. By 1793, only 4 mutineers remained alive, and all the Polynesian men had been killed. By 1800, 3 more men had died from a variety of causes, leaving only John Adams, 9 women, and 19 children. Adams brought the children up according to strict, Puritanical morality. He was later pardoned by the British government and lived on Pitcairn till his death in 1829 at the age of 65.

MODERN TIMES

Pitcairn is a British colony governed by the British High Commissioner to New Zealand in Wellington. The highest resident official is the Island Magistrate, who is elected for 3 years; there's also an elected 10-member Island Council. The economy is heavily subsidized by the British government, which spends almost NZ$1 million annually on Pitcairn. All the men work in the administration, mainly part-time. The fertile soil supports a variety of fruits and vegetables for local consumption, but the sale of postage stamps is the greatest source of revenue. The islanders make baskets, small wooden carved sharks, and tiny models of the *Bounty*.

the people: Of the present 54 inhabitants of Pitcairn, 47 are direct descendants of the mutineers and their Tahitian wives. In 1831, there was an attempt to resettle them on Tahiti due to fears of drought, but the Pitcairners returned to their island the same year. In 1856, all 194 islanders were taken to Norfolk I., 1,500 km E of Australia, where many of their descendants still live. Two families returned to Pitcairn in 1858, followed by 4 more in 1864. The present population is descended from these six families. Half the people bear the surname Christian; Youngs and Warrens are also numerous. The people speak a local patois of English and Tahitian. The population peaked at 230 early this century but most are now in New Zealand. There's a primary school with a N.Z. teacher, but children must go to N.Z. for any secondary education. Many fail to return and nearly a quarter of the present population is over 65, who fear that soon it may not be possible to

John Adams was the only mutineer to survive the bloodshed of the first years on Pitcairn. In 1819, just 4 years prior to his death, he wrote these words to his brother in England: "I have now lived on this island 30 years, and have a Wife and four Children, and considering the occasion which brought me here it is not likely I shall ever leave this place. I enjoy good health and except the wound which I received from one of the Otaheitens when they quarreled with us, I have not had a day's sickness... I can only say that I have done everything in my power in instructing them in the path of Heaven, and thank God we live comfortable and happy, and not a single quarrel has taken place these 18 years."

man the diesel-powered longboats that are the only connection to ships offshore. It may come to a sad choice between emigration to New Zealand or an airport and tourism.

PRACTICALITIES

getting there: There is no airport or harbor on Pitcairn. All shipping anchors in the lee, moving around when the wind shifts. This is why most passing ships don't even drop anchor but only pause an hour or so to pick up and drop mail. There are 2 open anchorages: Bounty Bay when winds are blowing from the SW, W, and NW; Western Harbor when there's an E wind. Both have landings but Bounty Bay is tricky to negotiate through the surf and Western Harbor is far from the village. A new jetty was contructed at Bounty Bay by the Royal Engineers in 1976. The anchorage at Down Rope could be used in case of N or NE winds, but there's no way up the cliff except by the proverbial rope. Dangerous rocks lie off the S coast. The wind is irregular, so yachts must leave someone on board in case it shifts. From 1970-1979 only 64 yachts called at Pitcairn. The islanders come out to meet boats anchored in Bounty Bay and ferry visitors ashore. The British High Commission in Wellington, N.Z., would have information on infrequent supply ships to Pitcairn.

tours: Unless you own a yacht, the only practical way of visiting Pitcairn is on an organized yacht cruise arranged by Ocean Voyages Inc.,

the landing at Bounty Bay, Pitcairn Island

1709 Bridgeway, Sausalito, CA 94965, USA. They have several 5-week trips a year from Tahiti to Pitcairn, with about 2 weeks spent living on the island with the Pitcairners. A wood run may be made to Henderson during this period. En route from Tahiti a stop is usually made at Mangareva and a few of the Tuamotus. The price is nearly US$5,000 if you join the group at Tahiti. Bookings must be made far in advance. This trip merits a number-one rating as the best of its kind in the world. Society Expedition Cruises, 723 Broadway East, Seattle, WA 98102, USA, calls at Ducie, Henderson, and Pitcairn on their annual run between Easter I. and Tahiti (from US$4,690 OW), but only a few hours are spent on each. It's also possible to charter a yacht such as the *Galaxie* or *Kebir* from Tahiti Mer et Loisirs (Box 3488, Tahiti, Polynesia) and sail from Tahiti to Pitcairn via Mangareva in about 20 days RT. The charge will be upwards of US$100 pp a day for 8 people including all meals, or US$2,000 pp for the trip. A French crew goes with the yacht.

accommodations: If you want to stay on Pitcairn for an extended period you must first obtain permission of the Pitcairn Island Council through a British diplomatic mission. Considering the great difficulty in just getting to the island, it's unlikely anyone will take you seriously unless you have a particular reason for going. You should apply about a year in advance. Visiting yachties, however, are welcomed into the Pitcairners' homes in a most hospitable fashion. If you're headed for Pitcairn, take along a good supply of tinned foods and butter, plus books for the library, to repay the kindness you'll inevitably encounter. They'll feed you mammoth meals. There is a great dependency on imported food. Since no freight is charged to Pitcairn, food is as cheap there as in New Zealand. Since an American missionary converted them in 1887, all Pitcairners are Seventh-day Adventists, so pork, cigarettes, and alcohol are not allowed.

information: The *Pitcairn Miscellany* is a delightful monthly newsletter sponsored by the Pitcairn Island School. One may become a

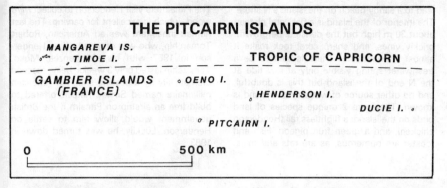

THE PITCAIRN ISLANDS

MANGAREVA IS.
TIMOE I.

TROPIC OF CAPRICORN

GAMBIER ISLANDS
(FRANCE)

○ *OENO I.*

○ *HENDERSON I.*

DUCIE I. ○

○ *PITCAIRN I.*

```
0                              500 km
```

subscriber for US$5 per year. Send cash or an undated check to: *Pitcairn Miscellany,* Pitcairn Islands, via New Zealand.

THE PITCAIRN ISLANDS

Pitcairn Island: On a plateau 120 m above the landing at Bounty Bay (good surfing here) is Adamstown, the only settlement. At the top of the hill over the bay is "The Edge," a restful spot with benches, shady trees, and a great view of everything. The original Bible from the *Bounty* is in the church at Adamstown. The Bible was sold in 1839 and was eventually acquired by the Connecticut Historical Society which returned it to Pitcairn in 1949. The 4-m anchor of the *Bounty,* salvaged in 1957 by the yacht *Yankee,* now lies in the square outside the courthouse. Local postage stamps may be purchased at the post office between the courthouse and church. Mail takes several months to reach Pitcairn. The library is adjacent. A bell on the square is used to announce church services and the arrival of a ship. There are 6.5 km of roads on Pitcairn and, although the quaint Pitcairn wheelbarrows are still used to move supplies, the islanders prefer to ride around on Honda 90s. There are also cars, tractors, and video—electricity is on from dusk to 2300. On the ridge W of Adamstown is a cave in which Fletcher Christian stayed during the period of strife on the island. He was finally killed by 2 Tahitians. Local place names are derived from historical events: "Upside-Nunk-Fall" is the cliff from which Un-

cle Alfonso Christian fell to his death while chasing pigs; "Where Minnie Off" is the rock where tragic Minnie was swept out to sea.

Oeno: Grouped together with Pitcairn under the same administration are the uninhabited islands of Oeno, Henderson, and Ducie, annexed by Britain in 1902. Oeno, a tiny atoll (less than one sq km) about 120 km NW of Pitcairn, is visited by the Pitcairners from time to time to collect shells, coral, and pandanus leaves to use in their handicrafts. **Ducie:** Ducie atoll, the smallest of the 3, is over 500 km E of Pitcairn, and due to its inaccessiblity is rarely approached. Unlike Pitcairn and Henderson, both Ducie and Oeno have central lagoons.

Henderson: Henderson, a 30-sq-km elevated atoll, is largest of the Pitcairn Islands. The island measures 4.5 by 8.5 km and is flanked by 15-m-high coral cliffs on the W, S, and E sides. Henderson is surrounded by a fringing reef with only 2 narrow passages: one on the N, the other on the NW coast. The passages

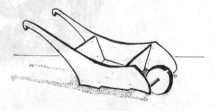

a Pitcairn wheelbarrow

lead to a sandy beach on the island's N shore. The interior of the island is a flat coral plateau about 30 m high but the dense undergrowth, prickly vines, and sharp coral rock make it almost impenetrable. There is said to be a freshwater spring visible only at low tide at the N end of the island but this is doubtful, and no other source of water on the island is known. There are 2 unique species of land birds on the island: a flightless rail (Henderson chicken), and a green fruit pigeon. Fish and lobster are numerous, as are rats and mice.

The Pitcairners visit Henderson to collect *miro* wood, which is excellent for carving. The last human inhabitant was an American, Robert Tomarchin, who was dropped off on Henderson in 1957 with his chimpanzee, Moko. Tomarchin lasted only 3 weeks, being rescued dramatically by a passing ship. An American millionaire named Smiley Ratcliff offered to build free an airstrip on Pitcairn if the British government would allow him to settle on Henderson. Luckily, he was turned down in 1983.

EASTER ISLAND

The mystery of Easter Island and its indigenous inhabitants, the Rapanui, has intrigued travelers and archaeologists for many years. Where did these ancient people come from? How did they transport almost 600 giant statues from the quarry to their platforms? What cataclysmic event caused them to overthrow what they had erected with so much effort? And most importantly, what does it all mean? With the opening of Mataveri airport in 1967, Easter I. became more easily accessible, and many visitors now take the opportunity to pause and ponder the largest and most awesome collection of prehistoric monuments in the Pacific.

the land: Barren and isolated, Easter I. lies midway between Tahiti and Chile, though over 3,500 km from either. Pitcairn I., 1,900 km W, is the nearest inhabited land. It measures 23 by 11 km, totaling 166 sq km. Easter Island is triangular, with an extinct volcano at each corner. The interior consists of high plateaus and craters surrounded by coastal bluffs. The highest peak is Maunga

Terevaka (530 m); its ancient lava flows cover the island, creating a rough, broken surface. Pua Katiki and Rano Kao, to the E and S, approach 400 m high. Many parasitic craters exist on the southern and SE flanks of Maunga Terevaka. Three of these, Rano Aroi, Rano Raraku, and Rano Kao, contain crater lakes; the largest (in Rano Kao) is a km across. The lakes feature thick, floating bogs of peat, and *totora* reeds of S. American origin, which surround and completely cover their surface. There are small coral formations, but the lack of any continuous reef has allowed the sea to cut cliffs around much of the shoreline: high where the waves encounter ashy material, low where they beat upon lava flows. Lava tubes and volcanic caves are another peculiarity of the coastline. The only sandy beaches are at Ovahe and Anakena on the NE coast. The native trees of Easter I. were all cut by the indigenous inhabitants long ago, and grasslands now cover the green, windswept surface.

climate: Temperatures which average 28.7 degrees C in Feb., 17.8 degrees C in July and

a Rapanui drawn by William Hodges, Capt. Cook's illustrator

Aug., and 20.5 degrees C annually, are moderated by the cool Humboldt Current. The SE Trades blow continuously from Sept. to May; the rest of the year N and NW winds are more common. The climate is moist, with some rain 200 days a year. March to June are the rainiest. Driest and coolest is July to October. Drizzles and mist are common and a heavy dew forms overnight. Snow and frost are unknown, however. The porous volcanic rock dries out quickly so the dampness need not deter the well-prepared hiker/camper.

HISTORY

the South America theory: The most comprehensive explorations of Easter Island to date were by the Norwegian Archaeological Expedition (1955-56) led by Thor Heyerdahl. Heyerdahl postulated that the first inhabitants arrived from S. America about A.D. 380. They dug a 3-km-long defensive trench isolating the Poike Peninsula, and built elevated platforms of perfectly fitted basalt blocks. Heyerdahl noted a second wave of immigrants (also from

S. America) who destroyed the structures of the first group, and replaced them with long platforms *(ahus)* which bore the famous slender statues *(moai)* known around the world. The *ahus* are generally found near the coast, and have long retaining walls facing the sea. Each carried 4-6 statues towering 4-8 m high. These statues or *aringa ora* (living faces) looked inland towards the village, to project the *mana* (protective power) of the *aku-aku* (ancestral spirits) they represented. The statues were all cut from the same quarry (at Rano Raraku), the yellowish volcanic tuff shaped by stone tools. Some statues bore a large cylindrical topknot *(pukao)* carved from the reddish stone of Punapau. Eyes of cut coral were fitted into the faces. Internecine fighting among the islanders began around 1680, and by 1840 all the *moai* had been thrown off their *ahus.* Heyerdahl sees this conflict resulting from the arrival of Polynesian invaders from the Marquesas who conquered the original inhabitants. The birdman cult, centering on the sacred village of Orongo, is believed to have been initiated by the victors. Heyerdahl's theory is partially corroborated by the legend of the long-eared people, who were annihilated by the short-ears at a battle on the Poike Peninsula. However, while most of the original *moai* have long ears, more recent woodcarvings of naked emaciated figures also have long ears, though they're clearly products of the later group.

other theories: Traditional archaeologists discount the S. American theory and see the statues as having developed from the typical backrests of Polynesian *marae.* The civil war would have resulted from a population growth beyond the island's slender means, leading to starvation, cannibalism, and collapse of the old order. The Poike "trench" is only a natural earth slump which was modified to grow crops, probably taro. Heyerdahl's detractors have less success in explaining the perfectly fitted, polished stonework. The stone wall of Ahu Tahira (Vinapu) is amazingly similar to Incan stone structures in Cuzco and Machu Picchu. The strange canoe-shaped house foundations with holes for wall supports are unique. Another mystery is the still undeciphered, incised wooden tablets *(rongo*

A rongo-rongo tablet of incised driftwood, figures darkened. Although the exact meaning remains a mystery, these boards were used as prompters by priests reciting religious chants. The hieroglyphic rongo-rongo are the only known examples of writing in ancient Polynesia. Since every other line is upside down, a reader would have had to rotate the board continually.

rongo), the only ancient form of writing known in Oceania. Although there have been several scholarly attempts to read these neat rows of symbols, their meaning remains unknown. Some romantic dreamers have envisioned Easter I. as the last remaining evidence of the sunken continent of Lemuria, the haunting stone statues carved by a people forced to flee their sinking homeland. Scientific study has now proven conclusively that there has been no emergence or submergence whatever on the island since the end of the Pleistocene, so visitors have at least one less theory to choose from. Or you can join Erich von Daniken (*Chariots of the Gods*) and attribute the strange happenings to beings from outer space!

European penetration: The European impact on Easter I. was among the most dreadful in the history of the Pacific. When Jacob Roggeveen arrived on Easter Sunday, 1722, there were about 4,000 Rapanui. Roggeveen's landing party opened fire and killed 12 of the islanders; then the great white explorer sailed off. Contacts with whalers, sealers, and slavers were sporadic until 1862 when a fleet of Peruvian blackbirders kidnapped over 1,000 Rapanui to work in the coastal sugar plantations of Peru and dig guano on the offshore islands. Among those taken were the last king and the entire learned class. Missionaries and diplomats in Lima protested to the Peruvian government, and eventually 15 surviving islanders made it back to their homes, where they sparked deadly tuberculosis and smallpox epidemics. French Catholic mis-

sionaries took up residence on Easter I. in 1865 and succeeded in converting the survivors; businessmen from Tahiti arrived soon after and acquired property for a sheep ranch. Both groups continued the practice of removing Rapanui from the island: the former sent followers to their mission on Mangareva, the latter sent laborers to their plantations on Tahiti. Returnees from Tahiti introduced leprosy. By 1870 the total population had been reduced to 110. One of the business partners, Jean Dutrou-Bornier, had the missionaries evicted in 1871 and ran the island as he wished until his murder by a Rapanui in 1877. The estate then went into litigation which lasted until 1893.

the colonial period: In 1883 Chile defeated Peru and Bolivia in the War of the Pacific. With their new imperial power the Chileans annexed Easter I. in 1888, erroneously believing that the island would become a port of call after the opening of the Panama Canal. Their total lack of knowledge about the island is illustrated by plans to open a naval base where no potential for harbor construction existed. When this became apparent, they leased most of the island to a British wool operation which ran it as a company estate until the lease was revoked in 1953. During this long period, the Rapanui were forbidden to go beyond the Hanga Roa boundary wall without company permission to deter them from stealing the sheep. In 1953 the Chilean Navy took over and continued the same paternal rule. In 1965 the moderate Christian Democratic government of Chile permitted the election of a local mayor and council. Elections were terminated by the 1973 military coup and Easter I., along with the rest of Chile, has suffered autocratic rule ever since.

government: Easter I. is part of the Fifth Region of Chile, with Valparaiso (Chile) as capital. All positions of authority on the island are held by *continentales* (mainlanders). The Chilean government names a military governor; the appointed mayor and council have little power. Chile heavily subsidizes services on the island, and a large military and official staff are present. Most of the land is held by the Chilean State. On several occasions various Chilean governments have offered to give the Rapanui clear title to certain areas but these offers have been consistently refused. The islanders fear such titles might eventually pass out of their hands and besides, they never ceded the land to anyone in the first place, they say.

the people: The original name of Easter I. was Te Pito o Te Henua, "navel of the world." The Rapanui believe they are descended from Hotu Matu'a, who arrived by canoe at Anakena Beach from Te Hiva, the ancestral homeland. The statues were raised by magic. The original inhabitants wore *tapa* clothing and were tattooed like Marquesans; in fact, there's little doubt these forefathers arrived from Eastern Polynesia about A.D. 500. The language of the Rapanui is Austronesian, closely related to all the other languages of Polynesia, with no S. American elements. The Rapanui have interbred liberally with visitors for over a century, but the Polynesian element is still strong. The 1,600 Rapanui keep gardens around Hanga Roa, the only settlement, growing sweet potatoes, corn, bananas, pineapples, and melons. Many earn money from tourism as innkeepers, guides, and craftspeople. More are employed by the Chilean government. Some 500 *continentales,* mostly government employees, also live on the island. The Rapanui are Chilean citizens and many have emigrated to the mainland.

PRACTICALITIES

getting there: Lan Chile Airlines flies to Easter I. twice a week from Tahiti and Santiago. They have a history of changing schedules at a moment's notice and will sometimes simply cancel a flight. Book your onward flight well ahead as the plane is often overbooked—a week is enough time to see everything. See the "Introduction" to this book for fares. Lan Chile's Circle Pacific Fare (US$1,450) puts you in Miami-Santiago-Easter I.-Tahiti-Los Angeles and is valid up to a year. Their Visit Chile Pass (US$449) allows 21 days unlimited air travel in Chile, including Punta Arenas and Easter I., but must be purchased before your arrival in Chile. In the U.S. call Lan Chile toll-free at 800-225-5526. Mataveri Airport (IPC) is walking distance from the places to stay in Hanga Roa. There is a US$5 departure tax.

This expressive toromiro *woodcarving of an ancestral figure* (moai kavakava) *was done around the middle of the Nineteenth Century. The eyes are inlaid with circles of bone and obsidian.*

getting around: Although guided tours and rental vehicles (US$100 daily—International Driver's license required) are available, the best way to get around is on foot or horseback. Horses rent for about US$10 a day. You can walk right around the island in 3 days (take water). Camp at the national park attendant's posts near Rano Raraku or Anakena where you can replenish your water. (The areas around Maunga Terevaka and Rano Kao have been set aside as the Parque Nacional Rapa Nui.)

accommodations: The cheapest is to stay with the locals, easily arranged upon arrival. A board near the airport information desk lists people who accept paying guests; most of the guest house owners meet the flights. Count on US$15-25 pp including all meals. In this price range is Residencial Tahai near the museum. The manager, Edmundo Edwards, speaks fluent English—a rarity here. Edmundo charges campers US$6 (no meals). More expensive is Residencial Pedro Atan (owner Juan Atan Perouse), where you often get

lobster. Also recommended is Rosita's, exceptionally well-run with excellent food—US$50 pp. Others include Residencial Roa Reka (US$20 pp), Residencial Meme (US$25 s, US$45 d), Residencial Manutara, Maison Taharaa, and Residencial Orongo. There is a 20 percent hotel tax. The government-owned, mainlander-operated Hotel Hanga Roa is greatly overpriced. Beware of hidden extras such as US$3 for hot water.

food and entertainment: Although several general stores sell groceries, bring some tinned food with you from Tahiti or Chile. There's only one supply ship a year, in Dec., meaning high prices and limited selection. The local market has fruit and vegetables. There's an impromptu handicraft market at the airport on arrival days. Bring jeans, windbreakers, T-shirts, sneakers, cosmetics, and rock music cassettes to trade for woodcarvings. The locals gather at the disco in Hanga Roa on Fri. and Sat. nights: US$6 for a coke. The local currency is the Chilean peso (fluctuating); U.S. dollars are easily exchanged. Credit cards are nowhere accepted.

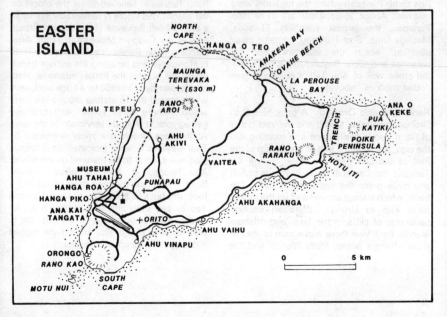

information: There's a tourist office in Hanga Roa. Those going on to Chile can obtain the *South American Handbook* (see booklist) at Libreria Eduardo Albers, Merced 320, Local 7, or Ave. 11 de Septiembre 2671, both in Santiago. Eduardo Albers also stocks this *Handbook,* if you're going the other way. The best books about the island are *The Island at the Center of the World* by Father Sebastian Englert, and *Aku-Aku* by Thor Heyerdahl.

SIGHTS

vicinity of Hanga Roa: Visit the small museum on the N side of Hanga Roa. Near this, at Ahu Tahai just outside the town, are 3 *ahus,* one bearing 5 restored *moai,* and a large restored statue complete with a red 10-ton topknot. The islanders launched their canoes from the ramp leading down to the water between the *ahus.* Quite a distance farther NE and inland is Ahu Akivi (Siete Moai), with 7 restored statues. On the way back to Hanga Roa climb Punapau where the topknots were quarried. About 25 topknots are in or near Punapau, the largest weighing 11 tons. Maunga Orito, S of Punapau, contains black obsidian, which the islanders used for weapons and tools. Beyond this is the splendid stone wall of Ahu Tahira at Vinapu (see "other theories" above).

Rano Kao and Orongo: A brisk hike S to Orongo (admission US$2) and the vast crater of Rano Kao is easily done in a morning. On the way, just past the end of the airstrip at the foot of the cliff near the water, is Ana Kai Tangata, the Cannibal Cave. Paintings of fish and birds grace the walls of this cave. The track, which swings around and up the side of Rano Kao to Orongo, offers an exciting panorama of cliffs, crater lake, and offshore islands. Each year there was a race to the farthest offshore island, Motu Niu, to find the first egg of a species of migratory sooty tern *(manutara).* The winning swimmer was proclaimed birdman and thought to have supernatural powers. There are many high-relief carvings of bird-headed men on rock outcrops near Orongo. The 40 cave-like dwellings at Orongo were used by participants and island chiefs during the festival.

around the island: Take the road along the S coast towards Rano Raraku. The first king of the island is buried at Ahu Akahanga. The stone walls seen at various places date from the English sheep ranch. Although many of the statues are concentrated at Rano Raraku, they are also found on the coastline all around the island. Work on the statues ended suddenly, and many were abandoned. About 200 are still in the quarry at Rano Raraku in various stages of completion; one unfinished giant measures 21 m long. Others were left en route to their *ahu;* from the top of Rano Raraku you can see them scattered along the roadway to the coast. Some 70 statues stand on the slopes of the volcano; another 30 lie on the ground. A seated statue on the W side of Rano Raraku is believed to be the oldest on the island. This figure is remarkably similar to a statue from Raivavae in the Austral Group, now at the Gauguin Museum in Tahiti. After climbing Rano Raraku, circle around to Hotu Iti (Tongariki) and up along the ancient trench which still isolates the Poike Pensinsula. Hotu Iti was destroyed in 1960 by a huge tidal wave which tossed the 15 statues around like cordwood. There are some extraordinary petroglyphs at Hotu Iti, very close to the road. At Anakena Beach is a *moai* re-erected by Thor Heyerdahl, as is indicated on a bronze plaque — the first to be restored on the island. Ahu Naunau at Anakena bears 7 *moai.* Beyond Anakena the road deteriorates into a footpath, but you should try to reach Hanga o Teo to see the ruins of a large village, including several oval houses. It's possible to walk back to Hanga Roa around the rugged NW slopes of Maunga Terevaka.

GALAPAGOS

INTRODUCTION

Ever since Charles Darwin visited the Galapagos in 1835, these islands have fired the imagination of naturalists worldwide. Perhaps nowhere else on earth (except Antarctica) has the ecosystem been so little altered by man. Indeed, the unique wildlife here is the main reason for visiting the Galapagos. Here you can swim alongside sea lions and fur seals; nesting boobies and frigate birds will casually watch as you pass, and hawks will swoop down and land beside you to get a closer look at their strange visitor. Some species survived in the Galapagos while their continental ancestors faded into extinction. Others diverged in form to adapt to the local environment. Certain Antarctic animals found here even stand alone as the only examples of their kind on the equator. The islands take their name from the Spanish word for land tortoise, *galapago*. There are in all 5 large islands (over 500 sq km), 8 medium-sized islands (14-to-500 sq km), and many smaller islets. It's 350 km from Darwin I. to Espanola. You'll need a minimum of 2 weeks to fully appreciate the Galapagos.

the land: Located 1,000 km off the coast of South America, the Galapagos are 2,000 km due S of El Salvador and 1,600 km SW of Panama City. The equator cuts directly through Wolf Volcano (1,707 m), highest peak in the archipelago. The islands were never connected to the mainland. They sit directly over a weak spot in the earth's crust and their formation and structure have much in common with the Hawaiian Chain. All the islands (except Darwin and Wolf) rest on the Galapagos Platform, an underwater mesa covering several thousand sq km, which was formed by repeated extrusions of molten basaltic rock (magma). The oldest of these lavas began to be laid down below the sea only 4 million years ago—very recent geologically. The volcanoes of Galapagos are the shield type: their fluid lava spreads far before solidifying and building up mountains in layers. This creates gentle slopes at the lower levels, becoming steep near the top, with a wide, flat summit. The islands are also pocked with over 2,000 secondary craters, giving the landscape a lunar aspect. Espanola, Santa Fe, Baltra, Seymour, and the NE part of Santa Cruz have a different origin. Here, volcanic material spread and cooled underwater, later to be uplifted out of the sea. Some of this uplifted rock may be up to 2 million years old, but none of the volcanic rock spewn out and cooled above sea level is older than 300,000 years. The uplifted islands are generally low and flat, traversed by parallel ridges and sea cliffs caused by faulting.

climate: The climate is hot and dry in the coastal areas, humid and temperate higher up.

There are 2 seasons. During the cool season (June to Dec.), brisk winds from the SE follow the cold Humboldt Current, and the contact of these waters with the warm tropical air causes cloudy conditions and mist. A fine, misty rainfall known as *garua* falls on the mountainsides during this time. From Jan. to May, gentle NE winds bring warm waters down from the N to begin the hot season. There are occasional heavy showers during these months. The highlands receive most of their rainfall during the cool season, the lowlands during the hot. Rainfall varies from about 350 mm annually at sea level to 1,200-2,500 mm on the mountains. The best agricultural lands are 200-250 m above sea level; the southern slopes are better watered than the northern. The smaller, lower islands get very little rainfall. The hot

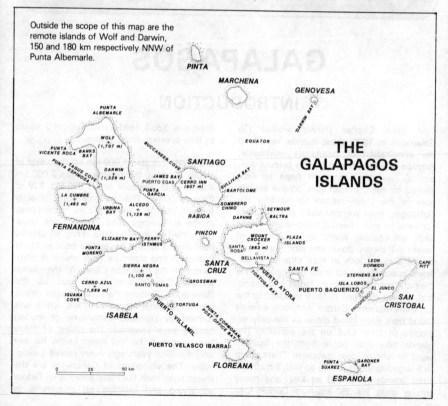

Outside the scope of this map are the remote islands of Wolf and Darwin, 150 and 180 km respectively NNW of Punta Albemarle.

THE GALAPAGOS ISLANDS

season is best for visiting because the water is warmer for swimming, there are fewer ocean currents to impede navigation, no strong winds, and the sky is generally clear, making it optimum for photography (bring enough film). The seas are roughest from July to September. From Feb. to April the surface water is always warmer than 25 degrees C, while from May to Dec. it's cooler than 25 degrees. Although 32 species of coral are found in the Galapagos, relatively low water temperatures resulting from the Humboldt Current inhibit the creation of large reefs.

FLORA AND FAUNA

Thanks to its isolation, close to half of the land birds are endemic, as are 32 percent of the plants and 23 percent of the coastal fishes. All the reptiles (except the sea turtles) are also unique to the Galapagos. The meeting of cold and warm currents has led to an amazing proliferation of marine life. What impresses the visitor most is the animals' tameness and lack of fear. Most of this fascinating flora and fauna originated in S. America, brought to the islands by the prevailing winds and currents, or on the wings of birds. The reptiles and some of the plants are believed to have arrived on logs or floating masses of vegetation. Some Antarctic fauna, such as penguins and fur seals, rode on the Humboldt Current and were able to adapt and survive on the equator due to the cooling effect of these polar waters.

evolution in the Galapagos: Charles Darwin spent 35 days in the Galapagos in 1835 as naturalist aboard the HMS *Beagle* and his observations here were crucial to the elaboration of his theory of evolution. Twenty-four years later in 1859 he published *On the Origins of Species* which gave the islands universal fame. What especially attracted Darwin's attention were the diversely shaped beaks of the 13 species of the island finches, each adapted to its own food supply, yet all evidently descended from a single ancestral species. The woodpecker finch, for example, uses cactus thorns to extract insects or worms from holes and crevices inaccessible to its

beak—one of the only birds in the world known to use a tool. Darwin deduced that isolation and new conditions lead to rapid evolution. The new environment exerts selective pressures on the insular population which gradually diverges from their ancestors. The lack of competition and the availability of unoccupied niches also contribute to this process. An example of divergence is the flightless cormorant, the largest cormorant in the world, which because it had no natural enemy was able to sacrifice its ability to fly in order to be able to dive into the water with greater ease and skill.

the giant tortoise: In the Galapagos, reptiles dominated the land in a way which hadn't been seen on the continents since the passing of the dinosaurs. The giant tortoise appeared some 80 million years ago, but had become extinct from most of the rest of the world 100,000 years ago. Today, one species survives on certain islands in the Indian Ocean and 11 species (of an original 15) are found in the Galapagos. The giant tortoise can have a shell up to one m wide, weigh as much as 230 kg, and live to be 200 years old. In humid areas where the vegetation is plentiful and accessible, such as Santa Cruz I., the shell is dome-shaped; on drier islands like Espanola where the terrain is rough and the vegetation hard to reach, the tortoises have evolved a longer neck and legs, and a saddle-backed shell which permits them to stretch higher.

Charles Darwin

reptiles: The marine iguana of the Galapagos is the only lizard in the world which feeds in the sea. Very agile in the water, they undulate their long tails for propulsion with legs and feet clutched closely to their sides. Their food is marine algae which they seek as the tide goes out. The rest of the time they spend sunning themselves on rocks by the seashore. They are found on all the islands in numerous colonies and aren't endangered. The land iguanas of Galapagos, on the other hand, are becoming increasingly rare, largely due to attacks by packs of wild dogs. They are larger and heavier than the marine type, have a conical instead of a flat tail, and are yellow/brown instead of black and red. They eat leaves and cactus fruits. The land iguana of Santa Fe I. is considered a separate species. There are also several species of non-poisonous snakes. Many small lava lizards are seen scampering about; the female has red cheeks. **other fauna:** Colonies of sea lions are common on all the islands. The male frigate bird inflates a bright red sack under its beak during the mating season to attract females.

an endangered environment: Today man is learning to live with his fellow creatures, but it has not always been so. From 1790 to 1870 whalers were active in the area, and during the 19th C. fur seals were hunted almost to extinction. Pirates and whalers carried off the tortoises for food, and Ecuadorian concessionaires arrived to process them into oil. It's believed that as many as a quarter-million giant tortoises were killed or removed from the islands during this period. Today the tortoises' worst enemies are the animals introduced by man which eat their eggs and young, and destroy their food supply. Only on Santa Cruz and northern Isabela are they still numerous. Introduced goats and pigs also destroy the vegetation and facilitate erosion. A continuing program eliminates the goats—they've already been removed from Rabida, Plaza, Santa Fe, and Espanola, and are greatly reduced on other islands. The flightless cormorants and penguins are threatened by a potential spread northward of wild dogs on Isabela. Large numbers of green sea turtles were killed by a Japanese refrigerator ship in 1971-72. Four of the 6

species of native rice rats have been eliminated through competition and diseases carried by the introduced black rats.

flora: Galapagos' flora is closely related to that of adjacent S. America, although many plants have adapted to local conditions and evolved into new forms. The most striking feature of the vegetation are cacti, found on all the islands, which grow up to 12 m high. The thick trunk has a wax-like bark to retain moisture in the spongy interior. On Floreana is a cactus without thorns. These cacti provide the tortoises with food and moisture on the arid islands, and they evolved their tall shapes to escape the lumbering creatures. Observe the dry zone vegitation on Santa Cruz on the hike up to Media Luna.

HISTORY AND GOVERNMENT

The Galapagos is one of the few areas of the world never reached by primitive man (although Thor Heyerdahl found pottery here in 1953, raising the possibility of visits by American Indians). The islands were discovered in 1535 by Tomas de Berlanga, Bishop of Panama, who was accidentally carried there by a strong ocean current during a calm. Of little interest to the Spaniards, the islands were left to pirates, who used them during the 17th C. as a refuge and supply base from which to attack shipping between Peru and Panama. The pirate William Dampier gave many of the islands English names in 1684. It was not until 1832 that newly independent Ecuador claimed them and established a colony on Floreana. Among the first group of colonists were 80 rebel soldiers exiled from the mainland. By 1835 Floreana had 300 inhabitants, but the settlement was unsuccessful and in 1882 it was abandoned. Three years later, an administrative center was established on San Cristobal. Colonization on southern Isabela began in 1897. The widespread use of convict labor in the 19th C. settlement schemes led to sporadic murders and revolts, first on Floreana (1878), then on San Cristobal (1904). An unscrupulous entrepreneur, Manuel Cobos, established a sugarcane plantation and mill on San Cristobal, which ended

GALAPAGOS AT A GLANCE

ISLAND	OTHER NAMES	AREA (sq km)	HIGHEST POINT (m)	HUMAN POP.	TORTOISE POP.	LAND IGUANAS	FUR SEALS
San Cristobal	Chatham	558	730	1,810 (1980)	500 (1975)	— —	— —
Espanola	Hood	61	206	— —	14 (1975)	— —	— —
Floreana	Santa Maria, Charles	173	640	53 (1980)	Extinct	— —	— —
Santa Fe	Barrington	24	259	— —	Extinct	Yes	— —
Santa Cruz	Indefatigable, Chavez	986	863	1,958 (1980)	3,000 (1975)	Yes	— —
Baltra	South Seymour	27	100	51 (1980)	— —	Extinct	— —
Seymour	North Seymour	1.9	30	— —	— —	Yes	— —
Pinzon	Duncan	18	458	— —	150 (1975)	— —	— —
Rabida	Jervis	5	367	— —	Extinct	— —	— —
Santiago	San Salvador, James	585	907	Extinct	500 (1975)	— —	Yes
Bartolome	Bartholomew	1.2	114	— —	— —	— —	— —
Tortuga	Brattle	1.2	186	— —	— —	— —	— —
Isabela	Albermarle, Santa Gertrudis	4,588	1707	538 (1980)	6,000 (1975)	Yes	Yes
Fernandina	Narborough	642	1494	— —	Extinct	Yes	Yes
Genovesa	Tower	14	76	— —	— —	— —	Yes
Marchena	Bindloe	130	343	— —	— —	— —	Yes
Pinta	Abingdon	59	777	— —	1 (1975)	— —	Yes
Wolf	Wenman	1.3	253	— —	— —	— —	— —
Darwin	Culpepper	1.1	167	— —	— —	— —	— —
TOTAL		**7,877**			**4,410**	**10,165**	

abruptly with his murder by a convict in 1904; little sugarcane has since been grown. In 1944 a penal colony was set up on Isabela and it soon gained a reputation for the cruelty of its guards. Finally, in 1958 a revolt and spectacular escape to the mainland by 21 prisoners led to its closing a year later.

government: Galapagos was declared one of the 20 provinces of Ecuador in 1973 by military decree. The capital is Puerto Baquerizo on San Cristobal and the provincial governor is appointed in Quito. The attainment of provincial status was not an especially positive development as it opened the islands to uncontrolled migration from the continent, which has caused the population of Santa Cruz to double and led to rapid inflation. This explosion is now the greatest danger facing the islands' delicate ecosystems. The local economy is based solely on tourism, agriculture, and fishing, in roughly that order of importance. INGALA (Instituto Nacional de Galapagos) is the development agency in the province.

protection and conservation: The first protectionist legislation was signed into law by the Ecuadorian government during the 1930s, but was never enforced. In 1959 the entire archipelago was declared a national park, excluding those areas already colonized. Galapagos National Park, which includes 88 percent of the land area of the islands, has become one of the finest in the world, of which Ecuador is rightfully proud. The secret of its success has been a symbiotic relationship with the Charles Darwin Foundation, an international, non-government scientific research organization formed in 1959 under the auspices of UNESCO and the International Union for the Conservation of Nature. In 1964 the Foundation established the Charles Darwin Research Station near Puerto Ayora on Santa Cruz. Its purpose is to study and help preserve the flora and fauna of the islands. Without the Darwin Station the National Park would never have been able to establish its authority so quickly and effectively, and without the National Park the ideals of the Foundation might never have been implemented. All native animals, birds, and reptiles are now fully protected, and the spirit of conservationism which the people at the National Park and the Darwin Station have been able to instill is impressive.

GETTING THERE

by air: TAME (Transportes Aereos Nacionales Ecuadorianos) has 5 flights a week (14 kg baggage allowed) between Guayaquil (Ecuador) and the Galapagos. The fare is about US$300 RT, but it's better to buy a OW ticket (US$150) since you may be able to find a boat back. TAME also quotes fares from Quito, but it's much cheaper to travel to Guayaquil by road or rail and board the flight there. TAME's reservation system is chaotic: they tell you the next 2 flights are booked, but at the airport you find the plane half empty. What happens is the tour companies corner all the seats and have you believe that the only way to get to the Galapagos is to join one of their tours. If you get this story it might be a good idea to go to the airport and try traveling standby. Unless you hit a real tour, your chances of getting on are good. Be sure to reconfirm your return reservations in the Galapagos, as reservations made in Guayaquil are often lost. Note, however, that it's difficult to change reservations once they're made. Note too that Ecuadorians pay less than half as much as you for the same ticket. You can save money by having one buy your ticket and check in your luggage. Only buy a OW ticket this way, though, as they ask for ID at check-in and your local friend has to be there to pretend he's you. You use "his" boarding pass to get on the plane. The Ecuadorian Air Force has occasional logistic flights to the Galapagos. Though these can be very cheap (US$30 OW), they're also unreliable, and it's nearly impossible to get on unless you know somebody. It may be easier to get a *logistico* (Air Force flight) back to Guayaquil or Quito, but you'll have to struggle with a throng of pushy locals who have priority over you.

by boat: TRAMFSA (Transportes Maritimos y Fluviales S.A.), Ste. 110, Villamil 315, Guayaquil (tel. 51-4264 or 51-6987) runs a passenger-carrying freighter, the *Pinzon,* to Galapagos every 3 weeks. The 8 passengers are carried in 4-berth cabins and pay US$300 for the 15-day RT or about US$100 OW. The *Pinzon* calls only at the ports on the 4 inhabited islands (not the wildlife areas). Since the *Pinzon* stops at Puerto Baquerizo first, you can get off there, visit San Cristobal, and continue on to Puerto Ayora on the weekly mail boat. The *Pinzon* doesn't have an agent in Puerto Ayora, so for a return passage you have to wait and talk to the captain. Another cargo/passenger boat plying between Guayaquil and the Galapagos is the *Iguana.* There is a trip every 15 days and foreign passengers pay about US$78 OW. Contact the ship's agent: MARITUR (Maritima de Turismo Compania Limitada), Casilla 3552, Guayaquil (tel. 38-5996). A third possibility is the *Calicuchima,* a 64-passenger cargo ship owned by the Ecuadorian Navy. This boat leaves Guayaquil every 3 weeks on an 11-day cruise of the islands, 5 of which are spent at sea. Unlike the *Pinzon* and the *Iguana,* the *Calicuchima* does stop at some of the wildlife areas and passengers are escorted ashore by a Spanish-speaking guide. Trouble is, the food on the *Calicuchima* is lousy, the crew uncooperative, and the tour groups large and rushed. The all-inclusive RT fare is US$360 in 2nd class (6-berth cabins) or US$450 in 1st class (double cabins), 15 percent less for Ecuadorians. A RT on *Calicuchima* is not recommended, so try to book OW. Reserva-

tions must be made in advance by writing Departamento Logistico, Comandancia de la Primera Zona Naval, Jefatura de Operaciones Navales, Armada del Ecuador, Canar y 5 de Junio, Guayaquil, or tel. 34-5317 or 34-5318, ext. 2. Without an advance reservation it could be difficult to get on in Guayaquil, although perhaps easier to catch coming back. In Puerto Ayora you may be able to get departure information by asking at the Cooperativa de Turisimo or the National Park Information kiosk.

tours: If your time is limited and you want to book an organized tour in advance, Economic Galapagos Tours (Galasam), Calle Pinto No. 523 y Ave. Amazonas, Quito (tel. 55-0094), or Gran Pasaje Building, 11th floor, 9 de Octubre Av., Guayaquil (tel. 30-6289), has the cheapest package. For US$340 (airfare extra) you cruise up around Santiago and back down the side of Santa Cruz to Puerto Ayora for 6 days, all inclusive. Galasam also sells air tickets without the tour. Scuba diving trips are arranged by Metropolitan Touring (Box 2542, Quito), but they're not cheap. For example, a 10-passenger luxury yacht charter costs US$8,200 (airfare extra) a week for the group all-inclusive. Divers pay an additional surcharge of US$125 pp per week. A qualified diver/guide comes along, but participants are expected to bring their own regulators, wet suits, and weight belts. Only tanks and backpacks are supplied. Both medical and diving certificates are mandatory. Non-divers in the group are not allowed to go ashore while the others are underwater. Much of the diving is done around Floreana and a night dive is possible. Other packages offered by Metropolitan Touring put you on crowded luxury cruise ships such as the *Santa Cruz* (90 passengers) or the *Iguana* (68 passengers) — hardly an appropriate way to experience these islands. Not recommended. Make sure your tour of the Galapagos does not put you in a group larger than 15 participants and spends no more than 2 nights in a Puerto Ayora hotel. Only small groups in small boats get close to the islands and their wildlife. Ocean Voyages Inc. (1709 Bridgeway, Sausalito, CA 94965, USA) offers 15-day yacht cruises, while Wilderness Travel (1760 Solano

Ave., Berkeley, CA 94707, USA) has scuba and hiking trips. Both companies charge about US$100 a day plus airfare. Recommended. Note that the pre-arranged tours always cost more than you would spend organizing your own on the spot, and you have no control over the itinerary. See "from Puerto Ayora" for alternatives. Travel agents outside the Galapagos usually want to sell their tours and will say anything to make you believe it's the only way to go.

MONEY AND VISAS

The official currency is the fluctuating Ecuadorian *sucre,* although U.S. dollars are accepted at a discount. All visitors must pay a US$30 Galapagos National Park admission fee. Spanish is the main language in the islands, although English is generally used by foreign visitors among themselves. Tourists are allowed to stay in Ecuador 90 days a year (no visa required). The only official in the Galapagos who can give you an extension is the chief of police at San Cristobal, in person. Ask for enough time when you arrive in Ecuador.

yachts: Foreign yachts are allowed only 72 hours in the Galapagos. It's also impossible to arrange for a longer stay by visiting an Ecuadorian diplomatic mission abroad, unless you happen to be a "VIP" sponsored by some official organization such as a university or a conservation group. In any case, it would take 3-4 months to obtain this kind of clearance. To get an extension your boat has to be damaged (they'll check). It's very unlikely they'll allow you to tour the islands in your own boat, even if you hire a local guide (US$35 a day), though you could try to convince them to let you leave your yacht in Puerto Ayora while you visit the islands on a charter boat. No other ports of call are permitted beyond Puerto Ayora and Puerto Baquerizo. The fine for stopping at an outer island without permission is about US$300 plus 5-90 days imprisonment. Yachts are charged an entry/clearance fee of US$35 (US$70 if you arrive outside office hours—0800-1700 weekdays). Forrest Nelson, manager of the Hotel Galapagos in Puerto Ayora, is helpful to visiting yachties; he'll top off your tanks with the only pure drinking water available in the Galapagos at 5 cents a gallon, and help you arrange daytrips.

airports: Guayaquil airport (GYE) is serviced by city bus no. 2 from the Malecon. The bank at Guayaquil airport changes travelers cheques at an honest rate. There is no airport tax on flights to Galapagos. On your way over sit on the L-hand side of the aircraft near the front for the best views. Baltra airport (GPS) is N of Puerto Ayora. A National Park information stand at the airport has a map/brochure and a list of Park rules. It is 6 km from the air terminal to the ferry across Itabaca Canal, then another 42 km into town. The airport transfer by bus and boat costs a total of US$3.

blue-footed boobies

SANTA CRUZ

Located near the center of the archipelago, Santa Cruz is Galapagos' second largest island and the main center of activity for visitors. It's also the most attractive and varied of the islands, with every type of vegetation. Tropical fruit and vegetables, along with cattle and some coffee, are grown in the humid upper portion of Santa Cruz. Academy Bay opens in front of Puerto Ayora, the main town, with Santa Fe I. visible in the distance. Marine iguanas are often seen sleeping on the public wharf at Puerto Ayora. A prosperous German community lives across the bay from Puerto Ayora toward the Delfin Hotel, where there's a bathing beach at high tide. Ask to see Gusch Angermeyers' cave.

SIGHTS OF SANTA CRUZ

vicinity of Puerto Ayora: Just a short walk E of the hotels is the Charles Darwin Research Station (open Mon. to Fri. 0700-1200/1300-1600). Although this is primarily a scientific research center, the exhibits for visitors and students make the visit a must. Notice the splendid desert vegetation. A large exhibition hall, a tortoise hatchery and nursery, and several tortoise pens are all open to the public. The work being done here has saved several species from extinction. Walk E along the coast from the Darwin Station over rocks black with iguanas (be careful not to step on any!) and red with crabs to the broken sea cliffs beyond. You may pass an occasional sea lion resting by the shore.

Tortuga Bay: The wide, perfect, white sand beach here, best in the islands, is separated from the warm water of the bay by high sand dunes. To get there take a bus (US$0.15) or walk the 2 km from town to the trailhead beyond the power plant (signposted), then hike for an hour (6 km) along a very rough, rocky trail. Good shoes are essential, and bring water, suntan lotion, and a hat—there's

little shade. If you're lazy and have a group of 10, hire a boat for the trip for about US$30 RT. The beach is very beautiful, despite the lack of coconut trees. Beware of undertow on the ocean side. Camping requires a permit (US$1) from the National Park. Tortuga Bay could be good for surfing when the waves are right (June-December).

vicinity of Bellavista: Bellavista is 7 km inland from Puerto Ayora by bus. A very impressive lava tube, big as a subway tunnel, is found about one km E of Bellavista. Take the road E from the main square and turn L at the first fork. A little beyond some large rocks beside the road, look for an overgrown trail to the R, on the other side of the barbed-wire fence; the lava tube is hidden among the trees about 60 m from the road. There's no sign, so if you have trouble finding things like this, have a boy guide you from Bellavista.

the highlands: The road N from the square at Bellavista leads to the highlands near the center of the island. It takes about an hour to get to Media Luna, a semicircular volcanic cinder cone. Beyond this, avoid the path to the green hut to the R behind Media Luna. Instead, veer a little to the L and up to the high, pointed spatter cone known as Puntudo. Scramble up to its rocky top for a view of both coasts, as well as vast empty grasslands and the *Scalesia* forest to the north. A hut on the side of Mount Crocker (863 m) is visible from Puntudo and you can climb up to it in 15 min. for a different view. The *Miconia* belt on the way to Media Luna adds to the botanic variety. The path up the mountain is good with almost no rocky sections, but it can be slippery if wet (bring rain gear). If the area is covered in fog and mist, there's a chance of getting lost, so take care. During clear, dry weather the hike to Puntudo is the best on Santa Cruz. Allow 5 hours RT. If you want to rent a horse (US$6), ask for Senor Cadena in Bellavista.

vicinity of Santa Rosa: Take the airport bus up to Los Gemelos (The Twins) for US$0.75, 4 km beyond Santa Rosa. These enormous pits, one to each side of the road, aren't craters; they were formed when the earth's surface collapsed into subterranean cavities. There is a trail around the N side of the western Gemelo—note the endemic *Scalesia* forest and birdlife. From Los Gemelos it's a pleasant downhill walk back to Santa Rosa, where the trail to the Giant Tortoise Reserve begins. Hire a horse from Rosa or Ramon in Santa Rosa for about US$5, or you can walk. The trail gets a little muddy and slippery when it's been raining. You hike S, downhill from the village for about 45 min. until you reach a large tree

where the trail divides. The ranger post at La Caseta is about a 30-min. walk to the L and there's a small pond 10 min. beyond that. To the R a less-frequented path leads to Cerro Chato, where tortoises lounge in muddy pools at the foot of the hill. You'll need at least 4 hours to visit both places but don't expect to see large groups of tortoises during the hot season (Jan.-May) when they spread out into the woods. Still, it's a chance to see a giant tortoise in the wild. **note:** All of the above places may be visited on your own without a guide. The cove at Tortuga Negra on the N side of Santa Cruz, excellent for observing green sea turtles, is accessible only by boat.

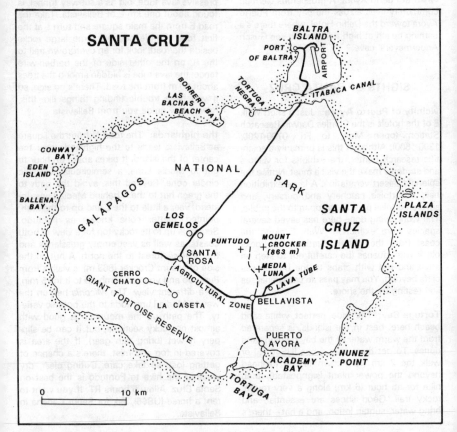

Baltra: Separated from Santa Cruz by the green waters of the Itabaca Canal, Baltra I. was converted to a U.S. Air Force base from 1941-48 to protect the Panama Canal. Practice bombing runs by the Americans destroyed the flora and fauna in some areas, and the base led to the extinction of Baltra's land iguanas. Concrete platforms remaining from the base are still evident among the cactus and lava rock. On the way to the ferry you cross an abandoned airstrip, which complemented the wartime airstrip presently used. Ten thousand men were stationed here during the war. **small adjacent islands:** South Plaza I. has land and marine iguanas, sea lions, plus swallow-tailed gulls along its southern cliffs. Frigate birds and blue-footed boobies nest on Seymour Island. Daphne is a very picturesque, cone-shaped island with extensive nesting areas for boobies in the craters.

PRACTICALITIES

accommodations: About the cheapest place for budget travelers is the Angermeyer Hostel, where a dormitory bed costs only US$1.50 and a double room in the new section US$3 pp. Harmless but huge Galapagos spiders protect you from the insects. There's a pleasant garden where you can sit and talk, and a primitive kitchen at the back for cooking over an open fire—an excellent place to meet other travelers with whom to charter a boat. Recommended. Nearby, the Hotel Europeo has 4 rooms at US$3.60 pp (ask for a receipt). A grocery store and bar adjoin. Pension Gloria (US$2) is popular with backpackers. The Hotel Colon Insular is a 2-story concrete building near the center of town with 12 rooms at US$3 pp (shared bath). In the same area is the Hotel Elizabeth with 20 rooms at US$2.40 pp, but this one is noisy and insecure—not recommended. The Hotel Darwin near the high school has a row of triples at US$4.50 pp with bath, but it could get noisy if your Ecuadorian neighbors turn up their radios. Inquire at the house behind the units. Better than the Darwin is Residencial Palmeras with 8 double rooms, all with private bath and shower, at US$4.50 pp—clean and friendly. The Hotel

Lobo del Mar behind the market has a sun roof, bar, and restaurant. All rooms, at US$6 pp, have private bath. The Residencial las Ninfas is clean and attractive, 17 rooms with private bath at US$6 pp. Nearby, the Hotel Castro charges US$9 pp—very poor value. The best of the medium-range hotels is the Solymar. A pleasant terrace overlooks the bay and the 8 rooms go for US$9 pp (fan and private bath)—good value, but often full. The Hotel Galapagos near the cemetery has a pleasant lounge with a panoramic view of Academy Bay. The 12 spacious bungalows have private facilities and inner-spring mattresses, and hot water is available—Forrest A. Nelson, the manager, knows how to take care of his guests. The charge is US$25 s, US$45 d, US$60 t—recommended if you are willing to pay for the very best. Note that most of the higher-priced hotels add a 16 percent service charge to their rates. There can be mosquitoes at night, so bring coils.

camping: There are 3 official campsites on Santa Cruz: near the Darwin Station, at Tortuga Bay, and at La Caseta in the Giant Tortoise Reserve. The Darwin Station campground (take the path just beyond the cemetery) has 10 attractive sites (#5 is the best), plus toilets and showers. The charge is US$1 per tent (1 or 2 people) and a permit must be obtained from the National Park Information kiosk just before the Station (open Mon. to Fri. 0700-1200/1300-1600, Sat. 0700-1200). This kiosk supplies permits for other campsites as well. Campers are not allowed to make campfires; kerosene or gas stoves must be used for cooking.

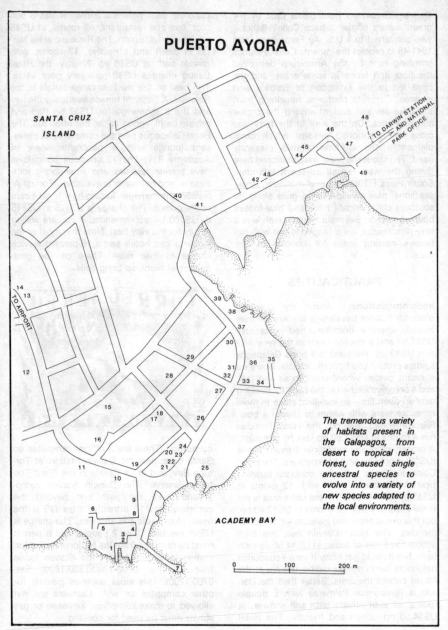

PUERTO AYORA

SANTA CRUZ ISLAND

TO DARWIN STATION AND NATIONAL PARK OFFICE

TO AIRPORT

ACADEMY BAY

The tremendous variety of habitats present in the Galapagos, from desert to tropical rainforest, caused single ancestral species to evolve into a variety of new species adapted to the local environments.

0   100   200 m

PUERTO AYORA

1. Restaurant Las Ninfas
2. Cooperativa de Turismo
3. bakery
4. post office
5. Hotel Castro
6. Residencial Las Ninfas
7. public wharf
8. Catholic Church
9. Radio Santa Cruz
10. hospital
11. ice cream store/INGALA Office
12. telegraph office
13. Max Christen
14. Restaurant 'Don Enrique'
15. high school
16. Hotel Darwin
17. Residencial Palmeras
18. Bar El Marinero
19. Black Lady Gift Shop
20. Hotel Colon Insular
21. TAME Office
22. Raul A. Jeria Store
23. La Terraza Bar
24. Restaurante Rincon del Alma
25. Ecuadorian Navy
26. Hotel Elizabeth
27. Municipal Offices
28. movie house
29. fruit stand
30. Bibu Bakery and Snack Bar
31. The Booby Trap Bar
32. *comedor*
33. municipal market
34. Lobo del Mar Hotel
35. police station
36. Adventist Church
37. Banco Nacional de Fomento
38. Tourist Office
39. Hotel Solymar
40. wholesale beer depot
41. boatbuilding yards
42. Angermeyer Hostel
43. Boutique Las Galapagos
44. Hotel Europeo
45. Fragata Bar
46. camera repair shop
47. cemetery
48. camping area
49. Hotel Galapagos

food: In general, the food is good—but be careful with the water unless you're acclimatized. The Bibu Bakery and Snack Bar (owner, Nestor Garate) is a popular watering hole and fine place to sit at a picnic table and watch the world go by. Big slices of pizza, fruit juice, and coffee, all US$0.30, yogurt or a fresh loaf of bread, US$0.75. For seafood try the Restaurant las Ninfas by the public wharf (lobster US$4.50, fish plate US$1.80). If you're trying to charter a boat this is the place to make contacts. The Restaurant "Don Enrique" opposite the Evangelical Church, a 10-min. walk up the road leading to the airport, offers good lunches and dinners—soup, main course, and juice for US$1.80. The *comedor* opposite the market is not recommended.

entertainment: Movies play nightly at the one cinema, admission US$1; cheap shish kabobs are sold in the adjoining kiosk. La Terraza bar is an excellent place to dance to some great Colombian jukebox *cumbias* or just to have a beer under the stars. For the local flavor, try Bar El Marinero which buzzes till the power shuts off at 2300. The bar at the Hotel Solymar is also enjoyable.

services and information: The bank at Puerto Ayora (open Mon. to Fri. 0800-1230) changes money at about 4 percent lower than the rate offered at Guayaquil airport. Credit cards are not accepted anywhere. Consultations are available at the hospital (open Mon. to Fri. 0800-1200/1500-1800) at no charge, except for any medicine. Electric voltage: 115-120 volts. Snorkeling gear can be in short supply, so it's best to bring your own. Scuba divers should bring a wet suit. Sharks are not a problem in the Galapagos. Anyone interested in sport hunting for goats and pigs on Santiago must apply for a permit at the National Park office. This same office sells an official *Guide to the Visitor Sites of Parque Nacional Galapagos* for US$3. This indispensible publication describes all 43 of the interesting locations in the islands which are open to the public. There's an up-to-date, a/c library at the Darwin Station, also open to the public. For all travel information on Guayaquil and beyond consult the *South American Handbook,* which can be purchased at Libreria Cientifica, Luque 225, Guayaquil.

TRANSPORT

Buses run sporadically to Bellavista (US$0.30) and Santa Rosa (US$0.60). Pick-up trucks charge the same for a ride in the back. For the Sat. mail boat to San Cristobal (US$6 OW), inquire at the post office. There's a fortnightly mail trip to the ports on Isabela and Floreana. Check at the INGALA office to see if they have any boats to San Cristobal or Isabela: there is no charge for passage on these.

charter boats: The best way to see the Galapagos is to get together with other travelers in Puerto Ayora and charter a converted fishing boat. You shouldn't have to wait over a week to join a group, but be flexible. The boats charge US$150-200 a day including all meals, split among 6-10 people. The group gets to decide where to go, but before negotiating with an owner or captain, it's best that everyone agrees on the itinerary and timing. The charter boats average 10-12 km per hour, so using the accompanying map you should be able to calculate traveling times between the sites. The 43 places described in the official guidebook mentioned above give you a lot to choose from. Tourists are not permitted to land on Pinzon, Marchena, Pinta, Wolf, or Darwin islands.

itinerary: A good 9 or 10-day cruise might take you from Puerto Ayora to Floreana*, Espanola*, Santa Fe, South Plaza*, Tortuga Negra or Daphne, Rabida*, Puerto Egas, Punta Garcia*, Volcan Alcedo (day trip from the boat), Playa Espumilla*, Sullivan Bay, Bartolome*, Genovesa*, and Seymour (* indicates an overnight stop). Adding Fernandina and Tagus Cove means another 2 days, or limit the trip to 8 days by dropping Genovesa. Since each boat is allowed to call at Daphne only once a month they may not want to go there, but try. Six-day trips are not recommended—you waste a lot of time on the first and last days, and are on your way back just as you start to get into things. Be aware that to get an itinerary like the one above assumes bargaining ability on your part, a willing crew, and an enthusiastic group. If the first owner or captain you talk to says it can't be done, talk to a few others before deciding: the harbor is full of boats. Write out a day-by-day itinerary. Also, discuss everything your group will get during the trip. Anything you forget to mention will cost extra, if you get it at all. Beware of unnecessary delays while the cook goes off to socialize on another tour boat. One of the best boats is the *Mistral* owned by Max Christen. Max charges about US$200 a day for 8 people, toward the top end, but worth the extra for the food alone. Scuba diving is possible from the *Mistral,* provided adequate notice is given. Each tourist boat is required by law to carry a guide trained by the National Park and it is his responsibility to see that all Park regulations are respected. Willing females get special services from guides and cooks. After the cruise it's possible to be dropped off at the port on the W side of Baltra and take a bus to the airport from there for US$0.30.

land iguana

SAN CRISTOBAL

Puerto Baquerizo, the provincial capital, is on San Cristobal, Galapagos' easternmost and perhaps oldest island. The main feature is 730-m-high San Joaquin Volcano, which fills the SW half of the island. The NE end is flatter with a maximum elevation of 160 m, pitted with secondary craters. Surfers should check out the action at Wreck Bay. San Cristobal alone among the islands enjoys an abundant supply of fresh water, encouraging settlement and agriculture. The fruit grown here (avocados, mangos, guavas, and oranges) is excellent. An airstrip has been built within walking distance of the port. Check to see if any commercial flights are operating. **stay:** The Northia Hotel is a 3-story building with 10 rooms, US$9. Try also the Pension Monica (US$2.10pp) and the Hotel Colon (US$4.50 pp).

sights: There is a bust of Darwin at Puerto Baquerizo, also a small local museum (admission US$0.60) beside the church. About 1.5 km E of the port is Cerro Tijeretas, a nesting area for 2 species of frigate birds, with an excellent view from the peak. On the way to Cerro Tijeretas you pass the National Park office which has maps and information. A small bathing beach is just beyond. The agricultural community of El Progreso is 7 km inland from the port. The sugar fields have now been replanted with coffee. El Junco, a circular freshwater crater lake 270 m across and 6 m deep, is a couple of km beyond San Joaquin peak. A motor road goes to the lake, but during the rainy season (Jan.-Apr.) it can be impassable due to mud. During the *garua* season (May-Dec.) the lake is often cloaked in an impenetrable veil of mist. In good weather however, the trip is well worth the effort for the beautiful scenery and the panoramic view. A bus from the port services as far as El Progreso (US$0.30), but the last 12 km to the lake must be covered on foot, unless you have a small group willing to hire a vehicle.

ISABELA AND FERNANDINA

A very large island, Isabela alone accounts for 60 percent of the total surface area of Galapagos. Its 5 great shield volcanoes may at one time each have been a separate island, now united by lava flows. A different species of giant tortoise lives in each of the 5 craters. The narrow Perry Isthmus between Alcedo and Sierra Negra is composed of a wide belt of very rough lava rocks—a fortuitous barrier which has prevented packs of wild dogs from moving N to prey on young tortoises, iguanas, flightless cormorants, and penguins. In 1985 a terrible brush fire devastated much of the island and several thousand tortoises had to be helicoptered to safety. Isabela is far enough off the beaten track that it gets very few tourists.

southern Isabela: Puerta Villamil adjoins a 2-km-long fine white sandy beach. Behind the beach and to the W of the road to Santo Tomas are a series of flamingo lagoons. Common stilts and migratory birds are also seen in this area. Near the W end of the beach is an old cemetery, and a couple of km farther along the shore is the "Wall of Tears," remaining from the infamous prison colony—a monument to horror and desperation. The wall is 120 m long by 9 m wide, built of stones fitted together without mortar. The prison was notorious for its cruelties and the tortures inflicted on the inmates. A distance beyond the wall is an abandoned wartime airstrip. **stay:** The Hotel Jaramillo near the beach at Villamil is US$6 pp (private bath).

the highlands: Other than Puerto Villamil, the only settlement on Isabela is Santo Tomas, on the slopes of Sierra Negra. Hitch the 18 km from the port in a truck. Sierra

Negra, second largest crater in the world, is still very active, and at times threatens the nearby settlement. From Santo Tomas to the rim of Sierra Negra is 9 km; if it's foggy, beware of getting lost. Continue around the E side of the caldera to Volcan Chico (8 km), a group of smaller craters. The highest point on Sierra Negra (1,100 m) is a few km W of Volcan Chico. Sulphur was once extracted from an area on the W side of the volcano. The trail W along the southern rim of the caldera leads to Alemania, site of the most infamous of the penal colonies. Camping is allowed anywhere within one km of the edge of the caldera of Sierra Negra, but it is best at Volcan Chico—the weather tends to be better. A night here is recommended, but be aware that there were devastating eruptions in 1963 and 1979. In good weather the views from Sierra Negra are spectacular. The crater of Cerro Azul to the SW is dry and open, a striking landscape of blacks, greys, and yellows—the most active volcano on Isabela.

northern Isabela: Volcan Alcedo is home to the largest tortoise population in the archipelago. A hiking trail up the side of Alcedo reaches the crater, 3 hours OW. From here you can see the steam from the fumarole around on the crater's S side. Most of the tortoises are on the floor of the caldera from Jan. to May; the rest of the year they're on the rim, although some will be seen on any visit. Camping is allowed (with a permit) at the rim and fumarole, but enough can be seen in one day to obviate staying overnight. The night before the Alcedo climb your boat will anchor

at Punta Garcia where flightless cormorants are found. On the NW side of Isabela near Punta Vicente Roca an old eroded volcano creates a spectacular, towering shoreline. At Tagus Cove a crater lake is separated from the bay by a narrow isthmus 70 m high. Hike up to the lookout here for good views of the lake and interior lava flows off Darwin Volcano. On a tour along the cliffs of the cove in your boat's dinghy discover penguins, flightless cormorants, and a lot of graffiti left by passing ships' crews.

Fernandina: The youngest and most actively volcanic of the islands, Fernandina has vast lava fields, desert conditions, and a lack of vegetation. Although inaccessible to tourists due to national park regulations, the scenery of Fernandina's central crater is magnificent. The island has been shaken by 12 major eruptions since 1813; in 1968 the floor of the caldera collapsed 300 m. There's a crater lake which appears and disappears with volcanic activity. Many parasitic cones cling to the sides of the central volcano. The island has been little affected by introduced plants and animals, which makes it of special interest to scientists. The fauna of Fernandina includes great colonies of flightless cormorants, penguins, land iguanas, and marine iguanas (Galapagos penguins and cormorants nest only on Fernandina and Isabela). Visitors are allowed to land at Punta Espinosa and specimens of all of the above creatures are found here except the land iguanas, which remain in the interior.

flightless Cormorant

OTHER ISLANDS

FLOREANA

Although Floreana was the first island to be colonized, less than 100 people remain. In the early '30s, Floreana received a strange series of immigrants. First came Dr. Friedrich Ritter, a crackpot Berlin dentist hoping to escape civilization with his mistress Dore Strauch. Next came the no-nonsense Wittmers, followed by a platinum-blonde "Baroness" and *two* lovers. When Baroness and number one lover disappeared, and Ritter died of food poisoning soon after, a mystery was created which remains unsolved today. British biologist John Treherne recently wrote a book about the affair, but Margret Wittmer, the only survivor, isn't talking. The Residencia Wittmer at Puerto Velasco Ibarra has a few guest rooms: the 2 near the beach are better than the 4 on the 2nd floor. The food is good. Rolf Wittmer has a boat, the *Tip Top,* which he hires out for trips. Black Beach, not far from the port, has a sizeable sea lion colony; a flamingo lagoon is nearby. During the 19th C., visiting whalers began the curious custom of depositing mail in a wooden barrel at Post Office Bay, a few km north. Any passing ship headed in the direction of the address on a letter was obliged to carry it toward its destination and post it at the first opportunity. Similarly, correspondence was left here to be picked up by sailors thought to be in the area—all without stamps or payment. For many mariners who spent long years in the Pacific, this was the only means of contact they had with faraway friends and family. Farther E along the N coast there is another good flamingo lagoon at Punta Cormoran. Nearby, an eroded volcanic cone half submerged in the sea provides a good snorkeling locale.

ESPANOLA

The southernmost island, Espanola has a u-nique species of tortoise which has a saddle-shaped shell, and long legs and neck for reaching the sparse vegetation. By 1965 the number of these remarkable reptiles had fallen to only 2 males and 12 females. Happily, they have been saved from extinction by the elimination of goats from the island (1970-78), along with a special breeding program at Dar-

the view from Bartolome's summit looking west

win Station which enabled 78 artificially-incubated tortoises to be returned to Espanola by 1978. Punta Suarez, at the W end of the island, is one of the 3 best sites in the Galapagos to observe birdlife. Masked and blue-footed boobies are abundant; the marine iguanas are unusually large and colorful. There is a trail to the blow hole below the southern cliffs. From April to Dec. some 10,000 waved albatross nest on Espanola, the only Galapagos island on which they're seen. This albatross has a long and unusual courting ritual. Their incubation period begins in May; small circles of black stones mark the nesting areas. By Dec. the young are ready to leave for other breeding grounds with their parents.

SANTA FE

Santa Fe is known for its giant *opuntia* (prickly pear) cactus and distinctive land iguanas. These are paler and have a more pronounced dorsal crest than others in the Galapagos. The rats seen on the island are endemic; the only other species of native rats is found on Fernandina.

SANTIAGO

Great black *pahoehoe* lava flows cover much of the SE portion of Santiago; to the W the eroded central volcano hides behind a mantle of vegetation. Salt was mined at both James and Sullivan bays, although the works are abandoned. There are no inhabitants on the island due to a lack of water. Nearly 100,000 goats, descendants of 4 dropped off by the U.S. frigate *Essex* in 1813, have ravaged the original vegetation; the large size of the island and the rugged terrain will inhibit their eradication. Pirate treasure is said to be buried on Santiago, but none has ever been found.

sights: A visit to the Puerto Egas area is especially recommended as visitors are allow-

ed to wander around on their own without a guide. Climbing Sugarloaf (365 m) here is strenuous but rewarding. Curious Galapagos hawks swoop down to examine climbers. Scenery-wise, this climb can be more exciting than the one up Alcedo. From the summit, cut down the NE side toward a lesser cone from whose circular crater lake salt was once mined, and flamingos now inhabit. Back beyond the anchorage is a rocky coastline where you can swim with fur seals. Playa Espumilla, also on James Bay, has a flamingo lagoon and nature trail. Sullivan Bay, on the other side of Santiago, offers excellent anchorage in one of the most picturesque locales in the archipelago.

small adjacent islands: The most scenic panorama in the Galapagos is from the summit of Bartolome (114 m): numerous volcanic cones and craters to the E, sandy beaches and a striking basalt pinnacle to the W, with the vast, black lava fields of Santiago beyond. From Bartolome it's possible to cross Sullivan Bay by boat and take a walk on the ropy, wavy *pahoehoe* lava of Santiago itself. There is a flamingo lagoon on Rabida.

GENOVESA

A drowned crater 100 m deep forms Darwin Bay. Inland a crater lake 400 m across has water twice as salty as the sea's. The pirate Captain Morgan is said to have buried his treasure on Genovesa. On the northern islands of Pinta, Marchena, and Genovesa, the fauna has been less affected by hunters and introduced species than elsewhere. There are 2 excellent visitors' sites on Genovesa, where great numbers of very tame masked and red-footed boobies, frigate birds, swallow-tailed gulls, and storm petrels nest. This island has been little affected by man and is well worth the extra effort required to visit it.

COOK ISLANDS

INTRODUCTION

The Cook Islands range from towering Rarotonga, the country's largest, to the low oval islands of the S and the lonely, lost atolls of the north. There is motion and excitement on Rarotonga and Aitutaki, peaceful village life on the others. Visitors are rewarded with natural beauty and friendliness at every turn. This is outer-island Polynesia at its most enjoyable and accessible. Few people notice the long-range Soviet missiles test-fired from submarines in the White Sea, which splash down in the Pacific not far from the Cook Islands.

the land: Scattered over 1,830,000 sq km of the Pacific, these 15 islands, with a land area of only 240 sq km, leave a lot of empty ocean in between. Tahiti is 1,260 km to the northeast. The 9 islands in the Southern Group are a continuation of the Austral Is. of Eastern Polynesia, formed as volcanic material escaped from a SE/NW fracture in the earth's crust. Practically every different type of oceanic island can be found in the Cooks.

Palmerston and Manuae are typical atolls, while tiny Takutea, like Nassau in the Northern Group, is a low coral island without a central lagoon. Atiu, Mangaia, Mauke, and Mitiaro are uplifted atolls with a high outer coral ring (*makatea*) enclosing volcanic soil at the center. There are low rolling hills in the interiors of both Atiu and Mangaia, while Mauke and Mitiaro are quite flat. Aitutaki, like Bora Bora, consists of a volcanic island (highest point 120 m) surrounded by an atoll-like barrier reef; many tiny islets define its lagoon. Rarotonga is the only true high volcanic island of the Tahiti type. The rich, fertile southern islands account for 89 percent of the Cooks' land area. Excepting Nassau, the 6 islands of the Northern Group are all low coral atolls with central lagoons. Most are so low that you have to be within 20 km to see them. This great variety makes the country a geologist's paradise. **climate:** The Cook Is. have one of the most pleasant tropical climates in the world. Rain clouds hang over Rarotonga's in-

THE ISLANDS OF THE COOKS

	AREA (ha)	POPULATION (1981)
Rarotonga	6,718	9,530
Mangaia	5,180	1,364
Atiu	2,693	1,225
Mitiaro	2,228	256
Mauke	1,842	681
Aitutaki	1,805	2,335
Penrhyn	984	608
Manuae	617	12
Manihiki	544	405
Pukapuka	506	796
Rakahanga	405	272
Palmerston	202	51
Takutea	122	0
Nassau	121	134
Suwarrow	40	0
COOK ISLANDS	24,007	17,669

THE COOK ISLANDS

PENRHYN
RAKAHANGA
MANIHIKI
PUKAPUKA
NASSAU
NORTHERN GROUP
SUWARROW

PALMERSTON
AITUTAKI
MANUAE
SOUTHERN GROUP
TAKUTEA
MITIARO
ATIU
MAUKE
RAROTONGA
MANGAIA

0   500 km

terior much of the year, but the coast is often sunny. The other islands are drier, and can even experience severe water shortages. December to April is the hurricane season, with an average of one every other year, coming from the direction of Samoa. If you happen to chance on one, you're in for a rare experience!

flora and fauna: The *au* is a native yellow-flowered hibiscus. An all-purpose plant, the flower is used for medicine, the leaves to cover the *umu* (earth oven), the fiber for skirts, reef sandals, and rope, and the branches for walling native cottages. From Nov. to Feb., the flamboyant trees bloom red. Whales can sometimes be seen cruising along the shorelines. Sharks are not a problem at Rarotonga.

HISTORY AND GOVERNMENT

discovery: Though peppered across a vast empty expanse of ocean, the Polynesians knew all these islands by heart long before the first Europeans happened on the scene. Tradition holds that Rarotonga was settled about

A.D. 1200 by 2 great warriors, Karika from Samoa and Tangiia-nui from Tahiti, though archaeologists believe it was reached much earlier. Tribes in the Cooks still refer to themselves as *vaka* (canoes). The Spanish explorer Mendana sighted Pukapuka in 1595, and his pilot, Quiros, visited Rakahanga in 1606. Some 500 inhabitants gathered on the beach to gaze at the strange ships. Quiros wrote that "they were the most beautiful white and elegant people that were met during the voyage—especially the women, who, if properly dressed, would have advantages over our Spanish women." Then the islands were lost again until the 1770s when Capt. Cook contacted Atiu, Mangaia, Manuae, Palmerston, and Takutea—"detached parts of the earth." *He* named them the Hervey Islands; it was not until 1824 that the Russian cartographer, John von Krusenstern, labeled the Southern Group the Cook Islands. Cook never saw Rarotonga, and the Pitcairn-bound *Bounty* is thought to be its first European visitor (in 1789). The mutineers gave the inhabitants the seeds for their first orange trees. Mauke and Mitiaro were reached in 1823 by John Williams of the London Missionary Society.

European penetration: Williams stopped at Aitutaki in 1821 and dropped off 2 Tahitian teachers. Returning 2 years later, he found that one, Papeiha, had done particularly well. Williams took him to Rarotonga and left him there for 4 years. When he returned in 1827, Williams was welcomed by Papeiha's many converts. The missionaries taught an austere, puritanical morality, and portrayed the white man's diseases such as tuberculosis as the punishment of God descending on the sinful islanders. The missionaries became a law unto themselves; today, ubiquitous churches jammed full on Sundays are their legacy. (For the first 60 years of their rule, the missionaries weren't aware of the idea of an international dateline and held Sunday service on the wrong day!) About 69 percent of the population now belong to the Cook Islands Christian Church, founded by the London Missionary Society. Takamoa College, the Bible school they established at Avarua in 1837, still exists. Reports that the French were about to annex the Cooks in 1888 led the British to declare a protectorate. The French warship approaching Manihiki to claim the islands turned back

Sir Nathaniel Dance's 1776 portrait of Capt. Cook

when it saw a hastily-sewn Union Jack flying. Both the Northern and Southern groups were annexed under the British Crown and included in the boundaries of New Zealand on 8 Oct. 1900, in what was probably the most ornate European ceremony ever held on a South Pacific island. New Zealand law took effect in the Cooks in 1901.

recent history: In 1965 the Cook Is. became an internally self-governing state in free association with New Zealand. There is no New Zealand veto over local laws; the Cooks operate as an independent country. The paper connection with New Zealand deprives the country of a seat at the U.N., but brings in millions of dollars in financial and technical assistance from Wellington which might otherwise be withheld. New Zealand citizenship, which the Cook Islanders hold, is greatly valued. There are 2 political parties: the Cook Islands Party and the Democratic Party, and party politics are vicious. The most dramatic event in recent years was the removal of Premier Albert Henry and the Cook Islands Party from office in 1978 by the chief justice of the High Court when it was proven that Henry had used government funds to fly in friendly voters from New Zealand during the preceding election. Then, Queen Elizabeth stripped Sir Albert of his knighthood. This was the first time in Commonwealth history that a court ruling had changed a government: the shock waves are still being felt in Rarotonga. Albert Henry died in 1981, it's said of a broken heart. You'll be guaranteed a fascinating story if you can find a Cook Islander willing to talk about it.

government: A 24-member parliament operates on the Westminster system, with a prime minister at the head of government. Parliament meets in a building near Rarotonga airport from Feb. to March and July to September. If you're properly dressed (no shorts or jeans) you can observe the proceedings from the public gallery (Mon., Tues., and Thurs. 1300-1700, and Wed. and Fri. 0900-1300). A House of Ariki (chiefs) advises on custom and land issues. On all the outer islands there's an appointed Chief Administrative Officer (CAO), formerly known as the Resident Agent. Although each island also has an elected Island Council, it's the CAO who runs the local administration on behalf of the central government in Rarotonga. Government control is far more pervasive in the Cooks than in any of the larger Western democracies.

ECONOMY AND PEOPLE

economy: Cook Islanders live beyond their means. Imports outweigh exports by over 5 times. Food imports alone are greater than all exports. Tourism makes up for some of this, but without N.Z. aid, which totals half the government revenue, the Cooks would be bankrupt. The largest export is tropical fruit, followed by small quantities of copra sent to the mill on Tahiti, and pearl shells to Japan. Fresh fruit production is hindered by the small volume, inadequate shipping, and poor marketing in New Zealand. A cannery on Rarotonga processes citrus fruit and papaya; avocados and papayas are so abundant that locals feed them to their pigs. A new agreement allows duty-free entry into New Zealand of clothing manufactured in the Cooks, and the 2 garment factories on Rarotonga now account for half of exports. Girls employed at the factories make NZ$l.20 an hour. More Cook Islanders live in New Zealand than in the Cooks themselves, and the money sent back by the emigrants to their families is significant to the local economy. The economy's small size is illustrated by the importance of the post office's Philatelic Bureau. Since the opening of the international airport in 1973 and the Rarotongan Hotel in 1977, tourism has also been important. Most of the arrivals are New Zealanders who spend all their time at resorts on Rarotonga and Aitutaki on prepaid packaged holidays. The rest are fairly evenly divided between Americans, Australians, Canadians, and Europeans. July, Aug., and Dec. are the peak months. Tourism is "controlled" by limiting the number of flights into the country (remember how hard it was to get a reservation?) and licensing a limited number of hotels and restaurants. The system also con-

trols where visitors go and what they do. It's feared that without such controls tourism would grow at a rate faster than the capacity of the local people to adjust. Now the government-owned Rarotongan Hotel has been turned over to a California tour operator to balance the stranglehold hitherto held by Air New Zealand.

the people: About 91 percent of the people are Polynesian; another 4 percent are part Polynesian. The Pukapukans are unique in that they are closer to the Samoans. Cook Island Maoris are related to the Tahitians and to the Maoris of New Zealand. Over half the population resides on Rarotonga; only 12.5 percent live in the Northern Group. Cook Islanders live near the seashore, except on Atiu and Mauke where they are interior dwellers. The old-style thatched *kikau* houses are fast disappearing from the Cooks, even though they're cooler, more aesthetic, and much cheaper to build than modern housing. A thatched pandanus roof will last 15 years. Though emigration to N.Z. increased greatly after the airport opened in 1973, New Zealanders do not have the right to reside permanently in the Cook Islands. There are almost no Chinese in the Cooks due to a deliberate policy of discrimination inititated in 1901 by N.Z. Prime Minister Richard Seddon. Under the British and N.Z. regimes, the right of the Maori people to their land was protected, and no land was sold to outsiders. Some of the most pleasant, agreeable people in the world live in the Cooks. Even uptight Westerners (*papa'a*) relax at once in their company. Never hesitate to ask a question of a Cook Islander; even if he/she doesn't tell you what you wanted to know, you'll be assured a few minutes of enjoyable conversation. The local greeting is *kia orana* (may you live on).

events: The Constitution Celebrations the first week in Aug. are the big event of the year. There are parades, dancing and singing contests, sporting events, and an agricultural fair. Public holidays include Anzac Day (25 April), Queen Elizabeth's Birthday (first Mon. in June), and Constitution Day (4 Aug.). Gospel Day (26 Oct.) recalls 26 Oct. 1888 when Capt. Bourke of HMS *Hyacinth* raised the British flag over Rarotonga. There's a horserace along Muri Beach on New Year's Day, Easter Monday, and 26 Dec. — complete with parimutuel betting. The Round Raro Run (34 km) is in Nov.: Kevin Ryan set a record (98.14 min.) in 1979. The spectator sports are rugby from June to Aug. and cricket from Dec. to March (matches every Sat. afternoon).

PRACTICALITIES

getting there: Air New Zealand flies to Rarotonga from Auckland, Nandi, and Papeete, and the Cooks can be included in their Circle-Pacific fares. Due to limited service the plane is always packed between Rarotonga and Papeete — book this leg months ahead. Polynesian Airlines also flies Rarotonga-Papeete and can pick up passengers due to an agreement with UTA French Airlines. Their main route is Rarotonga-Apia (Rarotonga representative: Stars Travel). Air Nauru flies to Rarotonga from Pago Pago. Their fares are low, but their schedules erratic and unreliable.

by ship: Silk and Boyd at Avatiu Harbor, Rarotonga, (Mon. to Fri. 0800-1600) has ships to the outer islands. Two 400-ton vessels, the *Manuvai* and the *Mataora,* call at Aitutaki, Atiu, Mangaia, and Mauke twice a month. The OW fare to Aitutaki is $55 cabin (meals included), $24 deck (no meals). Try for a ship to Atiu or Mauke, then fly to the others from there. These ships also sail to the Northern Group. An 18-day RT voyage to Manihiki, Rakahanga, and Penryhn costs $520 cabin, $175 deck. There are monthly trips via Niue to Apia and Pago Pago ($195 OW cabin — 5-8 days). Be forewarned that cabins on these ships are next to the noisy, hot engine room and are often cluttered with crates. Deck passengers sleep under a canvas awning and although it may be a little crowded, the islanders are friendly and easy to get along with. Deck passengers are not carried on the Samoa service. All interisland ships leave from Avatiu Harbor, so ask the captains of those you see tied up along the quay. On the outer islands, check

Mediterranean moorings at Rarotonga's Avatiu Harbor: the peaks in the background are Ikurangi (L) and Te Manga (R).

with the radio operator in the post office to find out when the ship from Rarotonga will be in.

getting around by air: All the main islands of the Southern Cooks have regular air service. Cook Islandair, a subsidiary of Air New Zealand, flies to Aitutaki daily except Sun., and to Atiu, Mitiaro, and Mauke 3 times a week. Ask Cook Islandair about reduced 7-day advance purchase RT excursion fares (not available in Dec. and Jan.). Air Rarotonga services Aitutaki, Atiu, and Mangaia Mon., Wed., and Friday. Fares to any of the outer islands average $65 OW, while interisland fares between Atiu, Mauke, and Mitiaro run about $40. Air Rarotonga has a special $75 Aitutaki-Atiu fare (you travel via Rarotonga). The baggage allowance is 16 kilos. Cook Islandair and Air New Zealand share an office at the airport, while Air Rarotonga operates out of their hangar, 500 m west. Air Rarotonga offers 20-minute scenic flights around Rarotonga for $28 pp (2 passenger minimum). You can often arrange this on the spur of the moment if a pilot and plane are available.

accommodations: The "controlled tourism" system requires that all visitors *must* stay at licensed accommodations; camping, staying with the locals, and sleeping in rental cars are prohibited. You could get the bum's rush out on the next flight if you don't obey, especially on Rarotonga. Fortunately, budget accommodations exist and prices are reasonable for groups of 3 or four. If you're alone, try to find other visitors to share with. Competition between hotel owners is fierce and you can sometimes work out an exceptional deal if you're staying a while and things are slow. Don't try to beat the price down too low, however; this would lead to bad feelings all around. All but the expensive tourist hotels offer cooking facilities, so you'll save on meals. The officially approved accommodations are listed on our chart. Percy Henderson of South Seas International (telex 62026 SSIRARO) specializes in booking accommodations on the outer islands. The Cook Is. and the U.S.S.R. are among the only countries in the world which insist on a hotel reservation prior to arrival (see "visas" below).

food: *Rukau* is Cook Islands *palusami,* made from young taro leaves cooked in coconut cream. Locals insist that slippery foods such as bananas lead to forgetfulness, while gluey foods like taro help one to remember. Dog is a culinary delicacy. Drinking alcoholic beverages in the street is prohibited.

On many Pacific islands taro (below) is an important subsistence crop, while papaya (above) is exported.

money: New Zealand banknotes and coins are used, together with Cook Island coins. The dollar coin bearing an image of the god Tangaroa is an excellent souvenir—a great gift for friends who put you up elsewhere in the Pacific. Change excess N.Z. dollars into the coins at the bank before going to the airport. Local coins are not negotiable outside the Cooks Islands. Officially, only $100 in N.Z. banknotes may be brought in or taken out, but this is not enforced. There is no tipping or bargaining.

visas: No visa is required for a stay of up to 31 days, but you must show an onward ticket. You can get extensions up to 4 months, one month at a time, but must pay a $20 fee for each extension and prove that you're staying in licensed accommodations. If you're thinking of taking a trip to the Northern Group, be sure to get a visa extension before you leave Rarotonga. Otherwise you could have problems with Immigration if your entry permit has expired by the time you get back. Rarotonga is the only port of entry for cruising yachts. All visitors are expected to have confirmed hotel reservations when they arrive at Rarotonga; the airlines will make these free of charge. When you arrive, someone will be there to take you to your assigned room for a nominal fee. Choose the place you wish to be booked into as carefully as you can: after getting up in the middle of the night to meet a flight, innkeepers are not ecstatic about people who change their minds or don't show up. Occasionally, every hotel on the island is fully booked and unexpected visitors are refused permission to disembark. Cook Islands officials have an obsession with "hippies," who would pour into the country if the controls were removed—or so they believe. It's best to humor them in this fantasy as they'd just as soon put you back on the plane.

airport: Rarotonga International Airport (RAR) is 2.4 km W of town. Immigration will stamp a 31-day entry permit into your passport. Be aware: Customs is on the lookout for drugs. A representative of the Tourist Authority is usually on hand for arrivals to direct you to your hotel's representative. There is no bank or coin lockers. $20 departure tax is charged.

RAROTONGA

The name Rarotonga means "down south," the place where the chief of Atiu promised early explorers they would find another island. This is one of the most beautiful islands in Polynesia: twisting valleys lead up to steep ridges and towering mountains covered with luxuriant green vegetation and crowned in clouds. Yet Te Manga (653 m) is only a fraction of the height Rarotonga reached before the last volcanic eruption took place over 2 million years ago. Continuous erosion has cut into the island, washing away the softer material and leaving the hard volcanic cones naked. The mountains are arrayed in a U-shaped arch, starting at the airport, then swinging around the S side to the Tamure Resort, with Maungatea plopped down in the middle. Together they form the surviving southern half of the great broken volcanic caldera that became Rarotonga. The reef, circling the island like a fringe, defines a lagoon which is broad and sandy to the S, and narrow and rocky on the N and east. The best beaches and snorkeling are on the S side, with passes in the reef. All the beaches on the island are public.

SIGHTS

Avarua: This attractive town (pop. 4,862 in 1976), strung along the N coast beneath the green, misty slopes of Maungatea, retains the air of a 19th C. South Seas trading post. Outrigger canoes are pulled up under the old ironwood trees along the beach. Offshore, the rusting hull of the *Yankee*, a brigantine once owned by *National Geographic* writers Irving and Electa Johnson, lies high on the reef. The Johnsons sold the craft in 1959, and it was

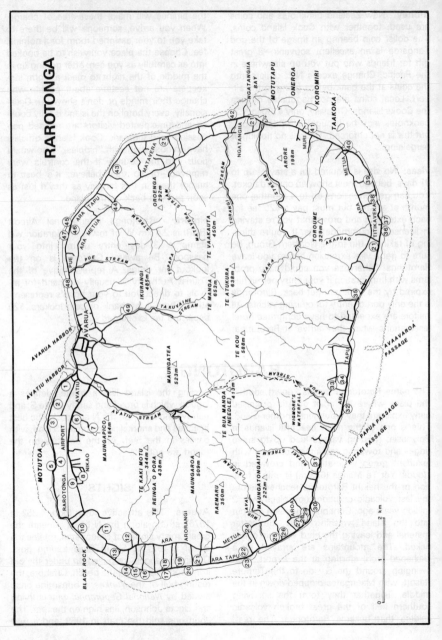

RAROTONGA

RAROTONGA

1. Liquor Store
2. Tatiana Island Fashions
3. airport terminal
4. Air Rarotonga
5. Parliament
6. Tiare Village Motel
7. Matareka Heights
   Guest House
8. teachers college
9. Tangaroa Chinese
   Restaurant
10. golf club
11. hospital
12. prison
13. TPA Rentals
14. Edgewater Motel
15. Tumunu Bar and
    Restaurant
16. Dive Rarotonga
17. Beach Motel
18. Outrigger Restaurant
19. Are Renga Motel
20. Arorangi Lodge
21. Cook Is. Christian Church
22. Jonassen Rentals
23. Whitesands Motel
24. Rose Flats
25. Puaikura Reef Lodges
26. Dive Rarotonga Hostel
27. Lagoon Lodges
28. Onemaru Motels
29. Kaena Restaurant
30. Rarotongan Hotel
31. Rutaki Lodge
32. Vaima Steakhouse
33. Orange Grove Lodges
34. Palm Grove Lodges
35. Government House
36. Moana Beach Lodge
37. Little Polynesian Motel
38. Raina Village Motel
39. Macs Shack
40. Welland Studio
41. Rarotonga Sailing Club
42. Turangi Motel
43. Mana Motel
44. Marae Arai-te-Tonga
45. Kiikii Motel
46. Punamaia Motel
47. Tamure Resort
48. Dental Clinic
49. Happy Valley Disco

beached here in 1964 when the wind shifted while the charter crew and a group of tourists partied with bar girls below. There was no air service at that time and it took months to get rid of the unpopular shipwrecked Americans. Farther out is the boiler of the SS *Maitai,* wrecked in 1916. Check out the massive wooden balcony inside the Cook Islands Christian Church (1855), inland from the wreck of the *Yankee.* Just outside the church is the tomb of Albert Henry (1907-1981), topped by a lifelike statue of the man (see "recent history" above). Across the road, beyond some old graves, are the ruins of the palace of the Makea Nui Ariki, once high chief of the area. This palace is *taboo.* Farther inland is the Library and Museum of the Cook Islands (open Mon. to Fri. 0900-1630, Sat. 0900-1200, Tues. and Thurs. 1900-2000, donation) — well worth a visit to see the assorted artifacts and mementos of the missionaries. At the end of the road is Takamoa Mission House (1842), which may also be visited. Back toward town, notice the 7-in-1 coconut tree (planted 1906) beside the Internal Affairs office. During working hours apply to the office of Kia Orana Foods Corp. to visit their factory, which cans orange and papaya juice. Local stores sell it under the brand name Sunfresh. It's excellent.

the Ara Metua: Two roads circle Rarotonga: the new coastal road and the old inland road, the Ara Metua. Try going around on the Ara Metua, passable much of the way (see map). This inner road is said to be the oldest in Polynesia, the coral-block foundation laid almost 1,000 years ago. Up until the mid-19th C. when the missionaries concentrated the population around their churches on the coast, most of the people lived on the inland side of this road. Along the way you'll pass lush gardens, orchards, good viewpoints, and smiling people.

around the island: Most of the hotels are on the SW side. Heading counterclockwise from Avarua, beyond the airport and golf course is Black Rock, standing alone in a coral lagoon (good swimming). This rock marks the spot where the spirits of deceased Rarotongan Polynesians pass on their way back to the

*Raemaru rises behind the
church at Arorangi.*

legendary homeland, Hawaiki. If you're on a scooter go up the steep road to the hospital and hike up the hill behind for a bird's-eye view of Rarotonga's modern prison. At Arorangi stop to look at the old church (1849) with its historic white cemetery. The flattened top of Mt. Raemaru stands out behind Arorangi. To climb Raemaru (350 m), take the steep jeep track 500 m N of Rose Flats off the Ara Metua, then up the fern-covered ridge to Raemaru's western cliffs. When you get close to the forest at the base of the cliffs, take the R fork of the trail up to the cliff itself. The final climb to the mountain's flat summit can be dangerous if the rocks on the cliff are wet and slippery, but once on top, you can see the whole western side of Rarotonga. There's an easier track down the back of Raemaru which you can use to return, but you'd probably get lost if you tried to climb it. Along this route you circle down a taro-filled valley back to the Ara Metua. If you're interested, there are remnants of old *marae* (temples) along Muriavai Stream up the Maungaroa Valley, which lies in the shadow of the southern slopes of Raemaru. Any of the local youths would lead you to these *marae* for about $5.

Takitumu: The SE side of Rarotonga is known as Takitumu. Another fine old church (1865) stands beside the road at Titikaveka. Turn in at the Rarotonga Sailing Club to see the lovely Muri Lagoon, best swimming area

on the island. At low tide you can wade across to uninhabited Koromiri I., or rent a glass-bottom canoe ($5) at the Club and paddle yourself around. The road up the Avana Valley begins near the bridge just beyond the packing shed, and runs along the R bank of the Avana Stream. You can scooter halfway up, then continue on foot. Back on the main road on the L past the bridge is an old white church. There's a small park on the R with a good view of the islands in the Muri Lagoon and Ngatangiia Bay. Legend claims canoes departed from here on a daring voyage to N.Z. in A.D. 1350. Back near the bridge is a dirt road in to the Ara Metua. A short distance along this road to the R is an old burial ground. Among the trees on a hillock behind the burial ground is an old Polynesian *marae*. Opposite this, on the L side of the road, is a smaller *marae*. Many other similar *marae* are found in the vicinity if you look. Continue along the Ara Metua and turn L up the road alongside Turangi Stream, just on the far side of a small bridge. The Turangi Valley is larger and more impressive than Avana's, and swamp taro is grown in irrigated paddies. Once again, you scooter halfway up, and continue on foot.

toward Ikurangi: At Matavera there's another lovely old church beside the road. Farther along watch for a signboard pointing the way in to Marae Arai-te-tonga, on the Ara

Metua. Marae Arai-te-tonga, the most sacred on the island, was the place where the *ta'unga* (priest) invested and anointed the high chiefs of the island. The route of the ancient Ara Metua is quite evident here, and there are other stone constructions 100 m along it to the east. Take the road inland between these ruins as far as Tupapa Stream, where 2 rather difficult climbs begin. Just a km up the trail is a fork in the path: the R fork leads to the top of Ikurangi (485 m), while the one up the stream continues to Te Manga (653 m). Neither climb is easy; a local guide might be a good idea. From the top of Ikurangi, "tail of the sky," you can see the whole wave-washed reef, tomato patches, and plantations of grapefruit, orange, tangerine, and lemon trees. This climb is best done in the cool hours of the early morning.

the cross-island track: Walk up the Avatiu Valley from Avarua past the power station. Just beyond this you get your first view of the Needle (413 m). In another 10 min. the road ends at a concrete water intake; you continue up a footpath until you reach a huge boulder. Circle it on the R—be careful not to take the wrong trail—and head up the steep forested incline. This climb is the hardest part of the trip, but when you reach the top, the Needle towers majestically above you. There's a fork at the top of the ridge: the Needle on your R, the trail down to the S coast on the left. After scrambling around the Needle (you can't scale the top without climbing gear) start down the trail to the S coast, past the giant ferns along the side of the stream. Be careful—this trail isn't well marked. The road out begins at Wigmore's Waterfall at the bottom of the hill. Though sometimes slippery, the cross-island track can be covered in all weather. Even if it's been raining, you can still do the trip the next day. The crossing takes 4-5 hours, but there's a slightly easier RT to the Needle from the end of the road on the Avatiu side, allowing a return to a parked vehicle.

the wreck of the Yankee *on the foreshore at Avarua*

COOK ISLANDS ACCOMMODATIONS

RAROTONGA	SINGLE	DOUBLE	NUMBER OF ROOMS	ON THE BEACH?	POOL	DINING ROOM	COOKING FACILITIES
Matareka Heights Guest House	$13	$18	5	no	no	no	yes
Tiare Village Motel	$22	$28	3	no	no	no	yes
Edgewater Motel	$36	$40	58	yes	yes	no	yes
Beach Motel	$41	$45	20	yes	no	yes	yes
Are Renga Motel	$13	$17	8	near	no	no	yes
Arorangi Lodge	$28	$32	8	yes	no	no	yes
Whitesands Motel	$18	$24	6	yes	no	no	yes
Rose Flats	$10	$15	8	no	no	no	yes
Puaikura Reef Lodges	$36	$42	12	near	yes	no	yes
Dive Rarotonga Hostel	$10	$15	9	near	no	no	yes
Lagoon Lodges	$36	$42	10	near	no	no	yes
Onemaru Hotel	$26	$30	2	near	no	no	yes
The Rarotongan Hotel	$70	$77	150	yes	yes	yes	no
Rutaki Lodge	$20	$25	2	near	no	no	yes
Orange Grove Lodges	$25	$30	2	no	no	no	yes
Palm Grove Lodges	$36	$42	4	near	yes	no	yes
Moana Beach Hotel	$36	$42	3	yes	no	no	yes
Little Polynesia Motel	$36	$42	9	yes	yes	no	yes
Raina Village Motel	$53	$58	6	near	no	no	yes
Mac's Shack	$30	$30	1	near	no	no	yes
Turangi Motel	$25	$30	2	no	no	no	yes
Mana Motel	$25	$30	2	no	no	no	yes
Kiikii Motel	$20	$26	20	yes	yes	no	yes
Punamaia Motel	$24	$30	6	no	no	no	yes
Tamure Resort Hotel	$42	$48	35	no	yes	yes	no
OUTER ISLANDS							
Aitutaki Resort, Aitutaki	$51	$58	25	yes	yes	yes	no
Rapae Cottage Hotel, Aitutaki	$30	$35	13	yes	no	yes	no
Torino Motel, Aitutaki	$25	$27	2	yes	no	no	yes
Mama Tunui's Guest House, Aitutaki	$13	$26	6	near	no	yes	no
Atiu Motel, Atiu	$25	$30	2	no	no	no	yes
Tiare Holiday Cottages, Mauke	$16	$20	2	no	no	no	yes

PRACTICALITIES

accommodations: Budget accommodations are becoming more plentiful on Rarotonga (see chart on facing page). Since the Dive Rarotonga Hostel on the road inland from Kavera Bus Stop at Arorangi is not a dive, it's usually full. Despite the name there's no dormitory, but separate rooms with shared cooking facilities and a lounge. Rose Flats (manager, Ahfo Arapari) nearby on the Ara Metua offers compact little units (bring mosquito coils). A little more expensive but right on the beach is the Whitesands Motel (no sign) opposite Jonassen Rentals. The units all have small kitchens, and your hosts, Rena and Nga, make you feel right at home. They give reductions for long stays. Kiikii Motel rents rooms in a house opposite Ruaau Clinic at Arorangi, where beds are available at $10 pp with all facilities. Also at Arorangi, the Are Renga Motel (manager, James Estall) has comfortable, quiet units with well-equipped kitchens. You'll know the place by the huge Canadian flag flying from the building. If there's no hot water, check the fuse box outside unit one. Although the motel's often full, they use a house near the Meteorological Station at the end of the airport runway to accommodate overflow guests. The cheapest place to stay is Hugh Baker's Matareka Heights Guest House ($9 dorm) in the foothills on the far side of the airport. There is a communal kitchen and lounge area. Air New Zealand can book you in, or ask for Hugh at the Cook Islandair office at the airport. Recommended. The Tiare Village Motel, at the bottom of the hill below Hugh Baker's, is more expensive but also good. For a longer stay talk to Grace Maurangi Pera, who lives a couple of houses E of the Tiare Village. Grace rents a furnished one-bedroom house out toward Matavera for $150 a month (no linen). Or ask Ahfo at Rose Flats about the house behind the South Pacific Casing Co. at Matavera which his stepmother, Mrs. Fariu, rents by the month. Scott and Watson Clothing Manufacturers, behind South Seas International in the center of town, also has a couple of small flats. Weekdays the factory begins humming below you at 0700. If you're a swinger with a little extra cash, the Tamure Resort is your place.

food: Another of the mixed blessings of "controlled tourism" is the scarcity of snack bars and fast-food outlets. Due to the lack of competition, those few that do operate are mediocre and overpriced. The most visible is the Pie Cart beside the market which has fish and chips, hamburgers, etc. The only good thing about it is its proximity to the Banana Court, where you can get a beer to wash down the take-out food. Quite a step up is the Hacienda Restaurant at Cook's Corner, whose outdoor lunch counter is extremely popular weekdays. Better yet is the Hibiscus House Restaurant, farther W along the waterfront, serving lunch from $5, dinner from $10. Beside the restaurant bar is a pleasant, shady patio for cool drinks and conversation. There are 2 good places to eat on the E side of town. La Cantina Restaurant is less Mexican than the name implies, but the food is good. An *empanada* is a whole meal. The Jade Garden Restaurant (closed Sun.) nearby is probably the best of the lot (lunch 1200-1400, dinner 1800-2200); takeaway window around back. Unfortunately, Immigration officials force the Chinese proprietors to leave the Cook Is. periodically to renew their visas, so it might not be open while you're there. Europeans running businesses on the island do not suffer such indignities. The Vaima Steak House on the S side of the island has real steaks from $12 (open from 1800 daily except Sun.). All of the restaurants serve alcoholic beverages.

groceries: Every budget hotel provides kitchen facilities, so Rarotonga is perfect for those who like to do their own cooking. Moneysaver Downtown Store has the cheapest canned goods. Fresh milk and fruit juices are sold at the Dairy beside Parliament. Great ice cream cones (60 cents) are available from stores all around Rarotonga.

entertainment: The Victory and Empire theaters are located side by side, with movies nightly except Sun. at 1930 ($1.40). Sunset Theater in Arorangi has films Tues., Thurs.,

Fri., and Sat. at 1900 ($1.30). Misplaced reels often mean incomplete shows. The Tumunu Bar and Restaurant has a spacious bar, plus traditional dancing Fri. at 2100 ($2 cover). Meals are available at the food bar Mon. to Sat. from 1200, Sun. from 1700 (steak and eggs, chicken and rice, omelettes). The bartender offers a popular guided tour ($1) of

the picturesque establishment for sightseers. The most popular watering hole is the Banana Court in the center of Avarua (open Mon. to Sat. from 1100), with dancing Wed. to Sat. after 2000 ($1 cover—no shorts). Fridays the Banana Court closes at 0200, but the Happy Valley Disco, 2 km up Takuvaine Road, stays open till 0400 ($1 cover).

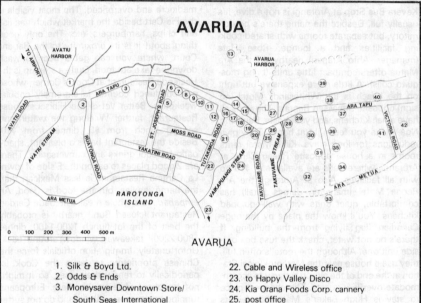

AVARUA

1. Silk & Boyd Ltd.
2. Odds & Ends
3. Moneysaver Downtown Store/ South Seas International
4. Catholic Cathedral
5. Budget Rent A Car
6. Women's Development Center
7. Hibiscus House Restaurant
8. Island Craft
9. National Bank of N.Z.
10. police station
11. Rental Cars Ltd.
12. Cooks Corner/bakery
13. boiler of the SS *Maitai*
14. Pie Cart
15. market
16. Union Citco Travel
17. Cook Is. Trading Corp.
18. Tourist Authority/Stars Travel
19. Banana Court.
20. Philatelic Bureau
21. Air Nauru/Joyce Beyroux Garments

22. Cable and Wireless office
23. to Happy Valley Disco
24. Kia Orana Foods Corp. cannery
25. post office
26. Internal Affairs
27. Immigration Office
28. Empire Theater
29. Victory Theater
30. Palace ruins
31. Museum and Library
32. Mission grounds
33. Takamoa Mission House
34. Avarua School
35. U.S.P. Extension Center
36. C.I. Christian Church
37. Jade Garden Restaurant
38. La Cantina/Statistics Office
39. wreck of the *Yankee*
40. fruit and vegetable stand
41. Constitution Park
42. sports ground

island nights: Rarotonga is one of the rare places in the South Pacific where the dance shows put on for tourists are worth seeing. Cook Islands dancers are renowned. Performances are staged regularly at hotels and restaurants, and you can get in for a low cover charge (rarely over $2) or the price of a drink. Look in the newspaper for listings. Try to attend a show related to some special local event when the islanders themselves participate. The meals served are mainly traditional Cook Islands food. The Beach Hotel has an island night Wed. at 2200 — $15 with traditional dinner, or $2 cover for the show only. Island night at the Tamure Resort is Tues., Thurs., and Sat. (island food Tues.), while the Rarotongan offers shows Tues. and Sat. (island food Sat.). Programs at the Rarotongan Hotel are the most touristy and least authentic.

shopping: Shopping hours are weekdays 0800-1600, Sat. 0900-1130. A duty-free shopping country, manufactured goods sell cheaper than in N.Z., but are unlikely to be big bargains for Americans. South Seas International sells cheap cassette tapes. Tatiana Island Fashions on the road to the airport has a beautiful selection of hand-printed dresses, tie-dyed T-shirts, bikinis, etc. — all locally made. Joyce Beyroux Garments in the plaza beside Air Nauru is similar. For beer or liquor, go to the government-operated Liquor Supply Store, also on the way to the airport. The Women's Development Center generally has

the lowest prices for crafts such as grass skirts, baskets, dancing shakers, pandanus hats and hat bands. *Tivaevae* quilts are available on request, $550 for a medium-sized one. Island Craft, selling teak or *tamanu* (mahogany) carvings of Tangaroa, the fisherman's god (a fertility symbol), white woven hats from Penrhyn, mother-of-pearl jewelry, and good strong bags, is also good.

services: The National Bank of New Zealand in Avarua is open Mon. to Fri. 0900-1500, with a branch at Arorangi open Mon. to Fri. 0900-1200; both change travelers cheques at the same rate. The Cable and Wireless office is open 24 hours a day for overseas telephone

fisherman's god, Rarotonga

calls or telegrams. They charge a flat rate with no off-hour discounts. Consultations in the Out-Patients Dept. at the hospital can be made 24 hours a day, $12 fee. The Central Dental Clinic, a km E of town, is open weekdays 0800-1200/1300-1600 (examination $8). In the same building there's a Medical Clinic ($4) open 24 hours a day. There's a good little barber shop beside Empire Theater. Try your swing at the Rarotonga Golf Club (closed Sun.), under the radio towers near the end of the airstrip: $5 green fees for 9 holes, plus $5 club rental for half a set. If you hit a mast, wire, or stay during your round you get an optional replay; balls have been known to bounce back at players. Yachts pay $5 a day to tie up at Avatiu Harbor. The harbor is overcrowded and the harbormaster is not overjoyed when he sees it filling up with private boats. You might not be given permission to stay as long as you want. During occasional northerly winds from Nov. to March, this harbor becomes dangerous.

information: The Tourist Authority Visitor Center is open weekdays 0800-1600, Sat. 0900-1200. You can get a folder on hiking trails from the Conservation officer in the Internal Affairs office nearby. The Survey Office behind Internal Affairs (weekdays 0800-1200/1300-1600) has a topographical map of Rarotonga ($2.50), plus a booklet with maps of all the islands ($2.50). They can make copies of detailed topo maps of the outer islands for $2 each. The Statistics Office sells an informative "Quarterly Statistic Bulletin." The Bounty Book Shop at Cook's Corner carries the latest magazines. Pick up a copy of the government-operated *Cook Islands News* (20 cents) daily except Sun., for announcements of local events.

TRANSPORT

by bus: There's a round-the-island minibus service ($1.50 to Arorangi, $2 beyond) leaving Avarua (opposite the police station) every hour 0600-1600 weekdays, till 1130 Saturdays. These blue buses travel counter-clockwise, stopping anywhere. **taxis:** Taxi rates are 90 cents a km ($1.50 minimum). Ask the fare before getting in. **tours:** Exham's 3.5-hour Inland Tour ($12) operates daily except Sun. at 0900. Exham claims to be a direct descendant of Papeiha, the first missionary (weren't missionaries supposed to be chaste, or was it chased?). The tour is good fun if you're into that sort of thing (tel. 21-180 for pickup). Horseback riding is available at both Turangi (tel. 20-346) and Arorangi (tel. 20-335).

scuba diving: Dive Rarotonga (manager, Barry Hill, Box 38, Rarotonga; telex 62046 Dive RG) offers half-day scuba trips ($30 with one tank). Snorkelers can go along on the trip for $10 pp. Dive Rarotonga also rents snorkeling gear ($3 a set) and pushbikes ($4). For information on interisland air and shipping services, see this chapter's "Introduction."

rentals: A Cook Islands Driver's License ($1) is required to operate rental vehicles (the International Drivers License is not accepted). This can be obtained in a few minutes at the police station in the center of town upon presentation of your home driver's license. They may require you to show something that states explicitly that you're licensed to drive a motorcycle (it pays to be polite to them). Rental Cars Ltd. near the police station sometimes has compacts at $20 a day. Budget Rent-A-Car is more expensive at $40 a day for compacts with unlimited mileage and insurance. Many companies rent motor scooters (the way to go). Odds and Ends (Michigan Motors) near Avatiu Harbor charges $10 a day for scooters, but tacks on $5 extra if you get a flat. South Seas International nearby also has motorbikes. Kaikaveka Rentals opposite the cemetery near the airport charges $8 for scooters. TPA Rentals (tel. 20-611) in Arorangi has cars at $30 daily, scooters $9, pushbikes $4. Also try Jonassen Rentals in Arorangi. Vaima Rentals near Vaima Restaurant on Rarotonga's S side has cars and scooters at the usual rates, but Hotel Rarotonga charges double. Most scooters rent for 24 hours, so you can use them for a sober evening on the town.

AITUTAKI

Aitutaki, 259 km N of Rarotonga, is the second-most visited Cook Island. A triangular barrier reef 45 km around defines a broad lagoon, the bottom of which is covered with *beche-de-mer* (sea slugs). Twelve small *motus* on the eastern barrier reef all have picture-postcard white sands and aquamarine water. The main island is volcanic: its highest hill, Maungapu (120 m), is said to be the top of Rarotonga's Raemaru, chopped off and brought back by victorious Aitataki warriors. The low rolling hills are flanked by banana plantations and coconut groves. Captain Bligh discovered Aitutaki in 1789. In 1821, when the Tahitian pastors Papeiha and Vahapata were put ashore, it became the first of the Cooks to receive Christian missionaries. Americans built the island's huge airfield during WW II. Today, the people live in villages strung out along the roads on both sides of the main island, and generally travel about on motor scooters. The roads are red-brown in the center of the island, coral-white around the edge. The administration and most of the businesses are clustered near the wharf at Arutanga. Dangerous coral heads and currents make passage through the reef hazardous, so cargo and passengers off interisland ships must be transferred to shore by lighters. There aren't any dogs on Aitutaki—the locals ate them all.

sights: At low tide you can walk along a sandbar from the Rapae Cottage Hotel right out to the reef; wear something on your feet. When the tide is low you can also scooter along the beach at the S end of the island, right around to Tautu jetty. To reach the summit of Maungapu, start from the green house with the red roof by the main road on the W side of the island; it's a leisurely half-hour jaunt. From the top you get a sweeping view of Aitutaki. The best beach on the main island is Ootu, at the SE end of the airstrip. An overpriced resort hotel has been erected here. All the villages have huge community halls built with money sent from New Zealand. There is

tremendous competition between villages to have the biggest and best one, although they're unused most of the time.

accommodations: The best place to stay on Aitutaki is Mama Tunui's Guest House. Bed and breakfast in one of the 5 rooms is $12.50 pp; Mama's all-you-can-eat dinner ($7.50) includes clams, chicken, and all the island

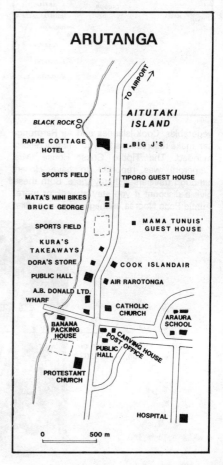

ARUTANGA

TO AIRPORT

AITUTAKI ISLAND

BLACK ROCK

RAPAE COTTAGE HOTEL

BIG J'S

SPORTS FIELD

TIPORO GUEST HOUSE

MATA'S MINI BIKES
BRUCE GEORGE

SPORTS FIELD

MAMA TUNUIS' GUEST HOUSE

KURA'S TAKEAWAYS

DORA'S STORE

COOK ISLANDAIR

PUBLIC HALL

AIR RAROTONGA

A.B. DONALD LTD.
WHARF

CATHOLIC CHURCH

ARAURA SCHOOL

BANANA PACKING HOUSE

CARVING HOUSE

POST OFFICE

PUBLIC HALL

PROTESTANT CHURCH

HOSPITAL

0   500 m

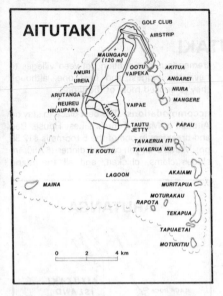

AITUTAKI

GOLF CLUB
AIRSTRIP

MAUNGAPU
(120 m)

OOTU
VAIPEKA   AKITUA
AMURI
UREIA   ANGAREI
NIURA
ARUTANGA   MANGERE
REUREU   VAIPAE
NIKAUPARA
TAUTU   PAPAU
JETTY
TAVAERUA ITI
TE KOUTU   TAVAERUA NUI

AKAIAMI
LAGOON
MURITAPUA
MAINA
MOTURAKAU
RAPOTA
TEKAPUA

TAPUAETAI

MOTUKITIU

0   2   4 km

vegetables. Cook Islandair and Air Rarotonga can make reservations for you — highly recommended. The Tiporo Guest House (Mrs. Cameron) was reported to have closed, although travelers still stay there. Both these give a discount if you stay a week or more. Auntie Pepe Noorea, manager of Torino Villa,

has 2 houses for rent: the larger one costs $25 s or $27 d, the other negotiable, weekly rates available. Two men or 2 women count as 2 singles! Both have cooking facilities, but the smaller house on the inland side has no fridge. Also, you get electric shocks when you touch the taps and there's often no water. **food:** Big J's opposite the Rapae Hotel is good. Kura's Takeaways is open for dinner Mon. to Sat., with steaks, fish and chips, hot dogs, hamburgers, etc. Ice cream is available at many of the shops. The wavy-shelled clams (*pahua*) abundant in the lagoon make good eating.

entertainment: Ask if there's a movie scheduled at one of the community halls. Aitutaki dancers are famous and the big event of the week is Friday's island night at the Rapae Cottage Hotel. Excellent atmosphere —don't miss it. There's a beachside barbecue at the motel Sun. from 1900-2100. **services:** Travelers cheques can be changed at the post office, but it's smarter to do it in Rarotonga. Outpatients are accepted at the hospital Mon. to Sat. 0800-1000. The golf course beside the airport welcomes visitors. The sixth par 4 involves a play across the airstrip. If your ball lands on the runway, make a tee from the crushed coral to avoid breaking your club on the next shot to the green.

This is how they looked on Aitutaki in 1903.

transport and tours: John Baxter represents Cook Islandair; Peter Wearing is the Air Rarotonga agent. Airport transfers are $2 pp. The shipping companies have no local agent, but the people at the banana shed near the wharf know when a ship's due in. Scooters can be rented from Mata's Mini Bikes, Bruce George, and Dora's Store. John Baxter (Tapaki Tours) has a circle-island tour (3 hours, $15). The lagoon trip ($18, lunch included) operated by the Rapae Cottage Hotel and others to a *motu* in the lagoon is highly recommended. Ben Grummels of Lagoon Sailing Tours does this trip every afternoon in a Hobie sailboat ($39 pp), and offers sailboat hire ($22 an hour), windsurfer and surfski rental (both $8), and scuba diving ($42). If you go to Akaiami or Tapuaetai (One Foot Island), you'll have an unforgettable swim in clear deep-green water.

ATIU

The old name of the island was Enuamanu, which means "land of birds." While neighboring Mauke and Mitiaro are flat, Atiu has a high central plateau (71 m) surrounded by low swamps and then an old raised coral reef *makatea* 20 m high. The poor volcanic soil on the plateau is planted with pineapple which, despite shipping difficulties, is supplied fresh to the N.Z. market. Some coffee (*arabica* type) is grown. Taro patches occupy the swamps along the inner edge of the *makatea* and, higher up, orange trees have been planted. Many scenic viewpoints from the roads of Atiu look down across the *makatea* to the blue ocean beyond. Lake Tiroto is clearly visible from a number of these points. According to legend, the eel Rauou dug this lake, and when he was finished, traveled to Mitiaro to dig the lakes there. A tunnel runs under the *makatea* from the lake through to the shore. You can enter it with a lamp and guide, if you're willing to wade through the muddy water. Local school teacher Vaine Moeroa takes advantage of visits to catch eels by organizing teams which herd the creatures up dead-end tunnels — a rare experience.

the people: Atiu is one of the only islands in Polynesia where the people prefer the center to the shore. Once fierce warriors who led cannibal raids on Mauke and Mitiaro, today they live peacefully in 5 adjacent villages on the high central plain. The post office, hospital, PWD workshops, stores, and government offices are at the plain's center, cooled by the ocean breezes. Taunganui Landing (built 1973), with a striking zigzag configuration, can dock barges in all weather. Large ships must anchor offshore. Flying fish swarm off Atiu at half moon, June to November. The local fishermen catch large quantities in butterfly nets. Although the swarming may last for as little as an hour, a single man can catch as many as a dozen sackfuls in that time. The women of Atiu meet throughout the week to work on handicrafts in their community halls.

sights: Teapiripiri Marae, where John Williams preached in 1823, is just across the field from the post office. This large rectangle, with its dramatic stalactite and stalagmite boundaries and crushed-coral floor, is easy to spot. Just off the road down to Matai Landing is Arangirea Marae (to the R behind the citrus plantation). There are a few large stones in the shape of a seat here, and places where pigs were killed for festival celebrations, but not much else. The most important *marae* on Atiu was Orongo Marae at Mokoero — obtain permission from Mr. Takapo of Ngatiarua village to visit. Those who go without permission, or behave badly, will be cursed and stricken by a terrible disease. The best beach on Atiu, and one of the finest in the Cooks, is Taungaroro. High white sands descend far into the quiet blue-green lagoon, protected from ocean breakers by the surrounding reef. The cliffs of the *makatea* frame this scenic masterpiece. A short footpath from the road leads to the spot where Capt. Cook arrived on 3 April 1777. Dense *puka* forests fill the shore along Atiu's

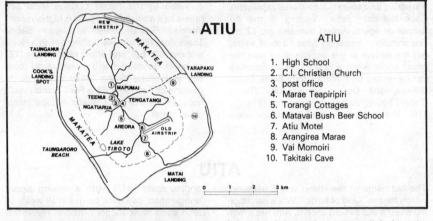

ATIU

ATIU

1. High School
2. C.I. Christian Church
3. post office
4. Marae Teapiripiri
5. Torangi Cottages
6. Matavai Bush Beer School
7. Atiu Motel
8. Arangirea Marae
9. Vai Momoiri
10. Takitaki Cave

0   1   2   3 km

W coast, with low, bird-nest ferns making a thick green cover. These leaves are used to wrap fish for cooking in the *umu.* Oneroa Beach, near the end of the road NW of Matai Landing, is the largest on Atiu, but you must scramble down a cliff to get to it. The only place to snorkel on Atiu is about 500 m up the Oneroa road from Matai. Look for an old pig fence, then go down to the beach where there are 2 sink holes draining the reef. At low tide when the sea is calm many varieties of fish may be seen in the holes and among the coral nearby. A stretch of reefless shoreline on the NE coast lets breakers roll right in to the cliffs. Beside the track from Tarapaku Landing to Tengatangi village is Vai Momoiri, a large water-filled cave which tunnels under the trail then opens up on both sides.

Takitaki Cave: This cave is the only one in the Cooks inhabited by birds: little *kopekas,* a type of swallow, nest in the roof. Their huge saucer-like eyes help them catch insects on the wing. They never land nor make a sound while outside the cave; inside they make a cackling, clicking sound, the echoes of which help them find their way through the dank dark. Visitors to the cave should try not to disturb the birds nor allow their guide to catch any. Takitaki is in the middle of the *makatea,* E of the old airstrip, a taxing 40-min. hike in from the road. A guide ($6 plus $2 pp) is required, as are good boots. The main part of the cave

is large and dry, and you can walk in for quite a distance. Many stalactites, broken off by previous visitors, lie scattered about the floor. The story goes that Ake, wife of the hero Rangi, lived many years alone in this cave before being found by her husband, led to the spot by a *ngotare* (kingfisher) bird.

accommodations and food: The Atiu Motel (manager, Roger Malcolm) near the old airstrip (a new airstrip has been built on Atiu's N side) offers 3 comfortable self-contained units, each capable of accommodating 4 persons. Motor scooters are available ($12), and horseback riding is also offered. Roger is a very attentive host and will arrange everything for you, if you wish. Recommended. Mr. Tearai Mokoroa of Teenui village takes guests willing to share meals and activities with his family for $20 a night. John Akava can sometimes arrange accommodations at Areora village with Mr. George Mateariki ($10 pp including a meal). Two bakers make bread on Atiu, and the Cook Islands Trading Corp. store is well stocked with grocery items. Bottled liquor and beer are sold at the post office.

entertainment and refreshment: See movies in the community hall near the post office at 1900. Videos abound on the island: watch for chalkboards advertising what's on (50 cents admission). Friday or Sat. night at 2200 there's a dance in the community hall near the post office. Tennis is popular on Atiu, with nets made of hanging *au* fibers. One venerable institution of note is the bush beer schools, of which there are 8 on Atiu. Bush beer is made locally from imported yeast, malt, hops, and sugar, fermented in a *tumunu,* a hollowed-out coconut tree stump about a m high. Orange-flavored jungle juice is also made. The mixing usually begins on Wed., the resulting brew ferments for 2 days, and is ready to drink on the weekend. A single batch will last 3 or 4 nights; the longer it's kept, the stronger it gets. Gatherings at the school resemble the *kava* ceremonies of Fiji and other islands. Only the barman is permitted to ladle bush beer out of the *tumunu* into half coconut-shell cups. The potent contents of the cup must be swallowed in one hardy gulp. Those who've developed the taste refer to regular beer as "lemonade." Village men come together at dusk and after a few rounds, the barman calls them to order by tapping a cup on the side of the *tumunu.* A hymn is sung and a prayer said. Announcements are made by various members, and work details assigned to earn money to buy the ingredients for the next brew. After the announcements, guitars and ukeleles appear, and the group resumes drinking, dancing, and singing for as long as they can. The barman, responsible for maintaining order, controls how much brew each participant gets. Non-members visiting a school are expected to bring along a kilo of sugar, or to put a couple of dollars on the table as their contribution. They may also be asked

an eel trap: *Eels are found in the swamps and lakes of Atiu, Mitiaro, and Mangaia; the locals catch them in traps or with hooks. The eel traps* (inaki) *are made of bush vines woven in long basket-like form, which the eel can easily enter but cannot get out of. Pieces of chicken, crab, or bee's wax are used as bait.*

to work in the taro patches the next day. This is no place for casual sightseeing: either join in wholeheartedly or stay away.

MITIARO

Mitiaro is a low island with 2 lakes and vast areas of swampland. Of the lakes, Rotonui is much longer and broader than Rotoiti. This surprisingly large lake is surrounded by the unlikely combination of pine trees and coconut palms. The eastern shore of the lake is firmer than the western. On one side of the lake is the small, coconut-studded island of Motu. Large banana plantations grow in the interior of Mitiaro. Old tin cans are planted below young coconut trees to provide the trees with minerals to absorb as the cans rust

away. As on the neighboring islands, Mitiaro has a severe water shortage.

the people: Before the arrival of Europeans, the people occupied the center of the island near their gardens. Today they all live in one long village on the W coast. The village is neat and clean, with white sandy roads between the Norfolk pines and houses. European-style dwellings predominate, though thatched cottages are still common on the backroads. Four different sections of the village maintain the names of the 4 original villages, and each has a garden area inland bearing the same name. Because the *makatea* cannot support crops, it's used for keeping pigs or growing coconuts. The fine outrigger canoes of Mitiaro are made of hollowed-out *puka* logs, held together with coconut-husk rope. They are used for long-line tuna and *paara* fishing outside the reef.

sights: The small church is quite exquisitely decorated; you might find it worth a look and a quiet moment of reflection on the European influence that still pervades island life. Cut over to the beach when you reach the graveyard and football field S of the village. This long stretch of white sand is the best close to the village, and has many small pools in the reef where you can relax when the tide is out. The restless rhythm and flow of the waves beating against the reef at low tide is almost hypnotic. If you're looking for secluded coves, you'll find many farther S along the coast. Walking along the reef at low tide all around Mitiaro is an incomparable experience.

inland: Vai Marere on the road to Takaue, is an easy 10-min. walk inland from the village.

MITIARO

The locals enjoy swimming in the green, sulphur-laden waters of this cave (*vai*). Take the road to the end, then carry on down the trail to Teunu. To the W of the trail is an old Polynesian fort (*tepare*), but you'll probably need a guide to find it. The Mitiaroans once used this fort to defend themselves against raids from Atiu. On a high crest in the *makatea* on the coast just NE of Teunu are several stone *marae* platforms with slabs of coral propped upright at the ends. At Parava there's an easy trail in to the E side of Lake Rotonui, and Vai Naure and Vai Tamaroa are off the road to the airstrip. Inland again on the northernmost road is Vai Ai, the Sandalwood Cave, a 40-min. walk from the road along a twisting, winding track through the bush. This cave is a large open hole in the *makatea* filled with clear water, good for swimming and diving—refresh yourself. Back on the road, continue on through Tourangi to the W side of Lake Rotonui. The dry, upper mud on the W bank will spring up and down on the deeper layer below as you walk on it. These mud flats stretch so far out into the water that it's hard to board a canoe. Lake Rotoiti is harder to reach than Lake Rotonui. You'll need a guide to lead you through the swamp. Small, edible black *tilapia* fish (introduced from New Caledonia) are abundant; they have a red streak along their back fins, and average 15 cm long. Black eels can also be seen undulating by the shore. The lake water is fresh and clear, although the bottom is muddy. The low-lying surroundings are peaceful and serene, but the mud will make you forget about swimming.

practicalities: Two small stores sell canned foods, but no bread is made, so bring some along. Weekday nights the 2 bands on the island can be hired—$10 each to play in the community hall, which costs an additional $10 rental. Thus you can arrange your own dance for a mere $30. There's often a volleyball game near the church in the afternoons, which you're welcome to join. It's easy to make friends among the local fishermen and go out with them in their outriggers. At low tide many people fish from the edge of the reef with long bamboo poles.

MAUKE

Mauke, the easternmost of the Cooks, is a flat raised atoll. As on its neighbors, the crops grow in the center; the *makatea* ringing the island is infertile and rocky. Both the *makatea* and the central area are low; you barely notice the transition as you walk along the road, inland from the coast, to the taro swamps and arrowroot plantations. In addition to citrus trees, the government is experimenting with beef cattle. Some ginger is still grown, but production has largely ceased due to marketing difficulties. Pigs and chickens run wild across the island, and occasional goats can be seen. The men fish for tuna in small outrigger canoes just offshore. The women weave fine pandanus mats with brilliant borders of blue, red, yellow, and orange along one end. There are also wide-rimmed pandanus hats, and *kete* baskets of sturdy pandanus with colorful geometric designs. The men carve the attractive white-and-black *miro* wood into large bowls shaped like breadfruit leaves. They also carve large spoons and forks, miniature models of chiefs' seats, and small replicas of the legendary Uke's canoe.

sights: The Cook Islands Christian Church (1882) has an almost Mohammedan flavor with its long rectangular courtyard, tall gateways, perpendicular alignment, and interior decoration of crescents and interlocking arches. Due to an old dispute between Areora and Ngatiarua villages, the church was divided across the center and each side decorated differently. The dividing partition has been removed, but dual gateways lead to dual doors, one for each village. The soft pastels (green, pink, yellow, and white) harmonize the contrasting designs, and the pulpit in the middle unifies the two. Inset into the railing in front of the pulpit are 9 old Chilean pesos. Look carefully at the different aspects of this building; it's one of the most fascinating in the Cook Islands.

inland: Vaitaongo Cave, a 10-min. walk from Ngatiarua, is fairly easily found. A large circular depression with banyan trees growing inside, it has a clear freshwater pool under overhanging stalactites. The locals swim and bathe here. To reach this cave follow the road to the R along a row of hibiscus and across the citrus plots. Beyond Vaitaongo there are other caves for swimming (Vai Ou, Vai Tunamea, and Vai Moraro), but a guide is necessary to find them. Moti Cave is a large, open cave beyond the airstrip, and farther into the *makatea* is Motuanga Cave, the "Cave of 100 Rooms," with freshwater pools. Limestone growth has made all but the first 3 rooms inaccessible. A powerful lamp and willing guide are necessary to explore this one. Just behind the queen's palace at Makatea village is Koenga Well, a source of fresh drinking water. The area behind the government residency is known as Te Marae O Rongo, a

Cook Islands Christian Church, Mauke

breadfruit leaf-shaped
bowls carved from miro
wood, Mauke

sacred place to the people of Mauke. All that remains is the large stone once used as a seat by the chief.

around the island: It's only 18 km around Mauke. There's a good beach on the E side at Arapaea landing, but the best beaches are on

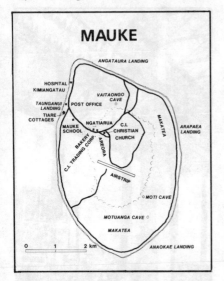

MAUKE

ANGATAURA LANDING

HOSPITAL
KIMIANGATAU

VAITAONGO
CAVE

TAUNGANUI
LANDING • POST OFFICE
TIARE
COTTAGES NGATIARUA

MAUKE
SCHOOL C.L.
CHRISTIAN
CHURCH ARAPAEA
LANDING

BAKERY
C.J. TRADING CORP.
AREONA

MAKATEA

AIRSTRIP

• MOTI CAVE

MOTUANGA CAVE ○

MAKATEA

0   1   2 km ANAOKAE LANDING

the S side of the island. Especially inviting is the beach at Anaokae, where a long stretch of clean white sand rings a green lagoon. This piece of paradise is flanked by rugged limestone cliffs, and backed by palm, pine, and pandanus. A short track leads down to the beach. No one lives on the S or E sides of Mauke, so these fine secluded beaches are ideal for those who want to be completely alone. There's good reef walking at low tide on the W side of Mauke.

accommodations and food: Tautara Purea, the Cook Islandair agent, has a few pleasant cottages (are *rau*) for visitors. Tautara is very helpful and makes you feel like one of the family. There's a cookhouse near the cottages for guests to use, or ask them to put on a beach barbecue. Discounts are given for long stays. Bread is made on the island and fresh tuna can be purchased directly from the fishermen at the landing. Try the meat along the top of the backbone near the fin—raw, with ginger, onions, and salt—for a tastebud orgasm. The brown insides of sea urchins, collected along the reef, are also eaten raw (the egg cases are the most delicious part—the texture of raw liver and a strong taste of the sea). The electricity supply cuts off at 2230 nightly.

MANGAIA

Mangaia, 200 km SE of Rarotonga, is the southernmost Cook. One of the major geological curiosities of the Pacific, Mangaia has a *makatea* or raised coral reef forming a 60-m-high ring around the island. The volcanic earth inside the *makatea* is the only fertile soil on the island; this rises in rolling hills of pineapple-planted slopes. Hopes to develop pineapple production have been disappointed. Near the inner edge of the *makatea*, where water is caught between the coral cliffs

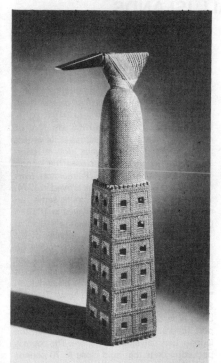

A decorated adze from Mangaia. This consecrated object was not used as a tool but may represent the craftsmen's god, Tane. Many of these adzes seem to have been made specifically for trade with passing ships.

and the hills, low taro swamps are flanked by banana fields and miscellaneous crops. Nothing but bush and coconut palms grow on the *makatea* itself, and pigs are kept there in makeshift pens. The people live in the 3 coastal villages, Oneroa, Tamarua, and Ivarua, but the population is declining rapidly due to migration to New Zealand. A 30-km road rings most of the coastal strip. It's 10 km from the airstrip to Oneroa, the main village.   **crafts:** Mangaia is represented in museum collections around the world by large ceremonial adzes, the exact use of which is not known. They may, in fact, have only been made to sell to collectors. The yellow *pupu* shell necklaces (*ei*) of Mangaia are unique. There are also white *pupu* shells; these have been bleached.

sights: Oneroa has an old church with fine sennet rope bindings in the roof. An impressive cut leads up through the *makatea* from Oneroa. Hike up to the flat summit of Rangimotia (169 m), the highest point on the island, where you get a great all-around view. A water-filled cave at Lake Tiriara is the legendary hiding place of the island hero Tangiia. Water from the lake runs through the cave under the *makatea* to the sea, and rises and falls with the tide. Tuatini Cave near Tamarua village has a huge gaping entrance, but gets narrower toward the back. George Tuara of the Cook Islands Trading Corp. will guide people through Teruarere Cave, once used as a burial ground. Old skeletons add a skin-crawling touch of reality. The opening is small and you have to crawl in, but the cave goes on for a great distance. A lamp is necessary. Below Teruarere on the cliff is Touri Cave. Use indicators to find your way back out—be careful not to get lost inside! There are 2 streams in this cave: one freshwater, the other salty. In a large stone near Avarua landing are the footprints of the legendary giant, Mokea, and his son; both jumped across the island in a race to this spot. The huge stones on the reef to the N were thrown there by Mokea, to prevent a hostile canoe from landing. The queen of Mangaia still has a large flag given to her grandfather by Queen Victoria. **accommodations:** A few of the inhabitants, Mrs. Karero included, take in paying guests at about $20, meals included. Air Rarotonga can arrange this.

OTHER SMALL ISLANDS

Manuae: This small island consists of 2 islets, Manuae and Te Au O Tu, inside a barrier reef. The unspoiled wealth of marinelife in this lagoon has prompted the government to offer the atoll as an international marine park. There is no permanent habitation, but copra-cutting parties from Aitutaki use an abandoned airstrip to come and go. Captain Cook gave Manuae its other, fortunately rarely-used name, Hervey Island.

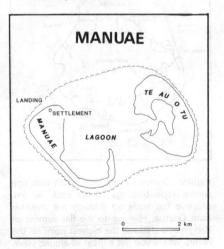

MANUAE

LANDING
SETTLEMENT
MANUAE
LAGOON
TE AU O TU

0   2 km

Takutea: Clearly visible 16 km off the NW side of Atiu. Until 1959 the people of Atiu called here to collect copra, but Takutea gets few visitors now. There are a few abandoned shelters and a freshwater collection tank. The waters along the reef abound with fish; many gannets and frigate birds live on the land.

Palmerston: Palmerston, 366 km NW of Aitutaki, is an atoll 11 km across at its widest point. Some 35 tiny islands dot its pear-shaped barrier reef which closes the lagoon completely at low tide. Palmerston was uninhabited when Capt. Cook arrived in 1774. William Marsters, legendary prolific settler, arrived with his 3 Polynesian wives in 1862 to manage the coconut plantation. He died in 1899 and is buried near the remains of his original homestead. The Marsters family on Palmerston was once as numerous as 150, but is now down to about 50. Thousands of Marsters' descendants also live elsewhere in the Cooks and throughout New Zealand. Ships visit Palmerston 3 or 4 times a year to bring ordered supplies and take the only export, copra. Although unable to enter the lagoon, they can anchor offshore. The copra is packed in bags that hold close to 70 pounds each, 30 bags to the ton, so there's no need for weighing, only counting.

THE NORTHERN GROUP

Suwarrow: In 1814 the Russian explorer Mikhail Lazarev discovered an uninhabited atoll which he named for his ship, the *Suvarov*. A mysterious box containing US$15,000 was dug up in 1855; remains of ancient occupation have also been unearthed. Early this century Lever Bros. attempted unsuccessfully to introduce to the lagoon gold-lipped pearl shell from Australia's Torres Straits. In the '20s and '30s A.B. Donald Ltd. ran Suwarrow as a copra estate, until the island became infested with termites and the export of copra was prohibited. During WW II New Zealand coastwatchers were stationed here—the few decrepit buildings on Anchorage I. date from that time. At various times from 1952 onwards, a New Zealander, Tom Neale, lived alone on Suwarrow and wrote a book, not surprisingly titled *An Island to Oneself*, about his experiences. Tom died of cancer in 1977 but his few possessions are as he left them, although someone has stolen his visitors' book. An entry in a logbook at Tom's house places a lifelong curse on anyone who removes any of his things from the island, and encourages visitors to leave unneeded supplies on Suwarrow for the use of those who become shipwrecked. Pearl divers from Manihiki and Penrhyn visit occasionally. Yachts often call on their way from Rarotonga to Samoa: Suwarrow and Penrhyn are the only atolls in the Cooks with a lagoon which can be entered by ships. The lagoon entrance is just E of Anchorage Island. A 40-m-long coral-rock jetty points to the deep anchorage. In the past hurricanes have washed 4-m waves across the surface of the island; during one in 1942 those present survived only by tying themselves to a large tree. Thousands of seabirds nest on this historically strange and still mysterious Cook Island.

Nassau: Egg-shaped Nassau has no inner lagoon; instead, taro grows in gardens at the center of the island. The American whaler *Nassau* called in 1834. Europeans ran a coconut plantation here until 1945, when the

government bought the island for 2,000 pounds. In 1951 the chiefs of Pukapuka, 88 km to the NW, purchased it from the government for the same amount and have owned it ever since. Korean fishermen from Pago Pago stop illegally at Nassau to trade Oriental canned foods, fishing gear, and cheap jewelry for love. The children of these encounters add an exotic Oriental element to the local population.

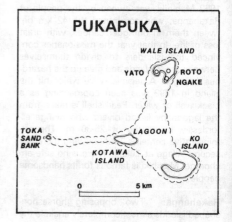

Pukapuka: An island sits at each corner of this unusual triangular atoll. Because of its treacherous reef where no anchorage is possible, Pukapuka was formerly known as "Danger Island." The only landing place for small boats or canoes is on the W side of Wale. Discovered by Mendana in 1595, Pukapuka was outrageously victimized in the mid-19th C. Peruvian slaver raids. Three villages on Wale I. (pronounced "wah-lay") have coexisted since pre-contact times, each with its own island council. They compete enthusiastically with each other in singing, dancing, contests, and cricket. The people make copra collectively, each receiving an equal share in the proceeds. Bananas and papaya also grow here in limited quantities; their harvesting is controlled by the councils.

Pukapuka's Catholic church is beautifully decorated with cowrie shells. The best swimming and snorkeling are off Kotawa Island. Pukapuka is closer to Samoa than to Rarotonga, so the people differ in language and custom from other Cook Islanders. Thus, viriginity is considered more of a handicap than a virtue. Robert Dean Frisbie tells the story in *The Book of Pukapuka*.

Manihiki: One of the Pacific's most beautiful atolls, Manihiki's reef bears 39 coral islets, enclosing a closed lagoon 4 km wide—no sharks are present. The dark green *motus* are clearly visible across the blue waters. Until 1852 Manihiki was owned by the people of Rakahanga, who commuted the 42 km between them in outrigger canoes, with great loss of life. In that year the missionaries convinced the islanders to divide themselves between the 2 islands and give up the hazardous voyages. A seismic wave which hit the island in 1899 was seen approaching as a black wall of water. Pearl shell is taken from the lagoon by island divers who plunge effortlessly to depths of 25-30 m. The administrative center is Tauhunu, and there is a second village at Tukao. There is no safe anchorage. Manihiki is famous for its handsome people.

Rakahanga: Two opposing horseshoe-shaped islands almost completely encircle the

MANIHIKI

lagoon of this rectangular atoll. There are several small *motus* which can be reached on foot at low tide. Breadfruit and *puraka* (a taro-like vegetable) are the staples here, and copra is made for export. So that too many coconuts are not taken at one time, the island councils regulate visits to the *motus*. These usually take place only 2 or 3 times a year, to give nature a chance to regenerate. Coconut crabs, a delicacy in Rakahanga, are mostly caught on the small uninhabited *motus*. The village is at the SW corner of the atoll. Although unable to

This 19th C. model of a double-hulled Manihiki sailing canoe is inlaid with mother-of-pearl.

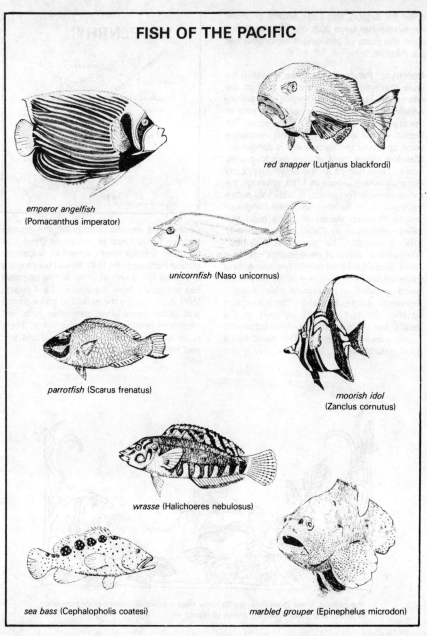

FISH OF THE PACIFIC

red snapper (Lutjanus blackfordi)

emperor angelfish
(Pomacanthus imperator)

unicornfish (Naso unicornus)

parrotfish (Scarus frenatus)

moorish idol
(Zanclus cornutus)

wrasse (Halichoeres nebulosus)

sea bass (Cephalopholis coatesi)

marbled grouper (Epinephelus microdon)

enter the lagoon, ships can anchor offshore. An airstrip has been built on the islands, but since the costs of servicing it are prohibitive, it's inactive.

Penrhyn: Penrhyn's turquoise lagoon is so wide that you can just see the roof of the church at Tautua from Omoka, the administrative center. The *motus* at the far end of the lagoon are too far away to be seen. The lagoon is thick with sharks, mostly innocuous black-tips; only the black shark is dangerous. Islanders ignore them as they dive for pearls. Penrhyn was named for the British ship, *Lady Penrhyn,* which arrived in 1788, although the native name is Tongareva. In 1863 four native missionaries on Penrhyn sold their congregation to Peruvian slavers for $5 a head and sailed with them to Callao as overseers at $100 a month. The blackbirders dubbed Penrhyn the "Island of the 4 Evangelists" as a result. Since the entire chiefly line was among those taken, Penrhyn today is the only Cook Island without a paramount chief (*ariki*). Remnants of old graves and villages abandoned after the raid can still be seen on the *motus,* and the ruins of an unfinished church crumble away at Akasusu. The island has a good natural harbor, one of the few in the

Cooks, and vessels can enter the lagoon through Taruia Passage, just above Omoka, to tie up at Omoka wharf. American forces occupied Penrhyn from 1942-46 and built a giant airfield at the S end of Omoka. The islanders use aluminum from the wreck of a 4-engine WW II bomber by the airfield to make combs and other items. Fine pandanus hats and mother-of-pearl jewelry are also made. There is no air service from Rarotonga (1,364 km) and charter costs are prohibitive.

The passion flower (passiflora) *got its name from a symbolic resemblance between its flower and Jesus' wounds, crown of thorns, etc.*

NIUE

A single 259-sq-km island 386 km E of Vava'u, Tonga, Niue is the world's smallest self-governing state (in association with New Zealand). The name comes from *niu* (coconut tree) and *e* (behold). This little-known island boasts the finest coastal limestone crevices and chasms in the South Pacific, all open to visitors and freely accessible. Each is unique—you'll need a week to do them justice. Niue is for the explorer who likes to get out and make discoveries on his own, for the skindiver in search of clean clear water, colorful coral, fish, and sea snakes, plus good facilities, and for those who want to relax in a peaceful, uncommercialized environment among charming people, yet still have the conveniences of modern life at their disposal. Niue is *not* for tourists who require beach resorts, nightlife, shopping centers, etc. Niue is perhaps the most unspoiled island in the Pacific—it's still an island of adventure.

the land: Niue is an elevated atoll shaped like a hat with 2 terraces. The lower terrace rises sharply from the sea, and 20-m cliffs virtually surround the island. Inland, the second terrace rises abruptly from this coastal belt to a central plateau some 60 m above the ocean. A fringing reef borders much of the coast, but at places the ocean breakers smash directly into the precipitous cliffs. Faulting during uplifting has created the chasms and crevices which are Niue's greatest attraction. Water dripping from above has added a touch of the surreal to the chasms and caves in the form of stalactites and stalagmites.

climate: December to March are the hottest, and the hurricane, months. The SE trades blow from April to November. Rainfall is fairly well distributed throughout the year. There is good anchorage at Alofi, except during strong westerly winds.

flora and fauna: The waters off Niue are clear as can be, with countless species of colorful fish. There are also many varieties of sea snakes—though poisonous, their mouths are too tiny to bite, and divers handle them with impunity. Underwater sightseers also spot white-tip reef sharks on most dives, but these aren't dangerous and add to the thrill. Butterflies are everywhere, as are orchids, hibiscus, frangipani, and bougainvillaea. A profusion of huge "crow's nest" (*nidum*) and other ferns, rhododendron, and poinsettia grow wild. The birdlife is rich; white long-tailed terns, weka, swamp hens, and parakeets abound.

history: Although Niue was first colonized by Samoans, the Tongans later invaded several times. Captain Cook made 3 landings in 1774. He called it Savage Island (as opposed to Tonga, the Friendly Islands) for the hostile reception he received. (The U.S. post office still requires that you include "Savage Island" in the address when writing to Niue!) In 1830 the redoubtable missionary John Williams was also thrown back by force. A Samoa-trained Niuean named Peniamina managed to convert some of the islanders to Christianity in 1846, but it was a series of Samoan pastors beginning in 1849 who really implanted the faith on the island. This paved the way for the first resident English missionary, George Lawes, who arrived in 186l. Much of the early hostility to foreigners was motivated by a very real fear of European diseases. The islanders' reputation for ferocity had always kept the whalers away, but then came the Peruvians and Bully Hayes who were able to entice Niuean men to leave their island voluntarily to work phosphate for years at a time on distant Malden Island. Appealing to Britain for protection, Niue was finally taken over by the U.K. in 1900 and transferred to New Zealand a year later.

government: In 1959 the appointed Island Council was replaced by an elected Legislative Assembly. Niue became internally self-governing in free association with New Zealand in 1974. The assembly has 20 members, 14 from village constituencies and 6 elected from a single island-wide constituency. Among the members is the premier and 3 cabinet ministers. They meet in the impressive Fale Fono next to Burns Philp in Alofi. Local government is provided by the 14 village councils.

economy: Imports run 6 times as high as exports, and Niue is totally dependent on official

Togia, the last king of Niue, addressing a gathering in 1903.

aid from New Zealand, which supplies two-thirds of the local budget. About 87 percent of the workforce is government-employed. Most of the money is used to support the infrastructure which maintains an artificial, consumer-oriented standard of living. Although the Niue Development Board and other agencies have attempted to stimulate agriculture, the economy is continually undermined by emigration of working-age Niueans for the higher wages in New Zealand (to which Niueans have unhindered entry). So little is produced that there isn't even a market building in Alofi; wage earners buy imported foods in the stores. Many of the landowners have left—you'll never see as many empty houses and near-ghost towns as you see here. Periodic hurricanes and droughts have also taken a heavy toll. Only taro and bananas are actively cultivated in bush gardens for personal consumption by the grower. Small quantities of passion fruit, lime juice, coconut cream, and honey are exported. Remittances from Niueans in New Zealand is a more important source of income. A visiting U.N. "expert" recently recommended expansion of the Niue Hotel, which has never had an occupancy rate of over 15 percent, as a way of attracting tourism. Dismal advice of this kind explains why Niue's economy is almost non-existent. Of course, this is one of the island's principal charms.

the people: Niueans are related to Tongans and Samoans rather than Tahitians. There are about 3,000 people on Niue. Another 10,000 Niueans reside in New Zealand (all Niueans are N.Z. citizens), and every year more people leave to seek employment and opportunity abroad. The inhabitants live in small villages scattered along the coast, with a slight concentration near the administrative center, Alofi, on the W coast. The villages on the E coast give an idea of how Europe must have looked in the Middle Ages after a plague, as direct Air Nauru flights to Auckland drain the population. Half the population was touched by a dengue fever epidemic in 1980 and 5 died. All land is held by families. Everyone on the island knows one another. There are no longer any chiefs and lineage means little. A major event for a teen-age boy is his haircutting ceremony, when the long tail of hair he has kept since childhood is removed. Invited guests to the concurrent feast each contribute hundreds of dollars to a fund which goes to the boy after expenses are paid. For girls there's a similar ear-piercing ceremony. These gatherings are usually held on a Sat. in private homes and you may be allowed to observe if you know someone.

events: Public holidays include Anzac Day (25 April) and Queen Elizabeth's Birthday (a Mon. in early June). The main event of the year is the Constitution Celebrations, which last 3 days around 19 October. There is traditional dancing and singing, parades, sports, and a display of produce and handicrafts at the high school grounds, 2 km inland from Alofi. A highlight is the exciting outrigger canoe race off Alofi wharf. Peniamina Day falls on the Mon. during the Constitution Celebrations. Sporting events such as soccer (March to June), rugby (June to Aug.), and netball (June to Aug.) take place on the high school grounds. Cricket (Dec. to Feb.) and softball matches are usually held in the villages on alternating Saturdays. The locals will know what is happening. Saturday is bush day when people go inland to clear, plant, and weed their gardens. Fishing on Sun. is taboo.

PRACTICALITIES

getting there: Polynesian Airlines has an unusual OW flight from Apia to Niue and on to Nukualofa (there is no service in the other direction). Since the portion of this flight to Tonga goes on to Auckland it's often full (book early). Air Nauru flies to Niue from Pago Pago and Auckland, but they have a history of cancellations without notice. If you're lucky

This impressive stairway at Motu is used to lower dugouts to the reef.

and get on, the erratic service is compensated by the low fare. Reconfirm your reservations at the Treasury Dept. in Alofi. This office might also have information about the irregular Warner Pacific Line ship from Niue to Rarotonga (about $120 OW). Large ships must anchor offshore; their cargo is transferred by lighters.

getting around: Russell Kars at K-Mart rents motorbikes at $12 for the first day, $10 successive days, petrol extra. They are sometimes in short supply, so don't wait till the last minute. The chief of police in the Administration bldgs. also rents motorbikes at the same rates. There's no bus service. Hitching is possible along the W coast, but you could get stranded on the east. Don't underestimate the size of the island: it's a long, long way to walk. The road around the island is 64 km.

tours: Niue Adventures (Box 141, Alofi) offers scuba diving and guided bush hikes. The diving is usually off Alofi wharf and costs $20 for a half day, $40 full, lunch included. Featured are dives through caves to drop-offs, and Niue's unique sea snakes. If you've never dived before you can do a resort course in the hotel pool for $25 (3 lessons), then get underwater. Bush hikes go to hard-to-reach attractions such as Vaikona Chasm, Ulupaka Cave, and "the wreck." Ulupaka (near Lakepa) is over a km long and coated with dirty black fungus. These trips cost $10 pp (half day). Niue Adventures is Kiwi-operated and the service is good.

accommodations: The Niue Hotel between the airport and Alofi is $24 s, $34 d for one of the 20 rooms. It has a dining room, bar, and swimming pool. Russell Kars operates the Hinemata Motel between the hotel and Alofi: $10 s, $15 d, with cooking facilities. The

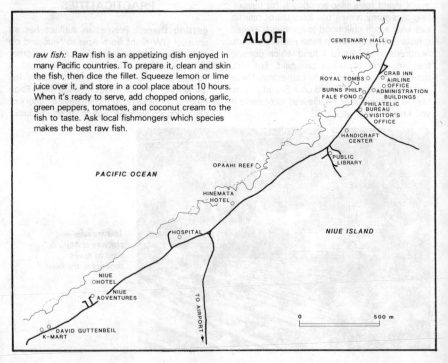

raw fish: Raw fish is an appetizing dish enjoyed in many Pacific countries. To prepare it, clean and skin the fish, then dice the fillet. Squeeze lemon or lime juice over it, and store in a cool place about 10 hours. When it's ready to serve, add chopped onions, garlic, green peppers, tomatoes, and coconut cream to the fish to taste. Ask local fishmongers which species makes the best raw fish.

ALOFI

CENTENARY HALL
WHARF
CRAB INN
ROYAL TOMBS
AIRLINE OFFICE
BURNS PHILP
ADMINISTRATION BUILDINGS
FALE FONO
PHILATELIC BUREAU
VISITOR'S OFFICE
HANDICRAFT CENTER
PUBLIC LIBRARY
OPAAHI REEF

PACIFIC OCEAN

HINEMATA HOTEL

HOSPITAL

NIUE ISLAND

NIUE HOTEL
NIUE ADVENTURES

TO AIRPORT

0   500 m

DAVID GUTTENBEIL
K-MART

The Handicraft Center in Alofi is the place to pick up a distinctive souvenir.

Hinemata has a spacious veranda with an ocean view. There are only 3 rooms, but you'll probably get one. Ask for the Kars family at the airport kiosk. Russell knows all there is to know about Niue. If you'd rather stay at a private home, David Guttenbeil, who lives next to the K-Mart just down from the hotel, rents rooms at $12 pp, breakfast and dinner included. David owns a charter bus which is sometimes at the airport, so ask. For a longer stay, ask around about renting a house by the month. There are usually plenty available. Camping would be possible on the E coast.

food and entertainment: There's a snack bar at Burns Philp, but the dining room at the hotel is better: breakfast, $3.50, lunch $5.50, dinner $9. Lunch is from 1200-1300 sharp. Tuesdays at 1900 the hotel has a buffet ($7), followed by disco dancing to recorded music. The Crab Inn Coffee Shop/Bar above the wharf serves light lunches and is a good place for a beer with the boys. You can buy passion fruit plus lime juice (take your own container), and papayas at the government Food Processing Factory near the airport. Liquor is sold by the Treasury Dept. near the post office, $20 for a 24-can case of beer. On paydays its hours are restricted; alcoholism is a problem here. Drinking alcohol in the street is prohibited. You can socialize a little at the hotel bar which picks up in the afternoon as people get off work. They close early if nobody's around, even on Fri. night. The Niue Sports

Club (better known as the Top Club) near the airport is nominally private, but visitors are welcome. Tap water is safe to drink.

shopping: Burns Philp and K-Mart are the largest stores, but both close at 1530 weekdays and don't open at all weekends. Be sure to buy a bottle of Niue honey ($2) while you're here. The Philatelic Bureau next to the Visitors Office sells beautiful stamps which make excellent souvenirs. The people make very fine, firmly-woven baskets of pandanus wound over a coconut-fiber core — among the best in Polynesia. Fine pandanus and coconut leaf-bud hats are also made. Visit the Handicraft Center in Alofi.

services and information: The administration buildings in Alofi contain the post office, Treasury Dept., Telecommunications Office, and police station. Change money at the Treasury Department weekdays 0800-1200/1230-1430. New Zealand currency is used (due to devaluation, prices in this chapter may have increased). The Telecommunications Office handles overseas calls and wires. See a doctor at the hospital 0730-1500 for $10. The Niue Visitors Office (weekdays 0730-1500) in Alofi supplies brochures. The public library (weekdays 0730-1500) at the Dept. of Education has a good Pacific section. Farther back in the same complex is the USP Extension Center which sells a few books on Niue. An excellent "Map of Niue" ($2) can be purchased at the hotel or Handicraft Center.

airport: Hanan International Airport (IUE) is 3 km SE of Alofi. No visa is required for a stay of up to 30 days. There's no bank or duty-free shop. Airport departure tax is $10. There's no airport bus, but a taxi should be under $2, if someone doesn't offer to drive you.

SIGHTS

exploring Niue: Virtually all of Niue's scenic attractions are within earshot of the ocean, but while sites on the W coast are easily accessible in a few minutes from the road, those on the E coast are only reached over rough trails requiring up to a 40-min. hike. Some of these trails, such as those through fantastic petrified coral forests at Vaikona and Tongo, are not well marked. Sturdy shoes are required to go almost anywhere off the road on Niue. If you're a good walker you could visit the sites S of Alofi on foot in less than a day. Those to the N can be covered by a combination of walking, hitching, and good luck, but

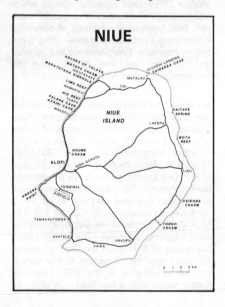

NIUE ISLAND

to get to the places on the NE and SE coasts and return to Alofi the same day, you'll need your own transport. Alternatively, camp in one of the E coast villages and visit the area at more leisure. Take your own food with you as little is available in the villages. Photographers should note that conditions on the E coast are best in the morning, on the W coast in the afternoon. Vaikona and Tongo are definitely not afternoon trips as the declining light in the forest makes the trails hard to discern. Also, limestone makes for slow walking.

near Alofi: According to popular tradition, Capt. Cook landed at Opaahi Reef opposite the Mormon church in Alofi. It's a scenic spot, well worth the short detour. Two kings of Niue, Tuitoga (r. 1876-87) and Fataaiki (r. 1888-96), are buried in front of the LMS church opposite Alofi's post office. Nearby, adjoining the war memorial, are 2 stone slabs against which these kings rested their backs. The last king of Niue, Togia (died 1917), ceded his kingdom to Britain on 21 April 1900, just 4 days after the Americans annexed Eastern Samoa. He's buried in front of the church at Tuapa. It's fascinating to walk on the reef SW of Alofi wharf at low tide. Crevices, cliffs, and coral abound, and there are natural pools on the reef where you can swim safely. Beware of waves heralding the incoming tide, however.

south of Alofi: Juices of passion fruit, limes, and papaya are extracted and exported in bulk from the Food Processing Factory near the airport on the road from town. You're welcome to have a look. The Niue Honey Plant is adjacent. Down the road beyond the airport is a large Dept. of Agriculture passion fruit plantation. The road drops to Tamakautonga, where you'll find a couple of small beaches behind the church. Farther S at Avatele (pronounced Avasele) there's another poor excuse for a beach at the canoe landing. Return to Alofi along the coastal road with a stop at Anaana Point, where you can sit atop a cliff by the road and watch as tons of water are thrown at your feet.

north of Alofi: Houme Chasm at Alofi North, about 4 km from the hotel, is behind the house across the street and just to the N of the Catholic Mission. A flashlight is required to reach the pool. Avaiki Sea Cave is another 6 km N, and an easy 5 min. from the road. The pool in the main cave just N of the landing contains a variety of marine life and is a great place to swim, but this is often prohibited. The limestone formations are outstanding. Just 200 m N of the Avaiki sign is the trail down to Palaha Cave with stalagmites and stalactites. Hio Reef, a little over a km farther N just before the point where the road divides, is a nice secluded sandy beach best for swimming at high tide. Farther N again just beyond Namukulu is the trail to Limu Reef, a perfect snorkeling locale with colorful coral and fish. A natural stone bridge over the lagoon is just a little N of here across the rocks. The trail to Makalea Cave is 200 m N of the Limu signboard. Makatutaha is a large pothole containing a pool connected to the sea near the road just opposite the southernmost house in Hikutavake. Two of Niue's highlights are Matapa Chasm and the Arches of Talava, reached along an extension of the coastal road just N of Hikutavake. Follow the road straight down to Matapa, a wide sunken chasm which was once the bathing place of Niuean royalty—very good swimming and snorkeling. The Arches of Talava are harder to find. The trail branches off the Matapa track to the R just before the beginning of the descent. Keep straight on the trail about 15 min., then watch for yellow marks on the trees which indicate the branch trail on the L to Talava. The site itself is entered through a cave. A great series of stone arches above the sea complement side caves with red and green stalactites and stalagmites in fantastic flowing formations. Behind the outermost arch is a large cave best entered at low tide with a flashlight. The constant roar of the surf adds to the overwhelming impression of the place.

the southeast coast: Niue's wild E coast has some of the most fantastic limestone features in the entire South Pacific. About 4 km NE of Hakupu, second largest village on the island, is the trail to Tongo Chasm. After a 20-min.

Matapa Chasm is a former bathing spot for royalty.

walk you reach a wasteland of coral pinnacles much like the interior of Nauru Island. The path leads down to a wide chasm with coconut trees growing on the golden sandy bottom. Lower yourself down the rope to the sand, and swim in the pools at each end of the chasm. The green of the coconut trees combined with the sand contrasts sharply with the rocky wasteland, creating an almost N. African effect—until you hear the ocean crashing into the cliffs just meters away: one of the scenic wonders of the Pacific. From the Tongo trailhead, travel NE another 4 km through the Huvalu Forest, with its many species of mahogany, to the Vaikona trailhead. The trail to Vaikona Chasm is partly marked with red paint, but careful attention is required as there is a good chance of getting lost. This trip is for experienced hikers only, or come with a group from Niue Adventures. As you approach the coast through pandanus brush over the jagged limestone, you pass a sudden opening straight down into the chasm. Wind your way around the back and drop into a deep cave grasping the stout orange rope provided for the purpose. You enter the chasm over huge rocks from the cave. There are 2 crystal-clear pools to swim in, one at each end of Vaikona; tiny freshwater crayfish and black carp live here. It would take a major expedition to explore all this chasm has to offer. Like a ruined Gothic cathedral the walls soar 30 m to a canopy of vegetation, the huge blocks of the collapsed roof littering the floor. The stalagmites and stalactites of the entrance cave are like images on a broken medieval portal; by plunging into the cool clear water of the pools one has communion with the bowels of the earth. The crashing of the breakers into the coast nearby is the expurgation of sin—a spectacular visual experience. This awe-inspiring chasm is outstanding even for Niue. Hopefully Vaikona, Tongo, and the Huvalu Forest will someday be set aside as a national park.

the northeast coast: The trail to Motu Reef is about a km S of Lakepa. There's a wide wooden stairway down to the reef from the cave where canoes are stored. It's a 25-min.

walk along an easy-to-follow trail from the trailhead to Vaitafe Spring, a couple of km N of Lakepa. Fresh water bubbles into a pool where you can swim from a crevice at the foot of a sheer cliff, but the area is only accessible at low tide. You can reefwalk here. At the N end of the island opposite the church in Mutalau village is a monument commemorating the arrival of the first Christian missionaries, Peniamina (1846), first Niuean convert, and Paulo (1849), first Samoan teacher. A jeep track across from the monument leads down to Uluvehi Landing, an easy 5-min. walk. This was the main landing on the island in the early days; the islanders' sleek outrigger canoes are still stored in caves on the cliffs. To reach Vaihakea Cave look for an overgrown trail just 100 m inland from the streetlight at Uluvehi on the E side of the track. Once you get on it it's only a 5-min. walk to this fantastic submerged cave full of fish and coral, but you must climb down a sharp limestone cliff near the end. There's excellent swimming and snorkeling at low tide. The sites mentioned above are only the *highlights* of Niue; there are many other caves for the avid spelunker to explore.

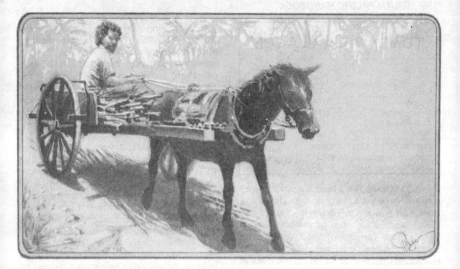

KINGDOM OF TONGA

INTRODUCTION

The ancient Kingdom of Tonga, Polynesia's oldest and last remaining monarchy, is the only Pacific nation never brought under foreign rule. Though sprinkled over a vast area of ocean from Niuafo'ou, between Fiji and Samoa, to Minerva Reef 290 km SW of Ata, the total land area of the kingdom is only 691 sq km. Tonga is divided into 3 main parts: the Tongatapu Group in the S with the capital, Nuku'alofa; the Ha'apai Group, a far-flung archipelago of low coral islands and soaring volcanoes in the center; and in the N the Vava'u Group with its immense landlocked harbor. There's over a 100 km of open sea between Tongatapu and Ha'apai, then another 100 between Ha'apai and Vava'u, then *another* 400 km N are the Niuas, including isolated Niuafo'ou and Niuatoputapu. In all, Tonga is comprised of 170 islands, 37 inhabited. Even though they're some of the most densely populated in the Pacific, the Tonga Islands are set quite apart from the 20th century. Due to its position just W of the

International Dateline, Tonga is the first country in the world to usher in each new day. In fact, the Dateline seems to have so confused the local roosters that they crow constantly just to be safe.

the land: Tonga sits on the eastern edge of the Indo-Australian Plate, which is forced up as the Pacific Plate pushes under it at the Tonga Trench. This long oceanic valley running from E of Tonga to New Zealand is one of the lowest parts of the ocean floor, in places over 10 km deep. Tonga is on the circumpacific "Ring of Fire" which extends from New Zealand to Samoa, then backtracks into Vanuatu and the Solomons. Where Tongatapu (a raised atoll), Lifuka (a low coral island), and Vava'u (another uplifted atoll) are today, towering volcanoes once belched fire and brimstone. Then they sank, and coral polyps gradually built islands. Study the map of Tonga and you'll distinguish 4 great atolls in a

TONGA AT A GLANCE

	POPULATION (1984)	AREA (sq km)
Eua	5,011	87
Tongatapu	63,847	259
Ha'apai Group	12,028	109
Vava'u Group	16,738	119
Niuas *	2,606	72
TONGA	**100,230**	**646****

* Niuafo'ou, Niuatoputapu, Tafahi
** inhabited islands only

line 350 km long. The 2 central atolls (Ha'apai) are now largely submerged, with Lifuka and Nomuka the largest remaining islands of each. As Ha'apai sank, the outermost groups, Vava'u and Tongatapu tilted toward the center, creating cliffs on their outer edges and half-submerged islands facing in. The crack in the earth's crust which originally built Tonga has moved NW, and the active volcanoes of today are in a line 50 km W of Ha'apai-Vava'u. Fonuafo'ou, Tofua, Lateiki, Late, Fonualei, and Niuafo'ou have all erupted over the last 200 years.

climate: The name Tonga means south; it's cooler and less humid here than in islands closer to the equator such as Samoa. December to April is the hot, rainy season, with especially high humidity from Jan. to March. Tonga gets an average of 2 tropical cyclones a year, usually between Nov. and March, although they can occur as late as May. Rainfall, temperatures, and the probability of cyclones increase the farther N you go. The SE trades prevail; in Tonga, W and NW winds herald bad weather.

HISTORY AND GOVERNMENT

prehistory: According to myth, the demigod Maui acquired a fishhook from Samoa with which he yanked the Tonga Islands out of the sea. The Polynesians reached Tonga from Fiji over 3,000 years ago. Tangaloa, the creator god, descended from the sky and had a son, Aho'eitu, by a beautiful Tongan maiden named Va'epopua. This child became the first

hereditary king, or Tu'i Tonga, perhaps around A.D. 950. Fierce Tongan warriors traveled throughout Western Polynesia in large double-hulled canoes (*kalia*), each capable of carrying up to 200 people. In the 13th C. the empire of the Tu'i Tonga extended all the way from Rotuma in the W through part of the Lau Group, Wallis and Futuna, Samoa, and Tokelau, to Niue in the east.

European contact: Although the Dutchmen Schouten and LeMaire sighted the Niuas in 1616, Abel Tasman was the first European to visit Tongatapu and Ha'apai. Arriving on 19 Jan. 1643, as Tongans approached his ship in narrow canoes, Tasman fired a gun—terrifying the chief. A trumpet, violin, and flute were then played in succession to this chief's further astonishment. Tasman received sorely-needed food and water to carry on with his journey. At one point he escaped disaster by charging full-tilt over the Nanuku Reef, which was luckily covered with sufficient water to

King George Tupou I: In 1831 this young chief of Ha'apai was baptized by Wesleyan missionaries. With their help he supplanted the Tu'i Tonga on Tongatapu and in 1845 was proclaimed king, taking the name of England's monarch. The present royal line is descended from him. In 1862 George I freed the Tongan slave class and in 1875 he gave his country the Constitution which is in effect today.

traverse. When Capt. Cook visited Tonga in 1773, 1774, and 1777, he and his men were received with lavish friendliness—pyramids of food were offered them, and dances and boxing matches in which little girls and women took part were staged in their honor. (The skillful Tongan pugilists made short work of Cook's crew in a competition.) Some say the islanders intended to roast and eat Cook and his men as part of the feast, but Cook's profuse thanks at his reception prompted them to change their minds. Cook presented the Tu'i Tonga with a male Galapagos tortoise, which was left to wander blind in the royal garden right up until 1966, when it died at the ripe old age of over 200. Ever since Cook's visit, Tonga has been known as "The Friendly Islands." Cook never visited Vava'u, which was only "discovered" by the Spaniard Mourelle in 1781.

the formation of a nation: European contact led to a decline in population as warring chiefs turned newly acquired muskets and cannons on each other. Members of the London Missionary Society arrived in 1797 in the middle of these wars, but unable to attract a following, by 1804 all had left. Wesleyan (Methodist) missionaries returned in 1822. Their most noteworthy convert (in 1831) was Taufa'ahau, chief of Ha'apai, who with their help in 1845 became King George Tupou I, ruler of a united Tonga. In 1862 he freed the Tongan people from forced labor on the estates of the chiefs, while making hereditary nobles of the chiefs. King George decreed that each of his subjects be allotted a *tax'api* consisting of a town lot and 3.34 ha of farm land for only $3.20 annual rental. This system continues today, although there's no longer enough land to go around. At the same time the king established constitutional government with a Privy Council of his choice and representation for both nobles and commoners in a Legislative Assembly. This system, institutionalized in the Tongan Constitution of 1875, remains in force today. A year later Germany concluded a Treaty of Friendship which recognized Tongan independence and the sovereignty of the king. Similar treaties were signed with England

KINGDOM
OF
TONGA

FONUALEI I.

NIUAFO'OU I.

TAFAHI I.
NIUATOPUTAPU I.

TOKU I.

VAVA'U GROUP VAVA'U I.
LATE I. NEIAFU

LATEIKI I.

HA'APAI GROUP
PANGAI
KAO I. HA'ANO I.
TOFUA I. FOA I.
LOFANGA I. LIFUKA I.
KOTU I. UIHA I.
HA'AFEVA I.
FONUAFO'OU I. NOMUKA I.
HUNGA HUNGA KELEFESIA I.
HA'APAI I. TONGA I.
NUKU'ALOFA TONGATAPU GROUP
EUAIKI I.
TONGATAPU I. EUA I.
KALAU I.

ATA I.

0   100 km

(1879) and the U.S. (1888). King George died in 1893 at 97 years of age, the creator of a unified Christian Tonga and one of the most remarkable men of the 19th century.

Queen Salote

the twentieth century: Tonga (along with Japan, Thailand, Nepal, and a few Middle East states) is one of the few countries in the world which has never been colonized by a European power. Germany had strong influence in Tonga during the late 19th C. and wanted to include it in their colonial empire, but bowed out to the British in exchange for a free hand in Samoa. In 1900 Tonga signed a new Treaty of Friendship with Britain, which gave the latter control of Tonga's foreign affairs as a means of forestalling encroachments by other colonial powers. British protection remained in effect until 1970, but the rule of the royal family continued unbroken. The pervasive influence of the missionaries, who dominated Tonga from the early 19th C. onwards, can still be experienced any Sunday. Magnificent, much-loved Queen Salote ruled Tonga from 1918 until her death in 1965. In 1953 she won the hearts of millions by riding through London in an open coach despite torrential rain at Queen Elizabeth's coronation. In fact, she was only observing the Tongan custom of showing respect for royalty by appearing before them unprotected in bad weather. Her son, His Majesty King Taufa'ahau Tupou IV, the present monarch, re-established Tonga's full sovereignty in 1970. Although just short of his mother's 2-m height, King Tupou is a 1.9-m, 210-kg giant who looks every bit the Polynesian king he is. In 1972 when right-wing American millionaires attempted to seize Tonga's Minerva Reef and convert it into a taxless utopian state, the king intervened per-

sonally and ousted the opportunists. The same bunch surfaced in 1980 as backers of subversion in Vanuatu (see the "Introduction" to the Vanuatu chapter for details).

government: Tonga is a constitutional monarchy in which the king actually rules. He appoints the 7 members of his Cabinet, who retain their posts until retirement (as in the British House of Lords). They and the governors of Ha'apai and Vava'u (both appointed by the king) sit in the 23-seat Parliament, along with 7 members who represent the 33 Nobles of the Realm, and another 7 elected to represent Tonga's 100,000 commoners. The elected members run as independents (there are no political parties). The prime minister is the king's younger brother. There are no municipal councils; Nuku'alofa is administered directly by the central government. Tonga has a small but efficient army with facilities behind the royal palace and at the airport. The press and radio are government-owned, and although no formal criticism of the king is permitted, as the number of landless Tongans increases and outside influences lead to rising expectations, the power of the privileged few is beginning to be called into question. However, most Tongans appreciate the stability and security the present system offers and have few illusions about the ability of politicians to make great changes for the better. To judge Tonga by British or American standards of democracy is to miss the point.

ECONOMY

trade and development: With an exploding population forced by a lack of land and resources to emigrate, and food imports alone running higher than all exports, Tonga has all the problems it needs. From a favorable trade balance prior to 1960, today it imports 4 times as much as it exports. External aid compensates for only about 10 percent of the deficit. Australia and New Zealand profit most from the trade imbalance, selling food, fuels, machinery, and manufactured goods to Tonga. Exports are coconut oil, dessicated coconut, bananas, vanilla, and taro. Ominously, the market value of these commodities is declining in relation to the prices charged for imports. As yet Tonga has managed to avoid the sort of extreme financial crises which have gripped Samoa in recent years, but both countries are very much part of the Third World. Tourism, and money returned from Tongans living abroad are crucial in maintaining the balance of payments. Tonga's educational system is preparing too many young people for the too few white-collar jobs, leading to discontent and emigration to more developed Pacific Rim countries. Labor unions don't exist. Rural areas are neglected as newly established light industry and government facilities become concentrated in Nuku'alofa. Unemployment is becoming critical in the rapidly growing town. A quarter of all Tongans now live in the capital and hundreds more commute daily from outlying villages.

agriculture and land: In Tonga's feudal system, all land is property of the crown, but administered by nobles who allot it to the common people. The king and nobles retain 27 percent of the land for their own use, while the government owns another 18 percent. Foreigners cannot purchase land, and even leasing requires Cabinet approval. This system has not been altered substantially since 1862, yet Tongan society has changed drastically. Frustrations with the system are relieved by migration to N.Z. and the U.S. If those avenues were to close, Tonga would face serious unrest. Still, there remains a baffling problem of underemployment. Only half the population is involved in the cash economy; the rest live from subsistence agriculture, fishing, and collecting. Here again, however, the danger in evaluating Tonga on the standard Western models is illustrated. Subsistence production of food, fish, housing, and handicrafts consumed by the producer is more than twice the value of all goods sold for cash—this situation is rarely reflected in official statistics. The staples are yams, taro, manioc, and sweet potato. Crops are rotated and up to two-thirds of a garden are left fallow at any time.

This magnificent statue of His Majesty King Taufa'ahau Tupou IV can be seen at Fua'amotu International Airport.

Tongans demonstrate great enthusiasm for events involving the royal family: these ta'ovala-clad women were attending a royal wedding in 1984.

THE PEOPLE AND THEIR ARTS

the people: Tonga is typical of developing countries with its large families and young population. The growth rate is an explosive 3 percent annually. With 145 people per sq km, Tonga is one of the most densely populated countries in the Pacific (twice as dense as the Cooks, 4 times as dense as Fiji). This puts pressure on the limited resources, and at least 10,000 Tongans have left, many for good. Some 35,000 ethnic Tongans now reside overseas. Tongans live in small villages near their bush gardens. Except in Europeanized areas, isolated houses along the roads are rare. Tongans have a long traditional history and many can name up to 39 generations by heart. There is little social mobility: a commoner can never become a noble, though a noble or a member of the royal family can be stripped of his title. Commoners have been appointed Cabinet ministers through education and ability, however. To a Tongan, great physical size is the measure of beauty—

Tongan women begin increasing prodigiously in beauty from age 15 onward. Families without female offspring may raise a male child as a girl, to do female chores, etc. The name *fakaleiti* literally means "like a lady." These male transvestites may revert to male status in adulthood. Tongans are more Westernized than Samoans. Say *"malo"* for "thank you," and greet people on the street with *"malo e lelei"* and a smile. Also note that in Tongan, "ng" is pronounced as in longing, not as in longer, making it Tong-a, rather than Tong-ga.

traditional dress: The *ta'ovala* is the distinctive Tongan traditional skirt. Made of a finely woven pandanus-leaf mat, it's worn around the waist. The men secure it with a coconut-fiber cord, while the women wear a *kiekie* waistband. The sight of a group of Tongan women on the road, each with a huge mat tied around them, is truly striking. Worn especially on formal occasions, these mats are often prized heirlooms. Tongan women dress in black when mourning. The King and Queen wear European dress to a European function, but dress in their plaited *ta'ovala* tied around the waist over the *vala* (skirt or kilt), and wear sandals or go barefoot to a Tongan ceremony or entertainment.

religion: Tongans are devout; their Constitution (drafted by a Methodist missionary) declares the Sabbath Day forever sacred: it's unlawful to work, hold sporting events, or trade on Sunday. Contracts signed that day are void. Police permission is required to drive a car on Sun. (although the nobles are exempt). Most tours are also prohibited, though picnic trips do run to Pangaimotu and other small islands off Nuku'alofa. The Sabbath is so strong that even the Seventh-day Adventists observe Sun. here as the Lord's Day (not Saturday). They claim this is permissible because of the "bend" in the International Dateline, but it would be intolerable to have 2 Sundays in Tonga! Great churchgoers, most Tongans are Wesleyan, but there are also Catholic, Anglican, Seventh-day Adventist, and Mormon congregations. Attend the service at Centenary Methodist Church in Nuku'alofa Sun. at 1000 to hear the magnificent church choir and perhaps catch a glimpse of the royal family. Gentlemen are expected to wear coats and ties. After church, the rest of the day is spent relaxing, strolling, and visiting friends—what Tongans like to do anyway, so it wasn't hard for the missionaries to convince them to set aside a whole day for it. Tourists lodged in a bare room with no local friends are at a disadvantage and can even go hungry on Sunday. All shops and most restaurants will be closed. **the Mormons:** Mormon churches (with their inevitable basketball courts) are popping up in villages all over Tonga as the children of Israel convert in droves to be eligible for the free buildings, schools, sporting facilities, and children's lunches paid for by American members of the Church of Latter Day Saints. Many Tongans become "school Mormons," joining as their children approach high school age and dropping out when they complete college in Hawaii. It's low profile in Nuku'alofa, however, as the king, a Wesleyan, is reputed to be uncomfortable with the new fast-faith religion. The building behind the Dateline Hotel now occupied by the Tong-Hua Restaurant was a Mormon church until it was judged too close to the palace for comfort. The Mormon Temple, the largest building in Tonga, is now beside Liahona High School near Houma on the opposite side of the island. **cemeteries:** Tongan cemeteries are unique. Usually set in a grove of frangipani trees, the graves are strange, sandy mounds marked with flags and banners, surrounded by inverted beer bottles, artificial flowers, seashells, and black volcanic stones.

Beer bottles are recycled into grave markers in cemeteries such as this one at Makave, Vava'u.

Miniature wooden statues of this kind were the only graven images made in Tonga. In 1830 the missionary John Williams witnessed the desecration by hanging of 5 of these at Ha'apai.

crafts: Tongan handicrafts are among the best in the Pacific. There is no mass production: virtually every item is handmade and unique. For the amount of work that goes into the articles, prices are surprisingly reasonable. Plan on buying most of your South Pacific gifts and souvenirs in Tonga and mail home what you don't wish to carry. Most of the traditional handicrafts are made by women: woven baskets, mats, or *tapa* cloth. The weaving is mostly of tan, brown, black, and white pandanus leaves. The large sturdy baskets have pandanus wrapped around coconut-leaf mid-ribs. A big one-m-high laundry basket makes an excellent container to fill with other smaller purchases for shipment home. (Remember, however, that the post office does not accept articles more than a meter long or weighing over 10 kilos.) The soft fine white mats from the Niuas, often decorated with colored wool, are outstanding. The famous *tapa* cloth of Tonga originates mostly on Tongatapu where the paper mulberry tree (*Broussonetia papyrifera*) grows best. The bark of this tree is stripped and beaten into pieces up to 200 m long and 6 m wide, then hand-painted with natural brown and tan dyes. These big pieces make excellent wall hangings or ceiling covers. In the villages, listen for the rhythmic pounding of *tapa* cloth mallets. The women are always happy to let you watch the process, and you may be able to buy something directly from them, about $25 for a very large piece. Unfortunately, Tongan woodcarving is now oriented toward producing imitation Hawaiian or Maori "tikis" for sale to tourists. Some are carved from sandalwood. Buy them if you wish, but know that they're not traditionally Tongan. Beware too of tortoise-shell jewelry, which is prohibited entry into many countries to protect sea turtles, an endangered species. Black coral jewelry is a good substitute. The beautiful war clubs one sees in museums are rarely made today, perhaps out of fear they might be used! Surprisingly, the best places to buy handicrafts are the impromptu markets which materialize whenever a cruise ship is in—by far the lowest prices in Polynesia as country folk bring their handicrafts to town.

dance: Traditional Tongan dances are stories sung by the singers and acted out by the dancers. The hands and feet convey the message, not the hips. The graceful movements of the female dancers contrast with the males, who dance with great vigor. The *'ma'ulu'ulu'* is a sitting dance usually performed by groups of women on formal occasions. Male groups often do the *lakalaka*. Unlike these, the *kailao* or war dance has no accompanying song. The feet-stamping, the shouts of the leader, and the insistent rhythm of the drums combine to make this dance popular among visitors. Very different is the dignified *'tau'olunga'* in which a girl dances alone, knees held closely together, at weddings or village functions. Your best chance to see real Tongan dancing is at fund-raising events (watch how the Tongans contribute, then give your share), national holidays, and visits by important personalities.

events: Public holidays include Anzac Day (25 April), the Crown Prince's Birthday (4 May), Emancipation Day (4 June), the King's Birthday (4 July), Constitution Day (4 Nov.), and King Tupou I Day (4 Dec.). The Heilala Festival, with beauty contests, parades, and sporting competitions, occupies the week coinciding with the king's birthday. Agricultural shows are held throughout Tonga during Aug. and Sept. with the king in attendence at each. The ferry *Olováha* makes special trips at these times, so ask and book early.

PRACTICALITIES

getting there: Air Pacific flies to Tonga from Nandi, Suva, and Auckland, while Polynesian Airlines arrives from Apia, Niue, and Auckland; the plane does not return from Tonga to Niue. Air New Zealand has flights from Apia and Auckland. The most direct connection from Hawaii is via Pago Pago on South Pacific Island Airways (SPIA), or via Fiji. SPIA also has a local service from Pago Pago to Tongatapu via Niuatoputapu, Vava'u, and Ha'apai — a whole trip in itself if you stop over

a stylized turtle on a piece of Tongan tapa

at each one, and you can do this for little additional airfare. Polynesian Airlines also flies to Vava'u direct from Apia. There are no commercial flights within or to Tonga on Sundays. For information on domestic interisland air and sea service see "Transport" in the "Tongatapu" section below.

accommodations and food: Inexpensive accommodations are easier to find in Tonga than anywhere else in the Pacific. There is no hotel tax or service charge. (Sadly, the main reason Tonga is inexpensive is because the people are so poor.) There are no real campgrounds, though some of the beach resorts such as the Good Samaritan Inn on Tongatapu and Evaloni Beach Resort at Ha'apai will let you pitch your own tent. Very few of the guest houses provide cooking facilities, but restaurant meals are cheap. In rural areas fresh fruit can be purchased at market prices from people you meet working in their gardens. Some stores sell horrendous fatty mutton flaps called *sipi,* which unfortunately constitute the diet of many Tongans. More inviting are Tonga's gargantuan feasts. The most spectacular of these, marking such important events as King Tupou's coronation or Queen Elizabeth's visit, feature a whole roasted pig for *each* of the thousands of guests. Literally tons of food are piled on long platters (*polas*) for these occasions. Less earth-shaking feasts are put on for visitors to Tongatapu and Vava'u. Try to attend at least one.

money and visas: The currency is the *pa'anga,* worth about the same as the Australian dollar. Change money at Bank of Tonga branches in Nuku'alofa, Pangai (Lifuka), and Neiafu (Vava'u); shopkeepers and market vendors give a much lower rate.

Visitors in possession of a passport and onward ticket do not require a visa for a stay of one month. Extensions up to 6 months are possible. Ports of entry for cruising yachts include Niuatoputapu, Vava'u, and Nuku'alofa.

conduct: Appearing in public without a shirt on is punishable by a $20 fine. Of course, this doesn't apply at the beach. Female travelers will feel more accepted in skirts or long pants than in shorts. In Tonga the possession of dope is a serious offense and the word soon gets around. Customs watches for yachts with drugs aboard. If you're busted they'll toss you in a tiny flea-ridden cell and throw away the key. Make no mistake—they mean business. Be careful with your gear in Tonga as there have been reports of thefts—don't tempt people by leaving valuables unattended. Beware if someone on the street (near the Dateline Hotel especially) attempts to give you a "gift" such as a shell necklace. You'll end up paying for it. Don't give money to beggars you may encounter in the heavily touristed areas. If you see a 6-door Mercedes with a police escort coming your way, get off your bicycle and remove your hat. You're about to see the king and queen.

airport: Fua'amotu International Airport (TBU) is 21 km SE of the capital, Nuku'alofa, across Tongatapu. There's no tourist information or bank, but there is a duty-free shop. Notice the large bronze statue of King Tupou IV next to the VIP Lounge. Departure tax is $5; airport bus is $3. Private cars hanging around the terminal will often take you for the same. Ask the price of taxi (not over $10) or bus before getting in. To return to the airport take the infrequent Fua'amotu bus (30 cents) right to the airport or any Mu'a bus to the crossroads near Malapo, then walk or hitch 6 km.

TONGATAPU

Tongatapu's 259 sq km are just over a third of
the kingdom's surface area, yet nearly two-
thirds of the total population live here. Of coral
origin, Tongatapu is flat with a slight
tilt—from 18.2-m cliffs S of the airport to partly submerged islands and reefs to the north.
Some 20,000 years ago Tongatapu was
blanketed with volcanic ash from the explosion of Tofua I., creating rich soil which today
supports intensive agriculture. Horsedrawn
carts appear on country roads Sat. as people
go to their gardens to collect food for Sunday.
Nuku'alofa, the capital, is just N of the azure
Fanga Uta Lagoon, now sterile as sewage
from adjacent Vaiola Hospital eliminates the
fish and other marine life. Tourism, industry,
commerce, and government are all concentrated in the town, which retains its slow-
paced South Seas atmosphere. Nuku'alofa
means "Abode of Love." Tongatapu is
famous for its *tapa* cloth, but it also contains
some of the mightiest archaeological remains
in the Pacific. Captain Cook was enthralled by
Tongatapu and you will be too.

SIGHTS

Nuku'alofa: Pick up the excellent "Walking
Tour of Central Nuku'alofa" brochure at the
Tonga Visitors Bureau office on the waterfront. The Royal Palace (1867) and Chapel
(1882), viewable from outside their grounds,
are handsome reminders of their Victorian
past, and most memorable sights. The Royal
Palace, where the king and queen live, is a
gingerbread house: gables, scalloped eaves,
and white frame buildings crowned by bright
red roofs are surrounded by Norfolk pines.
Since 1893 Tongan royalty has been buried in
the field opposite the striking new Catholic
Basilica (1980). Parliament meets in a small
wooden building (1894) near Vuna Wharf
from early June to early September. **the
coconut industry:** If you're in the vicinity,
visit the Coconut Oil Mill behind the Shell and
BP oil tanks just beyond Queen Salote Wharf
3 km E of downtown. The mill operates 24

the Royal Palace
at Nuku'alofa

Because the flying fox or fruit bat (Pteropus tonganus) is tapu in Tonga, this is the only place in the Pacific where the animal may be easily seen. Elsewhere islanders hunt the bats for food.

hours a day (except Sun.) squeezing copra into oil for export to Australia and the U.S.; coconut meal, a byproduct used for animal feed, is also obtained. They'll explain the process in a quick tour if you ask nicely. For the desiccated coconut, snack foods, and laundry soap factories of the Tonga Commodities Board, take a bus to Vaiola Hospital then walk one km west. Go in the truck entrance and wander around at will. Since Tongatapu is virtually one large coconut plantation, the processing plants are always humming.

western Tongatapu: Surf forced through naturally-formed air vents creates spectacular blowholes on the rocky, terraced SW coast near Houma, 15 km from Nuku'alofa. Waves batter the coral cliffs and spout water up to 30 m in the air through eroded tunnels. These impressive blowholes number in the hundreds—come at high tide on a windy day! Bus service to Houma is fairly frequent and continues W to Fahefa. From Fahefa it's a pleasant 5-km walk (or hitch) to the Flying Fox Sanctuary at Kolovai. Here countless hundreds of the animals (*Pteropus tonganus*) hang in many casuarina trees for about a km along the road. Flying foxes are actually bats (the only mammals which can fly) with foxlike heads and a wingspan of up to a meter across.

Nocturnal creatures, they cruise after dark in search of food, and hang upside down during the day. Legend says the bats were a gift from a Samoan maiden to an ancient Tongan navigator. Considered sacred, they may be hunted only by the royal family. Just beyond Kolovai is the turnoff for Kolovai Beach (see "accommodations" below); farther along, near the end of the island, turn L to Ha'atafu Beach. Some of the best reefbreak surfing in Tonga, and there's excellent snorkeling here, even at low tide—see at least a hundred species of fish. Buses from Ha'atafu head straight back to town.

vicinity of Mu'a: Across the lagoon from town, just outside Mu'a is a monument marking the spot where, in 1777, Capt. Cook landed from his ship the *Endeavor* and rested under a banyan tree. He then continued into Lapaha, capital of Tonga at the time, to visit Pau, the Tu'i Tonga. Retrace Cook's footsteps into this richest archaeological area in Western Polynesia. For over 600 years begin-

The Houma Blowholes are an impressive sight at high tide as the waves crash into the coral terraces, sending the surf soaring skyward.

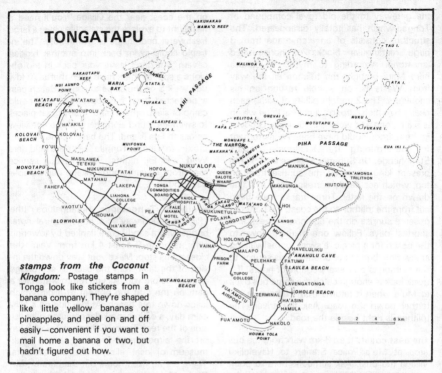

TONGATAPU

stamps from the Coconut Kingdom: Postage stamps in Tonga look like stickers from a banana company. They're shaped like little yellow bananas or pineapples, and peel on and off easily—convenient if you want to mail home a banana or two, but hadn't figured out how.

ning around A.D. 1200, Lapaha (Mu'a) was the seat of the Tu'i Tonga dynasty. Nothing remains of the royal residence today but some 28 *langi* (burial mounds of ancient royalty) have been located in or near Mu'a. Due to local objections none has yet been excavated. Several of these great rectangular platforms, with recessed tiers of coraline limestone, are clearly visible from the main road, including the *langi* of the last Tu'i Tonga (1865), a Catholic, which has a cross on top. The finest of the terraced tombs are hidden down a side road leading to the Paki Moe To'e Handicraft Center (open Mon. to Fri. 0900-1700). The best one of these is the Paepae 'o Tele'a, built during the early 17th C. for the 28th Tu'i Tonga. Notice in particular the gigantic L-shaped monoliths at the corners, the slanting upper surfaces, and the feet that extend under the ground. In its context this mighty monument has all the power and emotional

impact of a classical Greek temple. Adjacent to the Paepae 'o Tele'a is the Namoala, a 3-tiered pyramid with the stone burial vault still intact on top. The Hehea mound opposite Namoala bears another 2 vaults. The *langi* of Lapaha are the most imposing ancient tombs in the South Pacific and rank with the *moai* of Easter I. and Ponape's Nan Madol as major archaeological sites. The beating of *tapa* mallets from houses all around the *langi* adds an otherworldliness to this magical place. Bus service from Nuku'alofa to Mu'a (20 km) is frequent throughout the day (until 1500), making it easy to visit.

Ha'amonga 'a Maui: Catch the Niutoua bus to this famous trilithon 32 km E of Nuku'alofa, Tonga's most engaging relic. Called "The Burden of the God Maui," it was erected around A.D. 1200 by the 11th Tu'i Tonga. This massive 109-ton stone archway is said to be the gateway to the old royal compound of Tonga, which has totally disappeared. The structure consists of an arch made from 3 huge rectangular blocks of nonstratified limestone. According to myth, the culture hero Maui brought the trilithon all the way from Wallis Is. on a pole resting on his shoulders. The 2 upright pillars of coral, each nearly 5 m high, support a central lintel which is 5.8 m long and weighs 8,165 kilos. Grooves in the trilithon could have been an instrument for determining the seasons—Tonga's Stonehenge. On Summer Solstice in 1967 the present king observed the sunrise from on top, which accurately corresponded to a line drawn on the lintel. Three tracks have been cut from the trilithon to the coast, the better to observe sunrise on the equinox, longest, and shortest days. Follow one of them down to the beach for a picnic, a swim, or reefwalking at low tide (bring your booties). Bus service to the trilithon is only every couple of hours. If a quick look is enough catch the same bus back to Mu'a when it returns from Niutoua, a km farther down the road. Ask the driver. The trilithon is right beside the road.

the east coast: It's a 3-km walk from the bus stop at Mu'a Police Station to Haveluliku village (no bus). Ask someone here to point out the *makatolo,* huge stones which the demigod Maui reputedly threw across from Eua I. at an errant chicken. 'Anahulu Cave is on the coast near the village. You'll need a flashlight to explore the stalactite cave; a large freshwater pool inside is swimmable. The intrepid could swim back into another hidden cavern, but don't leave your pack in too obvious a spot as there have been thefts. At low tide walk S on the slope to Laulea Beach past a protected coral outcrop where you could camp or sleep on the sand. Many great places to swim are found along here, plus a fine view across to Eua Island. The beach continues unbroken to 'Oholei; Tongan feasts are held here Wed. and Fri. nights. Sporadic bus service runs from Lavengatonga village near 'Oholei back to town.

southern Tongatapu: Hufangalupe (the "Pigeon's Doorway"), a huge natural coral bridge with a sandy cove flanked by towering cliffs, is on th S coast 4 km from Vaini, the closest bus stop. Make your way down the inside of the fault from the back to see bridge and sea before you. As you return watch for a path on the L at the bottom of a dip which leads down to a beach. At low tide on a very calm day, a daring snorkeler could go over the side of the reef. Tupou College at Tuloa, 3 km off the airport road (no bus), has a small museum of local relics, crafts, and artifacts. There are no fixed hours but the curator, Mr. Paula Mu'a, is less occupied with classes weekdays 1500-1700, Sat. 0900-1200. Ask at the college office for permission to visit.

The cornerstones of the Mu'a's Paepae'o Tele'a, burial place of the 28th Tu'i Tonga, are massive L-shaped blocks of limestone.

dive spots: Hakaumama'o Reef, 14 km N of Nuku'alofa, is a sea reef populated by large numbers of brilliant parrotfish. Malinoa I. to the SE features a great variety of marinelife on the surrounding reef, plus a lighthouse and some old graves on the island itself. Both of the above are marine reserves and taking fish, clams, or coral is prohibited ($200 fine).

PRACTICALITIES

accommodations: Although it's a little out of the way, Sela and Atolo's Guest House has long been a favorite stopping place for both visitors and resident volunteers. There are 16 rooms at $5 pp a day or $28 pp a week; 3 ample meals run $10 extra daily. Breakfast is especially good. Near Sela's is Kuluni's Guest House. Also known a K's, it features an upstairs balcony and is only $3.50 pp, plus $9 for all meals. Three more good places to stay are clustered along Beach Road close to the center of town. Kimiko's Guest House is $5 s, $7 d (discounts for long stays)—fridge but no cooking facilities. It's a good place to meet other travelers. The Beach House, just a minute away, is one of the last of the old South Seas guest houses fast disappearing in the wake of self-catering flats and plastic motels. For $15 pp you get a room, 3 meals, morning and afternoon tea. Somerset Maugham would have stayed here. The Fasimoe-afi Guest House next to the Visitors Bureau is $5 s, $8 d for an inside room, $7 s, $12 d for an outside room. The manager, Herman the German, seems to be mellowing. The adjacent cafe (closed Sun.) is great for coffee on the terrace, as you watch the world go by. Langafonua, the handicraft outlet on the main street, has pleasant rooms at $3.50 pp, meals available. Farther W on the waterfront beyond the palace is Sunrise Guest House where a decent room with all meals is $15 s, $29 d: so good it's often fully booked. All the above accommodations have shared bath and a family atmosphere. For private bath and standard hotel facilities (restaurant, lounge, etc.) try Joe's Tropicana Hotel, $12 s, $16 d bed and breakfast. The government-owned International Dateline Hotel is $32 s, $38 d.

bungalows: If you're catching the 0630 ferry to Eua I., the Moana Hotel opposite Faua Jetty is convenient. There are 3 small *fale* units with private facilities at $5 s, $9 d, but it can be noisy due to the adjacent bar (pool table). The only lodging in Nuku'alofa which offers cooking facilities is the Fale Maama Motel beside the lagoon on the road from the airport, 4 km from town. Eight spacious *fales* sit in a garden setting, $60 d a week (no daily rates, monthly-rate discount). Guests are expected to comport themselves as Christians. If you're planning a long stay, ask at the Visitors Bureau for their list of apartments and houses for rent.

island living: Several of the small islands off Nuku'alofa are being developed for tourism. Pangaimotu I., the closest, has 3 *fales* at $7 pp, or camp for $3 pp (cooking facilities). A daytrip (1100-1600) to Pangaimotu is $11 including lunch, snorkeling gear $2 extra. The reef around the island is good and there's even a half-sunken ship sticking up out of the water for snorkelers to explore. Provided the weather cooperates, this trip is an excellent way to spend Nuku'alofa's pious Sunday. The resort has an office next to the Dateline Hotel. Fafa I., quite a distance farther out than Pangaimotu, is upmarket (German management): one of their 8 *fales* will run $15 s, $20 d (shared bath), plus about $25 extra for all meals in the restaurant/bar. A full range of sporting activities is offered in the emerald lagoon surrounding this delightful palm-covered island. The initial RT boatride is $6, but once you're staying they'll ferry you into town and back when you want at no extra cost. Call 22-800 to arrange a pickup.

at the beach: If you came to Tonga for the sand, tan, and salt, you can't go wrong at the Good Samaritan Inn on Kolovai Beach, 20 km W of Nuku'alofa. Take the Hihifo bus to Kolovai, then walk 1.5 km to the Inn. Accommodation is in small *fale* units, $5 pp, or for $2 pitch your tent on the grounds. Shared facilities, and the Inn has its own electric generator. A very pleasant restaurant/bar overlooks the beach. The meals offered are outstanding, a must for the jaded palate—about $5-7 each for lunch and dinner

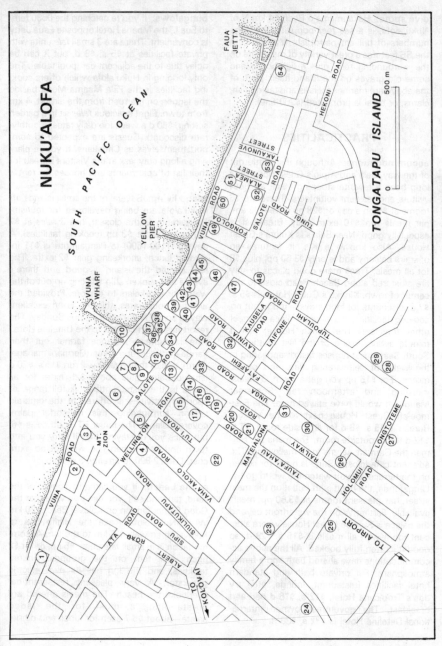

NUKU'ALOFA

SOUTH PACIFIC OCEAN

TONGATAPU ISLAND

FAUA JETTY

HEKONI ROAD

VUNA ROAD

FONGOLOA ROAD

TAKAUNOVE STREET

ALAMEA STREET

SALOTE ROAD

TUNGI ROAD

YELLOW PIER

VUNA WHARF

VUNA ROAD

SALOTE ROAD

TUPOULAHI ROAD

LAIFONE ROAD

KAUSELA ROAD

LAVINIA ROAD

FATAFEHI ROAD

UNGA ROAD

MATEIALONA ROAD

TAUFA'AHAU ROAD

RAILWAY ROAD

LONGOTEME ROAD

HOLOMUI ROAD

MT. ZION

WELLINGTON ROAD

TUI ROAD

VAHA'AKOLO ROAD

SIULIKUTAPU ROAD

SIPU ROAD

ALBERT ROAD

ATA ROAD

TO KOLOVAI

TO AIRPORT

0   500 m

NUKU'ALOFA

1. Sunrise Guest House
2. Seaview Restaurant
3. British High Commissioner's residence
4. Centenary Methodist Church
5. Vilai Army Barrack
6. Royal Palace and Chapel
7. Pangai Soccer Field
8. Bank of Tonga
9. post office
10. fish and meat markets
11. Treasury/Philatelic Bureau
12. police station/jail
13. Langa Fonua Handicraft Center
14. Fale Fakalato Restaurant/T. Jagroop
15. Tali'eva Cinema/German Consulate
16. John's Place Snack Bar
17. Ramanlal Disco/SPIA/Tungi Arcade
18. Friendly Islands Bookshop
19. Hau Hau Cinema
20. Catholic Basilica
21. banana shed
22. Royal Tombs
23. USP Center Library
24. Immigration office
25. Teufiava Rugby Field
26. Kulunis Guest House
27. Sela and Atolo's Guest House
28. Munioa Dance Hall
29. Fakatouato Community Center
30. Titilupe Disco Palace
31. bus stop
32. Baha'i Headquarters
33. Loni's Cinema
34. Talamahu Market and bus station
35. Vovo'a Pilolevu Restaurant
36. Parliament
37. Shipping Corporation of Polynesia
38. Ministry Block
39. Prime Minister's residence
40. laundry service
41. Fa'onelua Tropical Gardens
42. Tonga Visitors Bureau
43. Fasi-Moe-Afi Guest House
44. Pangaimotu Island Office
45. Dateline Hotel
46. Tong-Hua Chinese Restaurant
47. Australian High Commission
48. Tonga Club
49. Beach House
50. Kimiko's Guest House
51. Yacht Club
52. Joe's Hotel
53. Cable and Wireless office
54. Moana Hotel

(French cuisine). Highly recommended. Surfers head for the Ha'atafu Beach Motel near the end of the road, 3 km N of Kolovai. Ha'atafu experiences water shortages, but it's on the better beach. Thatched *fales* (shared facilities) begin at $6 s, $11 d, with 10 percent off if you stay a month (many do). Beware of mice if you bring food. The restaurant specializes in seafood served Aussie-style, about $7 a meal. Dining is by candlelight and the motel's kerosene lighting adds to the charm. They'll organize boat trips for snorkeling, fishing, or surfing on outlying reefs if enough people are interested (about $5 pp). The motel is right on Tonga's most popular surfing beach, just a 5-min. walk from the Ha'atafu bus stop. Both Kolovai and Ha'atafu are *palagi* beaches, which means there's no hassle about swimming on Sunday. Both fill up on Sat. night so call the Good Samaritan Inn (tel. 41-022) or Ha'atafu Beach Motel (tel. 41-088) for reservations before heading out to them.

food: The Fale Fakalato Restaurant upstairs serves American food, $2-3. Next door the T. Jagroop Fale Kai has real Tongan meals at $1, drinks 10 cents. Vovo'a Pilolevu Restaurant near the market also has Tongan food. John's Place Snack Bar (open Sunday!) on the main street dishes out the familiar hamburgers and chips. The Tong Hua Chinese Restaurant (lunch 1200-1400, dinner 1830-2130) behind the Dateline Hotel features hot Szechuan food. Their daily specials are good value and even the regular menu is not unreasonable. Chinese tea is served free. The best place to eat in Nuku'alofa is Akiko's Japanese Restaurant (open Mon. to Fri. 1130-1400/1830-2030) in the basement of the Catholic Basilica. You get a good special lunch for $1.50; there's a more extensive menu at dinner. Try the Japanese dishes posted on the wall. It's so popular there's often a lineup to get in (come early). For that special dinner out to pick the Seaview Restaurant (Mon. to Sat. 1700-2200). Under German management, it's not cheap, but the food and atmosphere are excellent. **others:** A cold beer by the pool at the Dateline Hotel is the perfect way to top off an afternoon. Talamahu Market (closed Sun.) is a colorful

The Basilica of St. Anthony of Padua At Nuku'alofa is popular among travelers for its library and Japanese restaurant in the basement.

place for fruit and vegetable shopping. You can buy bananas at wholesale rates in the green-and-white shed just S of the Catholic Basilica. Sunday at 1630 get fresh bread at the bakery near Tali'eva Cinema. For something different, ask for *loi hosi* at the fish market beside Vuna Wharf. You'll pay only $1 for a nice leaf package of horse meat cooked in coconut cream.

entertainment: The best cinema is Loni's (70 cents, showtime 2000); others are the Hauhau and Tali'eva. Local teenagers make the scene at Titilupe Disco Palace or Muniao Dance Hall, Fri. and Sat. at 2000. Only soft drinks are sold but the cover charge is low, so you don't have much to lose. You'll meet young Tongans rather than other tourists. Occasionally there's even a local band doing '60's rock. It's great fun if you're gutsy enough to be there. Tourists are *expected* to go to Ramanlal Disco Bar which offers live music Thurs., Fri., and Sat. at 2000 ($1 cover). Even more conventional is the barbecue ($8) by the pool at the Dateline Tues. at 1930. Also at the Dateline, see Tongan dancing Sat. at 2030 ($2 cover). Wednesday and Fri. evenings there's Oscar's Tongan Feast at 'Oholei Beach. Traditional dancing in the Hina Cave follows dinner. The price is $12 for transportation, dinner, and the show; alcoholic drinks are extra. Book at the Dateline's tour desk. There's good drinking at the Tonga Club; you're supposed to be a

member but you'll be admitted if you look right. **sports:** Catch a game of rugby (April to June) at the Tenfaiva Rugby Field on Fri. or Sat. at 1500. During the soccer season (May to July) you can watch them play at the Pangai Soccer Field on the waterfront next to the Bank of Tonga Sat. at 1500.

shopping: The best place to shop for baskets, *tapa,* mats, and shellwork is Langafonua, the Tongan Women's Assn. Handicraft Center (open weekdays 0800-1300/1400-1700, Sat. 0800-1200). Good-quality crafts are also available at the Tonga Cooperative Federation shop opposite the German Consulate. They'll wrap your purchases for mailing. After you've browsed in these, check Talamahu Market where you buy direct from the craftspeople. The Philatelic Bureau in the Treasury Bldg. on the waterfront sells pure gold coins at face value and striking commemorative medals bearing the image of the king. The beautiful first-day covers from Niuafo'ou make excellent gifts and souvenirs. Camera film is expensive and hard to find in Tonga, so bring a supply. In a pinch Tulua Bros. Rainbow Studio in the Tungi Arcade might have some.

services: The Bank of Tonga is open Mon. to Fri. 0930-1530; they don't accept Western Samoan *tala.* The bank stores valuables for you in their vault for $1 per sealed envelope. Outside banking hours the Dateline Hotel will change money for just slightly less. The Cable and Wireless office is open 24 hours a day for long-distance calls and telegrams. You can get an extension of stay at no charge from the Immigration office (weekdays 0830-1230/1330-1530). Medical consultations are $2.50 at Vaiola Hospital (daily 0830-1230/1330-1630), just outside town on the way to the airport. The women in the house on the E side of the bus station will do your laundry (pants $1, shirts 25 cents). You'll know the place by the wash hung up to dry. You can use the pool at the Dateline Hotel for only 60 cents.

information: The Tonga Visitors Bureau (weekdays 0830-1630), Sat. 0900-1200) is the best in the South Pacific — be sure to drop by. Get good maps from the Lands and Survey Dept. in the Ministry Block (3rd floor). The 'Utue'a Public Library (open weekdays 1130-1330/1600-2100, Sat. 1000-1300) in the Catholic Basilica is only $2 annual membership. There's also a good library in the University of the South Pacific Center (weekdays 0900-1230/1330-1630, closed Thurs. morning); ask to see their collection of antique Tongan war clubs. The Friendly Islands Bookstore is well worth a visit. Pick up a copy of *The Geography of Tonga* by E.A. Crane for excellent shipboard reading. There's a used book exchange at the Pangaimotu Island Office next to the Dateline. The *Tonga Chronicle* comes out on Friday. The bench on the waterfront opposite the Beach House is a good place to make contacts.

Island athletes play rugby with a passion. Here Tonga meets Samoa at the annual Three-Nations Tournament in Suva, Fiji.

time for a nap on the rough boat ride from Nuku'alofa to Eua

TRANSPORT

by air: In theory Tonga Air operates between the islands; in practice they're not flying. South Pacific Island Airways (SPIA) has flights from Nuku'alofa to Eua ($13), Ha'apai ($42), and Vava'u ($60). The plane often overflies Ha'apai if they've got a full load between Nuku'alofa and Vava'u—confirmed ticket holders waiting in Ha'apai may be out of luck. In emergencies they "bump" those with reservations for priority passengers. This doesn't happen often, but be forewarned. Domestic air service has deteriorated since SPIA was grounded by the U.S. Federal Aviation Administration in 1985 over alleged infractions of their rules.

by ship: The Shipping Corporation of Polynesia offers the safest, most reliable boat service among the Tonga Islands. Their large car ferry, the MV *Olovaha*, departs Nuku'alofa for Ha'apai ($13) every Tues. at 1800 arriving

Wed. morning, then on to Vava'u ($18) which it reaches Wed. evening. It leaves Vava'u again Thurs. evening, arriving at Ha'apai early Fri. morning and Nuku'alofa Fri. evening, schedules subject to change, of course. Cabins cost double the deck fare and you must book an entire twin room. No meals are included. The Warner Pacific Line (weekdays 0830-1230/1330-1630, Sat. 0830-1200) in the Fakafanua Center near Queen Salote Wharf has monthly sailings to Vava'u ($12), Apia ($40), and Pago Pago ($50), and occasional trips to Niue, Rarotonga, Fiji, Wallis, Tuvalu, and Kiribati. Bring your own food. The M. Tu'ihalamako Shipping Co. (office on the waterfront side of the market) runs the MV *Nanasipau'u* twice a month to Ha'apai ($9), Vava'u ($13), Niuatoputapu ($20), Niuafo'ou ($22), and Pago Pago ($50). Fie'eiki and Sons (office near John's Place Snack Bar) operates the MV *Ata* to Ha'apai ($6), Vava'u ($8), and sometimes Niue and Pago Pago. The *Ata* offers your best chance to see the outer islands of the Ha'apai Group.

to Eua: The Shipping Corporation of Polynesia's boat departs Faua Jetty Tues. to Sat. at 0630 ($3). You pay on board. Small private boats leave Faua Jetty for Eua ($2.50) daily except Sun. at 1300, but they're not renowned for their safety. Still, the time is convenient. Be prepared for an extremely rough 4-hour trip.

by bus: Buses (with taped rock music) leave from Nuku'alofa market for all parts of Tongatapu. Those from the East Terminal go to the E side of the island (Mu'a 40 cents, Ha'amonga 50 cents); those from the West Terminal go to the W (Houma 25 cents, Kolovai 30 cents). Local buses also leave from the West Terminal. The last bus back to Nuku'alofa from Kolovai and Ha'amonga is at 1500, and no buses on Sunday.

others: There are no scooter rentals. Rent bicycles ($5 a day) at the Pangaimotu Island Office next to the Dateline Hotel. You can sometimes get them from guys in the street for less. If you're going to be in Tonga long, buy a bicycle ($110) at the shop beside the

Tong Hua Chinese Restaurant. Cycling is likely to be tiring and dusty, but friendly Tongans are quick to smile and wave at a pedaling visitor. Ask at the Visitors Bureau about horseback riding ($5 an hour), but make sure the saddle is properly secured before you mount. Mini-moke taxis at the market are $1 for a trip in town, $2 for a longer trip in the vicinity. There is no reliable scuba operator in Nuku'alofa.

EUA ISLAND

A rough, 40-km boat ride from Nuku'alofa, Eua is a good place to go for the weekend. Its hills are a contrast to flat Tongatapu. The thickly forested spine down the E side of Eua drops to perpendicular cliffs, while the W half is largely taken up by plantations and villages. Bony bareback horses are available at $4 a day, but nowhere is too far to walk. Facilities on Eua are extremely basic; this is the best way to get off the beaten tourist track and see real Tongan life. Three full days are enough to get the feel of the island.

SIGHTS

Matalanga 'a Maui: Legend tells how the demigod Maui thrust his digging stick into Eua and pulled it back and forth in anger at his mother, threatening thereby to upset the island. To visit the great pothole that remained, head S of the sawmill and Ha'atua Mormon Church, take the third bush road on the L, and walk inland about 10 minutes. You'll need intuition or a guide to locate the pit hidden in the middle of a plantation on the R, although the lower level of the trees growing in it are an indicator. Holding onto vines, you can get right down into Matalanga 'a Maui itself for an eerie view of jungle-clad walls towering around you.

southern Eua: Most of the people in Pangai and farther S are refugees (and their children) evacuated from Niuafo'ou I. after a devastating volcanic eruption there in 1946. The road S from the wharf terminates in 10 km at Ha'aluma Beach. The deserted beach is a weathered reef with sandy pools to swim in. It's safe as long as you hug the shore. There are some small blowholes and a view of Kalau Island. Just before the descent to the beach

take the road to the L and keep straight one hour almost to the S tip of the island. When you enter a cow pasture, the track veers L and starts going N up the E coast. The first cliff you come to, across the field from the track, is Lakufa'anga, where Tongans once called turtles from the sea. So many have been slaughtered that none appear anymore. Look down on the grassy ledges below the cliffs and you'll spot the nesting places of sea birds. Continue N on the track a short distance, watching on the L for a huge depression partly visible through the trees. This is Li'angahuo 'a Maui, a tremendous natural

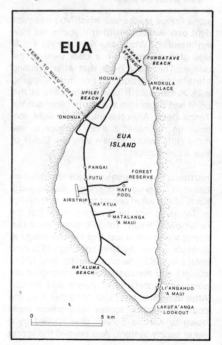

Legend tells how Li'angahuo 'a Maui on Eua I. was formed when the demigod Maui hurled his spear across the island.

stone bridge by the sea which you can pass right over without realizing if you're not paying attention. Work your way around the N side of the pothole for a clear view of the bridge. The story goes that after creating Matalanga, Maui threw his digging stick across Eua. It pierced the cliffs at this point and drove into the sea to carve out the Tonga Deep. After this impressive sight continue up the coast a short distance to see more cliffs, which explain why the E side of Eua is uninhabited.

northern Eua: The safest place to snorkel on Eua is in 'Ononua harbor. Ufilei Beach, just 2 km N of the wharf across the only river bridge in Tonga, is fine for a sunset stroll, but the undertow is deadly. Tonga's most spectacular scenic viewpoint is just E of Houma village at Anokula where the king built himself a new palace in 1983. The soaring cliffs drop 120 m straight into the coastal strip, creating an unsurpassed panorama of power and beauty. After this visual blast look for a trail N up the coast to another access road which leads down to Kahana Spring, now spoiled by a water supply system. Just beyond the spring

is a second magnificent viewpoint over the E coast, directly above inaccessible Fungatave Beach.

the interior: Tonga's finest tropical forest is on the slopes just above Futu. Take the road inland a little S of Haukinima Motel toward the Forestry Experimental Farm. Continue along the main road about 30 min. till you reach the Forestry Office, which has a map on the wall. Hafu Pool is near the office, down a trail which continues straight ahead from the road on the R—it isn't much. The forest, on the other hand, is well worth exploring for the many exotic species planted by the Forestry Dept. and the abundant birdlife, especially kingfishers and giant parrots.

PRACTICALITIES

accommodations: Two small guest houses are a couple of km S of 'Onohua wharf, closer to the airstrip. Leipua Lodge at Pangai is $10 pp including breakfast and dinner. Owner Lilo Vaka'uta also runs a store across from the wharf (not the one on the L), and the lackadaisical female clerks will arrange a free truck ride to the lodge if you hang around long enough. You share the facilities with Lilo's family. The other place is Haukinima Motel at Futu, a km S of Leipua Lodge. It's $4 pp with primitive cooking facilities (watch your food!). The manager, Sione Manukia, sells warm beer by the bottle to locals who drink it out back. His slogan is "Help Me and I Help You." At last report neither guest house had electricity; still, it's a roof over your head. Beware of rip-offs if you're camping on the beach.

events: The best time to come is late Aug. or early Sept. during the Eua Agricultural Show. The showgrounds are just above the hospital at Futu. The only nightlife on Eua unfolds at Maxi Disco Hall just across from Haukinima Motel. A live band plays Sat. at 2000, plus possibly a couple of other nights a week. The hall was built by Axel and Taina from Dusseldorf, Germany, who named it after their cat, Maxi. Dance nights the place is packed.

THE HA'APAI GROUP

This great group of low coral islands between Nuku'alofa and Vava'u is a beachcomber's paradise. Perfect white sandy beaches run right around the mostly uninhabited islands. Treacherous shoals keep cruising yachts away. There are 2 clusters: Nomuka is the largest of the seldom-visited southern islands, while Lifuka is at the center of a string of islands to the north. Captain Cook made prolonged stops at Nomuka in 1774 and 1777; on a visit to Lifuka in 1773 he coined the term "Friendly Islands," unaware of a plot by Tongans on Lifuka to murder him. Later, on 28 April 1789 off Tofua, Fletcher Christian and his mutineers lowered Capt. William Bligh and 18 loyal members of his crew into a rowboat, beginning one of the longest voyages (6,500 km) in an open boat in maritime history, from Tongan waters to Timor in the Dutch East Indies—a fantastic accomplishment of endurance and seamanship. Bligh's group suffered its only casualty of the trip, John Norton, quartermaster of the *Bounty,* when they landed on Tofua just after the mutiny and clashed with Tongans.

Tofua: Tofua (56 sq km) is a flat-topped volcanic island about 500 m high. The shoreline is steep and rocky right around. The few buildings near the coast are used by villagers who come to harvest Tofua's potent *kava.* Otherwise the island and its neighbor Kao are uninhabited. The large steep-sided, 4-km-wide caldera in the interior is occupied by a crater lake. Tofua is still active: steam and gases issue from a cone on the N side of the lake. Flames can be seen from passing ships at night.

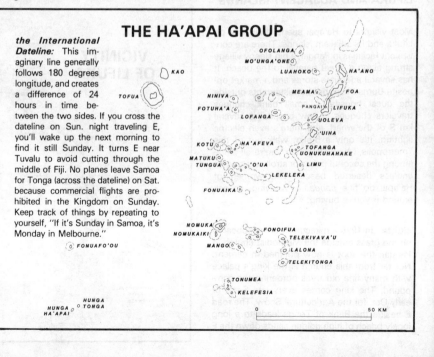

THE HA'APAI GROUP

the International Dateline: This imaginary line generally follows 180 degrees longitude, and creates a difference of 24 hours in time between the two sides. If you cross the dateline on Sun. night traveling E, you'll wake up the next morning to find it still Sunday. It turns E near Tuvalu to avoid cutting through the middle of Fiji. No planes leave Samoa for Tonga (across the dateline) on Sat. because commercial flights are prohibited in the Kingdom on Sunday. Keep track of things by repeating to yourself, "If it's Sunday in Samoa, it's Monday in Melbourne."

KAO

TOFUA

FONUAFO'OU

OFOLANGA

MO'UNGA'ONE

LUAHOKO   HA'ANO

NINIVA   MEAMA   FOA

FOTUHA'A   PANGAI LIFUKA

LOFANGA   UOLEVA

'UIHA

KOTU   HA'AFEVA   TOFANGA
UONUKUHAHAKE

MATUKU
TUNGUA   'O'UA   LIMU

LEKELEKA

FONUAIKA

NOMUKA   FONOIFUA
NOMUKAIKI   TELEKIVAVA'U

MANGO   LALONA

TELEKITONGA

TONUMEA
KELEFESIA

HUNGA
HUNGA TONGA
HA'APAI

0   50 KM

Kao: This extinct 1,046-m-high volcano is the tallest in Tonga; on a clear day the classic triangular cone is visible from Lifuka. There is no anchorage, but it's possible to land on the S side in good weather. The lower slopes are well wooded, becoming barren higher up. Kao can be climbed in a long day.

Fonuafo'ou: One of the world's outstanding natural phenomena, this geographical freak 72 km NW of Tongatapu was first observed in 1865 by the crew of HMS *Falcon*. Jack-in-the-box Fonuafo'ou ("new land") alternates between shoal and island. Sometimes this temperamental volcanic mound stands 100 m high and 3 km long, other times it's completely under water. If you walk on it you're ankle deep in hot, black scoria (shaggy lava), an extremely desolate, blackened surface. At last report Fonuafo'ou was submerged again for the fifth time in the past 120 years.

LIFUKA AND ADJACENT ISLANDS

Most visitors to Ha'apai spend their time on Lifuka and its adjacent islands. There are convenient facilities in Pangai, a big sleepy village strung along a street parallel to the beach. It has several adequate stores and a market opposite Burns Philp, but no restaurants outside the guest houses. A small bank changes travelers cheques, a new hospital is several km S of the wharf, and there's even electric lighting. It's only a 5-min. walk out of this "metropolis," however; then you're all alone among the coconut palms or strolling along an endless deserted beach. The women of Ha'apai do fine *pandanus* weaving, so ask around if you're buying.

sights: In 1975 a miraculous cross appeared on the grass outside the Methodist church at Pangai; the spot is now outlined in cement. Not far from this church is the king's palace with many fine old trees bordering the compound. The king comes every late Sept. or early Oct. for the Agricultural Show. The road E beside the Bank of Tonga leads to a long lonely beach of high golden sands down the E side of Lifuka, only a 5-min. walk from the guest houses. Just N of Pangai is the grave and monument of Reverend Shirley Baker (1836-1903), an adviser to George Tupou I, who helped frame the Emancipation Edict of 1862 and the 1875 constitution. When Baker went too far and became involved in religious strife, a British warship was sent to take him to Fiji in 1890 for an accounting. He was later allowed to retire to Ha'apai. From the S end of Lifuka, 3.5 km from town, you can wade across the reef at low tide to uninhabited Uoleva Island.

Foa Island: A causeway has been built between Lifuka and Foa. Buses (30 cents) run unpredictably throughout the day from Pangai to Faleloa village, Foa's northernmost. Continue on foot to the N tip to look across to Nukunamo I., owned by the king. Strong currents make it risky to try wading across. Outboard motorboats bring villagers from Ha'ano I. to the landing at Faleloa, and you can go

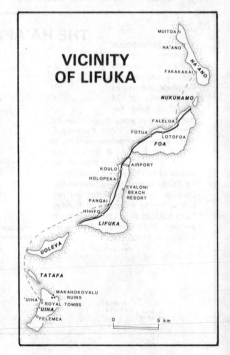

VICINITY OF LIFUKA

MUITOA
HA'ANO
FAKAKAKAI
HA'ANO
NUKUNAMO
FALELOA
FOTUA
LOTOFOA
FOA
KOULO
AIRPORT
HOLOPEKA
EVALONI
BEACH
RESORT
PANGAI
HIHIFO
LIFUKA
UOLEVA
TATAFA
MAKAHOKOVALU
RUINS
'UIHA
ROYAL TOMBS
'UIHA
FELEMEA

0   5 km

This distinctive monument at Pangai, Lifuka, marks the tomb of Rev. Shirley Baker, one-time advisor to King George Tupou I.

back with them most afternoons for about $1 OW. Ask permission to camp or stay in the village.

'Uiha Island: 'Uiha I., S of Lifuka, is fairly easy to get to on small boats departing the old wharf or beach at Pangai (50 cents OW), but at best the service is only once a day, so you'll have to spend the night. And don't be in a hurry to get back from 'Uiha or the 50-cent trip will become a $25 charter. There's a primitive guest house (no beds, only foam rubber pads on the floor) on Texas Beach near the dock; ask for Sunia. The burial ground of the Tongan royal family was on 'Uiha until the move to Nuku'alofa. Visit the Makahokovalu, an ancient monument comprised of 8 connecting stones, about an hour's walk from 'Uiha village. A cannon from the British privateer *Port-au-Prince,* sacked off the NW end of Lifuka in 1806, can be seen in the middle of the village at 'Uiha.

excursions: The Catholic Mission at Pangai owns a clean, 10-m interisland boat, the *Folau Moe'Eiki,* capable of transporting up to 20 passengers. There are 2 small cabins belowdeck. If you can get a group together, consider a visit to Tofua and Kao. A 3-day charter would run about $230 for the boat if you bring your own food. Father Falenaka at the Catholic Mission may be able to arrange guides for hiking on Tofua and Kao, plus overnight stays in villages on remote islands of the Ha'apai Group.

PRACTICALITIES

accommodations: One of the best places to stay at Pangai is Evaloni Town House (Mrs. Sitali Hu'akau) in the village back behind the bank. Rooms are $3 pp, or $10 including all meals. There's no cooking. Food prices are posted in the kitchen. It's better (if more expensive) to order specific dishes rather than take the all-inclusive price and risk getting tinned food. Lobster dinner (alas, never served in its shell) is $5. Rent bicycles for $2.50 a day. The Fonongava'inga Guest House (Mr. Pita Vimahi) nearby is similar. Seletute's Guest House (Mr. Seletute Falevai) beside the Catholic Mission (daybreak Mass) charges about the same, but there's a bar attached and video movies are shown nightly at 2000. The Government Rest House beside the bank is $2 pp and you can cook. **at the beach:** If you came to Ha'apai to get away from it all, Evaloni Beach Resort is just the place. Small *fales* constructed of local materials are set in a coconut plantation just a minute from the beach on the E side of Lifuka. You can walk to town in about 15 min., but here you're on your own to experience the wild natural beauty of the place. There's no electricity, the water supply is limited, and it can get windy, but the price is right: $4 s, $6 d with a discount if you stay a week or more. Or pitch your tent here for $2 pp and use the cooking facilities, etc. Book in at Evaloni Town House. **entertainment:** Wednesday and Fri. evenings from 1900-2400 you can drink *kava* in Tataki'aho Hall near the Methodist church for a flat fee of $1.

getting there: The Shipping Corp. of Polynesia has a regular weekly ferry from Nuku'alofa ($13) and Vava'u ($8). The ferry calls at Ha'afeva between Nuku'alofa and Pangai. The wharf at Pangai is near the center of town; turn R as you disembark. SPIA flies 4 times a week between Ha'apai and Vava'u ($30 OW), a useful supplement to the boat

service if you only want to spend a couple of days at Pangai. If you're sure you'll be doing this, it's best to book your flight before you leave Nuku'alofa. The plane will only land at Ha'apai if there are at least 2 people to pick up or set down. The SPIA office will be able to advise you. Koulo airport is 5 km N of Pangai but transport is easily arranged.

THE VAVA'U GROUP

This elevated limestone cluster tilts up to cliffs in the N, then submerges into a myriad of small islands to the south. A labyrinth of waterways plies between plateaus thrust up by some subterranean muscle-flexing. In Vava'u one superb scenic vista succeeds another, all so varied you're continually consulting your map to discover just what you're seeing. Only the Rock Is. of Belau are more magnificent. Of the 34 elevated, thickly forested islands, 21 are inhabited. Vanilla plantations now abound on Vava'u itself. Ships approach Vava'u up a fjord-like 11-km channel. The attractive main town, Neiafu, 275 km N of Nuku'alofa, looks out onto a picturesque, landlocked harbor, one of the best in the Pacific. A Spanish vessel en route from Manila to Mexico under Capt. Mourelle chanced upon Vava'u in 1781 and christened Neiafu harbor Puerto de Refugio, the name it still bears. The many protected anchorages in the

bays make Vava'u a favorite of cruising yachties. Beaches are harder to find, although there are some on the small outlying islands. Be careful walking barefoot in Neiafu. Large centipedes here deliver a painful bite.

sights: One of the burials in the cemetery on the corner a block back from the Bank of Tonga is of the ancient *langi* type. For a splendid view of Port of Refuge and much of the archipelago climb Mt. Talau (131 m), the flat-top hill that dominates Neiafu to the west. Take the road between the police station and market and follow it high above the shoreline until it begins to descend and you see a trail on the right. Turn R at the top of the hill. This is an easy trip from town. At Toula village, a half-hour walk S of Neiafu beyond the hotel, is a large cave by the shore with a freshwater pool where you can swim. Go through the village and up the hill past a cemetery to the

looking E along Vava'u's wild N coast from 'Utula'aina Point near Holonga

cave. At low tide walk back to town along the beach in about an hour. Another excellent walk at low tide is along the shore from the Stowaway Village Motel to Makave, passing a freshwater spring. The road S from Neiafu crosses 2 causeways before reaching Nga'unoho village (10 km) which has a lovely clean beach.

Vava'u Island: For a splendid view of the N coast travel due N from Neiafu to Holonga. About 2 km beyond the village turn L when the trail begins to descend to the beach, then R some 500 m farther along. With a little luck you'll come out on 'Utula'aina Point, a sheer cliff a couple of hundred m above the sea. You could spend a whole day exploring this area. At Feletoa village ask to see the burial

place of Finau Ulukalala II behind the house opposite the primary school. The large rectangular *langi* is surrounded by big stone slabs. Finau was the tyrant king of Vava'u who held Will Mariner prisoner and conquered Tongatapu. Two centuries ago Feletoa was the center of power on Vava'u, and a Polynesian fortress was built here in 1808. Little remains today. From Tuafa Church Farm at the W end of the island there's a good view of Hunga and many small islands trailing southward. The Ngofe Marsh near Lake Ano is totally overgrown with reeds.

offshore islands: The classic tour at Vava'u encompasses Mariners Cave, Swallows Cave, and Nuku Island. Mariners Cave is a hollow in Nuapapu Island, SW of Neiafu. You can ap-

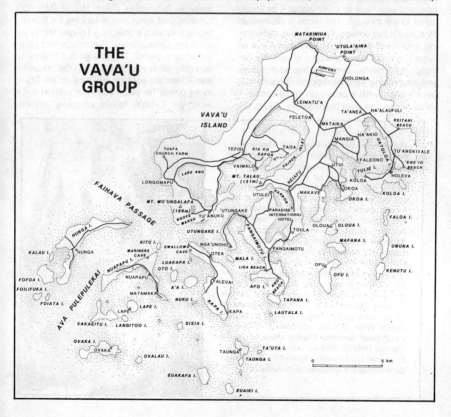

THE VAVA'U GROUP

MATAKINIUA POINT

'UTULA'AINA POINT

AIRPORT

HOLONGA

'LEIMATU'A

VAVA'U ISLAND

FELETOA

TA'ANEA

HA'ALAUFULI

TUAFA CHURCH FARM

TEFISI

SIA KO KAFOA

TAOA

MATAIKA

MANGIA

HA'AKIO

KEITAHI BEACH

VAIMALO

VAIHAU INLET

UATOLOA

TU'ANEKIVALE

LAKE ANO

MT. TALAU (131m)△

UTUI

TULIE

'ENE'IO BEACH

LONGOMAPU

UTULEI

KOLOA

HOLEVA

MT. MO'UNGALAFA △ (186m)

'UTUNGAKE

HARBOR

MAKAVE

OKOA

OKOA I.

KOLOA I.

NGOFE MARSH

TU'ANUKU

PARADISE INTERNATIONAL HOTEL

FAIHAVA PASSAGE

HUNGA I.

KITÚ I.

UTUNGAKE I.

TOULA

OLOUA

OLOUA I.

FALOA I.

KALAU I.

HUNGA

MARINERS CAVE

SWALLOWS CAVE

NGA'UNOHO

OTEA

PANGAIMOTU

MAFANA I.

UMUNA I.

FOFOA I.

NUAPAPU I.

LUAKAPA I.

OTO I.

MALA I.

LISA BEACH

OFU

OFU I.

KENUTU I.

FOILIFUKA I.

NUAPAPU

A'A I.

'FALEVAI

AFO I.

ANO BEACH

FOIATA I.

MATAMAKA

NUKU I.

KAPA I.

KAPA

TAPANA I.

VAKAEITU I.

LAPE

LAPE I.

LANGITOO I.

SISIA I.

LAUTALA I.

OVAKA I.

AVA PULEPULEKAI

OVAKA

OVALAU I.

TAUNGA

TA'UTA I.

TAUNGA I.

0   5 km

EUAKAFA I.

EUAIKI I.

proach it through an underwater tunnel in the island's stone face. The story goes that a young noble, fearing a despotic king would kill his sweetheart, hid her in this secret cave, coming back each night with food and water. Finally the young man and his friends built an ocean-going canoe and spirited the girl away to safety in Fiji. The cave gets its name from Will Mariner, who told the story to the world. To find it, go W along the cliff about 300 m from the NE tip of Nuapapu, watching for a patch of dark, deep water. White calcium deposits speckle the rocks to the R of the underwater opening; a single coconut tree high above also marks the place. Full snorkeling gear is recommended for entry, though a strong swimmer could go in without. The opening is about one m below sea level at low tide, and you have to swim about 4 m underwater to get through. The water is illuminated by sunlight but come up slowly to avoid banging your head on a ledge. Swallows Cave on Kapa I. is more obvious and a small boat can motor right inside. There are sea snakes here and an exciting vertical drop-off. This daytrip usually ends with a picnic on Nuku Island. If you'd like to camp on Nuku ask for Siketi, the driver at Mailefihi College in Neiafu. He can arrange transportation, food, and water. Otherwise find an outboard headed to Falevai on Kapa I., an easy swim from Nuku. They'll charge about $2 pp to drop you there. Don't litter this lovely little island or do anything else which might deprive others of its special beauty.

PRACTICALITIES

accommodations: Stowaway Village Motel on the Old Harbor offers peaceful accommodations with shared bath at $5 s, $9 d, or private bath for just slightly more. No cooking facilities, but a restaurant/bar provides meals. Island tours are arranged Thursdays. A few minute's walk up the waterfront from Stowaway is Tufumolau Guest House (Mrs. Ofa Lafaele); just what you're looking for if you'd like to stay with a charming Tongan family yet still have some privacy. Play chopsticks on an out-of-tune piano! The charge is $3.50 pp or you may pitch your tent behind the house for less. There are cooking facilities, or ask Ofa to make dinner for you—you won't regret it. On Sun. the Lafaele family prepares an *umu*

the story of Will Mariner: *Will Mariner was a well-schooled 15-year-old Londoner who embarked on the English privateer Port-au-Prince. In 1806 this ship stopped at Lifuka, Ha'apai, for repairs; they had been given a friendly reception but suddenly the vessel was attacked on all sides by war canoes and about half the ship's crew was killed. The youth Mariner was taken prisoner. Since the chief of Ha'apai, Finau 'Ulukalala II, took a liking to him, his life was spared and he became the chief's adopted son and a chief himself. Mariner spent 4 years in Tonga, wholeheartedly adapting himself to the 19th C. Tongan way of life. He was at last given the chance to depart on a passing brig. Back in England, Mariner wrote a 2-volume account of his life in Tonga, in collaboration with an English doctor. When this was published in 1816 it enjoyed great success. Mariner drowned in the Thames in 1853. Four cannon from the Port-au-Prince can still be seen in front of the British High Commissioner's residence in Nuku'alofa.*

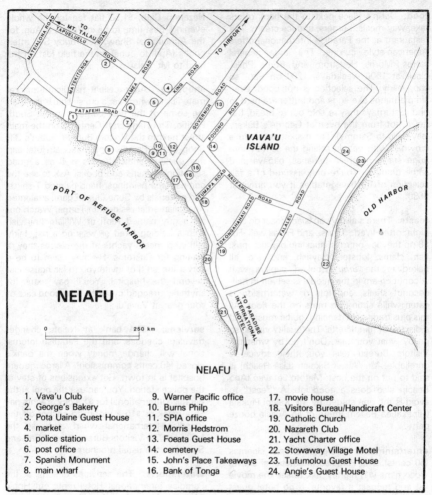

NEIAFU

1. Vava'u Club
2. George's Bakery
3. Pota Uaine Guest House
4. market
5. police station
6. post office
7. Spanish Monument
8. main wharf
9. Warner Pacific office
10. Burns Philp
11. SPIA office
12. Morris Hedstrom
13. Foeata Guest House
14. cemetery
15. John's Place Takeaways
16. Bank of Tonga
17. movie house
18. Visitors Bureau/Handicraft Center
19. Catholic Church
20. Nazareth Club
21. Yacht Charter office
22. Stowaway Village Motel
23. Tufumolou Guest House
24. Angie's Guest House

($3.50 pp). Angie's Guest House, just up the hill from Tufumolau, is similar and also recommended. More of the same is found at Pota Uaine Tu'iniua Guest House and Foeata Guest House, both near town center. The Foeata was built by a guy who designed water tanks, as you'll gather. For those who like luxury without having to pay for it, the Vava'u Guest House (also known as "Heini's" — Mr. Mikio Filitonga) is right across the street from the plush Paradise International Hotel and almost acts as an annex. Mikio's guests pay $4.50 s, $8 d for a room with shared bath in the old building, or $10 s, $12 d for a new *fale* unit with private facilities. It lacks cooking facilities, but meals in the restaurant are good (non-guests welcome). The place is often full-up with people immersed in the social scene at the Paradise. Rooms there start at $24 s, $30 d — good value by American standards.

food: John's Place next to the bank offers takeaway meals, burgers, and ice cream. The restaurant at the Paradise International offers American-style cuisine. The large general stores, Morris Hedstrom and Burns Philp, close at 1600 weekdays, 1200 on Sat., so shop early. The selection is not good: even simple things like eggs and butter are hard to find. Saturdays they're sold out of bread, but get it hot from the oven at George's Bakery (say hello to Sammy). The market at Neiafu is crowded with people selling the same thing: huge stalks of green bananas, papaya, and some oranges. You're only assured of a fair selection of fresh vegetables if you arrive at 0630.

feasts: There's always an island feast on Sat. night; often Wed., Thurs., and Fri. as well. For $8 pp they lay on roast suckling pig, octopus, fish, clams, lobster, crayfish, and taro; all baked in the *umu.* Cooked papaya with coconut cream in the middle is served in half-coconut shells, and lots of watermelon is eaten while sitting on mats on the floor. All this plus traditional dancing, guitar music, and a display of handicrafts. The quality varies, so go by what you hear. Don't go by what the Visitors Bureau tells you; their advice is unreliable. Mr. 'Aisea Sikaleti (Lisa Beach) is said to put on the best; Matoto Lotavao (Ano Beach) also does a good job. A "feast" to avoid is the one staged by Mr. Kelepi Piukala (Hinakauea Beach), more of an Aussie booze party.

entertainment: There are 2 local cinemas (50 cents). The Paradise International shows video films ($1) nightly; ask to see the movie list and request a favorite, if no hotel guest has already done so. The bar at the Paradise International is a good place to meet yachties and other visitors. Most nights there's a dance at the Paradise International; things pick up after 2200. Best place to socialize is the Vava'u Club (large beer $1.40). They have an enormous pool table where snooker and other such games are played; the bartender keeps a set of balls for 8-ball (Hi-Lo) pool. There are also video games for the young at heart. For real earthy interplay, drink *kavatonga* at the Nazareth Club, $1.50 flat fee for the whole evening. Best time to be in Vava'u is Aug. for the Agricultural Show. See rugby Sat. afternoons (April to June) on the field just off the road to Mt. Talau.

shopping: An excellent handicraft market materializes whenever a cruise ship is in, offering some of the best bargains in the South Pacific. The Handicraft Center is on the main street next to the Visitors Bureau. Robin's Gift Shop at the Paradise International Hotel carries quality handicrafts, as well as a good selection of maps and books. Ask to see the original *tapa* paintings, hand-painted T-shirts, and materials by Sune (June Egan), a talented Australian artist resident in Tonga. Watch out for a guy named Alofi or William (thirtyish with a balding head or wearing a hat, fairly tall) who meets yachts at the pier as they're waiting for Customs. He may claim to be a carver (he isn't) or invite you to his house just beyond the hospital. You'll pay extra for anything arranged by Alofi. Take good care of your gear at Vava'u.

services: The bank at Neiafu changes travelers cheques, and the Paradise International will change money when the bank's closed (40 cents commission). A large modern hospital is in town. Get extensions of stay at the police station. You can use the pool at the Paradise International for $1 a day. Yachts pay $5 a week or $15 a month to anchor off the Paradise International wharf and use the facilities. The Visitors Bureau (closed Sat. and Sun.) has the usual brochures.

watersports: The activities director at the Paradise International Hotel rents out Hobie 14 catamarans, Sunfish sailing dinghies, and windsurfers at reasonable rates. Use these to visit Swallows Cave and Mariners Cave if you know what you're doing. Otherwise join a motorboat trip to the caves, also arranged at the hotel and not expensive if enough people go—ask how many have already signed up. Scuba diving is also offered, but only for small groups. If you're serious you'd better book ahead (Box 11, Neiafu, Vava'u). Dives on the wreck of the *Glen McWilliam,* a copra steamer

Vava'u's Mt. Talau overlooks Port of Refuge Harbor as a Warner Pacific Line freighter unloads cargo at Neiafu's main wharf.

which burned and sank in 1917, are popular. Huge fish and clams hang around the wreck 20 m down, marked by a buoy just out past the yacht anchorage. Many other good dive sites are only 30 min. by speedboat from the hotel. An activities pass is available at $22 s, $30 d per day, which gives you all of the above plus motorbikes. Weekly rates are less. Hotel guests get priority on all rentals and activities, although non-guests are welcome to join in when there's room.

TRANSPORT

by air: SPIA flies to Vava'u 4 times a week from Ha'apai ($30) and Nuku'alofa ($60), 3 times a week from Pago Pago ($115), and weekly from Niuatoputapu ($65). The flights are often heavily booked. The airport (VAV) is 10 km N of Neiafu. The Paradise International bus is $4 (free for guests), the SPIA and Tonga Air buses $2, and local passenger trucks (if any) 50 cents. Alternatively, walk 3 km to Leimatu'a where public transport is easier.

by ship: Ships tie up to the wharf. For information on the weekly ferry to Nuku'alofa see "Nuku'alofa—Transport" above. The Warner Pacific Line has a passenger-carrying freighter to Apia ($30), Pago Pago ($40), and Nuku'alofa ($12) monthly. Information on ships to the Niuas is hard to get. Try the MV *Nanasipau'u* office opposite the police station. It's usually closed, but the people who live behind the building may know something.

others: To crew on a yacht put up a notice at the Paradise International, and ask around the bar at the Vava'u Club and at the hotel. The yachting season is March to October. Until Sept. try for a watery ride to Fiji; later most boats will be thinking of a run S to New Zealand. Catch rides with the locals in their outboard motorboats from Neiafu wharf; they return to their villages in the afternoon (about 50 cents OW). Passenger trucks and mini-buses departing Neiafu market cover most of the roads on an unscheduled basis. Leimatua is fairly well serviced, as is Tu'anekivale. If you want to go to Holonga you must take a bus as far as Mataika or Ha'alaufuli then walk. Hitching is easy but offer to pay if it looks like a passenger truck. They'll never ask more than $1. Rent motorbikes at the hotel for $14 per day petrol included; 5-speed bicycles are $4 a day.

THE NIUAS

NIUATOPUTAPU

Niuatoputapu and Tafahi were the first Tongan Islands to be seen by Europeans (by Schouten and Le Maire in 1616). Niuatoputapu I., 300 km N of Vava'u, is closer to Samoa than to the rest of Tonga. Unlike Niuafo'ou, however, it's a very accessible island with SPIA flights from Vava'u ($65) and Pago Pago ($80). The supply ships *Ata* and *Nanasipau'u* call between Nuku'alofa and Pago Pago monthly ($18 to Vava'u, $40 to Pago Pago). Niuatoputapu is also a port of entry and clearance for cruising yachts. As yet the number of visitors has been negligible, but the island has a lot to offer and is well worth including as a stopover on any Samoa-Tonga trip.

the land: Niuatoputapu is a triangular island with a long central ridge 150 m high which can be climbed from Vaipoa village in the north. Bush trails criss-cross the ridge which has small garden patches on it. A plain surrounds the ridge like the rim of a hat, fringed with lovely white sandy beaches. There's a sheltered lagoon on the N side, and on the S pounding surf. Much of the island is taken up by bush gardens producing copra and exquisite limes, but some native forest remains in the S (quickly disappearing).

facilities and sights: Hihifo, the administrative center, is about 3 km N of the airstrip. The Produce Board maintains an adequate general store at Hihifo; travelers cheques can be cashed at the post office. The Fita Motel nearby has 3 small *fale* units at $4.50 s, $8 d (shared facilities). Countless pigs forage on the beach at Hihifo. The best

A wide white beach on Tonga's remote Niuatoputapu.

NIUATOPUTAPU

HAKAU
TAPU

HAKAUTU'UTU'U

HIKUNIU

HAKAU
TAPU

WHARF

FITA
MOTEL

FALEHAU

HUNGANGA

VAIPOA

HIHIFO   RIDGE

TAVILI
TAFUNA
NUKUSEILALA

AIRSTRIP

NIUATOPUTAPU ISLAND

0   2 km

NAMOLIMU
POINT

beaches are on Hunganga I., accessible by wading at low tide. The channel between Hihifo and Hunganga is strikingly beautiful with clean white sands set against curving palms, and the majestic cone of Tafahi I. looming in the distance. The waterways S of the village are not only scenic, but also idyllic swimming areas. Within Hihifo itself is Niutoua Spring, a long freshwater pool in a crevice—perfect for an afternoon swim. Farther E there's a bakery near the Mormon church at Vaipoa. The wharf at Falehau offers good anchorage for yachties, good swimming for everyone. Niuatoputapu is a traditional island where the horse and cart are still widely used and fine pandanus mats are made. The best time to come is mid to late Aug. when the king arrives for the annual Agricultural Show.

Tafahi Island: Fertile, cone-shaped Tafahi I., 9 km N of the Niuatoputapu wharf, produces some of the best *kava* and vanilla in the South Pacific. Only a few hundred people live on the island; access is by small boat at high tide from Niuatoputapu ($1 pp if they're going, $24 for a charter). There are 154 concrete steps from the landing to clusters of houses on Tafahi's N slope. The climb to the summit (555 m) of extinct Tafahi volcano takes only 3 hours—get fresh water from bamboo stalks on top. On a clear day Samoa is visible from up here! You can also walk around the island on the beach in half a day.

NIUAFO'OU

Niuafo'ou is Tonga's northernmost island, 574 km from Nuku'alofa. It's actually closer to Samoa and Fiji than it is to the rest of Tonga. Despite the new airstrip (charter flights only), Niuafo'ou remains one of the remotest islands in the world. It's only connection with the outside is the supply ship *Nanasipau'u* which calls once a month on its trip from Nuku'alofa to Pago Pago. There is no wharf on the island, and the only anchorage is reportedly off Futu, on the W side of the island. For many years Niuafo'ou received its mail in kerosene tins wrapped in oilcloth thrown overboard from a passing freighter to waiting swimmers, giving it its other name, Tin Can Island.

the land: Niuafo'ou is a collapsed volcanic cone once 1,300 m high. Today the N rim of the caldera reaches 210 m. The center of the island is occupied by a crater lake, Vai Lahi, nearly 5 km wide and 84 m deep. From this lake rise small islands with crater lakes of their own—lakes within islands within a lake within an island. Greyish *lapila* fish live in the sulfurous waters. Presently Niuafo'ou is dormant, but the southern and western sides of the island are covered by bare black lava fields

Niuafo'ou megapode

from the many eruptions earlier this century. Lava flows emanating from fissures on the outer slopes of the caldera destroyed the villages of 'Ahau (1853) and Futu (1929). After Angaha disappeared under lava in 1946, the government evacuated the 1,300 inhabitants to Eua I., where many live today. In 1958 some 200 refugees returned to Niuafo'ou and by 1976 there were 678 people on the island once more. Signs of the 1946 eruption are apparent in the vicinity of the airstrip. Apart from the lava fields the island is well forested. Incubator birds (*Megapodius pritchardis*) lay their eggs in burrows 2 m deep in the warm sands of the hotsprings by the lake. Natural heating from magma close to the surface incubates the eggs, and the megapode chicks emerge fully feathered. Access to the lake is via a track on the E side.

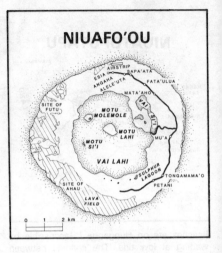

AMERICAN SAMOA

INTRODUCTION

American Samoa, 3,700 km SW of Hawaii, is the only U.S. territory S of the equator. Pago Pago Harbor (pronounced "Pango Pango"), made famous in Somerset Maugham's *Rain*, is by far the finest in the South Pacific, a natural hurricane shelter for shipping. It was this feature which attracted American attention in the late 19th C., as Germany built a vast commercial empire based around the coconut plantations of neighboring Western Samoa. Until 1951 American Samoa was run as a naval base, but as U.S. military needs moved closer to the Asian mainland, it came under civilian administrators who created the welfare state of today. Traffic constantly winds along Tutuila's narrow S coast highway, and gun-toting American-style cops prowl in big blue-and-white cruisers. American Samoa is a fascinating demonstration of the impact of American materialism on a communal island society. Although the Samoans have eagerly accepted the conveniences of modern life, the

fa'a Samoa, or Samoan way, remains an important part of their lives. Thus far the Samoans have obtained many advantages from the U.S. connection, without the loss of lands and influx of aliens which have overwhelmed the Hawaiians. While this part of Samoa will always be American, the Samoans are determined to prevent it from going the way of Hawaii.

the land: American Samoa is comprised of 7 main islands. Tutuila, Aunu'u, and the Manu'a Group (Ofu, Olosega, Ta'u) are high volcanic islands; Rose and Swains are small coral atolls. Tutuila is by far the largest, with a steep N coast cut by long ridges and open bays. The entire eastern half of Tutuila is crowded with rugged jungle-clad mountains, continuing W as a high broken plateau pitted with verdant craters of extinct volcanoes. The only substantial flat areas are in the wide southern plain between Leone and the airport. Fjord-like

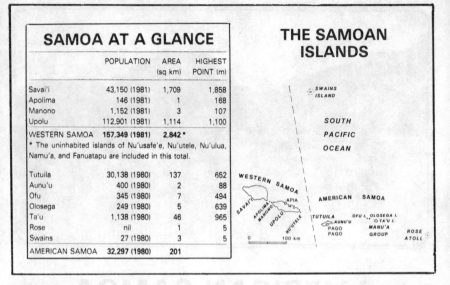

SAMOA AT A GLANCE			
	POPULATION	AREA (sq km)	HIGHEST POINT (m)
Savai'i	43,150 (1981)	1,709	1,858
Apolima	146 (1981)	1	168
Manono	1,152 (1981)	3	107
Upolu	112,901 (1981)	1,114	1,100
WESTERN SAMOA	157,349 (1981)	2,842 *	
* The uninhabited islands of Nu'usafe'e, Nu'utele, Nu'ulua, Namu'a, and Fanuatapu are included in this total.			
Tutuila	30,138 (1980)	137	652
Aunu'u	400 (1980)	2	88
Ofu	345 (1980)	7	494
Olosega	249 (1980)	5	639
Ta'u	1,138 (1980)	46	965
Rose	nil	1	5
Swains	27 (1980)	3	5
AMERICAN SAMOA	32,297 (1980)	201	

THE SAMOAN ISLANDS

Pago Pago Harbor, which almost bisects Tutuila, is a submerged crater, the S wall of which collapsed millions of years ago. Tutuila is about midway between the far larger islands of Western Samoa and the smaller Manu'a Group.

climate: Although the climate is hot and humid year-round, it's hotter and rainier from Nov. to April (hurricane season). The exact amount of rain in any given month varies greatly from year to year. Temperatures are usually steady, but the stronger winds from May to Oct. ventilate the islands. The prevailing tradewinds are from the E or SE, with W or NW winds and long periods of calm during the wetter season. As warm easterlies are forced up and over Tutuila's Rainmaker Mountain, clouds form which drop their moisture on the bay area just to the west. Apia, Western Samoa, receives only half the annual rainfall of Pago Pago. You can hear a recorded weather report by calling 639-9333 on Tutuila.

history: The Polynesians emerged in Samoa some 3,000 years ago. By 600 B.C. they'd established a settlement on Tutuila at Tula.

This nucleus (or a similar one in the Manu'a Group) may have been the jumping-off point for colonizing Eastern Polynesia (Tahiti and the Marquesas) about A.D. 300. The Samoans maintained regular contact by canoe with the other island groups of Western Polynesia, Tonga and Fiji. Both Samoas belong to a singular cultural area: the chiefs of Tutuila were subordinate to those of Upolu. The first European was Jacob Roggeveen, who visited the Manu'a Group in 1722. In 1786 Bougainville christened Samoa the Navigator Islands for islanders in canoes he observed chasing schools of tuna far offshore. Another Frenchman, La Perouse, called in 1787 and had a bloody encounter with the islanders. Protestant missionaries arrived in the 1830s. Nearly 40 years later, American businessmen chose Pago Pago Harbor as an ideal coaling station for their new steamship service from San Francisco to Sydney. In 1872 the U.S. Navy sent a ship to negotiate a treaty with local chiefs. Though never ratified by the U.S. Senate, this agreement became the excuse to keep other powers out of Tutuila. In 1900 the U.S. annexed Tutuila and Aunu'u, adding the Manu'a Group in 1904. This act was not formally ratified by the U.S. Congress until 1929.

From 1900 to 1951 American Samoa was under the Navy Dept.; since then it has been the responsibility of the Dept. of the Interior. Tutuila hosted thousands of U.S. Marines throughout WW II. Concrete pillboxes built at that time still punctuate much of the island's coastline. The only action experienced, however, was a few shells lobbed from a Japanese sub on 11 Jan. 1942, which ironically damaged the store of one of Tutuila's few Japanese residents, Frank Shimasaki.

the Americanization of Samoa: Outside the war years, little happened to alter the centuries-old lifestyle of the Samoans, until 1961 when President Kennedy appointed Governor H. Rex Lee, a Mormon, to dispense a giant infusion of federal funds. A massive public works program financed construction of roads, schools, housing, port facilities, electrification, a new hospital, tuna cannery, modern hotel, and international airport. Lee's

The Tu'i Manu'a, highest ranking chief of Eastern Samoa, was the last to sign a cession agreement with the U.S. (in 1904, 4 years after the chiefs of Tutuila signed). Before he died he willed that his title die with him and to this day there has not been another Tu'i Manu'a. This photo was taken at Ta'u circa 1904.

most publicized innovation was educational television, introduced in 1964; by the mid-'70s, however, the emphasis had shifted to the usual commercial programming. This excessive government spending has created an artificial American standard of living. The Samoans became so dependent that 3 times they voted down proposals to increase home rule for fear it would mean less subsidies from Uncle Sam. Only in 1976, after a short tenure by unpopular Gov. Earl B. Ruth, did they finally agree in a referendum to elect their own governor.

government: While Western Samoa received independence from New Zealand in 1962, American Samoa remains an "unincorporated" territory of the United States, meaning the U.S. Constitution and certain other laws don't apply. The territory is also defined as "unorganized" because it doesn't have a constitution sanctioned by the U.S. Congress. In 1966 federal officials authorized a Samoan constitution which included a bill of rights and gave legislative authority to the Fono, a body composed of 21 representatives (2-year term) elected by the public at large and 18 senators (4-year term) chosen by the customary Samoan *matai* (chiefs), but none of this has yet been made U.S. law by Congress. The powers of the Fono increased during the '70s; it now exercises considerable control over budget appropriations and executive appointments. Every 4 years since 1977 American Samoans have elected their own governor and Lt. governor. The governor can veto legislation passed by the Fono. Local government is conducted by 3 district governors, 15 county chiefs, and 55 *pulenu'u* (village mayors), all under the Secretary of Samoan Affairs, a leading *matai* himself. The territory is represented in Washington by a non-voting congressman. It's interesting to note, however, that Washington officials retain the right to cancel any law passed by the Fono, remove elected officials, and even cancel self-government itself without reference to the Samoans. Political development is now aimed at the attainment of a congressionally-approved Samoan constitution and the phasing out of the Dept. of the Interior. The Samoans have

*These San Diego helicopter-equipped purse seiners based at Pago Pago
each sweep millions of dollars in tuna from the South Pacific.*

no desire to be brought under the jurisdiction of the U.S. Constitution as this would mean an end to their system of chiefs and family-held lands, and would open the territory to un-controlled migration and business competition from the U.S. mainland. On the other hand, neither are they interested in independence so long as Washington is holding the purse strings and a majority of their people reside in the U.S. itself.

economy: Government, the largest employer, accounts for 46 percent of the workforce. The government of American Samoa receives an annual $50 million subsidy from Washington, well over half its income. In fact, the territory gets more money in U.S. aid than the entire budget of Western Samoa, although American Samoa has one-fifth the population. This, and diverging living standards, insures that the 2 Samoas will never be reunited. American Samoa's primary industry is tuna processing and packing by Starkist Samoa and Van Camp Seafood, a subsidiary of H.J. Heinz. The first cannery opened in

1954. Canned fish and pet food now account for 99.2 percent of exports. Canneries thrive in this tiny U.S. territory because they allow Oriental fishing companies to avoid high U.S. import tariffs on processed fish. Federal law prohibits foreign fishing boats from off-loading tuna at U.S. ports, however American Samoa is exempted. Thus the greater part of the South Pacific tuna catch is landed here. The canneries also receive substantial tax concessions from the local government. They provide jobs for 4,000 Oriental fishermen and 1,300 local cannery workers, most of them Tongans and Western Samoans en route to the U.S.; American Samoans themselves prefer to work in business or the easier, more lucrative government jobs. The trend, away from Korean and Taiwanese long-line tuna boats, is now toward large California purse seiners worth a million dollars apiece. Starkist has 35 purse seiners under contract, Van Camp about 15. A total of 82 Korean and 23 Taiwanese long-line boats also work out of Pago Pago. The government-owned Marine Railway near the canneries can dry-dock vessels up to 3,500 tons. Harbor facilities have been upgraded through government investment in recent years in an effort to make Pago Pago a transshipment center for surrounding countries. As a result, small cargo ships from Tonga, Western Samoa, and the Cook Is. now call frequently to pick up imported goods, bulk fuel, and often, passengers. There's also an industrial park at Tafuna near the airport. Tourism has declined sharply since Continental Airlines discontinued its through-service from Honolulu to Auckland via Pago Pago.

the people: The people of the American and Western Samoa groups are homogeneous in blood, speech, and traditions. There has been considerable migration from W to E and much intermarriage: about 10,000 Western Samoans now live in American Samoa. Another 10 percent of American Samoa's 34,940 (1984) residents are Tongans. American Samoans are U.S. "nationals," not citizens, the main difference being that nationals can't vote in U.S. presidential elections. They have free entry to the U.S., however, and some 60,000 of them now live in Hawaii and California, most in the lower income bracket. Nearly 70 percent of high school graduates leave American Samoa for the States within a year of graduation, many of them to join the Armed Forces. Although the young have largely forgotten their own culture in their haste to embrace that of the U.S., the *fa'a Samoa* is tenaciously defended by those who choose to remain in their home islands. For a complete description of the *fa'a Samoa,* see the Western Samoa "Introduction." The innate strength and flexibility of the Samoan Way has permitted its survival in the face of German, New Zealand, and American colonialism. On Tutuila the people live in 60 villages along the coast. After a hurricane in 1966 the U.S. government provided funds to rebuild the thatched Samoan *fales* in plywood and tin, resulting in the hot, stuffy dwellings one sees today. The most farsighted act of the former naval administration was to forbid the sale of Samoan land to outsiders. Except for a small area owned by the government, almost all land in the territory is communally owned by Samoan extended families *(aiga)*. The

Family *matai* assigns use of this land to different members of the *aiga*. If American citizens were allowed to buy land the Samoans would undoubtably be exploited: they have little knowledge of property values. Aliens can lease land however.

events: All standard U.S. public holidays are observed in American Samoa: President's Day is the third Mon. in Feb.; Memorial Day is the last Mon. in May; Independence Day is 4 July; and Labor Day is the first Mon. in September. Although Samoa wasn't even "discovered" until 230 years after Christopher got to America, Columbus Day, the second Mon. in Oct., is also a public holiday. April 17th is American Samoa's Flag Day, commemorating the first flying of the Stars and Stripes in 1900. This enthusiastic 2-day celebration features *fautasi* (long boat) racing, plus song and dance competitions in Fagatogo. The second Sun. in Oct. is White Sunday, when children dress in snow-white clothes and walk to church in procession, singing as they go. The children take the seats of honor and lead the service. After church there are family feasts,

the monument to John Williams at Leone on Tutuila

and the kids are given gifts. Another important event is the rising of the *palolo* (coral worm) in late Oct. or early November. When the moon and tide are just right and the *palolo* emerges to propagate, Samoans are waiting with nets and lanterns to scoop up this cherished delicacy, the caviar of the Pacific. Swimming at most beaches is prohibited Sundays.

PRACTICALITIES

getting there: South Pacific Island Airways (SPIA) services Pago Pago from Hawaii, Apia, and Tonga, while Polynesian Airlines has flights from Apia, Rarotonga, and Tahiti. Due to currency differences, tickets for the Pago Pago-Apia flight are much cheaper when purchased in Apia than in American Samoa or elsewhere. Air Nauru has service from Nauru, Niue, and Auckland, as well as a reputation for cancelling flights on short notice. If you're flying to Nuku'alofa you can stop on the Tongan islands of Niuatoputapu, Vava'u, and Ha'apai at little additional cost. Since American Samoa is considered a domestic gateway, airfares from Hawaii are generally lower than those to any other South Pacific destination. Note however that it's usually cheaper to buy separate tickets for Los Angeles-Honolulu and Honolulu-Pago Pago, to take advantage of bargain airfares to Hawaii. Compare.

money: U.S. dollars are used. Western Samoan currency is not exchangeable in American Samoa. Even though this is an American territory, tipping is not encouraged.

Because U.S. postal rates apply, American Samoa is a cheap place for mailing parcels home. Long-distance telephone calls to the U.S. are also relatively inexpensive. **visas:** No visa is required for a stay of 30 days, and extensions up to 90 days (maximum) are possible. Everyone except Americans requires a passport for entry; Americans *will* need one to visit Western Samoa. All visitors must report to the Immigration office beside the courthouse for an exit permit from American Samoa as soon as they know their exact departure date. Although Americans are not supposed to reside in Samoa for long periods of time or take jobs away from Samoans, many do; some of the yachts in the harbor have been there for years. Before departing Hawaii for American Samoa, cruising yachts must obtain a U.S. Customs clearance. Tutuila is infected with the Great African snail. Customs officials in neighboring countries know this and carefully inspect baggage and shipping originating in Pago Pago.

airport: Pago Pago International Airport (PPG) is at Tafuna, 11 km SW of Fagatogo. Call the airport information number (699-9906) to check that your flight's on time. There's no tourist information desk, but there is a duty-free shop. If you're hungry, try the fish and rice with gravy in the coffee shop. No departure tax. Transport to town is 75 cents by public bus or $6 by taxi. Public buses stop occasionally in front of the terminal, or walk 2 km up to the main highway where there are plenty (except on Sun. or after dark). Or hitch to town.

Samoan girl: The thick lips, moderately broad nose, and wavy hair are characteristic Samoan traits; the epicanthic fold at the corner of the eye is not.

TUTUILA

Few visitors ever get beyond Tutuila, the main island of American Samoa. Fagatogo, the largest town, looks out onto elbow-like Pago Pago Harbor. Government is centered at Utulei, just E of Fagatogo. Despite the oil slicks and continual flood of pollution from canneries, shipping, yachts, and residents, this harbor is still one of the most breathtaking in the South Pacific. There are many fine hikes in the surrounding hills, and the windsurfing is unsurpassed. There's good reef-break surfing along the S coast of Tutuila, especially from Dec. to March, and good snorkeling when it's calm. Tutuila is the showcase of American life in the South Pacific: garbage collectors have trouble keeping up. The piles of debris which lie scattered in the populated areas at least help feed the packs of stray dogs.

SIGHTS

Utulei: Overlooking the mouth of Pago Pago Harbor at Blunt's Point are 2 huge 6-inch naval guns emplaced in 1941 but now almost covered in vegetation. Start walking SE on the main road past the oil tanks. Just before the 2 houses on the bay side of the road look up to the R at a large green water tank. The track begins here — the guns are directly above the tank. Back toward town is the Lee Auditorium

(1962); the adjacent television studios may be visited weekdays at 1030. Three channels broadcast to the elementary schools from 0730-1330; evenings (1530-2330) channel 2 is educational (PBS), 4 is NBC, and 5 is ABC. The TV tapes are broadcast with Hawaiian advertising; no local advertising is accepted due to copyright contracts and there is little Samoan content in the programming. From the studios a road leads up to the cable-car terminal where a monument recalls the 1980 air disaster in which a U.S. Navy plane hit the cables and crashed into the Rainmaker Hotel, killing the 6 servicemen aboard and 2 tourists at the hotel. The hotel manager refused to allow the memorial to be erected on the hotel grounds. The cableway, one of the longest single-span aerial tramways in the world, was built in 1965 to transport TV technicians to the transmitters atop Mt. Alava (491 m). The car sways for 1.5 km over Pago Pago Harbor above the docks, with mountains such as rugged Rainmaker (524 m) in full view, making this the most spectacular aerial ride in the Pacific. You'll get the best views in the early morning or late afternoon (open daily 0800-1600, $1.25 each way).

Fagatogo: Just W of the entrance to the Rainmaker Hotel, a stairway leads up to

Pago Pago Harbor as it looked in 1939 before roadbuilders broke out of the Bay Area.

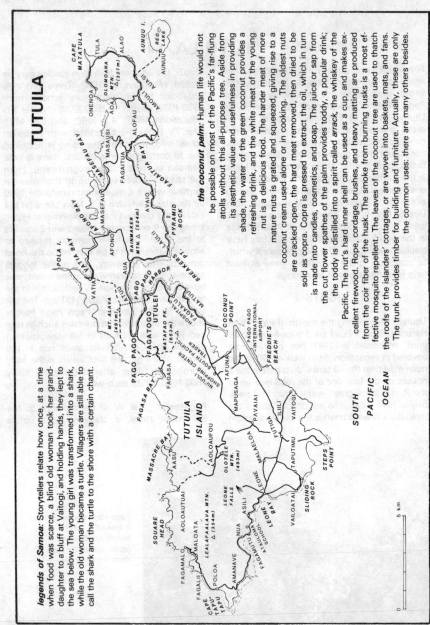

TUTILA

legends of Samoa: Storytellers relate how once, at a time when food was scarce, a blind old woman took her granddaughter to a bluff at Vaitogi, and holding hands, they lept to the sea below. The young girl was transformed into a shark, while the old woman became a turtle. Villagers are still able to call the shark and the turtle to the shore with a certain chant.

the coconut palm: Human life would not be possible on most of the Pacific's far-flung atolls without this all-purpose tree. Aside from its aesthetic value and usefulness in providing shade, the water of the green coconut provides a refreshing drink, and the white meat of the young nut is a delicious food. The harder meat of more mature nuts is grated and squeezed, giving rise to a coconut cream used alone or in cooking. The oldest nuts are cracked open, the hard meat removed, then dried to be sold as copra. Copra is pressed to extract the oil, which in turn is made into candles, cosmetics, and soap. The juice or sap from the cut flower spathes of the palm provides toddy, a popular drink; the toddy is distilled into a spirit called *arrack*, the whiskey of the Pacific. The nut's hard inner shell can be used as a cup, and makes excellent firewood. Rope, cordage, brushes, and heavy matting are produced from the coir fiber of the husk. The smoke from burning husks is a most effective mosquito repellent. The leaves of the coconut tree are used to thatch the roofs of the islanders' cottages, or are woven into baskets, mats, and fans. The trunk provides timber for building and furniture. Actually, these are only the common uses: there are many others besides.

Government House (1903), the governor's residence. Although the building itself is private you may walk through the grounds. The old Navy commissary (1917) now houses the Jean P. Haydon Museum (open Mon. to Fri. 1000-1600, Sat. 1000-1200, admission free). Facing the Malae-O-Le-Talu field, where local chiefs ceded the island to the U.S. in 1900, is the Fono Building (1973), in which the territory's legislature meets in Jan. and July. The police station across the field from the Fono was originally the barracks of the Fitafita Guard, the former Samoan militia. Farther W just before the market is the old courthouse (1904), in the U.S. Deep South-style. Just past this is the former guest house where Somerset Maugham stayed in 1916, now a grocery store. Maugham's tale of Sadie Thompson and the tormented missionary is set here.

Pago Pago: Continue W to Pila F. Patu Co. Inc. store where a road runs up the hill into Happy Valley. On this sideroad you pass 6 WW II bomb shelters on the L before reaching a dirt road, also on the L, which leads to a large concrete bunker used during the war as a naval command headquarters. Many of these military structures are now inhabited, and you'll need to ask permission before approaching the bunker, which is in a back yard. At the W end of the harbor is Pago Pago village, this whole area's namesake. Korea

House in Pago Park is a center for Oriental fishermen. The canneries are around the N side of the harbor. To visit the Van Camp plant call 633-1770 and make an appointment. You could also ask at the gate near the Ralston Purina sign; the tongue-twisting Van Camp Can Plant is nearby. Starkist is less amenable to visitors. Just W of these canneries is the Marine Railway, which provides maintenance and repair facilities to the fishing fleet.

the east end: Two more 6-inch WW II guns are on the hillside near Breakers Point. Walk up past Mr. Paleafei's house, the large 2-story dwelling at the high point in the road. The hill directly opposite the guns bears a small lighthouse with a view, while by the water at the bottom of the hill on the bay side is a concrete ammunition bunker now used for dynamite storage. At Alao and Tula at the E end of Tutuila are wide sandy beaches. Mr. Lesolo at Tula puts up visitors in his house for a reasonable rate—great if you'd like to be near the beach, but beware of the undertow. The road continues around to the N side of Tutuila as far as Onenoa. There are empty golden beaches all along the N coast.

Aunuu Island: There's a single village on Aunuu I. off the SE end of Tutuila. Motorboats shuttle constantly between the small boat harbors at Auasi and Aunuu, taking passengers

Fagatogo's Hotel Sadie Thompson as it looked prior to WW II

for $1 pp or $5 OW for a charter trip. Go over first thing in the morning and you shouldn't have any trouble getting back. Aunuu's eel-infested Red Lake in the sprawling crater is difficult to approach. Cliffs along the S coast and thick bush make hiking around the island heavy going. Aunuu's notorious stretch of quicksand is fairly close to the village, but you may have to wade through a swamp to get to it. The taro swamps just behind the village are easier to see, and a walk around to the new elementary school reveals an appealing slice of island life. A couple of hours are enough.

the west end: At Leone, ancient capital of Tutuila, visit the monument to Samoa's first missionary, John Williams, who landed here on 18 Oct. 1832. The ceiling of the adjacent LMS church is worth a look. Two km up a road beginning beside the Catholic church is Leone Falls (closed Sun.) where there's freshwater swimming. The former Atauloma Girls School (1900), a couple of km W of Leone, is inhabited by *palagis*—Samoans refuse to live here for fear it's haunted. There's surfing off the beach at Atauloma and nearby Fagamutu, plus beautiful scenery along the road farther west. Go around as far as you can.

inland and the north coast: Buses run fairly frequently between Pavaiai and Aoloaufou, high in the center of the island. It's a short walk up a paved road from Aoloaufou to the radio towers on Mt. Olotele (493 m) for the view. A muddy trail leads from Aoloaufou down to Aasu village on Massacre Bay, about an hour each way. In front of a house in the village is a monument (photos $2) erected in 1883 and surmounted by a cross. This memorializes 11 French explorers from the *Astrolabe* and *Boussole* of the ill-fated La Perouse expedition, killed in an encounter with the Samoans on 11 Dec. 1787. A Chinese member of the expedition and 39 Samoans who also died are not mentioned. Another trail from Aoloaufou goes down to Aoloautai; the trailhead is behind a house on the L near the NW end of the road. Aoloautuai is a deserted village site on a lovely bay where you could camp for a few days if you took enough food.

hiking: Mt. Matafao (653 m), Tutuila's highest peak, can be climbed from the pass on the Fagasa Road in half a day. Scamble up onto the ridge S of the road as best you can; the trail is much more obvious on top. It'll take about 3 hours up through a beautiful rain-forest—stay on the ridge all the way. No special gear is required for this climb and you could even go alone, but avoid rainy weather when it gets slippery. Take food and drink. In clear weather the view is one of the best in the South Pacific. On the other side of the pass a jeep track leads NE to the TV towers on Mt. Alava. You can also scale Mt. Alava standing in a cable car. From Mt. Alava follow the trail down to Vatia, a picturesque village on the N coast. Look across to unforgettable Pola I. with its sheer 100 m cliffs. There are pickup trucks from Vatia back to the market ($1.50) or you could walk back via Afono and Aua. All this is too much for one day, so split it up.

water sports: There are some quiet places to snorkel off Utulei and Fagaalu beaches. The closest points outside the harbor are the open reefs opposite Aveina Bros. Retail at Matuu, or One Stop Market at Laulii. These can be treacherous in the usual fresh tradewind and rather heavy break. If the water is fairly quiet

the monument at Aasu to La Perouse's massacred crew members

get into one of the *avas*—the channels going out—and enjoy undersea caves and canyons. But beware of sneak bumper waves and strong undertow in the channels: you might have to come back in over the reef. The break varies considerably in a few yards. Neither spot is outstanding, however, and you might see more trash than fish. Chuck Brugman (Box 3927, Pago Pago 96799) at Atamai Marine in Fagaalu runs scuba trips using his own boat: $30 pp (minimum of 2) for one tank, $45 pp for 2 tanks. All gear is supplied and the longer trip includes 4 hours of fishing. Call Chuck at 633-1701 (business) or 633-2183 (home)—recommended. The windsurfing in Pago Pago Harbor is excellent year-round, although from June to Oct. it's only for experts. Contact Bill Hyman at Island Printing behind the courthouse (tel. 633-4444) if you'd like to surf the wind.

PRACTICALITIES

accommodations: Budget accommodations are scarce in American Samoa. If you're only there a couple of nights, best is Herb and Sia's Family Motel (tel. 633-5413) in the heart of Fagatogo. The attractive a/c rooms, 5 with shared bath ($15 s, $20 d) and 2 with private bath ($25), have a fridge in each, but no cooking facilities. Guests are invited to a complimentary Sunday brunch at 1200. Dinner is not bad here. The only other official place to stay is the 183-room Rainmaker Hotel (tel. 633-4241), erected in the mid-'60s by Pan American Airways but now government-owned. Rates start at $46 s, $52 d—quite pleasant if you can afford it. If you're transiting American Samoa and airline connections force you to stay overnight in Pago Pago, the lobby of the Rainmaker is a better place than the airport to sit and wait. Rooms at Rosa's Grocery Store (tel. 633-4537) at Fagaalu, just across from the beach park, are about $5 a night. For a longer stay, check out Frank Manuma's house (tel. 633-5519) in Pago Pago village. Go up Fagasa Road, turn L after the second church, and cross the bridge over the stream. The facilities are extremely basic, but it's a quiet location and the rates are right: about $40 a month, prices negotiable with

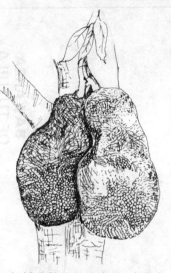

jackfruit (Artocarpus heterophyllus): This unusual relative of the breadfruit can weigh over 20 kilos. Like the durian its smell belies its taste. The roasted seeds taste like chestnuts.

Frank. Camping is not allowed in public parks. Mrs. Matiea (tel. 622-7568) at Avaio lets campers pitch their tents on her beach for $5 per tent per day.

food: Te'o Bros. Kitchen and Snack Bar, the pink building by the market, has the cheapest meals in town—recommended. Star of the Sea Fish Market adjacent offers salad, *oka* (cooked) taro, rice, and cooked bananas for 50 cents a scoop. Get hamburgers, etc., at the Icewich Fale nearby. Mike Bird's Restaurant, also in Fagatogo, has teriyaki steaks for $5, but lousy rice. The dining room at the Rainmaker Hotel has a good $4.50 lunch special weekdays; Fri. it's a buffet ($5). Also try the fish and chips in the surprisingly good hotel snack bar (open daily till 2300). Vegetarians might like to know about Matai's Pizza Fale in the Nu'uuli Shopping Center near the airport turnoff. Occasionally they sell out of pizza!

entertainment: Friday evenings at 2000 don't miss the Samoan feast ($8) with a

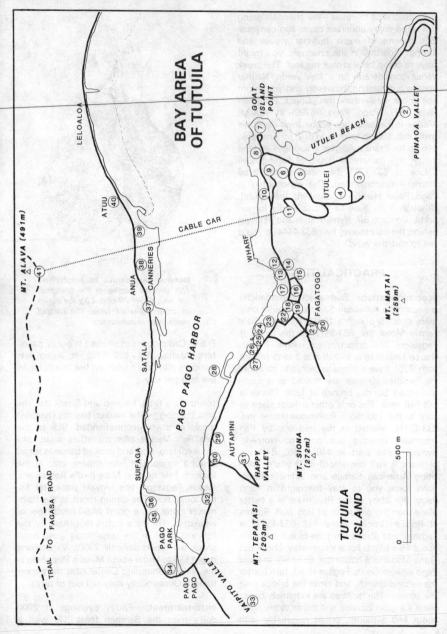

BAY AREA OF TUTUILA

Polynesian show and dancing at Herb and Sia's Motel. Another Polynesian variety show accompanies the nightly buffet dinner ($10.50) at 2000 at the Rainmaker Hotel. The Seaside Garden Club near the market is a great place for a beer. The hostesses at the Welcome to Pago Bar across from the Office of Communications will pump you for drinks

but are forbidden to sleep with you—give them a miss. American Samoa has the third highest beer consumption per capita in the world (after Australia and W. Germany). The drinking age is 21. **sports:** The best place for spectator sports is Pago Park at the W end of the harbor. See cricket (Jan. to April), softball (May to July), rugby (Aug. to Sept.), or soccer (Oct. to Dec.) any Sat. at the Park, with practice weekday afternoons at 1630.

shopping: The Public Market is busiest on Saturdays. Watch Samoan artisans at work at the Senior Handicraft Market (weekdays 0800-1600) near the end of the harbor; *tapa* cloth, shells, and basketry are for sale. The Samoan Women's Handicraft Fale beside the Fono is also worth a stop. Crafts are often made in the *fales* in front of the museum. The largest department store is South Pacific Traders at Tafuna near the airport turn-off—supermarket across the street and coin laundromat nearby. The Transpac Duty-Free Shop at the Rainmaker is not bad, but the selection is better at their main store by the highway near the hospital. Returning U.S. residents are allowed a duty-free exemption of US$800 (instead of US$400) on goods acquired in American Samoa. The next US$1000 worth is liable to only 5 percent flat rate duty (instead of 10 percent). Four liters of alcoholic beverages may be brought back from American Samoa (instead of 1 liter). You can mail home gift parcels worth up to US$100 (instead of US$40). Keep invoices or bills of sale in case it's necessary to prove where you purchased the articles. Downtown closing time is inconveniently early at 1630, on Sat. 1200.

services: The crowded Bank of Hawaii (weekdays 0900-1500) is next to the post office. Place long-distance calls at the Office of Communications diagonally across from the Fono Building. The LBJ Tropical Medical Center is one of the best hospitals in the South Pacific. You can see a doctor almost anytime at the Outpatients Dept. for a $2 fee. Inpatient rates are $60 a day. Get a cholera vaccination ($1.50) from the Public Health Dept. (weekdays 0730-1130/1300-1500) at the hospital. The Passport and Visa Office

PAGO PAGO

1. WW II naval guns
2. T.V. Laundrymat
3. Administration Building
4. Public Library
5. Lee Auditorium
6. T.V. studio/Office of Public Information
7. Rainmaker Hotel
8. Office of Tourism
9. Government House
10. Feleti Pacific Library
11. cable car terminal
12. museum
13. Inter-Island Shipping
14. post office/Bank of Hawaii/airline offices
15. police station
16. Malae-O-Le-Talu
17. Fono building
18. Office of Samoan Affairs
19. Office of Communications
20. Herb and Sia's Motel
21. Mike Bird's Restaurant
22. Courthouse
23. Te'o Bros. Kitchen
24. market/bus station
25. Icewich Fale
26. Seaside Garden Club
27. Sadie Thompson's Market
28. yacht anchorage
29. Burns Philp Dept. Store
30. Pila F. Patu Co.
31. wartime concrete bunker
32. Senior Handicraft Market
33. Frank Manuma's house
34. food stalls
35. Pago Park
36. Korea House
37. Marine Railway
38. Starkist Foods
39. Van Camp canning plant
40. Korean Restaurant
41. Mt. Alava T.V. transmitters

(weekdays 0830-1200) in the Administration Bldg. can issue U.S. visas, though you're supposed to apply in your home country. Mary's Laundromat opposite Herb and Sia's Motel charges 75 cents each to wash and dry.

information: The Tourist Office (weekdays 0730-1600) in the Convention Center near the Rainmaker has the usual brochures. The Development and Planning Office near the courthouse sells the *Atlas of American Samoa* ($150). Island Printing behind the courthouse sells USGS topographical maps of American Samoa ($4). There's good reading at the Feleti Pacific Library (weekdays 0800-1200/ 1300-1530), and the public library at Utulei (weekdays 0730-1600). The Office of Public Information in the TV studio (bright red door) behind Lee Auditorium puts out a free *News Bulletin* weekdays. The *Samoa Journal* comes out on Thurs., the *Samoa News* on Fridays.

TRANSPORT

by air: SPIA has daily flights from Tutuila to Ofu and Ta'u ($26); the flight *between* Ofu and Ta'u is $13. Manu'a Air Transport (tel. 699-9416) also has flights to the group. The local airlines often have price wars: those offering cheaper rates advertise in the weekly papers.

by ship: Inter-Island Shipping in the old white building near the wharf opposite the post office has ships to the Manu'a Group and Apia which occasionally accept passengers. The booking office for the Western Samoa Shipping Corporation ferry *Queen Salamasina* to Apia ($12 OW, $20 RT=8 hours) is below Burns Philp Dept. Store. Kneubuhl Maritime Services above the post office represents the monthly Warner Pacific Line sailings to Tonga ($50). The Tongan ships *Ata* and *Nanasipau'u* depart Pago Pago monthly for Niuatoputapu, Vava'u, and Nuku'alofa; call Mr. Vani Atafua (tel. 639-9277) for information. Polynesian Shipping is agent for the monthly Silk & Boyd passenger-carrying freighter to Rarotonga. They will know when the ship is due in, but you must buy your ticket from the captain.

by bus: For an American territory, bus services are extremely good. None of the buses are marked with a destination, however; also, there's no service after 1400 Sun. and very little after dark any day. Fares are reasonable. A trip anywhere in the congested zone from the canneries to the hospital is 25 cents. Westbound to the airport intersection is 50 cents, 75 cents to Leone, $1 to Amanave, $1.25 to Fagamalo; eastbound it's 50 cents to Laulii, 75 cents to Amouli or Fagasa, $1 to Tula. A pickup to Vatia is $1.50.

THE MANU'A GROUP

The 3 islands of Manu'a Group, 100 km E of Tutuila, offer spectacular scenery in a quiet, village environment. Ta'u is the territory's most traditional island. In 1925 as a young woman of 24, Margaret Mead researched her book, *Coming of Age in Samoa,* at Luma village on Ta'u. Beaches are far better and more numerous on Ofu and Olosega than they are on Ta'u. All these islands feature hiking possibilities and an opportunity for the adventurer to escape the rat race of Tutuila. The only hassle is canine: a real or pretended stone will keep the dogs at bay. Although there are a couple of small hotels, few tourists make it this far. If you'd like to immerse yourself in Sa-

moan life, the Office of Samoan Affairs in Fagatogo can arrange for you to stay with a family in a village if given enough lead time. With regular air service now operating from Tutuila, Manu'a has become more accessible. Book early as local commuters fill the flights.

Ofu and Olosega: Some of the best snorkeling is around the bridge that links these soaring volcanic islands. There's a small boat harbor just N of Alaufau. The airstrip is by a long white beach on the S side of Ofu, about an hour's walk from Olosega village. Don and Ilaisa's Motel at Olosega village has 5 rooms at $18 s, $20 d. **hiking:** To climb Piumafua Mountain on Olosega follow the shoreline S almost to Maga Point, then cut back up along the ridge to the 639-m summit. The forest atop the steep hill *after* you think you've hit the peak is like the Old Forest in *The Lord of the Rings.* No goblins, only mosquitoes, but be very careful not to get turned around as the trees cut off the view. There is no trail along Olosega's forbidding E coast. For Ofu's Tumu Mountain (494 m), take the road up the hill behind the big church in Ofu village and continue up to the ridge top, then over the mountain to a spectacular lookout on Leolo Ridge (458 m) above the airstrip. The forests on Ofu and Olosega are open and easy to cross after the trails give out.

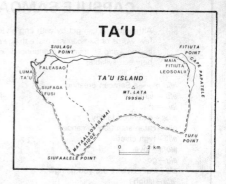

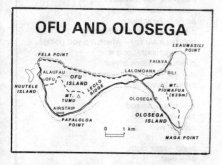

Ta'u: Ta'u is only 11 km SE of Olosega, with a submarine volcano between the two. The most sheltered anchorage for yachts is at Faleasao, while the small boat harbor is at Fusi. The airstrip at Siufaga is considered hazardous due to sudden air currents: 2 SPIA Twin Otters have already piled up here. The Niumata Mailo Hotel at Luma village has 8 rooms at $20. **sights:** Most inhabitants live in villages at the NE and NW corners of Ta'u. At Luma village see the tomb of the Tui Manu'a and other chiefly burials near the Sacred Water or "royal pool" (dry). Also of interest is the cave of Ma'ava, the legendary giant. Craters punctuate the island's wild, thickly forested interior, known for its cliffs and gulleys. Terrain and bush can change suddenly from easy hiking to difficult. Lata Mountain (995 m) is the highest point in American Samoa.

CORAL ATOLLS

Rose Island: To protect the turtles and seabirds found there, uninhabited Rose atoll, 100 km E of Ta'u, has been declared a wildlife refuge. Special permission is required to land. There is a reef of pink coral on the 3 by 3-km atoll. There are 2 small islands on the reef, one covered with coconut trees.

Swains Island: Swains Island, 340 km NW of Tutuila, is a circular coral atoll about 2 km across and 13 km around the fringing reef. There's a large lagoon in the center not connected to the sea. Swains is far closer to Tokelau than to the rest of Samoa. In fact, its customary owners were the Tokelauans of Fakaofo, who knew it as Olohega. In 1856 a New England whaling captain, Eli Jennings, arrived to set up a coconut plantation with the help of Polynesian labor; his descendants still run it as a private estate today. Olohega was included in the Union Group (Tokelau) which Britain incorporated into the Gilbert and Ellice Islands Colony in 1916. In 1925, when Britain transferred Tokelau to N.Z. administration, the U.S. took advantage of the opportunity to annex Swains to American Samoa. Finally, in 1980 the U.S. government bullied the Tokelauans into signing a treaty recognizing American sovereignty over Swains as a condition for the withdrawal of U.S. "claims" to the entire Tokelau Group and recognition of Tokelau's 200-nautical-mile fisheries zone.

CAPSULE SAMOAN VOCABULARY

Although one can get by with English in both American and Western Samoa, a few words of Samoan will make things more enjoyable. Always pronounce "go" as "ng," and "t" may be pronounced "k." An apostrophe indicates a glottal stop between syllables.

afio mai—a Samoan greeting
afu—waterfall
'ai—eat
aiga—extended family
alia—catamaran fishing canoe
ali'i—high chief
alofa—love
alu—go
alu i fea?—where are you going?
'ata—laugh

fa'afafine—transvestite
fa'afetai—thank you
fa'afetai tele—thank you very much
fa'amolemole—please
fa'apefea mai oe?—how are you?
fa'a Samoa—the Samoan way
fa'a se'e—surfing
fafine—woman
fa'i—banana
faia—sacred
fai se miti lelei—have a nice dream
failauga—orator
fale—house.
fautasi—a Samoan long-boat
fiafia—happy; a Samoan feast
fono—council

i—to, toward
i'a—fish
inu—drink
ioe—yes

lafo—a ceremonial exchange of gifts
lavalava—traditional men's shirt
le—the
leai—no
leaga—bad
lelei—good
lelei tele—very good
le tau—the cost, price
lotu—religion

malae—meeting ground
malaga—journey
maamusa—girlfriend
manaia tele Samoa—Samoa is very beautiful
manogi—smell
manuia!—cheers!
manuia le po—good night
matafaga—beach
matai—head of an *aiga*
mau—opposition

mea alofa—gift
moe—sleep
musu—to be sullen

niu—coconut
nofo—sit
nu'u—village

oi fea—where is
ou te alofa ia te oe—I love you
ou te toe sau—I shall return

palagi—a non-Samoan
paopao—canoe
pe fia?—how much?
pisupo—tinned corned beef
poo fea a alu iai?—where are you going?
pule—authority, power
pulenu'u—village mayor
puletasi—traditional woman's dress
pupu—blowhole

sa—taboo, sacred
sau—come
savali—walk
sene—a cent
siapo—*tapa* cloth
sili—best
siva—dance
soifua—good luck

taavale—car
tai—sea
tala—dollar
talofa—hello
talofa lava—hello to you
tama—a boy
tamaloa—a man
tamo'e—run
tanoa—kava bowl
taupou—ceremonial virgin
tautau—untitled people, commoners
tele—much
tofa—goodbye
tofa soifua—fare thee well
tulafale—talking chief, orator

ula—lei (flower necklace)
uma—finished
umu—earth oven

va'a—boat

WESTERN SAMOA

INTRODUCTION

The verdant, luxuriant islands of Western Samoa, 2,272 km W of Tahiti, are the very heart of the South Pacific. Despite a century of colonial interference, the Samoans retain their ancient customs as nowhere else in Polynesia. The *fa'a Samoa*, or Samoan way, continues to flourish in the face of extreme pressures. This society has attracted poets rather than painters. Robert Louis Stevenson spent the last 5 years of his life here, and Rupert Brooke was enraptured by the islands and their people: "You lie on a mat in a cool Samoan hut, and look out on the white sand under the high palms, and a gentle sea, and the black line of the reef a mile out, and moonlight over everything . . . And then among it all are the loveliest people in the world, moving and dancing like gods and goddesses, very quietly and mysteriously, and utterly content. It is sheer beauty, so pure that it's difficult to breathe it in." Travelers inbound from a dreary industrial world may be forgiven if they imagine they've returned to paradise, but there's more to it. In a series of

provocative novels, Samoan author Albert Wendt has portrayed the conflicting pressures of *palagi* (foreign) life on his people. The protagonist in *Sons for the Return Home* finds that he can no longer accept the *fa'a*-sanctioned authority of his mother, while *The Banyan Tree* explores the universal themes of a changing Samoan society. Wendt's books bring us closer to the complexity of a non-aligned, Third World Samoa, shaken by economic crises and searching desperately for a way to reconcile timeworn traditions to consumer needs. Samoa is not a passive place: you'll be challenged to define your own role as an outsider looking in.

the land: Western Samoa is made up of 4 inhabited and 5 uninhabited islands. Upolu, the most developed and populous, contains the capital, Apia; Savai'i is a much larger island. Between these sit well-populated Apolima and Manono, while the 5 islets off SE Upolu shelter only seabirds. Samoa's volcanic islands increase in age from W to east. Savai'i, though dormant, spewed lava this century; the now-extinct cones of western Upolu erupted much more recently than those farther east. Well-weathered Tutuila and Manu'a are older yet, while 10-million-year-old Rose Island is a classic atoll. Savai'i is a massive shield-type island formed by fast-flowing lava building up in layers over a long period. The low coast gradually slopes to a broad 1,858-m center of several parallel chains. Upolu's elongated dorsal spine of extinct shield volcanoes slopes more steeply on the S than the north. The eastern part of the island is rough and broken, while broad plains are found in the west.

climate: Although Samoa is hot and humid year-round, from May to Oct. (winter) the days are cooled by the SE trades. Winds vary from W to N in the rainy season (summer), Nov. to April. Practically speaking, the seasonal variations are not great and long periods of sun are common even during the "rainy" months. January to March is hurricane time; ships at Apia should put to sea at the first warning as the harbor is unsafe when a storm blows out of the north. Southern Upolu gets more rain than northern, but most of it falls at night.

flora and fauna: Rainforests thrive in mountain areas where heavy rainfall nurtures huge tree ferns and slow-growing, moss-laden hardwoods. The vegetation is sparse in the intermediate zones where more recent lava flows fail to hold moisture or soil. The richer coastal strip is well planted in vegetable gardens and coconut plantations. Birdlife is less disturbed in the interior: 16 of 34 species are unique to Samoa. One such species, the toothbilled pigeon or *manumea* (*Didunculus strigirostris*), is thought to be a living link with toothbilled birds of fossil times. Due to overhunting, all native species of pigeons and doves are approaching extinction. There are no snakes on Tutuila or Upolu, although several species are found on Savai'i.

HISTORY AND GOVERNMENT

prehistory: The Polynesians settled in Samoa by 1000 B.C. and here they evolved

their distinctive culture. It was a beautiful, comfortable, productive place to live. Their vegetables thrived in the rich volcanic soil and the lagoon provided ample fish. They had found their true home; not for another millennium did small groups push farther E from this "cradle of Polynesia" to colonize Tahiti and the Marquesas. The ancient Samoans maintained regular contact with Fiji and Tonga; Tongan invaders ruled Samoa from A.D. 950 to 1250. The *matai* or chiefly system was well-developed for almost 1000 years before Europeans arrived in the late 18th century.

Christianity and commercialization: The Rev. John Williams of the London Missionary Society called at Savai'i aboard the *Messenger of Peace* in 1830. Despite the influenza which Williams' ship carried, most Samoans had been converted by 1840. The missionaries taught the need for clothing, and right on schedule white traders arrived to sell cotton cloth. The first copra trader in Samoa was John Williams, Jr., son of the Rev., who exported 6 tons in 1842. In the late 1850s German businessmen landed and established coconut plantations with Chinese and Melanesian labor. The German traders Godeffroy and Sons opened a store at Apia in 1855. Germany, Britain, and the U.S. soon appointed consuls. In 1873 an American, Col. A.B. Steinberger, assisted the Samoan chiefs in creating a constitution; 2 years later he had himself appointed premier. His role was not supported by the U.S., however, although he was an official government agent. After 5 months in the premiership Steinberger was arrested and taken to Fiji by the captain of a British warship who suspected him of German sympathies. He never returned.

instability and intrigue: The new Samoan government fumbled on and signed treaties of friendship with the U.S. and Germany. An intermittent civil war between the chiefly orator groups Pule and Tumua over the 4 highest ceremonial titles dragged on through most of the late 19th century. Rival Europeans sided with the different factions, but no one was able to establish a single, stable government. In 1879 the European residents of Apia took advantage of the situation to enact a municipal convention which put control of the

Wreckage from the 16-17 March 1889 hurricane at Apia: the large wreck in the center is the USS Trenton; *the USS* Vandalia *is partially submerged alongside the* Trenton *to the R; the bow of the German* Eber *lies washed up on the beach, while the overturned hull of the* Adler *is visible in the background high on the reef to the left. The ship at anchor beyond the* Trenton *may be the USS* Nipsic, *after being hauled off and fitted with the* Vandalia's *stack. Only the British* Calliope *escaped by valiantly fighting its way out to sea in the face of the storm. None of the above is visible today.*

town in their hands. In 1887 the Germans, tiring of the vicissitudes of native government in an area where they controlled 80 percent of the business, staged an unofficial coup. The nominal "king" was forced to flee and the Germans installed a puppet in his place. The German regime, supported by German naval units but not sanctioned by Berlin, soon alienated Samoans, British, and Americans. In 1889 an armed Samoan rebellion brought the warships of Germany, Britain, and the U.S. to Apia's port in a major international confrontation. This came to a ludicrous pass when the 7 men-of-war refused to abandon Apia Harbor in the face of a hurricane, leaving the field to the opponent Great Power. This colonial stupidity and arrogance caused the wreck of 4

ships; 2 others were beached and damaged; 200 lives were lost. The Samoans saw it as an act of God. Instability and open factional warfare alternated with ineffectual government until 1899. On 2 Dec. that year a Tripartite Treaty signed in Berlin partitioned Samoa between Germany and the U.S. (see "American Samoa"), while Britain withdrew completely in exchange for German concessions in Tonga and the Solomons.

the colonial period: On 1 March 1900 the German flag was raised over Western Samoa. Several despotic governors followed; Samoan resisters to German rule were deported to the Mariana Is. in 1909. On 29 Aug. 1914 at the beginning of WW I, the last German governor

Members of the Mau, a Samoan resistance movement to foreign domination, met in this German-period bandstand.

surrendered without a fight to a New Zealand Expeditionary Force. The vast German plantations seized at the time are still held by the government-owned Western Samoa Trust Estates Corporation. The inept N.Z. administrators weren't much improvement over the Germans. In Nov. 1918, they allowed the SS *Talune* to introduce influenza to the territory and 8,000 Samoans—22 percent of the population—died; a stricter quarantine kept the epidemic out of American Samoa. In 1929 a strong opposition movement, the Mau, was crushed by military force, although it continued to enjoy the support of most of the villages, chiefs, and European businessmen. Only in 1949 was there a concrete step toward independence when a Legislative Assembly was created with some members elected from among the *matai* (chiefs). In 1960 a constitution was adopted; a year later both constitution and independence were approved in a plebiscite by universal ballot (the only such election that has ever taken place in Samoa—today only *matai* can vote). In 1962 Western Samoa became the first Polynesian nation to reestablish its independence in the 20th century.

government: Western Samoa has a parliamentary system with a prime minister elected by Parliament from its ranks. The prime minister chooses an 8-member Cabinet, also from among Parliament. Since independence His Highness Malietoa Tanumafili II, Paramount Chief of Samoa, has been ceremonial head of state, a position he may hold for life. The next head of state will be one of the 4 paramount chiefs, chosen by Parliament for a 5-year term. Of the 47 members of Parliament, 45 are elected by the traditional Samoan *matai* (chiefs) and 2 by non-Samoan residents on the Individual Voters Roll. Only the 14,000 registered *matai* may vote or stand as candidates for the 45 *matai* seats. The 1985 elections were won by the Human Rights Protection Party, led by Tofilau Eti Alesana. The Christian Democratic Party is the opposition. As elsewhere in Anglophone Oceania, political parties revolve around personalities rather than policies. Western Samoa has no army and very few police: most of their responsibilities are assumed by the *matai.*

ECONOMY

trade: Western Samoa is a typical Third World country with a high birth rate, agricultural economy, lack of industry, and severe balance-of-payments deficit. Imports run 6 times higher than exports; food imports alone exceed all exports. The most important export item is coconut oil, followed by taro and cacao. Smaller amounts of timber and bananas are also traded. During the 1950s Samoa exported 1.2 million cases of bananas a year to New Zealand. Unfortunately, shipping problems, hurricanes, disease, and inefficiency cost them a large share of this market, which is now supplied by Ecuador. New Zealand, Japan, and Australia profit most from the trade imbalance—a classic case of neocolonialism. The Samoan government has attempted to control the situation by devaluing the *tala,* thereby making imports less attractive while increasing the amount of local currency paid to exporters. But as Western Samoa attempts to implement an austerity program dictated from Washington by the International Monetary Fund, Samoan families are bombarded nightly with insipid Hawaiian TV advertising broadcast from Pago Pago.

Almost none of the consumer junk they see in the ads is available locally.

other income: Western Samoa receives considerable development assistance from a well-diversified group of donors: Japan, W. Germany, N.Z., the Asian Development Bank, Australia, the European Economic Community, and the U.N. Development Program, in about that order of importance. Since the mid-1970s when N.Z. moved to slow immigration, unemployment has increased in Samoa. Today Samoans continue to emigrate to N.Z., but more go to the U.S. via Pago Pago. Remittances from Samoans abroad are an important source of revenue for the country. The tourist industry is getting more attention, and Faleolo Airport has been upgraded—all the better to land your jumbo jets on. Like the U.S., Western Samoa has fostered cordial ties with the People's Republic of China. Despite alarmist cries of "communist penetration," this relationship has had no effect whatsoever on domestic policy.

domestic policy: The government of Western Samoa operates on the verge of bankruptcy, and repeated rescue operations by the International Monetary Fund and other agencies have been necessary. The desperation for hard currency is evident in the $20 departure tax levied on tourists (Samoans pay only $5). Sixty-six percent of wage earners are government-employed; bribery and corruption are widespread among civil servants. Wages are low: a schoolteacher with 16 years' experience makes just over 50 *tala* a week. Two-thirds of the workforce, however, are involved in subsistence agriculture. Although smaller than Savai'i, the rich volcanic soil of Upolu supports 72 percent of the population of Western Samoa; much of Savai'i is barren due to recent lava flows and the porousness of the soil which allows rapid runoff of moisture. Local fishermen go out in locally made aluminum *alia* catamaran fishing boats. Most of Western Samoa's light industry is at Vaitele, on the airport highway 5 km W of Apia. Most prominent is the coconut oil mill opened in 1982, which now accounts for almost half the country's export earnings. The German-operated Vailima Brewery adjacent produces excellent beer.

THE PEOPLE

Samoans are the second largest group of full-blooded Polynesians in the world, behind the Maoris. Eighty percent of Western Samoa's land is owned communally by family groups (*aiga*). The Samoan approach to life is almost the opposite of the European: property, wealth, and success are all thought of in communal rather than individual terms. The *matai* work to increase the prosperity and prestige of their *aiga*. Samoans are very conservative and resist outside interference in village affairs. The Samoans have an almost feudal concern for protocol, rank, and etiquette. They lead a highly complex, stylized, polished way of life. Today, however, they are being forced to reconcile the *fa'a Samoa* with the competitive demands of modern society where private property and the individual come first. The greatest burden of adjustment is on the young; theirs is the highest suicide rate in the world.

social structure: Since ancient times Samoan society has been based on the *aiga*, a large extended family group with a *matai* as their head, who is elected by consensus of the clan. The *matai* is responsible for the *aiga's* lands, assets, and distribution. He ensures that no relative is ever in need, settles disputes, sees to the clan's social obligations, and is the *aiga's* representative on the district or village council (*fono*). Blood relationships count to a large extent in the elections of the *matai*, but even untitled persons can be elected on merit. Only Samoans can become a *matai*. This semi-democracy gives Samoan society its enduring strength. In this formalized, ritualized society the only way a man can achieve place is to become a *matai*. A number of *aiga* comprise a village (*nu'u*) under an orator or talking chief (*tulafale*) and a titular or high chief (*ali'i*). The *tulafale* conduct eloquent debates and give ceremonial speeches.

villages: The Samoans live in 362 villages near the seashore. Families share their work and food, and everyone has a place to live and a feeling of belonging. Each immediate family

a Samoan.

has its own *fale* (house) which may be round or oval. Without walls, it's the least private dwelling on earth. The only furniture may be a large trunk or dresser. A *fale* is built on a stone platform with mats covering the pebble floor. Mats or blinds are let down to shelter and shield the *fale* from storms—a very cool, clean, fresh place to live. Most food is grown in village gardens and cooking is done in an earth oven (*umu*). Families are large, 8 children being "about right." The men wear a vivid wraparound skirt known as a *lavalava*. The women of the village are often seen work-

ing together in the women's committee *fale* making traditional handicrafts. The *fono* meets in the *fale taimalo*. Also a part of each village is the cricket pitch—looking like an isolated stretch of sidewalk. Notice too the *tia*, stone burial mounds with several stepped layers under which old chiefs are buried.

customs: Though missionaries a hundred years ago predicted its demise, tattooing is still widespread among Samoan men. The tattoos, extending from waist to knees, are a visual badge of courage as 16 or more highly painful sessions are required to apply a full *pe'a*. Once the tattooing begins it cannot end until completed, or the subject will be permanently marked with dishonor. The designs originally represented a large fruit bat, although this is only recognizable today in the lines of the upper wings above the waist. Unlike Fiji and Tonga, the Samoan *kava* ceremony is an exceptional occasion held at important gatherings of *matai*, seldom witnessed by visitors. A *taupou* prepares the drink in a traditional wooden bowl; in the old days she was a fiercely guarded virgin daughter of a village high chief, a ceremonial princess. Chanting and dancing usually accompany this serving ceremony.

religion: Ever since Rev. John Williams landed in 1830, the Samoans have taken Christianity very seriously. Samoan missionaries have gone on to convert residents of many other island groups (Tuvalu, the Solomons, and New Guinea). Many believe that Samoa was the biblical Garden of Eden. About half the population belong to the Congregational Church (successor of the London Missionary Society), a quarter are Catholic, and the rest fairly evenly divided between Methodist and Mormon. Each village has one or more churches, and the pastor's house is often the largest residence. Some villages have regulations which *require* villagers to attend church as many as 3 times on Sun. and choir practice weekly. There's a daily vespers called *sa* around 1800 for family prayers. All movement is supposed to cease at this time; some villages are rather paranoid about it. It only lasts about 10 minutes, so sit quietly under a tree or on the beach until you hear a gong, bell, or somebody beating a pan to signal "all's clear." Many of the schools are church-operated. Attendance is not compulsory and tuition must be paid, even at the elementary-school level.

arts and crafts: The Samoan love of elaborate ceremony is illustrated in the fine mat (*ie toga*). Exquisitely and tightly plaited from finely split pandanus leaves, a good example might take a woman a year of her spare time to complete. Fine mats are prized family heirlooms used as dowries, etc.: they acquire value as they're passed from person to person at ceremonial exchanges (*lafo*). Mats of this kind cannot be purchased. Samoan *tapa* cloth (*siapo*) is decorated by rubbing the *tapa* over an inked board bearing the desired pattern in relief. In Samoa the designs are usually geometric, but with a symbolism based on natural objects. In Tonga and Fiji *kava* bowls have only 4 circular legs, but Samoan bowls may be circular with 6 or more round legs, circular with 4 square legs, or turtle-shaped. Apart from these, if what is seen in the craft shops of Samoa seems poor in comparison with other Pacific countries remember that oratory and tattooing were the maximum expressions of Samoan culture, followed by the *kava* ceremony itself. **dance:** The *sa-sa* is a

synchronized group dance to the beat of a hand-gong. The slap, knife, and fire dances are done solo or in small groups, and the last 2 can be dangerous to the performers. Tradition holds that only men who are afraid will be burned during the fire dance. The *siva* is a graceful, flowing dance in which the individual is allowed to express him/herself as he/she sees fit.

events: The big event of the year is the Independence celebrations during the first week of June: dancing, feasting, speeches by *tulafale* (talking chiefs), horse races, and other sporting events. A highlight is the *fautasi* race on the Sat. closest to Independence Day, with teams of dozens of men rowing great longboat canoes. Note that there are 3 public holidays in a row at this time which means that banks, offices, and most stores will be closed for 5 consecutive days! Other public holidays include Anzac Day (25 April), White Sunday (the Mon. after the second Sun. in Oct.), and Arbor Day (the Fri. of the first full week in November). On White Sunday children dressed in white parade to church; after the service they take the places of honor and eat first at family feasts. Once a year the *palolo* reefworm (*Eunice viridis*) rises from the coral before dawn according to a lunar cycle (Oct. on Upolu, Nov. on Savai'i). The Sa-

weaving mats in a fale

moans wait with lanterns and nets to catch this prized delicacy.

PRACTICALITIES

getting there: Apia is well-connected to the rest of the South Pacific. Polynesian Airlines, Samoa's national carrier, flies to Pago Pago, Vava'u, Nuku'alofa, Niue (OW only), Rarotonga, Papeete, Auckland, Nandi, and Port Vila. They give a 25 percent discount to students under 26. Their "Polypass" allows 30 days unlimited travel over their entire network (a RT to/from Sydney included) for a flat US$999 fee. Note, however, that since many of their flights are weekly and Polynesian's network extensive, it would take 2 Polypasses to stop at all their destinations. Polynesian is the *only* Pacific airline that actually serves Pacific food (congratulations!). Air Pacific has flights to Apia from Suva and Nandi, Air New Zealand from Wellington, Auckland, and Nuku'alofa, and Air Nauru from Nauru. South Pacific Island Airways (SPIA) operates a frequent shuttle between Pago Pago and Apia. For travel by ship see "Transport" under "Upolu."

accommodations: The higher-priced hotels quote their rates in U.S. dollars to make them seem lower. The only budget accommodations are in Apia. There are a couple of small places to stay on Savai'i and one on the S coast of Upolu, but only the Safua Hotel on Savai'i is worth recommending. It's also possible to stay with the people, though since the Visitors Bureau hasn't started a regular homestay program yet, you'll have to arrange this for yourself. Samoans are among the most hospitable people in the world, proud that a stranger can go to any house and request food or shelter, and rarely be turned away. This admirable characteristic should not be abused, however. It's part of their culture that a gift will be reciprocated—if not now, then sometime in the future. Tourists who accept gifts (such as food and lodging) without reciprocating undermine the culture and cause the Samoans to be less hospitable to the next tourist who arrives. For this reason

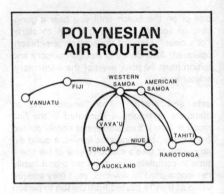

POLYNESIAN AIR ROUTES

it's strongly recommended that you look for a way of repaying their kindness. Thanks is not enough and a casual offer of payment might be offensive. Samoans are a very proud people, perhaps the proudest in the Pacific, and you must phrase this carefully to avoid misunderstandings. If your attitude is wrong they will sense it. Upon departure sit down with your hosts for a formal thank you. Say something like "Hospitality is not something that can be paid for, and I don't know how to show my appreciation fully, but I would like to leave a *mea alofa* (gift)." Then tender about $10 pp per night, more if they've been especially helpful by taking you out fishing, guiding you through the mountains, etc. If you ask them to buy something for the children with the money, they'll smile and accept. Otherwise, you could give a gift other than money (maybe cloth, or a shirt). But as in Fiji, it's essential that hospitality not be abused. Talk this over with your traveling companions before you set out, and don't go on a trip with one of the insensitive few. At times the Samoans will refuse to accept anything from you, in which case you might take a roll of photos of the family and mail them prints when you get home. Thus at least you'd be able to reciprocate in a small way.

other tips: It's best to make known the approximate length of your stay as soon as a family invites you. If one of your hosts' neighbors invites you to come stay with them, politely refuse. This would bring shame on the first family. It's a Samoan custom that travelers may spend the night at the pastor's house. If you do, make an appropriate contribution to the church. The pastor's views on religion, values, and development in general will fascinate you. Samoans are still unfamiliar with camping and might be offended if they feel you're refusing their hospitality. A tactful explanation of your desire to be near the sea or alone in a coconut grove might be accepted, but Samoans are naturally suspicious of those who try to remain apart from the group. Always ask permission of a responsible adult, or camp well out of sight of all roads, trails, and villages. To do otherwise is to place yourself beyond the protection of village law.

food: Try *palusami*—thick coconut cream, onions, tinned corned beef, and young taro leaves, wrapped in a breadfruit leaf, then baked on hot stones and served on slices of baked taro—a very tasty dish when well prepared. Other traditional Samoan specialties include *taofolo* (kneaded breadfruit and sweet coconut cream wrapped in taro leaves and baked), *fa'ausi* (grated taro and coconut cream pudding), *suafa'i* (ripe bananas with coconut cream), and *oka* (raw fish). **home cooking:** If you spend a night in a village notice how almost everything you eat is locally grown. Taro and breadfruit are the staples, but there's also pork, fish, chicken, *ta'amu,* and bananas. Mention at the outset how you're tired of tinned food and would like to try the food Samoans themselves eat. After a

meal with a family linger a while; it's considered rude for a guest to get up and abruptly leave. Samoans are big people. Most of us eat till we're full, but Samoans eat till they're tired.

money: The Western Samoan *tala* (divided into 100 *sene*) is close to the N.Z. dollar in value. *Tala* are not convertible outside the country, so change only what you think you'll need. If you overestimate, excess *tala* can be changed back into hard currency at the bank in Apia without question. Pick up some Tongan or Fijian money if you're headed that way. The export of *tala* is officially prohibited, but you'd have to be crazy to do it regardless. Repeated devaluations have led to a high rate of inflation (20.3 percent in 1981), but locally produced goods and services have become cheaper for visitors. High duties make most imported goods prohibitively expensive, so bring what you'll need as gifts for local hosts from Fiji or Pago Pago. Camera film is very expensive and the selection poor, so bring a good supply. Even simple things like tea bags, laundry soap, and toiletries are far more expensive in Samoa—if you can find them. Don't give money to beggar children on Apia's streets. Tipping is discouraged. **visas:** No visa is required for a stay of up to 30 days. You *must* have a ticket to leave. They stamp your passport to the date of your flight out, but you can get the 30 days without a struggle.

CONDUCT AND CUSTOM

custom fees: In many parts of Western Samoa it's an established village law that outsiders pay a set fee to swim at the local beach or waterhole, visit a cave, lava tube, waterfall, etc. Sometimes the amount is posted on a sign, but more often it's not. Although it may seem to Westerners that the Samoans have no *right* to charge for these things, what *right* do visitors have to enjoy them free of charge? The best solution, if you don't wish to pay, is just carry on quietly to some other beach or waterhole which is free or where no one's around. Don't argue with them; it's their country. Be aware, however, that a few rip-offs have been associated with this—sometimes an unauthorized person will demand payment, and you can't really tell if it's for real. The charge should be 50 cents to $2 maximum. If someone asks more, try bargaining. Some tourists stupidly pay whatever is charged, so the locals feel there's no harm asking. We recommend that you only pay customary fees of this kind if there's a sign clearly stating the amount or someone asks for the money *beforehand,* thus giving you the choice of going in or not. Resist paying anything if someone tries to collect as you're leaving (unless there's a sign), and *never* give the money to children. If there's a dispute or you're in doubt about the authenticity of a custom fee, say politely you want to pay the money directly to the *pulenu'u* (village mayor). He will straighten things out quickly. Keep your cool in all of this—Samoans respect courtesy far more than anger or threats. All customary fees we know about are listed in this book. Let us know if we missed any.

requests: Samoan culture is extremely manipulative, and there's a saying that you can buy anything with a *fa'amolemole* (please). Samoans are constantly asking each other for things; it's not just a game they play with foreigners. If you're staying in a village for long, somebody from another household will eventually come and ask you for money, or something you're carrying. It's important that you be firm with them. Explain that you're

sharing what you have with your hosts, and you simply don't have money to give out. Some naive young Americans come back from 5 days on Savai'i looking like they've been through a black hole, stripped of practically everything they own, as a result of this *fa'amolemole* bit. You have to form appropriate defenses in Samoa.

theft: Nobody means any harm and violent crime is almost unknown, but be careful: the concept of individual ownership is not entirely accepted by the Samoans. Don't leave valuables unattended. Someone might even steal your laundry off the line, so it's better to hang it up in your room. **rental cars:** Many Samoans in remote areas resent sightseers who drive through their village in a rented automobile. Cases of local children shouting insults, baring their bottoms, and even stoning passing motorists are not uncommon. Sometimes even *palagis* on buses get this reaction if they're thought to be intruding. Try to smile and keep your cool.

children: At times village children can be a bit of a nuisance, calling to you and crowding excitedly around in an almost mocking way. You can forestall much of this by smiling and saying *talofa* (hello) as soon as you see them. Just keep smiling, keep going, and you'll soon leave them behind. It's important not to show any anger or irritation at their behavior as this will only delight them and make them all the more unmannered with the next visitor who happens by. If you're resting somewhere and don't really want to move on, the only way to get rid of them is to complain very politely to the parents. Remember, *you're* the outsider so you've no right to lecture them or order them away. Tourists who thought they could use village property (such as a beach) without taking the reaction of local residents into account have been stoned by village children many times, so take care. As always, a kind smile is your best defense. Of course, if you're a guest in the village you'll be treated with great respect at all times. Be worthy of it.

a word to the wise: After a few days in the country it'll become fairly obvious to male visitors that Samoan women like to marry

Western men. Age is not an important factor here: teenagers smile invitingly at middle-aged bachelors. Samoans associate Europeans with the sort of affluence they see on American television. When a girl marries a *palagi* her economic situation, and that of her entire *aiga*, suddenly improves, or so they think. If you're really smitten with a Samoan, you'll be expected to satisfy much more than just her needs. Be aware too that Samoan women are expert at stopping just short of lovemaking before they're married, and their brothers can be very hard on an insincere man who thinks he can play the game to his own advantage. Note too that marriage to a Samoan woman does not imply any legal right to stay in Samoa; in fact, the idea is that you take the woman *and* her family back and support them in your own home country.

others: Don't eat while walking through a village. Don't talk or eat while standing in a *fale*. Sit down crosslegged on a mat, *then* talk and eat. Don't stretch out your legs when sitting: it's impolite to point your feet at anyone. Some villages object to the use of their beach on Sun., and some object anytime. If someone's around, ask or find one that's secluded. Public nudism is prohibited; cover up as you walk through a village. Don't wear flowers to church. Samoans are extremely courteous people and will answer affirmatively to almost any question. Check this by asking them to confirm something you know to be incorrect!

important note: If some of the above (proud, courteous Samoans throwing stones, committing suicide, etc.) seems confusing, consider how even "world authorities" such as Margaret Mead and Derek Freeman (see "Booklist") can create diametrically opposed theories as to just what Samoan customs were and are. For anthropologists, Samoa is the most fascinating island group in the Pacific.

airport: Faleolo Airport (APW) is 35 km W of Apia. There's a bank changing money at the usual rate and a counter with a rack of tourist brochures. There's also a small duty-free shop. The departure tax is $20 for tourists, $5 for Samoans. You don't have to pay the tax if you stay less than 24 hours (transit), but write TRANSIT on your arrival card and mention it to the Immigration officials as you come in. They'd just as soon charge you as not. The trip to town costs US$3 by airport bus or 80 *sene* if you wait on the highway for a public bus (very few after 1600 or on Sunday).

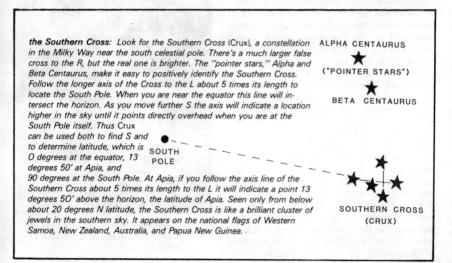

the Southern Cross: Look for the Southern Cross (Crux), a constellation in the Milky Way near the south celestial pole. There's a much larger false cross to the R, but the real one is brighter. The "pointer stars," Alpha and Beta Centaurus, make it easy to positively identify the Southern Cross. Follow the longer axis of the Cross to the L about 5 times its length to locate the South Pole. When you are near the equator this line will intersect the horizon. As you move further S the axis will indicate a location higher in the sky until it points directly overhead when you are at the South Pole itself. Thus Crux can be used both to find S and to determine latitude, which is 0 degrees at the equator, 13 degrees 50' at Apia, and 90 degrees at the South Pole. At Apia, if you follow the axis line of the Southern Cross about 5 times its length to the L it will indicate a point 13 degrees 50' above the horizon, the latitude of Apia. Seen only from below about 20 degrees N latitude, the Southern Cross is like a brilliant cluster of jewels in the southern sky. It appears on the national flags of Western Samoa, New Zealand, Australia, and Papua New Guinea.

ALPHA CENTAURUS

("POINTER STARS")

BETA CENTAURUS

SOUTH POLE

SOUTHERN CROSS (CRUX)

UPOLU

APIA AND ENVIRONS

Though growing fast, Apia (pop. 33,170 in 1981) is still only a cluster of villages. Churches and trading companies line the waterfront in the traditional South Seas manner. Visit the colorful market to see villagers arrive to sell taro, bananas, and cacao. It'll take the better part of a week to enjoy all Apia has to offer. Fortunately the facilities are good, so take a break in your transpacific odyssey and see the city one step at a time. The people are friendly and have lots of time to talk to you. Get into the culture as much as you can and prepare yourself for that big trip around Savai'i. Samoa is the most Polynesian place in the Pacific and Apia is the exciting bright light around which Samoa revolves.

market to Mulinu'u: Begin your visit in Apia's colorful market, best in the South Pacific. The market throbs with activity 24 hours a day—families spend the night here rather than abandon their places. You'll see a marvelous array of local produce, all with prices clearly marked, plus handicrafts, local foods, a fish market out back, and a great variety of classic Polynesian people. Walk through the bus station and across the street to the government-owned Tusitala Hotel. Go inside to appreciate the great hand-tied roofs of the main *fale*-like buildings. Continue out on Mulinu'u Drive past 2 monuments on the L commemorating the disastrous 1889 naval debacle (see "History" above). The German cruiser *Adler,* which sank during the hurricane, is now buried under the reclaimed area in central Apia. There's also a monument on the R which recalls the raising of the German flag on 1 March 1900 (*"die deutsche Flagge gehisst"*). The large beehive-style building on the L farther along is the Parliament of Samoa (1972). The old Fono House is across the field opposite the Independence Memorial (1962) which declares that "The Holy Ghost, Council of all Mankind, led Samoa to Destiny." The

white building between this memorial and the Apia Yachting Club is the National Museum (weekdays 1000-1200/1300-1600). At the end of the Mulinu'u Peninsula is the Apia Observatory, founded by the Germans in 1902. Note the many impressive royal tombs here and down the road to the left. Mulinu'u is the heartland of modern Samoan history.

sidetrip southwest: Take a TAFAIGATA or SEESEE bus and ask the driver to drop you at the closest point to Papase'ea Sliding Rocks. You'll still have to walk 2 km and pay 40 *sene* admission. You slide down 3 rocks into freshwater pools—don't forget your trunks. On the way back to Apia stop off at the Mormon Temple on the airport highway. The golden angel Moroni trumpets The Word

This monument to the German victims of the 1889 naval disaster stands on Apia's Mulinu'u Peninsula.

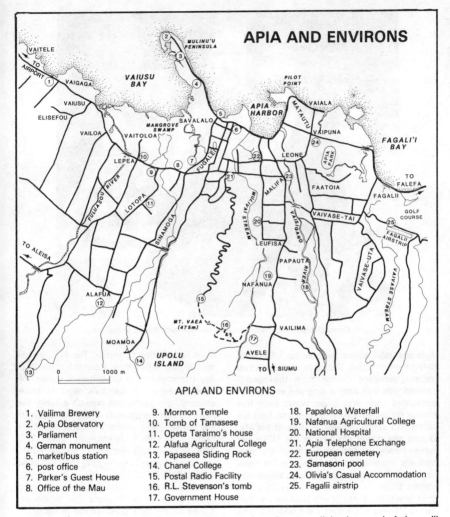

APIA AND ENVIRONS

1. Vailima Brewery
2. Apia Observatory
3. Parliament
4. German monument
5. market/bus station
6. post office
7. Parker's Guest House
8. Office of the Mau
9. Mormon Temple
10. Tomb of Tamasese
11. Opeta Taraimo's house
12. Alafua Agricultural College
13. Papaseea Sliding Rock
14. Chanel College
15. Postal Radio Facility
16. R.L. Stevenson's tomb
17. Government House
18. Papaloloa Waterfall
19. Nafanua Agricultural College
20. National Hospital
21. Apia Telephone Exchange
22. European cemetery
23. Samasoni pool
24. Olivia's Casual Accommodation
25. Fagalii airstrip

from above. Tourists are not allowed inside, but an information center adjoins if you'd like to hear the story. Just a few minutes walk W along the highway is the impressive 4-tier tomb of Tupua Tamasese Lealofi III, leader of the Mau Movement (see "History" above). Tamasese and 8 Samoan compatriots were killed on 29 Dec. 1929 by the New Zealand Constabulary for opposing the colonial regime. As you walk back towards Apia you'll pass on the L the "Office of the Mau," a bandstand in which the revolutionaries met, dating from the German period.

Vailima: In 1889 Robert Louis Stevenson, author of the adventure classic *Treasure Island,* purchased approximately 162 ha of bushland at the foot of Mt. Vaea, inland from

Fanny Osborne and Robert Louis Stevenson with friends at Vailima.

Apia and high above the sea, for US$4,000. Being near a stream, the place was known as Vailima, meaning "water from the hand." Legend tells that after a long sea voyage, an exhausted chief was given water from this stream by his wife. Here Stevenson built his home and spent the last 5 years of his life. During the power struggle in the 1880s between newly imperialistic Germany and sporadically imperialistic America, the Germans imprisoned some Samoan chiefs. Stevenson visited them in confinement, and to show their gratitude, these chiefs built him a road below Vailima when they were released. The Samoans called Stevenson *Tusitala,* or "teller of tales." On 3 Dec. 1894, Stevenson suffered a fatal brain hemorrhage while helping his wife Fanny fix dinner. He's buried just below the summit of Mt. Vaea overlooking Vailima, as he'd requested. The mansion with its beautiful, tropical gardens was first sold to a retired German businessman, then bought by the German government as the official

residence of their Governor. The N.Z. regime took it over when they assumed power. Today the structure is Government House, official residence of Samoa's head of state, although the gentleman doesn't actually live here. To visit the grounds of Vailima (bus from the market), first obtain a pass at the Prime Minister's Office (weekdays 0800-1200/1300-1635) in Apia. Inscribed "Samoa 1889," the old-fashioned mahogany hand-steering wheel of the British ship *Calliope,* the only one to survive the naval debacle of that year (mentioned earlier under "History"), is temporarily stored on the back porch of the building.

Mount Vaea: An almost obligatory pilgrimage for all visitors to Samoa is the 60-min. climb along a well-marked winding trail to the tomb of Robert Louis Stevenson just below the 475-m summit of Mt. Vaea. The area at the bottom of the hill adjoining Vailima has been tastefully developed with botanical gardens, swimming hole, and waterfall (dry except during the wet). The path to the top was cut by 200 sorrowful Samoans as they carried the famous writer's body up to its final resting place in 1894. From the tomb there's a sweeping panorama of Apia. The blue roof of Vailima directly below is clearly visible. To the E lies a verdant valley, with the misty mountains of Upolu beyond and, in the distance, the white line of surf breaking endlessly on the reef. It's utterly still—a peaceful, poignant, lonely place. Stevenson's requiem reads:

> Under the wide and starry sky,
> Dig the grave and let me lie.
> Glad did I live and gladly die,
> And I laid me down with a will.
>
> This be the verse you grave for me:
> Here he lies where he longed to be;
> Home is the sailor, home from the sea,
> And the hunter home from the hill.

Stevenson's wife Fanny died in California in 1914. Her ashes were brought back to Samoa and buried at the foot of her husband's grave. The bronze plaque bears her Samoan name, Aolele, and the words of Stevenson:

> Teacher, tender comrade, wife,
> A fellow-farer true through life
> Heart-whole and soul-free,
> The August Father gave to me.

bushwhacking: A longer, more difficult route across Mt. Vaea begins behind the Apia Telephone Exchange. Keep going up past a navigational light and continue on a jeep track (excellent views of Apia and the sea) all the way to the Postal Radio Facility at the end of the road. Go around the fence on the L side and push down onto the ridge directly behind. This part of the way is badly overgrown; you'll need long pants to protect your legs. If you try to keep to the highest ground right around to the L you'll eventually come out just before Stevenson's tomb. This hike affords a close view of the vegetation and is much more adventuresome than the usual tourist route. Take food and water.

central Upolu: Take the Vailima bus to the end of the line, somewhere near Island Styles Factory Showroom (see "shopping" below). A half-hour's walk above Island Styles is the new Baha'i House of Worship (opened 1984), Mother Temple to all Baha'is in the region and one of the most impressive modern buildings in the South Pacific. The monumental dome soars 30 m above the surrounding area and has 9 sides, symbolizing the unity of the 9 major religions of the world. Inside, the latticework of ribs forms a 9-pointed star at the apex of the dome. The seating is arranged facing the Holy Land (Israel) because this is the final resting place of Baha'u'llah (1817-1892), Prophet Founder of the Baha'i Faith. This great building was funded by Baha'is around the world and is open to all for prayer and meditation. Also visit the Information Center, to the L as you approach the temple, where a library, audio-visual program, and refreshments are at your disposal. Another 30-min. walk up the Cross Island Highway brings you to a road to the L for Lake Lanoto'o, high in the center of Upolu at 590 m above sea level. You could also catch a Siumu pickup ($1) from in front of the Dept. of Economic Development right to this turnoff, then visit the Baha'i Temple on the way back. At a small store near the turnoff you could ask directions to "Goldfish Lake." Walk straight W on the road for just under an hour till you see the power lines end abruptly at a transformer on a pole, plus several radio towers down the road to the left. Continue 500 m straight ahead to the next junction where a road runs S into the forest, and a small plantation with a tin-roofed shack set back from the road W is just ahead on the right. Look SW and you'll be able to distinguish a badly overgrown road cutting into the jungle diagonally between the 2 present roads. This is the way to the lake. The trail begins just a few steps down the S road; it'll take you 45 min. OW from here to Lake Lanoto'o. For the first 15 min. you push through long grass on the old roadbed, then the trail improves. When you arrive at a large rectangular microwave reflector on top of a hill, the lake is just below you. The opaque green water of this seldom-visited crater lake is surrounded by a mossy green forest drip-

the palm arrives in Samoa: Tuna, a young Fijian, once fell in love with Sina, a lovely visitor from Samoa. He asked her to marry him, but she could not decide and returned home. Tuna changed himself into an eel and followed her to Savai'i, taking refuge in a pool. Sina came to visit Tuna regularly there, but alas, he forgot the chant required to change back into a man. Eventually, her brothers discovered the affair, and came to kill him. Before Tuna died, he asked Sina to bury his head, from which a wonderful life-giving tree would grow. The fruit would contain his eyes and mouth, and every time Sina lifted one to drink, she would be able to kiss her lost lover. That's how the coconut tree came to Samoa.

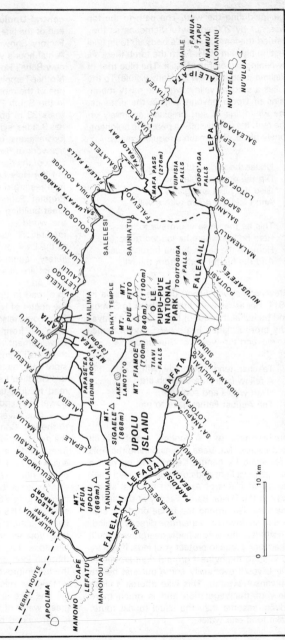

UPOLU

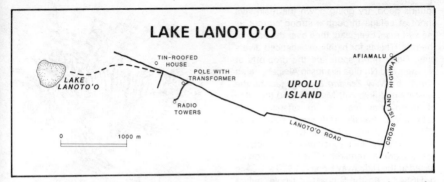

LAKE LANOTO'O

TIN-ROOFED
HOUSE
POLE WITH
TRANSFORMER

AFIAMALU

LAKE
LANOTO'O

RADIO
TOWERS

UPOLU
ISLAND

LANOTO'O ROAD

CROSS ISLAND HIGHWAY

0   1000 m

ping with the ever-present mist. Swimming in it is an eerie experience. To add to the otherworldliness of the place, Lake Lanoto'o is full of goldfish, but you'll have to wait patiently if you want to see any from shore. Bread crumbs might help. This hike is ideal for seeing high-altitude vegetation without going too far, and on a clear day there's a good view from the top of the reflector, but sturdy shoes and long pants are essential. If you're still keen when you return to the main highway ask directions to Tiavi Falls on the R near the road farther south.

sidetrip east: Buses depart Apia market every hour or so for Falefa, 29 km east. You get many fine views of Upolu's N coast, and pass right along surfing beaches Laulii and Solosolo (beware of undertow). Get off at Falefa Falls (free), impressive during the rainy season but too murky to swim. Walk back the way you came 2 km through beautiful Falefa village to Piula College. The Piula Cave Pool (open Mon. to Sat. 0800-1630, admission $1) is a natural freshwater pool fed by a spring directly below the large Methodist church. The water is unusually clear despite all the locals soaping up and washing clothes in it. Swim into the cave below the church. This is connected to a second cave by a small underwater opening on the L near the back. The second cave is long, dark, and deep, but can be explored with a mask and snorkel. After your swim (there are change rooms), catch a bus or hitch back to Apia. All this can be done in a morning. If you've got more time, there's good snorkeling at high tide around Albatross

I. in Saluafata Harbor (good anchorage for yachts) between Piula College and Solosolo.

where else to swim: There's a poor beach at Vaiala not far from Olivia's Casual Accommodation (beware of undertow). Opposite the church at Matautu is the signposted entrance to Palolo Deep Marine Park (admission $1) where there are toilets and change rooms, a bar, plus a platform out on the reef itself from which to explore the coral and good variety of fishlife in the Deep. The Deep's main attraction, however, is its convenience to Apia. Snorkeling gear is available for hire ($4 a set). Make an afternoon of it. Just a short distance up Falaelili Street from the waterfront, a road to the E leads to the Samasoni Bathing Pool where you can dive from the rocks into a clear, deep pool. Papaloloa Waterfall is farther upstream on the same river. Ask which road leads in to the falls just after passing the Nafanua Agricultural College.

scuba locales: Five Mile Reef, an ocean reef 8 km straight out to sea from Apia Harbor, was one of Samoa's best dive sites, until the locals started using dynamite to bring up the fish. Now the S coast of Upolu is favored for its good facilities, calmer seas, and variety of attractions. The reef channels off the Hideaway Hotel teem with fish, best seen on an incoming tide. Nu'usafe'e Island just off Poutasi is a favorite for its coral heads, wavy coral, and variety of fishlife (including harmless sand sharks). You can hand-feed the tame fish. Five lava shoots penetrate from 10-25 m and open into clear water. If that sounds good, try going down the main lava shoot at Lefaga through a strong current as the surf roars overhead, then over the edge of the reef. This is for highly experienced divers only. Other good spots are the drop-offs at Nu'utele and Nu'ulua islands in Aleipata (rated "tops" by *New Zealand Dive* magazine), the western reef areas off Manono, and the edge of the barrier reef, 3 km offshore from Lalomalava, Savai'i. Hideaway Tours (Box 891, Apia) offers one-tank (US$17.50) and 2-tank (US$32, lunch included) dives, equipment extra if required. Their operation is based at the Hideaway Hotel (US$28 s, US$36 d, US$43 t) on the S coast of Upolu, only a half hour drive from Apia. Certified divers can also rent scuba equipment in Apia for about $25 a day and organize their own trips. Contact Ken Power at Cander Engineering (no sign) behind Tivoli 2 Cinema, or call Peter Meredith (tel. 23-253). Peter lives near Apia Park. Another way to get out is to ask around at the Apia Yachting Club on the Mulinu'u Peninsula in the late afternoon. Some of the members dive regularly and are willing to take visitors who share the cost of gasoline and air. As the diving is on the open sea, beware of seasickness.

AROUND UPOLU

eastern Upolu: Some 8 km S of Falefa Falls the road works its way up to Mafa Pass (276 m). Five km farther along, deep in the interior, are Fuipisia Falls ($1 admission), signposted on the W side of the road. Just a 300-m walk inland, the falls plunge 56 m down into a fern-filled valley of which you get a good view from on top. Three km S the same river plummets over 53-m-high Sopo'aga Falls (admission charged). The viewpoint is behind the first house on the R just a few hundred m beyond the junction with the westbound road to O Le Pupu-Pu'e National Park. A trail heads down to the falls from the viewpoint. If you walk a short distance down the National Park road to the bridge across the river, you'll find a path on the E side which leads upstream to a good swimming area. Buses along the S coast from Sopo'aga to the National Park are rare, but your chances of getting a lift improve ap-

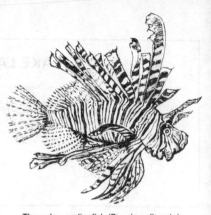

The zebra or lionfish (Pterois volitans) is among the most toxic in the Pacific. Its striking red coloration and long spines may be nature's warning.

preciably if you walk 4 km W to the Salani turnoff. Most buses turn E toward Aleipata District with its many excellent and unspoiled white sand beaches. The S coast of Upolu is more traditional than the north. Visit the beautiful offshore islands at high tide with fishermen from the easternmost house in Lalomanu (contribute for gas). Nu'utele I., once a leper colony, is now uninhabited. Two beautiful beaches flank the steep forested slopes. There's a footpath along the steep N coast from Ti'avea to Fagaloa Bay (good anchorage for yachts), also buses straight back to Apia.

O Le Pupu-Pu'e National Park: This large, 2,850-ha national park, one of the only ones in the South Pacific, stretches on the insular divide from the summits of Mt. Le Pu'e, the double-cratered peak E of Afiamalu, and Mt. Fito (1100 m), highest point on Upolu, right down to the lava fields of O Le Pupu and the coast. An informative Visitor Center is at Togitogiga, 28 km S of Apia via the Cross Island Highway. Near the Center and just a short walk from the main road are beautiful Togitogiga Falls, good for swimming, wading, and diving (middle pool). There are toilets, change rooms, and shelters at the falls; camping is allowed. A trail from the Visitor Center leads up to Peapea Cave, 2 hours RT. Good views of the lava fields and the coast are obtained on the O Le Pupu Trail, which begins a couple of km W of the Center. The easiest way to get to the park is ask for a pickup in front of the Dept. of Economic Development in Apia. There's a daily bus service W from the park to Lefaga District.

western Upolu: Lefaga District, 36 km W of Apia, is known for the white sand, black rocks, and clear water of Return to Paradise Beach, 2 km off the main road. The Lefaga bus goes all the way, while the Safata bus stops up at the crossroads 2 km away. Leave Apia early if you want to come back the same day. A woman charges $1 admission to the stretch of beach made famous by the 1952 movie "Return to Paradise," which starred Gary Cooper. There's a track SE along the coast from Lefaga to Salamumu passing a deserted beach where you could camp. Ownership of this area is in doubt — you may be charged $1 admission twice, by the people from Lefaga and again by the Salamumu people. Actually, it's a small price to pay to enjoy this beautiful area. There are *fales* on the beach near Salamumu village which you can rent for about $5 pp. At Mulifanua, site of the largest coconut plantation in the Southern Hemisphere, is the terminal for the ferries to Savai'i.

Manono Island: Catch an outboard from Manonouta to Manono I. for 50 *sene*. Go early or spend the night there. A trail around the island can be covered in about an hour. There are no cars on Manono: it's a delightful place to rest. See the grave with 99 stones, one for each of the dead man's wives. There's a monument to the first Methodist missionary to arrive in Samoa (1835), and a few beaches. If you look worried, they may try to charge you $20 for a special charter back. Wait instead for the regular trip.

PRACTICALITIES

accommodations: There are 3 good inexpensive places to stay in Apia. One of the best is Parkers' Guest House at Fugalei, a 10-min. walk from the market. For $8 pp you share a double room on the airy second floor of a pleasant European-style building. Showers, kitchen, and TV room are downstairs, but no "visitors" are allowed in the rooms. Across town on Matautu St. (take the LETOGO bus from the market) are the other two. Just before the Shell station nearby is Betty Moor's Guest House, where cubicles are good value at $8 pp (you'll probably get one to yourself). Betty will let you share her kero burner if she likes you, but beware of noisy dog fights at night. Checkout time is 1200 sharp. Farther along in the same direction, behind the B.P. gasoline station beyond the bank, is Olivia's Casual Accommodation ($8 pp). Extremely casual and friendly, the comfortable 6-bed Samoan-style units are set in spacious, land-scaped grounds a stone's throw from Apia Park. Each *fale* has its own kitchen, sitting room, toilet, and shower. There's no crowding and the atmosphere is excellent.

others: If you don't mind paying a little more, the Seaside Inn opposite the wharf at Matautu offers bed/breakfast for $14 s, $24 d (fan and shared bath), or $20 s, $28 d (private bath). There's a small bar attached. For a homestay contact Mr. Opeta Taraimo (tel. 20-955) who takes guests in his large 2-story house on Tokelau Road near Samoa Wood Products up from the Mormon Temple; or look for him at the Office for Tokelau Affairs where he works. One local institution of note is Aggie Grey's Hotel, which began in March 1942 as a hamburger stand for U.S. servicemen stationed in the area. Despite the surly staff and mediocre food, American tourists still flock to the place, now a pretentious 131-room hotel (US$51 s, US$76 d. The mixed bag of guests circulate freely at tea, and the "living legend" herself, now into her 80s, sometimes puts in an appearance at night. Aggie's is a trip in itself.

food: Wong Kee's Restaurant in a ramshackle building behind Otto's Reef has some of the best Chinese food in town at the lowest

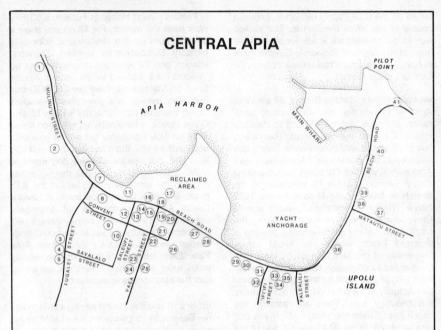

CENTRAL APIA

1. Air Nauru
2. Tusitala Hotel
3. Soul Train Disco
4. Savalalo Cinema
5. Office for Tokelau Affairs
6. local bus station
7. market
8. Thomsen's Bookshop
9. Starlite Cinema
10. Tivoli 2 Cinema
11. Dept. of Economic Development
12. Gold Star Agency
13. Le Bistro
14. SPIA
15. Polynesian Airlines
16. library
17. county buses
18. clock tower
19. Burns Philp
20. Chief Post Office
21. Donavons Reef
22. Betty's Restaurant
23. bus stop
24. The Chicken Parlor
25. Wendt's Bookshop
26. Feiloaimauso Hall
27. Wesley Book Store
28. Catholic Cathedral
29. Copy Center/Rent-a-Bike
30. Otto's Reef/Wong Kee Restaurant
31. Immigration office
32. police station
33. Prime Minister's office
34. Dept. of Statistics
35. Handicrafts Corp./Lands and Surveys
36. Aggie Grey's Hotel
37. Betty Moor's
38. S & T Guest House/Vatco Car Rentals
39. Western Samoa Shipping Corporation
40. Seaside Inn
41. Palolo Deep Marine Park

prices—too good to stay like this for long. Meanwhile try their $2 *aiga* lunch, or fresh lobster meat for $9.50. Several good places are on Vaea St., the road running inland from the clock tower. Betty's Restaurant (closes at 1800) offers $1.50 lunches of noodles, vegetables, curry, and eggs. Get cheap chop suey at the Chicken Parlor, farther down the road from Betty's. There are no tables so ask for a takeaway meal which will go great with a large Vailima beer in the Matai Bar up the stairway next door. The *matai* tend to get a little rambunctious. Amigos Restaurant nearby stays open later, serves a wicked hamburger, and has an American-style lounge attached. Other places to know about are Burns Philp Coffee Shop (good for breakfast and lunch weekdays) and Josie's Coffee Shop in the arcade beside Polynesian Airlines. Josie's is just right for a coffee break. One treat not to miss is a hot cup of real Samoan cocoa with donuts or pancakes at the market. Also look for the shop halfway back on the far E side of the market hall which sells gigantic ice cream cones. The food stalls at the back of the market are the cheapest place to eat, if you've got a strong stomach.

entertainment: There are 3 cinemas: Tivoli 2, Starlite, and Savalalo. Find swinging nightlife at the Mount Vaea Club—the place to pickup or get picked up. It's loud, rough, and fast, and there are lots of girls. Go-Go Night Club on Beach Road is good if there's a band. Soul Train Disco beside Savalalo Cinema features American pop with occasional break dancing—for the younger set. Things get going after 2100. Donavons Reef, hidden away behind the post office, is good for video or an afternoon beer. Thursday evenings you can see Polynesian dancing while enjoying a buffet dinner at Aggie's Hotel ($25 pp) or at the Tusitala ($20 pp), both good value. But the best show of all can be seen free by the market late Fri. night as evangelists preach and a choir sings joyful religious songs, all the hands moving gracefully just as they did at the Tusitala. Don't miss it. Church choirs are good Sun. mornings too (dress neat).

sports: See exciting rugby (March to June) or soccer (July to Sept.) at Apia Park Sat. at 1600. Admission to the grandstand is cheap. The gymnasium at Apia Park was a gift of the People's Republic of China for the 1983 South Pacific Games. You can observe basketball (Tues. and Thurs. at 1700), badminton (Wed. and Fri. at 1900), and volleyball (Sat. from May to July) in the gym. The tennis courts at Apia Park are open to the public daily. Cricket *(kirikiti)* is played mostly in rural villages at 1400 on Sat. throughout the year. There are often practice matches afternoons on the grassy area behind the clock tower opposite Burns Philp. Have a workout at the Squash Center beside the Seaside Inn, $3 pp for half an hour, bring your own partner.

shopping: Apia market is fascinating anytime, but best on Sat. morning. Buy genuine handicrafts here. Western Samoa isn't the place to shop for consumer goods, but the clothing and craft shops are good. The Western Samoa Handicraft Center on Beach Road has woodcarvings, baskets, handbags, and *tapa* cloth. Traditional woodcarving is limited to *kava* bowls, drums, and war clubs. It's interesting to note that the *tikis* are mock Maori or Hawaiian, not Samoan—don't buy the grotesque, grimacing little devils. Also beware of turtle shell jewelry which is prohibited entry into the U.S., Australia, and many other countries. Some of the best traditional handicrafts in the Pacific are available at the Office for Tokelau Affairs, especially high-quality coconut-fiber hats and handbags, fans, and exquisite model canoes. Some of the handbags have a solid coconut-shell liner—handy for women wishing to tranquilize over-enthusiastic males! The coconut-shell water bottles are authentic and unique. The most distinctive article on display is the *tuluma,* a wooden watertight box used to carry valuables on canoe journeys; its bouyancy also made it an ideal lifesaver. All the above are genuine collectors' items. The same office sells Tokelauan postage stamps and souvenir coins. The Western Samoa Philatelic Bureau is upstairs in the Chief Post Office—beautiful stamps at face value.

clothing: Go native in Samoa by changing into some colorful, eye-catching clothing. Female travelers especially will enhance their appearance and acceptance by wearing a long *mu'umu'u* gown, a 2-piece *puletasi* (with *lavalava*), or a simple wraparound *sarong*. Island Styles produces lovely hand-printed fabrics ready-made into the above and more. Visit their factory showroom on the Cross Island Highway (VAILIMA bus) for the best selection. They also have a small shop in the arcade behind Wesley Book Store. However, Pekas, across from the Nelson Library, has a better selection. Carol 'n Mark boutique beside Gold Star Agency has an outstanding variety of knockout dresses which have to be seen to be appreciated. Consider too just buying the cloth and having something made at one of the small tailor shops around town.

services: Avoid the long lines at the main office of the Bank of Western Samoa by changing your travelers cheques at the Gold Star Agency (weekdays 0930-1500) of the same bank for the same rate. On weekends changing money can be a problem, though a hotel might be able to help. Make long-distance telephone calls from the International Telephone Bureau (daily 0800-2230) behind the Chief Post Office. You can see a doctor at the National Hospital almost anytime for $15, but if you've got anything seriously wrong, catch a flight to Pago Pago. The Public Health Clinic in the dilapidated section of the same complex offers vaccinations weekdays 0800-1200/1300-1630. (Body lice and intestinal parasites are widespread among Samoan villagers.) Chemists in Apia are closed weekends and holidays, and the Pharmacy at the National Hospital is useless. Faupepe's Laund-Ro-Mat opposite the National Hospital is open daily 0900-2300, charging $1.20 to wash, $1.60 to dry, and 60 *sene* for powder. The barber shop beside Tivoli 2 Cinema is $1 a cut.

information: There are 2 sources of tourist information. The Visitors Bureau in the Dept. of Economic Development building (weekdays 0800-1200/1300-1630) has good brochures. If you have any questions, try the Visitors Information Desk in the Polynesian Airlines office which is very helpful and has slightly different brochures. The Dept. of Statistics behind the prime minister's office sells an *Annual Statistical Abstract* for $1. Get large maps of Apia and Samoa at the Lands and Survey Dept. for $2 each. The Pacific Room of the Nelson Memorial Public Library is worth browsing. The works of Samoa's leading novelist, Albert Wendt, plus excellent books on the Pacific, are available at Wendt's Bookshop opposite The Chicken Parlour on Vaea Street. There's also the Wesley Bookshop on Beach Road. Thomsen's Bookshop, upstairs opposite the Treasury, exchanges used pocketbooks. There are 2 English-language weekly papers, *The Samoa Observer* and *The Samoa Times.*

TRANSPORT

by ship: The Western Samoa Shipping Corp. has a car ferry, the *Queen Salamasina,* to Pago Pago Tues., Thurs., and Sun. at 0800, $12 OW (6 hours). The schedule varies from week to week, so ask. An international ser-

The louse (Pediculus capitis) *is a small, wingless insect which can infest the hairy areas of all warm-blooded beasts. It's untrue that personal cleanliness prevents lice. Anyone can get them, whether clean or dirty. The parasite attaches its egg securely to the side of hair shafts. By applying a solution available at any drugstore you can zap the varmints in minutes.*

vice, you must book before 1200 the previous day. Change excess *tala* back into dollars at the bank also the day before—no facilities on the wharf. The Warner Pacific Line has a monthly sailing to Nuku'alofa ($60 OW, no meals included). Pacific Forum Line is the agent for monthly Silk & Boyd freighters to Rarotonga. They won't sell you a ticket but will advise you when the ship is due in, then you must talk to the captain. For information on the supply ship to the Tokelau Is. contact the Office for Tokelau Affairs. There's one about every 2 months and a cabin would run $190 RT, but reservations are not accepted and tourists may travel on a "space available" basis only. (For information on the Savai'i ferry see "Savai'i" below.)

by bus: Buses around Apia cost 20 *sene,* 80 *sene* to Mulifanua Wharf (PASI OLE VAA), $1 to Lefaga, 60 *sene* to Falefa, $1.20 to Mafa Pass, $1.50 to Lalomanu. There's no service between Falelatai and Lefaga. For buses to the ends of the island, be at the market bus station by 0700 at the latest if you intend to return to Apia the same day. Many long-distance buses leave from the field opposite Burns Philp. Saturday is a good day for buses, but evening and Sun. service is limited. The buses are without cushions, but they do have destination signs and set fares. For pickup trucks to Siumu ($1.30) look in front of the Dept. of Economic Development (Visitors Bureau) building.

others: You have to be 25 to rent a car and must get a local driver's license ($5) at the Ministry of Transport next to the Seaside Inn. The International Driver's License is not recognized. Vatco Car Rentals below S & T Guest House rents Suzuki jeeps for $50 a day, unlimited mileage and insurance included. A $250 deposit is asked, and you're not permitted to take the vehicle to Savai'i. Don't accept a car from Vatco without checking it care-

Apia's Catholic Cathedral is a landmark for ships entering the harbor.

fully—there have been bitter complaints. Don't under any circumstances leave your passport as security on a car rental from Vatco, although they have the cheek to suggest it. Rent a Suzuki 80 cc motorcycle at the Copy Center on the waterfront near Otto's Reef. The charge is $15 a day plus $2 for insurance (gas is extra). A $100 deposit is asked. **taxis:** Taxis have license plates bearing the prefix T. They're fairly cheap to get back to your hotel after a night on the town, but agree on the price first. The Visitors Bureau publishes a list of all taxi and bus fares. It claims there's no additional charge for luggage, and tipping is unnecessary. Beware of the taxis parked in front of Aggie Grey's Hotel—they tend to be a rip-off.

SAVAI'I

The big island of Savai'i offers ancient Polynesian ruins, waterfalls, clear freshwater pools,
white beaches, vast black lava fields, massive
volcanoes, and traditional Samoan life. Robert
Flaherty's classic *Moana of the South Seas*
(1926) was filmed on Savai'i. Most of the
villages are by the seashore, strung along the
circuminsular highway. They're a pleasure to
stroll through so long as you don't let a little
teasing from the children ruffle you. Most of
the N side of this high volcanic island was
transformed in the great eruptions between
1905 and 1911, which buried much fertile land
and sent refugees streaming across to Upolu.
Today it's wildflower country. Also, vast
tracts of virgin rainforest are threatened by
logging and agricultural clearings. Coral reefs
are present along the E coast from Salelologa
to Pu'apu'a, on the N coast from Saleaula to
Sasina then Asau to Vaisala, and on the S
coast at Palauli. There's safe though exposed
yacht anchorage in Matautu Bay from May to
Oct.; the entrance to Asau Harbor is subject to
silting, so seek local advice before attempting
to enter.

SIGHTS

Letolo Plantation: Catch a bus from the
Salelologa ferry wharf 8 km to Letolo Plantation in Palauli District, just beyond Vailoa. The
largest remaining prehistoric monument in
Polynesia is here, as well as an idyllic waterfall
and pool. Turn R just 100 m N of the copra
sheds and walk straight E between coconut
trees 400 m to the edge of the ravine. The
path down to the pool is fairly obvious—you'll
notice imprints in the grass where vehicles
have turned and parked. The crystal-clear
waters of the river running down the E side of
the plantation plunge over a cliff into a large
deep pool—dive from the sides. Brown
prawns live in the pool: drop in bread crumbs
and wait for them to appear. After a refreshing
swim return to the farm road and continue
north. This road soon divides; the track to the

L leads up to the huge Pulemelei stone
pyramid *(kia)* on a steep slope to the L about 3
km from the main circuminsular highway.
Concealed by thick undergrowth until the
1960s, this immense stone platform, on a
hillside in the middle of the coconut plantation, rises 9 m (the summit measures 45 m by
27 m). Stone seats used in religious
ceremonies are scattered around it. The structure is similar to the stone temple platforms of
Tahiti, and is possibly their predecessor,
though its origins have been completely eras-
ed from the memory of present-day Samoans.
Return to the fork in the road just N of the
copra sheds. The other track leads up though
the plantation passing a much smaller stone
platform also on the left. During your visit
here, keep in mind that you're on private property, courtesy of the Nelson family. Politely
ask permission to proceed of any people you
meet along the way.

Savai'i's Taga blowholes are a memorable sight.

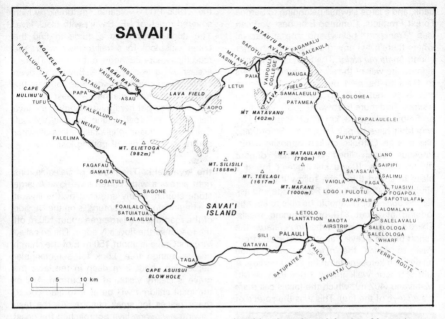

SAVAI'I

FAGALELE BAY

FALEALUPO-TAI

MATAUTU BAY

AIRSTRIP

AVAO

FAGAMALU

ASAU BAY

VAISALA BAY

SAFOTU

SALEAULA

MATAVAI

CAPE
MULINU'U

TUFU

PAPA

SATAUA

ASAU

MATAVAI
SASINA

PAIA

VAIPOULI
COLLEGE

MAUGA

LAVA FIELD

LETUI

LAVA
FIELD

SAMALAEULU

PATAMEA

SOLOMEA

FALEALUPO-UTA

NEIAFU

AOPO

MT MATAVANU
(402m)

FALELIMA

PAPALAULELEI

MT. ELIETOGA
(982m)

PU'APU'A

FAGAFAU
SAMATA

MT. SILISILI
(1858m)

MT. MATAULANO
(790m)

LANO

SAIPIPI

FOGATULI

MT. TEELAGI
(1617m)

SA'ASA'AI

SALIMU

SAGONE

MT. MAFANE
(1000m)

VAIOLA

LOGO I PULOTU

FAGA

TUASIVI

FOGAPOA

SAFOTULAFAI

FOAILALO
SATUIATUA

SALAILUA

SAVAI'I
ISLAND

LETOLO
PLANTATION

SAPAPALII

LALOMALAVA

SELELAVALU

SILI

MAOTA
AIRSTRIP

PALAULI

SALELOLOGA
SALELOLOGA
WHARF

GATAVAI

TAGA

VAILOA

CAPE ASUISUI
BLOWHOLE

SATUPAITEA

TAFUATAI

FERRY ROUTE

0   5   10 km

the southwest coast: There's a series of rather spectacular blowholes *(pupu)* along the coast near Cape Asuisui just a short walk from Taga village, some 40 km W of the wharf. You may be charged $2 admission. The blowholes are at their best when high tide is at sunset. Throw in a coconut and watch the roaring jet propel it skyward, usually smashed into tiny pieces. There's good surfing in winter (May to Aug.) at high tide just off the point behind the large store at Salailua, 13 km NW of Taga. Ask permission of the locals to camp on the beach at Satuiatua nearby. Local fishermen may offer to take you out with them if you show an interest.

Falealupo: It's 9 km on a dirt road from Falealupo-uta on the main highway to Falealupo-tai, a traditional Samoan village of thatched *fales* along a white sandy beach. Transport is limited to a bus at 0300 every morning and the occasional pickup. Two km before Falealupo-tai on the road from Falealupo-uta is Moso's Footprint on the R near a banyan tree *(aoa).* The print, 3 m long,

is said to have been left when Moso, the war god, leaped from Samoa to Fiji. A few hundred m W is the trail on the R to deserted Fagalele Beach, where you can camp. As you proceed in to Falealupo-tai you'll notice a cave on the L just beside the road with a concrete stairway inscribed "welcome." As you stroll through the village, look to see if the woodcarvers are working in a shed adjoining the Catholic church. You may be asked to contribute $2 to the village if you spend the night in Falealupo-tai. A half-hour's walk beyond the village is palm-covered Cape Mulinu'u, shaped like an arrow aimed against Asia and the spirit land of Pulotu. This is Samoa's westernmost tip. No people live here so you could camp out on the lovely white beach. The track continues past Tufu, one km from the cape, to Neiafu on the main highway which you can walk in a couple of hours.

the north coast: The paved road ends at Asau, the main center on the N side of Savai'i. Attractive Asau has an airstrip on the breakwater enclosing Asau Bay, a wharf, a bank, and a large sawmill belonging to Samoa Forest Products. Continue E as best you can (see "Transport" below) and stop at Matavai where there's swimming in a large freshwater spring (mata ole alelo). The Samoan-language sign on the wall of the adjacent building refers to fines to be paid by villagers for certain misdeeds, not fees to be collected from visitors. Find more freshwater pools (vaisafe'e) at Safotu village, 3 km E of Matavai; you shouldn't have to pay for a look. Safotu also has a large Catholic church opposite a picturesque beach lined with small dugout fishing canoes. If you still haven't found a place to spend the night, follow the road inland from Safotu 3 km to Paia village and ask for the pulenu'u. He should be able to arrange lodging at about $10 pp including meals. There's a good lava tube (nu'uletau), the "short people's cave," about 3 km inland from Paia, to which the pulenu'u will provide guides and kerosene lamp for $2 admission. A stiff 2.5-hour walk inland from Paia is Mt. Matavanu (402 m), which the locals call mata ole afi (eye of the fire). This was the source of

the 1905-1911 volcanic outbreak which covered much of NE Savai'i with black lava. You don't really need a guide to find the crater—just look for a trail to the L where the road dips about 2.5 hours out of Paia. There's a slash on a tree opposite. Beware of deep crevices and crumbling edges as you near the crater which have claimed at least one life. You can also get here by walking up the lava field from the road inland beyond Vaipouli College, but this involves taking lots of water and running the risk of getting lost.

the lava field: The road S of Saleaula runs right across a wide barren lava flow. A large stone church, nearly engulfed by the lava at the beginning of the century, is on the NE side of the road under a large tree about 100 m off the road near the flow's N edge. The so-called Virgin's Grave is about 150 m E of the church near a mango tree. Look for a rectangular depression about 2 m deep in the lava; the grave is clearly visible at the bottom. Any of the local children will be able to lead you to these places for small change. As the fast-flowing pahoehoe lava approached the coast here, it built up behind the reef and spread out in both directions. The highway now runs across it for 8 km. Walk across the lava to get a feel of this awesome geological event. Mauga village is built around the edge of an ancient crater which itself was almost engulfed by the lava. There's a deep well in the crater's central depression.

the east coast: Picturesque villages and intermittent white beaches run all the way S from Pu'apu'a to the wharf. Lano is a favorite surfing beach in summer (Dec. to March), and there's good snorkeling at Faga. At Sapapalii is a large monument to John Williams in front of the large Congregational Christian Church. This marks the site where the missionary arrived in 1830 and was able to convert the local chiefs to Christianity in a couple of days. Not far beyond is the Safua Hotel (see "Accommodations" below), where you could stop for a well-deserved rest after your exciting journey around Savai'i.

ACCOMMODATIONS

There are 5 hotels on Savai'i. The Salafai Inn ($18 s, $25 d) is a European-style building beside Salelologa market/bus station, just a few minutes' walk from the wharf. Far better is the Safua Hotel at Lalomalava, 6 km N of the wharf, with 9 Samoan *fales* with private facilities in a garden setting. The rates (US$27 s, US$45 d, US$63 t) include all meals, served family-style at a long table bringing together guests and the gracious owner/hostess Moelagi Jackson. The food is excellent and Samoan specialties supplement the varied international cuisine at dinner. Sunday dinner is especially good. An informal bar faces a shady garden, a large library, and best of all, the hotel also caters to budget travelers. One of the units has been converted into a 4-bed dormitory *fale* at US$5 pp (meals extra); campers may pitch their tents at the hotel for US$2.50 pp and use the facilities. Just a few minutes' walk from the hotel is a large freshwater pool where you may swim (no charge). Moelagi's mother owns the large *fale* overlooking the pool, so hotel guests may take a siesta there. If you'd like to snorkel, take a bus 6 km N to Faga, depicted in many travel brochures. Motorscooters are available at US$15 a day, negotiable for shorter periods. Island tours by minibus are arranged, or just ask to be shown around the plantation. Moelagi, one of the very few female *failauga* in Samoa, is an expert on *tapa*-making and she usually keeps a few high-quality pieces on hand to sell.

others: The Savaiian Guest Fales, a 5-min. walk from the Safua Hotel, is marginally cheaper but nowhere comparable in quality and service—the food is inedible. Not recommended. At Salimu, 7 km N of Lalomalava, is the Amoa Hotel, under the same management as the Safua and similar in structure and price (but no dorm). There's another lovely freshwater pool across the road from the Amoa. The *fale* units are spacious and airy, each with a small stove and fridge. The Amoa Hotel is best for those considering a long stay—there's 20 percent off on a weekly basis, 30 percent off for a month. In Apia, telephone 920 and ask for the Safua Hotel to check bookings at either the Safua or the Amoa. Just 4 km W of Asau on the N coast of Savai'i, the Vaisala Hotel offers rooms in a European-style building overlooking the beach for $18 s, $25 d (they'll tell you all the singles are full). Although the double rooms are good with private bath and fridge (no cooking), meals in the restaurant are exorbitant, and the rental scooters and nautical gear unreliable. This place is hardly worth more than a one-night stand.

TRANSPORT

by air: Polynesian Airlines has several flights a day from Apia's Fagali'i airstrip (on the E side of town) to Maota ($16 OW), just W of Salelologa, and Asau ($32 OW). There are also frequent flights from Faleolo International Airport to Maota ($12 OW).

by ship: The Western Samoa Shipping Corporation operates car ferries between the wharfs at Mulifanua (Upolu) and Salelologa (Savai'i), departing from each end at about 0600, 0900, 1300, and 1600 daily, $2 pp each way. The actual departure times vary according to the weather, number of passengers, and whims of the crew, so arrive early and be prepared to wait. The trip takes 1.5 hours. On the way across you get a good view of Apolima Island's single village in the broken N side of its classic volcanic crater.

by bus: Bus service on Savai'i focuses on the wharf at Salelologa, with morning departures to almost any point on the island. They leave soon after a ferry arrives and you'll see as many as 5 buses all going the same way, one right after another, then none till another ferry comes in. Going back toward the ferry is even more inconvenient as middle-of-the-night departures from villages in the NW corner of Savai'i seem standard. For example, the only bus leaving Asau for the wharf via Matavai (N coast) starts out at 0300! A new paved highway from the wharf to Asau via Salailua

(S coast), built with Australian aid, makes travel up that side of the island easier. The E coast road is paved as far as the lava field near Samalaeulu, then still good as far as Sasina. Bus service between Sasina and the wharf is also reasonable. From Sasina to Asau there's only a steep gravel road, extremely rough in places. Getting across this stretch is the biggest challenge of a round-the-island excursion. One useful thing to know is that flatback trucks jammed with plantation laborers leave the sawmill at Asau for Sasina and beyond weekdays at 1600, and they're usually willing to give you a lift. Offer the driver a pack of cigarettes and you're on for sure. You can go right around Savai'i, visiting most of the places described above, in 3 or 4 days.

hitchhiking: There's no such thing as hitchhiking on Savai'i: truck drivers expect their passengers to pay. They only ask the equivalent of bus fare and make getting around a lot easier, so don't spoil things by not offering. There are already a few drivers who won't stop for *palagis* because of previous unpleasant encounters, which is rather tragic. To avoid any misunderstandings, however, ask the price as soon as the truck stops.

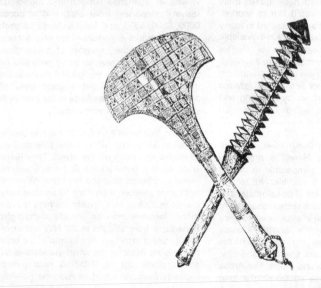

WALLIS AND FUTUNA

This little-known corner of Polynesia lies 600 km NE of Fiji and 300 km W of Samoa. Smallest of France's 3 South Pacific territories, Wallis and Futuna is isolated from its neighbors geographically, culturally, and politically. All the marks of French colonialism are here, from overpaid white officials controlling functionless staff to little French *gendarmes* in round peaked caps and shorts. Although weekly flights and a regular shipping service make the islands accessible from Noumea and Fiji, the lack of moderately priced facilities and resorts limits visitors to French officials, the eccentric, the adventuresome, and yachts' crews. Wallis and Futuna is still well off the beaten track.

the land: The islands of Wallis and Futuna, 250 km apart, are quite dissimilar. Wallis (150 sq km) is fairly flat, with gently sloping verdant hillsides rising to Mt. Lulu (145 m). There are freshwater crater lakes (Lalolalo, Kikila, and Lanutavake). The main island, Uvea, is surrounded by a barrier reef bearing 22 smaller islands, many with fine beaches.

Ships bound for Mata Utu wharf enter the lagoon through Honikulu Pass, the southernmost. Few fish remain in the broad lagoon—the locals have been fishing with dynamite. Futuna and Alofi, together totaling 115 sq km, are mountainous, with Mt. Puke on Futuna reaching 760 m. Though there are many freshwater springs on Futuna, Alofi, 2 km SE, is now uninhabited due to a lack of water. A reef fringes the N coast of Alofi; the

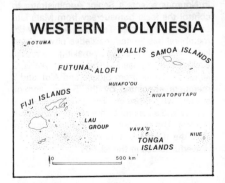

S coast features high cliffs. Futuna is completely surrounded by a narrow fringing reef. **climate:** The hurricane season on the islands is Nov. to March, and many form in the area between Wallis and Samoa. During the drier season, May to Oct., the islands are cooled by the refreshing SE trades.

history: Although these islands were discovered by the Polynesians thousands of years ago, not until 1616 did the Dutch navigators Schouten and Le Maire arrive at Futuna and Alofi. They named them the Hoorn Islands after their home port of Hoorn (now filled in) in the Zuider Zee. The name Cape Horn, S. America, is derived from the same old port. Captain Samuel Wallis of HMS *Dolphin* was the first European to contact Wallis (in 1767). American whalers began to visit from 1820 onward. Marist missionaries arrived on both Futuna and Wallis in 1837, and today the inhabitants are Catholic. Wallis was declared a French protectorate in 1886, Futuna in 1887. In 1924 the protectorate officially became a colony. Wallis was an important American military base from 1942 to 1944, with 6,000 troops on the island. Hihifo airport dates from the war, as does an abandoned airstrip just S of Lake Kikila. In a 1959 referendum, the populace voted to upgrade their status to that of an overseas territory, granted by the French Parliament in 1961.

government: The French high commissioner in Noumea selects a Senior Administrator to control the local bureaucracy from Mata Utu on Wallis. An elected Territorial Assembly (20 members) has limited legislative powers over local matters. The policy-making Territorial Council is comprised of the king of Wallis, 2 kings of Futuna (from Sigave and Alo), and 3 members appointed by the French administrator, who presides. The territory elects a deputy and a senator to the French Parliament in Paris. The traditional Polynesian monarchy and the Catholic Church continue to be powerful forces in the islands.

economy: The only exports are a maximum of about 50 tons of trochus shells a year. Of the 900 people employed on the island, 750 work for the French government. What they produce is perhaps the most invisible export of all—the illusion of colonial glory. The US$10 million annual budget mostly comes out of the pockets of French taxpayers, although some is collected in customs duties. French civil servants on Wallis make 3 times as much as they'd get back in France, plus a respectable lump sum upon completion of their 3-year contract. All prices on Wallis are set accordingly. The locals get free medical and dental care, and free education (in French) up to university level: with such French largesse, independence is unthinkable. Money also arrives in the form of remittances from Wallisian emigrants in New Caledonia. A plan to bring television and Club Med tourism to the territory was vetoed by the kings as dangerous outside influences. The locals grow most of their own food in the rich volcanic soils. Taro, manioc, and banana plantations are everywhere. All of the coconuts are used to feed the pigs. The coconut plantations on Wallis were destroyed by the rhinoceros beetle in the 1930s; this pest has now been brought under control. The plantations of Futuna were saved, but they only produce a couple of hundred tons of copra a year (also fed to pigs). Handicrafts are so expensive that it's actually profitable to bring things like *kava* bowls from Tonga or Fiji to sell *to* the Wallisians.

the people: The 8,000 people on Wallis and 6,000 on Futuna are Polynesian: the Wallisians descended from Tongans, the Futunans from Samoans. The Wallis Islanders are physically huge, bigger than Tongans. Another 12,000 people from both islands live and work in Noumea. These Wallisians and Futunans, recognizing the great difficulty of reintegrating themselves into their home islands, are strong supporters of French colonialism. Whole families migrate to New Caledonia, adding their numbers to the anti-independence faction. The many partially constructed and uninhabited dwellings on Wallis also reflect

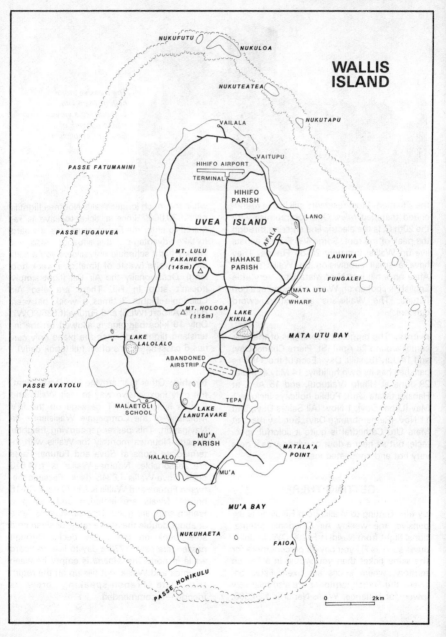

WALLIS ISLAND

NUKUFUTU

NUKULOA

NUKUTEATEA

NUKUTAPU

VAILALA

PASSE FATUMANINI

VAITUPU

HIHIFO AIRPORT

TERMINAL

HIHIFO PARISH

UVEA ISLAND

LANO

PASSE FUGAUVEA

AFALA

LAUNIVA

MT. LULU FAKAHEGA (145m)

HAHAKE PARISH

FUNGALEI

MATA UTU

WHARF

MT. HOLOGA (115m)

LAKE KIKILA

MATA UTU BAY

LAKE LALOLALO

ABANDONED AIRSTRIP

PASSE AVATOLU

TEPA

MALAETOLI SCHOOL

LAKE LANUTAVAKE

MU'A PARISH

MATALA'A POINT

HALALO

MU'A

MU'A BAY

NUKUHAETA

FAIOA

PASSE HONIKULU

0   2km

The massive stone hulk of Mata Utu Cathedral is a very visible bulwark of Gaulish Catholicism.

the situation. Most residents still live in round-ended thatched *fales*. One compromise with the 20th C. is the electric line entering through the peak of the roof. Some 400 French expats live on Wallis, but only 20 on Futuna. They have a small subdivision on Wallis named Afala on a hill just N of Mata Utu. Very little English is spoken on Wallis and none at all on Futuna. The Wallisians are expert sword dancers.

events: The biggest celebrations of the year center around 28 April (St. Pierre Chanel Day) and 14 July (Bastille Day). Each of the 3 Wallis parishes has its own holiday: 14 May at Mu'a, 29 June at Hihifo (Vaitupu), and 15 Aug. at Hahake (Mata Utu). Public holidays include 1 May (Labor Day), 1 Nov. (All Saints Day), and 11 Nov. (Remembrance Day). Sunday mass at Mata Utu Cathedral is quite a colorful spectacle, but sit near a door or window as it gets very hot and congested inside.

GETTING THERE

by air: Getting to Wallis from Fiji by air is expensive: the weekly Air Caledonie International flight from Nandi is F$208 OW. In dollar areas such as Fiji you pay 25 percent more for the same ticket than you would in a French territory, where prices are fixed. Fares between the French territories are also relatively lower: for instance, Wallis-Nandi is f.24,500,

while the much longer Wallis-Noumea flight is only f.30,600. Since a ticket-to-leave is required to enter the French territories, it's hard to take advantage of this situation. Also, the weekly flight schedule only allows you a half-day on Wallis (waste of time) or a week (too long). Occasionally the Air Cal flight simply doesn't stop in Fiji. There are also Air Caledonie flights 3 times a week between Hihifo Airport (WLS) and Futuna (f.6350 OW). Only 10 kilos baggage is allowed on the interisland flight and, since the plane only carries 6 passengers, it's often full (book early).

by ship: Other than arriving by private yacht, the only inexpensive way to visit Wallis and Futuna is to book RT passage on the MV *Moana II* of the Compagnie Wallisienne de Navigation. This passenger-carrying freighter departs Noumea monthly for Wallis with intermediate stops at Suva and Futuna. Fares are reasonable: Noumea-Wallis is f.14,610 deck, Suva-Wallis f.8348 deck. Passage between Futuna and Wallis is f.1170 deck (14-16 hours). Meals are included and, being a French ship, are good. One cabin is available at about double the above rates, or sleep on a steel bunk on the upper deck. Through passengers pay f.1770 a day to live on board while in port. The *Moana* is empty between Noumea and Wallis, but fills up on the return trip. The French-speaking crew is friendly—recommended.

PRACTICALITIES ON WALLIS

accommodations: Both hotels on Wallis are graceless concrete buildings with inflated rates. The Hotel Lomipeau beside the hospital has 15 a/c rooms with private bath at f.5500 s, f.6000 d, slight reduction if you stay a week. A super-expensive restaurant is on the premises. At f.4000 s, f.4500 d the Hotel Albatros near the airport is grossly overpriced. These places are meant for official visitors whose bills are paid by French taxpayers; they have little to offer anyone else. About the only alternative is

to camp in the interior; the Wallisians are hospitable, and a request for permission to camp sometimes leads to an invitation to stay.

food and shopping: Together, the 2 general stores at Mata Utu offer a reasonable selection of goods. Fresh meat is flown in from Noumea weekly. Drop in to the Bar Hatutori Molihina to meet Simi, a friendly Fijian, and Mele, his Wallisian wife. This is about the only place in town where you can speak English. There's a Centre Artisanal near the hospital selling handicrafts such as *tapa* cloth and handbags with plastic liners, and colored mats. The Philatelic Bureau adjoining Mata

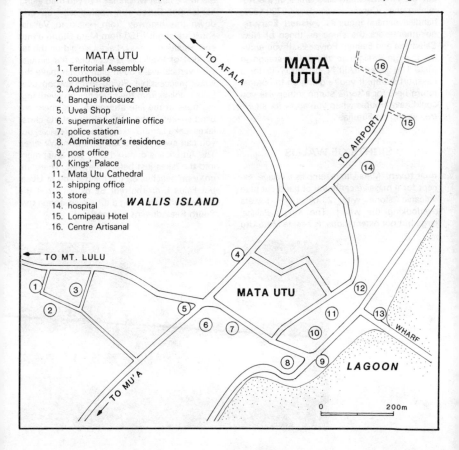

MATA UTU

1. Territorial Assembly
2. courthouse
3. Administrative Center
4. Banque Indosuez
5. Uvea Shop
6. supermarket/airline office
7. police station
8. Administrator's residence
9. post office
10. Kings' Palace
11. Mata Utu Cathedral
12. shipping office
13. store
14. hospital
15. Lomipeau Hotel
16. Centre Artisanal

WALLIS ISLAND

TO AFALA

MATA UTU

TO AIRPORT

TO MT. LULU

TO MU'A

MATA UTU

WHARF

LAGOON

0   200m

Utu Post Office sells first-day covers. Wallis and Futuna issues its own colorful postage stamps. Ask at the Uvea Shop in Mata Utu for cassettes of the music of the well-known Wallisian singer/composer Palisio Tuauli.

services: The Banque Indosuez at Mata Utu opens Mon., Tues., Thurs., and Fri. 0900-1200/1300-1500; why they close Wed. is anyone's guess. New Caledonian currency is used. Place long-distance calls at the post office near Mata Utu wharf. Mata Utu hospital offers free consultations from 0800-1000/ 1500-1600. The airline office is next to the supermarket. There's no tourist information but the Affaires Culturelles office in the Administrative Center (weekdays 0730-1330) handles general inquiries. **visas:** Entry requirements are the same as those of New Caledonia and Eastern Polynesia. If you arrive by ship go straight to the police station in Mata Utu (open 0700-1130/1500-1700) for a passport stamp. If you're going on to Futuna, return here for a *sortie* stamp, otherwise you could have trouble when you apply for an *entree* stamp on Futuna.

SIGHTS OF WALLIS

near town: Mata Utu resembles a village, except for a massive cathedral of hand-cut blue volcanic stone with 2 block-like towers overlooking the wharf. The King's Palace, large but not ostentatious, is beside Mata Utu

Cathedral. There are other massive stone churches at Mu'a and Vaitupu; the interior decoration of the one at Vaitupu is the best. A track up to the tiny chapel atop Mt. Lulu Fakahega (145 m) brings you to the highest point on the island. Take the road W from Mata Utu to the main N-S road in the center of the island: the track is on the L about 500 m N of the crossroads. From the summit the jungle-clad crater is fairly obvious, and you can descend to the taro plantation below along an easy trail. The view from Mt. Lulu Fakahega is good.

farther afield: Most of the villages are on the island's E coast which has a paved road along its length. Buses run sporadically up and down this highway from Halalo to Vailala. Fares are about f.150 from Mata Utu to either end. Hitching is easy. Lake Lalolalo on the far W side of Wallis is spectacular: it's circular with vertical walls 30-m high which make the water inaccessible. Flying foxes swoop over Lake Lalolalo from their perches on overhanging trees in the late afternoon, and there are blind snakes in the lake. Another of the crater lakes, Lake Lanutavake, is less impressive, but you can swim (approach it from the W side). The Americans dumped their war equipment into the lakes just before they left. There are no good beaches on the main island of Uvea, but Faioa I. on the reef SE of Mu'a has the white sands bordering a turquoise lagoon that South Seas dreams are made of.

Most Wallisians live in cool thatched fales of this kind.

FOOD PLANTS OF THE PACIFIC

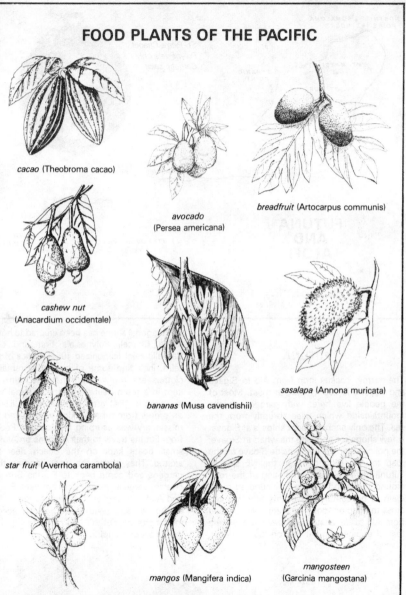

cacao (Theobroma cacao)

avocado
(Persea americana)

breadfruit (Artocarpus communis)

cashew nut
(Anacardium occidentale)

bananas (Musa cavendishii)

sasalapa (Annona muricata)

star fruit (Averrhoa carambola)

guava (Psidium guajava)

mangos (Mangifera indica)

mangosteen
(Garcinia mangostana)

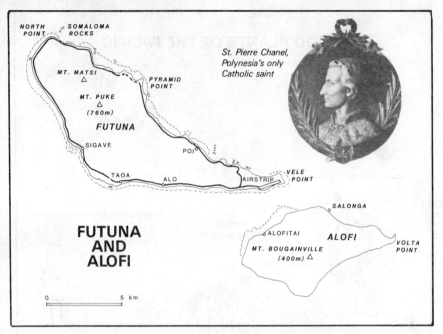

St. Pierre Chanel,
Polynesia's only
Catholic saint

FUTUNA
AND
ALOFI

0   5 km

FUTUNA

The narrow coastal strip from Alo to Sigave and beyond is 200 m wide at most. Most of the people live here, with gardens on the mountainside which rises abruptly from the sea. The only anchorage for ships is at Sigave. A few shops are opposite the wharf at Sigave; the police station is just outside Sigave on the road to Alo. High cliffs on the NE side of Futuna have delayed completion of the road around the island (only a few hundred m remain to be completed); at low tide you can cross the gap on foot. The steep, narrow road from Alo to the airstrip and beyond is quite a feat of engineering. At Poi, on the NE coast,

an octagonal shrine has been erected to honor Pierre Chanel, Polynesia's first and only Catholic saint (canonized 1954). Relics of the saint, including some of his bodily remains, clothes, and the war club that killed him, are kept in a room near the chapel. Chanel was martyred in 1841 after 4 years on the island, on orders from a native king who feared the missionary was usurping his position. People from Futuna travel to their gardens on Alofi in small boats kept on the beach near the airstrip. They spend the week tending their gardens and come back to Futuna Sun. for church. Large ships can pass between Futuna and Alofi, so long as they keep to the middle of the passage. With no organized accommodations on Futuna, plan on staying with the locals or camping.

TOKELAU

Tokelau, a dependency of New Zealand, consists of 3 large atolls 480 km N of Western Samoa (Tokelau means "north"). In British colonial times it was known as the Union Group. The central atoll, Nukunonu, is 92 km from Atafu and 64 km from Fakaofo. Swains I. (Olohenga), 200 km S of Fakaofo, traditionally belongs to Tokelau but is now part of American Samoa. Each atoll consists of a ribbon of coral *motus* (islets), 90 m to 6 km long and up to 200 m wide, enclosing a broad lagoon. At no point does the land rise more than 5 m above the sea. Together Atafu (3.5 sq km), Fakaofo (4 sq km), and Nukunonu (4.7 sq km) total only 12.2 sq km of dry land, but also 165 sq km of enclosed lagoons and 290,000 sq km of territorial sea. Life is relaxed in Tokelau. There are no large stores, hotels, restaurants, or bars, just plenty of sand and sun, coconuts, and a happy, friendly people. This is outer Polynesia at its best.

climate: There is little variation from the 28 degree C annual average temperature. Rainfall is irregular but heavy (2900 mm annually at Atafu); downpours of up to 80 mm in a single day are possible anytime. Tokelau is at the N edge of the main hurricane belt, and severe tropical storms are infrequent but occasionally devastating, sometimes sweeping through between Nov. and February.

history: Legend tells how the Maui brothers pulled 3 islands out of the ocean while fishing far from shore. Later the Polynesians arrived with taro, which supplemented the abundance of fish and coconuts. The warriors of Fakaofo brought the other atolls under the rule of the Tui Tokelau. The first European on the scene was Capt. Byron of HMS *Dolphin,* who saw Atafu in 1765. The U.S. Exploring Expedition of 1841 spent several days at Fakaofo. Catholic and Protestant missionaries arrived between 1845 and 1863. In 1863 Peruvian slavers kidnapped several hundred Tokelauans, including nearly all the able-bodied men, for forced labor in S. America. Those who resisted were killed. A terrible dysentery epidemic from Samoa hit Tokelau the same year. The British officially extended belated protection in 1877, but not until 1889, when it was decided that Tokelau might be of use in laying a transpacific cable, did Commander Oldham of the *Egeria* arrive to declare a formal protectorate. The British annexed their protectorate in 1916 and joined it to the Gilbert and Ellice Islands Colony. This distant arrangement ended in 1925 when New Zealand, which ruled Western Samoa at that time, became the administering power. With the Tokelau Act of 1948 N.Z. assumed full sovereignty and the islanders became N.Z. citizens.

government: The policy has been to disturb traditional institutions as little as possible. The Administrator of Tokelau is appointed by the N.Z. Ministry of Foreign Affairs and resides in Wellington. He works through the Office for Tokelau Affairs (the "Tokalani"), a liaison office in Apia, Western Samoa, and is represented on each island by a *faipule,* who is elected locally every 3 years. The Public Service on each island is controlled by an Administration Officer. All 3 atolls have a *pulenuku* (mayor), also elected for a 3-year term, who directs *nuku* (village) activities. Each island has a *taupulega* (island council) comprised of village elders or heads of families. Each *taupulega* chooses 15 delegates to the 45-member general *fono,* which meets twice a year on alternate islands. The *faipule* of the island on which the *fono* is meeting becomes chairman of that session. The *fono* has almost complete control over local matters. A Budgetary Advisory Committee of the *fono* decides how most N.Z. aid will be spent, subject to *fono* approval. There is talk of moving the Office for Tokelau Affairs from Apia to one of the atolls, but which? Although Fakaofo has an edge, there is great rivalry between the three. New Zealand would give Tokelau independence for the asking, but without a source of income it seems unlikely. Free association on the Niue model seems likely.

the changing village: The sandy soil and meager vegetation (only 61 species) force the Tokelauans to depend on the sea for protein. Coconut palms grow abundantly on the

motus: what isn't consumed is dried and exported as copra. *Pulaka* (swamp taro) is cultivated in man-made pits up to 2 m deep. Breadfruit is harvested from Nov. to March, and some bananas and papaya are also grown. Pandanus is used for making mats and other handicrafts, or thatching roofs; the fruit is also edible. Land and coconut crabs are a delicacy. Most land is held by family groups (*kainga*) and cannot be sold to outsiders. Now, as Tokelau enters a cash economy, imported canned and frozen foods are gaining importance. Aluminum motorboats are replacing dugout sailing canoes and when gasoline is scarce the islanders cannot travel to the *motus* to collect their subsistence foodstuffs. Also, the people now want appliances such as washing machines, electric irons, and freezers. European-style housing is becoming common as catchments from the tin roofs are used to alleviate water shortages. The changing values have meant a decline in traditional sharing. Outboard motors and electricity cost money: the rising standard of living has paralleled an increasing dependency on aid and remittances from New Zealand.

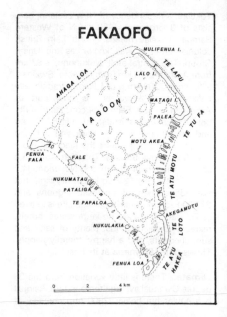

Passengers and cargo waiting to disembark from the supply ship Avondale *at Atafu.*

economy: In Tokelau today the 182 government jobs funded by New Zealand are the only regular source of monetary income. Almost all these jobs are held by Tokelauans—there are few resident expatriates. To avoid the formation of a privileged class, these positions are rotated among the community. Taxes collected from wage earners are used to subsidize copra and handicraft production, thereby further sharing the wealth. Island families provide for their old and disabled. Apart from copra and a trickle of handicrafts, Tokelau earns money from the sale of postage stamps and coins. Yet limited resources have prompted many islanders to emigrate to New Zealand. Tokelauans are not eligible for N.Z. welfare payments unless they live in New Zealand and pay N.Z. taxes. They may now receive their pensions in Tokelau, however, and this should stimulate return migration. Yet imports exceed exports by 5 times, and the N.Z. subsidy is 5 times greater than all locally-raised revenue. The U.N. Development Program also provides aid. The latest source of revenue is licensing fees from big American purse seiners which pull tuna from Tokelau's 200-nautical-mile Exclusive Economic Zone (EEZ). Inshore waters within 40 km of the reef are reserved for local fishermen. New Zealand has declared that all income from the EEZ will go to Tokelau.

the people: The Tokelauans are closely related to the people of Tuvalu. In 1983 there were 594 people on Atafu, 633 on Fakaofo, and 368 on Nukunonu, totaling 1,595. Another 3,000 Tokelauans live in New Zealand, the result of a migration which began in 1963 following overpopulation in Tokelau itself. To be in the lee of the SE trades, the villages are on the W side of each atoll. Due to the work of early missionaries, Atafu is Congregationalist (LMS), Nukunonu Catholic, and Fakaofo a combination of the two. Since the Samoan Bible is used, all adults understand Samoan. Young people learn English at school, but everyone speaks Tokelauan at home. In Tokelau, authority is based on age rather than lineage. Arguably, nowhere else in the world are senior citizens as respected.

PRACTICALITIES

getting there: The only way to go is on a ship chartered by the Office for Tokelau Affairs, leaving Apia, Western Samoa, for the 3 atolls every 2 months, taking about 2 days to reach the first island or 7-8 days RT. Cabin class is $190 RT, deck class $50 RT, including meals. Deck passengers can take cabin-class meals for a little extra. Tokelauans and officials get priority on these trips, and tourists are only taken if there happens to be any space left over. Advance reservations from tourists are not accepted and cabins will be confirmed only a week prior to sailing. Check with the Office for Tokelau Affairs when you reach Apia—you might get lucky. The seaplane service to Tokelau was suspended in 1983, but there's talk of building an airstrip on Fenua Fala (Fakaofo).

internal transport: Passages for small boats have been blasted through the reefs, but ships must stand offshore; passengers and cargo

are transferred to the landings in aluminum whale boats. In offshore winds there is poor anchorage at Fakaofo and Nukunonu, and none at all off Atafu. For safety's sake, interatoll voyages by canoe are prohibited. There are no cars or trucks in Tokelau, but most canoes are now fitted with outboards.

accommodations: Since there aren't any hotels or rest houses, you have to stay with a family. To stay on an island between ships you must first obtain an entry permit from the Office for Tokelau Affairs. They will cable the island council for permission, and you'll pay for food and accommodations, about US$5 pp a day minimum. You could also write in advance to the *faipule* or *pulenuku* of the island of your choice to let them know your intentions—having a contact or local friend makes everything easier. When you go, take along a bottle of spirits for whoever made the arrangements, as well as gifts for the family. Suggested items are rubber thongs, housewares, tools, fishing gear (galvanized fish hooks, fishing line, swivels, sinkers, lures, mask and snorkel, and spear-gun rubbers),

weaving preparation

reef fishing

canoe making

a kitchen

and perhaps a rugby or volleyball. The women will appreciate perfumes, deodorants, cosmetics, and printed cloth. Kitchen knives and enamel mugs are always welcome. Ask at the Office for Tokelau Affairs about agricultural import restrictions. You'll probably have to sleep on the floor and use communal toilets over the lagoon—there'll be little privacy. Most families own land on one of the *motus,* so you could spend a few days camping on your own if you have a tent and large enough water container.

food: There's only one cooperative store on each atoll, selling rice, flour, sugar, tinned fish and meat, spaghetti, gasoline, etc. Take as much food as you can— bags of taro, a sack of bananas, fruit such as pineapples and mangoes, garlic, instant coffee, and tea. Cigarettes are in short supply and camera film is not available. Only the coop on Nukunonu (and possibly Fakaofo) sells liquor. Instead, the locals drink sour toddy. This is obtained by cutting the flower stem of a coconut tree and collecting the sap in a half-coconut container. The whitish fluid (*kaleve*) has many uses. It can be drunk fresh, or boiled and stored in a fridge. If kept in a container at room temperature for 2 days it ferments into sour toddy beer. Boil fresh *kaleve* to a brown molasses for use in cooking or as a sauce. A tablespoon of boiled *kaleve* in a cup of hot water makes an island tea. You can even make bread out of it by adding saltwater, flour, and fat, as all Tokelauan women know.

money and health: Although the N.Z. dollar is the "official" currency, the Western Samoan *tala* is commonly used on the islands. A limited number of Tokelauan one-*tala* coins are issued each year. You can change money at the administration center on each island. There's a hospital on all 3 atolls and treatment is free. Take a remedy for diarrhea. **information:** The quarterly newsletter *Te Vakai Tokelau* contains a wealth of interesting information about the islands. To subscribe send US$5 to: Official Secretary, Office for Tokelau Affairs, Box 865, Apia, Western Samoa.

conduct and custom: In Tokelau, as elsewhere, conduct is mostly common sense.

Take care not to expect better service or facilities than anyone else. Avoid causing a disturbance. Keep in mind that you're a guest in someone's home. Bad reports or complaints could well deprive others of the opportunity to visit. Step aside for the elders and *never* tell them what to do. When passing in front of another person, bow slightly and say *tolou*. If people invite you into a house for a cup of coffee or a meal, politely refuse saying that you have just finished eating. Such invitations are usually only a form of greeting, and they may not even have what is offered. If they insist a second or third time, or it's someone you know quite well, then they probably mean it. Sit on the mat with your legs crossed or folded, not stretched out. Village men work together a day or 2 a week on communal projects. Join in with the group or you'll feel left out, not fitting into the community. You should also accompany your hosts to church on Sunday. Overt flirtations with members of the opposite sex are frowned on. If you feel an attraction, simply mention it to one of his/her friends and the word will be passed on. There's a 2300 curfew in the villages, although this can be flexible on Nukunonu.

THE ISLANDS

Atafu: The smallest of the atolls, Atafu's lagoon totals only 17 sq km (compared to 50 sq km at Fakaofo and 98 sq km at Nukunonu). This is perhaps the most traditional of the islands with the greatest number of dugout canoes. The village is at the NW corner of the atoll. There's a ceramic history of Tokelau on the side wall of Matauala Public School. Atafu is officially "dry," but a homebrew of yeast and sugar compensates. Be prepared for a $35 fine if you get caught partaking.

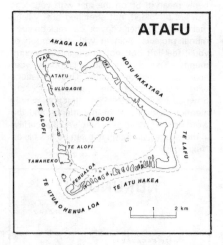

ATAFU

AHAGA LOA

VAO

ATAFU

ULUGAGIE

TE ALOFI

TE ALOFI

TAMAHEKO

FENUALOA

TE UTUA O HENUA LOA

MOTU HAKATAGA

TE LE FO

LAGOON

TE LAFU

TE ATU HAKEA

0   1   2 km

Nukunonu: This is the largest island in both land and lagoon area. Since Nukunonu is Catholic (see the large stone church), life is less restrictive than on the Congregationalist islands. The village is divided into 2 parts by a reef passage spanned by a bridge. No dugout canoes are left on Nukunonu; everyone has switched to aluminum outboards. The rhinoceros beetle, a pest which attacks coconut trees, has established itself here. Luhi'ano Perez, headmaster of the local school, can answer questions about the atoll.

Fakaofo: Some 400 people live on tiny 4.5-ha Fale I., which is well shaded by breadfruit trees. In 1960, a second village was established on the larger island of Fenua Fala, about 3 km NW, to relieve the overcrowding. At low tide you can walk across the reef between the two. The school and hospital are now on Fenua Fala. An ancient coral slab erected to the god Tui Tokelau stands in the meeting house at Fale. This stone may once have exercised supernatural power, but the head you see on it today is a recent addition. On the lagoon-side beach opposite the *hakava* (family meeting place) is a huge rock once used to crush wrongdoers, which takes a dozen men to lift. Guano, a fertilizer formed from bird droppings, is collected on Palea, a tiny *motu* on the E side of the atoll, for use in nearby taro pits. Pigs swim and forage for shellfish in pools on the reef near the settlements on Fakaofo (the only swimming pigs in the Pacific).

One of the largest of all insects, the rhinoceros beetle (Dynastinae) *menaces the coconut plantations of the South Pacific.*

above, clockwise: *yanggona (kava),* Fiji (D. Stanley); red ginger, American Samoa (U.S. Fish and Wildlife Service photo by Gerald M. Ludwig); silversword, Haleakala National Park, Maui, Hawaii (National Park Service photo); taro, Keanae, Maui, Hawaii (D. Stanley); dipladenia, Tahiti (Robert K. Yarnell)

above, clockwise: rainforest at Fuipisia Falls, Upolu, Western Samoa (Traugott Goll); Nu'utele I. seen from Upolu, Western Samoa (Traugott Goll); Pola I., American Samoa (U.S. Fish and Wildlife Service photo by Gerald M. Ludwig); Mouaroa (Shark's Tooth), Moorea, Eastern Polynesia (Paul Bohler); Lano Beach, Savai'i, Western Samoa (Traugott Goll)

TUVALU

One of the smallest independent nations in the world, Tuvalu was known as the Ellice Islands until quite recently. The name Tuvalu means "cluster of 8," although there are actually 9 islands in all. Niulakita, the smallest, was resettled by people from Niutao in 1949. This remote group of low coral atolls gets only about a hundred tourists a year, yet the outer islands of Tuvalu are among the most unspoiled and idyllic in the Pacific. For the culturally-sensitive visitor, Tuvalu might be as far from the worrisome modern world as you can get.

the land: Legend tells how an eel *(te Pusi)* and a flatfish *(te Ali)* were carrying home a heavy rock and began to quarrel. The eel killed the flatfish and fed on his body, just as the tall coconut trees still feed on the round flat islands. Then *te Pusi* broke the rock into 8 pieces and disappeared into the sea. The 9 islands that make up Tuvalu today total about 25 sq km in land area, curving NW-SE in a chain 579 km long. Funafuti, the administrative center, is over 1,000 km N of Suva, Fiji. All are true atolls under 4 m high with central lagoons, except Nanumanga,

Niutao, and Niulakita, which are without lagoons. Ships can enter the lagoons at Nukufetau and Funafuti; elsewhere they must stand offshore.

climate: The trade winds blow from the E much of the year. October to March, the hurricane season, experiences strong W winds and considerably more rain. Hurricanes are rare but not unknown, and most storms come out of the south. Otherwise, few seasonal variations disturb the warm, tropical weather.

history: The Polynesians colonized Tuvalu some 2,000 years ago; Samoans occupied the southern atolls, while Tongans were more active in the north. Groups of warriors also arrived from Kiribati, and their language is still spoken on Nui. Polynesian migrants reached the outliers of the Solomons and the Carolines from bases in Tuvalu. Although the Spaniard Mendana reportedly saw some of the islands in the 16th C., regular European contact did not occur until the 19th century. Blackbirders kidnapped about 500 people from Nukulaelae and Funafuti in 1863 to dig guano on the

TUVALU

NANUMEA

NANUMANGA NIUTAO

NUI

VAITUPU

NUKUFETAU

TUVALU AT A GLANCE

FUNAFUTI

	POPULATION (1979)	AREA (ha.)
Nanumea	844	361
Nanumanga	605	310
Niutao	866	226
Nui	603	337
Vaitupu	1,273	509
Nukufetau	626	307
Funafuti	2,120	254
Nukulaelae	347	166
Niulakita	65	41
	7,349	2,511

NUKULAELAE

NIULAKITA

0   175 km

islands off Peru. None returned. In 1863 a Cook Islander named Elekana was washed up on Nukulaelae. He taught Christianity to the islanders and, after reporting back to missionaries in Samoa, returned in 1865 with an organized LMS missionary party. Soon, most Tuvaluans were converted, and they remained under the spiritual guidance of Samoan pastors right up to 1969. To keep out American traders, Britain declared a protectorate over Tuvalu in 1892, upgrading it to colonial status in 1916. In 1896-98 scientists sent by the Royal Society of London conducted experimental drillings at Funafuti to test Darwin's theory of atoll formation. The colonial period was fairly uneventful, except for the American military bases established at Funafuti, Nukufetau, and Nanumea during WW II. Tuvalu was spared the trauma of a Japanese invasion, although Japanese planes did drop a few bombs.

recent history and government: Until 1975, Tuvalu was part of the Gilbert and Ellice Islands Colony. In the early '70s the Polynesian Ellice Islanders expressed their desire to

separate from the Micronesian Gilbertese and proceed towards true independence. In a 1971 referendum, the Tuvaluans voted overwhelmingly to become a separate unit. Britain acceded to the wish in 1975, and on 1 Oct 1978, after only 5 months of full internal self-government, Tuvalu became a fully independent nation. Tuvalu has a 12-member elected parliament headed by a prime minister. A Tuvaluan governor general represents the British Crown. Island councils provide local government on each island. In 1979, soon after independence, American real estate speculators arrived in Tuvalu. When they found they were prohibited by law from purchasing land, they decided to sell the natives land in the United States. Incredibly, several islands such as Nanumanga invested their entire savings in worthless Texas plots. A lot of good will left over from WW II went out the window in this outrageous swindle.

economy: About 84 percent of the population are engaged in subsistence agriculture and fishing. Only small quantities of copra are exported while most food, fuel, and manufactured goods are imported. This negative balance of trade makes Tuvalu totally dependent on outside aid, provided mostly by Britain and Australia. Remittances from Tuvaluans working in Nauru and elsewhere are also important. The economy is extremely simple: the sale of postage stamps to collectors, for example, provides a quarter of government revenue. There is great potential for a skipjack tuna industry but fisheries development has mostly been limited to the extraction of licensing fees from offshore Asian fishing boats. Nor has anything been done to promote tourism. Tuvalu seems in no hurry to join the 20th century.

the people: All 9 islands are inhabited, with a single village on each outer island. Over 80 percent of the people on the outer islands still live in traditional-style housing. The life of the people is hard—only coconuts and pandanus grow naturally, though bananas, pawpaws, and breadfruit are cultivated. A variety of taro *(pulaka)* has to be grown in pits excavated from coral rock. Reef fish and tuna add protein to the diet; pork and chicken are eaten on special occasions. The population density (294 persons per sq km) is one of the highest in the world and growing quickly. While some 8,364 people (1983) live in Tuvalu, another 1,500 Tuvaluans are employed overseas in the phosphate works on Nauru, or as crew on foreign ships. Mostly Polynesian, related to the Samoans and Tongans, their ancestry is evident in their language, architecture, and customs. Nui I. is an exception with some Micronesian influence. Some 50 expatriates live in Funafuti (compared to only 2 before independence). Most are advisers, missionaries, and Peace Corps. The Tuvaluan language is almost identical to that spoken on neighboring Tokelau, Futuna, and Wallis.

events: Public holidays include the Queen's Birthday (June) and Prince Charles' Birthday (Nov.). National Children's Day (4 Aug.) features kids' sports and crafts; dancing and a parade on Funafuti airstrip mark Independence Day (1 Oct.). Local Funafuti holidays include Bomb Day, which commemorates 23 April 1943, when a Japanese

bomb fell through Funafuti's church roof and destroyed the interior. An American corporal had shooed 680 villagers out of the building only moments before, thus averting a major tragedy. On 21 Oct., Hurricane Day, Tuvaluans recall 1972's terrible Hurricane Bebe.

PRACTICALITIES

getting there: Fiji Air flies to Funafuti (FUN) 3 times a week from Suva (F$250 OW). Local Europeans congregate at the airstrip when the flight comes in (a sure sign of the limited activities on Funafuti). The plane only carries 6 passengers; even if you're told it's fully booked months ahead, you've got a good chance of getting on simply by showing up at Suva airport. Beware of getting bumped in Funafuti, however. Air Tungaru has an on-off flight to Tarawa (A$300 OW), making Tuvalu a possi-

This Tuvaluan, strips of pandanus around head and waist, came aboard a ship of the U.S. Exploring Expedition which visited Nukufetau in 1841.

ble stopover between Fiji and Kiribati. Air Tungaru, however, is unreliable. Tuvalu collects a $5 departure tax. There's a ship to Tarawa 4 times a year. For details of the supply boat from Fiji ask at the Tuvalu High Commission in Suva. In Funafuti, ask about ships at the Fusi (Coop), 500 m S of the wharf.

getting around: The ship *Nivanga* makes the rounds of the islands roughly every 6 weeks. Meals are provided for cabin passengers (A$90 RT); the 60-odd deck passengers (A$30 RT) bring their own food. The ship only stops at each atoll for about an hour, depending on tides. If you decide to stop off at one of the islands, you may be there up to 2 months before the ship returns. A seaplane service was discontinued due to lack of funds (the Peace Corps withdrew from the outer islands at the same time). A minibus runs between the government center at Vaiaku and the new wharf on Funafuti: 20 cents pp for the 3 km. The taxi charges 50 cents per km.

accommodations: The only hotel in the country is the 7-room Vaiaku Langi Hotel near the Funafuti airstrip: $25 s, $36 d, plus $18 a day for bland meals (bring your own salt and pepper shakers). The Church of Tuvalu Guesthouse near the Fusi at Funafuti is $12 pp for up to 4 people. The Guesthouse is pleasant with good cooking and laundry facilities. All outer islands have guest houses run by the island councils where you can stay for $6 pp including meals. It is *essential* to announce your arrival by sending a telegram to the particular island council (you'd get there before a letter). Don't count on being able to buy *any* imported goods on the outer islands: take what you need with you.

food: The only restaurants are on Funafuti. The Supu Cafe offers such specialties as fish in coconut cream and heart of banana (from the purple leaf surrounding the flower). The Vaiaku Langi offers a good fish-and-chip lunch for a dollar. *Pulaka* (swamp taro) is eaten boiled, roasted, or made into pudding. Breadfruit, a staple, is boiled with coconut cream, baked, or fried in oil as chips. Plantain (cooking bananas) may also be boiled or chipped.

Sweet potatoes, though becoming popular, are still only served on special occasions. Fish is eaten every day, both white fish and tuna; pork, chicken, and eggs add a little variety. Reddish-colored fish caught in the lagoons may be poisonous. If you're interested in fishing, make it known and someone will take you out in their canoe. Imported foods such as rice, corned beef, and sugar are used in vast amounts. When eating on the outer islands ask for some of the local dishes such as *laulu* or *lolo* (a leaf in coconut cream, not unlike spinach and delicious), *palusami* (*laulu*, onions, and fish, usually wrapped in banana leaves), *uu* (coconut crab, only readily available on Nukulaelae and Nukufetau), and *ula* (crayfish). Quench your thirst with *pi* (drinking coconut), *kaleve* (coconut toddy, generally extracted morning and night), or supersweet coffee and tea. Water is scarce everywhere.

entertainment: Tuvaluans love dancing, be it their traditional *fatele,* more energetic than Gilbertese dancing, or the predictable twist.

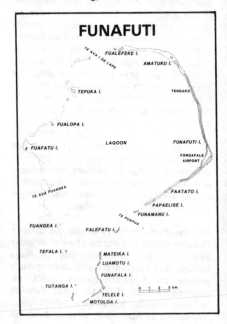

FUNAFUTI

Traditional dancing is performed on special occasions such as opening a building, greeting special visitors, or holidays. Get in on the singing, dancing, and general frivolity taking place at the *maneapas* (community halls) almost every night. On Funafuti migrants from each outer island have their own *maneapa,* so ask around to find out if anything is on. Or just listen for the rhythmic sounds and head that way. Many people wear flower garlands in their hair. On Funafuti movies are shown 3 times a week in 3 of these halls, admission 50 cents (good audience reactions). Catch the singing in the church on Sunday. Cricket and football are played on Funafuti airstrip on weekends, as is *te ano*—a sort of 50-a-side elongated volleyball.

shopping: Bring plenty of film as none is sold locally. Bring coffee too—it's priced out of reach here. The Fusi (Coop) carries staples such as rice, flour, and sugar, but on the outer islands they're often sold out. Local handicrafts such as baskets, mats, fans, necklaces, and model canoes can be purchased at a stall by the airstrip on Funafuti. Excellent maps of each of the atolls are available from the Lands Dept. above the Library and Archives building. **money:** Australian currency is used with Tuvaluan coins. Credit cards are not accepted. The National Bank of Tuvalu at Funafuti charges $1 commission to change travelers cheques. **communications:** A radio telephone links Tuvalu with the outside world through Fiji (open 0830-1530 weekdays). To call Funafuti, ask for the Fiji International Exchange. This can be difficult from the Northern Hemisphere at times, for they tend not to believe that there is such a place as Funafuti! **health:** There's a hospital on Funafuti but only dressers on the outer islands. Cholera, hepatitis, dengue fever, and tuberculosis are occasional problems. **visas:** Funafuti is the only port of entry. No visa is required but make sure you have an onward ticket, or it's a long swim back to Fiji. The maximum stay is 4 months.

conduct: If you're planning on stopping at an outer island, take along things like sticks of tobacco, cigarettes, matches, chewing gum, volleyballs, T-shirts, cloth, and cosmetics to give as gifts. Don't hand them out at random as if you're Santa Claus—give them quietly to people you know as a form of reciprocation. It's the custom. Scanty dress is considered offensive everywhere so carry a *sulu* to wrap around you. Women should cover their legs when seated. Never stand upright before seated people, and try to enter a house or *maneapa* shoeless, from the lagoon side rather than the ocean side. A lovely but nearly extinct custom is to carry a piece of green vegetation as you walk through the village to indicate that you're a friend. As one of the very few visitors you will be granted many privileges you do not deserve. Don't abuse the situation.

THE ISLANDS OF TUVALU

Funafuti: Over a quarter of the population of Tuvalu live on Funafuti and more arrive continuously in search of government jobs. Government offices (good library) are at Vaiaku, 200 m W of the airstrip; the Fusi (Coop) is a km NE; and the new (1981) deepwater wharf is a little over a km beyond that. Most of the homes are prefabs put up after the hurricane in 1972. The same storm left a beach of coral boulders along the island's E side. The Americans built the big airstrip during WW II. They excavated a lot of material from the N part of the atoll; quite a few wrecked cranes can still be seen. At the N end of Funafuti I. is a white sandy beach on the lagoon side (the hotel has bicycles for guests). Farther N is the Tuvalu Maritime Training School, which prepares young Tuvaluans for employment on ocean-going ships. If you wish to visit, radio the captain superintendent in advance from the Ministry of Social Services, Government Building. At low tide you can walk across the reef to Amatuku. Of the outlying *motus* on the atoll's coral ring, Funafala, Tepuka, and Fualefeke are inhabited. Te Ava Fuangea is the deepest (13 m) of the 3 passages into the Funafuti lagoon; the others are only about 8 m deep. Navigation within the lagoon is dangerous due to uncharted shoals, so yachts should proceed carefully along the marked channel to the anchorage off Fongafale.

Nukufetau: Unlike Funafuti's, the lagoon at Nukufetau is relatively safe for navigation. The Americans constructed a wartime airstrip and wharf on Motolalo, 8 km E of the present village. Quite a bit of debris remains.

Vaitupu: In 1905 the London Missionary Society opened a primary school at Motufoua on Vaitupu to prepare young men for entry into the seminary in Samoa. Over the years this has developed into the large church/government secondary school, the only one in Tuvalu. There are a few expatriates. In 1946 the *matai* (chiefs) of Vaitupu purchased Kioa Island in Fiji, where some 300 Vaitupu people now live.

Nanumea: A wartime U.S. landing craft still sits wrecked on the reef. Other aircraft wreckage (mainly B-24s) is strewn around the island. If you have a head for heights, climb the spire of the church—the view is worth it, but get permission from the pastor first.

Waterproof boxes of this kind kept a fisherman's valuables dry.

FIJI ISLANDS

INTRODUCTION

Fiji is the perfect place to go native. You begin to feel the happiness and warmth of this country as soon as you get beyond the airport. You immediately fall in love with Fiji's vibrant, exuberant people. In Fiji the smiles are always genuine and hospitality comes from the heart. Once notorious as the "Cannibal Isles," Fiji is now the multiracial crossroads of the Pacific: 5,000 km SW of Hawaii and 3,000 km NE of Sydney, in the middle of the main air route between N. America and Australia. There's a diverse beauty among the 322 islands that make up the Fiji Group. Over 100 are inhabited by Melanesians, East Indians, Polynesians, Micronesians, Chinese, and Europeans living in harmony, each with a cuisine and lifestyle of their own. *Mbula*, welcome to Fiji, everyone's favorite South Pacific country.

the land: The name Fiji is a Tongan corruption of the indigenous name "Viti." The Fiji Islands are arrayed in a horseshoe configuration with Viti Levu ("Great Fiji") and adjacent islands on the W, Vanua Levu ("Great Land") and Taveuni at the N, and the Lau Group on the east. This upside-down U-shaped archipelago encloses the Koro Sea, which is relatively shallow and sprinkled with more islands. Together the Fiji Is. are scattered over l,290,000 sq km of the South Pacific Ocean. The 2 largest islands, Viti Levu and Vanua Levu, together account for 87 percent of Fiji's l8,376 sq km of land. Most of the Fiji Is. are volcanic, remnants of a sunken continent. While fringing reefs are common along most of the coastlines, Fiji is outstanding for its many barrier reefs. The Great Sea Reef off the N coast of Vanua Levu is one of the largest in the world and the Astrolabe Reef N of Kandavu is one of the most colorful. The many cracks and crevices along Fiji's reefs are guaranteed to delight the scuba diver.

climate: The best time to go is June to Oct. when the SE trade winds prevail. In Feb. and March the wind often comes directly from the

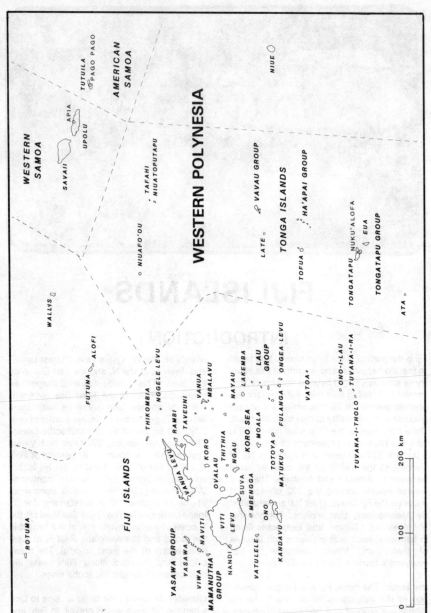

FIJI AT A GLANCE

ISLAND	AREA (SQ KM)	HIGHEST POINT (M)	POPULATION (EST. MID-1983)	PERCENT FIJIAN ★
Viti Levu	10,429	1,323	508,777	40.5
Vanua Levu	5,556	1,032	117,790	43.3
Taveuni	470	864	8,799	72.7
Kandavu	411	838	9,936	98.1
Ngau	140	747	3,054	99.4
Koro	104	522	3,654	98.5
Ovalau	101	626	6,660	88.3
Rambi	69	463	2,771	5.0
Rotuma	47	256	3,204	1.9
Mbengga	36	439	1,488	98.6

★ Viti Levu, Vanua Levu, and Taveuni have sizeable Fiji Indian populations, while Rambi is Micronesian and Rotuma is Polynesian.

east, and dumps 3,000 mm of annual rainfall on the SE coasts of the big islands, increasing to 5,000 mm inland. The NW coasts, in the lee, get only 1,500 to 2,000 mm. The official dry season (June to Oct.) is not always dry at Suva, although most of the rain falls at night. In addition, Fiji's winter (May to Nov.) is cooler than its summer, the best months for mountain trekking. December to March is hurricane season, with Fiji, Samoa, and Tonga receiving up to 5 storms annually. Even then the refreshing tradewinds relieve the high humidity.

flora: There are over 3,000 species of plants in Fiji, a third of them endemic. The wetter sides of the large islands are heavily forested, with occasional thickets of bamboo. On the drier sides open savannah predominates. Take care when evaluating the difficulty of climbing a grassy hill from a distance. Whereas in Europe the grass might be up to your knees, in Fiji it could be up to your neck.

fauna: One of the more unusual creatures found in Fiji and Tonga is the banded iguana, a lizard which lives in trees and can grow up to 70 cm long (two-thirds of which is tail). The iguanas are emerald green, and the male is easily distinguished from the female by his bluish-grey cross stripes. Banded iguanas change color to control their internal temperature, becoming darker when in the direct sun. Their nearest relatives are found in S. America and Madagascar, and no lizards live farther E in the Pacific than these. In 1979 a new species, the crested iguana, was discovered on Yanduatambu, a small island off the W coast of Vanua Levu. Two species of snakes inhabit Fiji: the very rare, poisonous *bolo loa,* and the Pacific boa, which can grow up to 2 m long. The land and tree-dwelling native frogs are noteworthy for the long suction discs on their fingers and toes. Because they live deep in the rainforest and feed at night, they are seldom seen. The only native mammals are the flying fox and the rat. Four of the world's 7 species of sea turtles nest in Fiji: the green, hawksbill, loggerhead, and leatherback. Nesting occurs from Nov. to Feb. at night when there is a full moon and a high tide. The female struggles up the beach and lays as many as 100 eggs in a hole which she digs and then covers with her hind flippers. The eggs are protected by law in Fiji, as are leatherback turtles, turtles with shells under 46 cm long, and all turtles during the nesting season. Persons who take eggs or turtles at this time are violating the Fisheries Act and face heavy fines. There are 22 endemic species of birds in Fiji and birds, eggs, and nests are fully protected.

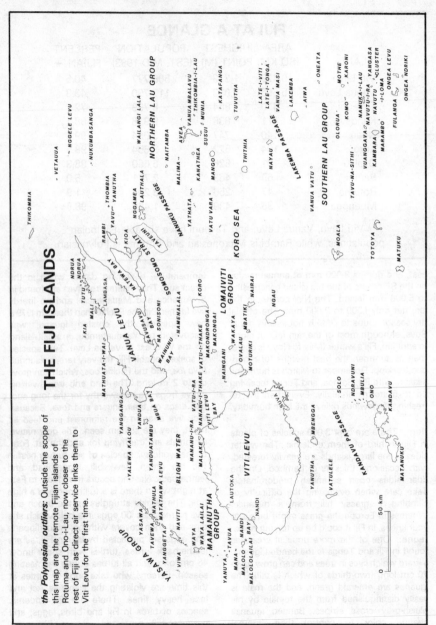

THE FIJI ISLANDS

the Polynesian outliers: Outside the scope of this map are the remote Fijian islands of Rotuma and Ono-i-Lau, now closer to the rest of Fiji as direct air service links them to Viti Levu for the first time.

THIKOMBIA

VETAUUA

NGGELE LEVU
NUKUMBASANGA

NDRUA
NDRUA

RAMBI
KIOA
TUTU

THOMBIA
YAVU
YANUTHA

NORTHERN LAU GROUP

NAITAMBA

WAILANGI LALA

AVEA
VANUA MBALAVU
THIKOMBIA-I-LAU
MUNIA

LATE-I-VITI
LATE-I-TONGA
VANUA MASI

ONEATA

MOTHE
KOMO
KARONI

OLORUA

NAMUKA-I-LAU
NAVUTU-I-RA
YANGASA
CLUSTER

VUANGGAVA
KAMBARA
MARAMBO

NAVUTU
-I-LOMA
ONGEA LEVU
ONGEA NDRIKI

FULANGA

SOUTHERN LAU GROUP

LAKEMBA PASSAGE
LAKEMBA
AIWA

NAYAU

TAVU-NA-SITHI

MASKA
MALIMA
KANATHEA
SUSUI
KATAFANGA

YATHATA
VATU VARA

NGAMEA
LAUTHALA

NANUKU PASSAGE

SOMOSOMO
STRAIT

TAVEUNI

SKIA
MALI
LAMBASA

MATHUATA-I-WAI

VANUA LEVU

SAVUSAVU
BAY
NA SONISONI

WAINUNU BAY

NAMENALALA

KORO

VANUA VATU
THITHIA

KORO SEA

MOALA

TOTOYA

MATUKU

NAINGANI
OVALAU
MOTURIKI

MBATIKI
WAKAYA

LOMAIVITI
GROUP

NGAU

MAKONGAI
MAKONDRONGA

NAIRAI

NAMEWA BAY
NDRUA

YANGGANGA

YADUA

YALEWA KALOU

YANDUATAMBU
YANDUATAHAWA LEVU

MBUA BAY

BLIGH WATER

NANANU-I-RA
MALAKE
VITI LEVU
BAY

NANANU-I-THAKE
VATU-I-THAKE
VATU-I-RA

LAUTOKA
NANDI
NADI

YASAWA
NAVITI
WAYA
WAYA LAILAI
YANGGETA
MATATHAWA LEVU
NATHULA
TAVEWA

VIWI

YASAWA GROUP

TAVUA

YANUTHA
MANA
MALOLO
MALOLOLAILAI BAY
NANDI

MAMANUTHA
GROUP

VITI LEVU

VATULELE

KANDAVU PASSAGE
MBENGGA

SOLO
NDRAVUNI
MBULIA
ONO

YANUTHA
MATANUKU
KANDAVU

0   50 km

HISTORY

pre-European period: Pieces of *lapita* pottery have been found in Fiji, indicating that it may have been first settled by Polynesians near 1500 B.C. Much later, about 500 B.C., the Melanesian people arrived, bringing with them their own distinct pottery traditions. Over the past 500 years there has been a back migration of Tongans into the Lau Group. Pre-European times were marked by cannibalism and continual warfare; this warfare became more ferocious with the beginning of the European musket trade. The native aristocracy practiced customs which today seem barbarous and particularly cruel. People were buried alive under the posts of new houses, war canoes were launched over the living bodies of young girls, and the widows of chiefs were strangled to keep their masters company in the spirit world. These feudal islanders were, on the other hand, guardians of one of the highest material cultures of the Pacific. They built great ocean-going double canoes up to 30 m long, constructed and adorned large solid thatched houses *(mbures)*, performed marvelous song-dances called *meke,* manufactured *tapa* (bark paper) and *sinnet* (coconut cordage), and skillfully plaited mats.

European exploration: The first European visitor was the Dutchman Abel Tasman; he sighted the islands in I643 but didn't land. In 1779, Capt. Cook anchored off Vatoa (Turtle I.) in Southern Lau. In 1789, after the *Bounty* mutiny, Capt. William Bligh was chased by canoe-loads of cannibals just N of the Yasawa Is. as he and his crew rowed through on their way to Timor; the section of sea where this happened is now known as Bligh Water. Bligh's careful observations gave Europeans an accurate picture of Fiji for the first time. But it was the American Exploring Expedition of 1840 led by Lt. Charles Wilkes which produced the first recognizable map of Fiji. When 2 members of the U.S. expedition were killed in a clash with Fijians on Malolo I. off Nandi, Wilkes ordered the offending village burned.

Fifty-seven of the inhabitants were murdered in the action. Capt. H.M. Denham of the HMS *Herald* prepared accurate navigational charts of the group in the I850s, making regular commerce possible.

European penetration: All of the early explorers stressed the perilous nature of Fiji's reefs which, combined with tales of cannibalism and warfaring natives, caused most travelers to shun the area. Then in I804, a survivor from the shipwrecked American schooner *Argo* brought word that sandalwood grew abundantly along the Mbua coast of Vanua Levu. This precipitated a rush of traders and adventurers to the islands. A cargo of sandalwood bought from the natives for $50 worth of trinkets could be sold to the Chinese at Canton for $20,000. By 1814 the forest had been stripped to provide joss sticks and incense, and the trade collapsed. From 1827 to 1850, off the coast, traders harvested *beche de mer,* a sea slug which, when smoked and dried, also brought a good price in China. The early 1830s saw the beginnings of whaling, and more important, the arrival from Tonga of the first missionaries.

the rise of Thakombau: For the next 30 years Christianity made little headway among these fierce, idolatrous people. A white missionary was killed and eaten as late as I867. During this period Fiji was divided among warring chieftains. The first Europeans to settle here were some escaped convicts from Australia who offered to instruct the natives in the use of firearms, and were thus well received. White beachcombers such as the Swedish adventurer Charles Savage took sides in local conflicts. In one skirmish he was separated from his allies, captured, and eaten. With outside help such as Savage's, Thakombau, the cannibal chief of Mbau I., extended his influence over much of Fiji. He was only seriously challenged by Ma'afu, the Tonga chief of Lau. In I854 Thakombau accepted Christianity. Part of the reason for this was a fire in the home of John Brown Williams, the American consul, on 4 July I849. Although the fire was caused by Williams' own over-enthusiastic celebration of his national holiday, he ob-

Thakombau of Fiji: A drawing from a photo taken in 1877, now in the possession of the Museum of Archaeology and Ethnology, Cambridge, England.

jected to the way Fijian onlookers walked off with items they rescued from the flames. His claims for damages against Thakombau eventually rose to $40,000 and he promised that American gunboats would soon arrive unless the money was paid. This threat continued to hang over Thakombau's head for many years and, together with growing disorder and difficulties in winning over Ma'afu's rival confederation of chiefs, convinced Thakombau in 1874 that he should cede his kingdom to Great Britain.

European colonization: During the 1860s, as Americans fought their Civil War, the world price of cotton soared, and sizeable groups of Europeans arrived in Fiji hoping to establish cotton plantations. They saw Thakombau as the only chance of maintaining a government. Levuka, the capital, boomed, but Thakombau was never strong enough to impose his authority over the whole country. The British were. The first resident British governor, Sir Arthur Gordon, created modern Fiji almost single-handedly. Memories were still fresh of the blackbirding era in the neighboring

islands, so Gordon ruled that Fijians could not be required to work on European plantations. Yet the colony had to be self-supporting. So when it was later decided that sugar would replace cotton, indenturing Indian laborers was seen as a solution. Many stayed on in Fiji after their 10-year contracts expired. Today their descendants outnumber native Fijians. Gordon further realized that the easiest way to rule was through the existing chieftain system. To protect the communal lands on which that system was based, he ordered that native land could not be sold, only leased. In addition to enlightened laws and stable government, the British also brought a deadly measles epidemic which wiped out a third of the Fijian population in 1874. At the beginning of European colonization there were about 200,000 Fijians, but by 1919 this number had been reduced to 83,000.

modern times: Although Fiji was a political colony of Britain, it was always an economic colony of Australia. The big Australian trading companies Burns Philp and W.R. Carpenters still dominate business today. The ubiquitous Morris Hedstrom is a subsidiary of Carpenters. Most of the Indian laborers were brought to Fiji to work for the Australian-owned Colonial Sugar Refining Company, which controlled the sugar industry from 1881 right up until 1973, when it was bought out by the Fiji government. Fijians were outstanding combat troops on the side of the Allies in the Solomon Island campaign in WW II, and again in Malaya from 1952-56 fighting Communist revolutionaries. So skilled were the Fijians at jungle warfare against the Japanese that it was never appropriate to list a Fijian as "missing in action" but to phrase it "not yet arrived." Until 1952, Suva, the present Fijian capital, was headquarters of the British Imperial Administration in the South Pacific. On 10 Oct. 1970 Fiji became a fully independent nation.

GOVERNMENT

The Fijian Parliament is composed of 2 houses: the House of Representatives has 52 members, 22 elected by the native Fijian community, 22 by the Indian community, and 8 by common roll, while the 22-member Senate includes 8 members appointed by the Great Council of Chiefs, 7 by the prime minister, 7 by the leader of the opposition, and one by the Council of Rotuma. Although the House of Representatives is by far the more important body, changes to the constitution and many laws require a 75 percent majority vote in both houses. The Fijian governor-general represents the British Crown. He has the right to dissolve Parliament and order new elections. While the ruling Alliance Party is predominantly Fijian, and the opposition National Federation Party is mostly Indian, both these political parties are multiracial. Prime Minister Ratu Sir Kamisese Mara, who led Fiji into independence in 1970 and through the first decade and a half of its national history, has been a strong moderating force in what could have been an explosive situation. The Great Council of Chiefs includes the high chiefs of Fiji, the members of Parliament, and others appointed by the Minister for Fijian Affairs. Government at the village *(koro)* level is led by a village herald (*turanga-ni-koro*) chosen by consensus. The villages are grouped into districts *(tikina)* and the districts into provinces *(yasana)*, of which there are 14. The Micronesians on Rambi and the Polynesians on Rotuma govern themselves through councils of their own. Fiji's Indian politicians have been realistic in their demands and slow progress is being made toward a more equitable society. However, a divisive chord has been struck by the Fijian Nationalist Party (not represented in Parliament) which has championed the cause of Melanesian racial extremism with such ideas as shipping the Indians back to India. Fiji was the first South Pacific country to play an appreciable and rather conservative role in international affairs.

ECONOMY

economic development: Fiji is the least dependent Pacific nation (excluding phosphate-rich Nauru). In 1982 overseas aid totaled only A$56 per capita (as compared to $1,091 per capita in American Samoa and $1,169 per capita in Tahiti); it accounts for just 10 percent of government expenditures.

Development aid is well diversified among 8 donors. Fiji's per capita gross domestic product (A$1,698 in 1981) is much higher than that of any other independent Pacific nation (again excepting Nauru). Sugar and tourism are the major earners of foreign exchange, with manioc, taro, yams, *kumara* (sweet potato), and corn the principal subsistence crops. Almost all of Fiji's sugar is produced by small independent Indian farmers on contract to the government-owned Fiji Sugar Corp., working land leased from native Fijians; some 20,000 farmers cultivate cane on holdings averaging 4.5 hectares. Most of Fiji's copra is produced by native Fijians in Lau, Taveuni, and Vanua Levu. Timber is becoming important as thousands of hectares planted by the Fiji Pine Commission and private landowners in the '70s reach maturity. Mining activity still centers on gold at Vatukoula on Viti Levu, and extensive copper deposits at Namosi are now being considered for development. Commercial fishing is becoming increasingly important and there is a major Japanese tuna cannery at Levuka. Fiji now grows almost half its own rice needs and is trying to become self-sufficient. Yet, in spite of all this potential, unemployment is turning into a major social problem as 4 times more young people leave school than there are jobs to take them. One of the most unique solutions has been employment with the U.N. peace-keeping forces in the Middle East, where hundreds of Fijian soldiers are now serving. The entire cost of this operation is met by the U.S. and other foreign governments. This has had certain repercussions, however. In 1980, Fiji declared a ban on nuclear-armed warships, but under intense American pressure, was forced to rescind it in 1983. France has also dramatically increased aid to Fiji as a means of dampening criticism of French nuclear testing at Mururoa Atoll in Eastern Polynesia. Fiji has decided to tap another singular source of finance by offering temporary citizenship to Hong Kong Chinese who invest $100,000 in government bonds or permanent residency to those who buy $200,000 worth of 15-year bonds. Although Fiji is still a Third World country with some of the attending problems, no one goes hungry and many people live better, quieter lives than most Europeans and N. Americans.

trade: Fiji is an important regional trading center. Although Fiji imports twice as much as it exports, much of this is later re-exported to smaller Pacific countries or sold to tourists who pay in foreign exchange. Sugar accounts for half of the nation's export earnings, followed by canned tuna, gold, molasses, coconut oil, and ginger, in that order. Fiji has long-term contracts to sell sugar to New Zealand, Singapore, Malaysia, and Europe at fixed rates. These contracts cover over 300,000 tons annually, with surplus sold on the world market. Mineral fuels have been Fiji's most expensive import item, but this is declining as the Monasavu Hydroelectric Project and other self-sufficiency measures come on line. Manufactured goods and food account for most of the remaining import bill.

tourism: Tourism is becoming the country's number one moneymaker as 200,000 visitors a year reach Fiji. This is twice as many as Tahiti gets and ten times as many as Tonga. Things appear in better perspective, however, when Fiji is compared to Hawaii, which is about the same size in surface area. Hawaii gets 4 million tourists, 20 times as many as Fiji. All the large resort hotels in Fiji are foreign-owned, and 80 percent of their purchases for food, beverages, linen, glassware, etc., are imported. Management is almost invariably European, with Fiji Indians filling technical positions such as maintenance, cooking, accounting, etc., and native Fijians working the high profile positions, such as receptionists, waiters, guides, and housekeepers. The Fiji government has diverted large sums from its capital improvements budget to provide infrastructure such as roads, airports, and other services to the foreign-owned resorts. Yet many of these same hotels have taken advantage of tax incentives and duty-free import allowances to escape paying any direct taxes back to the government. Clearly, this kind of tourism is not all its promotors claim. Development Plan 8, the government's 1980-85 5-year development program, called for "more local participation in all the various sectors of the industry" and "a network of smaller and less luxurious accommodation facilities in different parts of the country, offering to visitors an opportunity of seeing more of Fiji, its people and its culture." That is what this book is about. At present the main tourist resorts are centered along the S coast of Viti Levu and on the islands off Nandi/Lautoka. Tourism is changing in Fiji as a few of the big resorts recognize the youth market for the first time and have constructed dormitories and campgrounds. Even a million-dollar operation like Hide-A-Way on the Coral Coast now gets a third of its business from budget travelers. The difference in atmosphere between the places which cater to the young and young at heart and the conventional, computerized transnational hotels is striking. In this regard, Fiji is years ahead of Hawaii. A resort like Fiji's Beachcomber would be an instant success on Maui, with rave reviews in the travel sections of Sunday newspapers right across the U.S., but no developer has yet been able to shake off the straitjacket of American bourgeois tourism long enough to try it. It will come. Meanwhile, enjoy it now in Fiji.

Fijian boys, Singatoka Valley

THE PEOPLE

the Fijians: Fiji is a transitional zone between Polynesia and Melanesia. The Fijians bear more physical resemblance to the Melanesians, but in character they are much more like the Polynesians. In fact, the Polynesian influence in Fiji has been so strong that many historians now treat Fiji as part of Polynesia rather than Melanesia. Anyone who has traveled the Pacific will agree that a Fijian has much more in common with a Tongan than he does with a ni-Vanuatu. Native Fijians have interbred with Polynesians to the extent that their skin color is lighter than that of other Melanesians. However, the native Fijians have Melanesian frizzy hair, while most—but not all—Polynesians have straight hair. The Fijians live in villages of 50 to 400 people along the rivers or coast, or on the outer islands. Apart from the 2 big islands, the population is almost totally native Fijian. Most are Methodist. They work communal land, but individually, not as a group. Each Fijian is assigned his piece of native land. They grow most of their own food in village gardens. Only a few staples such as tea, sugar, flour, etc., are imported from Suva and sold in local coop stores. A visit to one of these stores will demonstrate just how little they import and how self-sufficient they are. The traditional thatched *mbure* is fast disappearing from Fiji as villagers rebuild (mostly following destructive cyclones) in tin and panel.

the Indians: Most of the Indians now in Fiji are descended from indentured laborers recruited in Bengal and Bihar a century ago. In the first year of the system (1879) 450 Indians arrived in Fiji to work in the cane fields. By 1883 the total had risen to 2,300 and in 1916, when the indenture system finally fell out of favor, 63,000 Indians were present in the colony. At that time the sugar fields were divided into 4-ha plots and the Indian workers became tenant farmers. In 1940 the Indian population stood at 98,000, still below the Fijian total of 105,000. But by the 1946 census Indians had outstripped Fijians 120,000 to 117,000

—making Fijians a minority in their own home. Now, of Fiji's total population of 645,000 (1981), 45 percent are Fijian while 50 percent are Indian. The relative proportions have stabilized somewhat as many Indians emigrate to N. America. Within the Fiji Indian community there are divisions between Hindus (80 percent) and Muslims (20 percent), North Indian versus South Indian, and Gujerati versus the rest. The different groups have kept alive their ancient religious beliefs and rituals. The majority of Indians are concentrated in the cane-growing areas and live in isolated farmhouses, small settlements, or towns. Many Indians also live in Suva, as do an increasing number of Fijians. Fiji's laws, which prevent Indians or anyone else from purchasing native communal land, have encouraged Indians to go into business, which they now almost monopolize at the middle levels. (Big business is the domain of Europeans.) If some Indians seem overly money-minded or business-oriented, it's because they have been forced into that role. When one considers their position in a land where they form a majority of the population and where most have lived for 3 generations, their industriousness and patience are admirable. The South Pacific has worked its magic on them, and anyone who has dealt with Indian communities in South Asia or elsewhere will affirm that Fiji's Indians are the friendliest, most open and hospitable of any.

the problem of land: When Fiji became a British colony in 1874, the land was divided between white settlers who had bought plantations and the Fijian inhabitants. The government assumed title to the balance. Today the alienated (privately-owned) plantation lands are known as "freehold" land, which accounts for about 10 percent of the total. Anyone can buy this land. If you've got a few million to spare and want to buy an island, contact Ragg & Associates, Box 861, Suva. Seven percent is Crown Land and the rest is inalienable native Fijian land which can be leased (about 8 percent is) but may never be sold. Compare this 83 percent with only 3 percent Maori land in New Zealand and almost zero native Hawaiian land and you'll understand the photos of the British royal family still pasted up in most native Fijian homes. Land ownership has provided the Fijian with a security which allows him to preserve his culture as almost nowhere else. However, even though native land can be leased for an average of 30 years, and Crown Land may be assigned on a 99-year basis, the difficulty in obtaining it has led to a serious squatter problem: people simply occupy unused areas without concerning themselves about who holds the title. Tenants are less likely to develop land than owners, and so the system is an obstacle to development. At the First Constitutional Conference in 1965, Indian rights were promulgated, and in l970 the Constitution for Independence asserted that *everyone* born in Fiji would be a citizen with equal rights. But land laws, up to the present, have very much favored "Fiji for the Fijians," and since any changes require a 75 percent favorable vote in both houses of the Fijian legislature, it's certain they will never be amended short of revolution. All groups in Fiji have accepted this with grace, though it's noteworthy that the Indians effectively occupy most of the best land, while Fijian villages are often seen adjacent to land of little agricultural use.

race relations: Visitors to Fiji can learn much about the country by listening to what their Indian and Fijian friends have to say about the preceding matters. The political and ethnic divisions built into modern Fiji continue to provoke nonviolent confrontations such as the protracted parliamentary boycott by the entire opposition in l983-84. Still, racial antagonism in Fiji has been exaggerated by superficial observers and certainly has none of the bitterness one encounters, say, in Guyana or Malaysia. Almost everyone realizes what a tragedy a breakdown in relations would be for the country. Fijians and Indians are often seen working and playing together, and a few Indian men have taken Fijian wives. (Most Indian women are too tradition-bound to marry a Fijian man—yet.) It would be hard to find another example of 2 so very different peoples living together peacefully in such numbers and such close quarters. That's what makes Fiji such a fascinating place to visit.

CUSTOMS

Native Fijians and Fiji Indians are very tradition-oriented people. Over the years they have retained a surprising number of their own ancestral customs, despite the flood of conflicting influences which has swept the Pacific over the past century. Rather than becoming a melting pot where one group assimilated another, Fiji is a patchwork of varied traditions. The obligations and responsibilities of native Fijian village life include not only the erection and upkeep of certain buildings, but personal participation in the many ceremonies which give their lives meaning. Hindu Indians, on the other hand, practice firewalking and religious processions, just as their forbears have for thousands of years in India.

Fijian firewalking: In Fiji, both Fijians and Indians practice firewalking, with the difference that the Fijians walk on heated stones instead of hot embers. Legends tell how the ability to walk on fire was first given to a warrior named Tui-na-vinggalita from Mbengga I., just off the S coast of Viti Levu, who had spared the life of a spirit god he caught while fishing for eels. Today, the descendants of Tui-na-vinggalita act as *mbete* (high priest) of the firewalkers: only members of his tribe, the Sawau, perform the ceremony. The Tui Sawau lives at Ndakuimbengga village on Mbengga, but firewalking is now only performed at the resort hotels on Viti Levu. Firewalkers are not permitted to have contact with women or to eat any coconut for 2 weeks prior to a performance. In a circular pit about 4 m across, hundreds of large stones are first heated by a wood fire until they're white hot. If you throw a handkerchief on the stones, it bursts into flames. Much ceremony and chanting accompanies certain phases of the ritual, such as the moment when the wood is removed to leave just the red-hot embers. The men psych themselves up in a nearby hut, then emerge, enter the pit, and walk briskly once around it. Bundles of leaves and grass are then thrown on the stones and the men stand inside the pit again to chant a final song. They seem to have complete immunity to pain and there's no trace of injury. The men appear to fortify themselves with the heat, to gain some psychic power from the ritual. Fijian firewalking is performed regularly at Nandi, Coral Coast, and Suva hotels, and at Pacific Harbor.

Indian firewalking: Fiji Indians brought with them the ancient practice of religious firewalking. In southern India, firewalking occurs in the pre-monsoon season as a call to the goddess Kali (Durga) for rain. Fiji Indian firewalking is an act of purification, or fulfilment of a vow to thank the god for help in a difficult situation. In Fiji there is firewalking in most Hindu temples once a year, sometime between May and September. The actual event takes place on a Sun. at 1600 on the Suva side of Viti Levu, and at 0400 on the Nandi/Lautoka side. In Aug. there is firewalking at the Sangam Temple on Howell Road, Suva. During the 10 festival days preceding the walk, participants remain in isolation, eat only vegetarian food, and spiritually prepare themselves. There are prayers at the temple in the early morning and a group-singing of religious stories at about 1900 from Mon. to Thursday. The devotees often pierce their cheeks or other bodily parts with spikes as part of the ceremony. The event is extremely colorful; drumming and chanting accompany the visual spectacle. Visitors are welcome to observe the firewalking but since the exact date varies from temple to temple according to the phases of the moon (among other factors), you have to keep asking to find out where and when it will take place.

the *yanggona* ceremony: *Yanggona (kava),* a tranquilizing, non-alcholic drink which numbs the tongue and lips, comes from the dried root *(waka)* of the pepper plant *(Macropiper methysticum).* This ceremonial preparation is the most honored feature of the formal life of Fijians, Tongans, and Samoans. It is performed with the utmost gravity according to a sacramental ritual. New mats are first spread on the floor, on which is placed a handcarved wooden bowl *(tanoa)* nearly a m wide. Cowrie shells decorate a long fiber cord fastened to the bowl, which leads to the guests of honor. To step over this cord during the ceremony is forbidden. As many as 70 men take their places before the bowl. The officiants are adorned with *tapa,* fiber, and croton leaves, their torsos smeared with glistening coconut oil, their faces usually blackened. The guests present a bundle of *waka* to the hosts along with a short speech explaining their visit *(sevusevu).* The *sevusevu* is received by the hosts along with a short speech of acceptance. The *waka* are then scraped clean and pounded in a *tambili* (mortar). Formerly they were chewed.

Cross-legged on a mat, Fijian men enjoy a bowl of grog.

a tanoa carved from a single block of vesi wood

Nowadays the pulp is put in a cloth sack and mixed with water in the *tanoa*. In the chiefly ceremony the *yanggona* is kneaded and strained through hibiscus *(vau)* fibers. The mixer displays the strength of the grog *(kava)* to the master of ceremonies *(matani vanua)* by pouring out a cupful into the *tanoa*. If the *matani vanua* considers the mix too strong, he calls for water *(wai)*, then says *"lose"* (mix) and the mixer proceeds. Again he shows the consistency to the *matani vanua* by pouring out a cupful. If it appears right the *matani vanua* says *"lomba"* (squeeze). The mixer squeezes the remaining juice out of the pulp, puts it aside, and announces *"sa lose oti saka na yanggona, vaka turanga"* (the *kava* is ready, my chief). He runs both hands around the rim of the *tanoa,* and claps 3 times. The *matani vanua* then says *"talo"* (serve). The cupbearer squats in front of the *tanoa* with a half coconut shell *(mbilo)* which the mixer fills. The cupbearer then presents the first cup to the guest of honor, who claps once, drains it, and everyone claps 3 times. The second cup goes to the *matani vanua* of the guest, who claps once and drinks. The man sitting next to the mixer says *"aa"* and everyone answers *"matha"* (empty). The third cup is for the first local chief, who claps once before drinking and everyone claps 3 times after. Then the *matani vanua* of the first local chief claps once, drinks, and everyone says *"matha"*. The same occurs for the second local chief and his *matani vanua*. After these 6 men have finished their cups, the mixer announces *"sa matha saka tu na yanggona, vaka turanga"* (the bowl is empty, my chief), and the *matani vanua* says *"thombo"* (clap). The mixer then runs both hands around the rim of the *tanoa* and claps 3 times. This terminates the full ceremony, but then a second bowl is prepared and everyone drinks. During the first bowl complete silence must be maintained.

social *kava* drinking: While the above describes one of several forms of the full *yanggona* ceremony which is performed only for high chiefs, abbreviated versions are put on for tourists in the hotels. However, the village people have simplified grog sessions almost daily. *Kava* drinking is important as a form of Fijian entertainment, and as a way of structuring friendships and community relations. Even in government offices a bowl of grog is kept for the staff to take as a refreshment at *yanggona* breaks. Some say the Fijians have *yanggona* rather than blood in their veins. Visitors to villages are invariably invited to participate in informal *kava* ceremonies, in which case it's customary to present 200 grams of *kava* roots or more to the group. Do this at the beginning, before anybody starts drinking, and make a short speech explaining the purpose of your visit (be it a desire to meet the people and learn about their way of life, an interest in seeing or doing something in particular on their island, or just a holiday from work). Don't hand the roots to anyone, just place them on the mat in the center of the circle. The bigger the bundle of roots, the bigger the smiles. (The roots are easily purchased at any town market for about $5 a half kilo. *Kava* doesn't grow well in dry, cane-growing areas or in the Yasawas, so carry a good supply with you when traveling there, as it can be hard to buy more.) Clap once when the cupbearer offers you the *mbilo,* take it in both hands and say *"mbula"* just before the cup meets your lips. Clap 3 times after you drink. Remember, you are a participant, not an onlooking tourist. Avoid taking photos during the ceremony. Even though you may not like the appearance or taste of the drink, try to finish at least the first bowl.

presentation of the *tambua*: The *tambua* is a tooth of the sperm whale. It was once presented when chiefs exchanged delegates, before alliance meetings, and before conferences on peace or war. In recent times, the *tambua* is presented during chiefly *yanggona* ceremonies, as a symbolic welcome for a respected visitor or guest, or as a prelude to public business or modern-day official functions. On the village level, *tambuas* are still commonly presented to arrange marriages, to show sympathy at funerals, to request favors, to settle disputes, or simply to show respect. Old *tambuas* are highly polished from continuous handling. The larger the tooth, the greater its ceremonial value. *Tambuas* are prized cultural property and may not be exported from Fiji without the permission of the prime minister. The Endangered Species Act prohibits their entry into the United States, Australia, and many other countries.

Fijian dancing (meke): Dances are performed at feasts and on special occasions. Their faces painted with charcoal and brandishing spears, the men wear frangipani leis and skirts of shredded leaves. The war club dance re-enacts heroic events of the past. Both men and women perform the *vakamalolo*, a sitting

Fijian women performing the seasea, *a dance which marks important occasions such as a meeting of high chiefs, the opening of a new church, or a royal visit.*

dance, while the *seasea* is danced by women flourishing fans.

stingray-spearing and fish drives: Stingrays are lethal-looking creatures with caudal spines up to 18 cm long. To catch them, 8 or 9 punts are drawn up in a line about a km long beside the reef. As soon as a stingray is sighted, a punt is paddled forward with great speed until close enough to hurl a spear. Another time-honored sport and source of food is the fish drive. An entire village participates. Around the flat surface of a reef at rising tide, sometimes as many as 70 men and women group themselves in a circle a km or more in circumference. All grip a ring of connected liana vines with leaves attached. While shouting, singing, and beating long poles on the seabed, the fishermen slowly contract the ring as the tide comes in. The shadow of the ring alone is enough to keep the fish within the circle. The fish are finally directed landward into a net or stone fish trap.

the rising of the mbalolo: Of all the Pacific Island groups, this practice takes place only in Samoa and Fiji. The *mbalolo (Eunice viridis)* is a segmented worm of the *Coelomate* order, considered a culinary delicacy throughout these islands. It's about 45 cm long and lives deep in the fissures of coral reefs, rising to the surface only twice a year to propagate and then to die. This natural almanac keeps both lunar and solar times, and has a fixed day of appearance—even if a hurricane is raging—one night in the third quarter of the moon in Oct., and the corresponding night in November. It has never failed to appear on time for over 100 years now. You can even check your calendar by it. Because this thin, jointed worm appears with such mathematical certainty, Fijians are waiting in their boats to scoop the millions of writhing, reddish-brown (male) and moss-green (female) spawn from the water when they rise to the surface, just before dawn. Within an hour after the rising the sacs burst and the fertile milt spawns the next generation of *mbalolo*. This is one of the most bizarre curiosities in the natural history of the South Pacific.

CRAFTS

The traditional art of Fiji is closely related to that of Tonga. Fijian canoes, too, were patterned after the more advanced Polynesian type, although the Fijians were timid sailors. War clubs, food bowls, *tanoas* (*kava* bowls), eating utensils, clay pots, and *tapa* cloth (*masi*) are considered Fiji's finest artifacts. The Government Handicraft Center behind Ratu Sakuna House in Suva has the most authentic designs. There are 2 kinds of wood-carvings: the ones made from *nawanawa* (*Cordia subcordata*) wood are superior to those of the lighter, highly breakable *vau* (*Hibiscus tiliaceus*). In times past it often took years to make a Fijian war club as the carving was done in the living tree and left to grow into the desired shape. The best *tanoas* are carved in the Lau Group.

Fijian masi (tapa)

pottery-making: Fijian pottery-making is unique in that it is a Melanesian artform. The Polynesians forgot how to make pottery thousands of years ago. Today the main center for pottery-making in Fiji is the Singatoka Valley on Viti Levu. Here, the women shape clay using a wooden paddle outside against a rounded stone held inside the future pot. A saucer-like section forms the bottom; the sides are built up using slabs of clay, or coils and strips. These are welded and battered to shape. When the form is ready the pot is dried inside the house for a few days, then heated over an open fire for about an hour. Resin from the gum of the *dakua* (kauri) tree is rubbed on the outside while the pot is still hot. This adds a varnish which brings out the color of the clay and improves the water-holding ability. The potters' wheel was unknown in the Pacific. This pottery is extremely fragile, which accounts for the quantity of potsherds found on ancient village sites. Smaller, less-breakable pottery products such as ashtrays are now made for sale to visitors.

tapa cloth: This is Fiji's most characteristic traditional product. *Tapa* is light, portable, and inexpensive, and a piece makes an excellent souvenir to brighten up a room back home. It's made by women on Vatulele I. off Viti Levu, and on certain islands of the Lau Group. First, bark is stripped from the paper mulberry tree and steeped in water. This material is then hand-beaten into a thin sheet with a wooden mallet. Four of these sheets are applied over one another and pounded together, then the *tapa* is left to dry in the sun. While Tongan *tapa* is decorated by holding a relief pattern under the *tapa* and overpainting the lines, Fijian *tapa* (*masi kesa*) is distinctive for its rhythmic geometric designs applied with stencils made from green pandanus and banana leaves. The only colors used are red, from red clay, and a black pigment obtained by burning candlenuts. Both powders are mixed with boiled gums made from scraped roots.

EVENTS AND SPORTS

Check with the Fiji Visitors Bureau to see if any festivals are scheduled during your visit. The best known are the Mbula Festival in Nandi (July), the Hibiscus Festival in Suva (Aug.), the Bougainvillea Festival in Mba (Sept.), and the Sugar Festival in Lautoka (Sept. or Oct.).

Public holidays in Fiji include Mohammed's Birthday (Dec. or Jan.), Queen Elizabeth's Birthday (June), Bank Holiday (Aug.), Fiji Day (around 10 Oct.), Diwali (the Hindu Festival of Lights in Oct. or Nov.), and Prince Charles' Birthday (Nov.). The dates vary from year to year. The soccer season in Fiji is Sun., Feb. to Nov., while rugby is played Sat. from April to September. Rugby is played only by native Fijians, while soccer teams are interracial. Cricket is played from Nov. to March, mostly in rural areas. Mercifully, Fiji is still without television, although video is becoming popular.

PRACTICALITIES

getting there: Fiji's geographic position makes it the hub of transport for the whole South Pacific. Nine major airlines fly into Nandi: Air Caledonie International, Air Nauru, Air New Zealand, Air Pacific, Canadian Pacific Air, Continental Airlines, Japan Airlines, Polynesian Airlines, and Qantas. Air Pacific also uses Suva's Nausori Airport. Nandi Airport is the most important international airport in the South Pacific, with long-haul services to points all around the Pacific Rim. Nausori Airport is a regional distribution centers, with flights to many of the Polynesian countries to the east.

getting around by air: Fiji Air is the main domestic carrier with flights several times a week from Nausori Airport to such out-of-the-way islands as Kandavu ($33), Ngau ($25), Koro ($32), Rambi ($51), Moala ($36), Thithia ($50), Lakemba ($54), Vanua Mbalavu ($54), and Rotuma ($116). More common destinations such as Levuka ($17), Savusavu ($36), and Taveuni ($41) are served several times daily (all fares OW). Fiji Air also flies to Funafuti in Tuvalu ($250 OW) 3 times a week. From Nandi they have a daily flight to Lambasa ($57). There are useful interisland flights between Levuka and Koro ($15) and Savusavu to Rambi ($15). Fiji Air offers a 2-week

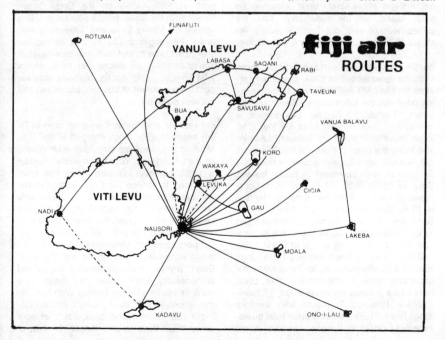

the crew of the Senikaloni unloading supplies at Ngaloa village, Kandava

unlimited travel Discovery Pass for $199 (Rotuma and Tuvalu not included), available at Fiji Air offices in Suva, Lautoka, and Nandi Airport. This is a good value and all flights may be booked ahead. Always reconfirm your return flight immediately upon arrival at an outer island, as the reservation lists are sometimes not sent out from Suva. Fiji Air allows 15 kg baggage. The service is reliable.

getting around by surface: Since most shipping operates out of Suva, passenger services by sea both within Fiji and to neighboring countries are listed in the "Suva" section under "Transport." Regular bus service is available all over Fiji and fares are low. The most important routes are between Lautoka and Suva, the biggest cities. Pacific Transport Ltd. has 8 buses a day along Queens Road (via Singatoka), with expresses (5 hours) leaving Suva at 0645, 0930, 1210, and l730. Local buses on Queens Road take 8 hours. The fare is $6.45 Suva-Lautoka for local or ordinary. Sunbeam Transport Ltd. services the northern Kings Road from Suva to Lautoka 6 times a day, with expresses (6 hours) at 0645, 1330, and 1715. The Sunbeam express along Kings Road is a comfortable way for those without a lot of time to see a little of the interior. Local buses take 9 hours on Kings Road, $7 Suva-Lautoka. Reliance Transport also services Kings Road. There are many other local buses, especially closer to Suva or Lautoka. Avoid

the a/c expresses which cost twice as much and are not as much fun as the ordinary expresses, whose big open windows give you a panoramic vision of Viti Levu. Note too that some expresses don't stop at isolated resorts such as Hide-A-Way on the Coral Coast. Check with the driver before you set out. Bus service on Vanua Levu and Taveuni is also good. Passenger trucks serving as carriers charge set rates to and from interior villages. If you're hitching, be aware that truck drivers who give you a lift on the highway may expect the equivalent of bus fare. Locals pay this without question.

car rentals and taxis: Car rental rates in Fiji are nearly double those charged in the U.S. Most of the roads are atrocious, with driving on the L-hand side. Your home driver's license is valid, however. Queens Road has been upgraded to service the Coral Coast resorts. Taxis are common within towns and relatively cheap, about $1 for a short trip. Meters are rare so ask the fare first. If in doubt, make sure it's understood the price is for the whole car, not per passenger, although not many drivers are unscrupulous enough to try this one. Don't tip your driver; tips are neither expected or necessary. Don't invite your driver for a drink or become overly familiar with him. He may abuse your trust. If you're a woman taking a cab in the Nandi area, don't let your driver think there is any "hope" for him or you'll be in trouble. Don't be intimidated by the taxi drivers waiting outside Nandi airport. They will do their jobs quite normally unless you, in the euphoria of arriving in such a wonderful country as Fiji, give them cause to do otherwise.

tours: Beachcomber Cruises Ltd. (Box 364, Lautoka) and Farthings International (100 Clarence St., Sydney, NSW 2000) combine to offer a unique 7-day "Adventure Cruise" out of Lautoka for $495 pp (all-inclusive) on the MV *Tui Tai*. Accommodations are a dormitory bunk, a bedroll on deck, or you may disembark and camp on the beach. There's a 35-year-old upper age limit. The absence of private cabins keeps obnoxious tourists away and ensures good amiable company. Shore excursions and snorkeling equipment are provided, along with cold showers and all meals. You'll cruise Bligh Water between the 2 big islands, and visit Levuka, Koro, and the Yasawas (among others). The *Tui Tai* sails from Lautoka only once a month, so book well in advance with a travel agent. If you prefer more comfort, Seafarer Cruises (Box 364, Lautoka) and Blue Lagoon Cruises (Box 54, Lautoka) offer 3-day-cruises of the Yasawa Is. beginning at $275 pp double occupancy, all-inclusive. Though expensive, these trips have a good reputation. There are daily departures but reservations are essential as they're usually booked solid months ahead—they're that popular. Lesi's Tours (GPO Box 1224, Suva) arranges hiking tours into Central Viti Levu for visiting groups at about $30 pp per day all-inclusive.

accommodations: Most of the transnational tourist hotels are found in Nandi, on small islands off Nandi/Lautoka, and along the Coral Coast on Viti Levu's S side. Budget accommodations are more spread out, with concentrations in Nandi, Suva, and Levuka. All are listed in this book. A few of the cheapies double as whorehouses, making them cheap in both senses of the word. Also, beware of rip-offs in a few of the hotels. A 5 percent hotel tax is added. If you want to spend time in the interior, consider "buying" a village house ($50-80 for as long as you need it). Resorts

with camping facilities (own tent) include Seashell Cove near Nandi, Rukuruku on Ovalau, Nukulau I. off Suva, and Reece's Place on Kandavu. Elsewhere, get permission before pitching your tent as all land is owned by someone. Some freelance campers on beaches such as Natandola near Nandi have been robbed, so take care. With the local property owners' permission, the chances of anything bad happening are slim.

staying in villages: A great way to meet the people and learn a little about their culture is to stay in a village for a few nights. Since the Fiji Visitors Bureau has not yet set up a regular homestay program, you'll have to arrange this for yourself. One way to do it beforehand is to pick any Fijian village off the map and write a letter to the *turanga-ni-koro* (village herald), requesting permission to visit. A careful reading of this book would suggest villages to write to. If you want to stay in a village in the Yasawa or Lau groups, this may be the only way to arrange it. In places off the beaten tourist track, you could just show up in a village and ask permission of the *turanga-ni-koro* to spend the night. Rarely will you be refused. Similarly, both Fiji Indians and native Fijians will spontaneously invite you in. The Fijian's innate dignity and kindness should not be taken for granted, however. All across the Pacific it's customary to reciprocate when someone gives you a gift—if not now, then sometime in the future. Visitors who accept gifts (such as meals and accommodations) from islanders and do not reciprocate are undermining traditional culture, often without realizing it. It is sometimes hard to know how to pay for hospitality, but Fijian culture has a solution: the *sevusevu*. This can be money, but it's usually a 400-gram bundle of *kava* roots (*waka*), which can be easily purchased at any Fijian market for about $5. The Fiji Rucksack Club recommends that its members donate $10 pp per night to village hosts, but $5 pp seems more standard. The *waka* is additional and anyone traveling in remote areas of Fiji should pack some (take whole roots, not powdered *kava*). If you give the money up front with the *waka* as a *sevusevu* you'll get better treatment. On the overland trekking routes through villages which get scores of overnight visitors a year, it is absolutely essential to contribute. You can always camp by the river if you'd rather not. The *sevusevu* should be placed before (but not handed to) the *turanga-ni-koro* or village chief so he can accept or refuse. If he accepts (by touching the package) your welcome is confirmed and you may spend the night in the village. It is also possible to give some money to the lady of the house upon departure with your thanks. Just say it's your goodbye *sevusevu* and watch the smile. A Fijian may refuse the money, but will not be offended by the offer. You could also take some gifts along such as lengths of material for the women, T-shirts, or a big jar of instant coffee. When choosing your traveling companions for a trip which involves staying in Fijian villages, make sure you agree on this before you set out. Otherwise you could end up subsidizing somebody else's trip, or worse, have to stand by and watch the Fijian villagers subsidize it.

village life: Staying in a village is definitely not for everyone. Most houses contain no electricity, running water, toilet, furniture, etc., and only native food will be offered. You should also expect to sacrifice most of your privacy, to stay up late drinking grog, and to sit in the house and socialize when you could be out exploring. The constant attention and lack of sanitary conditions may become tiresome, but it would be considered rude to attempt to be alone or refuse the food or grog. Remember that villagers are not paid performers to entertain tourists, but humans like you living their real lives, so put your heart in it or stay away. When you enter a Fijian village people will want to be helpful, and will direct or accompany you to the person or place you seek. If you show genuine interest in something and ask to see how it is done you will usually be treated with respect and asked if there is anything else you would like to know. Initially, Fijians may hesitate to welcome you into their homes because they fear you will not wish to sit on a mat and eat native foods with your fingers. Once you show them that this isn't true, you'll receive the full hospitality treatment. Consider par-

ticipating in the daily activities of the family such as weaving, cooking, gardening, and fishing. Your hosts will probably try to dissuade you from "working" but if you persist you'll become accepted. If the subject comes up, explain to the villagers how they could run a small business for themselves by setting up a simple guest house for travelers to use; businessmen and officials can't be relied upon to help with it. Staying in the villages of Fiji offers one of the most rewarding travel experiences in the South Pacific, and if everyone plays fair it will always be so.

food: Unlike other South Pacific nations, Fiji has many good, cheap eateries. Chinese restaurants are everywhere. On the western side of Viti Levu, Indian restaurants use the name "lodge," a place where you can always get some cheap curries. Real native dishes such as baked or fried fish, cassava, *ndalo,* and breadfruit, with *ndalo* and *kumala* leaves in coconut cream take a long time to prepare

preparing a lovo *(earthen pit oven) at Korovou on the Wainimala River, Viti Levu, to celebrate the opening of the primary school*

and must be served fresh, which makes it difficult to offer them in a restaurant. These are best enjoyed at special Fijian feasts at the hotels or, if you are lucky, in a private home. Basic Fijian food is served at the lunchtime food market beside Suva's Princes Wharf. Fijians have their own pace and trying to make them do things more quickly is often counterproductive. Their charm and the friendly personal attention you receive more than make up for the occasionally slow service. Note that drinking alcoholic beverages on the street is prohibited.

shopping: Shops in Fiji close at 1300 on Sat., except in Nausori town where they stay open all day Sat. but only half a day on Wednesday. Camera film is cheap and the selection good—stock up. Fiji's duty-free shops are not really duty-free as all goods are subject to a 10 percent fiscal tax. Bargaining is the order of the day, but only in Suva is the selection really good. To be frank, Americans can buy the kind of Japanese electrical merchandise sold "duty-free" in Fiji cheaper at any of the discount houses in downtown Los Angeles or through discount mail order at home, and get more recent models. If you do buy something get an itemized receipt and guarantee, and watch they don't switch packages and unload a demo on you. If you'd like to do some shopping in Fiji, locally made handicrafts such as *tapa* cloth, *kava* bowls, woodcarvings, etc., are a better investment (see "crafts" above).

money: The currency is the Fiji dollar, which is close to the U.S. dollar in value. Banking hours are Mon. to Thurs. 1000-1500, Fri. 1000-1600. There are banks in all the towns, but it's usually not possible to change travelers cheques on the outer islands; credit cards are strictly for the cities and resorts. If you need money sent, have your banker make a telegraphic transfer to any Westpac Bank branch in Fiji. When writing to Fiji use the words "Fiji Islands" in the address, otherwise the letter might go to Fuji, Japan.

visas: No visa is required of visitors from Europe, North America, or most Commonwealth countries for stays of 30 days or less, although everyone needs a ticket to leave and a passport. You'll also need to have been vaccinated against yellow fever or cholera if you're arriving from an infected area, which is unlikely unless you happen to be arriving straight from the Amazon jungles or banks of the Ganges River. Extensions of stay are given out 2 months at a time up to a maximum of 6 months at no charge. Apply to the Immigration offices in Suva or Lautoka, and at Nandi Airport, or to the police stations in Singatoka, Mba, Tavua, Levuka, Lambasa, Savusavu, or Taveuni. You must apply before your current permit expires. Bring your passport, onward or return ticket, and proof of sufficient funds. The Immigration people can sometimes be unreasonably sticky, insisting on a ticket back to your home country no matter how much money you show. Fiji has 3 ports of entry for yachts: Suva, Lautoka, and Levuka.

health: The climate is a healthy one and most tropical diseases are unknown. The tap water in Fiji is usually drinkable except just after a cyclone or during droughts, when care should be taken. If you're sleeping in villages or with the locals, you may pick up head lice—apply an emulsion available at any chemist or large general store. Be aware V.D. is rampant among the street people, and cases of herpes have been reported.

conduct and custom: It's a Fijian custom to smile when you meet a stranger and say something like "good morning" or at least "hello." Of course you needn't do this in the large towns, but you should almost everywhere else. If you meet someone you know, stop for a moment to exchange a few words. It's good manners to take off your hat while walking through a village, where only the chief is permitted to wear a hat. Don't point at people in villages. It's bad manners to touch another person's hair or head. Shorts and bathing suits are not proper dress in villages, so carry a *sulu* to cover up. Take off your shoes before entering a *mbure* and stoop as you walk around inside. Men should sit cross-legged, ladies side-ways. Sitting with your legs stretched out in front is insulting. Do you notice how Fijians rarely shout? Keep your voice down. When you give a gift hold it out with both hands, not one hand. If you wish to surf off a village or picnic on their beach, ask permission. Fijian children are very well-behaved. There's no running or shouting when you arrive in a village and they leave you alone if you wish. Also, Fijians love children, so don't hesitate to bring your own. You'll never have to worry about finding a babysitter.

AIRPORTS

Nandi International Airport (NAN): Most hotels have their rates listed on a board inside the Customs area, so peruse the list while you're waiting for your baggage. The Fiji Visitors Bureau office is to the left as you come out of Customs. They open for all international arrivals and can advise you on accommodations. There is a 24-hour bank (50-cent commission) in the commercial arcade just beyond the Visitors Bureau. Another bank is in the departure lounge. If you want to rent a car, Dominion Rentals is probably the cheapest. Many travel agencies (Rosie Reservations is one of the best) and airline offices are also located in this arcade, as is a post office with limited hours. Coin lockers are 20 cents a day over near the check-in counters, but half are broken and the other half taken. Check your change carefully if you buy anything at this airport as the clerks might try to pass Australian and N.Z. coins off on you. Tourists probably do the same to them. The airport never closes so you can sleep on the benches on the departures side if you're leaving in the wee hours. There's a large duty-free store in the departure lounge with the usual range of insipid luxury items—don't wait to do your shopping here. A departure tax of $5 is payable on all international flights but transit passengers connecting within 12 hours are exempt. There are frequent buses along the highway, just a short walk from the terminal, to Nandi town (8 km—37 cents) and Lautoka (22 km—75 cents).

Nausori Airport (SUV): The Bank of N.Z. counter opens Thurs. 1230-1400 only. There's the inevitable duty-free shop. The departure tax is $5 on all international flights, but no tax is levied on domestic flights. The airport bus costs $1 to the Air Pacific office in Suva (23 km). There's a local bus on the highway if you want to go to Nausori (26 cents). A taxi will run about $2 to Nausori, $11 to Suva.

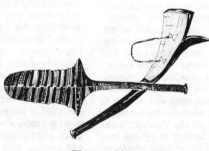

Fijian war clubs

SOUTHWEST VITI LEVU

NANDI

Nandi, on the dry side of Fiji's largest island, has little to offer the visitor other than a place to crash after a tiring transpacific flight; if you're not that exhausted you'd do better to head for Lautoka. Nandi has a km of concrete duty-free tourist shops, and mass-produced souvenirs are sold at the stalls behind the post office. But there's also a surprisingly colorful market (best on Sat. morning). Beware of the friendly handshake in Nandi for you may find yourself buying something you neither care for nor desire.

accommodations closer to the airport:
Most of the hotels offer free transport from the airport. As you leave Customs you'll be besieged by a group of Indian men holding small wooden signs bearing the names of the hotels they represent. If you know which one you want, call out the name: if their driver is there, you'll get a free ride. If not, the Fiji Visitors Bureau to the L will help you telephone them for a 20-cent fee. Don't be put off by the Indian hotel drivers at the airport. Question them about the rates and facilities, before you let them drive you to their place. The closest budget hotel to the airport is Johal's Motel, set in cane fields, a 15-min. walk in off the main highway past the Mocambo Hotel. There are 24 rooms that go for $10 s, $14 with private bath and fan, a $5 dorm, or camp by the pleasant swimming pool for only $3.50. The motel lawns swarm with toads at night. Recommended, but avoid the noisy rooms near the active bar. The Melanesian Hotel on the main highway is $16 s, $20 d, or

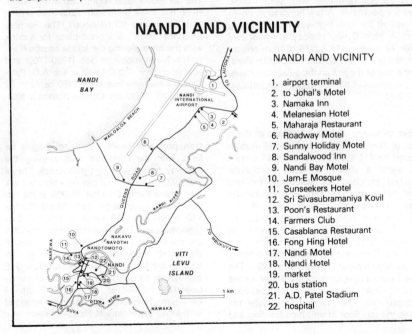

NANDI AND VICINITY

NANDI AND VICINITY

1. airport terminal
2. to Johal's Motel
3. Namaka Inn
4. Melanesian Hotel
5. Maharaja Restaurant
6. Roadway Motel
7. Sunny Holiday Motel
8. Sandalwood Inn
9. Nandi Bay Motel
10. Jam-E Mosque
11. Sunseekers Hotel
12. Sri Sivasubramaniya Kovil
13. Poon's Restaurant
14. Farmers Club
15. Casablanca Restaurant
16. Fong Hing Hotel
17. Nandi Motel
18. Nandi Hotel
19. market
20. bus station
21. A.D. Patel Stadium
22. hospital

$7 dorm (4 persons maximum), but it can be loud with a juke box playing all night. There's a swimming pool and restaurant (expensive) in the complex—not recommended. The cheapest place to stay in Nandi is the Namaka Inn near the Melanesian, $6 pp with breakfast or $3.50 dorm (no breakfast). It's plain, noisy, and has little to recommend it except the low price. You might want to try a meal in the restaurant downstairs however. Also very basic is the Roadway Motel, $8 s, $12 d, or $4 dorm (3 persons maximum)—all with private facilities. The Roadway partly makes up for the lack of a pool and bar by offering cooking facilities, a washing machine ($1), and luggage storage (20 cents a day). The Sandalwood Inn nearby doesn't have a dorm and is $16 s, $22 d for a room with shared bath in the old wing, but the layout is attractive with pool, bar, and restaurant. Video movies are shown nightly. The cheaper rooms may be full. Close by and less expensive is the Sunny Holiday Motel, $8 s, $12 d, $4 dorm (5 beds), all with breakfast included. Camping is $3 but take care with your things. There's a pool table. A few hundred m down the road off the main highway in the opposite direction from Sunny Holiday is Nandi Bay Motel. All rooms ($14 s, $15 d) have private bath, fan (a/c $4 extra), and cooking facilities, but the roar of the jets on the adjacent runway can be jarring. Still, it's clean, comfortable, and good.

closer to town: On Narewa Road at the N edge of Nandi is Sunseekers Hotel. Rooms here go for $11 s, $15 d, $6 dorm ($1 extra if you want ` a sheet), all with continental breakfast included ($1 surcharge for one night). Show your YHA card for a possible discount. There's a tiny pool out back, a cafe, and it's a good place to meet other travelers, but it can be noisy. There are 3 choices in the downtown area. The Fong Hing Hotel is a traditional Chinese commercial hotel offering a/c rooms with private bath at $16 s, $22 d. The other 2 places have confusingly similar names and are located side by side but have separate managements. The Nandi Town Motel occupies the top floor of an office building and

looks rather basic at first glance but the rooms are okay with fridge and private bath. The price ($11 s, $15 d, $18 t) is negotiable. Rates at the Nandi Hotel begin at $18 s, $22 d. For accommodations at the offshore resorts near Nandi, see "Lautoka and the Offshore Islands."

food and entertainment: For Chinese and European food try Poon's Restaurant upstairs on the main street on the N side of town across from the Mobil service station. The Pizza Hut nearby has 11 kinds of pizza ($1.60-7.50). There is a good Chinese restaurant in the Fong Hing Hotel with main plates averaging $3-4. Kwong's Refreshment Bar on the N side of the market is a good place to get a cheaper meal or a snack. The Maharaja Restaurant, out near the Melanesian Hotel, is more expensive but good. Special events in Nandi include the Tues. night barbecue ($8) at 1830 by the pool at the Nandi Hotel, followed at 2000 by a Fijian *meke* ($2). The Bamboo Palace Night Club at the Nandi Hotel has a live band from 2200-0100 on Fri. and Sat. nights ($2.50 cover). The Farmers Club near Poon's is a good place for a drink with the boys. During the sports season (Feb. to Nov.), see rugby on Sat. (1200-1700) and soccer on Sun. (1000-1600) at the A.D. Patel Stadium near the bus station (50 cents to $2 admission). There are 4 movie houses in Nandi.

transport and tours: You can bargain for fares with the collective taxis cruising the highway from the airport into Nandi. They'll usually take what you'd pay on a bus, but ask first. Khans Rental Cars (tel. 71-009) at the service station opposite the Nandi Motel charges $10 a day plus 10 cents a km for their cheapest cars. Their unlimited mileage rates are the lowest in Nandi. Tour Contractors in the Nandi airport arcade offers rubber raft trips on the Mba River daily except Sun. ($55 pp, lunch included). The same company operates helicopter tours ($100 pp—4 minimum). Horseback riding can be arranged with Inoke Derenalagi at Nawaka village near

Nandi (bus from market 35 cents; taxi $2). Inoke has 5 horses in so-so shape but they'll run if you insist. Prices begin at $5 and go up according to how much you seem willing to spend. Three-day trips begin at $30 pp and up. Inoke takes you out himself and makes stops to visit friends, so this is a great way to meet some local people.

THE SOUTH COAST

Seashell Cove: The first beach resort S of Nandi is Seashell Cove Resort, 28 km SW on Momi Bay. There are duplex *mbures* at $35 d, and a 5-bed dorm for $8 ($1 discount with a YHA card). Or pitch your own tent for $5—a good alternative to risky Natandola Beach (see below). Beware of prancing ponies around the tents. Baggage storage is available. The resort has a swimming pool, bar, and restaurant (expensive—bring groceries). The food is good, though the service is erratic. There's a *meke* ($3) Sat. evening. They do their best to keep you occupied with day trips to Natandola Beach ($10) and a deserted island ($10), tennis, water skiing ($1), and volleyball (free). Very popular. A public bus direct to Seashell Cove leaves Nandi bus station at 1545 Mon. to Saturday. There's a good onward connection from the resort by public bus to Singatoka ($1.40) Mon. to Fri. at 0900. **vicinity of Seashell Cove:** There are 2 huge WW II cannons on a hilltop overlooking Momi Bay. Take a bus along the old highway to Momi, then walk 3 km west.

Natandola Beach: The long, white, unspoiled sandy beach here has become popular for surfing and camping. You can camp on the beach, but be aware that thefts from both campers and sunbathers by locals are a daily occurrence here and the police make no effort to stop it. It might be better to stay at Sanasana village by the river at the far S end of the beach. There's a store on the hill just before your final descent to Natandola. Get there on the bus to Sangasanga village which leaves Nandi at 1630 (or catch one from Singatoka at 1130). You have to walk the last 3 km to the beach. Otherwise get off at the

The chambered nautilus (Nautilis pompilius) *uses the variable bouyancy of its shell to lift itself off the ocean bed, and jet-like squirts of water to propel itself along.*

Maro School stop on the main highway and hitch 10 km to the beach. The sugar train passes close to Natandola and, although it's officially for cargo only, they do pick up hitchhikers.

Singatoka: The S side of Viti Levu near Singatoka is known as the Coral Coast. With the upgrading of the Queens Road linking the area to Nandi and Suva, plans are underway for many new transnational resort hotels. Singatoka town is in a picturesque setting where the long highway bridge crosses the Singatoka River. There are the ubiquitous duty-free shops and a colorful local market (best on Sat.) with a large handicraft section. Strangely, the traditional handmade Fijian pottery, for which Singatoka is famous, is not available here. Find it by asking in Nayawa (where the clay originates), Yavulo, and Nasama villages near Singatoka. Better yet, take the 2-hour boat cruise ($9) up the river from Singatoka to Naithambuta and Lawai villages where the pottery is displayed for sale. **stay and eat:** The Singatoka Hotel is an older commercial establishment not far from the center of town. The 11 rooms range from $7-12 s, $12-18 d, but are often full. The hotel

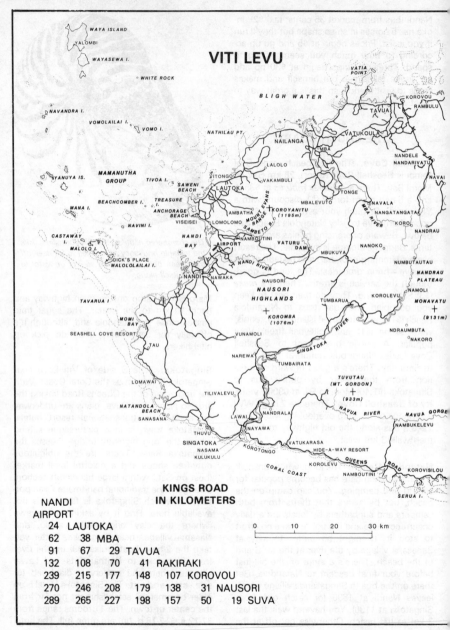

VITI LEVU

WAYA ISLAND
YALOMBI
WAYASEWA I.

WHITE ROCK

BLIGH WATER

VATIA POINT

KOROVOU
RAMBULU

NAVANDRA I.

VOMOLAILAI I.   VOMO I.

NATHILAU PT.

NAILANGA   TAVUA

VATUKOULA

MBA

NANDELE
NANDARIVATU

NAVAI

YANUYA IS.   MAMANUTHA GROUP   TIVOA I.

VITONGO

LALOLO

VAKAMBULI

SAWENI BEACH

LAUTOKA

AMBATHA   KOROYANITU (1195m)

MBALEVUTO

TONGE

MBA RIVER

NAVALA

NANGATANGATA

KORO

NANDRAU

BEACHCOMBER I.   TREASURE

ANCHORAGE BEACH

MANA I.

VISEISEI

LOMOLOMO   MOUNT EVANS RANGE

SAMBETO R.

MBUKUYA

NANOKO

NUMBUTAUTAU

NAVINI I.

NANDI BAY

AIRPORT   NAMBOUTINI   VATURU DAM

CASTAWAY I.

MALOLO I.

DICK'S PLACE MALOLOLAILAI I.

NANDI   NAWAKA

NANDI RIVER

NAUSORI HIGHLANDS

NANDRAU PLATEAU

NAMOLI   MONAVATU (9131m)

TAVARUA I

MOMI BAY

SEASHELL COVE RESORT

TAU

VUNAMOLI

KOROMBA (1076m)

TUMBARUA

KOROLEVU

SINGATOKA RIVER

NDRAUMBUTA

NAKORO

NAREWA

TUMBAIRATA

TUVUTAU (MT. GORDON) (933m)

LOMAWAI

TILIVALEVU

NANDRALA

NAVUA RIVER   NAVUA GORGE

NAMBUKELEVU

NATANDOLA BEACH

SANASANA

LAWAI

NAYAWA

THUVU

SINGATOKA

NASAMA

KULUKULU

KOROTONGO

VATUKARASA   HIDE-A-WAY RESORT

CORAL COAST   KOROLEVU

QUEENS ROAD   KOROVISILOU

NAMBOUTINI

SERUA I.

KINGS ROAD
IN KILOMETERS

0   10   20   30 km

NANDI AIRPORT							
24	LAUTOKA						
62	38	MBA					
91	67	29	TAVUA				
132	108	70	41	RAKIRAKI			
239	215	177	148	107	KOROVOU		
270	246	208	179	138	31	NAUSORI	
289	265	227	198	157	50	19	SUVA

NANANU-I-RA I.
VOLIVOLI PT.
MALAKE I.
NANANU-I-THAKE I.
VATU IRA I
WELLINGTON WHARF
KINGS ROAD
TONGOWERE
RAKIRAKI
VITI LEVU BAY
VATUKATHEVATHEVA
NANUKULOA
NASAU
NAKAUVANDRA RANGE
NAISERELANGI
NASEYANI
MATAWAILEVU
NAMARAI
MBURELEVU
NAYAVUTOKA
SILANA
NAINGANI I.
MT. TOVA
NANGGATAWA
NDAWASAMU
RUKURUKU
TOMANIVI (MT. VICTORIA) (1323m)
VANUAKULA
NATOVI
LEVUKA
OVALAU ISLAND LOVONI
NAMATA
SOA
VIRO
NDRAIMBA
WAILOA RIVER
NAIMBITA
NASAU
LONDONI
MBURETA AIRPORT
TOKOU
KORO-NI-O
WAIRUARUA
WAINIMBULA R.
NANGGUELENDAMU LANDING
LASELEVU
WAINIMALA RIVER
WAILOTUA
NAIVITHULA
MATATHAUTHAU
MOTURIKI IS.
MONASAVU DAM
NAVUNIYASI
KOROVOU
THANGALAI I.
LUTU
NAIRUKURUKU
VUNINDAWA
UTHUNIVANUA
KOROVOU
NAITAUVOLI
NALUWAI
SOTE
KUMI
NASAVA
SEREA
REWA RIVER
VIRIA
VIWA I.
WAINIKOROILUVA RIVER
WAINIMAKATU
NAMBUKALUKA
KASAVU
MBAU I.
SALIANDRAU
KOROSAMBA SANGA RANGE
WAINDINA RIVER
SAVU
MBAULEVU
THAUTATA
TOMBERUA I.
NAMOSI
WAIVAKA
WAMANU RIVER
NAUSORI
SAWANI
AIRPORT
NAKELO
MT. VOMA
THOLOISUVA
NUKU
NAMUAMUA
ORCHID ISLAND
MT. VOMA
LAMI
LOKIA
NASILAI PT.
KALOKOLEVU
TAMAVUA
LAUTHALA BAY
NAMBUKAVESI
SUVA HARBOR
SUVA
WAIYANITU
NAVUA
NUKULAU I.
PACIFIC HARBOR
NAITONITONI
NGALOA DEUMBA
NAVUA RIVER

QUEENS ROAD IN KILOMETERS

SUVA						
49	PACIFIC HARBOR					
96	47	KOROLEVU				
120	71	24	KOROTONGO			
127	78	31	7	SINGATOKA		
188	139	92	68	61	NANDI TOWN	
197	148	101	77	70	9	NANDI AIRPORT
221	172	125	101	94	33	24	LAUTOKA

Because it and its eggs are taken for human food, the green sea turtle (Chelonia mydas) is in danger of extinction. Fortunately the shell is too thin to be made into jewelry.

restaurant serves the best Chinese food on the S coast; there are 116 dishes to choose from. It's worth stopping for lunch—you'll be able to catch another bus later. Eat cheap but good Indian food at the Singatoka Lodge behind the market.

Kulukulu: Another favorite surfing beach is Kulukulu, 5 km S of Singatoka, where the Singatoka River breaks through Viti Levu's fringing reef. Incredibly high sand dunes separate the cane fields from the shore. There's good camping on the beach and plenty of firewood for evening bonfires, but no water. A group of American surfers (Marcus Oliver, (Box 3338, Lami) have opened a dormitory cabin ($5 pp) called "Club Masa" here (camping $3). The wind sometimes uncovers human bones from old burials and potsherds lie scattered along the seashore—these fragments have been dated up to 2,000 years old. Giant sea turtles sometimes come ashore here to lay their eggs. Altogether a fascinating, evocative place. About 4 buses a day run from Singatoka to Kulukulu village (26 cents); the one at 1400 is the most reliable.

Korotongo: There are 4 places to stay at Korotongo, 8 km E of Singatoka. Vakaviti Units and Cabins has a single dormitory with 5 beds, fridge, and use of the barbecue, at $5 pp. It's often full. Just a few hundred m E near the Reef Hotel is Waratah Lodge with 5 self-contained units—good value at $12 s, $22 d. A km farther E again is Tumbakula Beach Cottages, also with a 4-bed dorm ($4 pp) and kitchen. The Tambua Sands Beach Resort at Korotongo also has a $8 dormitory. All these hotels have swimming pools and Tumbakula is right on the beach.

Hide-A-Way Resort: The Coral Coast is studded with luxury transnational hotels catering to packaged tourists and the affluent. The only one which also makes itself available to budget travelers is Hide-A-Way Resort near Korolevu, 20 km E of Singatoka. Set on a palm-fringed beach before a verdant valley, Hide-A-Way offers everything the $100-a-night places nearby offer, but also 8-bed, $8-a-night dormitories. There's always room for travelers who just happen to drop in. If you're in a group, take one of the large *mbures* suitable for up to 5 people ($70) or smaller *mbures* for up to 3 ($56). Cooking your own food is not allowed; the restaurant is expensive but good, and there are no grocery stores nearby, but Hide-A-Way offers free live entertainment nightly, including a real *meke* Tues. and Fri. at 2100 and an all-you-can-eat Fijian feast ($11) Sun. night. Day excursions depart the resort regularly, if you want to hang out here a while. The trip to the hot spring and sliding falls ($6) should not be missed. Don Spencer, the manager, is a bit of a cave freak and will arrange to take you through a few if you show any interest. Even with the price of the meals, you'll still spend less than you would at Beachcomber Island. It's excellent value, and highly recommended as a stop on the way to Suva.

Vatulele Island: This small island, just S of Viti Levu, is famous for its *tapa* cloth. Vatulele reaches a height of only 34 m on its N end; there are steep bluffs on the W coast, and gentle slopes on the E face a wide lagoon. Both passages into the lagoon are from its N end. Five different levels of erosion are visible on the cliffs, as the uplifted limestone was undercut. There are rock paintings but no one

above, clockwise: Mele Peha preparing pandanus fruit *(fala)* for cooking, Nukunonu, Tokelau (Robert Kennington); Graciosa Bay, Nendo, Santa Cruz Is., Solomon Is. (Paul Bohler); a Tongan feast (Phil Esmonde); Luhi'ano Perez cleaning giant clams *(fahua),* Nukunonu, Tokelau (Robert Kennington); cleaning fish, Tapuaetai, Aitutaki, Cook Is. (D. Stanley)

above, clockwise: demonstrators on Noumea's Rue Anatole France, New Caledonia; Societe Le Nickel smelter, Noumea, New Caledonia (P. West); prime minister's office, Apia, Western Samoa (Traugott Goll); Waikiki seen from Diamond Head, Oahu, Hawaii (D. Stanley); church on Savai'i, Western Samoa (Traugott Goll)

knows when they were executed. Another unique feature of Vatulele are the red prawns which are found in 2 pools off its rocky coast. These scarlet prawns, which possess remarkably long antennae, become the same color as ordinary prawns when cooked. A forbidden Crustacea, it is strictly *tambu* to eat them or remove them from the pools. If one does, it will bring ill luck or even shipwreck. **getting there:** Village boats leave for Vatulele from in front of the Korolevu Beach Hotel on Tues., Thurs., and Sat. mornings if the weather is good ($6 OW). The Hide-A-Way people may also be able to arrange a daytrip to the island.

Deumba: The Coral Coast Christian Camp, 13 km W of Navua near Pacific Harbor, offers 5-bed Kozy Korner dormitories with communal kitchen and cold showers at $6 pp, or older dormitory cabins at $4 pp. The adjoining motel units go for $12 s, $15 d complete with private bath, kitchen, fridge, and fan. No alcoholic beverages or dancing are permitted on the premises; on Wed. and Sun. at 1930 you're invited to the Fellowship Meeting in the manager's flat. Call Deumba (tel. 45-178) to reserve. Recommended. Pacific Harbor, an American-style condo development complete cupied beach opposite. Pacific Harbor, an American-style condo development complete with golf course and tourist culture village, is within walking distance. Fijian dance theater or firewalking shows are put on here at 1530 daily except Sun. (admission $6). If you liked Waikiki and Surfers Paradise, then Pacific Harbor is for you.

Navua: This untouristed river town is the center of a rice-growing delta area near the mouth of the Navua River. The Navua Hotel is set on a hilltop just upstream from the bridge. The pleasant terrace overlooks the river. The 6 rooms ($10 s, $16 d) are rarely full, and this would be a nice place to stay while you're waiting for a boat. **from Navua:** Village boats leave from the wharf beside Navua market for Mbengga I. ($3), S of Viti Levu, and Namuamua village ($3), 25 km upstream. Boats may leave any day, but more depart on Saturday. For a description of Namuamua, see "Central Viti Levu."

Mbengga Island: Mbengga is the home of the famous Fijian firewalkers; Rukua, Natheva, and Ndakuimbengga are firewalking villages. Nowadays, however, they perform only in the hotels on Viti Levu. At low tide you can walk the 27 km around the island: the road only goes from Waisomo to Ndakuni. There are caves with ancient burials near Suliyanga, which can be reached on foot from Mbengga at low tide, but permission from the village chief is required to visit. Have your *sevusevu* ready. Climb Korolevu (439 m), the highest peak, from Waisomo or Lalati. Frigate Passage on the W side of the barrier reef is one of the best dive sites near Suva. There's a vigorous tidal flow in and out the passage which attracts large schools of fish, and there are large coral heads. Sulphur Passage on the E side of Mbengga is equally good. The best beach is Lawaki to the W of Natheva. Present the village chief of Natheva with a nice bundle of *waka* if you want to camp. The villagers could set up a great little resort here if they got it together. Kandavu I. is visible to the S of Mbengga.

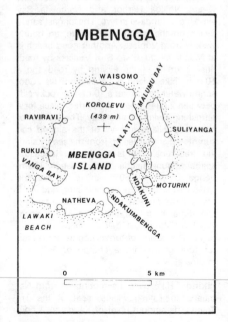

MBENGGA

WAISOMO

MALUMU BAY

KOROLEVU
(439 m)

RAVIRAVI

LALATI

SULIYANGA

RUKUA

VANGA BAY

MBENGGA ISLAND

NDAKUNI

MOTURIKI

NATHEVA

NDAKUIMBENGGA

LAWAKI BEACH

0   5 km

KANDAVU

This big, 50-by-13-km island 100 km S of Suva is the 4th largest in Fiji A mountainous, varied island with waterfalls plummeting from the rounded hilltops, Kandavu is outstanding for its vistas and beaches. The famous red-and-green Kandavu parrots may be seen and heard. In the 1870s steamers bound for New Zealand and Australia would call at Ngaloa Harbor to pick up passengers and goods, and Kandavu was considered as a possible site for a new capital of Fiji. Instead Suva was choosen and Kandavu was left to lead its sleepy village life; only today is the outside world making a comeback with the arrival of roads, planes, and visitors.

sights: The airstrip and wharf are each a 10-min. walk in different directions from the post office and hospital in the tiny government station of Vunisea. Vunisea is strategically located on a narrow, hilly isthmus where Ngaloa Harbor and Namalata Bay almost cut Kandavu in two. The longest sandy beach on the island is at Ndrue, an hour's walk N from Vunisea. Another good beach is at Muani village, 8 km S of Vunisea by road. Just 2 km S of the airstrip by road and a 10-min. hike inland is Waikana Falls. Cool spring water flows over a 10-m-high rocky cliff between 2 deep pools, the perfect place for a refreshing swim on a hot day. The women of Namuana village just W of the airstrip can summon giant turtles up from the sea by singing traditional chants to the vu (ancestral spirits) Raunindalithe and Tinandi Thambonga. On a bluff 60 m above the sea, the garlanded women begin their song and in 15 min. a large turtle will appear. This turtle, and sometimes its mates, will swim up and down slowly offshore just below the overhanging rocks. The calling of turtles can be performed for tour groups for a charge of $400 (no photos allowed).

hiking: Hike over the mountains from Namuana to Tavuki village, seat of the Tui Tavuki, paramount chief of Kandavu. A cou-

ple of hours beyond is the Yawe area where large pine tracts are being established. In the villages of Nalotu, Yakita, and Nanggalotu at Yawe, traditional Fijian pottery is still made. Carry on from Yawe to Lomati village, from where you begin the ascent of Nambukelevu (837 m). There's no trail—you'll need a guide to help you hack a way. Nambukelevu (Mt. Washington) dominates the W end of Kandavu and renders hiking around the cape too arduous. Petrels nest in holes on the N side of the mountain. There's surfing off Nambukelevuira village at the island's W point. Cut S from Lomati to Ndavinggele village, where another trail leads E along the coast to Mburelevu, end of the road from the airstrip. This whole loop can be done in 3 days without difficulty, but take food and be prepared to sleep rough.

the Great Astrolabe Reef: The Great Astrolabe Reef stretches unbroken for 30 km along the E side of the small islands N of Kandavu. One km wide, the reef is unbelievably rich in coral and marinelife; because it's so far from shore it still hasn't been fished out. The reef surrounds a lagoon containing 10 islands, the largest of which is Ono. There are frequent openings on the W side of the reef and the lagoon is never over 10 fathoms deep, which makes it a favorite of scuba divers and yachtspeople. The Astrolabe also features a vertical drop-off of 10 m on the inside and 1,800 m on the outside, with visibility of about 75 meters. There's a pine reforestation station at Nanggara on Ono.

accommodations: The only hotel on Kandavu is Reece's Place at the NW corner of Ngaloa I., a short launch ride ($6 OW) from Vunisea station. There are 8 beds ($10 pp) in Fijian mbures, or pitch your tent for $3 pp. Enjoy Mona's fantastic meals ($9 pp for ter to enjoy Mona's fantastic meals ($7 pp for all 3)—the best food in Fiji. Ask Joe if you can't sample his pineapple-and-papaya homebrew. The view of Ngaloa Harbor from the hotel is excellent. There's a long sandy beach and the snorkeling is good, though for $10 pp Joe will arrange for someone to take you to the Ngaloa Barrier Reef where snorkeling is exceptional (better than at Taveuni). Reece's Place is also a large, working, subsistence farm growing pawpaw and bananas. It's a lovely spot, the perfect place to get away from it all and have a quiet secluded stay with 2 of the most hospitable people in the South Pacific, Joe and Mona Reece. Albert's Plantation Hideaway at Langalevu at the E end of Kandavu is similar to Reece's Place but more remote and less crowded. The best way to come is by boat as the airport is half the island away!

practicalities: There are no restaurants at Vunisea, but a coffee shop at the airstrip opens mornings, and there are 2 general stores selling canned goods. A lady at the market serves tea and scones (50 cents) when the market is open, Tues. to Saturday. Buy *waka* at the Coop store for formal presentations to village hosts. Occasional carriers ply the roads of Kandavu: 50 cents pp to Wailevu.

getting there: Boats arrive at Vunisea from Suva ($20 OW) about twice a week, calling at villages along the N coast. The easy way to come is on Fiji Air from Suva ($75 RT), 3 times a week. Sunflower Airlines flies Nandi-Kandavu twice a week ($39 OW).

KANDAVU

dolphins: While most people use the terms dolphin and porpoise interchangeably, a porpoise lacks the dolphin's beak (although many dolphins are also beakless). There are 62 species of dolphins, and only 6 species of porpoises. Dolphins leap from the water and many legends tell of their saving humans, especially children, from drowning (the most famous concerns Telemachus, son of Odysseus). Because dolphins are often found in the vicinity of schools of tuna, many drown in purse-seine nets set by humans.

SUVA

Capital of Fiji since 1882, Suva is the pulsing heart of the South Pacific, the most cosmopolitan city in Oceania. The harbor is always jammed with ships bringing goods and passengers from far and wide. Busloads of commuters and enthusiastic visitors constantly stream into the busy market bus station nearby. In the business center are Indian women in saris, large sturdy chocolate-skinned Fijians, Australians and New Zealanders in shorts and knee socks, and wavy-haired Polynesians from Tonga and Samoa. This exciting multiracial city of 117,827 (1976), a fifth of Fiji's population, is also about the only place in Fiji where you'll see a building taller than a palm tree. The Fiji School of Medicine, the University of the South Pacific, the Fiji Institute of Technology, and the Pacific Theological College have all been established here. The city offers some of the best nightlife between Kings Cross (Sydney) and North Beach (San Francisco), plus shopping, sightseeing, and many good-value cheap places to stay and eat. Those sporting a sunburn from Fiji's western sunbelt resorts may even welcome Suva's tropical rains. The lovely *Isa Lei,* a Fijian song of farewell, tells of a youth whose love sails off and leaves him alone in Suva, smitten with longing.

SIGHTS OF SUVA

South Suva: The most beautiful section of the city is the area around Albert Park, where the aviator Kingsford Smith landed in 1928. To the N the stern and heavy lines of the Government Buildings (1939) reflect the tensions rampant in Europe at the time they were built. Parliament meets regularly in the Government Buildings and the public is welcome to observe (the budget debate each Nov. is the liveliest). To the W is the elegant, Edwardian-style Grand Pacific Hotel (1914) which dates from an earlier, more confident era; savor the interior for a taste of the old British *raj.* South of Albert Park are the fine Thurston Botanical Gardens, where tropical flowers such as cannas and *plumbagos* blossom. On the grounds of the Gardens is the Fiji Museum. Small but full, this museum is renowned for its maritime displays: canoes, outriggers, the rudder from HMS *Bounty,* and *ndrua* steering oars that were manned by 4 Fijians. The collection of Fijian war clubs is outstanding. The history section is being greatly expanded as artifacts in overseas collections are returned to Fiji. The museum is open daily 0830-1630, admission 50 cents. South of the Gardens is Government House (1928), residence of the governor general. Entry is allowed only between 1400-1700 on the first Sun. of each month. Visitors may, however, see the changing of the guard at the gates, usually enacted sometime during the first or second week of the month, when a cruise ship is in. The sentry on ceremonial guard duty wears a belted red tunic and an immaculate white *sulu* (kilt). The seawall just opposite the sentry box is the perfect place to sit and enjoy the view across Suva Harbor to Mbengga I. (to the L) and the dark, green mountains of eastern Viti Levu punctuated by Joske's Thumb, a high volcanic plug, to the right. Take the Nasese bus (20 cents) around its loop through South Suva and back for a glimpse of the beautiful garden suburbs of the city.

University of the South Pacific: Catch any bus eastbound along MacArthur or Gordon streets to reach this beautiful 78-ha campus on a hilltop at Lauthala Bay. The area E of the university was a Royal N.Z. seaplane base before the land was turned over to the USP. Leading educational institution in Oceania, the USP is jointly owned by 11 Pacific countries for the purpose of building the skills needed back home. Although over 70 percent of the 2,000 full-time students are from Fiji, the rest are on scholarships from every corner of the Pacific. There's a good library. The USP's In-

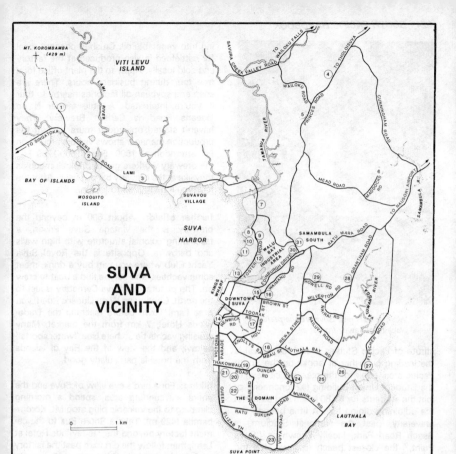

SUVA AND VICINITY

1. cement factory
2. Tradewinds Marina/Scubahire
3. Castle Restaurant
4. Fiji School of Medicine
5. Tamavua Reservoir
6. Queen Elizabeth Barracks
7. Suva Cemetery
8. Royal Suva Yacht Club
9. Suva Prison
10. Marine Department
11. Narain wharf
12. Carlton Brewery
13. Marine Pacific Ltd.
14. General Post Office
15. New Haven Motel
16. hospital
17. mosque
18. Suva Apartments
19. South Seas Private Hotel
20. Fiji Museum
21. Thurston Botanical Gardens
22. Government House
23. Pacific Theological College
24. South Pacific Bureau
    for Economic Cooperation (SPEC)
25. University of the South Pacific
26. National Stadium
27. Beach Road Park
28. Raiwangga market
29. Sangam Temple
30. Tanoa Guest House
31. Fiji Institute of Technology

Wailoku Falls near Suva are the perfect place to get away from it all.

stitute of Pacific Studies (Box 1168, Suva) is the leading publisher of books on the South Pacific area. Look for the pleasant canteen in the Student Union Building ($2 luncheon), or join the students for $1.80 lunch and dinner in the adjoining dining hall. A little beyond the university, past the National Stadium, is Beach Road Park, locally known as "Suva Point," the closest beach to town. It's too muddy and dirty to swim, but the view across Lauthala Bay is worth the stop. The Vatuwangga bus passes nearby.

North Suva: Suva's wonderful, colorful market is a good place to linger. If you're a yachtie or backpacker, you'll be happy to know that the market overflows with fresh produce of every kind. Worth some time looking around. Unfortunately fumes, noise, and pollution from the adjacent bus station buffet through the market. Continue N and turn R just before the bridge to reach the factory of Island Industries Ltd. Most of Fiji's copra is shipped to Suva for processing. At this plant the copra is crushed to extract the coconut oil which is then sent to the U.K. for further refin-

ing into vegetable oil. Crushed coconut meal for cattlefeed is also produced at the factory and sold locally. Apply to the plant office for a free tour during business hours. There are soap and soybean oil factories nearby to tour if you're interested. A little farther N on Queens Road is Carlton Brewery. They haven't started up regular tours yet but the production manager shows visitors around on Fri. afternoon at 1500. From 1600-1730 Fri., the brewery workers get to drink as much as they like at the brewery bar out back. After the tour you'll be invited to join in.

farther afield: About 600 m beyond the brewery is the vintage Suva Prison, a fascinating colonial structure with high walls and barbwire. Opposite is the Royal Suva Yacht Club where you can buy a drink, meet some yachties, and maybe find a boat to crew on. The picturesque Suva Cemetery is just to the north. Continuing W on Queens Road, you pass Lami Town before reaching the Tradewinds Hotel, 7 km from the market. Many cruising yachts tie up here (see "water sports" below), and the view of the Bay of Islands from the hotel is particularly good.

hiking: For a bird's-eye view of Suva and the entire surrounding area, spend a morning climbing to the volcanic plug atop Mt. Korombamba (429 m). Take a Shore Bus to the cement factory beyond the Tradewinds Hotel at Lami, then follow the dirt road past the factory up into the foothills. After about 45 min. on the main track, you'll come to a fork just after a sharp descent. Keep L and cross a small stream. Soon after, the track divides again. Go up on the R and look for a trail straight up to the R where the tracks rejoin. It's a 10-min. scramble to the navigational marker at the summit from here. There's a far more challenging climb to the top of Joski's Thumb, a volcanic plug 15 km W of Suva. Take a bus to Naikorokoro Road, then walk inland 30 min. to where the road turns sharply R and crosses a bridge. Follow the track straight ahead and continue up the river till you reach a small village. Request permission of the villagers to proceed. From the village to the Thumb will take just under 3 hours and a guide might be advisable. The last bit is extremely steep, but an experienced rockclimber could make it without ropes. Another good trip is to Wailoku Falls below Tamavua, one of the nicest picnic spots near Suva. Take the Wailoku bus from lane 15 at the market bus station as far as its turn-around point. Continue down the road, cross a bridge, then follow a footpath on the L upstream till you reach the falls. There's a deep pool here where you can swim among verdant surroundings.

Tholo-i-Suva Forest Park: With the lovely green forests in back of Suva in full view, this is one of the most breathtaking places in all of Fiji. Get there on the Sawani bus (47 cents) which leaves the market every hour. The park offers 3.6 km of trails (including a half-km nature trail) through a beautiful mahogany forest, plus waterfalls and natural swimming pools. The park is so unspoiled it's hard to imagine you're only 11 km from Suva. Enter the park from the Forestry Station along the Falls Trail. Unfortunately, there have been a few

ripoffs lately so keep an eye on your gear while you're swimming. Thefts from previous visitors have forced the rangers to prohibit camping in the park.

ACCOMMODATIONS

Most of the decent places for travelers to stay are clustered on the S side of the downtown area near Albert Park. The commercially-oriented hotels are near Marks St. and the market, while swingers gravitate to the establishments in the foothills up Waimanu Road. One of the most popular places near Albert Park is the Coconut Inn, 8 Kimberly St., which charges $4 for a bunk in the dorm. There's a small flat upstairs for couples, $5 pp. The Inn offers cooking facilities. Though it does get crowded this is just the place to meet other travelers and exchange experiences. Buy some *kava* powder and have an evening grog session in the lounge. Ask Tambua to do the honors as master of ceremonies. Another good choice, one block E of the Park, is the

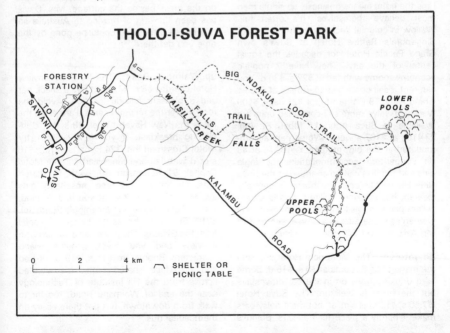

THOLO-I-SUVA FOREST PARK

FORESTRY STATION

TO SAWANI

TO SUVA

BIG NDAKUA LOOP TRAIL

WAISILA CREEK

FALLS TRAIL

FALLS

KALAMBU ROAD

LOWER POOLS

UPPER POOLS

0   2   4 km

⌐ SHELTER OR PICNIC TABLE

Fishing for matu and kaikai on the Nasese seawall, just S of Suva's Botanical Garden.

South Seas Private Hotel, 6 Williamson Road (tel. 22-195), which charges $5 pp in double rooms. There's a large kitchen and veranda, and guests may use the pool at the Grand Pacific Hotel, which is owned by the same company. The no-nonsense Tongan lady who runs the hotel means business, so single men must behave themselves. It's often full. Wallow in colonial decadence (in the style of Singapore's Raffles Hotel) at Suva's own Grand Pacific Hotel, for decades the social center of the city. They have 7 non-a/c economy rooms with fan at $22 s, $30 d. You can rent a self-contained apartment at Pacific Grand Apts, 19 Gorrie St., for $21 daily, $100 weekly. Twelve more self-contained units are available at Suva Apts, 17 Mbau St. (tel. 23-416), at $107 a week. Women are accommodated at the big, modern Y.W.C.A. at $8 pp. Longer-term accommodations for single girls and families can be arranged at the Suva Girls Hostel ($3 pp). The hostel is centrally located, has cooking facilities, and is an excellent place for visiting women to meet local women as it operates as a drop-in center. Call Mr. Aziz, tel. 311-546, for information.

downtown: The Metropole Hotel opposite the market has 9 rooms at $9 s, $15 d. Some hard drinking goes on in the bar downstairs but the hotel is well-run. The Suva Hotel ($7.50 s, $12 d) is similar, but the 4 noisy bars make it hardly a place for travelers. Bhindi's

Apts. nearby at 55 Toorak Rd. has a row of self-contained units at $72 a week. Try also Davis Accommodations, 20 Stewart St., for a homey, central place to stay. There are only 4 beds—$5 pp bed and breakfast (dorm)—so it's often full. They might let you pitch a tent on the grass beside the cottage. Mrs. Davis has been thinking of moving to Australia so this quaint little place could be gone by the time you get there.

up Waimanu Road: The Suva Oceanview Hotel charges $8 s, $12 d. It has a snack bar and a pleasant hillside location. Avoid the rooms over the reception area. Farther up the hill is the New Haven Motel, $8 s, $11 d including breakfast. If you're a swinger try Motel Crossroad Inn, 124 Robertson Rd., $10 s or d with fan and fun. Nearby is the Motel Capital, 91 Robertson Rd., with 10 shared apts, $5 for a short time, hospitality girls available. If this *isn't* what you had in mind, stay at Tanoa House in Samambula South (tel. 381-575), a guest house run by an ex-colonial from the Gilberts. The place has a garden with a view and you meet genuine island characters. Rooms are $11 s, $19 d for bed and breakfast (shared bath). It's situated across from the Fiji Institute of Technology near the end of Waimanu Road, too far to walk from downtown, but get there easily on the hospital bus.

camping: There's camping on Nukulau, a tiny reef island SE of Suva. For many years Nukulau was the government quarantine station where most of the indentured laborers spent their first 2 weeks in Fiji. Now it's a public park; get free 3-day camping permits from the Dept. of Lands, Room 39, Government Buildings, during office hours. The island has toilets and drinking water, and the swimming is good. Problem is, the only access is the $22 tourist boat (includes lunch) departing downtown Suva at 0930 when there are enough passengers. Call Coral See Cruises, tel. 361-258 or 361-592, for information. You're allowed to return to Suva a couple of days later at no extra charge.

FOOD

Suva has many excellent, inexpensive restaurants. Three of the best are on Cumming St. in the heart of the duty-free shopping area. All post their menus on boards outside. This author's personal favorite is the Shanghai Restaurant upstairs which serves Chinese and European dishes priced from $1.80 to $4.20. The staff and surroundings are pleasant, and the food good and ample. You get free tea or coffee with the meal, but beer isn't sold until after 1800. Next door to the Shanghai is Le Normandie (French), and across the street the Wan-Q (Chinese), both a little more expensive than the Shanghai. If you just want a snack check out Donald's Kitchen in the arcade at 45 Cumming Street. This is an excellent place to take a break. One block over on Marks St. are cheaper Chinese restaurants, but did you come all the way to Fiji to put up with mediocre meals just to save 50 cents? Several places offer good weekday lunchtime Chinese smorgasbords, especially the Bamboo Terrace opposite the Fiji Visitors Bureau and the New Peking Restaurant in the Pacific Arcade, both $3.50. Two of the best Indian restaurants in the entire South Pacific are side by side at the corner of Pratt and Joske streets downtown: the Hare Krishna Restaurant specializes in luncheon vegetarian *thalis* and sweets, while the Curry Place next door offers non-vegetarian food. Study the menu carefully the first time you go into Hare Krishna, as 2 distinct all-you-care-to-eat offers are available and the prices vary considerably. Both these restaurants are highly recommended. The Y.W.C.A. cafeteria (closed Sun.) is the place to try native Fijian food, such as fish fried in coconut milk. You have to come early to get the best dishes. Another place where you may find Fijian food is the Old Mill Cottage Cafe on the street behind the Golden Dragon nightclub. Stop by for afternoon tea. Snack bars around town often sell large bottles of cold milk (50 cents) — cheap and refreshing. The Castle Restaurant (Chinese) in the Lami Shopping Center is the best place to eat near the Tradewinds Marina. The very cheapest and most colorful places to eat in Suva are down near the market. At lunchtime Fijian ladies run a food market beside Princes Wharf, about $1 a plate. At night a dozen Indian food trucks park beside the market just opposite Burns Philp. Great curries.

ENTERTAINMENT

Movie houses are plentiful downtown; admission is $1-1.50. Have some *kava* at the *yanggona* kiosk in the market; it's $1 a bowl. There are many nightclubs, all of which have cover charges ($1 to $2.50) and nothing much happens until after 2200. The most interracial and relaxed of the clubs is Chequers, which has live music Tues. to Sat. after 2100 (no cover on Sun.). Gays will feel comfortable at Lucky Eddies above Fiji Air, but it's not really a gay bar, as the Fijian girls present try to prove. The Golden Dragon is similar. The teenage crowd frequents the disco at Screwz, opposite Sukuna Park. For really earthy atmosphere try the Bali Hai, the roughest club in Suva. Friday and Sat. nights the place is packed with Fijians (no Indians) and tourists are rare, so beware. If you're looking for action, you'll be able to pick a partner within minutes, but take care with aggressive males. The dancehall on the top floor is the swingingest, with body-to-body jive — the Bali Hai will rock you. Hookers work the street from Chequers to the Regal Theater: don't pay over $10 for a quickie (they'll usually stay

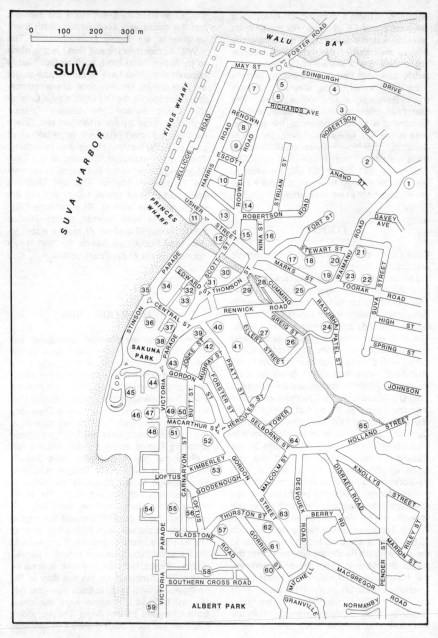

SUVA

0   100   200   300 m

the night for that). However, if this is what you're after, check in to the Flagstaff Boarding House, 62 Rewa St., $10 s or d. All the taxi drivers know it. Don't forget the penicillin and tetracycline when you're calculating the cost of your spree. Better yet, work off that excess energy at the roller skating rink on Greig St., only $1 weekdays, skate rental included.

sports: The Fijians are a very muscular, keenly athletic people, who send champion teams far and wide in the Pacific. You can see rugby and soccer on Sat. and Sun. afternoons at 1500 in season at the National Stadium near the University of the South Pacific. Rugby and soccer are played at Albert Park weekends, and you could also see a cricket game here.

The best time to be in Suva is around the end of Aug. or early Sept. when the Hibiscus Festival fills Albert Park with stalls, games, and carnival revelers. Yacht races to Suva from Auckland and Sydney occur in April or May on alternate years. There's a powerboat race from Suva to Levuka on the long weekend around 10 October.

SHOPPING

Items of the best workmanship are sold in the Government Handicraft Center behind the same building which houses Air Nauru. Familiarize yourself here with what is authentic in a relaxed fixed-price atmosphere before

---

SUVA

1. Oceanview Hotel
2. Crossroad Inn
3. Motel Capital
4. Island Industries Ltd.
5. Bali Hai Cabaret
6. Phoenix Theater
7. Union Maritime Ltd.
8. Health Office
9. buses for Lautoka
10. bus station
11. Kaunitoni Shipping (Maritime Checkers)
12. Metropole Hotel
13. market
14. Morris Hedstrom store
15. Burns Philp Supermarket
16. Wong's Shipping
17. Century Theater
18. Davis Accommodations
19. Suva Hotel
20. Handicrafts of Suva
21. Alankar Theater
22. Bhindi's Apartments
23. Lilac Theater
24. D. Chung Shipping
25. Chequers Nightclub
26. roller skating rink
27. Hart Craft Shop
28. Shanghai Restaurant
29. Morris Hedstrom Supermarket
30. Harbor Center
31. Fiji Visitors Bureau
32. General Post Office

33. Thomas Cook Travel
34. Curio and Handicraft Center
35. Coral See Cruise landing
36. Y.W.C.A.
37. Air Pacific office
38. Regal Theater
39. Hare Krishna Restaurant
40. Dominion Rent-a-Car
41. Catholic Cathedral
42. police station
43. Tuvalu High Commission
44. Overseas Telephone Office
45. Suva Civic Auditorium
46. Suva Olympic Pool
47. Suva Aquarium
48. Suva City Library
49. Fiji Air/Lucky Eddies
50. Pacific Arcade
51. Government Handicraft Center
52. Anglican Cathedral
53. Coconut Inn
54. Immigration Office
55. Golden Dragon
56. Old Mill Cottage Cafe
57. Lotu Pasifika Productions
58. Government Buildings
59. Grand Pacific Hotel
60. Fiji Arts Council
61. Pacific Grand Apartments
62. Gordon St. Medical Center
63. Forestry Dept.
64. The Playhouse
65. Hindu Temple

plunging into the hard-sell establishments. Another good place to start is the Fiji Museum shop, or try Handicrafts of Fiji (upstairs from the arcade), an outlet for a group of coops. There's a large Curio and Handicraft Center on the waterfront behind the post office; you can bargain here. The Hart Craft Shop is a boutique selling the rather artsy productions of the local charity associations. (Notice the WW II air raid shelters across the street.) Some of the most off-beat places in Suva to buy things are the pawn shops, most of which are in the vicinity of the Suva Hotel. Ask for the behind-the-counter selection. Cumming St. is Suva's duty-free shopping area, and the wide selection of goods in the large number of shops make this about the best place in Fiji to do it. Expect to receive a 10-40 percent discount with bargaining. Premier Electronic Co., 54 Cumming St., may offer the best prices, but shop around before you buy. Be wary when purchasing gold jewelry as it might be fake. Never buy anything on the day when a cruise ship is in port—prices shoot up. For clothing

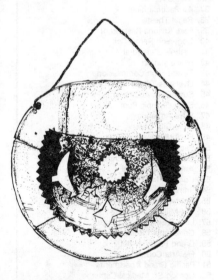

This Fijian breastplate of sperm whale ivory bears a pearl-shell plaque with perforated star and birds.

see the very fashionable hand-printed shirts and dresses at Tiki Togs across from the post office or their second location next to the Pizza Hut: you could come out looking like a real South Seas character at a very reasonable price. The Philatelic Bureau opposite the post office sells the stamps of Tuvalu, Pitcairn, and the Solomons, as well as those of Fiji. Lotu Pasifika Productions (Box 208, Suva) on Thurston St. near the Government Buildings sells books on island social issues and Nuclear Free Pacific posters ($1). In Suva beware of the seemingly friendly sword and mask sellers who will approach you on the street, ask your name, then quickly carve it on a sword and demand $15 for a set that you could buy at a Nandi curio shop for $3. Laugh at them.

PRACTICALITIES

health: You can see a doctor at the Outpatients Dept. of the Colonial War Memorial Hospital for $5 (tourists) or 50 cents (locals). It can be extremely crowded so take along a book to read while you're waiting for them to call your number. You'll probably receive better attention at the Gordon St. Medical Center, Gordon and Thurston streets (consultations $6 for tourists, $4 for locals). There is a female doctor here. The J.P. Bayly Clinic opposite the Phoenix Theater is a church-operated low-income clinic ($2 consultation). The Health Office (open Tues. and Fri. 0830-0930) past the market gives tetanus (free), polio (free), cholera ($1), typhoid ($1), and yellow fever ($8) vaccinations.

services: Thomas Cook Travel next to the post office will change foreign currency Sat. 0830-1200 at the usual rate. The Overseas Telephone Office is open 24 hours a day for trunk calls and telegrams. There is a row of public telephones outside the post office, most out of service. The Immigration office (for extensions of stay, etc.) is behind the Labor Dept. Building (open Mon. to Fri. 0800-1300/1400-1600). Cruising yachties wishing to tour the Lau Group must first obtain permission from the prime minister, who is customary high chief of the group. Fijian Affairs gives approval to cruise the other Fijian islands. This is mostly a formality, but they want to know who's out there. Australia, Britain, China, France, India, Japan, Korea, Malaysia, New Zealand, Papua New Guinea, Tuvalu, and the U.S. have diplomatic missions in Suva. A good local contact for house rentals, real estate, and the purchase of islands is Abdul Aziz, Box 2410, Govt. Bldgs., Suva (tel. 311-546). The Fiji Society (Box 1205, Suva) can help researchers on Fiji and the other Pacific islands. Contact them locally through the Fiji Museum. The Fiji Arts Council, 34 Gorrie St., can be of assistance to visiting musicians and artists. The Indian Cultural Center above the Bank of Baroda on Marks St. shows free films Thurs. at 1830 and arranges cultural events such as music and dance. The program is posted on the board downstairs. There are courses on Indian music, dance, etc., and cultural events can be arranged for visiting groups (write GPO Box 1134, Suva). The Center also has a library (open Mon. to Fri. 0830-1300/1400-1700). Suva's only laundromat (open Mon. to Fri. 0900-1700, Sat. and Sun. 0900-1200) is in the Raiwangga Market Shopping Arcade (catch the Raiwangga bus in front of Desai Books). The machines ($1 to wash, $1 to dry) are in Jeff's Pawn Shop.

water sports, diving, and yachting: The Suva Olympic Swimming Pool charges 40 cents admission; open Mon. to Fri. 1000-1800, Sat. and Sun. 0800-1800 (April to Sept.) or Mon. to Fri. 0900-1900, Sat. and Sun. 0600-1900 (Oct. to March). Scubahire (GPO Box 777, Suva; tel. 361-241 or 361-458) at the Tradewinds Marina arranges 2-tank diving trips ($35-40). Scubahire takes snorkelers out on all their dive trips for $10-15 pp, gear extra. Their full-day to the Mbengga Lagoon is outstanding. They also do certified one-week P.A.D.I. training courses at reasonable rates. Scubahire will ferry you over to Mosquito I., where the city maintains a beach and showers, for $7 RT per group. Admission to the island is 20 cents. Mooring charges for yachts at the Tradewinds are $30 a week per boat if you tie up alongside, otherwise $10 a week if you anchor offshore (includes all the

facilities of the hotel, plus water and electricity). There's a notice board by the pool for people seeking passage or crew for yachts. At the Royal Suva Yacht Club it costs $12 a week for such amenities as mooring privileges, hot showers, and the full use of facilities by the whole crew. A dormitory ($10 pp) for surfers has opened in Suva; the boat to the surf break is only $3 pp and takes 5 minutes to get there. For information write: Marcus Oliver, Box 3338, Lami, Fiji Islands.

information: The Fiji Visitors Bureau is in front of the post office, open Mon. to Fri. 0830-1630, Sat. 0830-1200. The Ministry of Information, Ground Floor, New Wing, Government Buildings, hands out a few booklets on the country. Across the parking lot in the same complex is the Maps and Plans Room of the Lands and Surveys Division which sells excellent maps of Fiji (open Mon. to Thurs. 0900-1300/1400-1530, Fri. 0900-1300/1400-1500). Carpenters Shipping in the Harbor Center sells navigational charts ($10 each). The Suva Public Library is worth a look (open Mon., Tues., Thurs., Fri., 1000-1900, Wed. 1200-1900, Sat. 0900-1300). The Desai Bookshop has the best selection of books on Fiji. There's a good second-hand book exchange upstairs in the building at 45 Marks Street. Suva has 2 daily papers: *The Fiji Times* (earliest newspaper published in the world today) and *The Fiji Sun*. There are also 2 tourist newspapers: the *Fiji Beach Press* (weekly) and *Fiji "Fantastic!"* (monthly). *The Krishna Sun* is a monthly publication of the International Society for Krishna Consciousness (ISKCON).

TRANSPORT

Although nearly all international flights to Fiji arrive at Nandi, Suva is still the most important transportation center in the country. Interisland shipping crowds the waterfront, and if you can't find a ship going your way at precisely the time you want to travel, Fiji Air flies to all the major Fiji islands while Air Pacific services Tonga, Samoa, and New Zealand, both from Nausori. A solid block of buses await your patronage at the market bus station near the harbor, with continuous local service to Lami and Raiwangga, among others, and frequent long-distance departures to Nandi and Lautoka. For a description see "getting around by surface" in the "Introduction" to this chapter. Most of the points of interest around Suva are accessible on foot. If you wander too far, jump on any bus headed in the right direction and you'll end up back in the market.

ships to other countries: Burns Philp Shipping (above Burns Philp Supermarket) are agents for the monthly Banks Line service to Lautoka, Noumea, Honiara, Kieta, Port Moresby, and on to Europe. They cannot sell you a passenger ticket. They can only tell you when the ship is due in and where it's headed. It's up to you to make arrangements personally with the captain. You may get on if there are any empty cabins. The Fijian Shipping Agency in the Honson Bldg. opposite the Fiji Visitors Bureau handles passenger bookings for the MV *Fijian* trip from Suva to Auckland every 3 weeks, about $295 OW. Union Maritime, 80 Harris Rd., are agents for the monthly Kiribati ship to Funafuti ($70 deck) and Tarawa ($94 deck). Meals are included in the fares. The Tuvalu High Commission has a ship to Funafuti 2 or 3 times a year, which then cruises the Tuvalu Group ($29 deck, $58 cabin to Funafuti). Marine Pacific Ltd., upstairs near the dry dock at Walu Bay, handles Warner Pacific Line ships to Tonga and Samoa. Passengers are accepted but you must bring your own food. Carpenters Shipping in the Harbor Center near the Fiji Visitors Bureau are agents for the MV *Moana II* which sails from Suva to Futuna and Wallis ($75 OW), then on to Noumea, about every 2 months. Again, they can't sell the ticket but will tell you when the ship is expected in and you book with the captain. This is a beautiful trip, not at all crowded between Fiji and Wallis. Book a cabin, however, if you're going right through to Noumea. Sofrana Line ships sometimes accept work-a-passage crew for New Zealand, Australia, or any other port when they need hands. You must arrange this with the captain. The Wed. issue of the *Fiji Times* carries a special section on international shipping, though most of the services listed don't accept passengers. You can also try to sign on as crew on a yacht. Try both yacht anchorages in Suva: put up a notice, ask around, etc.

ships to other islands: Wong's Shipping Co., Suite 6, 1st floor, Epworth Arcade off Nina St. (open Mon. to Fri. 0800-1700, Sat. 0800-1000) has 6 ships to different parts of Fiji with departures every other day. There are 2 ships a week to Savusavu, Taveuni, and Rambi ($25 deck, $35 cabin each); weekly departures for Koro ($20 deck, $30 cabin); plus a monthly service to the Lau Group ($38 deck, $48 cabin to Vanua Mbalavu). Wong's is the biggest domestic shipping company in Fiji, so check with them first. All fares include meals but cabin passengers get better food and facilities. Patterson Brothers opposite Wong's takes reservations for the Suva-Natovi-Nambouwalu-Lambasa bus-ferry-bus combination which departs Suva Post Office Mon. to Sat. at 0500 and Lambasa at 0700. The fare is $18 Suva to Nambouwalu, $24 right through to Lambasa, an excellent 10-hour trip. Ask about the Northwest Shipping ferry service to Savusavu at 0600 (be there early) Mon., Wed., and Fri. ($18 OW). The Fri. trip calls at Levuka. Another good place to try is D. Chung Shipping Co., 24 Raojibhai Patel St. (upstairs). Chung has weekly service to Kandavu ($17 deck) and Ngau ($15 deck), fortnightly to Moala ($20 deck), and every 6 weeks to Kambara, Namuka, and Komo in Lau ($67 RT deck). All fares include basic meals. Also check at the Narain Wharf in Walu Bay for private ships to different islands. Also at Walu Bay, the Marine Dept. handles government barges to all the Fiji islands, and passenger fares are generally lower than on the private ships but no meals are included. Departures are listed on a blackboard at their office. The government barge to Rotuma leaves approximately once a month ($22 OW deck). Kaunitoni Shipping at Princes Wharf handles the *Kaunitoni* which services the Lau Group to the east. There are different trips to the northern, central, and southern Lau islands, $234 for tourists and $156 for locals RT in a cabin, meals included. Tourists are not

pick of the produce at Suva's colorful market

allowed to travel deck class on this ship, due mostly to the complaining attitude of previous European deck passengers who expected red-carpet treatment while paying the least possible. Though not cheap, it's a good way to see a cross section of Lau in 7 to 9 days. A compromise would be to take the *Kaunitoni* as far as Lakemba ($54) or Vanua Mbalavu ($53) and fly back on Fiji Air. Ask on the smaller vessels tied up at Princes Wharf for passage to Nairai ($18), Ngau ($18), Kandavu ($20), etc. If you're planning a long voyage by interisland ship, a big bottle of Corruba to captain and crew as a token in appreciation of their hospitality works wonders.

to Ovalau Island: The most popular trip is the bus/launch combination to Levuka on Ovalau via Natovi. The bus leaves from behind the post office in Suva Mon. to Sat. at 0830, Sun. at 1330; you leave Levuka on the return trip Mon. to Sat. at 0800, Sun. at 1300. Bus Suva-Natovi is $2.33, launch Natovi-Levuka is $6. Reserve your seat on the bus at Budget Rent-a-Car (open daily 0730-1700) in

Queens Road near Carlton Brewery. Reservations are recommended on weekends and public holidays.

tours and trips: If your time in Fiji is limited, the Orchid Island Cultural Center, NW of Suva, offers a synopsis of Fijian customs with demonstrations, dancing, and informative exhibits. Although the visit is invariably superficial and rushed, Orchid Island does afford a glimpse into traditions such as the *kava* ceremony, *tapa-* and pottery-making, etc., and the historical displays and miniature zoo are good. See and photograph Fiji's rare banded and crested iguanas up close. There are 2-hour tours of the center every morning except Sun. and the $8.50 pp cost includes transportation, admission, and entertainment (Orchid Island can only be visited on the tour). Bookings can be made through any travel agency in Suva. More exciting are the whitewater rafting trips offered by Pacific Crown Aviation (tel. 361-532) on the headwaters of the Navua River with helicopter transportation to and from Suva. The price is $126 pp (minimum of 4); great if you can afford it. The Fiji Rucksack Club (Box 2394, Govt. Bldgs., Suva) offers non-commercial outings from Suva every weekend and visitors are welcome to participate upon payment of a $2 temporary membership fee. These trips offer an excellent opportunity to meet some local expats and see the untouristed side of Fiji. The Fiji Visitors Bureau will be able to put you in touch with the club. For information on scuba diving see under "Practicalities" above.

NAUSORI AND VICINITY

Nausori: The Rewa River town of Nausori, 19 km NE of Suva, was the site of Fiji's first large sugar mill which operated 1881-1959. In those early days it was believed incorrectly that sugarcane grew better on the wetter eastern side of the island. Today cane is grown only on the drier, sunnier western sides of Viti Levu and Vanua Levu. The old sugar mill is now a rice mill and storage depot as the Rewa Valley has become a major rice-producing area. Nausori is better known for its large international airport 3 km SE, and is a good place to stay if your flight leaves very early the next morning. The business area is compact so it's easy to attend to odds and ends like getting a haircut, last-minute shopping at the small stores and the few duty-free shops, and taking in a movie at one of the 3 cinemas. Rewa Pawn Shop opposite the Mobil station sells off-beat souvenirs such as large mats and old *tapa* cloth. You could have trouble getting these through Customs back home. **accommodations and food:** The Hotel Nausori beside the rice mill has rooms with private bath and hot water at $12 s, $16 d. Joe's Restaurant on the back street opposite the bus station is very reasonable. Have a beer in unaccustomed comfort at the Whistling Duck pub nearby. Better yet, have a bowl of grog at the Nausori Kava Saloon farther back from the bus station.

from Nausori: Buses to the airport (26 cents) and Suva (67 cents) are fairly frequent, but the last bus to Suva is at 2130. You can also catch buses here to Lautoka and Natovi (for Levuka). Take a bus to Nakelo Landing to explore the Rewa River Delta. Many outboards leave from here to take villagers to their riverside homes. Passenger fares are 20 cents each for short trips. Hop aboard and you'll probably be invited to spend the night with the villagers. Larger boats leave sporadically from Nakelo for Levuka, Ngau, and Koro, but finding one would be pure chance. Some also depart from nearby Wainimbokasi Landing.

Mbau Island: Mbau, a tiny, 8-ha island just E of Viti Levu, has a special place in Fiji's history: this was the seat of High Chief Thakombau who used European cannons and muskets to subdue most of western Fiji in the 1850s. At its pinnacle Mbau had a population of 3,000, hundreds of war canoes to guard its waters, and over 20 temples on the island's central plain. After the Battle of Verata on Viti Levu in 1839, Thakombau and his father Tanoa presented 260 bodies of men, women, and children to their closest friends and allied chiefs for gastronomical purposes. Fifteen

years after this slaughter, Thakombau converted to Christianity and prohibited cannibalism on Mbau. In 1867 he became a sovereign, crowned by European traders and planters desiring a stable government in Fiji to protect their interests. **getting there:** Take the Mbau bus from Nausori (40 cents) to Mbau Landing. There are punts to cross over to the island: $1 at high tide from the old landing, $2 at any time from the new landing. Note that Mbau is not considered a tourist attraction and from time to time visitors are prevented from going to the island. It helps to know someone. If you're told to contact the Office for Fijian Affairs in Suva forget it—they have no procedures for arranging visits and will only waste your time. If you really want to go, just wade across to the island at low tide about 20 m N of the telegraph poles. Bring a bundle of *waka* for the *turanga-ni-koro* and ask permission very politely to be shown around. You can see everything on the island in an hour or so.

sights of Mbau: The graves of the Thakombau family and many of the old chiefs lie on the hilltop behind the school. The large, sturdy, stone church, located near the provincial offices, was the first Christian church in Fiji. Inside its nearly one-m-thick walls, just in front of the altar, is the old sacrificial stone once used for human sacrifices, today the baptismal font. Now painted white, this font was once known as King Thakombau's "skull crusher." It's said a thousand brains were splattered against it. Across from the church are huge ancient trees and the Council House. Ratu Sir George Thakombau, governor general of Fiji from 1973-82, has a large traditional-style home on the island.

Viwa Island: To reach Viwa Island, where the first Fijian Bible was printed, hire a punt at Mbau Landing for about $5. If you're lucky, some locals will be going and you'll be able to get a ride for less. The Rev. John Hunt, who did the translation, lies buried in the graveyard beside the church which bears his name.

CENTRAL VITI LEVU

THE CROSS-ISLAND HIGHWAY

Vunindawa: If you have a few days to spare, consider exploring the river country NW of Nausori. The main center of this area is Vunindawa on the Wainimala River. There are 5 buses a day from Suva to Naluwai where you cross the river on a free government punt, then walk the last bit into Vunindawa. It's a big village with 4 stores, hospital, post office, police station, 2 schools, and a provincial office. Frederick Rakavono, a veteran of the Solomon Islands campaign during WW II, will probably be able to arrange your stay at Korovatu village, a 5-min. walk from Vunindawa. You could camp beside Frederick's house. (See "staying in villages" in the main "Introduction" for etiquette, which also applies to campers.) Go for a swim in the river or borrow a horse to ride around the countryside. Stroll 2 km down the road to Waindawara where there's another free punt near the junction of the Wainimbuka, Wainimala, and Rewa rivers. Take a whole day to hike up to Nairukuruku and Navuniyasi, and back.

getting there: Regular bus service covers the Cross-Island Highway, with routes from both Suva and Tavua at either end connecting at Monasavu in the middle. Buses depart Suva for Monasavu ($3.95) at 0900 and 1300 daily. If you want to make a connection at Monasavu for Nandarivatu or Tavua, you'll have to catch the 0900 bus. The 0900 bus to Monasavu passes Naluwai, across the river from Vunindawa, at about 1000. This bus passes Mbalea, trailhead of the Trans-Viti Levu Trek, about noon. A bus leaves Tavua for Monasavu at about 1500 daily, passing through Nandarivatu.

riverrunning: There's an exciting bamboo raft (*mbilimbili*) trip through the Waingga Gorge between Naitauvoli to Naivuthini, two villages on the Cross-Island Highway W of Vunindawa. Two men with long poles guide each raft through the frothing rapids as the seated visitor views towering boulders enveloped in jungle. The charge for the 2-hour ride is $20 pp, but reservations must be made in advance as an individual *mbilimbili* will have to be constructed for you. (There's no way to get a used *mbilimbili* back up to Naitauvoli.)

right: The yam (Dioscorea), a tropical tuber which requires heavy rainfall but good drainage, appears aboveground as a long trailing vine with heart-shaped leaves. A prestige food in some Pacific cultures, yams can grown to over 3 m long and weigh hundreds of kilos.

left: Each sweet potato (Ipomoea batatas) plant has 4 to 10 starchy tuberous roots joined by a long vine with lobed leaves and morning glory-like flowers. A native of South America, the means by which the sweet potato or kumara arrived in the South Pacific is still a mystery.

Write Mr. Joeli Bose, Naitauvoli village, Wainimala, Naitasiri, P.A. Naikasanga, Fiji Islands, at least 2 weeks ahead, giving the exact date of your arrival in the village and the number in your party. Mere Nawaqatabu at the Fiji Visitors Bureau in Suva can also arrange this trip for you in advance for a small consideration. No trips are made on Sunday. If you plan to spend the night at Naitauvoli specify whether you require imported European-style food, or will be satisfied with local village produce. If you stay overnight a *sevusevu* and monetary contribution are expected, in addition to the $20 pp for the raft trip.

Monasavu Hydroelectric Project: The largest development project ever undertaken in Fiji, this massive F$234 million scheme at Monasavu near the center of Viti Levu took 1,500 men and 6 years to complete. This earthen dam, 82 m high, was built on the Nanuka River to supply water to the four 20-megawatt generating turbines at the Wailoa Power Station on the Wailoa River, 625 m below. The dam forms a lake 17 km long and the water drops through a 5.4-km tunnel at a 45 degree angle, one of the steepest engineered dips in the world. Transmission lines carry power from Wailoa to Suva and Lautoka, and Monasavu is capable of producing double Viti Levu's needs for the rest of the decade. The project headquarters is at Koro-Ni-O, 5 km from the dam site.

Mt. Victoria: The two great rivers of Fiji, the Rewa and the Singatoka, originate on the slopes of Mt. Victoria (Tomanivi), highest mountain in the country (1,323 m). The climb begins near the bridge at Navai. Turn R up the hillside a few hundred m down the jeep track, then climb up through native bush on the main path all the way to the top. Beware of misleading signboards. There are 3 small streams to cross; no water after the third. Bright red epiphytic orchids (*Dendrobium mohlianum*) are sometimes in full bloom. There's a flat area up there where you could camp—if you're willing to take your chances with Mbuli, the devil king of the mountain. On

your way down, stop for a swim at the largest stream. Allow at least 5 hours for the RT. Local guides are available.

THE TRANS-VITI LEVU TREK

For experienced hikers there's a rugged 3-day trek from the Cross-Island Highway to the Navua River at Namuamua, up and down jungle river valleys through the rainforest. Although considerably longer and more difficult than the Singatoka River Trek described below, the Trans-Viti Levu Trek passes through 9 large, Fijian villages and gives you a good cross section of village life. On this traditional route, you'll meet people going down the track on horseback or on foot. Since you must cross the rivers innumerable times, the trek is probably impossible for visitors during the rainy season (Dec. to April), although the locals still manage to do it. If it's been raining, sections of the trail become a quagmire stirred up by horses' hoofs. Hiking boots aren't much use here; you'd be better off with shorts and an old pair of running shoes in which to wade across the rivers. There are many refreshing places to swim along the way. Some of the villages have small trade stores, but you're better off carrying your own food. Pack some *yanggona* as well. You can always give it away if someone invites you in. But remember, you are not the first to undertake this walk; the villagers have played host to track-walkers many, many times. Some previous hikers have not shown much consideration to local residents along the track. Unless you have been specifically invited, do not presume automatic hospitality. If a villager provides food or a service, be prepared to offer adequate payment. This applies equally to the Singatoka River Trek. Camping is a good alternative, so take your tent if you have one. Hopefully, the locals will soon recognize the popularity of these treks and set up simple rest houses along the way for trekkers to use.

the route: Take the Monasavu bus to Mbalea, which is just before Lutu. From Mbalea walk down to the Wainimala River which must be crossed 3 times before you

TRANS-VITI LEVU TREK

reach the bank opposite Sawanikula. These crossings can be dangerous and well-nigh impossible in the wet, in which case it's better to stop and wait for some local people who might help you across. From Sawanikula it's not far to Korovou, a fairly large village with a primary school, clinic, and 2 stores. Between Korovou and Nasava you cross the Wainimala River 14 times, but it's easier because you're farther upstream. Try to reach Nasava on the first day. If you sleep at Korovou you'll need an early start and a brisk pace to get to the first village S of the divide before nightfall on the second day. From Nasava, follow the course of the Waisomo Creek up through a small gorge and past a waterfall. You zig-zag back and forth across the creek all the way up almost to the divide. After a steep incline you cross to the S coast watershed. There's a clearing among the bamboo groves on top where you could camp, but no water. Before Nasau (Wainimakatu) the scenery gets better as you enter a wide valley with Mt. Naitarandamu (1,152 m) behind you, and the jagged outline of the unscaled Korombasambasanga Range to your left. Nasau is a large village with 2 stores. You continue down the Wainikoroiluva River. Around Saliandrau the scenery again becomes rewarding with high cliffs to the left.

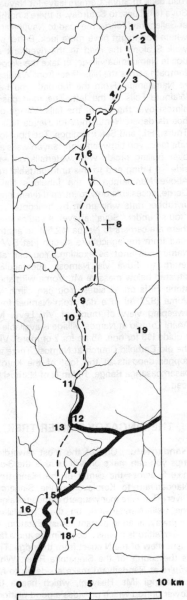

TRANS-VITI LEVU TREK

1. Lutu
2. Mbalea
3. Sawanikula
4. Korovou
5. Matawailevu
6. Nasava
7. Nasauvere
8. Mt. Naitarandamu
9. Nasau (Wainimakutu)
10. Nanggarawai
11. Saliandrau
12. Navunikambi
13. Wainitava
14. Wainuta Falls
15. Namuamua
16. Nuku
17. Nukusere
18. Sambata
19. Korombasambasanga Range

0   5   10 km

Namuamua: At Saliandrau there's a gravel road back to Suva. Carriers leave for Navua or Suva ($4) Tues. to Saturday. If there's nothing at Saliandrau, follow the road to Navunikambi where you might have more luck. Better still, walk S along the road to the riverbank opposite Namuamua village, or take the slippery footpath across the hills direct from Wainitava to Namuamua. From the footpath you'll see Wainuta Falls to the left. The road passes almost over the top of the falls. Village outboards depart Namuamua for Navua ($3) on Thurs., Fri., and Sat. mornings. The hour-long ride takes you between high canyon walls and over boiling rapids with waterfalls on each side—a fitting end to this unforgettable trek. Above Namuamua is the fabulous Navua Gorge, accessible only to intrepid riverrunners in rubber rafts who go in by helicopter (see "tours" under "Suva" above). If you're stuck, there are carriers to Navua ($2.50) on another road from the agriculture station just SW of Namuamua—not as exciting. You can also return to Suva via Namosi, spectacularly situated below massive Mt. Voma with sheer stone cliffs on all sides. You can climb Mt. Voma (927 m) in a day from Namosi for a sweeping view of much of Viti Levu. Mr. Anani Lorosio at Namosi village is available as a guide ($8 for one, $5 pp for 2 or more). Visit the old Catholic Church at Namosi. There are copper deposits at the foot of the Korombasambasanga Range, 14 km N of Namosi by road.

THE SINGATOKA RIVER TREK

Nandarivatu: One of the most rewarding trips you can make on Viti Levu is the 3-day hike S across the center of the island from Nandarivatu to Korolevu on the Singatoka River. There are many superb campsites along the trail. Nandarivatu, on the Cross-Island Highway, is an important forestry station; its 900-m altitude means a cool climate and a fantastic view of the N coast from the ridge. This is the source of the Singatoka River. While you're at Nandarivatu make a sidetrip to Mt. Lomalangi (Mt. Heaven), which has a fire tower on top which provides a good platform

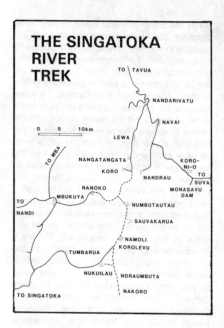

THE SINGATOKA RIVER TREK

for viewing Mt. Victoria. It's an hour's hike to the tower past the Forestry Training Center; pine forests cover the land. **practicalities:** Nandarivatu is a good place to catch your breath before setting out on the trek. The Forestry Rest House at Nandarivatu charges $4, but you must reserve in advance at the Forestry Dept. in Suva or Lautoka. When booking, explain that you don't mind sharing the facilities with other travelers, otherwise they might reserve the whole building (9 beds) just for you, or turn you away for the same reason. There's an excellent campsite at the viewpoint just above the District Officer's residence. Some canned foods are available at the canteen opposite the rest house. Bring most of the food you'll need for the hike from Suva or Lautoka. Cabin crackers are handy.

the route: Follow the dirt road S from Nandarivatu to Nangatangata (fill your canteen before proceeding). From Nangatangata walk about one hour. When you reach the electric high-power line, where the road turns R and begins to descend towards Koro, look for the well-worn footpath ahead. The trail winds along the ridge, and you can see as far as Mba. The primeval forests which once covered this part of Fiji were destroyed long ago by the slash-and-burn agricultural techniques of the Fijians. When you reach the pine trees, the path divides with Nanoko to the R and Numbutautau down to the left. The Rev. Thomas Baker, the last missionary to be clubbed and devoured in Fiji (in 1867), met his fate there. Numbutautau gets more than its share of hikers looking for a place to stay. A simple guest house would make things easier for all concerned and provide a little income for the villagers. Suggest it to them. Nangatangata, Namoli, and Korolevu have also been visited far too often for it to be pure Fijian hospitality anymore: a monetary *sevusevu* spiced with a bundle of *waka* are in order. Camping is an excellent alternative, but please don't spoil things by littering or causing fires. The Numbutautau-Korolevu section involves 22 crossings of the Singatoka River, which is easy enough in the dry season (cut a bamboo staff for balance), but almost impossible in the wet (Dec. to April). At this time it's best to turn R and head to Nanoko, where you may be able to find a carrier to Mbukuya or all the way to Nandi. There's a bus service between Mbukuya and Mba. Still, it's a fantastic trip down the river to Korolevu if you can make it. Hiking boots will be useless in the river so have a pair of old running shoes. From Korolevu you can take a carrier to Tumbarua, where there are 4 buses a day to Singatoka. A few hours' walk from Korolevu are the pottery villages, Ndraumbuta and Nakoro, where traditional, long Fijian pots are still made. The pots are not sold, but you can trade mats or salt for one.

NORTHERN VITI LEVU

Korovou to Natovi and beyond: Korovou is an engaging small town 31 km N of Nausori on the E side of Viti Levu at the junction of Kings Road and the road to Natovi, terminus of the Ovalau and Vanua Levu ferries. Its position makes it an important stop for buses plying the northern route around the island. (Note: since "korovou" means "new village" there are many places called that in Fiji—don't mix them up.) The very enjoyable Tailevu Hotel in Korovou has rooms at $7 pp. At Wailotua, 20 km W of Korovou, is a large cave (admission $2) right beside the village, easily accessible from the road. At Nanggatawa, 8 km N of Natovi, there's a camping area near a good beach (but no surf). Ask about this place at the Coconut Inn in Suva, which owns the property. For a sweeping view of the entire Tailevu area climb Mt. Tova (647 m) in a day from Silana village, 8 km NW of Nanggatawa.

near Rakiraki: The old Catholic Church at Naiserelangi on a hilltop above Navunimbitu Catholic School, on Kings Road about 25 km SE of Rakiraki, was beautifully decorated with frescoes by Jean Charlot in 1962-63. Typically Fijian motifs such as the *tambua, tanoa,* and *yanggona* blend in the powerful composition behind the altar. Father Pierre Chanel, who was martyred on Futuna I. in 1841, appears on the L holding the weapon which killed him, a war club. The church is worth stopping to see and you'll find an onward bus, provided it's not too late in the day. Ask the driver.

Nananu-i-ra Island: Off the northernmost tip of Viti Levu, this is a good place to spend some time amid perfect tranquility and beauty. Kontiki Island Lodge (Box 87, Rakiraki) offers bungalows with 4 beds each ($6 pp). All have fridge and full cooking facilities, but it's necessary to take all your own supplies as there is no store or village on the island. The boat to Nananu-i-ra costs $8 RT pp (20 min.). Contact Empire Taxi (tel. 94-320) in Rakiraki for transport to Volivoli Wharf ($5 for the car) or catch the twice-daily bus (at 1300 and 1700 Mon. to Sat.) to Volivoli (47 cents). Boats from Nananu-i-ra meet these buses. Enjoy the beach, snorkel, and rest—4 nights is the average stay. Highly recommended. Don't arrive in Rakiraki too late in the day, however, as the Rakiraki Hotel is expensive: $30 s, $38 d.

Tavua: Tavua is an important junction on the N coast, where buses on Kings Road and the Cross-Island Highway meet. Catching a bus from Tavua to Rakiraki or Lautoka is usually no problem, but buses to Nandarivatu are less frequent (one leaves at 1500). The Tavua Hotel, on a hilltop behind the town, offers rooms in the main building at $14 s, $18 d including private facilities and fan, or slightly more - expensive a/c units overlooking the pool. The hotel restaurant is pleasant and reasonable; there are also lounges and public bars. This old South Seas-style hotel is full of character, a fine place to break your journey if night is approaching.

Vatukoula: Gold was first discovered at Vatukoula, 8 km S of Tavua, in 1932 and the Emperor Gold Mine opened in 1935. Now owned by an Australian company, the Emperor employs 1,000 miners. The ore is mined both underground and in an open pit, and the mine presently extracts 100,000 oz. of gold annually from 300,000 tons of ore. Waste rock is crushed into gravel and sold. The ore comes up from the underground area through the Smith Shaft. There's also a crushing section, ball mill, and flotation area where gold and silver are separated from the ore. It is not possible to visit the mine.

Mba: The large Indian town of Mba on the Mba River is seldom visited by tourists. There's an attractive mosque in the center of town. Small fishing boats depart from behind the Shell service station opposite the mosque and it's fairly easy to arrange to go along on all-night trips. Mba is better known for the large Rarawai Sugar Mill, opened in 1886. To visit, apply to the Mill Personnel Office. The Mba Hotel is the only organized accommodations, 14 rooms at $20 s, $28 d; very pleasant with a swimming pool, bar, and restaurant. Have a meal at the Ming Wah Restaurant not far from the mosque. There's a local amusement park called Merryland at Mba, which includes a mini zoo (admission $1). If you'd like to stay in a village try Navala on the road to Mbukuya; ask for Semi and say the guy from the Peace Corps sent you.

LAUTOKA AND THE OFFSHORE ISLANDS

Fiji's second largest city (pop. 28,847—1976) and center of the sugar industry, Lautoka is an amiable place with a row of royal palms along its main street. Ferries to the nearby offshore resorts in the Malolo Group depart from Lautoka, and this is the gateway to the Yasawa Islands. Lautoka offers a rambunctious nightlife (though not as good as Suva's), but it's also a religious city with all the main religions of India (except the Jains and Buddhists) well represented. The mosque is also very prominent, located in the center of town.

SIGHTS OF LAUTOKA AND VICINITY

sugar mill: The Lautoka Sugar Mill (founded in 1903) offers free tours during the crushing season (June to Nov.). To get on one, apply to the Tourist Center next to the mill at 0930 and 1430 Mon., Wed., Thurs., and Friday. This mill, one of the largest in the Southern Hemisphere, is well worth a visit.

Sikh temple: Both males and females must cover their heads (handkerchiefs are all right) when they visit the Sikh Temple. Sikhism began in the Punjab of NW India in the 16th C. as a reformed branch of Hinduism much influenced by Islam: for example, Sikhs reject the caste system and idolatry. The teachings of the 10 gurus are contained in the *Granth,* a holy book prominently displayed in the temple. The Sikhs are easily recognized by their beards and turbans. There is a *dharamshala* (hostel) in the temple where sensitive visitors may spend the night, but cigarettes, liquor, and meat are forbidden. There's a communal kitchen. Make a contribution to the temple when you leave.

Hare Krishna Temple: The Sri Krishna Kaliya Temple on Tavewa Ave. (open daily until 2030) is the most prominent Krishna temple in the South Pacific. The images inside on the

R are Radha and Krishna, while the central figure is Krishna dancing on the snake Kaliya to show his mastery over the reptile. The story goes that Krishna chastised Kaliya and exiled him to the island of Ramanik Deep, which Fiji Indians believe to be Fiji. (Curiously, the native Fijian people have also long believed in a serpent god named Dengei.) The 2 figures on the L are incarnations of Krishna and Balarama. At the front of the temple is a representation of His Divine Grace A.C. Bhaktivedanta Swami Prabhupada, founder of the International Society for Krishna Consciousness (ISKCON). The big event of the week at the temple is the Sun. evening *puja* (prayer) from 1630-2030, followed by a vegetarian feast. Visitors are encouraged to join in the singing and dancing. Take off your shoes and sit on the white marble floor, men on one side, women on the other. The female devotees are especially

Lautoka stands out as a religious center, with Sikhs, Hindus, Moslems, Protestants, and Catholics all well represented.

stunning in their beautiful *saris*. Bells ring, drums are beaten, conch shells blown, and stories from the *Vedas, Srimad Bhagavatam,* and *Ramayana* are acted out as everyone chants, *Hare Krsna, Hare Krsna, Krsna Krsna, Hare Hare, Hare Rama, Hare Rama, Rama, Rama, Hare, Hare*. It's a real celebration of joy and a most moving experience. At one point children will circulate with small trays covered with burning candles on which it is customary to place a modest donation; you may also drop a dollar or 2 in the yellow box in the center of the temple. You'll be readily invited to join the feast later and no more money will be asked of you. If you are interested in learning more about Vedic philosophy, there are several spiritual teachers resident in the temple *ashram* who would be delighted to talk to you about the *Bhagavad-gita,* and who can supply literature for a nominal fee.

north of Lautoka: Timber is becoming important as Fiji attempts to diversify its economy away from sugar. One of the largest reforestation projects yet undertaken in the South Pacific is the Lalolo Pine Scheme, 8 km off Kings Road between Lautoka and Mba. There's a shady picnic area along a dammed creek at the forestry station where you could swim, but even if you don't stop, it's worthwhile to take the RT bus ride from Lautoka to see this beautiful area and learn how it's being used.

east of Lautoka: Ambatha, 10 km east, is the perfect base for hiking into the Mount Evans Range behind Lautoka. To stay in the village ($10 pp including meals) bring a *sevusevu* for the *turanga-ni-koro*. There are 4 waterfalls near the village and Table Mountain, with sweeping views, is only an hour away. Pay $1 hiking tax pp a day. Get there on the Tavakumba bus as far a Ambatha junction, then walk.

south of Lautoka: Popular legend holds that Viseisei village between Lautoka and Nandi (frequent buses) is the oldest settlement in Fiji. It is told how the first Fijians came from the W, landing their great canoe, the *Kaunitoni,* at

Vunda Point where the oil tanks are now. By chance, the first missionaries also disembarked at Viseisei; a Centennial Memorial (1835-1935) in front of the church commemorates the event. Opposite the memorial is the residence of the present king of Vunda—a traditional Fijian *mbure*. Near the back of the church is another monument topped by a giant war club. All this is only a few minutes walk from the bus stop, but you're expected to have someone accompany you (Fijian villages are private property). Ask permission of anyone you meet at the bus stop and they will send a child with you. You could give him/her a pack of chewing gum as you part. Nearby is a Memorial Cultural Center where souvenirs are sold to cruise ship passengers. There's a fine view of Nandi Bay from the Center. A couple of km on the airport side of Viseisei, just above Lomolomo Public School, are 2 big WW II cannons which once defended this coast. It's a fairly easy climb to them from the main highway and you get an excellent view from the top.

PRACTICALITIES

accommodations: The Sugar City Hotel on Nathula St. charges $5 pp in the dorm (4 beds) or $12 s, $16 d for a private room with bath. More appealing is the clean, quiet Sea Breeze Hotel on the waterfront near the bus station, $15 s, $20 d with private bath. Also recommended are the 8 economy rooms at the Cathay Hotel, which features a swimming pool. The charge is $15 s, $25 d with private bath. To be close to the action, stay at the Lautoka Hotel which has several good bars and night clubs on the premises. There's also a pool. There are 6 cheaper rooms (shared bath) at $10 s, $16 d. Lautoka's most colorful lodging without doubt is the Fiji Guest House, once the Lautoka Police Station (cells downstairs). Hookers on the beat outside now like to be brought in and the management is understanding. Peep holes between rooms! A reasonable snack bar is attached. It's hot and noisy, and at $10 s, $12 d (shared bath) not cheap, but swingers enjoy the diversions. Be

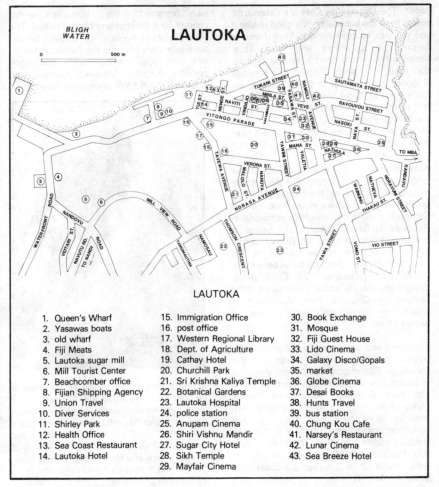

LAUTOKA

1. Queen's Wharf
2. Yasawas boats
3. old wharf
4. Fiji Meats
5. Lautoka sugar mill
6. Mill Tourist Center
7. Beachcomber office
8. Fijian Shipping Agency
9. Union Travel
10. Diver Services
11. Shirley Park
12. Health Office
13. Sea Coast Restaurant
14. Lautoka Hotel
15. Immigration Office
16. post office
17. Western Regional Library
18. Dept. of Agriculture
19. Cathay Hotel
20. Churchill Park
21. Sri Krishna Kaliya Temple
22. Botanical Gardens
23. Lautoka Hospital
24. police station
25. Anupam Cinema
26. Shiri Vishnu Mandir
27. Sugar City Hotel
28. Sikh Temple
29. Mayfair Cinema
30. Book Exchange
31. Mosque
32. Fiji Guest House
33. Lido Cinema
34. Galaxy Disco/Gopals
35. market
36. Globe Cinema
37. Desai Books
38. Hunts Travel
39. bus station
40. Chung Kou Cafe
41. Narsey's Restaurant
42. Lunar Cinema
43. Sea Breeze Hotel

prepared, after a night of revelry, for the *muezzin* of the mosque across the street who calls the faithful to prayer at the crack of dawn. Don't leave your luggage here while you go to the Yasawas.

at the beach: There are 2 beach hotels between Lautoka and Nandi airport, both 2 km off the main road. They are also alike in offering dormitory accommodations with good cooking facilities, fridge, swimming pool, and nearby stores. The Saweni Beach Hotel ($10 pp dorm) is quieter and has a better beach, while the Anchorage Beach Resort ($12 pp dorm) offers free pickups from the airport (tel. 62-099), a washing machine ($1), and panoramic views. Stay at the Anchorage if you like meeting people, at Saweni if you want to regenerate. The Anchorage Beach Resort is between Viseisei and Vunda Point, while the Saweni Beach Hotel is on the beach of that name a few km north.

food: The Chung Kou Cafe on Yasawa St. across from the bus station is a good choice if you roll into Lautoka hungry. Their menu is surprisingly extensive and reasonable. Narsey's Restaurant nearby has the best Indian food—very spicy. Enjoy ample servings of good Chinese food at the a/c Sea Coast Restaurant; $2.20-6.40 menu. For something a little earthier, have a bowl of grog (50 cents) at the Rabnia Pool Center, 32 Namoli Avenue. For dessert, try the ice cream at Gopals near the market.

entertainment: There are 4 movie houses with several showings daily. The disco scene in Lautoka centers on the Hunter's Inn ($3 cover) near the Lautoka Hotel. Next door is Cinderella's with a rougher atmosphere. Roughest is Galaxy Disco in the center of town. Nothing happens at Galaxy before 2200. The Captain Cook Lounge at the Lautoka Hotel is a safe place for an early evening drink (they close at 2100). Catch an exciting rugby (Sat.) or soccer (Sun.) game at the stadium in Churchill Park. Admission is reasonable—check locally for the times of league games.

shopping and services: Lautoka has a big, colorful market, open daily except Sun. but busiest on Saturday. The duty-free shopping in Lautoka is very poor compared to Suva. The Book Exchange, 36 Vitongo Parade, swaps books, or buy a Fijian geography textbook for facts and figures. There's an outpatient service and dental clinic at the Lautoka Hospital (Mon. to Fri. 0800-1600, Sat. 0800-1100). A consultation ($8) with Dr. Y. Raju, whose office is across the street from Desai Bookstore, is more convenient. Vaccinations for international travelers are available at the Health Office (Tues. and Fri. 0800-1200). The Forestry Dept. in the Dept. of Agriculture Bldg. takes reservations for the Nandarivatu Forestry Rest House (see "The Singatoka River Trek" above). The Western Regional Library nearby has a good collection of topographical maps you could use to plan your trip.

transport: Buses, carriers, taxis—everything leaves from the bus stand beside the market (see "Transport" in the "Introduction" to this chapter for a description of bus services). The Fijian Shipping Agency (tel. 63-940), behind the liquor store opposite the Beachcomber office, can book passage on a passenger-carrying freighter between Lautoka and Auckland ($295 OW), once every 3 weeks.

scuba diving: The closest scuba locale to Lautoka is Tivoa I. (20 km RT), which has clean clear water (except when it rains), abundant fish, and beautiful coral. Farther out is Vomolailai Island (50 km RT), a sheer wall covered with Gorgonian soft coral, visibility 30 m plus. The Mana Main Reef off Mana Island (65 km RT) is famous for its drop-offs. It has turtles, fish of all descriptions, plus the occasional crayfish. Visibility on this reef is never less than 25 m. At Yalombi on Waya I. (100 km RT) in the Yasawas see cabbage coral, whip coral, and giant fan corals in the warm, clear waters teeming with fish. Diver Services Fiji (Box 502, Lautoka) has a dive shop beside Union Travel where you can arrange scuba trips and rent snorkeling gear. A one-tank dive costs $28, 2 tanks $35. Tank air fills ($3) at offshore islands can also be arranged. Divers should phone 60496 for free pick-up at Nandi/Lautoka hotels.

THE OFFSHORE ISLANDS

Beachcomber Island: This is Club Med at half the price. The resort caters mostly to young Australians and it's a good place to meet travelers of the opposite sex. You'll like the informal atmosphere and late-night parties: there's a sand-floor bar, dancing, and entertainment. The island is small. You can stroll around it in 10 min., but there's a white sandy beach and buildings nestled amongst coconut trees and tropical vegetation. A beautiful coral reef extends far out on all sides. Snorkeling gear rents for $2 a day, or take the free glass-bottom boat trip to get oriented. Accommodations include all meals served buffet style. Most people opt for the big open dormitory where a bunk costs $35 a night, but you can also get a shared twin or triple in the lodge for $40 (shared bath). There's no hot water, but in this heat, who needs it? Occasionally there's no cold water either, but this is rare. There's also a $30-RT boatride from Lautoka to consider, but that includes lunch on departure day. You can make a day trip to Beachcomber (18 km) for the same price if you only want a few hours in the sun. There's a free shuttle bus from all Lautoka/Nandi hotels to the wharf; the ferry leaves at 1000 daily (1.5 hours). Beachcomber is heavily booked so reserve ahead at their Lautoka office or any travel agency.

Plantation Island: Plantation Island Resort on Malololailai I. offers dormitory (*mburelevu*) accommodations similar to Beachcomber and the price is also similar. There are separate dormitories for men and women (at Beachcomber it's coed). Snorkeling gear, row boats, and windsurfing are free, but boat trips cost $2-5. What Plantation has over Beachcomber is leg room. Malololailai is a fair-sized island 8 km around (a nice walk); there are beaches on the far side of the island where you can be alone. At low tide you can wade to Malolo I., which is bigger yet and has 2 Fijian villages. Plans to build 3 hotels, 700 villas, a golf course, restaurants, and shops on Malolo were vetoed by the villagers as it would have spoiled their fishing grounds, meant an end to their privacy, and besides, they didn't need the estimated million a year anyway. Malololailai is a favorite stopover for cruising yachts and there's a regatta race to Port Vila every September. Mabey you can hitch a ride! Fly to Plantation I. several times a day on Sunflower Airlines ($15 OW) or take the daily cruise boat for $12 OW (tel. 70-103 for free pickup).

Musket Cove Resort: Musket Cove Resort, also on Malololailai I. 16 km off Nandi, is another excellent choice. For $72 s, $92 d, you get a fully equipped *mbure* unit. While the single and double rates may be beyond the reach of most budget travelers, the price is $114 t, $124 for 4, $134 for 5, and that includes free RT airfare (6-night minimum stay) to Malololailai from Nandi airport on Island Air (3 flights daily). The 24 units are clean and have hot water. Small kitchenettes allow you to cook and a well-stocked grocery store selling fresh fruit and vegetables is on the premises. There's also a bar and restaurant by the pool near the beach. A package covering all meals is $25 pp daily. Musket Cove Resort is simple and unpackaged; you do your own thing. Activities such a snorkeling, windsurfing, waterskiing, line fishing, and boat trips are free for guests. Scuba diving is offered ($35 one tank, $50 two tanks.) The resort has an office in the Nandi airport arcade, or book through any travel agent. Day trips to Musket Cove on Island Air are $35, including lunch and activities.

surfing: Aquarius Tours (Box 1419, Nandi) runs a surfing base camp on Tavarua I., just S of Malololailai. There are both lefts and rights at Tavarua, although the emphasis is usually on the lefts. Only 6 surfers are on the island at a time and the $85 pp a day charge includes meals, accommodations, transfers from Nandi, and activities (3-day minimum stay). Non-surfers are accommodated at half price.

THE YASAWA ISLANDS

The Yasawas are a chain of 16 volcanic islands stretching 80 km in a NNE direction roughly 35 km off the W coast of Viti Levu; they offer beautiful, isolated beaches, cliffs, bays, and reefs. It was from the N end of the Yasawas that 2 canoe-loads of cannibals appeared in 1789 and gave Capt. William Bligh and his 18 companions a chase. Nearly 200 years later, increasing numbers of cruise ships ply the chain and it's becoming harder to visit as officials try to prevent eager tourists from really going native. Small village guest houses have appeared on at least 2 islands, but even here a visit still means taking along some *yanggona*, (which doesn't grow in the Yasawas), and observing the conditions outlined in "staying in villages" above. You'll also have to take most of your own food. To be prepared, your shopping list could include flour, rice, sugar, tea, milk powder, baking powder, cooking oil, fresh fruit, onions, canned corned beef, tinned fish, cigarettes, soap bars or powder, mosquito coils, rope, cloth, fishing gear, rubber-lined baby panties, disinfectant, Band-Aids, and candles. Unfortunately, a lot of culturally insensitive people have been going over without anything lately,

expecting to be fed by the locals for a week. This has created local food shortages and the reception has cooled. Do your part to reverse the trend by being as generous as your hosts.

Waya Island: A sheer 500-m mass of rock rises above Yalombi village on the island. This village has a beautiful beach. At low tide you can wade from here across to neighboring Wayasewa I.: there's good snorkeling here. A remarkable 354-m-high volcanic thumb overlooks the S coast of Wayasewa. Also from Yalombi, it's a 30-min. hike across the ridge to Natawa village on the E side of Waya. There's a deserted beach another 20 min. N of Natawa. For a place to stay at Yalombi ask for Miss Andje or her father Monasa who rent *mbures* at $5 pp.

Tavewa Island: Tavewa is a small island about 3 km long with a population of around 50 souls. There is no store or electricity and tall grass covers the hilly interior. There's a beach on the SE side where the bathing is excellent and there's a good fringing reef. Two families on the island regularly accept paying guests. Auntie Lucy Doughty has space for 6

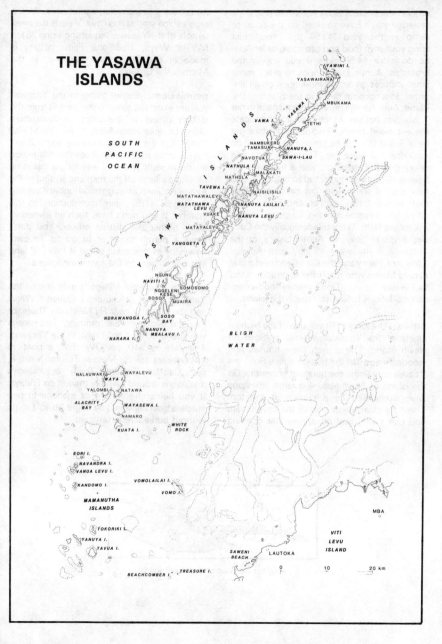

THE YASAWA
ISLANDS

SOUTH
PACIFIC
OCEAN

Y A S A W A   I S L A N D S

YAWINI I.

YASAWAIRARA

MBUKAMA

YASAWA I.

VAWA I.

TETHI

NAMBUKERU
TAMASUA   NANUYA I.
NAVOTUA   SAWA-I-LAU
NATHULA I.
NATHULA   MALAKATI
MATATHAWALEVU   NAISILISILI
MATATHAWA
LEVU I.   NANUYA LAILAI I.
VUAKE
NANUYA LEVU I.
MATAYALEVU

TAVEWA I.

YANGGETA

NGUNU
NAVITI I.
NGGELENI
KESE
SOSO
MUAIRA
SOSO
BAY
NDRAWANGGA I.
NANUYA
NARARA I. MBALAVU I.

SOMOSOMO

BLIGH

WATER

NALAUWAKI   WAYALEVU
WAYA I.
YALOMBI   NATAWA
ALACRITY
BAY   WAYASEWA I.
NAMARO

KUATA I.

WHITE
ROCK

EORI I.
NAVANDRA I.
VANUA LEVU I.

KANDOMO I.   VOMOLAILAI I.
VOMO I.

MAMANUTHA
ISLANDS

MBA

VITI
LEVU
ISLAND

TOKORIKI I.
YANUYA I.
TAVUA I.

SAWENI
BEACH   LAUTOKA

0   10   20 km

BEACHCOMBER I.   TREASURE I.

or 7 in her concrete block house ($6 pp); if it's crowded you'll have to sleep on the floor, or camp in the yard ($3.50 pp). You must bring your own food and can cook, or let Auntie do it for $4.50 extra if you supply the groceries. Auntie Lucy hopes to erect some small *mbures* so accommodations could improve. In a coconut grove at the S end of the island, Aunt Amelia provides floor space in her 2 wooden houses which also accommodate the extended family. Two lucky visitors get beds. Bring food, or be prepared to subsist on cold rice and black tea. There's singing and dancing in the evening under a tree near the houses. Guests are expected to help with odd jobs around the house, cut cassava, collect reef animals, fish, gather coconuts, make copra, and do some cooking. To get to Tavewa ask for the Nathula boats, specifically the *Calm Sea* if you're going to Auntie Lucy's, or the *Vatuvula* if you want to stay with Amelia/ Tom/Jack/Henry and the kids. Beware of a guy named Moses who may offer to arrange a trip to Tavewa for you. Don't prepay food or accommodations before you reach the island.

others: The King of Naviti, one of the highest chiefs of the Yasawas, resides at Soso on Naviti Island. The church there houses fine woodcarvings. On the hillside above Soso are 2 caves containing the bones of ancestors. On the island of Sawa-I-Lau is a large limestone cave illuminated by a crevice at the top. There's a clear, deep pool in the cave where you can swim, and an underwater opening leads back into a smaller, darker cave. All the cruise ships stop at this cave. Viwa is the most remote of the Yasawas, squatting alone 25 km NW of Waya. Traditional Fijian pottery is made in the village on Yanuya I. in the Mamanutha Group.

permissions: Before going to the Yasawas you are expected to get a free permit from the district officer in the Dept. of Agriculture Bldg., Lautoka (open Mon. to Fri. 0800-1300/ 1400-1600). He will only issue the permit if you have a letter of invitation from the village you intend to visit. The only way to get this is by picking a village off the map and writing to the *turanga-ni-koro* as suggested under ''staying in villages'' in the main ''Introduction'' to this chapter. If you don't have such an invitation, don't bother the district officer. You don't need a permit or letter to go to Tavewa, however, as this small island is freehold land and not subject to the same restrictions.

getting there: Village boats from the Yasawas arrive at Lautoka's Queen's Wharf and the old jetty near Fiji Meats on Thurs. or Fri., and depart on Sat. morning. This means you spend either 4 or 11 days in the Yasawas. The fare is $10 pp OW. For a boat to Yasawairara ask for Mosese Tui; for Naviti I., see Captain Robert. There are always Yasawans around Lautoka market on Fridays. If you befriend someone or manage to persuade a boat captain, you might be able to go without bureaucratic sanction.

long-horned cowfish (Lactoria cornuta)

THE LOMAIVITI GROUP

OVALAU ISLAND

Levuka: Ovalau, the large, 626-m-high volcanic island just E of Viti Levu, is well-known as the site of Levuka, capital of Fiji until the shift to Suva in 1881. Levuka was founded as a whaling settlement in 1830, and grew into a boisterous town with over 50 hotels and taverns along Beach Street. The cotton boom of the 1860s brought new settlers who joined traders already there. Escaped convicts and debtors fleeing creditors in Australia swelled the throng until it was said a ship could find the reef passage into Levuka by following the empty gin bottles floating out on the tide. On 10 Oct. 1874, a semblance of decorum came to Levuka with the annexation of Fiji by Great Britain. The lovely green hills which rise behind the town were, in fact, the cause of its downfall as colonial planners saw that there was no room for the expansion of their capital. When the copra trade also moved to Suva, Levuka seemed doomed. Today, the fishing industry and low-profile tourism keep it going; it's also a minor educational center. The pioneer atmosphere is still strong in this somnolent town of 1,400, a perfect base for excursions into the moun-tains, along the winding coast, or out to the barrier reef one km offshore. Levuka is one of the most peaceful, pleasant, and picturesque places in Fiji.

sights: Stroll along Levuka's sleepy waterfront. The old Morris Hedstrom Ltd. store near the wharf has been converted into a museum and library (closed Sun.). They arrange walking tours of historic Levuka Mon. and Fri. at 1000 ($1). When you reach the dilapidated movie house, turn onto the adjacent street, head inland on the L side of the creek to the Levuka Public School (1879), Fiji's first. Farther up, the creek has been dammed to create a pond. Continue straight and you'll eventually reach the source of the town's water supply. As you come back down the hill, the Ovalau Club is on your L across the small bridge. There's a framed letter from Count Felix von Luckner, the WW I German sea wolf, on the wall by the bar. The old Town Hall and Masonic Lodge adjoin the Club.

south of Levuka: The Japanese-run Pacific Fishing Company tuna cannery is S of the main wharf. The Cession Monument is a little farther along; the Deed of Cession which

The Ovalau Club at Levuka was once the reserve of British colonials. Although the sign by the door says PRIVATE— MEMBERS ONLY, the bartender will sign you in.

made Fiji a British colony was signed here in 1874. A traditional *mbure* used for Provincial Council meetings is on the other side of the road. When you reach Ndraimba village (2 km), take the road to the R before the 4 condominiums and follow a path for 4.5 hours through enchanting forests and across clear streams to Lovoni village in the center of the island. The trail is no longer used by the locals and requires attentiveness to follow. Swim and picnic, then catch the 1500 bus from Lovoni back to Levuka. If you forego this hike, you'll come to an old cemetery a little S of Ndraimba. A few km farther is the Devil's Thumb, a dramatic volcanic plug towering above Tokou village, one of the scenic highlights of Fiji. Catholic missionaries set up a printing press at Tokou in 1889 to produce gospel lessons in Fijian. In the center of the village is a sculpture of a lion made by one of the early priests. It's 5 km back to Levuka.

north of Levuka: Follow the coastal road N from Levuka to the second yellow bridge where you'll see the old Methodist Church (1869) on the left. In the small cemetery behind the church is the grave of the first U.S. consul to Fiji, John Brown Williams. For the story of Williams' activities see "the rise of Mbau Island" under "History" in the introduction to this chapter. Across the bridge and beneath a large *ndilo* tree is the tomb of an old king of Levuka. The large house in front of the tree is the residence of the present Tui Levuka. Directly above is Gun Rock, which was used as a target in 1849 to show Thakombau the efficacy of a ship's cannon so he might be more thoughtful of resident Europeans and perhaps reconsider the missionaries' message. The early Fijians had a fort atop the Rock to defend themselves against the Lovoni hill tribes. Ask permission of the Tui Levuka (the "Roko") or a member of his household to climb Gun Rock for a splendid view of Levuka. If a small boy leads you up and down, it wouldn't be out of place to give him 50 cents for his trouble. From the summit, let your eyes follow the horizon from R to L with the islands of Ngau, Mbatiki, Nairai, Wakaya, Koro, Makongai, and Vanua Levu respectively in view. Continue N of the road,

round a bend, pass the ruin of a large concrete building, and you'll come to a cluster of government housing on a cricket field where King George V played in 1878. There's a beautiful deep pool and waterfall behind Waitovu village, about 2 km N of Levuka. You may swim here but please don't skinnydip; this is offensive to the local people and has led to serious incidents in the past. Since they're good enough to let you use this idyllic spot which they own, it's common courtesy to respect their wishes.

accommodations: There are 3 good inexpensive places to stay in Levuka. The first one you come to after disembarking is the Old Capital Inn, a favorite of budget travelers who want to be with their counterparts where the action is. The Inn has double rooms at $5 pp, breakfast included, or a $3 dormitory without. Also recommended is the Mavida Guest House ($6 pp bed and breakfast) on the waterfront near the Levuka Club. Mavida is in a spacious colonial house with cooking facilities. Your host, George, is a retired government officer who can tell you anything you want to know about Fiji. For the Somerset Maugham flavor, stay at the Royal, Fiji's oldest operating hotel ($8 s, $12 d). **a beach resort:** The perfect escape from it all is rustic Rukuruku Resort, on the NW side of Ovalau 20 km from Levuka. There's a large campground ($3 pp) complete with toilets, showers, barbecue, kitchen, and an open pavilion with electric lighting. Dormitory-style accommodations are also available, or rent your own private *mbure* for $30 a day. The restaurant/bar is somewhat overpriced but basic groceries may be purchased in the adjacent Fijian village. The beach is only so-so, but the snorkeling out on the reef is good and there's a natural freshwater swimming pool in the river adjacent to the resort. A vanilla plantation and beautiful verdant mountains cradle Rukuruku on the island side. A small boat is available to charter for day trips ($25 for the boat) to Naingani I., the reef, or for fishing. Get to Rukuruku on a carrier from Levuka ($1 pp), no service on Sun. or late in the afternoon. When you're ready to return to Suva, the resort launch will shuttle you out to the

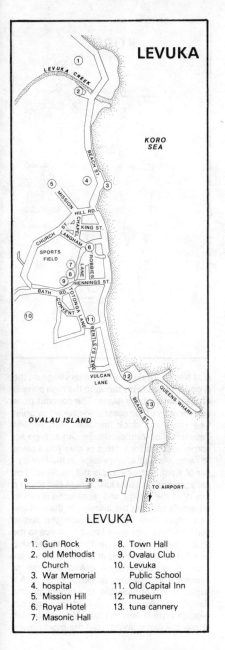

LEVUKA

1. Gun Rock
2. old Methodist Church
3. War Memorial
4. hospital
5. Mission Hill
6. Royal Hotel
7. Masonic Hall
8. Town Hall
9. Ovalau Club
10. Levuka Public School
11. Old Capital Inn
12. museum
13. tuna cannery

Natovi ferry ($4 for the boat), making a return to Levuka unnecessary. Don't expect a flashy tourist hotel like the ones near Nandi—Rukuruku is Fiji-style.

food and entertainment: There's a restaurant at the Old Capital Inn where everyone gathers for dinner. Otherwise try the curry house on the waterfront. Although the sign says MEMBERS ONLY, visitors are welcome at the Ovalau Club (cheap beer). Stop in for a drink at the Royal Hotel to absorb some of the atmosphere of old Levuka.

transport: Fiji Air has flights several times a day from Ovalau to Nausori ($17) and once a week direct to Koro ($15). Book the Koro flight well ahead. Fiji Air has a minibus from their Levuka office to the airstrip for $2 pp. There's sometimes a ship direct from Levuka to Nambouwalu, Vanua Levu, very early Mon. mornings. Ask at the Patterson Bros. office on the waterfront beside the market in front of the Royal Hotel. Ask about the Suva-Savusavu ferry which calls at Levuka on Fri. northbound and Tues. southbound. Village boats leave sporadically for Mbatiki, Nairai, and Koro. Small outboards to Moturiki I. depart Nangguelendamu Landing most afternoons (30 cents). You can charter one to take you over anytime for about $5. The best beaches are on the E side of Moturiki. (For details of the bus/launch service between Suva and Levuka see "Suva—Transport" above.) Book your seat on the express bus back to Suva at Gulabdas & Sons (recommended on holidays). Due to steep hills on the NW side of Ovalau there isn't a bus around the island. Northbound, they go as far as St. Johns College, while those headed S don't reach farther than Viro. Carriers run as far as Rukuruku village ($1) along a beautiful, hilly road. Go in the morning.

tours: Emosi, manager of the Old Capital Inn, offers many good trips. He does a land tour around Ovalau with lunch at Rukuruku for $6.50. His reef tour ($3 pp, $1 extra for gear) is great for swimming and snorkeling, and he'll show you sharks if you ask. Five people are required to do either of these tours. Ask Emosi about a visit to Thangalai I., a lovely isolated reef island with nothing but coconut trees and sandy beaches. He'll charge about $100 RT for a charter but up to 16 people can get in on it. Take food, water, and tents, and camp out for a few days. Emosi will also go to Naingani, Wakaya, or Makongai if enough people are interested. If you'd like to climb the peak which towers behind Levuka just ask; Emosi will arrange a guide for a nominal amount. Problem is, when Emosi's out of town on business, activities are suspended.

THE LOMAIVITI GROUP

Naingani: Naingani is a lush tropical island near Ovalau on the W end of the Lomaiviti Group with beautiful beaches and one Fijian village. Dormitory accommodations for 34 people ($10 pp) are available at the Islanders Village, a millionaires' resort, where private units begin at $60. Cooking facilities are provided, but bring food. The restaurant/bar is expensive. Windsurfing is $10 an hour, air mattresses on the beach $2. A launch leaves Natovi wharf daily at 1130 ($10 RT) for the resort. For reservations check with their office opposite the public library in Suva or tel. 44-364.

Makongai: Until 1969, This was a leper colony staffed by Catholic nuns. Today it's owned by the Dept. of Agriculture, which runs a sheep farm. Many of the old hospital buildings still stand. **Wakaya:** Wakaya has been purchased by the Pacific Harbor Corporation and stocked with deer and condo-tourists. The German raider, Count Felix von Luckner, was captured on Wakaya when his ship, the *Seeadler*, foundered on the reef during WW I. **Mbatiki:** Mbatiki has a large interior lagoon of brackish water surrounded by mud flats.

Koro: Koro is an 8-by-16-km island with 14 large Fijian villages. A ridge traverses the island from NE to SW, reaching 561 m near the center. High jungle-clad hillsides drop sharply to the coast. The best beach is along the S coast between Mundu and the lighthouse at Muanivanua Point. The government center with post office, hospital, and schools

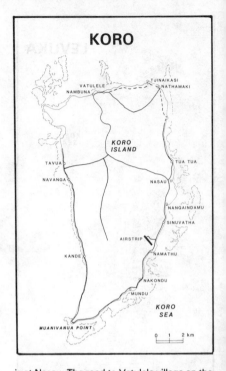

is at Nasau. The road to Vatulele village on the N coast climbs from Nasau to the high plateau at the center of the island. The coconut trees and mangos of the coast are replaced by great tree ferns and thick rainforest. Mr. Amena Tave, chief of Vatulele village, can arrange accommodations for visitors or give you a place to camp. At Nathamaki village, in the NW corner of Koro, turtle-calling is still practiced. The caller stands on Tuinaikasi, a high cliff about a km W of the village, and repeats the prescribed words to bring the animals to the surface. The ritual does work, although the turtles seem to have become a little bored due to the tour groups which arrive fortnightly by ship and get a performance; only one or 2 may appear. If anyone present points a finger or camera at a turtle, they quickly submerge. Actually, it is not possible to photograph the turtles as magic is involved (the photos wouldn't show any turtles). You're so high above the water you'd need the most power-

ful telephoto lens just to pick them out,
anyway. The track S between Nathamaki and
Tua Tua runs along a golden palm-fringed
beach. There's a cooperative store at
Nangaindamu where you can buy *yanggona*
and supplies. Koro *kava* is Fiji's best. A
30-min. hike up a steep trail from the coop
brings you to a waterfall and idyllic swimming
hole. Keep L if you're on your own, although a
guide would be preferable. The ship from
Suva anchors off Nangaindamu (no wharf).
Koro has an unusual inclined airstrip on the E
side of the island near Namathu village. You
land uphill, take off downhill. Several carriers
meet the flights ($1 to nearby villages, $2 to
the farthest).

Ngau: Ngau is the 5th largest island in Fiji,
with 16 villages and 13 settlements. There's a
barrier reef on the W coast, only a fringing
reef on the east. There's a hotspring swimming pool close to the P.W.D. depot at
Waikama. From Waikama hike along the
beach and over the hills to Somosomo village.
If you lose the way, look for the creek at the
head of the bay and work your way up until
you encounter the trail. There's a bathing pool
in Somosomo with emerald-green water. A
road runs from Somosomo to Sawaieke
village where the Takalaingau, high chief of
Ngau, resides. The remnants of one of the
only surviving pagan temples (*mbure kalou*)
in Fiji is beside the road at the junction in
Sawaieke. The high stone mound is still impressive. It's possible to climb Mt. Ndelaitho
(760 m), highest on the island, from Sawaieke,
in 3 or 4 hours. The first hour is the hardest.
From the summit there is a sweeping view.
MacGillivray's Fiji petrel, a rare seabird of the
albatross family, lays its eggs underground on
Ngau's jungle-clad peaks. Only 2 specimens
have ever been taken: one by the survey ship
Herald in 1855, and a second in 1984 by Dick
Watling of Nandi. The coop and government

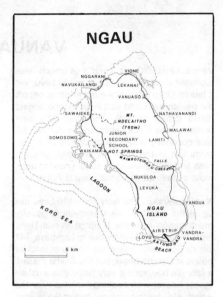

station (hospital, post office, etc.) are at Ng-
garani at the N end of Ngau. Two ships a
week arrive here from Suva on an irregular
schedule, but there is no wharf so they anchor
offshore. The wharf at Waikama is used only
for government boats. There are a number of
waterfalls on the E coast, the best known
behind Lekanai and up Waimboteingau Creek,
both an hour's walk off the main road. The
"weather stone" is on the beach, a 5-min.
walk S of Yandua village. Bad weather is certain if you step on it or throw a stone at it. To
arrange accommodations contact Taina
Ravutu in the Fiji Air office in Suva. Tom
Koroi, driver of the carrier ($2) serving the
airstrip, can provide accommodations in
Waikama village at $10 pp including all meals.
Tom connects with another carrier down the E
coast to Lamiti. The airstrip is on Katundrau
Beach at the S end of Ngau.

VANUA LEVU

Vanua Levu ("Great Land") is much less touristed and only half as big as Viti Levu, yet it has much to offer. Make the effort to get off the beaten track and visit Fiji's second largest island (5,556 sq km). The drier NW side features cane fields, while on the damper SE side coconut plantations predominate. Fiji Indians live in the large market town of Lambasa and the surrounding sugar-growing area; most of the rest of Vanua Levu is Fijian.

Nambouwalu: The ferry from Viti Levu ties up to the wharf at this friendly little government station near the S tip of Vanua Levu. From here it's 137 km by bus to Lambasa, 141 km to Savusavu. There are no restaurants or hotels at Nambouwalu, but Mr. Sukha Prasad, a jolly ole boy, runs a very basic *dharamshala* (guest house) with cooking facilities near the wharf. He doesn't charge, but make a contribution upon departure. Another possibility is the lovely Government Rest House on the hillside. They have 2 rooms where you can cook at $5 pp. Make reservations with the district officer, Mbua (tel. no. 6, Nambouwalu). If the Rest House is booked, ask the D.O.'s clerk if you may camp on the grounds. **getting there:** The large Patterson Bros. car ferry sails from Natovi on Viti Levu to Nambouwalu daily except Sun. around 0730, $16 for the 4-hour trip. From Nambouwalu the same boat departs for Natovi daily except Sun. at noon. Patterson Bros. runs an express bus from Nambouwalu to Lambasa (4 hours — $4) for ferry passengers. This bus is quicker and cheaper than the 4 regular buses to Lambasa (5 hours — $4.85) which make numerous detours and stops.

the road to Lambasa: This twisting, tiring bus ride takes you past Fijian villages, rice paddies, and cane fields. The early sandalwood traders put in at Mbua Bay. Nukungasi Beach on Ngaloa Bay is 3 km off the main highway just S of Lekutu postal agency (keep R). About 5 km N of Lekutu Secondary School, one km off the main road

(bus drivers know the place), are Fiji's most accessible yet least-known waterfalls, the Naselesele Falls. This is a perfect place to picnic between buses with a nice grassy area where you could camp. The falls are most impressive during the rainy season, but the greater flow means muddy water so swimming is best in the dry. There is a large basalt pool below the falls and nobody lives in the immediate vicinity. You'll probably have the place to yourself.

LAMBASA

Lambasa is a large Indian market town which services Vanua Levu's major sugar-growing area. Other than providing a good base from which to explore the surrounding countryside and a place to spend the night, Lambasa has little to interest the average visitor.

sights: There's a library in the Civic Center near the Lambasa bus station. The Lambasa Sugar Mill (1894), in operation from May to Dec., is a km E of town. Walk a little farther along the road for a view of the Three Sisters Hill to the right. Anyone with an interest in archaeology should take the short ride on the Nakoroutari bus to Wasavula on the southern outskirts of Lambasa. Parallel stone platforms bearing large monoliths are found among the coconut trees to the E of the road. This site is not well-known, so just take the bus to Wasavula, get off, and ask. Other easy sidetrips with frequent bus service include the Fiji Forests plant at Malau and the Wainggele hotsprings (no bathing) beyond the airport. **near Lambasa:** You can get a view of much of Vanua Levu from atop Ndelaikoro (941 m), 25 km S of Lambasa. There's no public transport, but you might swing a ride by asking the telecommunications engineer in the building behind the Lambasa Post Office if any of his staff is going to the summit to service the equipment. Only a 4-wheel drive vehicle can make it to the top.

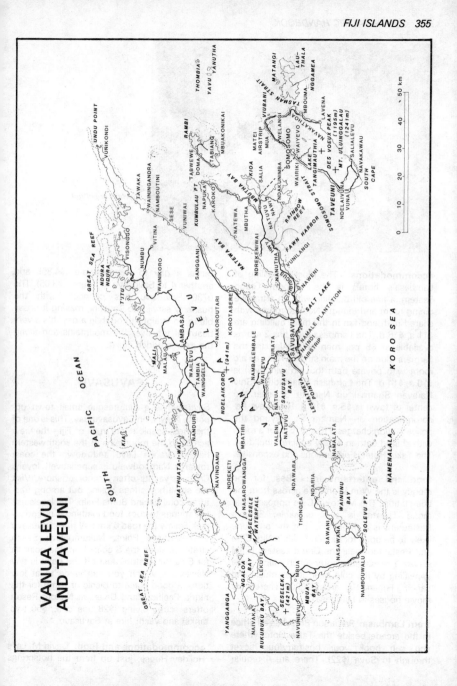

VANUA LEVU
AND TAVEUNI

peeling breadfruit

accommodations: The most appealing of Lambasa's hotels is the 17-room Grand Eastern, a fine old building with an attractive dining room and lounge. Non-a/c rooms with shared bath and fan in the main building are $11 s, $16 d. The Lambasa Club has 2 rooms available at $5 pp, men only. Also try the Farmers Club on the main street, where an a/c room with private bath (but no windows) is $10 s, $14 d. The Lambasa Guesthouse (Shiv Narayan Sharma) on Nanuku St. near the center of town is $5 s, $10 d. Riverview Accommodation on Namara St. beyond the police station charges $10 s, $15 d for a room with shared bath in a new concrete building. The Takia Hotel is pretentious and expensive.

food and entertainment: Best for the money is the Wun Wah Cafe across from the bus station. The Midtown Cafe opposite Diamond Theater is also passable. Singh's Restaurant is a poor third, but the only one likely to be open for dinner. Naidu's Nite Club and Restaurant near the Grand Eastern Hotel serves a reasonable curry lunch made more appealing by the cold beer; it has music and dancing Fri. and Sat. around 2200. There are 3 movie houses in Lambasa.

from Lambasa: Patterson Bros. has an office in the arcade beside the Takia Hotel where you can book your bus/ferry/bus ticket through to Suva ($22). There are 4 regular

buses a day to Nambouwalu ($4.85), and another 4 to Savusavu (3 hours — $3.05). The 0730 Savusavu bus connects with the bus/ferry service to Taveuni, making it possible to go straight through in a day. It's a very beautiful trip over the mountains and along the palm-studded coast.

SAVUSAVU

Savusavu is a picturesque small town opposite Nawi I. on Savusavu Bay. This is one of the most scenic spots in all of Fiji — the view across to the mountains of the southwestern half of Vanua Levu and down the coast towards Nambouwalu is superlatively lovely. Cruising yachts often anchor offshore. Visit the small hotsprings boiling out among fractured coral behind Burns Philp. The locals use the springs to cook food (bathing is not possible). Follow the road 6 km SW from Savusavu to Lesiatheva Point. Nukumbalavu Beach stretches along the S coast from the point as far E as the airstrip. Just off the point is tiny Naviavia I. which you can wade to at low tide — a good place to picnic or camp for the night. Pacific Island Divers at Nakoro Resort offers scuba diving ($28 one tank, $50 two tanks) and yacht hire at Savusavu.

accommodations and food: David M. Lal's Holiday House, just up from the hotsprings behind Burns Philp, has bed and breakfast for $10 s, $15 d (shared bath), and there's a well-equipped kitchen. The place is clean; no alcoholic beverages are allowed on the premises. Ask David if you may borrow his push bike. Two new hotels, Kontiki Resorts and Lesiaceva Point Beach Apartments, have opened at Savusavu, both $20 s, $25 d. If money is no problem, consider Namale Plantation (from $50 pp—meals extra), a secluded retreat with superb food and homey atmosphere amid exotic landscapes and refreshing beaches. Namale is only a couple of km E of the airstrip, but bookings should be made in advance: Box 244, Savusavu. (Your host, Robin Mercer, is the author of *A Field Guide to Fiji's Birds.*) This little jewel is still fairly unknown, but most who stay there go away ecstatic. Note, however, that Namale only caters to in-house guests. There is no provision for sightseers who'd like to stop for lunch. Have a meal at the Pingho Cafe opposite the market or try the more modern Wing Yuen Restaurant farther along. Drinkers can repair to the Planters Club toward the wharf.

from Savusavu: Fiji Air flies between Savusavu and Nausori twice a day. The airstrip is beside the main highway, 3 km E of town. There's no airport bus, but you could walk, or take a taxi for $2. Northwest Shipping has a ferry to Suva Tues., Thurs., and Sat. at 0700 ($18 OW). The Tues. trip calls at Levuka ($15 OW). There are 4 buses a day to Lambasa ($3.05). The 1030 Napuka bus connects with the daily ferry to Taveuni ($3), which departs Natuvu around 1300. This is a beautiful trip.

along the Hibiscus Highway: This lovely coastal highway runs 77 km E from Savusavu to Natuvu, then up the E side of Vanua Levu to the old Catholic mission station of Napuka. Large red prawns inhabit a saltwater crevice in the center of a tiny limestone island off Naweni village between Savusavu and Natuvu. The villagers believe the prawns are the spirit Urumbuta.

The island is accessible on foot at low tide, but a *sevusevu* must first be presented to the chief of Naweni for permission to visit (no photos). Local guides must also be compensated. Ask to be shown the weather stone on the beach and, perhaps, a second pool of prawns on the other side of the village. There are petroglyphs (*vatuvola*) on large stones in a creek near Ndakunimba village, 10 km S of Natuvu (no bus service). Look for a second group of rock carvings a couple of hundred m farther up the slope. The figures resemble some undeciphered ancient script.

THE OFFSHORE ISLANDS

Kioa: The Taveuni ferry passes between Vanua Levu and Kioa, home of some 300 Polynesians from Vaitupu I., Tuvalu (the former Ellice Islands), who purchased the island in 1949. Upon request the ferry will drop you at Salia, on the S side of Kioa (ask the captain if he'll pick you up on the next day's trip to Taveuni). To charter a speedboat from Natuvu to Kioa would cost about $8 each way. The women of Salia make baskets for sale to tourists, while the men go out fishing alone in small outrigger canoes. If you visit, try the coconut toddy (*kalevi*) or more potent fermented toddy (*kamangi*). Kioa and nearby Rambi are the only islands in Fiji where the government allows toddy to be cut.

Rambi: The British government purchased Rambi I. from Lever Bros. just after WW II to serve as a new home for the Micronesian Banabans of Ocean I. in Kiribati, whose home island was being ravaged by phosphate mining. Today the Banabans live among Lever's former coconut plantations at the NW corner of Rambi. Try coconut toddy (*te karewe*) or the fermented product (*te kaokioki*). There's a small guest house at Nuku. The island reaches a height of 472 m and is well-wooded. **getting there:** Fiji Air flies direct to Rambi from Nausori ($51) twice a week. Ask about flights from Savusavu to Rambi. A chartered speedboat from Karoko on Vanua Levu to Tabiang on Rambi costs $12-20 each way.

TAVEUNI

This long, green island covered with coconut trees is Fiji's third largest (470 sq km). Known as the Garden Island of Fiji for the abundance of its flora, Taveuni's 16-km-long, 1,000-m-high volcanic spine causes the prevailing tradewinds to dump colossal amounts of rainfall on the island's SE side and considerable quantities on the NW side. The almost inaccessible SE coast features plummeting waterfalls, soaring cliffs, and crashing surf. Because the island is free of the mongoose, there are many wild chickens and birds. The deep, rich volcanic soil nurtures indigenous floral species such as *Medinilla spectabilis* which hang in clusters like red sleigh bells, and the rare *tangimauthia (Medinilla waterousei)*, a climbing plant with red-and-white flower clusters 30 cm long. *Tangimauthia* grows only around Taveuni's 900-m-high crater lake and on Vanua Levu. It cannot be transplanted and flowers only in mid-December. The story goes that a young woman was fleeing from her father who wanted to force her to marry a crotchety old man. As she lay crying beside the lake, her tears turned to flowers. Her father took pity on her when he heard this and allowed her to marry her young lover. Taveuni today is about the most beautiful, scenic, and friendly island in Fiji.

southern Taveuni: The post office, hospital, and government offices are on a hilltop at Waiyevo above the exclusive Castaways Hotel. Tiny Korolevu I. off Waiyevo is haunted. The 180th degree of longitude passes through a point just S of Waiyevo, where there's a marker. Beyond this a couple of American-style condo developments stand out like pimples on the side of Taveuni. At Vuna the lava flows have formed pools beside the ocean which fill up with freshwater at low tide and are used for washing and bathing. Good snorkeling on the reef. Take a bus S to Navakawau village at the SE end of the island. Hike NE for an hour and a half along a dirt track through the coconut plantations from Navakawau to Salialevu, site of the Billyard Sugar Mill (1874-96), one of Fiji's first. Fiji's only magpies (large black and white birds) inhabit this plantation. A tall chimney, boilers, and other equipment remain below the school at Salialevu. From Salialevu, another road climbs over the island to Ndelaivuna, a tiring 2 hours. The bus comes up this road from the NW coast as far as Ndelaivuna, so you could also start from there and do the above in reverse.

northern Taveuni: Somosomo is the chiefly village of Taveuni: Ratu Sir Penaia Kanatabuta, the present governor general, hails from here. Take a bus around the N tip of the island to Mbouma to see the famous waterfall (admission $1 pp). The track to the falls leads along the R bank of the second stream S of Mbouma. The falls plunge 15 m into a deep pool where you could swim. The villagers at Mbouma are very friendly. Some of the Mbouma buses go on to Lavena, a beautiful area.

to the interior: The trail up to lovely Lake Tangimauthia, high in the mountainous interior, begins behind the Mormon church at Somosomo. The first half is the hardest. You'll need a full day to do a RT and a guide ($10) will be necessary for all but the most experienced as there are many trails to choose from. You must wade for a half hour through knee-deep mud in the crater to reach the lake's edge. Much of the lake's surface is vegetation-covered and the water is only 5 m deep. The adventuresome might try hiking to Lake Tangimauthia from Lavena on the SE coast, or SW from Lavena to Salialevu, lesser-known but feasible routes. An easier climb is up the jeep track from the Marist school, one km S of Waiyevo, to the telecommunications station on Des Voeux Peak. This is an all-day trip with a view of Lake Tangimauthia as a reward (clouds permitting). The less ambitious will settle for the short hike up to the cross above the Marist mission.

Taveuni's Mbouma Falls are among the most impressive in Fiji.

per night) at Mua, 2 km SW of Matei airstrip. There's a beach, spring water, and good snorkeling on the reef offshore. Clusters of small shops sell groceries at Somosomo and Wairiki, a couple of km N and S of Waiyevo respectively.

scuba diving: New Zealanders Ric and Do Cammick (CPO Matei, Taveuni) arrange scuba diving off Taveuni ($50 for 2 tanks including lunch). Divers are accommodated at Dive Taveuni's premises just SW of Matei airstrip. They'll take you to the fabulous Rainbow Reef off the S coast of eastern Vanua Levu where you'll see turtles, fish, overhangs, crevices, and corals, all in 5 to 10 m of water. This operation is the best of its kind in Fiji.

getting there: Matei airstrip at the N tip of Taveuni is serviced daily by Fiji Air from Nausori ($41) and by Sunflower Airlines from Nandi, but flights out of Taveuni can be heavily booked. A good compromise is to fly direct to Taveuni from Viti Levu and return overland to Suva via Vanua Levu. You get superb views of Taveuni from the plane. Sit on the R side going up, the L side coming back. The ferry to Natuvu on Vanua Levu leaves Waiyevo daily at 0800 ($3), connecting with a bus to Savusavu on the other side. Buses on Taveuni run N to Mbouma and S to Navakawau, leaving Waiyevo daily at 0900, 1230, and 1700.

offshore islands: Crabs are gathered in abundance on Nggamea I., just E of Taveuni, in Oct. and November. Lauthala Island, just E of Nggamea, is owned by the American multimillionaire Malcolm Forbes. The inhabitants of the one village on Lauthala work for him making copra. Outboards from villages on Nggamea land near Navakathoa village, on the NE side of Taveuni. Best time to try for a ride over ($2 pp) is Thurs. or Fri. afternoons, or you could charter a boat from Navakathoa to Naiiviivi village on Nggamea for about $10.

accommodations and food: Kaba's Guest House at Somosomo charges $8 s, $15 d for a bed in a double room with shared facilities. You can cook. Inquire at Kaba's Supermarket nearby. You may camp behind the guesthouse and use the facilities for half price. Trevor's Place, at Matei just E of the airstrip, is a Christian-oriented camp with several *mbures* and a tenting area. The best campsite is Thomas Valentine's compound ($3 per tent

THE LAU GROUP

Lau is by far the most remote part of Fiji, with its 57 islands scattered over a vast area of ocean between Viti Levu and Tonga. Roughly half of them are inhabited. Though all are relatively small, they vary from volcanic islands, to uplifted atolls, to some combination of the two. Tongan influence has always been strong in Lau, and due to Polynesian mixing the people have a somewhat lighter skin color than other Fijians. Once accessible only after a long sea voyage on infrequent copra-collecting ships, 4 islands in Lau (Lakemba, Vanua Mbalavu, Moala, and Thithia) now have regular air service from Nausori. There are organized accommodations on Lakemba and Vanua Mbalavu; the latter is the more rewarding of the two. Similarly, Moala is a large mountainous island with much to explore, while there is little for the average visitor on Thithia. Both government and private ships circulate through Lau, usually calling at 5 or 6 islands on a single trip. To experience what life in the group is really about, try to go at least one way by ship (see "Suva—Transport" for details).

NORTHERN LAU

Vanua Mbalavu: The name means the "long land." The southern portion of this unusual, seahorse-shaped island is mostly volcanic, while the N is uplifted coral. An unspoiled environment of palm-fringed beaches backed by long grassy hillsides and sheer limestone cliffs, this is a wonderful area to explore. There are varied vistas and scenic views on all sides. To the E is a barrier reef enclosing a lagoon 37 by 16 km. The Bay of Islands at the NW end of Vanua Mbalavu is a recognized hurricane shelter. The villages of Vanua Mbalavu are impeccably clean, the grass cut and manicured. Large mats are made on the island and strips of pandanus can be seen drying before many of the houses. In the days of sail, Lomaloma, the largest settlement, was an important Pacific port. The great Tongan chief

Enele Ma'afu made his bid to dominate Fiji from here. A small monument flanked by 2 cannon on the waterfront near the wharf recalls the event. Fiji's first public botanical garden was laid out here over a century ago, but nothing remains of it. History has passed Lomaloma by. Today it's only a sleepy big village with a hospital and a couple of general stores. Some 400 Tongans live in Sawana, the S portion of Lomaloma village, and many of the houses have the round ends characteristic of Lau. This is one of the few places in the world where you can't order a Coke.

sights: Copra is the main export and there is a small coconut oil mill at Lomaloma. A road runs inland from Lomaloma, up and across the island to Ndakuilomaloma. From the small communications station on a grassy hilltop midway, there's an excellent view. Follow the road S from Lomaloma 3 km to Narothivo

VANUA MBALAVU

village then 2 km beyond to the narrow passage separating Vanua Mbalavu and Malata islands. At low tide you can easily wade across to Namalata village. Alternatively, work your way around to the W side of Vanua Mbalavu where there are isolated tropical beaches. There is good snorkeling in this passage. There are hotsprings and burial caves among the high limestone outcrops between Narothivo and Namalata but you'll need a guide to find them. This can be easily arranged at Nakama, the tiny collection of houses closest to the cliffs, upon payment of a $2 pp fee. Small bats inhabit some of the caves. Rent a boat ($15) to take you over to the Raviravi lagoon on Susui I., the favorite picnic spot near Lomaloma for the locals. The beach and snorkeling are good and there's even a cave if you're interested.

events: A most unusual event occurs annually at Masomo Bay, W of Mavana village, usually around Christmastime. The Mavana villagers, clad only in skirts of *ndrauninggai* leaves, enter the waters and stir up the muddy bottom by swimming around clutching logs for a couple of days. No one understands exactly why and magic is thought to be involved, but this activity stuns the *yawi* fish which inhabit the bay, rendering them easy prey for the waiting spearmen. Peni, the *mbeti* (priest) of Mavana, controls the ritual. No photos are allowed.

accommodations: Mr. Poasa Delailomaloma and his brother Laveti operate a charming traditional-style rest house in the middle of Lomaloma village. A bed and all meals are $10 pp. If you'd like to camp ask Alfred Miller, the Fiji Air agent, if he knows of a place. **getting there:** Fiji Air flies in from Nausori ($54 OW) 3 times a week. Ask about connecting flights to Lakemba ($32). The bus from the airstrip to Lomaloma is 50 cents. After checking in at the airstrip for departure you'll probably have time to scramble up the nearby hill for a good view of the island. Several carriers a day run from Lomaloma N to Mualevu (40 cents), and some carry on to Mavana (70 cents).

Necklaces of whale's teeth were a badge of chiefly authority. At night men would use wooden headrests to preserve their carefully coiffured hairdo.

other islands of Northern Lau: Kanathea, to the W of Vanua Mbalavu, is owned by the Australian firm, Morris Hedstrom. Mango I. is a copra estate owned by the English planter, Jim Barron. In 1983 Naitamba I. was purchased from TV star Raymond Burr by the American spiritual group, Johannine Daist Communion (750 Adrian Way, San Rafael, CA 94903), for US$2,500,000. Johannine Daist holds 4-to-8-week meditation retreats on Naitamba for long-time members of the Communion. Baba Da Free John, the communion's founder and teacher, resides on the island. There's a single Fijian village on Yathata Island. Vatu Vara, to the S, with its soaring interior plateau, golden beaches, and azure lagoon is privately owned and unoccupied much of the time. The circular, 314-m-high central limestone terrace, when viewed from the sea, gave it its other name, Hat Island. There is reputed to be buried treasure on Vatu Vara. Katafanga, to the SE of Vanua Mbalavu, was at one time owned by Harold Gatty, the famous Australian aviator who founded Air Pacific is 1951.

SOUTHERN LAU

Lakemba: Lakemba is a rounded, volcanic island reaching 215 m. The fertile red soils of the rolling interior hills have been planted with pine, but the low coastal plain, with 8 villages and all the people, is covered with coconuts. To the E is a wide lagoon enclosed by a barrier reef. In the olden days the population lived on Delai Kendekende, an interior hilltop well-suited for defense. The original capital of Lakemba was Nasanggalau on the N coast.

The present inhabitants of Nasanggalau retain strong Tongan influence. When the Nayau clan conquered the island their paramount chief, the Tui Nayau, became ruler of all of Lau from his seat at Tumbou. He also happens to be the current prime minister of Fiji.

sights: A 29-km road runs all the way around Lakemba. Get a good view of Tumbou, an attractive village with a hospital, wharf, and several stores, from the Catholic church. The Tongan chief Enele Ma'afu (died 1881), king of Lau, is buried on a stepped platform behind the Provincial Office near the wharf. Alongside Ma'afu is the grave of Ratu Sir Lala Sakuna (1888-1958), an important figure in the colonial administration. The first Methodist missionaries to arrive in Fiji landed on the

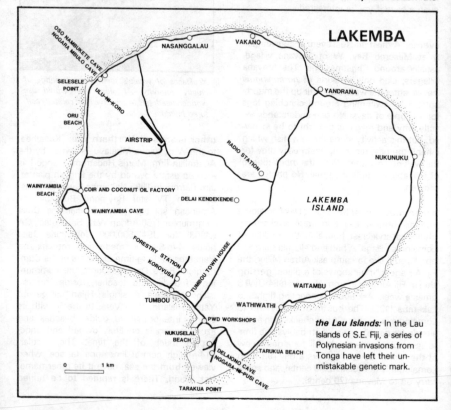

LAKEMBA

the Lau Islands: In the Lau Islands of S.E. Fiji, a series of Polynesian invasions from Tonga have left their unmistakable genetic mark.

0   1 km

beach just opposite the burial place in 1835. Tumbou was originally situated at Korovusa, just inland, where the foundations of former houses can still be seen. Farther inland on the same road is the forestry station and a nursery.

coconut factory: Four km W of Tumbou is the coir (husk fiber) and coconut oil factory of the Lakemba Cooperative Assn. at Wainiyambia. Truckloads of coconuts are brought in and dehusked by hand. The meat is removed and sent to the copra driers. The coconut oil is pressed from the copra and exported in drums. The dry pulp remaining after the extraction is bagged and sold locally as feed for pigs. The husks are flattened and soaked, then fed through machinery which separates the fiber. This is then made into twine, rope, brushes, and door mats, or bundled to be used as mattress fiber. Nothing is wasted. Behind the factory is Wainiyambia Beach, one of the most scenic on Lakemba.

Nasanggalau and vicinity: The best limestone caves on the island are near the coast on the NW side of Lakemba, 2.5 km SW of Nasanggalau. Oso Nambukete is the largest; the entrance is behind a raised limestone terrace. You walk through 2 chambers before reaching a small, circular opening about one m in diameter which leads into a third. The story goes that women attempting to hide during pregnancy were unable to pass through this opening, thus giving the cave its name, the Pregnant Women's Cave. Nearby is a smaller cave, Nggara Mbulo (Hidden Cave), which one must crawl into. Warriors used it as a refuge and hiding place in former times. The old village of Nasanggalau was located on top of the high cliffs behind the caves at Ulu-ni-koro. The whole area is owned by the Nautonggumu clan of Nasanggalau, and they will arrange for a guide to show you around. Take some newspapers to spread over the openings to protect your clothing.

east of Tumbou: Two less impressive caves can be found at Tarakua, SE of Tumbou. Nggara-ni-pusi has a small entrance but opens

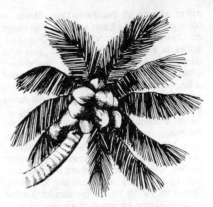

Every part of the coconut tree (Cocos nucifera) can be used. The husk provides cord, mats, brushes, and fuel, the leaves thatch, baskets, and fans, and the trunk building material. Food and oil from the nuts are the greatest prize. A healthy tree will produce 50 nuts a year for over 60 years.

up once you get inside. Delaiono Cave is just below a huge banyan tree; this one is easier to enter, and smaller inside. The best beach near Tumbou is Nukuselal, which you can reach by walking E along the coastal road as far as the P.W.D. workshops. Turn R onto the track which runs along the W side of the compound to Nukuselal Beach.

into the interior: Many forestry roads have been built throughout the interior of Lakemba. Walk across the island from Tumbou to Yandrana in a couple of hours, enjoying excellent views along the way. A radio station operates on solar energy near the center of the island. Aiwa I., which can be seen to the SE, is owned by the Tui Nayau and is inhabited only by flocks of wild goats.

accommodations: The Tumbou Town House has 4 rooms at $8 pp bed/breakfast, $3 extra for lunch or dinner. The locals at Tumbou concoct a potent homebrew (*umburu*) from cassava. **getting there:** Fiji Air flies to Lakemba 3 times a week. The bus from the airstrip to Tumbou is 50 cents. Buses around the island run 4 times weekdays, 3 times weekends ($1.20 RT).

other islands of Southern Lau: Mothe is famous for its *tapa* cloth, which is also made on Oneata, Namuka, Vatoa, and Ono-i-Lau. Komo is known for its beautiful girls and dances (*meke*), which are performed whenever a ship arrives. The Yangasa Cluster is owned by the people of Mothe, who visit it occasionally to make copra. Fiji's best *tanoa* are carved at Kambara. Fulanga is also known for its woodcarving; large outrigger canoes are still built on Fulanga, as well as Ongea. Over 100 tiny islands in the Fulanga lagoon have been undercut into incredible mushroom shapes. The water around them is tinged with striking colors by the dissolved limestone. Ono-i-Lau, far to the S, consists of 3 small volcanic islands, remnants of a single crater, in an oval lagoon. A few tiny coral islets sit on the barrier reef. The people of Ono-i-Lau make the best *mangi mangi* (sennet rope) and *tambu kaisi* mats in the country. Only high chiefs may sit on these mats. Structurally and historically, the high volcanic islands of Moala, Totoya, and Matuku have little to do with the rest of Lau, yet they are administered as part

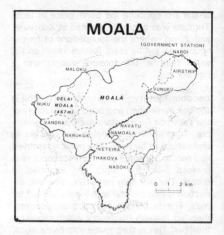

of the group. Totoya is a horseshoe-shaped high island enclosing a deep bay on the south. Unfortunately, the bay cannot be entered by ships due to reefs. Fiji Air flights from Nausori also call at Thithia I., between Northern and Southern Lau.

ROTUMA

This isolated volcanic island 500 km N of Viti Levu is surrounded on all sides by more than 322 km of open sea. In the beginning Raho, the Samoan folk hero, dumped 2 basketloads of earth here to create the twin islands joined by the Motusa Isthmus. He installed Sauiftonga as king. Tongans from Niuafo'ou conquered Rotuma in the 17th C. and ruled from

Noa'tau until they were overthrown. The first recorded European visit was by Capt. Edwards of HMS *Pandora* in 1791, while searching for the *Bounty* mutineers. Christianity was introduced in 1842 by Tongan Wesleyan missionaries, followed in 1847 by Marist Roman Catholics. Their followers fought pitched battles in the religious wars of

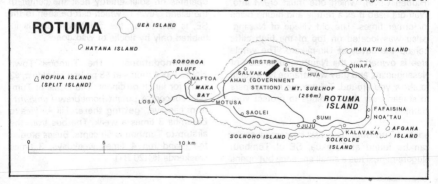

1871 and 1878, with the Wesleyans emerging victorious. Escaped convicts and beachcombers also flooded in, but mostly succeeded in killing each other off. Tiring of strife, the chiefs asked Britain to annex the island in 1881 and it has been part of Fiji ever since. European planters ran the copra trade from their settlement at Motusa until local cooperatives took over. Some 2,800 Rotumans presently inhabit the island, and another 4,600 of their number live in Suva. The light-skinned Polynesian Rotumans are easily distinguished from Fijians. Rotuma *kava* is noted for its strength and the women weave fine white mats. The climate is damp.

sights of Rotuma: Shipping arrives at a wharf on the edge of the reef, connected to Oinafa Point by a 200-m coral causeway which acts as a breakwater. There's a lovely white beach at Oinafa. The airstrip is to the W, between Oinafa and Ahau, the government station. At Noa'tau, SE of Oinafa, is a coop store; nearby, at Sililo, a hill with large stone slabs and old cannon scattered about which mark the burial place of the kings of yore. There's a large Catholic mission at Sumi on the S coast and inland near the center of the island is Mount Suelhof (256 m), the highest peak. Climb it for the view. Maftoa, across the Motusa Isthmus, has a cave with a freshwater pool. Sororoa Bluff (218 m), above Maftoa, should be climbed for the view. A km SW of Sororoa is Solmea Hill (165 m) with an inactive crater on its N slope. Hatana, a tiny islet off the W end of Rotuma, is said to be the final

resting place of Raho, the demigod who created Rotuma. A pair of volcanic rocks before a stone altar surrounded by a coral ring are said to be the King and Queen stones. Today Hatana is a refuge for seabirds.

getting there: Although Fiji Air flies to Rotuma from Nausori twice a week ($116 OW) and government barges call monthly ($22 OW deck), as yet there are no organized accommodations on Rotuma. Many Rotumans live in Suva, however, and if you have a friend he/she may be willing to send word to their family to expect you. Ask your Rotuman friend what you could take along as a gift.

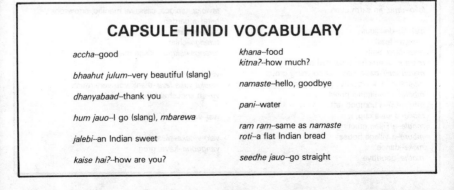

CAPSULE HINDI VOCABULARY

accha--good

bhaahut julum--very beautiful (slang)

dhanyabaad--thank you

hum jauo--I go (slang), *mbarewa*

jalebi--an Indian sweet

kaise hai?--how are you?

khana--food
kitna?--how much?

namaste--hello, goodbye

pani--water

ram ram--same as *namaste*
roti--a flat Indian bread

seedhe jauo--go straight

CAPSULE FIJIAN VOCABULARY

Although most people in Fiji speak English fluently, their mother tongue may be Fijian, Hindi, or another Pacific language. Knowledge of a few words of Fijian, especially slang words, will make your stay more exciting and enriching. Fijian has no pure *b*, *c*, or *d* sounds, as they are known in English. When the first missionaries arrived they invented a system of spelling with one letter for each Fijian sound. To avoid confusion, all Fijian names and words in this book are rendered phonetically, but the reader should be aware that, locally, "mb" is written "b," "nd" is "d," "ng" is "g," "ngg" is "q," and "th" is "c."

au lako mai Kenada--I come from Canada
au la o--Vanua Levu version of *mbarewa*
au lili--affirmative response to *au la o* (also *la o mai*)

duo oo--said by males when they meet a chief or enter a Fijian *mbure*

e rewa--a positive response to *mbarewa*

io--yes

kai--freshwater mussel
kambawangga--prostitute
kana--eat
kokonda--chopped raw fish and sea urchins with onions and lemon
ko lako ki vei?--where are you going?
koro--village
kothei na yathamu?--what's your name?
kumala--sweet potato
kumi--stencilled *tapa* cloth

lailai--small
lako mai--come here
lali--hollow log drum
levu--big, much
lolo--coconut cream
loloma yani--please pass my regards
lovo--umu, an earth oven

maleka--delicious
mangiti--feast
masi--tapa cloth
masa kesa--freehand painted *tapa*
matanggali--basic Fijian landowning group
mbarewa--a provocative greeting for the opposite sex
mbete--a traditional priest
mbilimbili--a bamboo raft
mbilo--a kava cup
mbula--a Fijian greeting
mbure--a village house
meke--dance
mothe--goodbye

ndale--taro
ndaru lako!--let's go!
ndrua--an ancient Fijian double canoe
nggara--cave
nice mbola--you're looking good
ni sambula--how are you? (answer is *an sambula vinaka*)

palusami--young taro leaves wrapped around coconut cream and baked
papalangi--foreigner
phufter--a gay male
ratu--high chief
rewa sese--an affirmative response to *mbarewa*

salusalu--garland, lei
sambula--hello (can also say *mbula* or *mbula vinaka*)
sayandra--good morning
senga--no, none
sevusevu--a presentation of *yanggona*
sulu--lavalava, sarong, a Fijian kilt

talatala--reverend
tambua--taboo, forbidden, sacred
tambua--a whale's tooth, a ceremonial object
tambu rewa--a negative response to *mbarewa*
tanoa--a kava bowl
tavioka--tapioca, cassava, manioc, arrowroot
teitei--a garden
tilou--excuse me
turanga--chief
turanga-ni-koro--village mayor

vinaka--thank you
vinaka vaka levu--thank you very much
vu--an ancestral spirit

wai--water

yalo vinaka--please
yanggona--kava, grog

NEW CALEDONIA

INTRODUCTION

New Caledonia is unique. In Noumea, the capital, the fine French restaurants, chic shops of Rue de l'Alma, and cosmopolitan crowds along Anse Vata all remind you that this is the Paris of the Pacific. Yet on the E coast of the main island and on all of the outliers, the Kanak languages and *la Coutume* (native custom) have survived a century and a quarter of repression, and the indigenous people are presently undergoing a dramatic social and political reawakening. For New Caledonia is not only a contradiction, but also an anachronism, the last surviving highly visible stronghold of white colonialism in Melanesia, and the world. (Most of the others — Guadeloupe, Martinique, Reunion, etc. — are also French.) This big territory just N of the Tropic of Capricorn, 1,500 km E of Australia, is quite unlike its neighbors and will surprise you in every respect.

the land: New Caledonia consists of the mainland (Grande Terre), the Isle of Pines, the Loyalty Group, and the small uninhabited dependencies of Walpole I. (125 ha), the d'Entrecasteaux Reefs (64 ha), and the more distant Chesterfield Is. (101 ha). The d'Entrecasteaux Reefs consist of 2 separate lagoons centered on tiny Huon and Surprise islands, with a deep strait 10 km wide between. Grande Terre is part of the great fold in the earth's surface which produced the Central Highlands of Papua New Guinea to the N and the northern peninsula of New Zealand to the south. Don't underestimate its size: Grande Terre is 400 km long and 50 km wide, the largest island in the South Pacific outside of P.N.G. and New Zealand. It's slowly sinking as the Australian Plate pushes under the Pacific Plate to the east. The winding, indented coastline is a result of this submergence. Ten km off both coasts is the second longest barrier reef in the world, which marks how big the island once was. Locals refer to Grande Terre as "Le Caillou" (The Rock). The interior is made up of row upon row of craggy mountains throughout its length, such as Mt. Panie (1,639 m) in the N

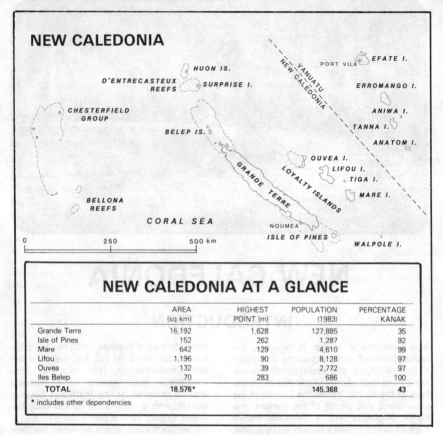

NEW CALEDONIA

HUON IS.

D'ENTRECASTEUX
REEFS

SURPRISE I.

CHESTERFIELD
GROUP

BELEP IS.

BELLONA
REEFS

CORAL SEA

GRANDE TERRE

NOUMEA
ISLE OF PINES

VANUATU
NEW CALEDONIA

PORT VILA   EFATE I.

ERROMANGO I.

ANIWA I.

TANNA I.

ANATOM I.

OUVEA I.
LIFOU I.
TIGA I.
MARE I.

LOYALTY ISLANDS

WALPOLE I.

0   250   500 km

NEW CALEDONIA AT A GLANCE

	AREA (sq km)	HIGHEST POINT (m)	POPULATION (1983)	PERCENTAGE KANAK
Grande Terre	16,192	1,628	127,885	35
Isle of Pines	152	262	1,287	92
Mare	642	129	4,610	99
Lifou	1,196	90	8,128	97
Ouvea	132	39	2,772	97
Iles Belep	70	283	686	100
TOTAL	**18,576***		**145,368**	**43**

* includes other dependencies

and Mt. Humboldt (1,634 m) in the S, and it contains 25-44 percent of the world's reserves of nickel, as well as profitable traces of other minerals such as tungsten, cobalt, copper, manganese, iron, and chromium. The landscape, you'll notice, is wounded in many locales by huge open-cut mines—the Great Red Menace. The verdant NE coast of this island is broken and narrow, cut by tortuous rivers with jagged peaks falling directly into the lagoon. The drier SW coast is low and swampy with wide coastal plains and alluvial lowlands. The Loyalty Is., on the other hand, are uplifted atolls with no rivers. Walpole I., 130 km E of the Isle of Pines, is also an uplifted limestone island 3 km long and 400 m

wide. There is no protective reef around its 70-m-high cliffs. Guano (fertilizer) was exploited from 1910-36. The Huon Is. consist of 4 tiny coral islands 275 km NW of Grande Terre, while the Chesterfields are 11 coral islets on a reef 550 km W-NW of the mainland. All of these dependencies are home to many species of seabirds.

climate: New Caledonia is farther S than most other South Pacific islands; this, combined with the refreshing SE tradewinds, accounts for its sunny, moderate climate, similar to that of the S of France. It can even be cool and windy from June to Sept. and campers will need sleeping bags. The ocean is warm enough for bathing year-round. December to March is warm and rainy; it's also the cyclone season. The cyclonic depressions can bring heavy downpours and cause serious flooding. The NE coast of Grande Terre catches the prevailing winds and experiences as much as 3,000 mm of precipitation a year, while the SW coast is a rain shadow with only 800 to 1,200 mm. Strong currents and heavy seas off the NE coast make the SW coast, where navigation is possible behind protective reefs, a better choice for cruising yachts.

flora: New Caledonia's vegetation has more in common with Australia's than it does with that of its closer tropical neighbor, Vanuatu. Eighty percent of the 2,500 botanic species are endemic. The most extensive floral feature is the *niaouli,* a relative of the eucalyptus, which covers 5,000 sq km of savannah in the N and W of Grande Terre. This tree has a white, almost completely fireproof bark which peels off in papery layers and is used for an excellent medicinal oil, somewhat like eucalyptus oil. By maintaining the continuity of the vegetation, the *niaouli* plays an important environmental role in this mountainous country where bush fires are so common. There are extensive areas of mangrove along the W coast. Along the E coast and in the S, the Norfolk pine (*Araucaria cooki*) is more common, towering 30-45 m high with branches only 2 m long. They stand on low hills, along the rockier shorelines, and on offshore islands.

fauna: The extreme richness of life on the reefs compensates for the lack of variety on land. The only native mammals are the flying fox and the rat. The deer which inhabit the savannahs of Grande Terre are descended from 2 pairs introduced in 1862. Some of the butterflies possess a rare beauty. Eighty-eight species of birds are found in New Caledonia, 18 of them endemic. Only a few hundred specimens of the Ouvea parakeet still exist. The national bird is the flightless *cagou* (*Rhynochetos jubatus*), about the size of a small rooster. This bird has lovely soft grey plumage, contrasted by striped brown and white wings. The crest on its head rises when

angered, and its cry is like the bark of a dog. It eats insects, worms, and snails. As it hatches only one egg a year and is slow on the ground, the *cagou* is approaching extinction. Dogs often outrun and kill it.

HISTORY

prehistory: New Caledonia has been inhabited for over 3,000 years; *lapita* sites have been found near Kone and on the Isle of Pines, carbon-dated at earlier than 1,000 B.C. The clans lived in small villages of 50 Kanaks (from *kanaka,* the Hawaiian word for "human") and farmed their own land, using sophisticated irrigation systems and terraced gardens. The center of the village was the *grande case,* a large conical house where the chief lived and ceremonies were performed. The collective was more important than the individual, and society was based around a relationship between the living and the ancestors, both of whom the chief represented in a sense. There was little contact between local tribes and many languages evolved; surprisingly, language groups extended across the main island rather than down the coasts. When Captain Cook, the first European, arrived in 1774, there were over 50,000 people living in these islands.

contact and conquest: Cook landed at Balade, on the NE coast of Grande Terre, and

The flightless cagou (Rhynochetos jubatus) *is the national bird of New Caledonia.*

gave New Caledonia its name—the mountainous island reminded him of the Scottish Highlands (Caledonia was the Romans' name for Scotland). After more navigators (d'Entrecasteaux and Huon de Kermadec), traders arrived looking for sandalwood and *beche de mer*. The first missionaries were Protestants from the London Missionary Society who established themselves on Mare (1841) and Lifou (1842) islands. French Catholic missionaries arrived in 1843 at Balade again but the Kanaks expelled them 4 years later. At this time France was watching enviously the establishment of successful British colonies in Australia and New Zealand. So in 1853, with the idea of creating a penal colony similar to that in New South Wales, Emperor Napoleon III ordered the annexation of New Caledonia. Ile Nou, an island in Noumea Bay, never attained the notoriety of its contemporary, Devil's Island off South America, but between 1864 and 1897 thousands of French convicts were transported here. They were used for public works and construction projects in the early days. Some 3,900 political prisoners from the Paris Commune were held on the Isle of Pines from 1872-79, including Louise Michel, the "red virgin," and Henri de Rochefort, who escaped in 1874.

the struggle for land: In 1864 Jules Garnier, a French mining engineer, discovered nickel at Diahot. Four years later the French government established a series of "indigenous reservations" for the confinement of natives in areas that didn't appeal to them and opened the rest of Grande Terre to mining and stock-raising. The reaction didn't take long. In 1878 High Chief Atai of La Foa launched a guerrilla war which cost 200 Frenchmen and l,000 Kanaks their lives. Eventually Atai was betrayed by a rival tribe and assassinated. His head was sent to a Paris museum for exhibit but has since been stolen. In the repression which followed, many clans were forced off their own lands onto that of other clans, leading to further rivalry and disruption. The abandoned taro terraces can still be seen. The French government assumed title to two-thirds of Grande Terre, another quarter was eventually given or sold to white settlers, and only 11 percent (in scattered, hilly areas) was

left to the original inhabitants. Title to even these crowded areas was uncertain and, right up until 1946, when the Kanaks were finally given French citizenship, they could not leave their reservations without police permission. The *colons* (settlers) brought in cattle and sheep and occupied the river valleys and coastal plains. In 1917 the high chief, Noel, appealed to his people to fight the French at home as well as Kanaka soldiers had fought the Germans abroad; although not as widespread as the 1878 revolt, 11 Europeans and 200 Kanaks died. Today the greater part of this alienated land is concentrated in large estates over 15 sq km in size, owned by a total of only 37 individuals. One French farm alone covers 367 sq km; another is 149 sq km. Land remains the basic issue behind the current discontent in New Caledonia. The Melanesian land-*using* culture continues to find itself confronted by a European land-*owning* culture which has usurped the rights it enjoyed for thousands of years. The French Socialists have now begun a cosmetic program of buying tracts of land from the *colons* and giving it back to the original owners.

military history: In June 1940, after the fall of France, the *Conseil General* of New Caledonia voted unanimously to support the Free French government, and the pro-Vichy governor was forced to leave for Indochina. The territory became an important Allied base, and the fleet which turned back the Japanese navy in the Battle of the Coral Sea (1942) was based at Noumea. Since WW II France has maintained its military presence in the territory; today some 4,000 French servicemen and police are present. Much of the army and all of the naval units are stationed in Noumea. There are 2 companies of infantry near Bourail and other army detachments at Plum, SE of Noumea. Air force helicopters are kept at Tontouta airport. Of 4 French overseas military commands, one is in New Caledonia and another in Eastern Polynesia—a considerable military commitment. Young Kanaks are forced to serve 11 months in the colonial army. In Jan. 1985 French President Mitterand announced that the military presence at Noumea is to increase.

Le St. Hubert, a favorite haunt of local French: someone has painted "colons assassins" on the wall.

the struggle for independence: The continuing struggle of a people to regain their identity against a colonial administration set on maintaining the status quo threatens the stability of the South Pacific as a whole. Nidoish Naisseline, a high chief of Mare, initiated the latest phase of the struggle by founding the *Foulards Rouges* (Red Scarves) in 1969. On 19 Sept. 1981 Pierre Declercq, secretary-general of the pro-independence *Union Caledonienne,* was shot through a window of his Mt. Dore home as he sat working at his desk. No one has ever been brought to trial for this act. The independence movement was united as never before by this crime, and in 1982 the *Front Independantiste* gained a majority in the Territorial Assembly. There is an extremist element among the French *colons,* reinforced by reactionary elements from Santo (Vanuatu) who fled to New Caledonia after the collapse of the French-inspired secession. This group is heavily armed. On 22 July 1982 these French right-wingers wearing paramilitary-style uniforms stormed the Assembly building and assaulted the pro-

independence members. Two French police were killed in a clash with Kanak villagers in 1983. Many other persons have died in recent incidents. In Nov. 1984, after Territorial Assembly elections in which thousands of transient French voted, but boycotted by the *independantistes,* a provisional government of Kanaky was established by independence supporters, now united as the *Front de Liberation National Kanake Socialiste* (FLNKS). Soon after, in the worst outbreak of violence in the South Pacific since the end of WW II, *colons* ambushed a group of unarmed Kanak activists at Hienghene with dynamite, killing 10 and wounding others. French gendarmes didn't arrive on the scene until the next day, although they were called shortly after the incident. Among the dead were 2 brothers of Jean-Marie Tjibaou, a former Catholic priest and vice-president of the previous Government Council of New Caledonia. In Jan. 1985, police sharpshooters murdered Eloi Machoro, minister of the interior in the provisional government, and Marcel Noraro, an aide, as they stood outside their rural headquarters near La Foa. In retaliation the giant French-owned Thio and Kouaoua nickel mines were blown up by saboteurs, as whites rioted against independence in Noumea. Amid growing disorder the struggle continues.

French policy: Before coming to power, Mitterand's socialists pledged support for Kanak self-determination. However, since becoming the French government all they have done is created an economic agency to promote development in Kanak areas through soft loans and outright grants, and offered a referendum on independence. There is a dispute about who should vote in this referendum. At present any French citizen can vote in local elections after 48 hours in the territory and thousands of French soldiers and police are on the rolls. Kanaks, on the other hand, who didn't get the vote until 1953, must return to their place of origin within New Caledonia in order to register to vote. The FLNKS is asking that only those likely to remain in New Caledonia after independence be allowed to vote. With voting regulations as they stand now it's likely a majority will vote *against* independence, probably leading to further chaos. Special French envoy Edgard Pisani has offered New Caledonia independence as a "state associated with France." It will be interesting to see whether he and Mitterand come through on their offer, or if it's just another smokescreen. Many white residents are concerned — quite

naturally — over their rights post-independence. France is determined to hold onto the territory for the mineral riches it possesses and its strategic role of protecting the French nuclear test zone in Eastern Polynesia (the domino theory). Many resident Polynesians, fearing the changes independence will bring, support the French position. The Kanaks have already been radicalized to the extent that independence will almost certainly result in a reduction of freedom in New Caledonia and an anti-white backlash. David Robie predicted in *Pacific* magazine that if independence is denied, the coming years could see a campaign of harassment against European farmers, along the lines of Kenya's Mau Mau movement. The struggle for political independence is becoming a struggle for the liberation of the Kanak people.

French power: In New Caledonia today, after more than 125 years of colonial rule, nearly all positions of authority in business and the administration are held by Europeans. It was not until 1951 that Kanaks were allowed anything more than primary education; none graduated from high school until 1960. The first Kanak university graduate returned from college in France as recently as 1971. Despite French enthusiasm to spread their culture, there is still no university in the territory although de Gaulle promised one decades ago; it's feared that such an institu-

Cite Pierre Lenquette, a low-cost housing project for Kanaks near Noumea

tion would soon become a hotbed of revolutionary activity. In the schools, the teaching staff is largely French. The curriculum is exactly the same as in France: Kanak children are taught that their ancestors are the Gauls. The teaching of political science to Kanaks is forbidden. There are no Kanak doctors, economists, or engineers, and only one architect. Yet the French government uses this fact as an argument that the Kanaks are not "ready" for independence. France has a bad track record in teaching democracy to its colonies or preparing them for independence; French withdrawals from Africa, Indochina, and Vanuatu led to chaos. A million deaths were needed to convince France it had to give up Algeria. It appears that Noumea, Papeete, and the native peoples of the French territories can expect some very difficult times. The FLNKS has called for the listing of New Caledonia on the agenda of the U.N. Decolonization Committee and this position has been supported by all neighboring countries. One of the more original proposals is to convert New Caledonia into New California, the 51st State of the Union. Pro-American graffiti painted on walls and hillsides appear incongruously alongside exhortations to socialist revolution and seem to have been painted by the same hand.

GOVERNMENT

New Caledonia is a dependent territory run by a high commissioner appointed by the president of France. The high commissioner controls all national government departments (including the military and police, education, finance, public works, and mines) and has veto power over the Territorial Assembly, which operates at his mercy and can be dissolved by him at any time, as has happened. The Territorial Assembly has 36 members elected for 5-year terms. They set local taxes, control the territorial budget (an insignificant amount compared to the money controlled by French civil servants, however), and provide social services. The assembly has no opportunity to make significant policy decisions and is little more than a showpiece institution

designed to give the illusion that New Caledonia is self-governing. The assembly elects a 7-member Government Council which is impotent. Everyone born in New Caledonia is legally a French citizen and can vote in French presidential elections. Two deputies are elected to the French Parliament, one from the E coast of Grande Terre and outer islands, one from the W coast and Noumea. A senator, elected by the municipal councils and Territorial Assembly, is also sent to Paris. Local government is organized into 32 communes, each with an elected mayor and Municipal Council. The communes are grouped into 4 administrative subdivisions with headquarters at La Foa, Kone, Poindimie, and We (Lifou). The appointed civil servants who head these subdivisions have veto power over the actions of the elected municipal officials in their area.

parties: There are 3 major political groupings in New Caledonia. The largest party is the Gaullist *Rassemblement pour la Caledonie dans la Republique* (RPCR), led by Noumea's Mayor Roger Laroque and Deputy Jacques Lafleur. The FLNKS is an alliance of 5 separate parties, of which the *Union Caledonienne* is the most important. The *Federation pour une Nouvelle Societe Caledonienne* (FNSC) favors autonomy for the territory and has allied itself with the FLNKS. *Liberation Kanak Socialiste* (LKS) is a revolutionary socialist party whose leader, Nidoish Naisseline, has boycotted his assembly seat. In the 1979 election it was estimated that 70 percent of the Kanak population voted for the independence parties. **the media:** Radio and television in the territory are a monopoly of the French government and 90 percent of the programming originates in France. The rest is mostly sports. There is only one daily paper in New Caledonia, the pro-French *Les Nouvelles Caledoniennes.*

ECONOMY

mining and business: New Caledonia has a classic colonial economy, being primarily a source of raw materials for France and a market for finished products from France. New Caledonia ranks third in world nickel production (after Canada and the U.S.S.R.); nickel accounts for 99 percent of territorial exports by volume and 70 percent of the gross national product. The nickel ore is high grade, being free of arsenic. The French government considers nickel a "strategic" metal and all mining permits must be approved by the Minister for Industrial Development in Paris. This, and the requirement that there be 50 percent French participation in any foreign investment in the territory, guarantees the exploitation of nickel by French companies. Societe Le Nickel, which owns the smelter at Noumea, is part of the Rothschild international mining conglomerate. There are large nickel mines at Thio, Poro, and Nepoui. While half the population enjoys the benefits of nickel mining, the other half suffers its effects. The industry has led to the importation of foreign labor, making the Kanaks a minority in their own land, while that very land has been expropriated from beneath their feet. Chrome and iron ore were formerly exported, but these operations have closed due to market conditions. France supplies a third of the territory's imports, followed by the U.S. and Australia. France takes over half of New Caledonia's exports; Japan gets another quarter. Tourism is being strongly promoted and Australia, France, and Japan provide the most visitors. The old *Caldoche* families—Ballande, Barrau, Lafleur, Laroque, Montagnat, and Pentecost—control the local economy, though their hold is currently being challenged by French newcomers such as Ravel. Together, Ballande and Laroque almost run Noumea. This powerful class is firmly committed to a continuing relationship with France: Lafleur and Laroque are leaders of the political movement to block independence.

agriculture: Yams are the main subsistence crop, followed by taro, manioc, and sweet potatoes. From 1865 to 1890 the cultivation of sugarcane was attempted; it failed due to labor costs and milling problems. Cotton was grown from 1860 right up until the 1930s when drought, disease, and the world depression brought it to an end. Coffee, introduced

a female fertility figure

in the first days of French colonization, is still grown today, mostly the robusta type. Kanaks participate in coffee growing, but the processing and marketing is in the hands of large French companies such as Ballande. Although production is limited, the quality is excellent (take a bag home with you). By far, beef cattle raising has always been the most important monetary agricultural activity, mostly large herds kept by Europeans on the W coast. Due to high demand meat still has to be imported, however. Pig farming is well-developed. Food still accounts for about a quarter of New Caledonia's imports by value.

THE PEOPLE

Of the 145,368 inhabitants of New Caledonia, 43 percent are Melanesian, 38 percent European, and 12 percent Polynesian. Vietnamese, Indonesians, other Asians, West Indians, and Arabs make up the remaining 7 percent. A little over half the Europeans were born in New Caledonia. The Vietnamese and Indonesians were brought in to work in the mines early this century; by 1921 some 4,000 of them were present. During the nickel boom of 1969-73 the European population increased in size by a third and the number of Polynesians doubled. French planners want to increase the population to 400,000 by inviting immigrants from France and other French territories; in fact, one of the strongest arguments in favor of independence is that it will stop this uncontrolled migration. Of the 21,630 convicts transported to New Caledonia from 1864 to 1897, just over a thousand stayed on as settlers (*colons*) on land granted them when they were freed. These and other early French arrivals are called *Caldoches,* while the present transients who come only to make money to take back to France are referred to as *les oreilles* (the ears). French expatriates holding government jobs in New Caledonia are notoriously overpaid. The 2,500 Frenchmen who migrated to the territory from Algeria are the *pieds noir* (black feet). The Kanaks are also known as *Ti-Va-Ouere,* the Brothers of the Earth. There is a striking contrast between the affluent French community around Noumea and the poverty of Kanak villages on the NE coast of Grande Terre and on the outer islands. **language:** There are some 28 indigenous languages, all Austronesian, which can be broadly organized into 8 related areas: 5 on Grande Terre and one on each of the Loyalties. The Kanak languages all developed

Stocking up with baguettes at a Noumea bakery.

from a single mother tongue but are today mutually incomprehensible. Lifou is the language with the most speakers: about 8,000 on Lifou itself, plus a few thousand in Noumea. French is the common language understood by everyone. Very few people in New Caledonia understand English.

la Coutume: In essence the present conflict in New Caledonia is a clash of cultures. For over a century the Kanaks have been obliged to adopt a foreign way of life which styled itself as superior to their own. Despite acceptance of a foreign language, religion, dress, and money economy, indigenous custom (*la Coutume*) continues to maintain a surprising strength just beneath the surface. Today the Kanak people struggle not only to regain their lands but also to reassert their own culture over another which they both embrace and reject.

events: Bastille Day (14 July) features a military parade through Noumea. New Caledonia Day (24 Sept.) recalls the day in 1853 when Admiral Despointes took possession of New Caledonia for France. The Agricultural Fair at Bourail in Aug. or Sept. features rodeos and other colorful activities. Don't miss it. There's a bicycle race around Grande Terre in Aug. or Sept., a car race about the end of November. If you're in Noumea around the second Sat. in Oct., ask about *Braderie,* a popular street fair to which the whole population turns out. Other public holidays include Labor Day (1 May), All Saints Day (1 Nov.), and Armistice Day (11 Nov.). The school holidays run from 15 Dec. till the end of February. **sports:** *Petanque* is a French bowling game, played with metal balls the size of baseballs, which are thrown at other balls, not rolled.

PRACTICALITIES

getting there: UTA French Airlines connects Noumea to France, Singapore, Sydney, Auckland, Tahiti, and Los Angeles. Their planes are heavily booked so don't forget to reconfirm your onward reservations not less than 72 hours prior to your departure time, otherwise they will be cancelled automatically. If you're already in the South Pacific, the easy way to get to New Caledonia is with Air Pacific's Triangle Fare which gives you Nandi-Noumea-Port Vila-Nandi for F$386. You can fly any day and take up to a year to complete the trip. This ticket can also be purchased from Air Pacific in Noumea, if you've arrived on a discount UTA ticket and want to see a little more of the Pacific before proceeding to New Zealand. Air Caledonie International connects New Caledonia to Vanuatu and Wallis Island. Air Nauru, Air New Zealand, Polynesian Airlines, and Qantas also have services from their home countries. All these flights operate from Tontouta airport.

getting around: Air Caledonie, the domestic commuter airline, uses Magenta Airport (GEA) near Noumea. They run daily flights to the Loyalty Is. (Mare, Lifou, and Ouvea), f.4750 OW, plus an interisland link between the 3 larger Loyalties and Tiga, about f.2300 per sector. This means that for f.15,900 airfare RT, you can visit all 4 Loyalty Is. from Noumea. There are 2 flights a day to the Isle of Pines, f.3200 OW. You can fly twice a week from Koumac to Belep, off the NW coast of Grande Terre, f.3100 OW. On all these flights, the baggage allowance is 10 kg pp, and there's a f.800 penalty if you change or cancel a reservation less than 48 hours in advance. If Noumea travel agents tell you the flights are fully booked, go out to the Air Caledonie office at Magenta Airport and check for yourself. Grande Terre has fairly good bus service and the prices are reasonable. Cheapest are the buses marked *subventionne,* subsidized mail runs. Inquire about these at local post offices. Hitchhiking is also possible.

accommodations: Prices at the hotels are manageable for 2, but sometimes too high for one. Hotel rooms are taxed at a flat rate which varies according to the category (about f.70-130 a day for those listed here). In the tribal areas a network of Melanesian-operated accommodations known as *gites* has been created. These are mostly small thatched cottages near a beach. Although many are overpriced and poorly run, the best are described herein. The Air Caledonie office at Magenta Airport can reserve a cottage for you at any of the *gites.* Noumea has the only genuine youth hostel in the South Pacific. **camping:** New Caledonia is also one of the few places in the South Pacific where camping is widely understood, practiced, and accepted. French soldiers on leave from Noumea do it all the time; bourgeois French locals consider it a legitimate way to spend a weekend. There are many organized campgrounds on Grande Terre. On the outer islands camp at a *gite.* Almost anyone you ask will readily give you permission to pitch your tent, but do ask. Otherwise you might be violating custom and could cause yourself a needless problem. Take care with your gear around Poindimie, where rip-offs have occurred. Otherwise it's hassle-free. Don't swim topless or naked in front of a Kanak village. There are lots of isolated beaches where you can do it and if you want to be seen, there's always Noumea.

food: French cuisine prevails in Noumea and the towns. Watch for the *plat du jour,* a reasonably-priced businessman's lunch. There are also excellent (though pricey) Chinese and Vietnamese restaurants. If you've never tried Vietnamese food, it's like Chinese food, only spicier. Curries are good value, as is *porc au sucre* (sweet pork), which comes with "sour" (vinegared) vegetables to maintain the Oriental *yin-yang* balance. A *bougna* is a native pudding made from sliced root vegetables soaked in coconut milk, wrapped in banana leaves with pork, chicken, or seafood, and cooked over hot stones in an earthen oven. Since New Caledonia is associated with the European Economic Community, the foods available in the supermarkets are totally different from those offered in most other South Pacific countries. Buy long crusty *baguettes* and flaky *croissants* to complement the *pate,* wine, and cheese. Together these are the makings of a memorable picnic. Note grocery stores are not allowed to sell bottles of wine on weekends. Note too how little local produce is available in the stores.

money: Currency is the French Pacific franc (CFP). This is linked to the volatile French franc: f.100 equals 5.5 French francs. You can determine how many CFP you will get by finding out how many French francs you get for your dollar/pound, then multiplying by 18.18. From 1980 to 1984, the CFP dropped from 83 to 140 to the US$ and prices rose accordingly. For this reason, prices in this chapter are relative approximations only. New Caledonia and Eastern Polynesia use the same currency, so although the notes may bear Noumea or Papeete mint marks, the two are freely interchangeable. Banks open early (0720) and close at 1545. In Noumea the Banque Indosuez on the Place des Cocotiers next to the old Town Hall is open Sat. 0800-1100. All banks charge f.250 commission for each foreign currency transaction, whether buying or selling, and usually give the same rate for cash or travelers cheques. There is no tipping in New Caledonia. Camera film is much cheaper in Fiji, Vanuatu, and Australia, so bring a good supply. New Caledonia's form of taxation—high import and export duties—inflates the cost of living.

visas and health: No visa is required for citizens of the U.S., Japan, Switzerland, and most Commonwealth countries for visits of less than a month. Citizens of European Economic Community countries get 3 months and French are admitted for an unlimited stay. Everyone (French included) must have an onward ticket. This requirement is strictly enforced and there's no chance of slipping through without one. Noumea is the only port of entry for cruising yachts. The government health service is run by the army and most of the doctors are military officers recruited in France. Tourists are usually referred to private doctors. There is no malaria in New Caledonia.

AIRPORTS

international airport: La Tontouta Airport (NOU) is 53 km NW of Noumea and 112 km SE of Bourail. Don't jump on the special airport bus: it costs f.2000 for the ride to Noumea. Wait instead for the blue interurban bus (f.350), to the L as you leave the terminal. They run hourly, but stop at an early 1800. Despite the posted schedule, the blue buses do run on Sun. and holidays, although less frequently; ask at the airport information counter. The blue bus follows the old road through picturesque towns and carries colorful local passengers, while the tourist bus zips along the toll road nonstop. The airport bank is open for most arrivals, but not all departures. They give about the same rate you'll get in town. If it's closed, there's another bank on the main highway near the airport. Coin lockers are f.40 a day. As your plane is taxiing up to the terminal, glance across the runway at the French air force hangars to see if their counterinsurgency helicopters or Neptune bombers are in. When checking in at Tontouta, pack your camera in your suitcase, otherwise the security guards will force you to put it through an X-ray machine, thereby spoiling your film. There is no airport tax.

domestic airport: Magenta Airport (GEA) is 5 km NE of downtown Noumea. City bus No. 7 will drop you right at the door. A taxi from the Place des Cocotiers costs about f.500. There are no coin lockers. Air Caledonie has their reservations office (open Mon. to Fri. 0730-1115/1400-1730, Sat. 0730-1115) at the airport.

NOUMEA

Noumea was founded in 1854 by Tardy de Montravel, who called it Port de France. A French governor arrived in 1862; convicts condemned to the penal colony on Ile Nou followed 2 years later. Robert Louis Stevenson, who visited in 1890, remarked that Noumea was "built from vermouth cases." The town remained a backwater until 1942 when American military forces arrived to transform this landlocked port into a bastion for the war against Japan. Admiral Halsey directed the Solomon Islands campaign from his headquarters on Anse Vata. Today this thriving maritime center near the S end of the New Caledonian mainland is a busy, crowded, cosmopolitan city of 69,000, made rich mostly by nickel. Fully half the population of the territory resides here. The city is predominantly French, but Melanesian women in their Mother Hubbard dresses add color to the market area. Bathing beauties bask at Noumea's chic Anse Vata beach, where most of the luxury hotels are found. Windsurfers and sailboats hover offshore and it's clear that this is a monied tourist's paradise. The city is especially beautiful from Nov. to Jan. when the flame trees (poincianas) bloom red. Only a couple of hours by jet from Australia or New Zealand, most tourists limit their visit to Noumea, but New Caledonia has much more to offer than just its capital city. You can't claim to have seen the territory until you get across to the NE coast or out to one of the islands.

SIGHTS

historic Noumea: The Place des Cocotiers, with its statues, fountains, and old trees, is the best place to begin your tour of New Caledonia. In the middle of this wonderful central square, the Monumental Fountain (1892) is point zero for all mileages in the territory. On the N side of the square is the old Town Hall (1880). Special exhibitions are often displayed inside. The graffiti-covered statue at the W end of the park is of Admiral Olry, governor from 1878-1880. Walk N on Rue du Gen. Mangin to the old military hospital, which dates from the 1880s and is still the main medical facility in the city. Go R on Ave. Paul Doumer and you'll come to the residence of the French high commissioner. Turn R, then L, and continue E to Blvd. Vauban. The Territorial Assembly is on the corner. Go R on Blvd. Vauban to the Protestant Church (1893) at the head of Rue de l'Alma. Continue S on Blvd. Vauban to St. Joseph's Cathedral (1894), which was built by convict labor. This fine old building overlooking the city has stained glass windows. Continue E from the cathedral along Rue Frederic Surleau to the French army barracks (*caserne*), which has changed very little since its construction in 1869. Return W along Ave. de la Victoire to Ave. du Marechal Foch, where you turn R to enter the Bernheim Library. In 1901 Louis Bernheim, a miner who made his fortune in the territory, donated the money for its first library (the only time a local mining mogul has ever given away anything and it's still the only real library in the territory). What had been the New Caledonian Pavilion at the Paris Universal Exposition of 1900 was used to house the collection. The original building still stands alongside the present reading room.

New Caledonia Museum: This outstanding museum 2 blocks S of the Bernheim Library on Ave. du Marechal Foch contains a great deal of material on Kanak culture: woodcarvings, masks, daily implements, canoe and house designs, and *lapita* pottery. The main shortcoming is that all the labels are only in French. There's an unusual botanical collection in the courtyard, and a traditional full-sized *grande case* (big house) behind the museum. Open Tues. to Sat. 0900-1100/ 1400-1730, admission free. Don't miss it. If you'd like to clear your head after the museum, climb Mont Coffyn for the sweeping view; there's a ceramic map at the top for orientation. Go S on Ave. Foch to Rue Duquesne, turn L and go up 2 blocks to Rue Guynemer where you turn R then L and up the hill. Use the map. As you stand beside the immense two-armed Cross of Lorraine, you'll be able to pick out Amedee Lighthouse (1865), 18 km to the south. This was prefabricated in Paris, and at 56 m high is still the tallest metal lighthouse in the world.

nearby beaches: Baie des Citrons and Anse Vata, Noumea's finest beaches, are near the southern end of the peninsula. Very attractive and easily accessible by bus, they're also cluttered with hotels, and tend to be crowded; elsewhere in New Caledonia you can usually have a beach all to yourself. Anse Vata is topless. Legally, all beaches in the territory are public so you're within your rights to use the

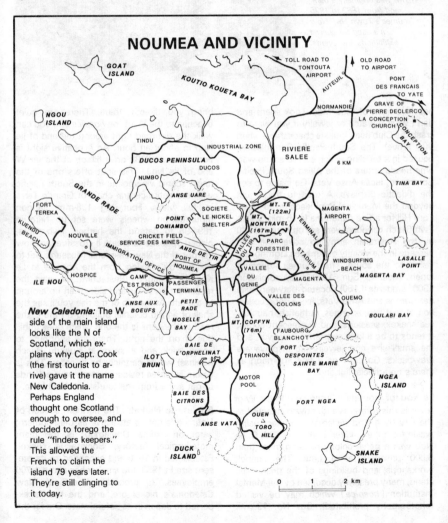

NOUMEA AND VICINITY

New Caledonia: The W side of the main island looks like the N of Scotland, which explains why Capt. Cook (the first tourist to arrive) gave it the name New Caledonia. Perhaps England thought one Scotland enough to oversee, and decided to forego the rule "finders keepers." This allowed the French to claim the island 79 years later. They're still clinging to it today.

0   1   2 km

The old Hotel de Ville (1874) was originally a bank and from 1882 to 1975 Noumea's Town Hall. Now it's used for special exhibitions and events.

beach in front of Club Med. Look sharp and don't wear a watch or jewelry if you want to crash the Club itself (guests check these when they arrive). The South Pacific Commission, housed in a building which served as the war-time headquarters of the Allied South Pacific Command, faces Anse Vata. Go inside to see the didactic displays. A road to the L just beyond the Municipal Pool leads up to Ouen Toro Hill for a fine panorama (a 15-min. walk). Two 6-inch cannons were set up here in 1940 by the Australian army to cover the reef passage in the vicinity of Amedee Lighthouse, visible to the south. The Noumea Aquarium (open Tues. to Sun. 1330-1630, admission f.300, students f.150), located between Baie des Citrons and Anse Vata, has a good collection of reef fish, sponges, cuttlefish, nautilus, sea snakes, seaslugs, and fluorescent corals. It tends to be a little overrated, however, and the small size and jewelry-like displays are drawbacks. Go early on a fine afternoon as there's no artificial lighting.

Ile Nou (or Nouville): Jutting out to the W of town is this former island, now connected to the city by a land reclamation project using waste from the smelter. In the late 19th C. Ile Nou was a penal colony housing more than 3,000 prisoners at a time. The chapel, workshops, and buildings of the prison still stand, many presently occupied by the Mental Institution (*hospice*) which may be visited (photography prohibited). Bus No. 13 will

bring you directly there. There are quiet beaches to the W of the *hospice* and you can walk the dirt road right around the end of Ile Nou in about an hour. An evocative sight is Fort Tereka (1878), on a hilltop at the far W end of Ile Nou. This spot offers one of the finest scenic viewpoints in the South Pacific with the entire central chain of Grande Terre in full view. Four big 138-mm cannon mounted on wheels were set up here in 1894-96 to defend the harbor. Two more, placed opposite to create a crossfire, are now in front of the New Caledonia Museum. Get to the fort by walking from the *hospice* to Le Kuendu Beach Bar/Restaurant. Go past the restaurant on the inland side, then up around to the left. At the top of the rise you'll see the shell of an old colonial building on the L; the road to the guns is the one which goes uphill due N on the right. There are shortcuts to come back and a swim at Kuendu Beach (topless) would certainly be in order. This is where Noumea residents come on weekends to get away from the tourists at Anse Vata.

Societe le Nickel: The northern section of Noumea is not as attractive as the southern; here, on Pointe Doniambo, is the giant metallurgical factory, Societe le Nickel. Established in 1910 and expanded to its present size in 1958, the smelter has about 1,700 employees. It processes most of New Caledonia's nickel ore, and the rest is exported to Japan in its natural state. Ore for the smelter is collected from a number of giant, open-cut mines around Grande Terre by the ore carriers *Nickel I* and *Nickel II,* leaving terrible scars in their wake, particularly on the NE coast of the island. Two distinct products are smelted: ferronickel and matte. The former, sold to a variety of industrialized countries, is 75 percent iron and 25 percent nickel, used in the manufacture of stainless steel. Matte, sent to the company's Le Havre (France) plant, is 80 percent nickel and cobalt, used in the making of high-quality steel products. If you're interested, the Service des Mines, located between the smelter and downtown, has a small collection of rocks on display Mon. to Fri. 0730-1130/1215-1600 (free).

Parc Forestier: Visit this botanical garden and zoo 5 km NE of downtown to see the flightless and rapidly disappearing *cagou* (*Rhynochetos jubatus*), New Caledonia's official territorial bird. The excellent ornithological collection also includes the rare Ouvea parakeet. There are a few mammals, of which the flying foxes stand out. The botanical collection continues to be disappointing, but growing. It's a 45-min. walk from the Noumea Youth Hostel. Follow the radio towers N and turn L up the signposted gravel road past the 3 towers of the Centre Recepteur Radioelectrique. There are many excellent scenic views along the way, the best from the summit of Montravel (166 m), accessible up a stairway 400 m before you reach the Parc. Amedee Lighthouse is visible once

Only a few hundred specimens of the Ouvea parakeet (Eunymphicus cornutus uveaensis) *still exist in the wild.*

again on the horizon S of the summit, just to the L of Ouen Toro. To the NE the twin peaks of Mt. Koghi (1,061 m) dominate the horizon, while due E the oval profile of Mt. Dore (772 m) stands alone. You can also get to the Parc by taking bus No. 12 to the Montravel low-cost housing area, then walk 1.5 km uphill. The zoo is open Mon. to Sat. 1330-1600, Sun. and holidays 1100-1600, admission f.200.

PRACTICALITIES

accommodations: The cheapest hotels are in the downtown area. The Hotel Caledonia, behind the museum in the Latin Quarter, is cheerful but noisy from traffic: f.1400 s, f.1800 d, f.2300 t, shared facilities. The Hotel Mon Logis, 55 Rue de Sebastopol, is one step down in quality and one step up in price: f.1800 s or d, f.2200 for a studio with bath. Monthly rates are f.25,000 s, f.35,000 for a studio. There are 2 medium-priced hotels near Anse Vata Beach. The Motel Anse Vata (tel. 26-2612) is only a short walk from the beach: f.2800 s, f.3200 d, f.3600 t, f.4000 quad. The Motel Chrislyne (tel. 26-1290) is a 10-min. walk farther inland: f.2410 s, f.2810 d, f.3630 t. The rooms at both hotels have private bath, fridge, and cooking facilities. Monthly rates are available. Not as appealing is the Hotel Bagatelle, above the pizzeria at Baie des Citrons right across from the beach: f.2000 s or d. The Hotel La Residence, also near Baie des Citrons, is f.2600 s, f.3000 d, f.3500 t with private bath—better value. Neither of these last 2 provides cooking facilities. In a pinch you could camp free in the park by the river at Dumbea, just N of Noumea; the Dumbea, Paita, and Tontouta buses all pass here. There is no obvious place to pitch a tent in Noumea itself.

youth hostel: The budget traveler's best headquarters is the Noumea Youth Hostel (*auberge de jeunesse*) on Colline de Semaphore (fantastic sunsets from here). There's a shortcut up to the hostel from behind St. Joseph's Cathedral—take the stairs up behind the Relais "Guillaume Douarre" next to the Virgin's Grotte. Not only

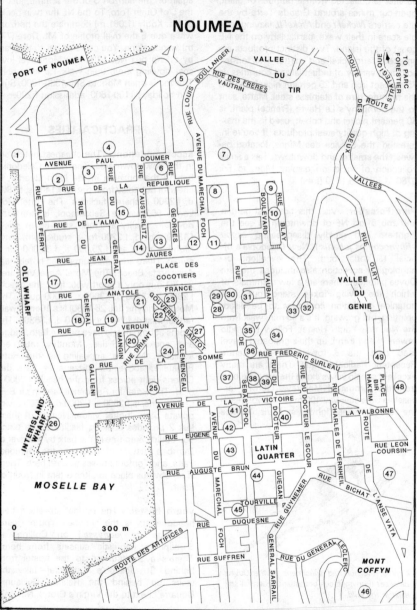

NOUMEA

PORT OF NOUMEA

VALLEE DU TIR

TO PARC FORESTIER

ROUTE STRATEGIQUE

ROUTE DES DEUX VALLEES

RUE LOUIS BOULANGER

RUE DES FRERES VAUTRIN

⑤

AVENUE DU MARECHAL FOCH

AVENUE PAUL DOUMER

②

③

④

⑥

⑦

RUE DE LA REPUBLIQUE

RUE DU

RUE D'AUSTERLITZ

RUE GEORGES

⑧

⑨

⑩

BOULEVARD

RUE BLAY

RUE JULES FERRY

RUE DE L'ALMA

⑮

⑬

⑫

⑪

⑭

JAURES

RUE DU GENERAL

RUE JEAN

PLACE DES COCOTIERS

RUE VAUBAN

VALLEE DU GENIE

RUE OLRY

OLD WHARF

RUE

⑰

ANATOLE

FRANCE

②①

GOUVERNEUR

㉓

㉒

㉙ ㉚

㉘

㉛

㉝ ㉜

⑯

⑲

⑱

GENERAL

RUE DE

VERDUN

RUE DRANT

②⓪

㉔

RUE DE LA

SUTOT

㉗

㉟

㉞

㊱ RUE FREDERIC SURLEAU

⑱

RUE MANGIN

CLEMENCEAU

SOMME

RUE DE

RUE DU

㊴ ㊵

RUE CHARLES DE VERNHEIL

PLACE BIR HAKEIM

㊽

㊾

RUE GALLIENI

㉕

AVENUE

DE

LA

SEBASTOPOL

㊲

㊳ ㊸

VICTOIRE

RUE DU DOCTEUR

㊵

LA VALBONNE

RUE LEON COURSIN

INTERISLAND WHARF

㉖

AVENUE DU MARECHAL

RUE EUGENE

㊸

LATIN QUARTER

RUE DOCTEUR LE SCOUR

㊼

DE L'ANSE VATA

MOSELLE BAY

RUE AUGUSTE BRUN

㊹

RUE GUEGAN

RUE GUYNEMER

RUE BICHAT

0   300 m

㊺

TOURVILLE

DUQUESNE

RUE FOCH

RUE SUFFREN

GENERAL SARRAIL

RUE DU GENERAL LECLERC

MONT COFFYN

㊻

ROUTE DES ARTIFICES

NOUMEA

1. Restaurant des Dockers
2. Amac Tours/S.C.E.A.
3. Bureau de Surveillance Sanitaire
4. General Hospital
5. Locamat
6. Service Topographique
7. Government House
8. Marine Corail
9. Territorial Assembly
10. Protestant Church
11. Australian Consulate
12. old town hall/Syndicat d'Initiative
13. Oceanie Dept. Store
14. Air Pacific/Air New Zealand
15. Ballande Dept. Store
16. City Hall
17. Budget Rent a Car
18. Compagnie Generale Maritime
19. Chamber of Commerce
20. Restaurant New Caledonie
21. Barrau Dept. Store
22. interurban bus station
23. market
24. Restaurant Orohena
25. city bus terminal
26. Solenav and Hanner agencies
27. Restaurant Hameau II
28. Center Voyages/American Express
29. tourist office
30. Le St. Hubert
31. La Perouse Restaurant
32. Cultural Center
33. youth hostel
34. St. Joseph's Cathedral
35. UTA French Airlines
36. Cafe de Paris
37. Bernheim Library
38. Hotel Mon Logis
39. Rex Theater
40. La Poule au Pot
41. police station
42. post office
43. New Caledonia Museum
44. Hotel Caledonia
45. Pressing Laundromat
46. Mont Coffyn viewpoint
47. Courthouse
48. Army Barracks
49. Chez Jeannette

does it provide inexpensive dormitory accommodations (f.600 for members, f.700 for nonmembers), but it's also a center for exchanging information with other travelers. Unlike hostels in many other countries, it's open all day and does allow alcohol. There's no age limit and you can stay as many nights as you like, but an up-to-date Y.H.A. card is required for the member's rate. You must do a housekeeping chore. One of the biggest advantages is the excellent cooking facilities which will save you money. The hostel will store excess luggage for you when you go to the outer islands, and will also exchange foreign banknotes without commission. It fills up fast when the cheap UTA flights from S.E. Asia arrive; you can crash in the ping pong room in a pinch. Warden Jacky Sorin runs a tight little ship—the best and only *real* youth hostel in the South Pacific.

food: Noumea is thick with restaurants serving dishes like *coq au vin* (chicken in wine sauce) and *champignons provencales* (mushrooms seasoned with garlic and parsley). The cuisine is *tres bon;* indeed, at the prices some places charge, it has to be! Many have a special set menu for a complete meal, varying anywhere from f.500 to f.1500 and up. For a filling, unpretentious French meal, try La Perouse's *plat du jour,* f.750 for 5 courses with wine. La Poule au Pot, 5 Rue du Docteur Guegan, is also very good for French cooking, especially at lunchtime, and the manager, Patrick Poulet, speaks good English. Recommended. Chez Nicolas, next to the Mon Logis Hotel, offers roast rabbit (f.750). For Chinese food it's Chez Jeannette on Place Bir Hakeim near the French army barracks. Main plates run under f.700. Port de France, in the Moana Center behind the post office, specializes in ice cream, and they offer 6 kinds of salads (f.180-480). Grilled dishes here run about f.550. **budget:** The cheapest places to eat are near the interurban bus station. The Restaurant Hameau II on Rue de Verdun serves filling meals at reasonable prices. Try the steak and *frites.* The Restaurant Orohena on Rue de la Somme posts their menu in the window. Also try the Restaurant New Caledonie, 8 Rue Col. Driant, which serves a good bowl of Chinese soup for f.300. For cafeteria-style service you can't go wrong at the Restaurant des Dockers, a few hundred m E of the Passenger Terminal near the wharf. Their hours (breakfast 0600-0730, lunch 1030-1300, dinner 1700-1900) are fairly standard—most establishments catering mostly to locals stop serving lunch at 1300 and dinner at 1900, so come early. The snack bar in Ballande Dept. Store on Rue de l'Alma offers milkshakes, sandwiches, and good coffee.

Anse Vata: As you'd expect, the places out at Anse Vata are high-priced, although the Santa Monica Restaurant (open 1100-1330/1900-2115, closed Sun.) offers excellent food at moderate prices. Their menu is posted outside. The San Remo, next to the Nouvata Hotel, has the best pizza in the Southern Hemisphere (f.600 and up). La Grande Muraille (Cantonese) beyond the swimming pool at Anse Vata is more expensive but good value. Try the Imperial Duck (f.680).

entertainment: The Rex Theater on Ave. de la Victoire is the best of the movie houses (showtimes are 1400 and 2000); however, all films are dubbed into French (no subtitles). For such a cosmopolitan city, the nightlife in Noumea is disappointing and the trends change fast—ask around for the current "in" club. Le St. Hubert on the Place des Cocotiers is the place for cold draft beer and local atmosphere. The Cafe de Paris is open 24 hours a day. Club Woody at the Mon Logis Hotel opens at 2100 daily (f.500 cover). There's a Tahitian show at the Santa Monica Cabaret at

Anse Vata (open 2200-0300); drinks are expensive but well worth it for the Polynesian atmosphere (no cover charge). Every couple of weeks there's Polynesian dancing at about 2000 at the Ile De France Hotel behind the South Pacific Commission; just enter the bar to enjoy it and the attempts of Japanese tourists to join in. Also on Anse Vata is the Casino Royale. Proper dress (black tie for gentlemen, evening gown for ladies) is mandatory to enter the gaming salon. You must show your passport at the door and persons under 21 are not admitted. Admission is charged. The casino is open daily except Sun. 2100-0200, slot machines operating 1400-0200. Not recommended.

cricket matches: Saturday afternoons from March to Nov. is the time for cricket—jolly good show! Both Melanesian men and women play on the gravelly surface just beyond the town center toward the nickel smelter and at Motor Pool near Anse Vata. Up to 3 people stand at each crease, brandishing bats high in the air, and it's anybody's guess who's supposed to do the hitting or running. There are no overs, and bowler and wicketkeeper swap roles as needs arise. Dress is informal, with fat old dames and spunky young wenches alike wearing Mother Hubbard dresses. Men wear jeans, football gear, and even Indonesian-style sarongs. The whole spectacle would horrify cricket purists, but it's great fun to watch—and you can get some good photos if you're brave enough to stand up close.

Melanesian women playing cricket

shopping: The public market (open daily 0500-1000) beside the interurban bus station is the place to buy fruit and vegetables. The adjacent fish market is almost as good as the aquarium. Noumea's best supermarket and department store, Prisunic Barrau (open Mon. to Fri. 0700-1800, Sat. 0700-1100/1400-1730, Sun. 0700-1100 for groceries only), is a block from the market; they have a good coffee bar. The other department store, Oceanie, has gone downhill and keeps limited opening hours. Rue de l'Alma, with its numerous flashy boutiques, is Noumea's most exclusive shopping street. There are several duty-free shops on Rue de l'Alma selling French luxury goods such as jewelry, perfume, cosmetics, lingerie, fashionable clothing, leather goods, bags, scarves, and shoes. Cameras and electrical goods are better purchased elsewhere. Several small shops on Rue Anatole France, just E of the Place des Cocotiers, specialize in locally-made handicrafts. One, in a basement below Le Coin du Cuir, sells authentic-looking Kanak war clubs made on the premises. Alisena, 48 Rue de Sebastopol, has Wallisian handicrafts. Among the best souvenirs are the stamps and first-day covers available at the Philatelic Bureau (Mon. to Fri. 0745-1115/1200-1430) in the main post office. They sell the stamps of all 3 French Pacific territories. Buy camping and snorkeling gear at R. Deschamps, 34 Rue de la Somme. You can also buy/sell used camping/hiking gear, etc., at the Coin des Affairs, 6 Rue F. Ecorchon, Orphelinat (bus No. 6). Rent a small 2-person tent from Locamat behind the Mobil station at the traffic circle on the N side of town: f.1200 for 2 days, f.400 each additional day (f.10,000 deposit). They also sell used tents.

services: When planning your day, remember that nearly everything closes for the 1100-1400 siesta—a 3-hour break! So get an early start. There are several banks along Ave. de la Victoire. You can change American Express travelers cheques without paying a commission at Center Voyages, 4th floor, 27 Ave. Foch (open Mon. to Fri. 0730-1100/1330-1730, Sat. 0800-1100). The post office's hours are Mon. to Fri. 0745-1115/1215-1530.

ceremonial jade mace, a symbol of chieftainship

They charge f.200 to forward mail, and overseas phone calls can be made from there as well. If you have a medical problem, ask the tourist office to recommend a private doctor; the General Hospital accepts only emergency cases. Get a cholera vaccination (f.200) from the Bureau de Surveillance Sanitaire (Mon. and Thurs. 1400-1645). The Australian Consulate General, 8th floor, Immeuble Foch, opposite the old Town Hall, issues tourist visas (open Mon. to Fri. 0800-1130/1330-1630). The attractive Municipal Pool just beyond Club Med at the far end of Anse Vata is open Mon. to Thurs. 0730-1230/1330-1700, Sat. 1300-1700, Sun. 1015-1600, admission f.120. Scuba diving is difficult to arrange individually in Noumea. Instead have a workout at Squash, opposite the marina on Baie de l'Orphelinat. Charges are f.450 pp a half hour, plus f.100 for a racket. There's a bar and restaurant on the premises. Pressing Laundromat on Rue Tourville charges f.650 to wash and dry up to 5 kilos. The Chamber of Commerce (B.P. 10, Noumea) can arrange French lessons for groups of 10 or more (f.3000 pp a week), but arrangements must be made at least a month in advance.

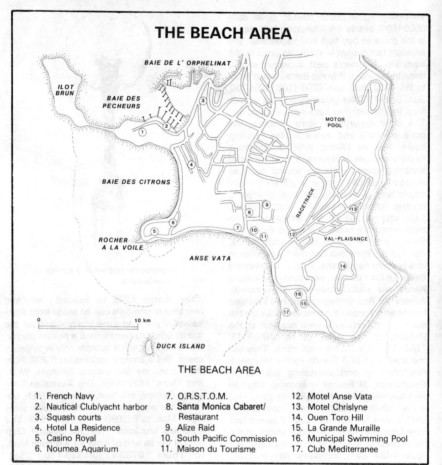

THE BEACH AREA

THE BEACH AREA

1. French Navy
2. Nautical Club/yacht harbor
3. Squash courts
4. Hotel La Residence
5. Casino Royal
6. Noumea Aquarium
7. O.R.S.T.O.M.
8. Santa Monica Cabaret/ Restaurant
9. Alize Raid
10. South Pacific Commission
11. Maison du Tourisme
12. Motel Anse Vata
13. Motel Chrislyne
14. Ouen Toro Hill
15. La Grande Muraille
16. Municipal Swimming Pool
17. Club Mediterranee

information: There are 2 separate tourist information offices in Noumea: the Territorial Tourist Office, 25 Ave. Mar. Foch, and the Syndicat d'Initiative in the old Town Hall. Both dispense free brochures and can answer questions. The privately operated Maison du Tourisme at Anse Vata provides travel agency-type help with tour arrangements. The Service de la Statistique, 2nd floor, Immeuble Gallieni, sells specialized publications. Up-to-date photocopied maps (f.500) of New Caledonia are available from the Service Topographique, Room 9, 4th floor, Centre Ad-

ministratif (open Mon. to Fri. 0730-1130). Most Noumea bookstores sell the excellent I.G.N. 1:500,000 "Carte Touristique" of New Caledonia. Pentecost, 34 Rue de l'Alma, sells colored I.G.N. topographical maps (f.870) of New Caledonia and Vanuatu. If this isn't enough, Nefo Diffusion, 26 Boulevard Vauban, sells the 9-volume *Encyclopedie de la Nouvelle-Caledonie* and Orstom's monumental and excellent (despite the lamentable English translations) *Atlas* (f.14,650). Study the *Atlas* for free at the Bernheim Library (Tues. to Fri. 1430-1830, Sat. 0900-1100/

1400-1730). They have a good reading room with a few English magazines. The Association pour la Sauvegarde de la Nature Neo-Caledonienne, 50 Rue Anatole France, organizes hikes every 2 months (f.200 for insurance) and visiting environmentalists are invited. Their office (open weekday afternoons) sells French books and Association T-shirts (f.1000).

TRANSPORT

by ship: See the agents at Ballande Agency, upstairs in the Dept. Store of Rue de l'Alma, for the date of the monthly Banks Line service to Port Vila. You must book directly with the captain. The same people represent the Compagnie Wallisienne de Navigation whose ship, the *Moana II*, makes the Noumea-Futuna-Wallis-Noumea trip monthly. Every second trip they call at Suva, Fiji. A bed in the dorm (sleeps 22) is f.13,645 to Futuna, f.14,610 to Wallis. Sofrana/Unilines has freighters to Port Vila and Fiji every couple of weeks; ask at the Sofrana office opposite St. Joseph's Cathedral when the next ship is due in, then go see the captain. For the Loyalty Is., take the *Cap des Pins* (agent: M. Hanner, S.A.) which leaves Mon. for Lifou, returning Tues., and leaves Wed. for Mare, returning Fri.; the fare is f.2400 OW on *tatami* mats, no meals. The *Boulari* (agent: Solenav) sails to Ouvea (f.2000 OW) and the other Loyalty Islands several times a week. The *Boulari* leaves for the Isle of Pines every 2 weeks, usually on a Thurs. (f.1500 OW). You must come back by plane. Check in person down at the wharf.

interurban buses: Most long-distance buses leave from the triangular bus station by the market to the side of the Place des Cocotiers. The schedules posted are not always complete, so you might have to communicate with the French-speaking female ticket sellers in the office. The bus to Tontouta Airport (f.320 weekdays, f.350 weekends) departs from the interurban bus station, hourly from 0530 to 1730 Mon. to Sat., every couple of hours from 0630 to 1700 Sun. and holidays. There is also a greatly overpriced S.C.E.A. airport bus

(f.2000), which will pick you up at your hotel. The bus to Yate (f.500) leaves at 0600 weekdays, 1200 weekends. Service to La Foa (f.550) and Bourail (f.700) is fairly frequent, and there are departures for Thio (f.600) and Canala from the interurban terminal. Koumac-bound buses (f.1200) depart Mon. to Thurs. at 1130, Fri. at 1200, Sat. and Sun. at 1030. There's a bus all the way to Poum (f.1300) at the NW end of Grande Terre on Tues. and Thurs. at 0800, Fri. at 1745. Weekdays at 1030 and weekends at 1130 you can get a bus to Poindimie (f.950). The Hienghene bus (f.1200) leaves at 0800 weekdays, at 1000 weekends. There's also a GEINC mail bus to Hienghene (f.760) Mon. to Sat. at 0500. To find out about the mail bus to Koumac (f.760) which leaves Noumea Mon. to Sat. at 0405, you must go to S.C.E.A., 3 Rue de la Republique (open weekdays 0900-1100).

city buses: Noumea's city bus system (*transport en commun*) is excellent; fares run f.65-95 depending on the distance traveled. There are 13 different routes serving such places as Anse Vata (Nos. 1, 3, 6), Baie des Citrons (No. 6), Magenta Airport (No. 7), and Nouville (No. 13). The buses run every 10-30 minutes from 0530-2030 daily. Catch them at the city bus terminal downtown.

rentals: Budget Rent-A-Car has vehicles at f.5000 daily with unlimited mileage (2-day minimum), full collision insurance f.500 extra daily. You could also choose to pay f.1900 a day plus f.21 per km. The Maison du Tourisme at Anse Vata rents bicycles (f.1400 daily) and mopeds (f.2900 daily, gas and insurance included). Any driver's license will do. **taxis:** The main Noumea taxi stand is in the Place des Cocotiers. **hitching:** Beside the Service des Mines just beyond the traffic circle on the N side of town is a good place to hitch. Otherwise take the Tontouta bus to the airport to get well out on the road to Bourail, or the Robinson, St. Louis, or Plum buses for the road to Yate; city bus No. 8 (PONT DES FRANCAIS) also goes out to the start of the road to Yate. Hitching up the SW coast is easy, but difficult elsewhere due to lack of traffic. Also, very few drivers speak English.

Tourist boats call daily at Noumea's Amedee Lighthouse.

tours and travel: Alize-Raid Excursions, 13 Rue Tabou, Anse Vata (tel. 26-26-41), offers outstanding one to 4-day camping trips by Land Rover to the very best of Grande Terre. The price is about US$50 pp a day but that includes everything (meals, transport, tent, snorkeling gear, and guide). This is organized adventure at its best. For details of horseback safaris across the mountains of Grande Terre, see the "Kone" section of this chapter. Several companies offer day-trips to Amedee Lighthouse for f.3650 pp including lunch — the cruise on the *Samara* is best. Two travel agencies book accommodations and flights to the Loyalty Is. and the Isle of Pines: Amac Tours,

3 Rue de la Republique, and the Maison du Tourisme (Agence Boyer) at Anse Vata. The Air Caledonie office at Magenta Airport also handles this. Don't buy a one-day package to Ouvea or the Isle of Pines. These are rushed, overpriced, and superficial, and will only appeal to those who like being herded by a Japanese-speaking guide. Hibiscus Tours, upstairs in the shopping arcade next to UTA, operates sightseeing tours to the countryside, and a 3-day yacht cruise (f.22,000 pp) to the islands S of Grande Terre. Ask Hibiscus about nudist camping at Club Naturiste on M'Ba I. near Noumea. Four-berth chalets are also available.

GRANDE TERRE

YATE AND THE SOUTH

Yate: Yate, 81 km E of Noumea, is a good place for a weekend out of the city. The bus goes as far as Touaourou Mission, and sometimes to Unia and Goro. The journey is through grandiose, empty country with good views. South is the Plain of Lakes with its amazing variety of plantlife. The road winds along the shore of Yate Lake (48 sq km) for quite a distance before descending to the NE coast. If you're a good hiker get off at the access road to the giant hydroelectric dam (*barrage*), just before the final pass. The dam, which produces about 270 million KWH a year (a quarter of the territorial requirements), is 2 km. A narrow old road continues past the dam, 7 km down to the powerhouse, passing a beautiful, high waterfall on the way. From Yate Generating Station, it's only 1.5 km E to the Unia ferry (*bac*), then another 2 km around to the bridge at the junction of the Noumea, Yate, and Goro roads. The coastal plain is narrow here and the alternate views of inlets, mountains, and sea are fine. Make a sidetrip to Goro at the S tip of Grande Terre, about 23 km from Yate bridge. Hitching there is easiest on the weekend and there are sporadic passenger trucks (f.200). Wadiana Falls is one km beyond Goro village. Climb to the top of the falls for a view across to the Isle of Pines and all the intermediate reefs, but beware of loose rocks. Two km beyond the falls are a pair of giant rusting cantilever loaders which once fed iron/chrome ore from conveyors directly into waiting ships. The scenery is superb. The bus back to Noumea leaves Yate around 1100 Mon. to Fri., Sun. at 1500. On your way back to Noumea stop off at La Conception Church (1874), just S of the highway a few km before you enter the city. Pierre Declercq, secretary-general of the *Union Caledonienne,* murdered on 19 Sept. 1981 by persons unknown, is buried in the graveyard beside the road leading to the church. His tombstone reads: *assassine dans le combat pour la liberation de peuple Kanak.*

accommodations: The most accessible is Chez Cornaille behind the Total service station at the river mouth, just a km beyond the Yate bridge; bare rooms (shared facilities) with beds and electric lighting at f.1000 s, f.2000 for up to 4 persons. Or camp on a grassy area among the pine trees for f.200. There's a general store and restaurant (breakfast f.200, meals f.800) on the premises. Best for budget travelers is San Gabriel Camping and Bungalows, 10 km S of Chez Cornaille or 4 km beyond Touaourou Mission. A basic room without linen or electricity is f.500 pp, but a nice little bungalow with linen (shared facilities) is only f.800 pp. Camping is f.200. Set in a coconut grove right on a lovely beach, the Melanesian staff is charming. Meals are available, or cook your own over an open fire (bring food). At low tide explore the pools and

Visitors to Yate are accommodated in these thatched cottages at San Gabriel Camping.

crevices in the raised reef just a km NW of San Gabriel along the beach. One deep pool full of eels appears to extend back into a submerged cave. Public Camping Chez Ambroise Atti, a km before San Gabriel, has no facilities other than running water, although the setting is nice. The Relais de Wadiana, beyond Goro 14 km S of San Gabriel, is overpriced at f.2000 s, f.2500 d (shared facilities). You may camp, however, for f.300 (small tent) or f.500 (large tent). There's a relaxing sitting room and a beach (murky water). Last but not least is Chez Hermann, an exclusive little resort 3 km N of the Unia ferry crossing. For f.1800 s, f.2000 d, plus f.130 tax, you get a room with private bath and shower (f.l500 for shared facilities). Tenters (f.450 pp) who agree to take either lunch or dinner in the dining room may camp free. The restaurant (breakfast f.250, lunch f.1350, dinner f.1200) overlooks the swimming pool, but note it may close on Tues. and Wednesday. Chez Hermann also features a reading room, sauna, solarium for nude sunbathing, and private topless beach. Hermann is a bit of an eccentric who makes no bones about his ultra-right, anti-independence views. Although popular with the Noumea bourgeoisie, Chez Hermann is still unknown to tourists—recommended.

THE CENTER

Thio: Thio, the most important mining center in New Caledonia, was the scene of a $3 million Kanak sabotage in Jan. 1985, to protest the murder of 2 of their leaders by French *gendarmes.* On arriving from Bouloupari, turn R to Thio Mission, Botamere Hill, and the beach. From the beach you can see the nickel workings on the plateau to the NW and the port to the southeast. The ore is brought down in buckets suspended from a moving cable, and loaded onto ships for Noumea and Japan. Thio village is 2.5 km NW of here at the foot of the plateau beside the Thio River. From Thio a scheduled one-way road, with a timetable (*horaire*) for traveling in each direction, leads 35 km NW to Canala.

Canala: The turnoff for Ciu Falls is 2.5 km SE of Canala, then it's another 4.5 km in to the

falls themselves. During the late 19th C., Canala was the hub of the NE coast. Canala Bay is the best hurricane refuge for shipping on the NE coast. At La Crouen, 14 km E of Canala, are thermal hotsprings where you can bathe. Farther E is the turnoff to Kouaoua to km NW of Canala. Although no road yet connects the two, you can walk from Kouaoua to Poro near Houailou via Koua Beach in 2 easy days. From here, the main highway cuts S across the mountains to La Foa, passing tons of cascading water from several fantastic waterfalls along the way.

La Foa: La Foa, 65 km NW of Tontouta Airport, is an alternative place to spend the night before catching a flight. Hotel Banu, opposite the post office in the center of town, charges f.1400 s, f.1600 d for a simple room with sink and shared bath. The hotel has a restaurant (expensive) and bar, but there are plenty of grocery stores in the vicinity. You may pitch your tent on the grass next to the Maison de la Culture (Centre Socio-culturel) nearby for a nominal amount. The Maison has a library, video room, ping pong, tennis, and snack bar. There are activities such as Tae Kwon Do, dance, weaving, etc. almost every evening, and campers are very welcome to attend. Just outside La Foa on the road to Bourail is the workshop of Remy Weiss, Sculpteur, who does woodcarving in the traditional Melanesian fashion. Horseraces take place at the track in La Foa the first or second weekends in September.

Bourail: Although this town, 167 km NW of Noumea, is the second largest in the territory, it's a disappointing little place after Noumea. There's nothing much to do in Bourail itself, although you could hike up to the cross on the hillside just E of town for the view. Use it as a stopover on a trip around the island or as a base for visiting the surrounding area. Bourail has an off-again, on-again youth hostel (cooking facilities) in a pleasant wooden building in Bellevue suburb, an easy 2-km walk from town. Ask at the Noumea Y.H. if it's on or off. Hotel Le Niaouli opposite the market and bus stop is f.1900 s or d for a room with shared bath, f.2200 s or d for private bath. There's a market in Bourail on Tues. and Sat. mornings

GRANDE TERRE

barrier reefs of the world: Dr. John W. Wells, Cornell University, and Dr. Armand Kuris, University of California, Santa Barbara, recently concurred in naming the world's longest barrier reefs: the Great Barrier Reef, Australia (1,600 km); New Caledonia's barrier reef (550 km), and the Great Sea Reef, Vanua Levu, Fiji (260 km). Since there's a barrier reef along both sides of Grande Terre, New Caledonia holds both second and third place. The fifth longest barrier reef in the world may be the S. Louisiade Archipelago Reef, P.N.G. (over 200 km), or the reef off Belize, Central America (250 km), depending on definition.

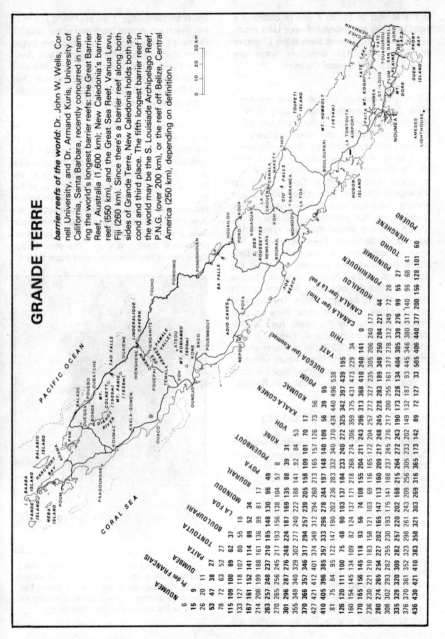

PACIFIC OCEAN

CORAL SEA

0   10   20   30 km

Distance chart cities (diagonal labels): NOUMEA, Pt. des FRANCAIS, DUMBEA, PAITA, TONTOUTA, BOULOUPARI, LA FOA, MOINDOU, BOURAIL, POYA, POUEMBOUT, KONE, VOH, KAALA-GOMEN, KOUMAC, POUM, OUEGOA (par Koumac), YATE, THIO, CANALA (par Thio), CANALA (par La Foa), HOUAILOU, PONERIHOUEN, POINDIMIE, TOUHO, HIENGHENE, POUEBO

at the N end of town. If you're catching a flight out you can reconfirm your UTA reservations with Mr. Felicien Barri at the Chambre du Commerce. Bus departure times are posted outside the Hotel Douyere.

vicinity of Bourail: Bourail was an important New Zealand training base during WW II; there's a N.Z. military cemetery 8 km SE of town right beside the main highway. A Moslem cemetery is nearby. One recommended sidetrip from Bourail takes in Pierced Rock (Roche Percee), 8 km west. This is a cliff with a tunnel right through it. Don't try to get through to the other side at high tide though; there's rough sea here. Nearby there's a very good beach for swimming and snorkeling. One km farther along the main road is the track up to Belvedere Viewpoint, with a fine view of Nera River, the coast, and Turtle Bay. Turtle Bay (Baie des Tortues) is just up the coast from Pierced Rock, accessible down a footpath from the viewpoint. Be there early in the morning to see any turtles. There's good camping here, but bring water. Nine km past Pierced Rock along the same road is Poe Beach, 17 km from Bourail. There's a well-managed campsite (f.200 per tent) with plenty of sand, banyan trees, fresh water, showers, toilets, and excellent surfing. There's a store at Poe, but the selection is better in Bourail.

THE NORTHEAST COAST

vicinity of Houailou: The winding road from Bourail follows sparkling rivers and crosses the Col de Roussettes (381 m), a pass named for the big red fruit bats of the region, with good views, especially of the abandoned Kanak taro terraces. A km off the main highway, 4 hours from Noumea by bus is the riverine town of Houailou. Norfolk pines are common here. If it's late in the day, there are several possibilities for campers. Mr. Mazurier, who lives 12 km before Houailou on the road from Bourail, graciously allows travelers to camp free on his land by the Houailou River. More adventuresome would be to camp on the wild, deserted beach adjacent to Houailou airstrip. The access road is 3

km N of the bridge, then another 2 km in to the beach (go around the S end of the airstrip). Plenty of driftwood for campfires here. Get water from a tap at the airstrip. If you don't have a tent or it's raining, you can rent a simple room with a sink (shared facilities) at Chez Paul Druminy (f.1000 s, f.1200 d) in Houailou itself, close to the town hall (*mairee*).

up the coast: As you continue up the coast your first stop will be spectacular Ba Falls, 15 km NW of Houailou bridge and only 1.5 km upstream from the highway on the mountain side. There's a large swimming area at the base of the falls. After a swim, climb to the top for the view. Ponerihouen, 44 km NW of Houailou, is a picturesque little town by the river of the same name. Coffee is the main cash crop in this area and there is an experimental station in town. The steel bridge just beyond Ponerihouen dates from WW II.

Masks such as these represented water spirits and were produced only in the N part of Grande Terre. With headdress and beard of human hair, the lower portion of the costume shrouded the body of the dancer in a net of feathers.

the Brooding Hen, Hienghene

Poindimie: This inviting little town, 308 km from Noumea, was founded during WW II, as the many Quonset huts attest, and today is the administrative center of the NE coast. Koyaboa Hill offers a fine overlook from its 390-m summit. There's a jeep track from beyond Hotel Le Tapoundari to the radio towers on top. The public swimming pool (hours variable) near the hotel features a 1961 Vasarely mosaic. **accommodations:** Hotel Le Tapoundari opposite the Poindimie River Bridge has triple rooms with cooking facilities and private bath for f.2700. The friendly manager, Gaudibert Herve, offers dormitory accommodations to Y.H.A. members at the usual hostel rates. Present your card on arrival. There's a free municipal camping area at Tieti Beach on the N edge of Poindimie. It's a nice spot and with running water, but don't go off and leave your things unattended as there have been rip-offs here.

Touho: This small settlement 27 km NW of Poindimie has a mission church (1889) typical of many on the island, plus mandarin orchards and coffee plantations. **accommodations:** There are 2 campgrounds. Camping Amenage Leveque, on the beach right in town, has small, clean bungalows with a table but no beds at f.500 a night for as many as can be crammed inside. Campers are charged f.150 per tent per day. Camping Gastaldi, 3 km from town, charges f.300 per tent, and there's a

beach and store. Take the Hienghene road over the hill, then turn R toward the Coco Beach Resort 1.5 km farther in.

HIENGHENE

Pronounced "yang-GAIN," the scenery around this small town 376 km from Noumea is unquestionably the finest in New Caledonia. Several km before Hienghene on the road from Touho you see high limestone cliffs on the R with a salt lake at their base. A road leading to huge Linderalique Cavern (*grotte*) on the far side of these cliffs is 3 km before Hienghene (donation). There's a free campsite with running water on the beach a little before the *grotte*. A little closer to Hienghene at the top of the pass is a turnoff to the viewpoint (*point de vue*) — one of the most beautiful spots on the island. From here, you'll see huge isolated rocks named Sphynx (150 m high) and Brooding Hen (60 m high) guarding the mouth of Hienghene Bay. Shades of the *Odyssey!* Such is the majestic beauty of the place that one can well imagine those ancient wanderers sailing in here on their way to some strange adventure. The town itself is on a rocky spur at the mouth of the river. Across the bay are nestled the tiny white buildings of Ouare Mission with the high coastal mountains behind. Several fine coral islets are seen offshore. From town the Brooding Hen looks more like the Towers of Notre Dame, its other name. As you come into Hienghene, between the viewpoint and the bridge is the Cultural Center, which should be visited for its mixture of modern and traditional architecture. A hundred years ago Kanaks under Bouarate struggled against French colonialists here; in Dec., 1984, 10 Kanaks were murdered just up the river by French terrorists because they supported independence.

amenities: You can camp free right in town on the beach below the football field. A better choice is the Hotellerie Maitre Pierre, up by the river 2 km from the bridge. Camping here is f.300 pp, facilities included (hot showers, TV room, and a lounge where they play Emmylou Harris records). If you don't have a tent, rooms at the hotel start at f.2600. Dinner in the restaurant is very good and very expensive. Breakfast is only f.350. This hotel has unique atmosphere and character—there's nothing else like it in the South Pacific. Borrow the hotel rowboat or canoe (free) and paddle yourself up the beautiful Hienghene River. You could easily spend an entire day this way—the vegetation and views are great. A good hike from Maitre Pierre is up to the TV relay station for a panoramic view. The only other hotel in Hienghene is the Relais de Koulnoue, a millionaires' resort in a spellbinding location on the beach beside Hienghene airstrip (charters only). The locals at Hienghene gather outside the Ballande store, popping bottles of cheap Number One beer on an opener attached to the wall by the door. Later they sleep it off in the cruiseship passenger pavilion across the street.

from Hienghene: Hike across the mountains from Hienghene to Voh along the "Chemin des Arabes" in a couple of days. The trail begins at Tiendanite, up the valley, and continues to Pouepai where there's a rough road to Voh. A mail bus leaves Hienghene for Pouebo on Mon., Tues., Thurs., and Fri. at 1400 (f.130), sometimes connecting in Pouebo with a bus to Koumac. The coastline NW from Hienghene features towering mountains with slopes falling right to the sea, empty beaches with fine coral just offshore, numerous high

waterfalls clearly visible from the road, and rivers full of small fish such as you've never seen before. This is also the most traditional area on Grande Terre, with the greatest number of *cases*. There's a free ferry at Ouaieme. It's possible to climb to the top of Mt. Panie (1639 m), New Caledonia's highest peak, from near Tao waterfall; there are several shelters on the mountain for hikers. At Pouebo, camp on St. Mathieu Beach. At Balade there's a monument (1913) commemorating the French annexation of New Caledonia in 1853. Captain Cook landed near this same spot in 1774. Just before the monument is the short access road to Mahamate Beach, where you may camp. Le Caillou Hotel near the Diahot River Bridge at Ouegoa is f.1200 s, f.1500 d.

THE SOUTHWEST COAST

Koumac: This town, 370 km NW of Noumea, has little to offer the traveler other than a place to spend the night. Have a look at the woodcarvings in the Catholic church. The road inland beside the church leads 7 km to some rather exciting limestone caves. The longest stretches 3 km underground, but there's no water in the vicinity. A campsite called Camping de Pandop (f.500 per tent) is windy, but beautifully situated by the sea only one km from Koumac (take the road opposite the church at the traffic circle and keep L). For a roof over your head try Hotel Le Grand Cerf on the traffic circle; bungalows with private facilities are f.1500 s, f.2000 d. Marginally cheaper but nowhere as good is Hotel Passiflore, 500 m up the road to the caves. Hotel Coppelia, just a short distance down the road to Noumea, is more expensive than either.

from Koumac: The coastal highway runs 56 km NW of Koumac to the town of Poum, with good views along the way. Tanle Bay, SE of Poum, is a recognized hurricane shelter for shipping. Twice a week there's a flight from Koumac to the Belep Is. (f.3100 OW), perfect if you want to get off the beaten track, but book ahead in Noumea. The road SE from

Your trusty steed dines on Hienghene's rich grasses.

Koumac to Poya offers only occasional gum trees to break the monotony—cattle country. The Adio Caves at Poya are 18 km off the main highway; there's little traffic so forget it unless you have your own transportation.

Kone: Kone is the administrative center of the NW coast, and though the town has some slight appeal, the only real reason for stopping are the horseback expeditions organized by 2 local companies. Both offer week-long excursions across the mountains from Kone to Hienghene and back, or shorter 3-day rides into the Pamale Valley. Kone Rodeo (contact Patrick Ardimanni, tel. 35-51-51, Kone) charges f.30,000 for a 7-day Hienghene ride, f.15,000 for a 3-day mountain ride. The price is all-inclusive (typical French Caledonian food, lodging, evening campfires, horses, etc.). A minimum of 6 persons is required to do a trip, but they do as many as 30 a year, and individuals can join one of them. Riders spend the night at a riverside dormitory lodge in the mountains, and in a dormitory at the Relais de Koulnoue in Hienghene. Patrick has 40 horses and speaks good English. The other horse-back company is Randonnee Equestre (contact Eric Tikarso, tel. 35-52-55, Kone) based in the Kanak village of Ateou. Eric lives beside the cemetery in Kone, but you'll need to know a little French. Randonnee charges f.3500 pp per day, 5 participants required. These rides must be arranged in advance either by phoning or through Center Voyages/American Express in Noumea. If you're looking to join a group, weekends are best. This is a great opportunity if you can spare the cash. There are several buses a day from Noumea to Kone (f.900). **accommodations:** Try the Escale de Kone (Madame Yoshida) right at the bus stop (rooms f.1800 with private bath), or the Hotel Madiana nearby (f.1500 s, f.2300 d with private bath). The restaurant at the Escale de Kone is good, as is the snack bar in the same building. Meet the locals at Bar Le Tabou down the road. The ultra-energetic can hike to Foue Beach (8 km OW) or climb Kone Peak (236 m) via Baco village (4 km OW), while awaiting their ride to begin. Note that the Koniambo Hotel/Motel is isolated at the airstrip and expensive.

THE ISLE OF PINES

Across a strait of shoals and coral banks 70 km SE of Grande Terre is the stunningly beautiful Isle of Pines. Famous for the former French penal colony here, in 1774 Capt. Cook named the 17-by-14-km island for its extraordinary *columnaris,* but the native name is Kunie. Protestant missionaries arrived in 1841, but were killed a year later when they became involved in a dispute between sandalwood traders and the Kunie natives. More recently missionaries of a different kind wanted to build a 600-bed Club Med on the island, but the locals torpedoed the project when they learned that it would have meant converting the entire Kanumera/Kuto area into an out-of-bounds pleasure resort for affluent outsiders. Their foresight means these fantastic cocaine-white beaches are still largely untouched—a tropical paradise of the first degree. Come during the Festival of the Yams in March or April.

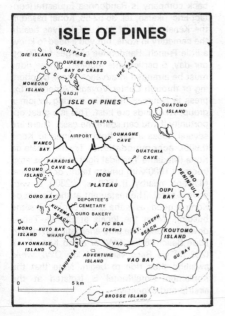

ISLE OF PINES

SIGHTS

Kanumera/Kuto: Kanumera/Kuto is one of the gems of the Pacific: Kuto with its long rolling surf, Kanumera with its gentle turquoise waters. The talcum-soft beaches curve around a narrow neck of sand which joins the Kuto Peninsula to the rest of the island. The shabby ruins of the bankrupt Relais de Kanumera is the only blot on this otherwise idyllic scene. Towering Norfolk pines contrast with curving palms, casuarinas, gum trees, ferns, wild orchids and other flowers to create an environment of exotic richness, separated from the sea by a wide strip of snowy white sand. Kanumera is a photographer's dream, although the snorkeling is second-rate. Follow the footpath from the main wharf right around the Kuto Peninsula for a series of scenic views. Another good walk is to the NW around Kuto Bay, then across the rocky headland on the trail to wild Kutema Bay. For a sweeping panorama of the entire island and a profile of Grande Terre on the horizon, climb to the cross atop Pic Nga (266 m) in an hour (easy). The trailhead is midway on the Kanumera/Kuto cutoff but it's poorly marked; look carefully to the E of the house with 2 pine trees in the front yard. You'll know you're going right when you start seeing red paint splashed on the trees.

farther afield: From 1871-1879 political prisoners from the Paris Commune were held on the Isle of Pines. Pigs now forage in the old prison yard and the narrow cheerless brick cells—snuffling scavengers in the gloomy and forbidding atmosphere. Some of the ruins are visible behind the bakery at Ouro, but the baker's vicious dogs deter visitors. One building can be reached via the track inland on the other side of the highway. To get to the Deportees' Cemetery continue one km N on the airport road and take the first turn on the right. The cemetery is to the L about 500 m inland; to the R is a track right across the island. The administrative center and largest village on the island is Vao, 7 km E of Kanumera. Catholic missionaries arrived here in 1848 and the present church dates from 1860. Unfortunately, its interior has been ruined by a heavy-handed restoration. Climb up to the chapel above the church for the view. The chief's house (*chefferie*) at Vao is surrounded by a driftwood palisade. Two km due E of the church is St. Joseph Beach, with as fine a collection of large dugout sailing canoes (*pirogues*) as you'll find anywhere in the Pacific. Oupi Bay is dotted with their sails. Gite Manamaky is on this beach too, but you're better off staying at Kunamera/Kuto. A 40-km road makes a loop all the way around the island.

speleology: The Isle of Pines boasts 3 important caves, each one different from the others. Using the map, Paradise Cave is very easy to find: take the obvious path to the R at the end of the access road. Much of the cave is flooded and there are refreshing pools where you can take a dip, but only experienced scuba divers with lamps and a guide should enter the dark areas. The Oumagne Caves (f.100 honesty box) are a 30-min. walk from the airport and these can also be done on your own—this is a cave for everyone. The cave floor is relatively level and a large opening at the far end provides lighting. A fast-flowing stream disappears into the cave as swarms of swallows circle overhead. The unmarked trail to Ouatchia Cave begins about a 40-min. walk SE of the Oumagne Caves. Watch for a cross on a hilltop to the R (the second cross you'll see) and a low ridge off to the left. The trail begins behind some houses a few hundred m N, where there are pine trees on both sides of the road. You'll probably have to find someone to ask, and a guide to lead you through the cave would be a very good idea. Give him a pack of cigarettes for his trouble. With a good flashlight you can go along through the narrow passage quite a distance underground past some sparkling white formations. Ouatchia Cave is by far the most difficult of these 3 caves, but it's also the best.

PRACTICALITIES

accommodations: The best places to stay are adjacent to one another on beautiful Kanumera Bay. Gite Oure (Chez Christine) at the E end of the beach is the perfect place to camp (f.300 per tent) or, for those without a tent, there are small bungalows in a garden-like setting. The charge is f.1200 with shared facilities, f.1800 with private facilities for native huts capable of accommodating up to 3 or four. Meals are f.900 each, but the service is pitiful (continental breakfast f.300). Gite Wilfrid nearby has fairly decent rooms with shared facilities, and 3 beds at f.1000 for the room, campers f.300 per tent. Gite Nataiwatch (Chez Guillaume) is in the same area but farther inland away from the beach. The accommodations are good, each with private bath and cooking facilities, and the prices are also higher: f.2000 s, f.2500 d, f.400 to camp. The restaurant at the Nataiwatch is pleasant; nonguests are welcome to wander in and order a meal or a drink, one of the few places on the island where you can do this. There are 2

Thick stalactites hang in the Oumagne Caves, a few km from the Isle of Pines' airport.

more places to stay near the far end of Kuto Bay—Gite Kunie Kaa (Chez Augustine) and Gite La Reine Hortense (Chez Eugene)—but these tend to get a lot of wind off the open sea. Prices at La Reine Hortense are similar to those at Nataiwatch. You may also camp free in the open, unfenced areas of both beaches, but you'll have to scrounge for water and your security will be less than if you were camping at a *gite*. Gite Kodjeue on Wameo Bay is isolated and expensive. **food:** There are well-stocked grocery stores at Ouro and Vao; the one at Ouro bakes bread, but both close on Sunday. Mr. Peterson operates a pavilion on Kuto Beach where Japanese daytrippers have lunch. Nearby is a French military vacation camp with a well-stocked bar, but you're not welcome. If you're a drinker bring your own supply from Noumea.

scuba diving: Nauticlub (B.P. 18, Vao, Isle of Pines), beside the Gendarmerie on the Kuto Peninsula, offers scuba diving at f.6500 pp (2 tanks), but there's a 4-person minimum so write ahead if you're serious. The best reef

diving is at Gadji Pass, off the N end of the island, especially the Gie Island Drop-off and fantastic Oupere Grotto. The strong tidal flow means abundant marinelife and spectacular coral and sponge coloration, which can be appreciated through rents in the reef. Nauticlub also offers freshwater diving into Paradise Cave with its huge stalactites and stalagmites—truly a unique experience.

transport: Air Caledonie flies to the Isle of Pines twice a day (US$23 OW), but Japanese daytrippers often pack the planes, so book well ahead. The airport sits on an 81-m-high plateau at the center of the island, 9 km from Kanumera. There's a bus (f.375) from the airport to the *gites,* or you can hitch. Air Caledonie has an office at Kuto open weekdays 1000-1100/1400-1600. At other times use the blackboard outside. The boat from Noumea (US$11 OW) ties up to the wharf on Kuto Bay, but it's not worth saving US$12 to wait for the infrequent ships. Try coming down from Noumea by ship, however.

Big dugout sailing canoes line St. Joseph's Beach on the Isle of Pines.

THE LOYALTY ISLANDS

This coralline group, 100 km E of Grande Terre, consists of the low-lying islands of Ouvea, Lifou, and Mare, plus several islets. Even though Capt. Cook never saw them, the Loyalties are visible from the tops of New Caledonia's mountains. The people are mostly Kanak, although Ouvea was colonized by Polynesians from Wallis I. hundreds of years ago. The lifestyle is still unhurried and many people grow their own yams, taro, and sweet potatoes in bush gardens. If you're here for the sand and sun, the Loyalties have some of the finest beaches in the world. The locals are friendly, camping is fine, and tourism is undeveloped. Be aware, however, that almost nobody speaks English.

OUVEA

Ouvea is everything you'd expect in a South Pacific island. Twenty km of unbroken white sands border the lagoon on the W side of the island and extend far out from shore to give the water a turquoise hue. The wide western lagoon, protected by a string of coral islands and a barrier reef, is the only one of its kind in the Loyalties. On the ocean side are rocky cliffs, pounded by surf, but fine beaches may be found even here. At one point on this narrow atoll only 450 m separates the 2 coasts. Traditional circular houses with pointed thatched roofs are still common in the villages. The compound of each village chief on Ouvea is surrounded by a high palisade of driftwood logs. Two of the best of these are at St. Joseph. The inhabitants of the far ends of the island (St. Joseph, Lekine, Mouli) speak the Wallisian language (Ua), while those in the center speak Iaai, the original Kanak tongue. Everyone speaks French as well. Ouvea produces 80 percent of the territory's copra.

northern Ouvea: A paved highway extends S from St. Joseph to Fayaoue (23 km), the administrative center, then on to Mouli (another

19 km). St. Joseph is a friendly village strung along the lagoon, with several general stores and a large Catholic mission. The Gite Loka is near the mission, just opposite the low stockade of the local chief's *case*. This chief also runs the adjoining store. Ask his permission to camp on the beach. The beach curves NW away from St. Joseph. Also, there are several fine protected beaches at Ognat, 8 km E of St. Joseph on the ocean side. To reach the large natural sinkhole (*trou d'eau*) near the coast several km SE of St. Joseph, take the Ognat road E and turn R at Weneki just after a curve. Keep straight ahead past an abandoned quarry. At the fork a km beyond this, go left. The sinkhole is near some coconut trees and a large garden at the end of the road. The Grand Chief of Weneki keeps turtles in the brackish water of the hole until they are required for his table but never mind, you can swim. No one has ever found the bottom of this deep dark hole. There is another sinkhole, the Trou d'Anawa, at Casse-Cou between St. Joseph and Wadrilla.

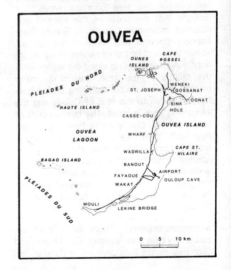

The undercut coral cliffs of Lekine, Ouvea, are an impressive sight.

southern Ouvea: Beyond the E end of the airstrip, near the center of the island, is a road leading straight to a high limestone cliff thick with stalactites and stalagmites. The entrance to Ouloup Cave is just opposite, a small opening at the back of the pit. Bones from old burials may be seen. The guide to the caves lives in the house at the end of the airstrip and, if he's around, ask his permission before proceeding. Midway between the house and the cliff is a banyan tree to the right. A deep hole under the tree contains water. It's thought that the roots of this banyan and those of another at Canala on Grande Terre connect through this "way of the spirits." Notice a water-filled cave farther along on the right. Fayaoue is strung along the lagoon near the middle of the atoll. Farther S, many tropical fish are visible from the bridge connecting Mouli to the rest of Ouvea and the swimming here is good. The famous cliffs of Lekine are also clearly visible from this bridge. Approach them by following the beach around. Long ago, before the island was uplifted, wave action undercut these towering walls of limestone. Massive stalactites tell of the great caverns for which this area is noted. On this island of superb beaches, the best is at Mouli.

accommodations: There are 6 *gites* opposite the beach at Fayaoue. Gite Lorano and Gite Beautemps-Beaupres are at Banout, just N of the junction of the airport and lagoonside roads. Gites Kauma (Banout), Whatau-Hapopa (Chez Suzanne), and Fleury are to the L of the junction near the site of the Ouvea Village Hotel. Gite N'Gei is S of the post office. At f.2000 s, f.2500 d, f.3000 t with private bath but no cooking facilities, they're a little overpriced. All will let you camp on their beach and use their water for f.300-500 per tent. Ask for Ebeneser at Gite Lorano. The *gite* at Mouli is isolated from everything but the beach. Ouvea has a water problem so use it sparingly. The plush Ouvea Village Hotel at Fayaoue has been burned 3 times due to a lack of understanding between the off-island owners, tourists, and local residents. The spark that ignited the latest conflagration was a female hotel guest who chose to sun herself in the buff in front of local schoolchildren, and a hotel management which neglected to make customary amends (*Coutume*). In 1984 the charred remnants of the hotel lay silent behind the palm-shaded beach.

transport: Air Caledonie lands at the airstrip 6 km from Fayaoue several times a day. A bus meets most of the flights from Noumea (except on Sun.) and charges f.50 for the ride to Fayaoue post office, or f.200 all the way to St. Joseph, where the driver lives. The interisland boat ties up to a wharf on the lagoon side between Fayaoue and St. Joseph.

LIFOU

Lifou, the largest of the Loyalties, is less visited than Ouvea, and *the* place for the adventurer to get very lost for a while. Like Mare, Lifou is a raised atoll. The cliffs and terraces of the various periods of geologic emergence are clearly visible from the air. Lifou was conquered by a French military expedition in 1864. We, the main town, is the administrative center of the Loyalty Is., but the 3 grand chiefs of Lifou reside at Nathalo, Doueoulou, and Mou. The local language is Dehu, the Kanak name for Lifou. Traditional round houses resembling beehives with conical roofs are still common on Lifou. During the cool season the locals light a fire in their *case* and sleep there. The rest of the year they're vacant, and you may be invited to occupy one.

sights: The *case* of the grand chief of Nathalo is the largest of its kind in New Caledonia. A low palisade surrounds this imposing structure, held aloft by great tree

an abandoned colonial church at We, Lifou

trunks set in a circle. Ask permission to go inside. Even more massive is Nathalo Church (1883), a monument to the zeal of early French Catholicism. The interior retains the original decoration. We is situated at the S end of a truly magificent white beach. Just a 5-min. walk from Gite Luecilla near We is a cave with a clear freshwater pool where you can swim. To get there, take the Nathalo road and look for a path near some wrecked cars on the left. A good modern highway follows the coast beside a cliff thick with stalagmites from We to Mou and Kode. There's a superb protected beach with talcum sand at Luengoni. A large cave with an underground pool is found between Mou and Kode, along with a fine beach on the coast here. There's another cave and underground pool near the highway on the E side of Chepenehe—in fact you'll find these everywhere on Lifou if you ask. One of the most picturesque spots on the island is the Chapel of Our Lady of Lourdes, perched atop a peninsula above Sandalwood Bay, 5 km E of Chepenehe. Take a bus or hitch to Eacho, then follow a poorly marked track on the R after the last house. The view from the chapel is breathtaking and there's a fair beach nearby (on any other island it would be considered excellent). Between the chapel and Chepenehe is a new wharf where your ship might decide to drop you.

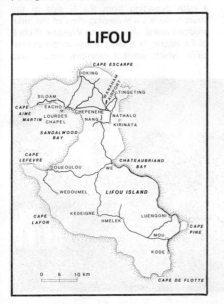

LIFOU

LIFOU ISLAND

CAPE ESCARPE
DOKING
SILOAM
CAPE AIME MARTIN
EACHO
LOURDES CHAPEL
CHEPENEHE
NANG
ANANAM AIRPORT
TINGETING
NATHALO
KIRINATA
SANDALWOOD BAY
CAPE LEFEVRE
DOUEOULOU
CHATEAUBRIAND BAY
WE
WEDOUMEL
CAPE LAFON
KEDEIGNE
HMELEK
LUENGONI
MOU
CAPE PINE
KODE
CAPE DE FLOTTE

0   5   10 km

accommodations: All organized places to stay are at We. The Relais des Cocotiers (tel. 45-11-36) is near the stadium, about one km from the wharf but far from the beach. Bungalows with private bath are f.1700 s, f.2500 d, f.3100 t, and there's a restaurant/bar. Airport transfers are f.400 pp, but you must phone ahead. The village you see across Chateaubriand Bay from the wharf at We is Luecilla. The Gite de Luecilla (tel. 45-12-43) is on the fine white beach near the village. A bungalow with cooking facilities and private bath is f.2500 s, f.3000 d, f.3500 t, or rent a Melanesian *case* with communal facilities for a flat rate of f.2000 (up to 6 persons). Camping is f.500 per tent. Recommended. Also try the Gite de Beau Rivage nearby. At the S end of the beach at We are the charred remains of another misplaced tourist hotel.

practicalities: Saturday mornings there's a market in the hall in front of Wanaham Airport, 2 km from Nathalo village. Near the airport terminal is a small store where you can get hot tea and coffee for f.60. The Banque Indosuez at We is the only bank in the Loyalties. Buses from We (f.150), Eacho (f.150), and other parts of the island connect with the afternoon flight to and from Noumea, which makes this the best time to arrive. The interisland ship arrives at the wharf behind the Ballande store at We.

Tiga: The Air Caledonie flight between Lifou and Mare stops on this tiny 2-by-6-km island twice a week. The one village is near the airstrip in the NE corner. The village (pop. 150) has a small store and a good beach. A N-S track approaches the cliffs at the S end of Tiga. You'll have to camp or sleep in the airport if you stop over.

MARE

Mare is the least-visited of the 3 main Loyalty Islands. Nengone is the local language. During the 19th C. Mare suffered a period of religious strife between Protestants (arrived 1841) and Catholics (arrived 1866). Oranges were once common on Mare (harvested in May and June), but the orchards have not been replanted. Mare Airport is only 2 km from a large Catholic mission at La Roche. Massive stone walls enclose the mission compounds and a tall white Gothic church towers above the settlement, itself dominated by a high limestone cliff topped by a cross. La Roche (the rock) got its name from this hill. You'll need sturdy shoes to climb up to the cross on a path departing from the N side of the church; there's a sweeping view of the pine-studded island. Just beyond Wakone, 7 km E of La Roche, is a deep abyss in the coastal cliffs which ancient warriors would leap

The case of the Grand Chief at Nathalo is the largest of its kind in New Caledonia.

*All Mare opens up from the clifftop cross overlooking
La Roche's airstrip and Catholic church.*

across to prove their bravery, giving the place its name, Saut du Guerrier (Warrior's Leap). A monument at the wharf at Tadine recalls the 126 persons who perished in the disappearance of the interisland trader *Monique* in 1953. No trace of the ship was ever found. At Netche, 8 km N of Tadine, is the residence of Nidoish Naisseline, grand chief of Mare and a leader of *Liberation Kanak Socialiste* (LKS). Several monuments near Nidoish's house, across from the adjacent church, commemorate early Protestant missionaries.

practicalities: A road leads from La Roche Mission 1.5 km to the picturesque cliffs on the coast (no beach). The house just before the final descent is Auberge "Chez Lucien," a rustic lodging with beds for f.750 plus another f.1800 for all meals. Clarify prices at the onset. The location is lovely and there's plenty of room to pitch a tent. Restaurant La Fourmi at Netche offers simple rooms with shared facilities at f.700, or the friendly proprietors will probably let you camp free on the grounds if you take a meal or 2 in their restaurant (no menu). Gite Wayemene is on

the beach at Wabao, 13 km S of Tadine. There's a market in the hall adjoining La Roche Airport on Wed. and Fri. mornings. The interisland ship arrives at the wharf at Tadine, the administrative center (no beach).

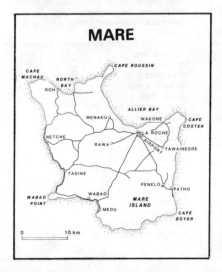

CAPSULE FRENCH VOCABULARY

bonjour — good day
bonsoir — good evening
salut — hello
Je vais a... — I am going to...
Ou allez-vous? — Where are you going?
Jusqu'ou allez-vous? — How far are you going?
traverser la chaine — to cross the mountains
Ou se trouve...? — Where is...?
C'est loin d'ici? — Is it far from here?
Je fais de l'autostop. — I am hitchhiking.
courrier — mail bus
A quelle heure? — At what time?
horaire — timetable
hier — yesterday
aujourd'hui — today
demain — tomorrow
Je desire, je voudrais... — I want...
J'aime... — I like...
Je ne comprends pas. — I don't understand.
relais, auberge — country-style hotel
gite — native-style accommodations
une chambre — a room
Vous etes tres gentil. — You are very kind.
Ou habitez vous? — Where do you live?
Il fait mauvais temps. — It's bad weather.
la Coutume — Kanak tradition
tribu — Melanesian village, tribe
niaouli — a Javanese immigrant
colon — settler
gendarmerie — police station
Quel travail faites-vous? — What work do you do?
la chomage, les chomeurs — unemployment, the unemployed
Je t'aime. — I love you.
une boutique, un magasin — a store
du pain — bread
du lait — milk
du vin — wine
bougna — native pudding
casse croute — sandwich
conserves — canned foods
fruits de mer — seafood
roussette — flying fox
cafe tres chaud — hot coffee
de l'eau — water
plat du jour — set meal
Combien ca fait? How much is it?
  Combien ca coute?
  Combien? Quel prix?
auberge de jeunesse — youth hostel

la clef — the key
la route, la piste — the road
la plage — the beach
la falaise — cliff
cascade — waterfall
grottes — caves
Est-ce que je peu camper ici? — May I camp here?
Je voudrais camper. — I wish to camp.
le terrain de camping — campsite
Devrais-je demander la permission? — Should I ask permission?
s'il vous plait — please
oui — yes
merci — thank you
cher — expensive
bon marche — cheap
merde — shit

un	1
deux	2
trois	3
quatre	4
cinq	5
six	6
sept	7
huit	8
neuf	9
dix	10
onze	11
douze	12
treize	13
quatorze	14
quinze	15
seize	16
dix-sept	17
dix-huit	18
dix-neuf	19
vingt	20
vingt et un	21
vingt-deux	22
vingt-trois	23
trente	30
quarante	40
cinquante	50
soixante	60
soixante-dix	70
quatre-vingts	80
quatre-vingt-dix	90
cent	100

VANUATU

INTRODUCTION

This string of lush, green islands, 2,250 km NE of Sydney, is the South Pacific's youngest country. Born out of the ponderous Anglo-French New Hebrides Condominium, the Ripablik Blong Vanuatu received worldwide attention in 1980 during its painful emergence into nationhood. Today, as the wounds are beginning to heal, travelers can avail themselves of an exciting new destination in Melanesia—a pastel land of many cultures and full of fascinating surprises. Vanuatu hasn't too many specific attractions in the way of museums or ruins, but rather a general beauty and relaxed way of life. Travelers here can make discoveries for themselves by asking any ni-Vanuatu (indigenous inhabitant) about the nearest cave, waterfall, swimming hole, hotspring, blowhole, cliff, or old burial place. Beginning with the capital at Port Vila, Vanuatu is a land of contrast and adventure.

the land: The 82 islands of Vanuatu stretch 1,300 km in a N/S line from the Torres Is. near Santa Cruz in the Solomons to miniscule Mat-thew and Hunter islands (also claimed by France) just E of New Caledonia. They are divided into 3 groups: the Torres and Banks islands in the N, the Y-shaped central group from Espiritu Santo and Maewo to Efate, and the Tafea islands (Tanna, Aniwa, Futuna, Er-romango, and Anatom) in the south. Together they total 12,189 sq km, of which the 12 largest islands account for 93 percent. Vanuatu is comprised of ash and coral: volcanic extrusion first built the islands, and limestone plateaus added to them through tectonic uplift. The islands form part of a chain of volcanic activity stretching from New Zealand up through Vanuatu and the Solomons to the islands off New Guinea. Besides Yasur Volcano on Tanna, there are active volcanoes on Lopevi, Ambrym, Aoba, and Santa Maria, plus a submarine volcano near Tongoa. Lopevi has a classic cone 1,413 m high with a 5-km base; when it last erupted in the early 1970s the population was permanently relocated to nearby Epi. Vanuatu sits on the W edge of the Pacific Plate next to

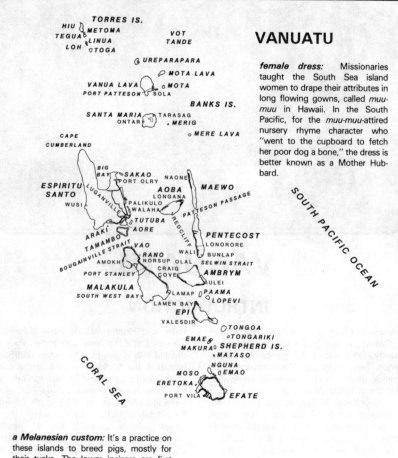

VANUATU

female dress: Missionaries taught the South Sea island women to drape their attributes in long flowing gowns, called *muu-muu* in Hawaii. In the South Pacific, for the *muu-muu*-attired nursery rhyme character who "went to the cupboard to fetch her poor dog a bone," the dress is better known as a Mother Hubbard.

a Melanesian custom: It's a practice on these islands to breed pigs, mostly for their tusks. The lower incisors are first knocked out so the upper tusks will grow inward, sometimes even penetrating the cheek. This upper pair, which would normally grind against the tusks in the lower jaw, thus curve into an almost spiral ring. The pigs are coveted by their owners, and the meat and tusks are prized at initiation rites and funeral feasts.

Map labels: TORRES IS., HIU, METOMA, TEGUA, LINUA, LOH, OTOGA, VOT, TANDE, UREPARAPARA, MOTA LAVA, VANUA LAVA, MOTA, PORT PATTESON, SOLA, BANKS IS., SANTA MARIA, ONTAR, TARASAG, MERIG, MERE LAVA, CAPE CUMBERLAND, BIG BAY, SAKAO, PORT OLRY, NAONE, MAEWO, ESPIRITU SANTO, LUGANVILLE, AOBA, LONGANA, PALIKULO, WALAHA, PATTESON PASSAGE, WUSI, TUTUBA, AORE, REDCLIFF, ARAKI, TAMAMBO, VAO, RANO, PENTECOST, LONORORE, BOUGAINVILLE STRAIT, AMOKH, NORSUP, OLAL, WALI, BUNLAP, SELWIN STRAIT, PORT STANLEY, CRAIG COVE, AMBRYM, ULEI, MALAKULA, SOUTH WEST BAY, LAMAP, PAAMA, LOPEVI, LAMEN BAY, EPI, VALESDIR, TONGOA, EMAE, TONGARIKI, MAKURA, SHEPHERD IS., MATASO, NGUNA, MOSO, EMAO, ERETOKA, PORT VILA, EFATE, CORAL SEA, SOUTH PACIFIC OCEAN, ERROMANGO, DILLON'S BAY, IPOTA, ANIWA, TANNA, WHITESANDS, LENAKEL, FUTUNA, TAFEA ISLANDS, ANELGHOWHAT, ANATOM

0   50   100 km

VANUATU AT A GLANCE

ISLAND (* includes offshore islands)	AREA (sq km)	HIGHEST POINT (m)	POPULATION (1979)
Espiritu Santo *	4,010	1,879	16,785
Malakula *	2,053	863	15,163
Efate *	887	647	17,799
Erromango	887	886	932
Ambrym	666	1,270	6,176
Tanna	561	1,084	15,397
Pentecost	499	946	9,361
Epi	446	833	2,597
Aoba	399	1,496	7,754
Vanua Lava	331	946	1,008
Santa Maria	330	797	824
Maewo	300	811	1,822

the 8,000-m-deep New Hebrides Trench. This marks the point where the Indo-Australian Plate slips under the Pacific Plate in a classic demonstration of plate tectonics. Its islands are pushed up 10 cm a year, to the accompaniment of earthquakes and volcanic eruptions. Although the new republic is also relatively young geologically, this uplifting has created the series of stepped limestone plateaus you'll see on many of the islands.

climate: Vanuatu has a hot, rainy climate—tropical in the N, sub-tropical in the south. The southernmost islands get less rain, but are prone to devastating hurricanes (Jan. to March). Though hotter, the far N is outside the main hurricane zone. The rainy season (Nov. to April) is also the low tourist season and there will be fewer other visitors crowding the tour buses, planes, etc. at that time. May to July are the best months for hiking—cooler and less rain. The SE tradewinds blow steadily from April to Oct.; the rest of the year there are strong westerlies or long periods of calm broken by storms caused by N winds and tropical cyclones.

flora: The windward, eastern sides of the islands are equatorial, with thick rainforests. The leeward, western sides, which get less rain, are often open tropical woodlands or savanna, especially in the south. Higher up on the mountains is a humid zone of shrub forest. A principal botanical curiosity of Vanuatu are giant banyan trees (*nabangas*), which often dominate village meeting places (*nakamals*), especially on Tanna. The banyan begins by growing up around another tree, which it eventually strangles out of existence. These massive twisting mazes of trunks and vines are among the earth's largest living organisms.

HISTORY

prehistory: Vanuatu may have been populated since before 3,000 B.C., although little from this era is known for certain. *Lapita* pottery found in the group indicates that Polynesians passed this way. Later arrivals from the Solomons brought a second type of pottery, which they carried on to Fiji and New Caledonia. Excavations on Eretoka I. off western Efate uncovered burials dated to A.D. 1300. The first inhabitants lived in small villages and had a remarkable variety of languages and customs. Each clan was autonomous; relations between them were often based on ceremonial gift-giving, while individuals related by drinking *kava*. Wives, considered property, were exchanged between villages. Spirits were controlled by magic. To work one's way up the graded societies and become a "big man," an individual had to supply pigs to be slaughtered at clan festivals. The borrowing and loaning of pigs between men created a complex system of bonds and obligations which strengthened the group. Only the most able men could rise in this system. Clans raided one another for gastronomical purposes; these cannibal raids being reciprocal, one never wandered far from his home village.

European contact: The first European to arrive was the Spanish explorer Quiros, who pulled into a big bay on 29 April 1606, believing he had found the "lost" southern continent. When he and his men landed, pious, God-fearing Quiros knelt and kissed the sand, naming the island Terra Australis del Espiritu Santo, after the Holy Ghost. He claimed

a Europeanized version of a woman of Tanna as seen by Wm. Hodges, Capt. Cook's illustrator on board the HMS Resolution

possession of it and everything to the S as far as the South Pole in the name of the king of Spain and the Catholic Church. Quiros planned to build a model Christian settlement on the site, but his treatment of the inhabitants soon led to open hostility which, together with sickness and dissent among his own men, drove this visionary mystic away after only 3 weeks. White men did not return for 162 years, when Bougainville sailed between Espiritu Santo and Malekula, disproving Quiros' theory that they were part of a southern continent. In 1774 Capt. Cook became the first European to really explore and chart the group, naming it New Hebrides, after the Scottish Hebrides.

Christianity and depopulation: The sandalwood traders operated in the islands from 1825 to 1865. Their methods created deep resentment among the islanders, so when the first white missionaries landed on Erromango (Martyr Island) in 1839, they were clubbed and eaten. Next Samoan missionaries were sent, many of whom were also killed or died from

malaria. Worse still, they introduced diseases such as measles, influenza, and dysentery, which devastated whole populations. Well-wishers in Australia and elsewhere sent second-hand garments to clothe the naked savages. Regrettably, these were also impregnated with disease. Since converts—who had the closest contact with missionaries—were the most affected by these epidemics, the newcomers were thought to be evil sorcerers, and the ni-Vanuatu resisted any way they could. Erromango remains relatively unpopulated and only after 1920 did Vanuatu's population begin to rise. Even today, many refuse to accept Christianity and regard all white men with suspicion. Although a majority had been "converted" by 1900, their understanding of doctrine was shallow and there have been mass defections from the church, especially on Tanna, since WW II. The Melanesian Mission (Anglican) and the Presbyterians divided the group into spheres of influence, with the Anglicans in the NE and the Presbyterians in the center and south. Catholicism became established in the central islands somewhat later, and little headway was made on Malakula and Santo until recently. The missionaries did manage to stop village warfare and cannibalism, facilitating the entry of the next 2 groups—the labor recruiters and European settlers.

the blackbirders: From 1863 to 1904 some 40,000 ni-Vanuatu were recruited to work in the canefields of Queensland, Australia, and another 10,000 went to Fiji and New Caledonia. Though many young men welcomed the chance for adventure and escape from the restrictions of village life, conditions were hard. The blackbirders sometimes kidnapped the natives, or herded them together by brute force. Outriggers were sunk and the survivors "rescued"; others were bought outright from chiefs for beads, tobacco, mirrors, and muskets. In the end most of the laborers were deported from Australia in 1906 when the White Australia Policy took effect, but a large percentage died abroad. Some of the returnees to Tanna were so irate about being evicted from Australia that they drove all whites off the island. One of the most lasting legacies of the labor trade was the evolution of a pidgin tongue called Bislama, the national language.

the planters and the land: The first impetus for establishing European plantations in Vanuatu was high cotton prices in the aftermath of the American Civil War. In 1882 the Compagnie Caledonienne des Nouvelles Hebrides began acquiring large tracts of native land, followed by Australian-based trading company Burns Philp in 1895. By 1980, when independence was achieved, 36 percent of the land of Vanuatu was foreign-owned, including the best tracts. Traditionally, land could not be sold in Vanuatu, only the *use* of the land temporarily assigned. Also, many sales had been instigated by a few individuals and not agreed upon by consensus as custom required. The ni-Vanuatu had little understanding of the alienation taking place; when they began to resist, British and French warships were sent to bombard coastal villages. Although the first traders and missionaries had been mostly English, the French recognized the agricultural potential of the islands and wanted another colony to strengthen their position in New Caledonia. This alarmed the Australians, who thought one French colony on their doorstep was enough, so in 1878 the British and French governments agreed not to annex Vanuatu without consulting one another. To protect the planters' interests and regulate the labor trade, the 2 nations established in 1887 a Joint Naval Commission with jurisdiction over the islands, but it could only intervene in the event of war. During the hurricane season, however, when the Naval Commission vessels had to be withdrawn, there was no law other than the musket.

the colonial period: In 1902, when the Germans began to show an interest in these "unclaimed" islands, the British and French quickly appointed Resident Commissioners. In 1906, 3 years after an auspicious visit to Paris by the francophile English King Edward VII, the Anglo-French New Hebrides Condominium was established. The arrangement was formalized in the Protocol of 1914, then proclaimed in 1923. The Condominium

system of government resulted in an expensive duplication of services and administration, as each colonial power implemented its own judiciary, police force, hospitals, schools, etc. Each power had jurisdiction over its own citizens and the natives, but the ni-Vanuatu were not permitted to claim either British or French nationality and in effect became stateless persons. A Joint Court was set up, and the Convention stipulated that land titles registered before 1896 could not be challenged. This institutionalized the large European plantations. In addition, the ni-Vanuatu didn't have the right of appeal from native courts to the Joint Court. This administration had little impact on the ni-Vanuatu, other than freezing an unjust social structure, and they could simply ignore the Condominium pandemonium if they wished. Education remained in the hands of the missionaries right into the 1960s. Despite the fact that the budget of the French Residency was twice that of the British, the latter were more effective, due to a long-standing policy of localization and advanced training for Melanesians. France wasted much of its money on a large staff of expatriates, failing to train a French-speaking native elite capable of assuming power—a mistake they are repeating in New Caledonia. During WW II there were major Allied bases on Espiritu Santo and Efate. These islands didn't suffer as much as the Solomons and New Guinea, however. The Japanese bombed Santo once but only managed to kill a cow. The Americans constructed crushed coral roads, bridges, and airstrips, so by the end of the war a whole communications infrastructure had been installed.

the road to independence: The independence of Vanuatu was not generously granted, as it has been elsewhere in the South Pacific, but had to be won through a long, bitter struggle against bungling colonial administrators, entrenched settlers, and opportunists. In 1971, the New Hebrides Cultural Association emerged to resist the large land purchases and subdivisions by an American businessman, one Eugene Peacock. Three months later the Association became the New Hebrides National Party, headed by Father

Walter Lini of Pentecost, the current prime minister. The party soon won grassroots support throughout the islands, mostly among English-speaking Protestants, by calling for a return of all alienated land to its custom owners. Several French-oriented parties (the "moderates") were soon created, which favored prolonged collaboration with the British and French governments. These factions forced the ruling powers to establish a Representative Assembly in 1975, but it was dissolved in 1977 following a boycott by the Vanuaaku Party (formerly the National Party) which demanded the elimination of appointed members as well as immediate independence. The crisis was resolved in 1978 when the creation of a Government of National Unity temporarily united the 2 factions. A constitution was signed in Oct. 1979, and in elections a month later the Vanuaaku Party won a two-thirds majority. Understandably, little of the above was popular with the French. Most of the plantations were owned by French nationals, who outnumbered British subjects 3 to one. Their influence was especially strong on Espiritu Santo. The French administration then adopted a disruptive policy of encouraging local divisions and disturbances, while the British, who just wanted to get out as soon as possible, hesitated to interfere with their European Economic Community ally.

the Republic of Vemarana: The leading figure in the independence disruption was Jimmy Stevens, a charismatic part-Samoan/Scottish half-caste with a large following on Espiritu Santo and some of the central islands. Basically he was a nonconformist, suspicious of the Vanuaaku Party leadership, composed mainly of ni-Vanuatu British civil servants and Protestant clergy. They in turn regarded Jimmy as a dangerous cargo cultist. His NaGriamel Party began as an agricultural reform movement centered at Tanafo village in the bush 20 km N of Luganville. NaGriamel represented a turning-away from European influence and return to native ways. In 1971 NaGriamel petitioned the United Nations to halt further sales of land on Espiritu Santo to American interests for development as hotel and investment properties. Ironically, by 1980 Stevens had come full

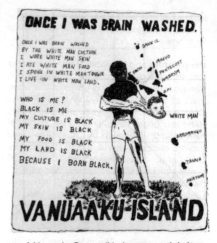

A Vanuaaku Party political poster used during the 1971-80 independence struggle.

circle, supplied with US$250,000 in aid, arms, and radio transmitting equipment by the Phoenix Foundation, an American right-wing organization that wanted to turn Espiritu Santo into a capitalist's paradise. By this time 4 areas of land on the island had been subdivided into 5,000 lots, of which 2,000 had already been sold to individual Americans. Aore Island, off Espiritu Santo, was to have become a health resort and casino. Stevens, who now styled himself "President Moly," declared Espiritu Santo the independent "Republic of Vemarana," and Vanuaaku Party supporters were driven off the island. The Coconut War had begun.

escalation: During it all, French police stood by and took no action. Stevens had visited and presumably received encouragement from French President Giscard d'Estaing prior to the rebellion. The French apparently intended to have Espiritu Santo continue alone as a French colony. Chief Minister Walter Lini responded by imposing an economic boycott on Espiritu Santo, but was unable to prod the British and French authorities into putting down the revolt. A simultaneous disorder on Tanna dwindled when Alexis Yolou, its "moderate" leader, was mysteriously shot dead. There was talk of delaying the scheduled independence (30 July 1980), but Father Lini announced that he would declare Vanuatu's independence unilaterally if Britain and France reneged on their promises. Additionally, neighboring countries such as Australia, New Zealand, and P.N.G. indicated that they would recognize such independence. So, the colonial powers were forced to adhere to their timetable and Vanuatu became an independent republic on the scheduled day. To prevent a bloodbath, the British and French sent military forces to Espiritu Santo to disarm Stevens' followers just a week before independence.

the outcome: In August, 1980, Papua New Guinea troops replaced these forces and arrested Jimmy Stevens, who was sent to Vila for trial, and Stevens' son Eddie was killed by a grenade when he tried to run a roadblock. Stevens was sentenced to 14.5 years imprisonment for his part in the rebellion, during which Luganville was looted and burned. He's now housed in a cell at the old French jail near the stadium in Port Vila, with no visitation privileges—he's greatly feared by the present administration. Documents captured at the rebel HQ at Tanafo implicated aides to former French Resident Commissioner Jean-Jacques Robert, as direct accomplices in the secession. Robert is now barred from re-entering

Vanuatu. The sins of the rebels are well known, but there were abuses on both sides. Many Frenchmen arrested on Espiritu Santo for participating in the revolt were clubbed and beaten as they got off the plane in Port Vila. Non-Melanesians, including some who have spent their whole lives in Vanuatu, are still expelled and their property forfeit with no explanation given. The only opposition newspaper, the *Voice of Vanuatu,* was recently closed and its editor forced to return to Australia because someone decided the paper went too far in its criticism of government officials. There has been little reconciliation between the factions and the English-speaking element is firmly in control. The French schools stay open only because the French government picks up the tab. A Vanuatu Mobile Force has been created to maintain order. The schizophrenic nature of Vanuatu's tragicomic colonial history will continue to overshadow the republic for many years to come.

government: The rebellion has led to a centralization of authority in Port Vila. Vanuatu has a parliamentary system of government; the prime minister is the leader of the majority party in Parliament. Its 39 members are elected for 4-year terms. The prime minister appoints his cabinet from among these members. A National Council of Chiefs advises on matters relating to custom. Parlia-

the protagonists meet: From L to R are Jimmy Stevens, the rebel leader; Gen. Ted Diro, PNG Defense Force Commander at the time; Sir Julius Chan, former Prime Minister of PNG; and Father Walter Lini, Prime Minister of Vanuatu.

ment and the heads of Regional Councils elect a president, who serves a 5-year term as ceremonial head of state. There are 11 Regional Councils, each with an elected president and Local Government Council. These local governments are supported by a head tax which averages v.1000 a year for men, v.500 a year for women. In 1982 Vanuatu closed its ports to American warships which refused to confirm or deny whether they were carrying nuclear weapons. In 1983 a law was passed which made Vanuatu the 1st totally nuclear-free nation in the Pacific: nuclear weapons, ships, power plants, and waste-dumping are all prohibited, although they have failed to enshrine this principle in their constitution. Vanuatu was the first South Pacific country to acquire full membership in the Non-Aligned Movement; to maintain its neutrality Vanuatu does not have diplomatic relations with the U.S.S.R. or the U.S.

ECONOMY AND PEOPLE

agriculture and land: Roughly 80 percent of the population live by subsistence agriculture. Root crops such as yams, taro, manioc, and sweet potatoes are grown, with a little copra produced for cash sale. The new constitution specifies that land can only be owned by indigenous ni-Vanuatu and by the government. At independence, all alienated land was returned to its custom owners; former landlords were given 5 years to go into partnership, lease the land, or otherwise dispose of it. Leases of up to 75 years are available. A problem has arisen in determining just who owns what land, as many ni-Vanuatu claim the same areas. The government is attempting to implement a system for deciding on the claims and registering titles, but there are many complications. One of the most ironic of these is the waterfront property in Luganville which was reclaimed by U.S. forces during WW II. This area has been taken over by the Santo Land Council and leased back to its former owners; as yet no one has suggested returning it to its earlier custom owner, the U.S. Government. Although about 40 percent of the land is arable, only 17 percent is presently utilized, mostly in coastal areas. The

coconut plantations are aging—many are 50 years old—and replanting is hampered by the uncertainty of ownership. Cattle bred with French Charolais and Limousin stock roam under the coconuts to provide beef for canning and export.

trade and tourism: Copra is the largest export, accounting for a half to a third of total exports by value, mostly shipped from Luganville to Belgium and Holland. Coconut oil exportation disappeared with the destruction of the oil mill at Luganville during the rebellion—it has yet to be rebuilt. Exports of fish from the Japanese plant at Palikulo on Espiritu Santo are second only to copra. Exports such as cacao, canned meat, and timber are less significant. Vanuatu imports twice as

taro **(Colocasia antiquorum** *or* **Colocasiae sculenta)***: The staple of many Pacific islanders, taro requires moist soil, and matures 8 to 15 months after planting. When ripe, the edible portion of this thick starchy root is cut off below the stalk, and the stalk is then replanted. The tender elephant ear-like leaves are eaten as greens after thorough cooking, and the root is boiled or baked until tender, then peeled. Cooked taro can be creamed, scalloped, sliced, or fried—even made into taro chips. In Hawaii, cooked taro is mashed and pounded, then water is added to make poi, a thick, sticky paste eaten with pork or fish.*

Tourists off the cruise ship Fairstar purchasing handicrafts on the remote island of Anatom, Republic of Vanuatu; the insensitive tour organizers failed to inform their passengers that this type of attire was considered utterly scandalous by the Seventh-day Adventist villagers.

much as it exports and has a huge trade imbalance with Australia, which supplies 31 percent of its imports but buys only one percent of its exports. A third of the total imports are foodstuffs. The local economy is dominated by 2 companies: the Comptoirs Francais des Nouvelles-Hebrides (C.F.N.H.) and Burns Philp Limited. Cooperatives predominate in rural areas. Tourism is being developed along conventional lines, focusing on transnational hotels centered in Port Vila, with Tanna serving as a daytrip destination. Since independence Espiritu Santo has been played down as a tourist destination. Most tourists are Australian, followed by French from New Caledonia. Cruise ships call frequently at Port Vila, and occasionally at Luganville. Tourism is largely in the hands of Ansett Airlines of Australia which runs Air Vanuatu; little has been done to encourage ni-Vanuatu to participate in tourism by setting up low-key indigenous resorts.

taxation and evasion: Although Vanuatu has pursued a confrontational left/center foreign policy, its domestic policies are ultra-right. Income tax has not been instituted, largely because government officials themselves would be the main group affected. There are also no direct or corporation taxes, estate duties, capital gains taxes, or exchange controls. Instead, revenue is obtained from customs duties, export taxes, local licensing fees, the 10 percent hotel and restaurant tax, and outside aid. Vanuatu offers excellent facilities to foreign corporations wishing to evade their own country's taxation, public auditing, and secrecy laws. In 1971 the British Companies Regulation was enacted, giving tax-free status to companies registered in what was then New Hebrides. Today some 1,000 foreign companies and 75 banks participate in the tax-haven scheme. A company sells products cheaply to its Vanuatu subsidiary, which then resells them at market prices to the destination country, thereby avoiding taxation, while the products never pass through Vanuatu. Vanuatu has also established a shipping registry or flag-of-convenience law similar to Liberia's, which allows foreign shipping companies to evade taxation, safety regulations, union labor, government controls, etc.

the people: Seventy of Vanuatu's 82 islands are populated, but most of the country's 128,000 (in 1984) people live on 16 main islands. After a century of depopulation due to warfare, blackbirding, and introduced diseases, Vanuatu now has one of the highest birthrates in the Pacific. Ni-Vanuatu continue to migrate to Port Vila from rural areas in search of jobs, excitement, and better services. One in 6 now lives in the capital, with

A Malakula Big Nambas man poses beside an image he carved.

people from the same outer island congregating in their own suburban communities. Although 93 percent of the population is Melanesian (ni-Vanuatu), there are also Europeans, Chinese, and Vietnamese. Thousands of indentured Vietnamese laborers were brought in earlier this century to work in the plantations, but most were repatriated in 1963. Although the Melanesians arrived in Vanuatu from the NW thousands of years ago, there was a "back migration" of Polynesians from the E less than a thousand years ago. Polynesian languages are still spoken on Futuna, Aniwa, and Emae islands, and in Ifira and Mele villages on Efate. The hierarchy of chiefs the Polynesians established is still evident in much of central and southern Vanuatu, while in physical appearance they have been almost totally assimilated by the surrounding Melanesian peoples, largely due to a custom requiring a young man to take his bride from a neighboring clan. The ni-Vanuatu possess an amazing variety of cultures, from the "land-diving" tribesmen of Pentecost I. to the festival-rich inhabitants of volcanic Tanna. Customs differ from island to island, and remain strong despite generations of missionary influence. In the interiors of the 2 largest islands, Malakula and Espiritu Santo, are some of the most traditional peoples in the Pacific. Penis-wrappers (*nambas*) are still worn by men in remote regions of Malakula, Ambrym, and Pentecost. Traditional magic is practiced on Maewo, Ambrym, and Epi. The payment of bride-price — currently about US$800 — is still common throughout Vanuatu. Traditional culture revolves around the pig; each tribe or leader tries to acquire the greatest number. In the N the ritual killing of pigs raises the social status of the individual in the village hierarchy *(nimangki)*, while in the S it signifies a competition for friendship between tribes *(nei)*. Traditional art objects were usually associated with graded secret societies; the best are from Malakula, Ambrym, Pentecost, and the Banks.

language: There are 115 local languages, most with several dialects, giving Vanuatu the most languages per capita of any country in the world. Many ni-Vanuatu are fluent in 5 or 6 languages: Bislama, English, French, and a few local languages. Although English and French are also official languages, Bislama is the national language. It developed as a traders' tongue in the 19th C. and took hold among the indentured native laborers in Queensland. This dialect of Pidgin English is now spoken by almost all ni-Vanuatu and is the main communication medium between persons of different tribes, although they speak their mother tongue at home. Bislama verbs have no tenses: finished and unfinished actions are defined by adverbs. Nouns are often a description of use. Bislama can sound deceptively simple to the untrained ear, but the meaning is not always what one would expect from a literal translation into English. The ability to speak correct Bislama is only attained through careful study (there are several dictionaries) and practice.

above: dancers, Rarotonga, Cook Is. (D. Stanley); below: Radha and Krishna in the Sri Krishna Kaliya Temple, Lautoka, Fiji (D. Stanley)

above, clockwise: male frigatebird, Kure I., Hawaii (Eugene Kridler); black crowned night heron, Hilo, Hawaii (R.J. Shallenberger); albatross concentration on North I., Pearl and Hermes Reef, Hawaii (Eugene Kridler); green sea turtle, Whale Scate I., Hawaii (Gerald M. Ludwig); Hawaiian monk seal, Hawaiian Islands National Wildlife Refuge, Hawaii (Ian Tait; all photos this page courtesy U.S. Fish and Wildlife Service)

events: Public holidays include National Chiefs Day (5 March), Labor Day (I May), Independence Day (30 July), Constitution Day (5 Oct.), All Saints Day (1 Nov.), National Unity Day (late Nov.), and Family Day (26 Dec.). Important annual events include the Jon Frum Festival at Sulphur Bay, Tanna, on 15 Feb., the Pentecost Jump in April/May, and the Toka Dance on Tanna at the end of August. The Vila Agricultural Show in Sept. or Oct. features cattle and horse exhibits, custom dancing, and a parade through downtown.

PRACTICALITIES

getting there: Air Pacific flies to Port Vila from Brisbane, Honiara, and Nandi, Fiji. Air Vanuatu provides a direct link from Sydney. Air Nauru flies in from Nauru, while Air Caledonie International has 4 flights a week Noumea-Vila (v.9000 OW). In Port Vila, Burns Philp Travel represents Air Pacific, while Air Caledonie International are agents for Air Nauru. Solair flies between Vanuatu and the Solomons twice a week: v.19,300 Vila-Honiara or v.17,200 Santo-Honiara. This excellent connection avoids an inconvenient backtrack from Santo to Vila. Trouble is, Solair tickets are difficult to purchase outside Vanuatu or the Solomons, yet you need one beforehand to show Immigration upon entry! Solair may also refuse to accept mileage tickets for their sectors. Note too that Solair's plane carries only 19 passengers. Start working on this one well ahead.

getting around: Air Melanesiae, owned by Talair of P.N.G., offers punctual daily service to all the main islands of Vanuatu. No stopovers are allowed—the fare from Vila to Santo is v.5000 direct, and v.5800 with a stopover at Lamap and Norsup (Malakula) on the way. Students get 25 percent discount. The Air Melanesiae network is extensive, and such out-of-the-way places as Anatom, Pentecost, Aoba, and Vanua Lava are also served. The baggage allowance is 10 kilos, though they might let you on with more. Reconfirm your onward reservations immediately upon arrival at an outer island.

accommodations: There's a 10 percent hotel tax; meals at licensed restaurants (which sell alcoholic beverages) are also taxed 10 percent. The only commercial accommodations

dancers from the Banks Islands

are at Port Vila, Tanna, and Luganville. Camping is possible and safe elsewhere, but always get permission from the landowner or chief. Some of the churches and Local Government Councils have basic rest houses; people from the particular island will have information, so ask around. Often people invite you into their homes, and in such cases it doesn't hurt to offer payment, especially if the host is a storekeeper, truck driver, etc. If their property is well situated, explain to them how they can start a small business by accommodating visitors on a regular basis. Give back as much as you receive and be polite.

food and drink: *Lap lap* is the national dish. Root vegetables such as yams, taro, and manioc are first pounded in a wooden bowl, grated, and kneaded to a paste, to which coconut cream and aromatic leaves are added. Pork or seafood can be included. The mixture is then wrapped in banana leaves and cooked over hot stones in an earth oven. The best *lap lap* is made in remote villages, though a plain variety is sold at the Vila market. Other local specialties include mangrove oysters (served cold) and freshwater prawns (steamed with young bamboo stalks and mayonnaise). Try coconut crab hot with garlic sauce. Vanuatu *kava* is the strongest in the world—it's narcotic rather than alcoholic. After a few cups you won't be able to lift your arms or walk, and your mouth will feel as if the dentist had just given you novacaine. Although it looks and tastes like dishwater, *kava* is pure relaxation, leaves no hangover, and never prompts aggression (unlike beer). Pentecost and Tanna are famous for their *kava*.

money: The *vatu* is the unit of currency in Vanuatu, US$1 = v.100 approximately. Since the *vatu* is now linked to special drawing rights (SDR) in the International Monetary Fund instead of the French franc, inflation has fallen considerably. Sometimes you can buy *vatu* cheaply at banks outside Vanuatu. *Vatu* are not well-known abroad and may be hard to get rid of, so change your excess back into Australian or U.S. dollars before you go to the airport. The Australian banks in Port Vila give better rates than the Banque Indosuez. As in most of the Pacific, there's no tipping in Vanuatu. If you need to hire a guide to take you through the bush, v.1000 a day is more than adequate payment (local expats pay only v.400-500). You should also supply canned food.

visas: Most nationalities (except Austrians) don't require a visa for a stay of 30 days or less, although onward tickets and sufficient funds are required. Extensions of up to 4 months are possible. The only Immigration offices are in Port Vila and Luganville. Elsewhere, take your passport to a police station; they'll send it to Port Vila for the extension. Both Port Vila and Luganville are ports of entry for cruising yachts.

health: Tourism officials don't like to warn their clients about it, but there is malaria in Vanuatu. This is more of a problem in the N than in Port Vila or the S, but malaria pills should be taken anyway to be safe. Begin a week before you arrive and continue for a month after you leave the infected area (Vanuatu, Solomon Islands, Papua New Guinea—though none in New Caledonia or Fiji). In Vanuatu you need a prescription to buy malaria pills—ask at the business office of the Central Hospital. They prescribe two 25 mg Daraprim tablets to be taken every Sunday. All minor cuts should be treated immediately: a little iodine at the right time can save you a lot of trouble later. The tap water in Port Vila is safe to drink.

airport: Bauerfield Airport (VLI) is 6 km N of Port Vila. Despite the scores of fake banks in the tax-haven scheme, there's none at the international airport. You can change small amounts of cash at the snack bar, however. A red public telephone (v.20) is outside the toilets in the terminal. There's no duty-free shop and souvenirs at the snack bar cost double what you'd pay for the same items in town. A departure tax of v.1000 is charged on international flights (no tax on domestic flights). Transit passengers staying under 24 hours are exempt. The tourist information counter at the airport may tell you there's no public bus (untrue), but both the airport bus and taxis charge v.300 for the trip into town, so it's cheaper to get a taxi and share the cost. Or you could walk 1.5 km to Tagabe and catch a public bus for v.30.

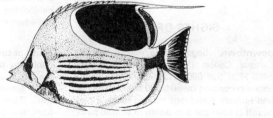

saddleback butterflyfish
(Chaetodon ephippium)

PORT VILA

Port Vila (pop. 14,598 in 1979) is the commercial, administrative, and tourist center at the strategic heart of Vanuatu, the crossroads of the islands to N and south. A cosmopolitan attractive town, with yachts moored Mediterranean-style along the waterfront, settle in for a week till you get your bearings. Havannah Harbor on the N side of 42-by-23-km Efate I. was the 1st European settlement. In the late 1870s, drought forced the settlers to shift to the site of Port Vila. Plantations were created in the area and a few traders set up shop, but only after establishment of the Condominium in 1906 did a town form. Commercial activities occupied the waterfront; the colonial administration settled into the hills above. The town expanded quickly during WW II and again during the New Caledonian nickel boom of the early 1970s as the French invested their profits. Today Vila is a modern capital with excellent facilities and great beauty. Add the French *joie de vivre,* which pervades the town, the shopping, the easy transport, the many things to see and do, and proximity to Australia, and you have one of the most exciting cities in the Pacific. Don't spend all your time in Port Vila, however, as Espiritu Santo, Ambrym, and the other islands also have much to offer.

SIGHTS OF VILA

downtown: Begin with a visit to the Vila Cultural Center (Mon. to Fri. 0900-1130/1400-1700, Sat. 0900-1130 — donation), with a library containing over 10,000 books in French and English, a pleasant reading room, a handicraft center, and a museum of stuffed birds, insects, and shells. Don't miss the native artifacts room, with a superb collection of articles from Malakula. Upon request they'll put on video films about local customs, the independence celebrations, etc. On the lawn outside the library is a large metal pot used by the natives to cook early missionaries. One of the best-known artists living in Vanuatu is

Aloi Pilioko, a Wallisian. Aloi created the reliefs on Pilioko House opposite the Banque Indosuez. Aloi's close associate, Nicolai Michoutouchkine, runs an exquisite dress shop in Pilioko House. In an Oceanic tradition of useable art, Nicolai has designed an absolutely shattering line of hand-printed clothing, with prices to match. Have a look at least. The road beside Pilioko House leads up to the prime minister's office, formerly the French Residency. There's an excellent view of Vila and Vila Bay from up here. The island you see nearest the town is Reriki, where the British Resident Commissioner once lived. Ifira I. is farther out. Back down on the main street are 2 more colorful murals by Aloi Pilioko, one on the front of the post office, the other on the side wall of the building across the street. The small pavilion across from the market with an attractive mural by students of the French *lycee* is the House of Parliament. Ask at the Visitors Bureau nearby for a pass to enter Parliament and listen to debates in Bislama by local personalities — earphones are provided for translation. To visit Ifira I. take a launch (v.40 OW) from the wharf a little past Burns Philp; this easy trip leaves every hour or so. The tombs of a few missionaries and the first Christian chief of Ifira, Kalsakau I, are behind the large Presbyterian church above the wharf on Ifira.

south of town: The beauty spot of Vila is undoubtedly the Erakor Lagoon, accessible by the Le Lagon Hotel bus (v.40) which you can catch across the street from the post office (ask). Take the free ferry (24-hour service) from the dock beside the hotel across to Erakor Island, the perfect place to sunbathe, swim, and snorkel. When you return to the mainland walk L along the beach as far as the point. A small sign shows the way to the ART GALLERY. The Atelier-Musee Michoutouchkine-Pilioko (open daily 1000-1700, free) is wonderfully set among trees and gardens. Here you can see many South Pacific artifacts and works of art arrayed in loving abandon. The 2 resident artists have studios on the grounds and their creations may be purchased. After visiting the Atelier, continue along the beach or road to Pango village. Look for the large stone fish traps offshore. If you're a surfer there are possibilities in this area. Tom will put you up in the village for a reasonable charge.

north of town: Take a bus (v.40) to Tagabe and walk one km E along the airport road to the Agricultural School Plots. A great variety of plants are kept here, especially cacao, coffee, and oil palms—see how many you can identify. Return to Tagabe and continue W on the Mele Road. Go 500 m W of the Tagabe junction, where a dirt road to the L leads 1.5 km to Blacksands Beach where the local people swim. You can walk W along this beach as far as Hideaway Island, but you'll have to wade or swim across several creeks. Otherwise hitch to Mele on the main road. Hideaway (good snorkeling) is a small tourist resort open to the public Tues. to Fri., and Sun. when they put on a buffet at 1230 (v.700). A launch (v.100) ferries tourists across to the island, although you can often wade across the shifting sandbar or swim. Mele village, on the mainland near here, is the largest village in Vanuatu and has a big Presbyterian church. People from Ambrym were resettled at Mele Maat, just NW of Mele, after a big eruption on their home island in

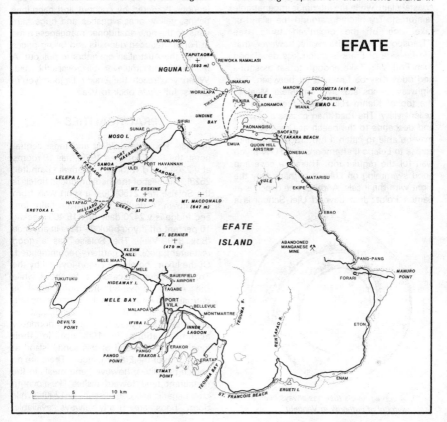

1951. There's a signposted CASCADE up from the bridge at the foot Klehm Hill, just beyond Mele Maat, where the locals like to swim. Wade up the river to a waterfall which tumbles down from the plateau like a miniature Iguazu into the beautiful jungle-green setting. There are many lovely pools near this upper falls.

AROUND EFATE

A 132-km road runs around Efate's 887 sq km. The American servicemen who built it during WW II dubbed the road "U.S. Route No. 1." Vast coconut plantations with herds of grazing Charolais cattle characterize much of the coastal plain, while the interior is impenetrable rainforest. Try hitching around the island or take one of the organized tours (see "Transport" below). Be aware, however, that the far side of Efate is much less developed than Port Vila. Take enough to eat as shops and rides may be few and far between. The highway climbs steeply from Mele Maat to the top of Klehm Hill, where there's an excellent view. The road then passes a sawmill and descends to the beach at Creek Ai. You may be able to catch a motorboat from here across to Lelepa I. afternoons, v.50 OW if you wait for the regular trip. There's a cave and good swimming on Lelepa; perhaps stay the night with the locals. Another fine beach is at Samoa Point. Just beyond Ulei School is a

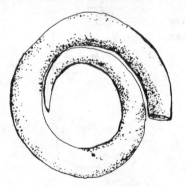

A curved boar's tusk has always been a symbol of authority in Vanuatu.

freshwater pool used by the U.S. Navy during WW II when they had a field hospital and base for the repair of damaged ships here. A km farther, 31 km from Vila at Port Havannah, is one of the oldest colonial buildings in Vanuatu, a remnant of the days before Vila became the capital. An abandoned American airstrip remains in the bush behind the building. Villagers commute to the large islands of Nguna and Pele from the wharf at Emua on the N coast of Efate. Try for a ride with them by motorboat (v.100 OW) weekday afternoons. Village outboards to Emao I. leave from Takara Beach farther E, 54 km from Vila. The U.S.-built Quoin Hill airstrip near here is kept usable. From Takara follow the road beside white sandy beaches and green lagoons bordered by coconut and pandanus palms, yellow acacia bushes and huge banyans, to the now-abandoned manganese mine at Forari. Reduced deposits and falling prices forced the Australian operators to pull out. A giant elevated cantilever still crosses the road. When you reach the Erakor Lagoon you're almost full circle back to Vila.

PRACTICALITIES

hotels: Port Vila's oldest and most central hotel, the Rossi (opened 1929), has 19 rooms at v.2200 s or d with a/c and private bath (tel. 2528). The best of the medium-priced hotels is the Solaise (tel. 2150), just a short walk from downtown. A double with private bath, fan, and fridge is v.2420 daily or v.15,400 weekly, 10 percent off if you book 21 days in advance (Box 810, Vila). The Solaise has a good restaurant, pool, and garden—recommended. Of the luxury hotels, Le Lagon (owned by the Tokyu Corporation) caters to Japanese, while the American-owned Intercontinental is patronized by Australians. Le Lagon is the better. Erakor Island Resort (tel. 2983), just opposite Le Lagon (free ferry), offers dormitory accommodations (v.1100 pp) in their longhouse at the end of this sandy island at the mouth of the Erakor Lagoon. There are no cooking facilities, however, and meals in the restaurant tend toward dishes like coconut crab in garlic and cream sauce (v.1200). While dorm beds are nearly always available,

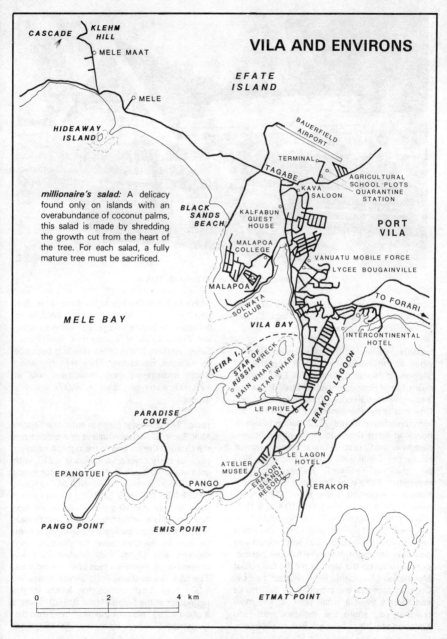

VILA AND ENVIRONS

CASCADE
KLEHM HILL
MELE MAAT
EFATE ISLAND
MELE
BAUERFIELD AIRPORT
TERMINAL
TAGABE
HIDEAWAY ISLAND
KAVA SALOON
AGRICULTURAL SCHOOL PLOTS
QUARANTINE STATION
PORT VILA

millionaire's salad: A delicacy found only on islands with an overabundance of coconut palms, this salad is made by shredding the growth cut from the heart of the tree. For each salad, a fully mature tree must be sacrificed.

BLACK SANDS BEACH
KALFABUN GUEST HOUSE
MALAPOA COLLEGE
VANUATU MOBILE FORCE
LYCEE BOUGAINVILLE
MALAPOA
SOLWATA CLUB
VILA BAY
TO FORARI
INTERCONTINENTAL HOTEL

MELE BAY

IFIRA I.
STAR OF RUSSIA WRECK
MAIN WHARF
STAR WHARF
ERAKOR LAGOON

PARADISE COVE
LE PRIVE

EPANGTUEI
PANGO
ATELIER MUSEE
ERAKORI ISLAND RESORT
LE LAGON HOTEL
ERAKOR

PANGO POINT
EMIS POINT

0   2   4 km

ETMAT POINT

fast food with a flair at Vila's Bloody Mary's

bungalow accommodations (v.4500 d) must be booked in advance through Magic Carpet Tours, Sydney, Australia.

hostels: Several of the missions in Vila provide accommodations. Most central is Sutherland House opposite Vila East School near Central Hospital (hospital bus). There are 3 apartments with cooking facilities, v.800 pp. Check in at the Presbyterian Church office on Independence Park (tel. 2722) during business hours; at other times go direct to the house. Nearby is the Church of Christ Seaside Transit House (tel. 2469) with 2 triple rooms at v.800 pp (cooking facilities). Kalfabun's Guest House (tel. 2930) near Tagabe, a 30-min. walk from the airport, is v.600 s, v.1000 d for a room in the main building, or v.1000 s, v.1500 d for a little bungalow with kitchen and veranda. There's a 10 percent discount if you pay a week in advance, and a v.100 surcharge if you only stay one night. If they're full, ask permission to camp on the lawn or try the Church of Melanesia (Anglican) Rest House nearby. Cooking facilities are provided at Kalfabun's and there's even a small pool. In the main building you share the facilities with Bob Kalfabun and his family; ask Bob to show you

where he hides the key to the front door. Bob also runs taxi tours to the Wed. night barbecue at Erakor village. For a longer stay, see Freda Giles at Investment Real Estate Sales, upstairs in the office building opposite Le Kiosque Bookstore. They rent furnished studio apartments near downtown Vila at v.20,000 a month (plus v.10,000 security deposit).

food: The cheapest place to eat is the Taporo Milk Bar in Chinatown, inland one block from the Cultural Center and to the right. A heaping plate of curry chicken and rice is v.210, with cold water to wash it down. Open for lunch and dinner. A sign reads NO ALCOHOLIC BEVERAGE IN THIS SNACK, so you don't have to pay the 10 percent restaurant tax. Another gastronomic tax haven is Bloody Mary's Fast Food beside the market. It's *namba wan kai kai quik taem*: hamburgers, fish, chicken and chips, thick shakes, and ice cream cones. There's a nice open eating area. The Milk Bar at Burns Philp serves coffee for v.30. Your best choice for lunch is the restaurant at the Solaise Hotel (taxed). There's a good v.250 "plate of the day" luncheon daily except Sunday. Pizza is v.200-450, beer v.110. A pleasant terrace overlooks the pool—good. If you want to splash out a little on a real Aussie steak (v.600 and up) try Ma Barker's (taxed) opposite the Cultural Center. Hotel Rossi (taxed) specializes in French cuisine. The BESA (British Ex-Servicemen's Association) Club, on the hill behind the post office, serves reasonably priced hot meals in the street-level dining room. Try an omelette for starters. For v.500 you can get a temporary one-month membership and use the club's facilities: video room, lending library, pool, snooker, billiards, squash courts, gambling machines, and bar.

entertainment: Both Vila's cinemas, Cine Pacifique (v.200) and Cine Hickson (v.250), show French films (nightly at 2000). Only the Drive-In (v.200, on Mon. v.100) shows English films (nightly at 1930). There's a covered seating area for those without cars. Le Prive Night Club, on the road to Le Lagon, gets going at 2300 (cover charge v.200). The girls are very timid. Check out the *kava nakamal* behind Le Prive, where that strong Vanuatu *kava* goes for v.50 a cup (open all day). Another *kava* saloon near Kalfabun's Guest House, down the road beyond the Church of Melanesia (Anglican), is open 1800-2100, v.50 for a small cup, v.100 for a large cup. The Solwata Klab at Malapoa is a local hangout (v.200 cover Fri. and Sat.). See soccer from the bleachers at the stadium every Sat. afternoon (v.100). The Sports Hut at the Intercontinental Hotel offers a Sports Pass (v.3200 pp a week) for windsurfing, sailboat, paddle boats, snorkeling gear, surf ski, catamaran, golf, and tennis. Nautical gear must stay within sight of the hotel, however, and the sailboat can only be taken out for an hour at a time.

shopping: Buy groceries at the large department stores, Hebrida, Ballande, and Burns Philp. Hebrida is especially well-stocked and has hard-to-find items such as gas refills for camping stoves, plastic bags of milk (v.55), snails, and Tanna coffee. Soft ice cream is dispensed at the back; there's an excellent grocery section with fresh croissants, and only Hebrida is open at lunchtime. Ballande is good for French wines, liqueurs, and cheeses. Try

Au Bon Marche for French Caribbean rums. The stores in Chinatown sometimes have cheaper canned goods. Vila's picturesque market operates Wed., Fri., and Sat.; in addition to economical fresh fruit and vegetables, you can buy lovely seashells and a few handicrafts. Live crabs are tied up with creepers to keep them from running away. No one will hassle you to buy anything, so look around as you please, but don't bargain—the prices are low enough to begin with. Vila is a duty-free port, so cameras, watches, jewelry, stereo equipment, calculators, cosmetics, French perfume, etc., are all good value. Camera film is also readily available and reasonably priced. Avoid shopping on a cruiseship day, however, as most prices are jacked up 15 percent. There's a notice board outside Burns Philp Shipping which lists the arrival days of all cruise ships, permitting you to avoid the Australian carnival hordes by heading for the hills.

crafts: The best place to buy authentic crafts is the Handikraf Blong Vanuatu boutique adjoining the Cultural Center. Here you'll find stone and woodcarvings, fern figures, slit gongs both large and small, bowls, war clubs,

a tapestry by Wallisian artist Aloi Pilioko

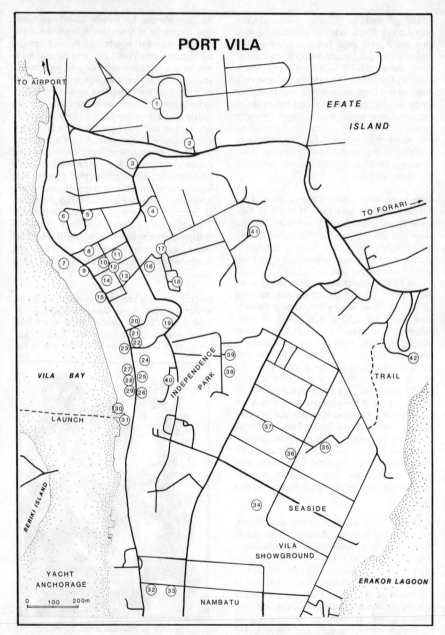

PORT VILA

TO AIRPORT

EFATE ISLAND

TO FORARI

VILA BAY

RERIKI ISLAND

LAUNCH

INDEPENDENCE PARK

TRAIL

YACHT ANCHORAGE

0   100   200m

SEASIDE

VILA SHOWGROUND

ERAKOR LAGOON

NAMBATU

spears, bow and arrows, fish traps, model canoes, masks, rattles, panpipes, combs, shell necklaces, grass skirts, shoulder bags, mats, native pottery, and curved boar tusks. The best articles come from Ambrym. Collectors will find an outstanding selection of artifacts from Vanuatu, the Solomons, and P.N.G. at Island Carvings opposite Hotel Rossi. Some of

Vila's finest shops are on Bougainville St., which runs from Hotel Rossi up to the Catholic Cathedral. L'Atelier Galerie d'Art, opposite Le Kiosque Bookstore, displays local paintings. You can buy one of those colorful Mother Hubbard dresses in the Chinese stores on the street running inland from Ma Barker's. These dresses are highly recommended for women who wish to visit remote areas.

services: As in Noumea, businesses and government offices in Vila open early, usually about 0730, and close for a long siesta lunch from 1130 to 1400. So get an early start. Banking hours vary: Barclay's, beside Hotel Rossi, is open 0800-1400, while the ANZ Bank opens 0800-1100/1330-1500. Exchange rates also vary, so check around if you're changing much. Barclay's Bank is usually good. The Philatelic Bureau is upstairs in the post office. Place long — distance telephone calls, telegrams, and telexes at Vanitel, behind the grandstand in Independence Park, 0700-2200 daily. The Central Hospital accepts outpatient consultations (v.500) weekdays 0700-0930. Fill prescriptions at the hospital dispensary. The Quarantine Station near the airport fumigates plants and plant products (fern carvings, grass skirts, etc.) and issues a phytosanitary certificate (v.200) for their export. A minimum of 2 working hours is required. Luggage can be left for the day at Frank King's Visitors Club opposite the market.

information: The Vanuatu Visitors Bureau (Mon. to Fri. 0730-1130/1330-1630) beside the market supplies maps and information sheets. If they can't answer your questions, go to the head office of the Department of Tourism to the R in the Government Office Building across the street. Otherwise try Frank King's Visitors Club across from the market. The Bureau of Statistics, 3rd Floor, Lolam House, sells informative reports on the economy. The Survey Department (weekdays 0730-1130/1315-1630) behind the courthouse sells excellent topographical maps (v.300) of all the islands of Vanuatu -- just the thing you need for getting out and exploring on your own. ORSTOM in the Oceania Building has a very detailed soil atlas of Vanuatu (v.9700) and a large *Atlas de la*

PORT VILA

1. stadium
2. prison
3. Ministry of Health
4. Catholic Cathedral
5. Cine Pacifique
6. Radio Vanuatu
7. Hotel Rossi
8. Le Kiosque Bookstore
9. Cultural Center
10. Taporo Milk Bar
11. British/Australian high commissions
12. Chinatown
13. police station
14. French Embassy
15. Immigration office/Banque Indosuez
16. town hall
17. War Memorial
18. Prime Minister's office
19. BESA Club
20. The Bookshop
21. Lelam House
22. post office
23. Air Melanesiae
24. Frank King's Visitors Club
25. Government Office Building
26. Burns Philp
27. open air market
28. Bloody Mary's Fast Food
29. Vanuatu Visitors Bureau
30. Burns Philp Wharf
31. Ifira Island launches
32. Cine Hickson
33. Solaise Hotel
34. Drive-In
35. Central Hospital
36. Seaside Transit House
37. Sutherland House
38. Vanitel
39. government ministries
40. Presbyterian church office
41. courthouse
42. Intercontinental Hotel

main street, Vila

Nouvelle Caledonie (v.8570). Pentecost Motors opposite the Cultural Center offers nautical charts at v.1360 a sheet. Vila has 2 good bookstores: Le Kiosque and The Bookshop. *Tam Tam* (Box 927, Vila), published weekly in Bislama, French, and English by the Government Office of Information, is the only newspaper. Visiting activists should contact Rex Rumakiek at the Vanuatu Pacific Community Center (Box 807, Vila) in Room 23 of the Oceania Building behind the Olympic Hotel. Rex can assist in making official contacts and answer questions on local issues. The Center publishes a monthly magazine, *Povai*.

TRANSPORT

ships to other countries: There are no regular passenger-carrying freighter services to any adjacent country, although Burns Philp Shipping puts out a monthly mimeographed sheet, "Shipping Movements," which lists when all large cargo boats will be in and where they're going. To arrange passage you must deal directly with the captain of the ship

concerned. The Banks Line has a monthly trip to Honiara. The French C.G.M. ships take passengers to Tahiti and France, but reservations are tight and the fare is the same as a plane ticket. Inquire at Ballande Shipping behind the perfume shop opposite the Banque Indosuez. Bookings can be made through Compagnie Generale Maritime agents worldwide.

local shipping: Regular scheduled passenger-carrying freighters depart Port Vila for Luganville 3 times a week (on Mon., Wed., and Sat. at 1900), with stops at Malakula, Epi, Paama, Ambrym, Pentecost, Maewo, and Aoba. The through trip takes 1.5-2.5 days depending on ports of call, and the deck fare (v.2200 to Ambrym, v.4000 to Luganville) includes meals. A bunk in a 4-bed cabin is v.500 extra a night (available only on the *Onma*). Both shipping companies operating this service have offices in Lolam House beside Vila Post Office, which is where you book: Issachar Dennis & Co. (1st floor), and David Edson and Company (2nd floor). Don't expect any luxuries on these ships—they're extremely basic. If you don't feel up to it, do yourself and the captain a favor by flying. For information on government boats (Marine Dept.) contact the Harbormaster at the Main Wharf. Burns Philp Shipping has several interisland trading ships such as the *Konanda* and the *Kismet*. A 2-week cruise on one of these would be a real adventure, taking you to places few tourists ever see. The B.P. Shipping office will be able to give you an approximation of when the next trip will depart, but you'll have to arrange passage with the captain or purser. If you're serious about going by ship, ask around the wharves opposite the Burns Philp warehouse on the main street.

by bus: No regular public buses travel all the way around Efate I., but fairly frequent citywide public transit runs along 3 routes for a flat v.30: Route I, Tagabe-Vila; Route II, Hotel Le Lagon-Vila; Route III, Hotel Intercontinental via the hospital to Vila. For a little extra the Tagabe bus will take you to the airport. The taxi drivers prevent minibuses from picking up at the airport, so walk down the road a short distance and flag one down. The public buses are the smaller 11-seat minibuses; the bigger 22-seat (usually white) buses are for tourists. Catch them from opposite the Cultural Center. Service is frequent, but the last bus to Tagabe leaves at 1900.

rentals: I.S. Moped Rentals (tel. 2470), near the start of the road to the Main Wharf, has 50 cc mopeds for v.1300 daily, 100 cc motorcycles v.1700 daily. Both rates include third-party insurance, but a v.3000 deposit and a motorcycle license are required. The mopeds may have difficulty on rough roads and steep slopes, so take the larger bike if you can.

tours: For organized sightseeing tours, go to Frank King's Visitors Club. Their prices are lower than the others, but they offer a wide variety of trips, friendly service, expert commentary, etc. Ask about their "7 Days Open Pass" which allows you take as many trips as you like during one week for a set fee. Included are boat cruises, horseriding, dinners, round-the-island tour, and more. Frank King's glass-bottom boat cruise to Hideaway Island (v.2200 including lunch) on the *L'Espadon 2* is the best of its kind in Vila. There are several opportunities to snorkel (gear provided) and Frank's commentary on coral and marinelife is unsurpassed. Tour Vanuatu, on the other hand, is not recommended.

scuba diving: Port Vila is an ideal base for serious scuba divers. Several efficient operators are based here, and the reefs are only half an hour away from the fine hotels and restaurants of a cosmopolitan city. Efate offers as much as Australia's Great Barrier Reef, but is far more accessible; in fact, Aussies flock to Port Vila to do their diving. And unlike the Barrier Reef, there's no big surf to break up the coral formations. Fresh nutrient seawater constantly cleans and feeds the sealife just offshore, and the visibility is excellent. See lava tubes, huge table corals, coral columns, clown fish, and feather starfish. Sharks are rare. The underwater photographer will go octopus here. **operators:** Dive Action (Box 816, Vila), on the waterfront opposite Burns Philp, offers morning and afternoon scuba trips (v.2000) to places like Mele Reef, Cathedral Cavern, and Outboard Reef. They'll also take you to the wreck of the *Star of Russia,* a fully-rigged clipper ship which burned and sank in 1874 near the main wharf. Snorkelers are welcome along for v.800, gear included. A complete PADI certification course is available for v.20,000. Dive Action takes you out on the *Island Trader,* a converted gun-runner used by Jimmy Stevens and the Australian pirate Ken Castle in their abortive 1982 escape to New Caledonia. Scuba Holidays (Box 875, Vila) at Hideaway Island and the Nautilus Dive Shop (Box 78, Vila) also offer diving trips and certification courses. All 3 companies come highly recommended.

MALAKULA

Shaped like a sitting dog, Malakula is a big 2,053-sq-km island of 15,163 inhabitants. The rugged interior of southern Malakula is inhabited by some of the most traditional tribes on Earth, while the island's E coast features the gentle beauty of continuous coconut plantations. Sharks can be a problem offshore, so get local advice before swimming. It's easy to visit Malakula on your way from Port Vila to Luganville. Air Melanesiae offers stopovers at both Lamap and Norsup for only v.800 extra airfare, or come by ship. Although there are a few basic rest houses, Malakula is more for the adventuresome traveler who requires few amenities.

crafts: Young hogs on Malakula have their upper canines knocked out to allow room for their tusks to grow round into full circles. The tusks sometimes force their way through the pigs' cheeks or even jawbones. These great spiral tusks are extracted and polished after the hog's death and used in crafting bracelets, anklets, pendants, and masks. Headdresses with bulging eyes and upcurving tusks, worn by initiates into men's fraternities, are formed from tree fern trunks. Some masks are 4-sided, all sides showing the same face. Death masks are made by molding vegetable paste over a skull. Painted masks with hair of bleached banana fiber are worn in rites to in-

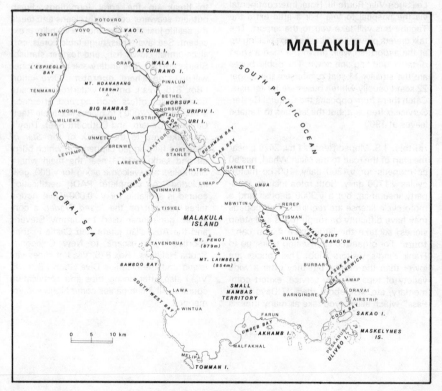

MALAKULA

a brightly-colored Malakula helmet mask worn during secret society initiation ceremonies to a higher grade

crease the yield of yams. Wooden puppets play a part in myths of death and resurrection. Carved figures stand before dwellings to show social rank.

Lamap: Lamap, at the SE corner of Malakula, adjoins Port Sandwich where Capt. Cook came ashore to a friendly welcome. Port Sandwich is the best harbor in Vanuatu, as it affords protection from all winds and has a good holding ground. There's a lovely view of the area from the wharf, 3 km W of the police station. You'll probably arrive at the airstrip near Dravai village, 5 km S of the police station. Lopevi Island's volcanic cone looms exotically behind Paama I. in the distance. Camp on the grass beside the airstrip or proceed N to Lamap, where a small Council Rest House (v.200 pp) adjoins the police station. Bread and other supplies are available from local stores. Ambrym I. is just NE of Lamap, but speedboats across are rare.

Norsup: Norsup airstrip is midway between Lakatoro and Norsup, the former British and French District Headquarters in N.E. Malakula. There's a Council Rest House (v.600) with cooking facilities at Norsup, but you may have to visit the council offices in Lakatoro, 7 km S, to be admitted. There's also a privately-owned tourist bungalow and restaurant, a Ballande supermarket, the PRV store, and a Coop. Market days at Norsup are Wed. and Saturday. There are many French-speaking villages on the coast N of Norsup and on small offshore islands: ships between Norsup and Luganville (v.1000) call at them several times a week. It's possible to walk along the shore from Norsup to Tautu village near the airport — beautiful white Aop Beach is right at the end of the airstrip. Visit Lakatoro where there's a traditional-style open-air courthouse near the government offices. A longer walk is from Norsup through the forest to the timber mill and cocoa project at Larevet (15 km OW). There's a trail S along the coast from Larevet to Vinmavis, where a new road cuts back across to the E coast. Many convivial and picturesque red-and-green parrots are seen around here.

THE BIG NAMBAS

These were the last tribesmen of Vanuatu to be touched by Western civilization. Now only about a dozen of the once-feared Big Nambas are left on the plateau at Amokh in the NW of the island; over the past 25 years the rest have moved down to the coastal villages of Tenmaru, Leviamp, and Brenwe to escape savage tribal fighting, and to take advantage of the expanded opportunities of the coastal areas. Up until the 1930s there was almost constant internecine warfare among the 500-odd tribesmen of that time, and cannibalism was frequently practiced (the last occurred about 35 years ago). Strange rites still remain: the men continue to barter yams and pigs for women, and if a man values his wife highly he may do her honor in an expensive, secret ritual. In this ceremony a selected tribesman knocks out the woman's 2 front teeth, considered great prizes by virtuous Big Namba

Chief Virhambat (left) rules the Big Nambas from Amokh village, N. Malakula.

women. These women still wear a large head-dress of red fibers, and the men wear a wide bark belt and a large red penis sheath (*namba*)—from which the tribe derives its name.

getting there: A 20-km road links Norsup to Amokh, where Chief Virhambat and his 7 wives reside. A taxi to Amokh will run v.5000

RT; even then you're not sure Virhambat and the others will be around to see you when you arrive. Of course you could walk, and the Chief is fairly friendly, allowing travelers to stay in his guest house in exchange for gifts of tinned food. You must pay for photos, however: v.500 for ordinary villagers, and v.1000 for Chief Virhambat himself.

THE SMALL NAMBAS

The jungles of the interior of S. Malakula are home to the Small Nambas. Because no missionaries penetrated here, the 400-500 tribesmen living in many scattered villages have retained their primitive customs right up to today. The men wear a small *namba* made of banana leaf. They are famous for their gaudy face-masks and body paint worn during funeral rites. No roads penetrate their territory, although they sometimes come down to Mbwitin and South West Bay to trade. There are many taboos, including one established by the Vanuatu Government which prohibits tourists from visiting them. Serious researchers are sometimes given permission, however. Apply to the Vila Cultural Center, Box 184, Vila, at least 6 months in advance. There will be a US$500 processing charge.

ESPIRITU SANTO

With 4,010 sq km, Espiritu Santo is Vanuatu's largest island. Mt. Tabwemasana (1,879 m) is the highest peak in the country. It's believed that still-uncontacted pygmy tribes reside in the impassable interior jungles. Espiritu Santo has played a central role in the history of the country, from Quiros' 1606 settlement on Big Bay to the giant support base set up by the Americans during WW II and the Bow and Arrow Rebellion of 1980. Wusi on the W coast (accessible only by ship) is the source of some of Vanuatu's only native pottery. The island possesses great economic potential and most of Vanuatu's exports of copra are shipped from Luganville, yet development has stagnated since independence. This beautiful island has much to offer the visitor, including untouched beaches, wild jungle hikes, friendly country villages, good communications, and an attractive, untouristed main town. A visit is recommended.

airport: Pekoa Airport (SON), between Luganville and Palikulo, is 5 km E of town. Pekoa is a reconditioned WW II airstrip, one of 5 remaining in the area. There's a v.1000 departure tax on flights to Honiara. There's no airport bus, but taxis (v.200) are sometimes available. If none are around, someone will offer you a ride—it's that kind of place.

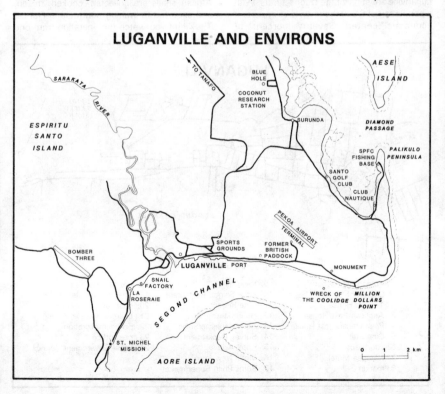

LUGANVILLE AND ENVIRONS

LUGANVILLE

Apart from Port Vila, Luganville is the only town of any consequence in Vanuatu. It lies at the SE corner of the island on the Segond Channel, a 13-km-long waterway which offers anchorages sheltered enough for a ship to ride out a hurricane. The locals call Luganville "Canal" because of this strait, while to people in Vila it's simply "Santo." Coconut crabs scamper through the plantations W of town at dusk. Magic mushrooms abound in the cow pastures E of Luganville and there's a small plot in the field where cattle are tethered past the Dept. of Lands near the post office. During WW II, 100,000 U.S. servicemen were stationed here, at 3 bomber airfields and 2 fighter strips, and a major dry dock functioned at Palikulo. Today many of the buildings in Luganville are still vintage Quonset huts. With a population of 6,000 the town is an important economic center. Seventy percent of

Vanuatu's copra passes through Luganville's docks, and there's a meat cannery. The 1980 independence disturbances seriously disrupted the local economy, however, and things have been slow getting back to normal.

sights: There's an attractive park along Segond Channel near the mouth of the Sarakata River; it adjoins the new town hall and market. Cross the metal bridge over the river and walk SW toward St. Michel Mission (1912), 4.5 km from town. Until WW II, Luganville occupied the W bank of the river; the E bank, site of the present downtown, was a marsh reclaimed by the Americans in 1942. You pass the French high school at Saint Louis and just before La Roseraie, 2 km from Luganville, is the access road to the town's strangest sight: the snail factory, where Giant African snails are collected, cooked, frozen, and exported to waiting gourmets in France. They'll let you watch the operation from one

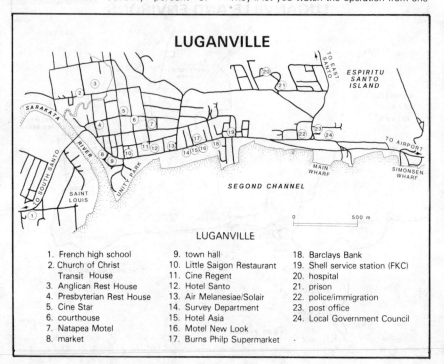

LUGANVILLE

1. French high school
2. Church of Christ Transit House
3. Anglican Rest House
4. Presbyterian Rest House
5. Cine Star
6. courthouse
7. Natapea Motel
8. market
9. town hall
10. Little Saigon Restaurant
11. Cine Regent
12. Hotel Santo
13. Air Melanesiae/Solair
14. Survey Department
15. Hotel Asia
16. Motel New Look
17. Burns Philp Supermarket
18. Barclays Bank
19. Shell service station (FKC)
20. hospital
21. prison
22. police/immigration
23. post office
24. Local Government Council

Abandon ship! Troops are taken off the USAT President Coolidge, *which hit a mine off Santo on 25 Oct. 1942. The wreck is now a favorite of scuba divers.*

side, so long as you don't interfere by distracting the employees. Two beached wrecks at La Roseraie are worth inspecting, but take care—they're rusted. Yachts often anchor near the old wharf here. The road inland just S of La Roseraie leads steeply up to Bomber Three (2 km), another abandoned WW II airfield.

Palikulo Peninsula: The area E of Luganville as far as the Palikulo Peninsula is usually done as a daytrip. About a km beyond the airport turnoff, near the monument to Capt. Elwood J. Euart, 103 Field Artillery Battalion (1942), is a road to the shore of Segond Channel. The wreck of the USAT *President Coolidge,* a 32,000-ton pre-war luxury liner converted into a troop ship, lies on an angle at the edge of the reef here, the bow 18 m underwater. The *Coolidge* sank in 1942 when it hit a mine in its haste to get into port without a pilot. Capt. Euart became the only casualty when he went below at the last minute to get something he had forgotten and the ship sank. A km farther along the coastal road is Million Dollar Point, where the U.S. forces dumped immense quantities of war materiel just before their departure from Espiritu Santo. The local planters refused an American offer to sell

them the equipment at a give-away rate, thinking they'd get it all for free. But a ramp was built out into the water and all rolling stock driven off the end. Today, rusting metal and Coke bottles litter the coast for hundreds of meters in both directions. After another 4.5 km on the coastal road, take the turnoff to the R which leads N to the plant of the South Pacific Fishing Company. A short distance up this road is the Club Nautique, with a beach, picnic area, toilet, and shower. The caretaker allows you to camp here for v.200 pp daily; cruising yachts pay the same to anchor offshore and use the facilities. The Japanese-owned fishing base, 2 km N of the club at the end of the road, freezes and exports large quantities of fish brought in by Taiwanese fishing boats. There are no tours of the large cold storage, 2 slipways, and repairing plant, although it's unlikely anyone will object to your looking around. The canteen across the field from the plant office sells big bottles of Japanese sake (v.550).

PRACTICALITIES

stay: Hotel Asia opposite Burns Philp looks basic, but at v.1000 d with private bath it's not bad. The rooms on the R are quieter than those on the left. Beware of weekends and holidays, however, when the adjacent disco roars until 0300, or go in and roar with 'em! Say you're a hotel guest and can't sleep—they'll probably let you in for free. The Motel New Look nearby has 6 rooms with cooking facilities at v.2000 s or d. Only half the rooms have a/c and private bath, yet the price is the same for all. Look for the manager behind the building if the store is closed. The Natapoa Motel near the courthouse is primarily for long stays, but pleasant rooms with kitchen, bath, and shower are sometimes available at v.2000 s or d. Several of the missions offer accommodations: the Church of Christ Transit House is v.600 pp and you can cook; the Anglican Church nearby has a similar arrangement; there's a Presbyterian Rest House (v.300 pp) about a block away with cooking but no electric lights. All 3 are just up from the market. For information on the Council Rest House, contact the Local Government Council office near the post office. Avoid pretentious, overpriced Hotel Santo.

food and entertainment: The best restaurant is the Little Saigon, opposite Unity Park. Prices are low and the Vietnamese dishes worth trying. The snack bar at Burns Philp offers meat pies, sandwiches, and cold drinks, but groceries are a better buy. The Chinese stores are much cheaper than Burns Philp however, and they stay open till sundown even weekends and holidays. Get a plate of beef and rice for v.70 at the back of

a tangle of vines on one of Vanuatu's mighty banyans

the market on market days (Tues., Thurs., and Sat.). Cine Regent (v.120), a reconditioned Quonset hut behind Hotel Santo, shows French films; Cine Star (v.140) near the courthouse runs English films. Apart from the disco beside Hotel Asia (Fri. and Sat. 2100-0300), the Rotona Bar is good for its cold beer and hot juke box, when it's not operating as a pool room.

services: There are several banks. The hospital accepts outpatient consultations weekdays 0700-1000. The Immigration office is at Police Headquarters near the post office. The Survey Department opposite Burns Philp sells topographical maps. The rough can be very rough on the front 9 holes at the Santo Golf Club; watch for crocodiles near the 7th tee.

TRANSPORT

by air: Air Melanesiae flies direct from Santo to Vanua Lava, Aoba, Pentecost, Malakula, and Port Vila. Solair has a twice-weekly flight from Espiritu Santo to Honiara. Book this one well ahead as the plane only carries 12 passengers. Solair doesn't accept international mileage tickets.

by ship: The shipping companies operating the Luganville-Port Vila passenger service don't maintain offices here, so you have to go on board and deal directly with the captain. There are 3 departures a week, stopping at many smaller islands along the way. Burns Philp Shipping beside the supermarket only handles cargo, but they'll be able to tell you when the various ships are due in port. You might get on the *Kismet,* a Burns Philp trading ship which does 2-week trips out of Santo collecting copra. Many other cargo ships tie up at the Simonsen Wharf, just E of Luganville, and something leaves almost every day. Just go down to the wharf and start asking.

by road: There is no bus service on Espiritu Santo. A taxi to the airport is v.200, to Palikulo v.500. The locals travel by trucks, which gather at Luganville market. Tuesday is market day for the S. Santo people, so you

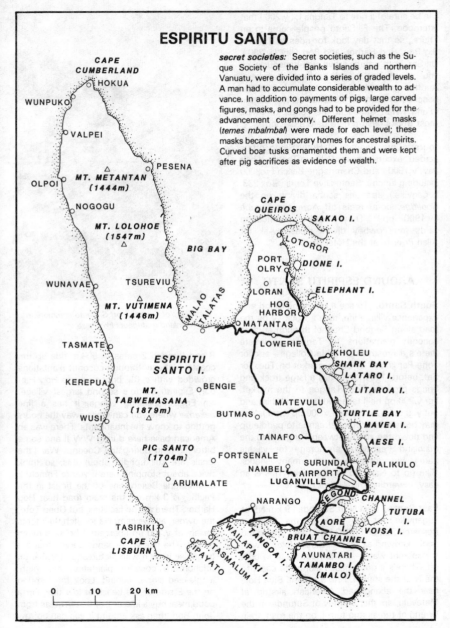

ESPIRITU SANTO

secret societies: Secret societies, such as the Suque Society of the Banks Islands and northern Vanuatu, were divided into a series of graded levels. A man had to accumulate considerable wealth to advance. In addition to payments of pigs, large carved figures, masks, and gongs had to be provided for the advancement ceremony. Different helmet masks (*temes mbalmbal*) were made for each level; these masks became temporary homes for ancestral spirits. Curved boar tusks ornamented them and were kept after pig sacrifices as evidence of wealth.

CAPE CUMBERLAND
HOKUA
WUNPUKO
VALPEI
PESENA
OLPOI
MT. METANTAN (1444m)
NOGOGU
MT. LOLOHOE (1547m)
BIG BAY
CAPE QUEIROS
SAKAO I.
LOTOROR
PORT OLRY
DIONE I.
LORAN
ELEPHANT I.
HOG HARBOR
MATANTAS
MALAO
TALATAS
TSUREVIU
WUNAVAE
MT. VUTIMENA (1446m)
LOWERIE
TASMATE
KHOLEU
SHARK BAY
LATARO I.
ESPIRITU SANTO I.
LITAROA I.
KEREPUA
BENGIE
MT. TABWEMASANA (1879m)
MATEVULU
TURTLE BAY
MAVEA I.
BUTMAS
WUSI
TANAFO
AESE I.
PIC SANTO (1704m)
FORTSENALE
SURUNDA
PALIKULO
NAMBEL
AIRPORT
ARUMALATE
LUGANVILLE
NARANGO
SEGOND CHANNEL
TUTUBA I.
AORE I.
VOISA I.
TASIRIKI
WAILAPA
TANGOA I.
BRUAT CHANNEL
CAPE LISBURN
TASMALUM
ARAKI I.
IPAYATO
AVUNATARI
TAMAMBO I. (MALO)

0   10   20 km

can be sure of a ride to Tangoa I. (v.200) that afternoon. The E. Santo people come in on Thurs., so that day look for rides to Tanafo, Big Bay, Hog Harbor, and Port Olry (v.200). On Sat. both groups arrive simultaneously, so you might get a ride almost anywhere. Another good place to wait for rides are the benches in front of the Shell service station (Fung Kwan Chee) in the center of town. Most trucks gas up here before leaving.

tours: Tour Vanuatu at Hotel Santo offers guided excursions to Palikulo/Tanafo (half day, v.1500) and Champagne Beach (v.3000 including lunch). Santo Dive Tours (Box 233, Luganville) arranges scuba diving on the *Coolidge,* or at reefs off Aore and Tutuba (v.1900 pp). They require certification cards—no cowboy divers please! Ask for Allan Powers at the Hotel Santo.

AROUND ESPIRITU SANTO

South Santo: To see a bit of the island and experience village life, take a truck W on the road along Segond Channel through endless coconut plantations to Tangoa I., where there's a Presbyterian Bible College—ask for John Pama Vari at Santo market on Tues. or Sat. before 1500. John has a large truck and brings produce from Tangoa to the market. For v.200 pp he'll take you back with him and put you up in his house (v.500 pp extra). You may borrow his outrigger canoe to paddle up and down the strait between Tangoa and the mainland (excellent anchorage for yachts here), but don't swim—too many sharks. Hike up to Narango for the view. This is an easy, rewarding trip—don't miss it.

East Santo: Just N of Surunda (9 km NE of Luganville) at the back of the Coconut Research Station (IRHO) is a deep, spring-fed pool known as the "Blue Hole," with transparent water—the perfect place to cool off. There's a good beach along the coast to the N of the station. Find a second Blue Hole near the abandoned American airstrip at Matevulu, another 9 km N of Surunda: at the W end of the airstrip turn L on the road, then

Residents of Tangoa I. off S. Santo commute to the mainland in dugouts like these.

R and through 2 gates. A 50-km ride up the coastal highway through coconut plantations crowded with cattle brings you to Hog Harbor, Espiritu Santo's second largest village. An English-speaking village, it has a fine *nakamal* where you can while away the hours getting to know the inhabitants. There was an American base here during WW II and some bitter fighting during the Coconut War (the locals are still uptight about this, so think twice about stopping here if you're French!). Champagne Beach, one of the finest in the Pacific, is 3 km off the main road near Hog Harbor. There are no facilities, but Obed Toto, the owner, allows campers to pitch their tents for about v.200 pp (bargain if he asks much more). The fine white sands curve around a turquoise lagoon with picturesque Elephant I. offshore, a coconut plantation and high, jungle-clad slopes behind. Look for a spring on the E side of the beach at low tide. For a good meal buy a kilo or 2 of frozen steak from John Bori, then ask around if you can borrow someone's kitchen to cook it in. Share with them. Or take it back to the campsite and have a beach barbecue, but please don't litter this wonderful place. At the end of the road 13 km N of Hog Harbor is the French-speaking community of Port Olry with its large Catholic mission. Ask the Father for permission to camp on the beach. This granted, he will ask you to also pay a courtesy call on Chief Pascal. The site is idyllic and there are 2 lakes on nearby Dione I., accessible on foot at low tide. Swim in a transparent, spring-fed pool, inland before the second gate on the track N from the village. Visit Rennet wharf for the view, or climb the bush track W of Port Olry for a panorama of the entire area.

into the interior: Tanafo, 22 km N of Luganville, was the center of the 1980 Santo Rebellion. The NaGriamel Custom Movement met in the thatched meeting house and Jimmy Stevens was captured as he sat under the immense banyan tree drinking *kava*. Today, it's quieter and tourists are even bused in to see traditional dances and similar activities. There is a large waterfall near here. A bush road continues N from Tanafo toward Big

Bay, but there's very little traffic. Just before the steep descent to Matantas, this road meets another road from the E coast near Hog Harbor through Lowerie. It was at Matantas on Big Bay that the Spanish *conquistador* Quiros established his "New Jerusalem" in 1606. A wall 8 m long with 2 gun openings, near the point where the Matantas River empties into the bay, is reputed to date from this time. If one is *very* keen (and a bit crazy), it's possible to walk from Big Bay to Wailapa in S. Santo in 6 hard days. It's damp and slippery, and you'll have to cross fast rivers up to your neck, but you'll see some of the most remote people in the Pacific. Don't go during the rainy season (Jan. to April) if you're not into drowning. You can buy food from villagers along the way, but you'll need a strong stomach. Take plenty of stick tobacco to give them. A guide, of course, would be required. Ask for Chief Robert at Talatas. Longer, but less rigorous, is the walk along the coast to Cape Cumberland. In fact, it's possible to hike right around Espiritu Santo this way if you're experienced and well-equipped. This is as far off the "beaten" track as you can get in the South Pacific.

The mature puffball (Calvatia gardneri) bursts when touched and discharges a brown powder. This edible mushroom tastes best when sliced and fried.

ERROMANGO

Although rugged and untouristed, Erromango is easily accessible as a stopover between Port Vila and Tanna. Better yet, there are 2 airstrips on Erromango, and flights in each direction land at Dillon's Bay twice a week and Ipota weekly. This makes it possible to arrive at one, hike across the island, and leave from the other. It's not easy though, and you'll probably need a guide part of the way. A minimum of 3 (preferably 4) days is required to do this. There are lots of ups and downs, so pack light. A tent is essential — you can't always count on staying with the locals. Water is available at villages, but bring your own food, as well as stick tobacco for gifts. Erromango has practically no roads: the one from Dillon's Bay airstrip to Unpongkor village is the only one regularly used. Maps show a network of logging roads spreading out from Ipota, but these are totally overgrown and difficult to follow even on foot. Besides, there are no motor vehicles at Ipota, and only 3 at Dillon's Bay. The locals travel around the island by outboard speedboat (expensive) or on trails through the bush. If you begin your hike from the Dillon's Bay side, you'll go to Ipota via Happy Land; from Ipota hike N to Potnarvin and W to Dillon's Bay. Either way,

you'll be able to do the first half of the walk on your own, and find a guide to take you across the island more easily at Happy Land or Potnarvin. Offer about v.1000 for this service. Tim Thorpe, who spent 2 years on Erromango, offers this advice, however: "Be warned of three things — first, not all 'guides' know the tracks as well as they claim; secondly, the Erromangan can go all day on a spoonful of water, no food and little rest; and thirdly, 'klosup' to and Erromangan generally translates as 'longwe' to non-Erromangan.

Dillon's Bay: A truck sometimes meets the flights at Dillon's Bay airstrip and carries passengers 8 km in to Unpongkor village for about v.200 pp. The road drops sharply into the William River Valley. Mr. William Mete has a native hut without electricity or running water in the center of the village, v.800 pp to stay, meals v.1000 extra, half price for locals and government employees. Make sure the price you pay is clearly understood before agreeing to stay here. If you're planning an early start the next morning, forget breakfast or you'll waste half the morning waiting. There's a small coop store nearby. You could also camp on the grass beside the

village housing at Rampunrungo, Erromango

river or just set out and camp up on the plateau. The village is beautifully situated in a deep valley at the river mouth. As the sun sets across the Coral Sea, you know you've reached one of the farthest ends of the earth. Plaques in the church at Dillon's Bay commemorate the martyrdom of John Williams and James Harris (1839), George and Ellen Gordon (1861), and George's brother, James Gordon (1872). On the other side of the river in the village cemetery are monuments to these well-meaning missionaries, killed in reaction to the abuses of the early 19th C. sandalwood traders, as well as to diseases the messengers of God themselves helped introduce. From a population of 6,000 in the early 1800s, Erromango plummeted to 400 by 1930 and has only 932 inhabitants today. Many Erromangans were carried off to labor in the Australian canefields and those few who returned brought back further disease and discord. Old burial caves dot the cliffs along the W and S coasts.

Dillon's Bay to Ponumbia: An experienced hiker should have little trouble going from Dillon's Bay to Ponumbia on his own. After a steep climb up a jeep track from Dillon's Bay, you travel S across an open plateau. Two hours along there's an obvious fork in the road. The track to the L goes up to the telecommunications tower atop Mt. Fetmongkum (636 m). Keep straight. About 10 min. beyond this junction there's a straight, level stretch for about 200 m, followed by a sharp R turn in the road, which descends to a lighthouse on the coast. The footpath to Happy Land is straight ahead at the curve. You go through an enchanted forest and after about an hour, climb up to Buniakup, the first settlement. Beyond Tamsel there's a steep descent to a hamlet at the mouth of the Pongkil River. Have a swim and rest up for the sharp climb back to the plateau. The terrain levels out on top and you walk for a couple of hours through a string of traditional settlements, all the way to Ponumbia. Sunday is a good day to visit this area as most people will be relaxing at home and happy to talk to you. There's a good view of the coast from the cow pasture at Potlusi.

onward to Ipota: Beyond Ponumbia the trail to Ipota is much more difficult to follow; consider hiring a guide. The villagers in this area have to walk that whole route to Dillon's Bay to buy soap and kerosene, so it shouldn't be too hard to convince someone to go to the coop at Ipota instead. It's a fairly strenuous 10-hour-walk from Ponumbia to Ipota with a guide, 1.5 days at least without. Only go alone if you're very experienced—even then at times you'll think you're lost. After a moderately steep descent 40 min. out of Ponumbia, you come to a dip in the trail. At the far top of the dip, just before the final descent to South River, look for the branch trail to Ipota leading up to the left. About 5 min. along this trail you come to a T-junction. Keep L and pass through a garden. After an hour there's an extremely steep descent to a tributary of the South River (knee deep). The climb on the other side is less severe. About 15 min. along the level trail on top there's a turnoff to the R to South River. Keep straight. After another 10 min. you reach Punmoungo, the only settlement between Ponumbia and Ipota. Keep R after Punmoungo and follow a creek to a small river. If you think you've lost the way, go upstream 500 m and keep looking on the right. About an hour out of Pun-moungo you enter a logged-out area, stripped of *kauri* and *tamanu* from 1966-73 by a French company. Between this point and Ipota you're on and off logging roads several times. Often you descend through the forest on shortcuts, and must cross 2 small rivers. Precise instructions are hard to give, as they would be lengthy and perhaps confusing. Even the 1:100,000 survey map is of little use. A compass and sense of direction are more helpful. If you think you're lost, backtrack a little or work your way up and down the river till you find a trail in the right direction. When you reach a burned-off area which has been sloppily replanted in *cordia,* you're near Ipota.

Ipota to Dillon's Bay: The E side of Erromango gets more rain than the W and there are lush forests and huge banyans. Visit the wreck of a tugboat carried 500 m up the river estuary during a hurricane, just S of Ipota airstrip, and find your way through the village to the coast for a good view of Urantop across Cooks Bay. A swimming hole has been blasted out of the raised reef here. At Ipota, camp on the grass beside the airstrip, right in the middle of the forestry settlement. There are 2 poorly-stocked stores. In a couple of hours you can do Ipota to death. If you've got a day to kill, hike S to Ifo village in 3 hours. The hike N to Potnarvin takes less than a day. You'll need someone to get you started, but the route generally follows the coast till you reach a river at the NW corner of Cooks Bay. Wade across the river and go along the beach about 15 min. where you find a trail leading inland to Potnarvin, one of the nicest spots on the island. There's a basic rest house (v.150) in Potnarvin, a pleasant beach, and a waterfall nearby. An excellent sidetrip can be made to the top of Urantop (837 m), though it's often cloud-covered. On a clear day the view is superb. Between Potnarvin and Dillon's Bay is "dark bush" — *tamanu*-dominated primary rainforest and no villages, so you'll probably need a guide to take you across. There are a few small rivers to ford. This is probably the best walk in Vanuatu for seeing many different types of vegetation. There are many other possibilities for hikers on Erromango, such as Potnarvin to Rampunalvat (guide unnecessary), Rampunalvat to Elizabeth Bay (guide essential), and Antioch to Ifo then on to Ipota (guide optional).

the wreck of the tug Angelique *at Ipota, Erromango*

dancers at Yaohnanen, Tanna

TANNA

Vanuatu's second most visited island (after Efate), Tanna is renowned for its active volcano, potent *kava,* custom villages, cargo cultists, exciting festivals, strong traditions, magnificent wild horses, long black beaches, gigantic banyans, and daytripping packaged tourists. There's an ancient Tannese myth that a great white ship will someday anchor offshore and the wealth of the world will be transfered to the beach for them to enjoy without working. Now this millennium seems to have arrived, as affluent white visitors line up and pay good money to look at anything and everything of interest on the island. Adventurers, trying to get away from the funfair, zoo-like environment of the world's tinsel strips, must contend with operators who consider them a resource to be exploited, and locals who are used to being paid fat bucks to smile for the camera. All is not lost, however, as tourists and their guides rarely walk far. Leave the roads and you'll enter a wonderland of charming, innocent people living close to nature as their ancestors did before them. The island is heavily populated and well-used trails crisscross the landscape. Here the real Tanna remains, almost untouched by a century and a half of traders, missionaries, officials, and other visitors.

politics: Tanna is divided into warring factions: the people on the E side of the island against those on the W, Protestants against each other and the Catholics, French-educated against English-educated, village against village. There is extreme jealousy of anyone who seems to be getting ahead. Villagers around Yasur Volcano argue over who is to get the tourists' money, and tour buses are often turned back by rival groups and prevented from seeing the volcano. Guides hassle visitors who decline to join their tours or stay in the tourist bungalows. One fellow named Sam is especially obnoxious. You'll be accosted more often around Lenakel on the W coast, however, so it's best to spend as little time there as possible and proceed directly to the E coast as soon as you arrive. Beware of crooked taxi drivers. Tanna is still well worth visiting, but be forewarned.

kava: Every village has its *nakamal,* an open area surrounded by gigantic banyan trees, where the men gather nightly to drink *kava.* Tanna *kava* is strong and sudden. One cup has the effect of a few tokes of hash. Two cups will knock you out. The roots are first chewed into a pulp, spit out on a green leaf, then mixed with a little water and squeezed

Sulphur Bay villagers before a Jon Frum cross

through a coconut frond into a cup to be drunk all at once. If one touches any part of the campfire during the ceremony, it's thought that his house will burn down. After finishing the *kava* one must speak only in a whisper; to do otherwise is extremely bad manners. Women are forbidden to take part in this gathering or even to see it. If they're caught, they must pay a fine of one large pig and one good *kava* root. In the old days they would have been put to death.

events: Custom dances are held on the occasion of marriages, circumcisions (many in July), etc. Ask around to find out where the next one will be held. The most important festival of the year is the Nekowiar Festival with its famous Toka Dance. This may be held in Aug. or around the end of the year. The Toka celebrates the circumcision of young boys, and is accompanied by pig-killing, feasting, and dancers with painted faces and grass skirts—the works. Admission is only v.3000 to attend this stirring event.

the Jon Frum cargo cult: Although the Tannese were declared converted to Presbyterianism in the early years of this century, in the '40s they invented their own religion. Three cults worshipping a god named Jon Frum have sprung up. Several theories attempt to explain the exact origin of the cults and the

meaning of the name Jon Frum, but all agree that the sight of huge quantities of war materiel and black soldiers in 1942 was catalytic. One theory holds that an American pilot, Jon Frum, unloaded supplies here. For reasons unknown, they were never used for the war effort, but given to the Tannese. Their animistic beliefs eroded and confused by rival Christian sects, the villagers assumed Frum was some kind of god coming from across the sea to bring them wealth in abundance. They did, however, learn that he was an American (John "from" America). A couple of years later an American medical officer comes into the story. The Tannese automatically connected him with Jon Frum, and took the Red Cross Medical Corps insignia on his uniform as the symbol of their new-found religion. Today the villages N of Yasur Volcano and elsewhere are dotted with little red crosses neatly surrounded by picket fences, bearing witness to this extraordinary chain of events. The priests and prophets of these cargo cults are called "messengers" and they foretell the return of the ships laden with cargo for *Man Tanna*, escorted by Jon Frum, the reincarnation of an ancient deity. Towers with tin cans strung from wires, imitating radio stations, were erected so Jon Frum could speak to his people. The movement declares that money must be thrown away, pigs killed, gardens left uncared for, since all material wealth will be provided in the end by Jon Frum. It's felt that missionaries and government administrators have interfered with this Second Coming, thus the movement sometimes manifests itself in non-cooperation with them. The authorities have arrested cult leaders from time to time and jailed them in Port Vila, but new devotees spring up to take their place. There's also a Prince Philip cult on Tanna, fostered recently by 2 strange acts: Prince Philip himself writing in support, and the Vanuatu government publishing a postage stamp bearing his image.

SIGHTS

Yasur Volcano: The chief attraction of Tanna, 30 km from the airstrip in the eastern part of the island, Yasur (361 m) is one of the most

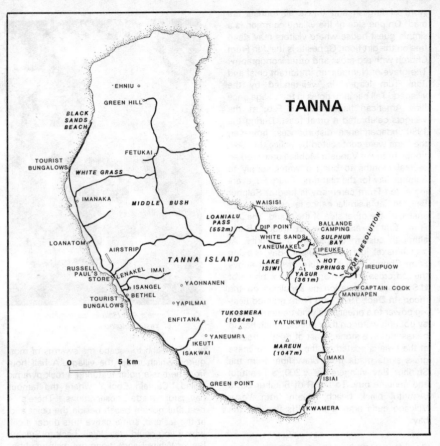

accessible of its kind in the world. A road goes almost to the summit on the mountain's S side to accommodate the tour groups, but it's a superior experience to climb the path up the N slope, to the L between the vegetation and the ashfield (40 min.). Either way, you'll pay v.240-500 or more to the "Volcano Committee." The slopes are scattered with boulders considered sacred by the Tannese, and black dust from the crater covers everything for kilometers. A barren ash plain surrounds it, with Lake Isiwi to the east. Views down into the crater are quite spectacular—steam and masses of black ash seethe furiously, discharging cinders and rocks, while gas

burns your throat. The sulphur fumes can be choking, the noise deafening. At 940 degrees C, it hisses, rumbles, and spits, constantly erupting in minor explosions which emit small filaments of volcanic glass called "Pele's Hair." Cargo cultists believe that Jon Frum lives beneath the fires of Yasur where he commands an army of 5,000 men. Some days are better for viewing than others, depending on smoke, wind, etc. Yasur is especially impressive at night.

Sulphur Bay: Just N of Yasur is Sulphur Bay village, stronghold of the Jon Frum cargo cult. The chief is a funny old guy who speaks not a word of English and thinks all tourists are mad! On one side of the village common is a simple guest house where visitors may sleep free on the dirt floor. Opposite is the Jon Frum Church with red cross and other iconography. The grave of Nampus, an important chief and Jon Frum leader, is well-tended by the villagers. Tall bamboo poles in the village once flew American flags each 15 Feb. as the villagers celebrated a great feast. During the 1980 independence disturbances, however, the flags were confiscated by police. In 1984, troops from the Vanuatu Mobile Force worked several months to bring a water supply to Sulphur Bay for the first time. Every Fri. evening a Jon Frum ceremony is held at Sulphur Bay. On Sat. a similar dance takes place at Imanaka, on the other side of the island. The Jon Frum Cult is also active at Middle Bush, although custom people are a majority. At Yaneumakel, just above Sulphur Bay, is a Jon Frum Church with a picture of Christ above the red cross and a magazine color photo of U.S. space exploration personalities on the moon. In Dec., 1976, Jon Frum granted healing power to a priest here who treated the sick by pouring water on their heads, which had to be resting on a stone. A list of people treated at the time is posted on the L wall. Purchase grass skirts made from *braw* fiber from the Sulphur Bay villagers for v.300, a beautiful and genuine buy. To the R of Sulphur Bay's beautiful black beach, steam from Yasur Volcano curls among the cliffs flanking the bay.

Port Resolution: Hike from Sulphur Bay straight over the mountains on a footpath to Port Resolution (2 hours). The hotsprings (v.100), which the locals use for cooking, are at the NW end of the beach near the cliffs. The locals can call a *dugong* (cowfish) named Chief Kaufis from the sea nearby for v.200. Captain Cook sailed into this bay in 1774 and named it after his ship. The locals wouldn't allow him to visit Yasur Volcano. Port Resolution is useless to shipping today because an eruption in 1878 raised the area 20 m, and silt blocked the anchorage. Continue in to Ireupuow village and have a look at the splendid high white beach. The locals sleep in huts

Tanna's Ash Plain in the shadow of Yasur Volcano

on this beach to escape the swarms of mosquitos which infest the village. A half hour from here is a point featuring a rock pyramid called "Captain Cook," where the famous navigator made observations. There's a beautiful golden beach beside the point and, at the far end, some native huts under a cliff where you could stay. Walk back to Sulphur Bay or White Sands along the main road between Lake Isiwi and Yasur. Immense banyan trees line the way.

across the island: There's little of interest in Lenakel, the administrative center on the W coast. If you get stuck there, just walk across the island to White Sands on village footpaths. One trail begins near the hospital, another near the Agriculture Station at Isangel (the "Melbourne" trail). The latter path follows a ridge and is an easy uphill walk for about 4 hours, the first half through villages and the second through dense jungle. The last 2 hours or so of the hike is downhill and across the ash plain to either White Sands or Sulphur Bay. These trails are well-known, regularly used, and easy to learn about and follow. A good hiker could make it across in a day. There are many such hikes in both S. and N. Tanna. You'll pass through some of the 92 villages where people still live in the traditional way (no Christians or Jon Frummers). Yaohnanen is the "Custom Village" where the people wear only small *nambas* or grass skirts. For v.300-500, they'll perform 2 or 3 dances involving 10 small teenage boys, plus 2 or 3 elderly men. The *kava* ceremony is about v.100. Ask about magic mushrooms in N. Tanna. The 1:50,000 topographical map is the only guide you need.

PRACTICALITIES

accommodations: The best place to stay on Tanna is White Sands Camping, behind the Ballande store at White Sands. You're within walking distance of all the attractions and there's a nice beach just below the breeze-cooled, grassy bluff which has an excellent view and no mozzies. It's v.250 to pitch your tent or v.500 for a small hut with shared facilities. Ask for Melfen Gideon who can arrange walking tours to the volcano (v.350), Port Resolution (v.300), and a waterfall (v.250). Another place to stay nearby is Semu's Hotel (v.300 pp) in the village behind the Presbyterian church near the Health Center at White Sands. There are 3 rooms in a native-style house where you may cook. Tour operators in Vila and Lenakel will try to prevent you from staying at White Sands and may threaten police action if you attempt to camp. How far they'll actually go is uncertain but be prepared for a heavy experience. On the W coast there are 2 clusters of tourist bungalows, one 5 km S of the airstrip (Russell Paul), the other 12 km N of Lenakel (Chief Tom Numake) on a "nudey" beach. Both have cooking facilities. Russell charges v.3000 d, and is the better of the two; Tom asks v.2000. Tom Numake also runs White Horse Tours, and owns the "wild" horses at White Grass, so pay him v.200 for photos. At either place, make sure there's water before you check in.

food: Apart from the well-stocked Ballande store at White Sands, you'll find a couple of stores at Lenakel near the airstrip. There's still no market building at Lenakel, but the village women spread out their produce on the ground at various locations weekdays. At v.20 a bunch for almost anything, it's the best buy on the island. The biggest market takes place beside Russell Paul's store on Mondays. The Lenus lapin Restaurant, at the corner of the Airport Road and the W coast highway, serves simple meals of rice and meat for v.100.

transport: Tanna's airport is a 15-min. walk from Lenakel. Only Tour Vanuatu passengers are permitted to use the toilets at the airport. Tour Vanuatu is not recommended. Minibus transfers to Russell Paul's bungalows are v.300 pp RT. You can also come from Port Vila by ship: look for a boat going direct to the E coast (Waisisi, White Sands, Port Resolution). A couple of minibuses offer unscheduled service between Lenakel and White Sands (v.150 pp) a couple of times every weekday. Be prepared to wait. It's essential to fix the price with taxi-truck drivers before setting out. Even then they may ask more when you arrive. Be polite but firm with them. There is quite a bit of traffic between Lenakel and White Sands, so if you suspect trouble just wait for the next one. Horses can sometimes be rented from the locals.

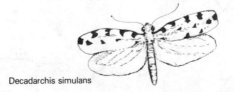

Decadarchis simulans

OTHER ISLANDS

AMBRYM

Ambrym, like Tanna, is famous for its highly active volcanoes and native culture, yet is much less developed touristically. The inhabitants live in the 3 corners of this triangular island, and their only links are by foot and sea. Two of these communities, Craig Cove in the W and Ulei in the E, have airstrips with flights from Port Vila 3 times a week, but N. Ambrym is accessible only by ship.

South Ambrym: Take a plane or ship to Ulei and hike W along the beach on the S coast between the end of the roads at Pawe and Bwele. From near Lalinda you can climb to the vast ash plain near the center of the island.

The village chief collects a v.200 custom fee and can supply a guide for another v.500. Allow 3 hours hard climbing to The Gate (750 m). From here you look across the vast ash plain to Benbow (1,159 m) and Marum (1,270 m).

North Ambrym: North Ambrym is one of the most traditional areas in Vanuatu. Paramount Chief Tofor resides at Fanla. Ask at Ranon about possibilities of climbing Marum from this side. There's a Catholic mission at Olal where you might be able to stay, but leave a donation. From N. Ambrym you can hike S to Ulei, but not SW to Craig Cove, as the way is blocked by lava flows. Vanuatu's best handicrafts come from N. Ambrym, especially the tall slit gongs known as *tam tams*. Craftsmen

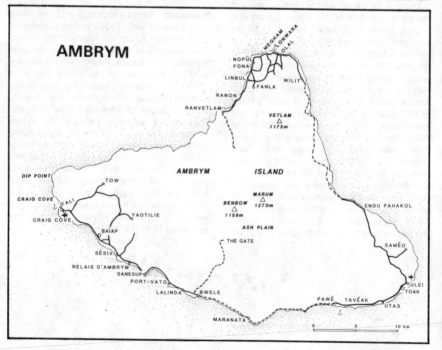

above, clockwise: Taeloa village, Malaita, Solomon Is. (Paul Bohler); saltwater girl, Takwa market, Malaita, Solomon Is. (Rod Buchko); Kanak girls, New Caledonia (New Caledonia Office of Tourism); stockmen, New Caledonia (New Caledonia Office of Tourism); girl of Indonesian descent, New Caledonia (New Caledonia Office of Tourism)

above, clockwise: sunset over Moorea, Eastern Polynesia (Paul Bohler); Paopao, Moorea, Eastern Polynesia (Traugott Goll); arches of Talava, Niue (Government of Niue photo); a *motu*, Eastern Polynesia (Tahiti Tourist Board photo by Tini Colombel); Kilauea Iki, Hawaii Volcanoes National Park, Hawaii (D. Stanley)

carve faces on 2-m logs, then slot and hollow them to be used as signal drums. Great fern figures and bamboo flutes with burnt-in geometric designs are also made. Storytellers on Ambrym use intricate sand drawings to illustrate their tales.

stay: The only hotel on the island is the Relais d'Ambrym, between Craig Cove and Lalinda, 10 km E of the airstrip. There are 6 native-style bungalows with private bath and shower at v.2500 s, v.3000 d, v.3500 t, airport transfer included. It also has a bar/restaurant. Horseback riding and trips to the volcano are arranged. Ask about the traditional sorcerers, who sometimes demonstrate their art to guests. The friendly proprietors, Jean-Pierre and Marie Jo, allow budget travelers to pitch their tents on the premises. There's also a rest house at Craig Cove where you get *lap lap* and rice in the evening, tea and bread in the morning, for a nominal amount.

PENTECOST

Pentecost is renowned for its land diving, a thrilling spectacle on this thickly forested island. Men tie liana vines to their ankles, then jump head-first from atop 25-m man-made towers built around tree trunks, jerking to a halt just centimeters from the ground. Slack in the lifeline vine eases the shock as it stretches to its limit and the jumpers are rarely injured. This daring feat is used to prove manhood, as part of the initiation ceremony for young boys. Even 8-year-olds prove their courage by hurtling themselves from these giddy heights. When the plunging diver is about to smash to the ground, the vines stretch full out. This slows and finally stops his fall just as his head brushes the spaded soil, symbolically refertilizing the earth for the next crop of yams. The diving takes place around April to June, soon after the yam harvest.

practicalities: Tour Vanuatu has taken over the land diving on Pentecost and everyone, even those not on the tour, must pay v.6000 to watch, v.8000 if you have a movie camera. A daytrip from Port Vila to see the show is v.25,000, all-inclusive. The jumps were originally held at Bunlap village, on the SE side of Pentecost, but now they're performed at Wali, about 7 km S of Lonorore airstrip, to spare tourists the exhausting 4-hour hike across the island. Maru Bungalows (Mr. Fargo) at Wali has 2 units with cooking facilities at v.500 s, v.800 d. Any visitors who do make it across to Bunlap are accommodated for v.2000. All flights to Pentecost are via Espiritu Santo.

OTHERS

Aoba: Aoba resembles a capsized canoe, with Maewo and Pentecost the broken outriggers. Three tribes—the Moli, Vira, and Tari—are found here. There are airstrips with service to Espiritu Santo and Pentecost at the 3 corners of Aoba. A good harbor at Lolowai, at the E end of the island, is where the Church of Melanesia headquarters and hospital are located. Longana airstrip is nearby and a Council Rest House is at Sarie Tamata, 5 km away. Aoba is noted for its massive volcanic peak (1,496 m), which contains 2 warm-water lakes in the extinct crater. The lakes are thought to be the eyes of the mountain. The god Tagaro took the fire from these craters and threw it across to neighboring Ambrym. There are 7 islands in the lakes and a fumarole beside one. The mountain is climbed from Ambanga in 3 hours, but it's often socked in by fog and there could be problems about taboos. You could hike 35 km along the N coast from Longana to Walaha and fly out from there.

Banks and Torres: The Banks Is. are noted for their handicrafts and traditional dancers. The main airstrip for the Banks, with service from Espiritu Santo, is at Sola on Vanua Lava. There's a Council Rest House here. Near the airstrip is Port Patteson, a natural harbor with safe anchorage year-round. Jets of steam rise from the hotsprings on the slopes of Mt. Sere'ama (921 m), at the center of Vanua Lava. Santa Maria, a circular island 22 km S of Vanua Lava, also has fumaroles and sulphur springs, as does Ureparapara I., a sunken volcano with a drowned crater that large ships can sail into. At the center of Santa Maria is a deep crater lake drained by a waterfall. Mere Lava and Mota have beautiful symmetrical cones. Surfers should go on to the Torres Is., a remote corner of the Pacific not explored until the mid-1800s.

Anatom: The fortnightly plane from Tanna lands on a sandy islet just off Anatom, and passengers are transfered to the beach by launch. The Rev. John Geddie, the first missionary to establish himself in Vanuatu, arrived in 1848 and built a 1,000-seat church. His efforts were in vain, however, as introduced diseases ravaged the population which soon fell to 800, only 350 of whom were Geddie's converts. Totemic petroglyphs and *kauri* stands are found on Anatom, the southernmost inhabited island in Vanuatu.

Matthew and Hunter: Although these small, uninhabited islands were administered from Port Vila in the Condominium days, then the Vanuatu flag was raised and sovereignty proclaimed on Independence Day, they are also claimed by France. Matthew, 350 km SE of Anatom, is an actively volcanic island a little over a km long. There are 2 peaks separated by a narrow isthmus of sand and ashes: the W peak is older and reaches 177 m, while the younger E peak (142 m) features smoking fumaroles in its rocky crater. Hunter is an abrupt basalt block 297 m high; no anchorage is possible due to great depths. There are sulphur-colored cliffs on the W side. Seabirds are the only inhabitants of both Matthew and Hunter.

CAPSULE BISLAMA VOCABULARY

gut moning — good morning
gut bai — goodbye
yu orait? — how do you do?
wanem nem bilong yu? — what's your name?
nam bilong mi... — my name is...
mi no harim — beg your pardon?
tenk yu tumas — thank you very much
yumi mit wea? — where can we meet?
me les lilbit — I feel a little tired
olgeta samting bilong mi hia — these are my things
wanem taim? — what time is it?
em i lait nau — it's late
tumora — tomorrow

yo no toktok — silence
em i hat smol smol — it's warm
taim i ren — wet season
pusim — push
go insait nating — admission free
em ia haumas? — how much is this?
mi mus paiim long hau mas? — how much should I pay?
em i nap long ten dolas — it's ten dollars
mi tekem emia — I'll take this one
karim olsem yu laik — help yourself
bilong baim — for sale
ol man — mens
ol woman — ladies

wooden mask from S. Pentecost

SOLOMON ISLANDS

INTRODUCTION

One of the last regions to fall under European religious and political control, the Solomon Islands remain today the best-kept secret in the South Pacific. The islanders think of them simply as the "Happy Isles." Government officials and powerful missionaries discourage tourism and, such is their distaste for publicity, that most foreign journalists were barred from the Solomons during the 7-hour 1984 visit of Pope John Paul II to Honiara, the capital, on Guadalcanal. The number of visitors is negligible. Most of those who do come stay only for a few days, mainly in Honiara. Flights into the country are few, accommodations sparse, and reliable information hard to obtain before you arrive. Even yacht traffic is discouraged by the imposition of a $100 "lighthouse fee." Solomon Islanders can be curious to the point of suspicion; you are constantly asked who you are, why you came, where you're going, and why. Unless you're on a tour, travel outside Honiara is an unstructured, make-your-own-arrangements

affair, which makes the Solomons a land of adventure. Travelers have an unparalleled opportunity here to get well off the beaten track and have a genuine South Sea paradise all to themselves. You're in for something totally original. Don't wait too long, however; the United Nations Development Program and various transnational corporations are pushing for the construction of 3 high-rise hotels in Honiara, and smaller resorts throughout the country. Ansett Airlines of Australia is waiting eagerly in the wings to take over tourism in the Solomon Islands, as they have in Vanuatu.

the land: With its 27,556-sq-km area, the Solomons is one of the major insular nations of the Pacific. This thickly forested, mountainous country, 2,000 km NE of Australia, is made up of 6 large islands in a double line (New Georgia, Guadalcanal, Makira, Malaita, Isabel, Choiseul), about 20 medium-sized ones, and numberless smaller islets and reefs—922 islands in all. The group stretches nearly 1,000 km from the Bougainville Strait in the W to Tikopia and Anuta in the E, and 692 km from Ontong Java atoll in the N to Rennell I. in the south. The Solomons are on the edge of the Indo-Australian and Pacific plates, which accounts for volcanic activity, past and present. Tinakula, Savo, Simbo, and Vella Lavella are part of the circumpacific Ring of Fire, and there's a submarine volcano called Kavachi just S of the New Georgia Group. The New Britain Trench, SW of the chain, marks the point where the Indo-Australian Plate is shoved under the Pacific Plate. This causes uplifting; therefore most of the Polynesian outliers are elevated or true atolls. Rennell is one of the best examples of a raised limestone atoll in Oceania. The other islands are mostly high and volcanic with dense rainforest

shrouding the rugged terrain. Under these conditions roadbuilding is difficult; only Malaita and Guadalcanal have fairly extensive networks. The wide coastal plain E of Honiara on Guadalcanal is the only area of its kind in the group. Geographically and culturally, the NW islands of Bougainville and Buka belong to the Solomons, but politically are part of Papua New Guinea.

climate: The Solomons are hot and humid year-round, but the heaviest rainfall comes Dec. to March. The SE tradewinds (*ara*) blow almost continually from the end of April to Nov. (force 4, sometimes reaching force 5-6). The rest of the year is uncertain, with long periods of calm punctuated by squalls (if you're lucky). Cyclones build up at this time

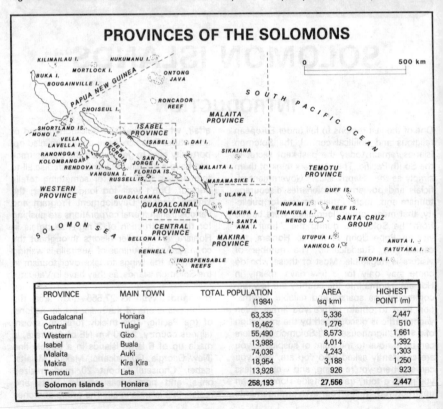

PROVINCE	MAIN TOWN	TOTAL POPULATION (1984)	AREA (sq km)	HIGHEST POINT (m)
Guadalcanal	Honiara	63,335	5,336	2,447
Central	Tulagi	18,462	1,276	510
Western	Gizo	55,490	8,573	1,661
Isabel	Buala	13,988	4,014	1,392
Malaita	Auki	74,036	4,243	1,303
Makira	Kira Kira	18,954	3,188	1,250
Temotu	Lata	13,928	926	923
Solomon Islands	**Honiara**	**258,193**	**27,556**	**2,447**

(Dec. to March), but move S and rarely do much damage here. Between Nov. and April winds are generally from the W or NW (*komburu*), though occasionally from the southeast. The most pleasant time to visit is July to Sept., when rainfall, humidity, and temperatures are at their lowest, and the cooling trades blow you away.

fauna: The endemic land mammals (opossum, bats, rats, and mice) are mostly nocturnal, so it's unlikely you'll see them. Birdlife, on the other hand, is rich and varied with as many as 140 species. The most unusual is the megapode, a flightless bird which lays large eggs in the volcanic sands of the thermal areas. There are many species of colorful parrots. Some of the moths and butterflies are magnificent. The 70 species of reptiles include crocodiles, lizards, snakes (nonvenomous), turtles, skinks, frogs, and toads. Sharks are common offshore, so ask local advice before swimming. These creatures earned a certain notoriety among sailors and airmen during WW II, but the problem seems to have receded. White beaches are safer than black. No shark attacks have been reported in the Santa Cruz Is. in recent memory. Many islanders have a curious rapport with the shark and believe that the souls of their ancestors live on in them. Shark worship has made Malaita relatively free of shark attacks.

HISTORY

pre-history: The earliest known human habitation, provided by the radiocarbon dating of remains from Fotoruma Cave near the Poha River (Guadalcanal), is 1300-1000 B.C. Due to the nature of the objects discovered in this excavation and the absence of pottery (the 19th C. inhabitants of the island still had no pottery), it's believed that the occupants of this quite sizeable cave were the direct ancestors of the present-day people of Guadalcanal. It's likely that even earlier sites await discovery and that man has lived on the island no less than 6,000 years. The many different languages currently spoken by the Melanesians illustrate this long period of isolated settlement. *Lapita* pottery has been

Alvaro de Mendana

found in the Santa Cruz Is., and New Britain obsidian was carried through the Solomons to Santa Cruz and New Caledonia some 3,000 years ago, probably by the first Polynesians. Today's Polynesian enclaves in the Solomons have no relation to these original eastward migrations, however. Their forebears arrived in a back-migration within the last 1,500 years to Anuta, Tikopia, Bellona, and Rennell from Wallis and Futuna, and to Taumako (Duff Is.), Pileni (Reef Is.), Sikaiana, and Ontong Java from Tuvalu.

the Spanish episode: There were 3 Spanish expeditions to Melanesia in the late 16th and early 17th centuries: 2 by Alvaro de Mendana (in 1568 and 1595) to the Solomon Is., and one in 1606 by Mendana's pilot Pedro Fernandez de Quiros to Vanuatu. Incan legends told of a rich land 600 leagues W of Peru, so the eager *conquistadores* prepared an expedition to find the elusive *Eldorado*. Mendana set out from Peru in Nov. 1567, and arrived on 7 Feb. 1568 at Estrella Bay, Isabel I., to become the first European to "discover" the Solomons. Mendana established a base on Isabel, where his men built a small, 5-ton, undecked vessel to explore reefs that would have destroyed a bigger, clumsier ship. At the beginning of March, a fleet of war canoes paddled near the Spanish ship, presenting Mendana with a

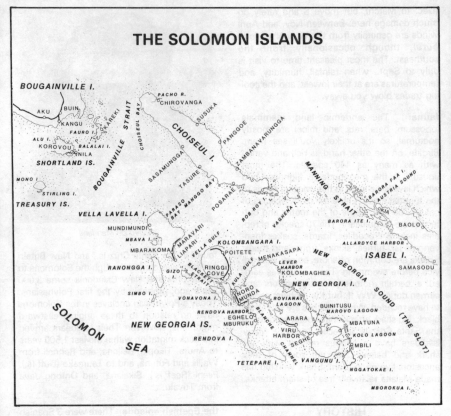

THE SOLOMON ISLANDS

quarter of boy, nicely garnished with taro roots. Mendana sailed his brigantine among the islands, giving them the Spanish names still used today. In retaliation for violence and treachery initiated earlier on Guadalcanal by a subordinate commander, the islanders massacred all 9 members of a watering party sent out by Mendana. The Spaniards then fired every village within reach, and when they departed, Guadalcanal was left in ashes and death. Mendana left Makira for Peru on the morning of 17 Aug. 1568. He returned in 1595 and landed on Nendo in the Santa Cruz Group, where he died soon after, and his crew carried on to the Philippines. Mendana found no gold in the Solomons, but he gave the islands their exotic name, implying to his royal

patrons that they were as rich as, or even the source of, King Solomon's treasure—an early example of a real estate salesman's trickery. The name soon appeared on maps and in formal reports, and was eventually adopted as official. Mendana placed the Solomons far to the E of their actual location, and for the next 200 years they were lost to European explorers.

recontact and exploitation: In 1767, Capt. Carteret rediscovered Santa Cruz and Malaita, followed a year later by Bougainville, who visited and named Choiseul and other islands to the north. This opened the door to traders, missionaries, and labor recruiters. The traders bought *beche-de-mer*, pearls, tortoise shell, and coconut oil, and by 1860 stone tools had been replaced almost everywhere with iron. Copra became important in the 1870s and labor recruitment for the canefields of Queensland and Fiji also began about this time. The treacherous methods of the blackbirders, who often kidnapped workers, sparked a wave of intense anti-European feeling which resulted in the murder of many honest traders and missionaries. Some blackbirders even dressed in priests' gowns to ensure a peaceful reception on an island. Between 1870 and 1910, some 30,000 people were removed from the islands; 10,000 never returned. In retaliation the natives killed Monseigneur Epalle, their first real Catholic bishop, on Isabel in 1845, Anglican Bishop John Coleridge Patteson on Nukapu, Reef Is.,

in 1871, and Commodore Goodenough on Nendo, Santa Cruz, in 1875. The recruiting became more voluntary in the latter 19th C., but it still amounted to economic slavery. This system died out in Queensland in 1904, when most blacks were expelled from Australia, and in Fiji in 1910.

the missionaries: The earliest attempts to implant Christianity in the Solomons were by Catholics: first Mendana in the 16th C., then the Society of Mary in the 1840s. Mendana failed, and the Marists withdrew in 1848. A decade later the Anglicans of New Zealand began to take an interest in the area. The Melanesian Mission of those days, covering both northern Vanuatu and the Solomons, has grown into today's Church of Melanesia

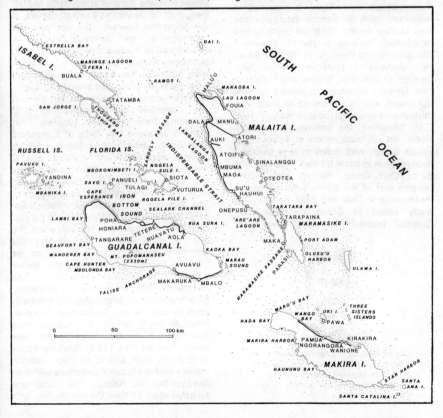

(Anglican). The Catholics returned at the end of the 19th C. and established missions on several islands. Around 1900, Solomon Island laborers returning from the cotton and sugar plantations of Queensland brought back the South Seas Evangelical Mission. Some who had worked in Fiji returned as Methodists; as a result the United Church (Methodist) is active in the Western Solomons. The Seventh-day Adventist Church here dates from 1914. Although the missionaries effaced many old traditions, they did pioneer education, health care, and communications, transforming the country from one of the most dangerous areas on earth to one of the most peaceful. Their influence remains strong today.

the colonial period: In 1884 Britain declared a protectorate over Papua in response to Australian alarm at German expansion into New Guinea. By the 1890s the Germans had established interests in the N. Solomons (Bougainville and Buka), so in 1893 the British also declared a protectorate over New Georgia, Guadalcanal, Makira, and Malaita to limit German advances, to protect resident Europeans, and as a response to pleas from missionaries to control the labor trade. In 1896 C.M. Woodford, the first resident commissioner, set up headquarters at Tulagi in the Florida Group, with orders to raise sufficient local revenue to cover his own expenses. The Santa Cruz Group, Rennell, and Bellona became part of the British Solomon Islands Protectorate in 1898 and 1899. In 1900 Germany ceded to Britain the Shortlands, Choiseul, Isabel, and Ontong Java in ex-

Charles Woodford, a naturalist sent to the Solomons in 1885 to collect specimens for the British Museum, created the first colonial administration almost single-handedly.

change for a free hand to annex Samoa. The first decade of the 20th C. saw the establishment of large coconut plantations by Levers (1905), Burns Philp (1906), and Fairymead (1909), as well as expansion of the missions. Government officials seemed to appear in villages only to collect taxes and punish people. Life led a sleepy course until the Japanese seized the Solomons in 1942.

the Pacific War: After Singapore fell in Feb. 1942, the South Pacific was fully exposed to attack. Stung by the Doolittle raid on Tokyo in April, the Japanese moved S and occupied Tulagi, Florida Group, in May, 1942. A Japanese invasion fleet sailed toward Port Moresby, P.N.G., but was turned back in the Battle of the Coral Sea. On 4 June another invasion fleet was stopped at the Battle of Midway, in which Japan lost 4 aircraft carriers. In the Solomons, however, the war was just beginning as the Japanese landed on Guadalcanal on 7 July and began constructing an airbase. A month later 10,000 U.S. Marines went ashore at Red Beach and quickly captured the partly-completed airstrip and unarmed Korean construction workers, but the next day Japanese planes prevented U.S. transports from unloading supplies. That night, a Japanese task force of 8 warships stole silently past a destroyer patrol near Savo I. and sank 4 Allied cruisers and 2 destroyers—one of the worst naval defeats ever suffered by the U.S. These savage attacks forced Allied naval forces to withdraw. The Japanese then began an intense campaign to push the 10,000 Marines into the sea. Supplies and troops were funneled down The Slot (a wide channel that divides the Solomons into 2 chains of islands) on the "Tokyo Express," and Japanese planes bombed Guadalcanal incessantly. The Marines held out for 6 months against malaria, blood-curdling banzai charges, and bombardment by land and sea. By this time, however, American reinforcements and supplies were pouring in, so in Feb. 1943, the Japanese secretly moved their 12,000 surviving troops to a newly built airfield on New Georgia, thereby shortening communications with their headquarters in Rabaul. The Americans followed them to New Georgia in July, with

*a B-17 bomber over-
the Solomons on 4
Oct. 1942: in the
background smoke is
rising from Gizo town*

major actions at Rendova and Munda, but a
few die-hard Japanese detachments held out
on Choiseul and the Shortlands until 1945.
Some 19,000 Japanese and 5,000 American
soldiers were killed or wounded on
Guadalcanal itself, plus many more in the surrounding sea and air. Official histories do not
mention how many Solomon Islanders were
killed. Thousands volunteered to work for the
Americans as porters, orderlies, and guides.
Many American lives were saved (including
that of John F. Kennedy) by villagers who risk-
ed their own to rescue downed airmen and
seamen. Also highly active was the coast-
watching organization, which used radio
transmitters to report on Japanese
movements from behind enemy lines. Many
of these coastwatchers were members of the
British administration who knew the area well,
but they were aided by militant churchmen,
nuns, planters, mission nurses, and hundreds
of loyal islanders.

the aftermath: World War II left deep scars
on the Solomons. The former capital, Tulagi,
was devastated when the Americans recap-
tured it, so the returning British administration
chose to establish a new capital at Honiara to
take advantage of the infrastructure installed
by the Americans during the war. A high
percentage of the Solomon's roads and
airstrips date from the war. Military dumps

and scattered wreckage can still be found in
the bush E of Henderson Airport, although
time and souvenir-hunters are beginning to
take their toll. Perhaps the most unexpected
outcome of the campaign was the rise of the
Ma'asina Ruru (The Brotherhood) movement,
dubbed "Marching Rule" by local expatriates.
Thousands of islanders who'd been forced into the bush to avoid the fighting returned and
found great American armies possessed of
seemingly limitless wealth and power. This
awakening, coupled with dissatisfaction in a
colonial system which treated natives like
naughty children, gave birth to the
widespread cargo cult on Malaita. Ma'asina
Ruru attempted to reorganize society on the
basis of "custom," but in 1948 the British administration decided that things were moving
in an undesirable direction and used police to
crush the movement. By 1949 some 2,000
islanders had been imprisoned for refusing to
cooperate with the government. This adversi-
ty united the Malaita people for the first time,
and the British were forced to respond. The
Malaita Council, formed as a compromise in
1953, was the beginning of the system of local
government followed in the Solomons today.
Unlike cargo cults in Vanuatu and New
Guinea, little remains of the original "Marching Rule," although Americans are still
popular. By 1964 the local government councils were handling all regional affairs. A
nominated Legislative Council was created in

1960; some elected members were added in 1964. In l974 this became a completely elected Legislative Assembly, followed by internal self-government in 1976, and full independence on 7 July 1978.

GOVERNMENT AND ECONOMY

government: The Solomon Islands has a 38-member National Parliament, which elects a prime minister from its ranks, who then appoints his top-heavy 15-minister cabinet from among the members. Most members belong to one of several political parties based more on personalities than issues; other members are independent. A governor general represents the British Crown. There are 7 provinces, each with a premier and Provincial Assembly. Honiara is administered separately from Guadalcanal Province by the Honiara Town Council. Although many powers have been transferred from the national to the provincial governments, the latter are largely dependent on the former for financing. The provincial governments are supported by the head tax, a colonial levy which forces people to sell part of their produce or work for planters. Within each province are various area councils, each with a president, which deal with local or village matters. The Solomon Islands government has banned nuclear-armed warships from the country's ports.

economy: Although 90 percent of the population rely on subsistence agriculture, the money economy in the Solomons is booming, based largely on the removal of raw materials by foreign corporations. Exports are reasonably diversified. Fish is the main export, followed by timber. Copra and palm oil are a distant third and fourth. Small quantities of cacao, gold, and shells are also exported. Imports are primarily machinery, manufactured goods, and mineral fuels. Trade is fairly balanced, with only a small deficit. Australia (copra) and Japan (fish) have the greatest economic interest in the Solomons; logging is done by both. One project which could affect light industry is the proposed Lungga River

hydroelectric scheme on Guadalcanal. Lack of financing is delaying the start of construction. Tourism is actively discouraged and plays only a small role in the economy. Those few tourists who come are mostly from P.N.G. and Australia.

primary products: Taiyo Fisheries has plants at Tulagi and Noro. To avoid the U.S. import duty on processed fish, Taiyo freezes 90 percent of its tuna catch and ships it to Puerto Rico and Pago Pago for processing. Only the lowest-quality tuna is canned in the Solomons. Smoked tuna is also produced. Solomon Islanders employed by Taiyo are paid less than expatriates in comparable positions, are housed in concrete bunkhouses segregated according to tribe, and offered no chance for advancement into management due to "language barriers." In 1984, when a U.S. purse seiner was caught poaching tuna deep inside the Solomons' 200-mile fisheries zone and ordered forfeit by a local court, the U.S. slapped an embargo on Solomons fish and threatened action against anyone purchasing the US$3.5 million ship and helicopter—a good example of U.S. "fish imperialism." The Japanese government is trying to help to stimulate coastal fishing by Solomon Islanders by establishing icemaking facilities throughout the country. On Kolombangara and New Georgia, some of the world's last untouched rainforests are falling to the chainsaw in a one-time exploitation by transnational timber companies which export rough logs to Japan. As the giant slow-growing trees disappear, many rare endemic species of birds and butterflies face extinction due to the destruction of their habitat. It's estimated that within 20 years this resource will be totally depleted. Villagers on Kolombangara have fought an ongoing battle against Unilever and the government for control of their lands. Only persons born in the Solomons may own land. Lever Bros. operates vast coconut plantations in the Russell Is. (now leased from the government as 75-year fixed-term estates), but village copra production exceeds that of the plantations. The palm oil plantations and modern oil mill on Guadalcanal are a joint effort of government (which owns 26 percent), land-owners (4 percent), and the Commonwealth Development Corporation (70 percent). The ricefields adjoining the palm oil tracts were originally organized by C. Brewer Co. of Hawaii, but were nationalized in 1982. The Solomons is one of the only countries in the Pacific self-sufficient in rice, although none is exported. Solomon Islanders have collected alluvial gold by panning methods at Guadalcanal's Gold Ridge since the early 1940s. There are undeveloped bauxite deposits on Rennell and Vaghena, and phosphates on Bellona.

THE PEOPLE AND THEIR ARTS

About 93 percent of the Solomon's 258,193 people (1984) are Melanesians. These islanders have an astounding variety of com-plexions—ranging from light tan to blue-black. Generally, the darker groups live in the W and N, becoming lighter to the southeast. Their features can be prognathous and heavy, or delicate and fine-boned. Bushy blond hair is often seen with chocolate-colored skin, especially on Malaita. To add to the variety, thousands of Micronesian Gilbertese were resettled near Honiara and Gizo in the early 1950s, where small European and Chinese communities are also found. The government maintains close relations with the Republic of China (Taiwan), and the number of Chinese residents is growing. Thousands of Polyne-sians live on Rennell and Bellona, Sikaiana, Ontong Java, Anuta, and Tikopia—the so-called "Polynesian Fringe."

village life: Nine out of ten Solomon Islanders live on shifting, subsistence agriculture in small rural villages, operating much as they did before the white man ar-rived. Most villages are near the shore so fresh fish play an important role in the diet, sup-plemented by wild pigs hunted with dogs and spears, plus the occasional chicken. On Malaita many people live in the interior and keep small herds of cattle for food. Everywhere native vegetables (taro, yams, sweet potato, and cassava) grown in small in-

Australian photographer J.W. Beattie took this photo of a man of the Florida Islands in 1913.

dividual plots provide the bulk of the diet. Villagers work collectively on community pro-jects and there's much sharing among clans, yet individuals keep their own gardens and can readily tell you what land they own. Land may be passed on by the mother or father, depending on local custom. Customary land accounts for 87 percent of the Solomons, another 9 percent is owned by the govern-ment, and the rest by individual Solomon Islanders. About 2 percent is leased to foreigners. Disputes over land and boundaries are common. The achievements of individuals are evaluated by their value to the community as a whole, and a villager who shows too much initiative or ability in his own affairs is more likely to inspire jealousy and resentment than admiration. Education is not compulsory and nearly half the population have no formal education whatever. There is strong opposi-tion to family planning and the population growth rate is fast (3 percent). About 65 per-cent of the inhabitants are aged 6 to 16. The Solomon Is. is one of the few countries in the world were the life expectancy of women is less than men; many are literally "worked to death."

language: There are at least 87 distinct indigenous languages, none with more than a few thousand speakers. Most of these derive from a single parent tongue, Austronesian. Small groups speaking Papuan languages are scattered throughout the Solomons and are perhaps remnants of an earlier population largely replaced or absorbed by the Austronesians. (Papuans entered New Guinea at least 2,000 years before the Austronesians.) Today, most Solomon Islanders use Pidgin, which takes its vocabulary largely from English, but the grammar is Melanesian. It's used mainly as a contact language between tribes and, although the vocabulary may be limited, there is a richness and freshness to the grammatical constructions which always delights newcomers. Solomon Islands Pidgin varies considerably from those of New Guinea or Vanuatu. Get hold of *Pijin Blong Yumi* by Linda Simons and Hugh Young. Trying to communicate in Pidgin will add enjoyment to your visit.

crafts: All traditional handicrafts are either ceremonial or functional. Representational carvings of fish, birds, or humans, although often good, are made solely to sell to visitors. Some traditional items such as war clubs, masks, and *nguzunguzu* are now made in miniature to increase their desirability to tourists. These articles are of little interest to serious collectors—try to get items of original size, if possible. The fantastic cultural diversity of this country is reflected in its artwork. The most distinctive local carving is the *nguzunguzu* of Western Province, depicted herein. The carved sharks and dolphins of the same area are made to European taste, but are of exceptional workmanship. The shark is a popular figure because it's believed that the soul of a successful fisherman is reincarnated in a shark. Carving in the W is done in brown streaked kerosene wood *(corsia subcordata)* or black ebony, both hardwoods, which may be inlaid with nautilus shell or mother-of-pearl. Another excellent purchase is the shell money of Malaita, made into beautiful necklaces. Handicrafts from Malaita are often useful

items like combs, bamboo lime containers (for use with betelnut), rattles, flutes, panpipes, and fiber carrying bags. Watch too for traditional jewelry such as headbands, earrings, nose and ear plugs, pendants, breastplates, and armbands, mostly made from shell. Bone and shell fishhooks make authentic souvenirs. Guadalcanal people excel in weaving strong, sturdy bags, baskets, and trays from the *asa* vine *(lygodium circinnatum)*. These items are known collectively as Bukaware. The Polynesians of the Solomons make fine miniature canoes. The small woven pandanus bags of Bellona are commonly used by the people. Santa Ana and Santa Catalina in Makira Province are another source of quality handicrafts, especially the

nguzunguzu: *Figureheads such as this were once attached to the prow of war canoes, just above the waterline, as they set out from the Western Solomons on headhunting expeditions. It was hoped that the dog-like spirit would guide them to success in the collection of heads. The mother-of-pearl shell inlay work is characteristic. A* nguzunguzu, *such as those sold at craft outlets in Honiara, makes an excellent souvenir.*

striking black ceremonial pudding bowls inlaid with shell. Solomon Island handicrafts tend to be more expensive than those of other Pacific countries, but the quality is worth it. Bargaining is not practiced, but if you feel the cost is too high, hesitate a few moments, then ask the seller if he has a second price. Consider, however, the amount of time which went into making the object. Outside Honiara you can often trade cassettes, radios, watches, jeans, and sunglasses for handicrafts. The superb Melanesian-style decoration in some of the churches (especially Catholic) is worth noting. Remember that any handicrafts incorporating the bodily parts of sea turtles or marine mammals (dolphin teeth) cannot be taken into the U.S., Australia, and many other countries.

events: Public holidays include the Queen's Birthday (June), Independence Day (7 July), Bank Holiday (early Aug.), Solomon Islands Day (Oct.), and Prince Charles' Birthday (Nov.). Most other events are church-oriented.

PRACTICALITIES

getting there: Air Pacific has service twice a week from Brisbane, Port Vila, and Nandi (Fiji), while Air Niugini has flights from Kieta and Port Moresby. Air Nauru flies in from Auckland and Nauru. Solair has 5 flights a week to Honiara from Kieta, P.N.G., and a weekly service from Espiritu Santo and Port Vila, as well as a backdoor service from Kieta to Balalae, Gizo, and Munda, which allows you to visit the Western Solomons between Bougainville and Guadalcanal. Note again that it's often difficult to purchase Solair tickets prior to arrival in the area, although Immigration insists that you have an onward ticket. Solair has the reputation of refusing international mileage tickets, which is probably why most travel agents won't touch them. In Hawaii, Nauru, and Fiji, for example, you may be unable to find anyone willing to issue a ticket on Solair services. In Australia contact Hideaway Holidays, 1071 Victoria Road, West Ryde, NSW 2114 (tel. 02-858-4100) for Solair tickets. Elsewhere try Air New Zealand. In Honiara itself, Guadalcanal Travel Service can handle complicated international itineraries.

Munda airport is a Quonset hut between the big wartime airstrip and the Roviana Lagoon.

getting around: The domestic air service is operated by Solair, a subsidiary of Talair of Papua New Guinea. They offer convenient, punctual service with more than 300 scheduled flights a month linking 24 airstrips in the Solomons, but their fares are 3 times higher than the cost of going by ship. Honiara-Santa Cruz, for example, is $167 OW. Ask about student fares, standbys, and advance purchase deals. Solair offices and agents on the outer islands are good sources of information about accommodations, transport, diving, etc., in their area. In Honiara they're less helpful, and can make catastrophic errors with your bookings, so check every detail carefully. But don't get angry lest they get unnerved and make more mistakes. Solair represents Air Pacific and Air Nauru in Honiara. The baggage allowance is 16 kilos on domestic flights, 20 kilos on international. Interisland travel by ship is preferable, both for color and economy, and there's frequent regular service to Malaita and Gizo. Take your own food on board. See "Honiara—Transport" for details.

accommodations and food: The only true hotels are in Honiara, the capital. There are tourist lodges at Auki (Malaita), Munda, Gizo, and Pigeon I. (Reef Is.), cottages at Marau Sound, and a laid-back resort at Tambea (both on Guadalcanal). All of these charge a 5 percent hotel tax. Otherwise try the government rest houses at Tulagi, Gizo, Kirakira, Malu'u (Malaita), and elsewhere. Camping is still rare in the Solomons and should only be done in remote areas. Before pitching your tent get permission from the customary land-owner, often the village chief. This is almost invariably granted, although you'll probably be asked to stay with them. If you accept their hospitality, it's proper to reciprocate with either cash or gifts, such as stick tobacco and matches, plastic bags of Spear course-cut tobacco, small kitchen knives, etc. Corned beef, tea, and sugar are also appreciated by village hosts, and are a nice way of saying "thank you" for hospitality received. Note, however, followers of the South Sea Evangelical Mission and Seventh Day Advent-ists don't smoke, chew betel or tobacco, or drink, so be prudent with your gifts. Note too that stepping over a sitting or sleeping person is considered a serious insult. You'll be given food in most villages you visit—including some you hadn't intended to eat in! Most coastal villages have small trade stores, so there's little need to carry much food with you unless you go "big bush" (inland). If you plan to stop on any isolated island for a period of time, be sure to take plenty of food with you so as not to become a burden.

money: The Solomon Islands dollar is linked to a trade-related basket of currencies and the rate is adjusted daily. All prices in this chapter are in the local currency. Banking hours in Honiara are Mon. to Thurs. 0900-1130/ 1330-1500, Fri. 0900-1500. Otherwise you can change money at the Mendana Hotel at a slightly lower rate. Small banking agencies where travelers cheques may be changed are at Gizo and Auki. Elsewhere you must have enough local currency to tide you over. There is no tipping in the Solomons.

visas: British subjects, Americans, and some European nationals (Denmark, Finland, Italy, Spain, Sweden, and Switzerland) require no visa for a stay not exceeding 2 months in any 12-month period. Almost everyone (except Israelis) with a confirmed onward reservation within 7 days is eligible for a transit visa upon arrival. If in doubt, contact a British diplomatic office or an Australian Foreign Affairs office to determine entry requirements. An onward ticket is mandatory for everyone. Upon arrival

you're given a passport stamp allowing you to stay 2 weeks. This can be extended up to a total of 2 months at the Immigration office in Honiara. You must bring along your air ticket with a confirmed reservation; the extension will be to the date of your flight out. Perma-nent immigration to the Solomons or even staying longer than 2 months is not usually possible. Male tourists are not permitted to marry local women, nor would such a mar-riage give them any right to stay in the coun-try. Female tourists who marry a local man, however, may be permitted to stay. Don't bother claiming that you're doing some kind of research as a way of getting more time, as this requires prior clearance, and anthro-pologists are especially loathed by ethno-centric local officials. Freelance mineral prospectors are deported. All immigration regulations are strictly enforced and a cooperative attitude on your part is essential. In addition to Honiara, Gizo, Munda, and Graciosa Bay are ports of entry for cruising yachts.

malaria warning: Guadalcanal is the most heavily malaria-infested island in the world; half the cases reported in the Solomons occur here. A full-scale eradication program began in 1970 with DDT house spraying, case detec-tion, and treatment, and by 1975 malaria seemed to be on the way out. Since then, un-fortunately, the number of cases has increas-ed steadily to almost epidemic proportions, and health officials no longer talk of eradica-tion, only control. From 1977 to 1983 the number of cases treated in the Solomons in-creased from 10,496 to 84,527 (a third of the population). It's found everywhere in the country, including Honiara. Since 1980 chloroquine-resistant malaria has established itself in the Solomons. Fansider and Maloprim are effective against this. There are certain contra-indications for taking these, however, so see a doctor before you arrive if you have problems with any particular medication. Start taking the pills (after a meal) a month before you arrive and more importantly, continue a month after you leave. The Pharmacy beside the Hongkong Bank in Honiara sells malaria pills without prescription. Transmitted by

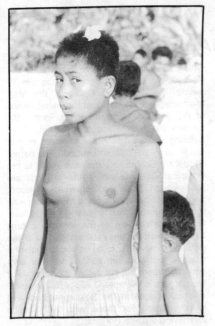

a girl on Tikopia (1969)

mosquitoes, malaria is a blood disease involving parasites which destroy red blood cells. Avoid being bitten by covering up at night. If you develop a fever, get a blood test as soon as possible, as malaria can kill. Later, if you become sick in another country, don't forget to tell the doctor you've been in the Solomons. Don't let this situation prevent you from visiting the Solomons, but do take the precautions.

important note: Certain traditional areas such as the Kwaio country on Malaita, the territory ruled by Chief Moro in S. Guadalcanal, and Tikopia and Anuta may be off limits to casual tourism to protect the local people from disruptive outside influences and diseases. The respective provincial authorities

are the people most likely to have information about this, but it's often hard to get a definite answer — you could even be turned back unless prior arrangements to visit have been made. A brief stopover on Tikopia or Anuta as a through passenger on a government ship should present no problems, but anything more than this is not something to be taken lightly. Sensitive visitors will appreciate the need for restraint here.

custom fees: From time to time you'll come upon a situation where the locals ask you to pay money to visit an archaeological site, see natural phenomena such as hotsprings or caves, or enter a traditional village visited regularly by tourists. The way they look at it, these things belong to them, so how can outsiders expect to be allowed in for nothing? Often they will start off by asking a ridiculously high amount ($15-20), but will come down after a little bargaining. Believe it or not, many tourists foolishly pay the first price, so the locals figure they have nothing to lose by trying. Try to avoid paying over $2. All custom fees we know about are mentioned in this book. Please help by sending us precise details of any others you encounter so we can publicize them, giving future visitors the opportunity to decide in advance whether it's still worth the expense and trouble.

airport: Henderson Airport (HIR) is 13 km E of Honiara. There's no tourist information desk, bank, or duty-free shop (allow one week for goods to be delivered to the airport by "duty-free" outlets in town). The pay phone (10 cents) is beside the Solair domestic check-in counter. Don't do anything suspicious (such as writing in a notebook) at the airport, as you risk being taken in the back room to be searched and interrogated. The airport bus costs $3 to your hotel. The drivers are friendly and help you with your luggage. Public buses and passenger trucks (40 cents) travel the highway several times a day. Taxi fare to town is $6-10. Departure tax is $10.

HONIARA

Honiara began as an American army base during WW II, then replaced the former capital, Tulagi, which had been devastated in the fighting. Honiara is also drier than Tulagi (it's protected from rains by high mountains to the S) and well-placed to serve the N. Guadalcanal plain. Its harbor is poor, however — only safe for yachts from April to October. Still, it's the major copra port of the group, and interisland ships bustle along the waterfront. Business and government crowd the narrow coastal strip behind Point Cruz, with residential areas covering the adjacent hillsides. Light industry is concentrated at Kukum, a suburb to the east. "Honiara" derives from the indigenous name for Point Cruz, *naho-ni-ara*, which means "facing the E and SE wind." Here in 1568 Mendana, the European discoverer of the Solomons, raised a cross and claimed the island for Spain. Almost 400 years later in Sept. 1942, the town area was the scene of heavy fighting, and the Mataniko River which runs through the city was the Japanese/American front line for several months. Quonset huts from the US base established after the Japanese withdrawal remain on the backstreets behind the Hongkong Bank. Today it's a booming mini-metropolis of 23,500 (1984), where wide lawns, tulips, fig, palm, and poinciana (flamboyant or flame) trees line the streets. Watch the sun set behind Guadalcanal from the breakwater beside the Quarantine Office on Point Cruz.

SIGHTS

the town area: A good place to start is the Solomon Islands Museum (open Mon. to Fri. 0900-1600; Sat. 0900-1300; Sun. 1300-1430; free) opposite the tourist office. The museum presents changing exhibits, but the permanent collection is in storage due to the inadequacy of the present building to display it and staff to protect it. Between the museum and police station is "Pistol Pete," a Japanese gun which caused havoc by shelling Henderson Field during the campaign. Just to the W beside the Mendana Hotel is the War Memorial, with Government House, residence of the governor general, behind. Farther W, beyond the post office, is the High Court building (1963-64) where Parliament meets. Continue W past Town Ground. Just before St. John's School take the road inland to the Botanical Gardens where the grounds are always open. There's an herbarium, lily pond, and orchid house, plus many attractive paths through the rainforest adjoining the gardens. Unfortunately, most of the identifying tags have fallen off the trees and plants. One of the gardeners may offer to guide you in hope of a gratuity, but you can easily find your own way. Upstream but still within the confines of the gardens is Watapamu village, fairly typical of rural villages in the Solomons, and well worth visiting for those who will not be journeying outside Honiara.

Chinatown and around: Return to the main road and take any bus E to Central Hospital. Go through the hospital grounds to the beach and proceed W to the mouth of the Mataniko River. In shallow water just off this beach is the wreck of a Japanese tank cut to pieces by American artillery and small arms fire on 23 Oct. 1942. The area behind the beach is Lord Howe Settlement, a large community of Polynesian people from Ontong Java. Beyond the settlement is Chinatown, an Oriental wild west of photogenic high-porched wooden buildings adjacent to the riverside. Cross the old Mataniko River bridge and proceed up Skyline Drive from the Catholic Cathedral. Keep L and up the ridge right to the top, an easy 15-min. climb, for a knockout view of the Mataniko Valley and the hills behind Honiara. You'll end up directly above a large village of Malaita people. Notice the sago palms they use to roof their houses. Skyline Drive, a WW II jeep track, meanders back into the boonies if you're keen.

PRACTICALITIES

hotels: The Honiara Hotel near Chinatown is the best place to stay if all you want is an inexpensive room with reasonable facilities. They have a few non-a/c rooms with shared bath for $16 s, $20 d, and there's a swimming pool, restaurant, and good bar. While it lacks the pool, popular bar, and atmosphere of the Honiara, the Hibiscus Hotel is centrally located. The 10 rooms with private facilities and fridge in the old wing are $21 s, $24 d. The government-owned Mendana Hotel is surprisingly unpretentious. Although the rates (from $42 s, $54 d in a standard room) are aimed more at businessmen on expense accounts, the continental buffet breakfasts, Fri. night barbecue, and Sun. night Gilbertese dancing should not be missed. The Mendana is close to a social center for resident expatriates—if the price doesn't bother you, by all means stay there. Note, however, that plainclothes police and Immigration men hang around the bar, so watch what you say.

hostels: Six rest houses and hostels in Honiara offer dormitory-style accommodations, most with cooking facilities. The most central is the friendly Church of Melanesia Transit House ($8 pp). Apply to the office, 2nd floor, Church House (Mon. to Fri. 0730-1200/1330-1630). Yelping dogs and sagging beds could be a problem, but it is convenient, and often full. The United Church Rest House nearby is a better bet. Go up the

Honiara's Chinatown is an authenic South Seas wild west.

These big leaf houses in Watapamu village at the upper end on Honiara's Botanical Gardens are typical of many in the Solomons.

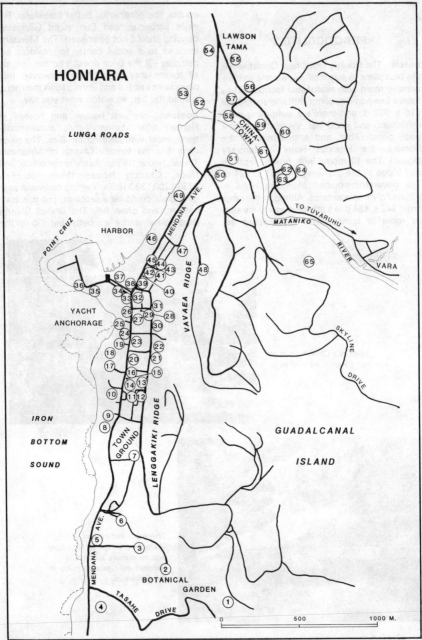

HONIARA

LAWSON
TAMA

CHINA-
TOWN

LUNGA ROADS

POINT CRUZ

HARBOR

MENDANA AVE.

TO TUVARUHU

MATANIKO

RIVER

VARA

YACHT
ANCHORAGE

VAVAEA RIDGE

SKYLINE

DRIVE

IRON

BOTTOM

SOUND

TOWN

GROUND

LENGGAKIKI RIDGE

GUADALCANAL

ISLAND

MENDANA AVE.

TASAHE

DRIVE

BOTANICAL
GARDEN

0   500   1000 M.

street beside South Sea Traders and turn R at the top of the hill. If they're full, the amiable pastor might even put you up in his house beside the hostel. The cost either way will be $7 pp. You'll have a better chance of finding a bed ($7 pp in a triple room) at the Kukum United Church Rest House near the Kukum Shopping Center. Though it's 3 km E of downtown, bus service is good and cheap. The pastor lives in the adjacent house so checking in is no problem. The South Seas Evangelical Church Transit House on Vavaea Ridge has 2 doubles and one 4-bed bunkroom downstairs ($7 pp). Smoking and drinking are not allowed. When there's space the Parliament Rest House will accommodate visitors at $12 pp. You get to meet local politicians. There's no cooking, however, and you must check in during business hours at the Parliamentary office near the High Court. They're not very eager to have you. The Y.W.C.A. across the field from the Guadalcanal Club offers accommodations for visiting women at $8 pp (less if you're a member), an excellent place for female travelers to meet local women—recommended. For long-term rentals check Triangle Realty in the Sun Alliance Insurance office behind Church House. Note that there's nowhere to camp in Honiara itself. The nearest

HONIARA

1. Watapamu village
2. Botanical Gardens herbarium
3. prison
4. Rove Clinic
5. Police Headquarters
6. radio station
7. Y.W.C.A.
8. Guadalcanal Club
9. Information Service
10. government offices
11. courthouse
12. Dept. of Lands and Surveys
13. Immigration office
14. post office
15. Soltel
16. National Bank
17. Government House
18. War Memorial/Open Air Theater/Canoe House
19. Mendana Hotel
20. police station
21. Hibiscus Hotel
22. National Archives
23. museum
24. tourist office
25. Yacht Club
26. The Bookshop/Solair
27. barge *Ulusaghe* office
28. Kingsley's Fast Food/Honiara Coin Center
29. Consumers Supermarket
30. Parliament Rest House
31. Wings Rent Cars
32. Lena Cinema
33. A.N.Z. Bank
34. Isabel Development Co./Adamasia Transport

35. Kai Bar
36. Quarantine office
37. Marine Division
38. Central Revenue Collection office
39. Hongkong Bank/Pharmacy
40. laundromat
41. Solomon Exporters/Joy Supermarket
42. Tom's Kitchen
43. Church of Melanesia Transit House
44. Church Store and Shipping Division
45. Church House/Coral Seas Ltd.
46. Village Crafts Ltd.
47. United Church Rest House
48. South Seas Evangelical Church Transit House
49. market
50. Catholic cathedral
51. public library
52. Lord Howe Settlement
53. submerged Japanese tank
54. Central Hospital
55. Community Center/University of the South Pacific Center
56. Squash Courts
57. Fast Food Bar
58. Mandarin Restaurant/Saloon
59. Super Video Cinema
60. Honiara Hotel
61. Mavis Leong Lunchroom
62. lunchroom
63. camera shop
64. Guadalcanal Bus Service office
65. Malaita village

possibilities are beyond the end of the road up the E bank of the Mataniko River or out at Kakambona. Get permission from the landowner and try to pitch your tent out of sight of passersby. Expect to arouse a lot of curiosity.

resort: If you came for a rest, Tambea Village Resort, on a sheltered black beach 45 km W of Honiara, is your best bet. There are 24 bungalows at $24 s, $32 d, $40 t, and facilities include restaurant, bar, boats, and scuba diving. The kerosene lighting lends a romantic air. There's a special feast and dancing at the resort on Sat. night. Don't buy handicrafts here, however; they're overpriced. Transfers from Honiara are provided free to those who have booked a bungalow—inquire at the tourist office.

food: The cheapest place to eat is the Central Market. The B-Kool Dairy Bar here sells milk shakes for 90 cents; the adjacent Honiara Fish Market offers big pieces of fried fish for 60 cents each. One piece is a complete meal. Also good is the Kai Bar (open 0900-1600) on Point Cruz, with a filling beef or fish plate. Kingsley's Fast Food Center beside Guadalcanal Travel specializes in barbecued chicken, hot meat pies, and noodle soup. Tom's Kitchen, a few blocks over, serves filling lunches for about $2 and coffee for 30 cents. Also try the Fast Food Bar in Chinatown for cheap fish and chips, or Mavis Leong Lunchroom by the bus stop near the bridge for a good cheap meal of curry beef and rice or chop suey. For that special Chinese dinner head for the Mandarin Restaurant (open 1830-2130 only), also in Chinatown. Prices are high, but the food is excellent. Next to the Mandarin is Honiara's roughest Wild West saloon, complete with swinging doors and wire grills protecting the bartender. Stop in for a Fosters if you've got guts. Weekdays, Honiara expatriates line up for a self-service lunch at the Casablanca Restaurant ("Rick's" Bar, Humphrey Bogart theme) in the Hongkong Bank Arcade (rear). Better is the restaurant at the Guadalcanal Club, open to the public daily for lunch (1130-1330) and dinner (1830-2100). An impressive Japanese field gun stands sentinel over the adjacent bowling green. The dining room at the Mendana Hotel is expensive and the quality variable, but the service is good and the portions large. Only European dishes are served. Pamper yourself with a filling continental breakfast ($3), served buffet-style at the Mendana 0700-0900, and don't miss the terrace barbecue ($7.50) Fri. at 1930. Fill up on the salad and meat, then gorge yourself on the lip-smacking desserts. There's sometimes entertainment.

entertainment: See 3 B-grade features daily at Lena Cinema ($2) in the center of town. The Yacht Club is the best place in Honiara for a beer—have the bartender sign you in. There's video Tues. night, and the usual notice board if you're looking for a ride/crew. For $1 daily or $3 weekly you can get a temporary membership in the Guadalcanal Club, once the reserve of British colonials. There's a swimming pool, tennis courts, billiards, video (Thurs. and Sun.), and a cheap bar (Tues. happy hour). The best event of the week is the Gilbertese dancing at the Honiara Hotel, Wed. at 2030 (admission $1, free for hotel guests)—a delightful, authentic performance with more locals in the audience than tourists. The dancers are not paid, and it's customary to show your appreciation by stuffing a banknote or two under the bra strap of the dancer who pleases you most *during* the dance. Watch how the locals do it. Beware if a dancer comes up and places a garland of flowers on your head. Next thing you know she'll have you dancing with her up on the stage! A different Gilbertese dance group peforms at the Mendana Hotel Sun. at 1930 (admission 50 cents). Catch a Sat. afternoon rugby (Oct. to March) or soccer (April to Aug.) game at the Lawson Tama Sports Ground opposite Central Hospital. The action starts about 1630 and the entrance fee is cheap.

shopping: The Central Market (open all day but best before 1030) is the place to buy fruit and vegetables, seashells, and shell money. Prices vary considerably from one stall to another, so shop around. Don't bargain, just keep looking. Village Crafts Ltd., behind the Guadalcanal Provincial offices, sells genuine handicrafts from many parts of the Solomons.

It's a cooperative, non-profit venture. Solomon Exporters is more commercially-oriented. Seashells and Buka baskets are sold at the Dive Center, up and across the road from the Yacht Club. For a better display of crafts and war relics than you'll see at the museum, visit the Honiara Coin Center across from Guadalcanal Travel. The American who set this place up was later booted out of the country. The Philatelic Bureau beside the post office sells beautiful stamps and first-day covers which make excellent souvenirs. Watch for pirate cassettes sold in Honiara at Singapore prices.

services: In addition to the mid-town banks, the National Bank branch in Chinatown changes travelers cheques. Place long-distance telephone calls at Soltel (Mon. to Fri. 0700-2200, Sat. 0800-1200) next to the post office. The old Central Hospital is impossibly overcrowded, so if you need medical attention, go to Kukum Clinic (Mon., Tues., Thurs., and Fri. 0730-1200) next to Kukum Cinema, or the Rove Clinic (Mon. to Fri. 0730-1200/1300-1600, closed Thurs. afternoon) beyond Rove Prison. Offer to contribute whatever you feel the service is worth. The Dental Clinic ($5) is at Central Hospital. The Immigration office is open weekdays 0900-1100/1300-1500. Get Australian visas free in 24 hours at the Australian High Commission (Mon. to Fri. 0830-1200/1300-1600). Papua New Guinea visas ($7) are available at the P.N.G. High Commission, 2nd floor, Hongkong Bank Building. They only accept applications on Mon. and Wed. mornings and you must present your passport, ticket out, and one photo (24-hour service). There's a shoe repair shop at the prison behind Police Headquarters. Sgt. Jack Manakera, one of the prison staff, is a good amateur painter who sells his work. A laundromat is beside REG Store near the Hongkong Bank ($3 to wash, soap included, and $2 to dry). Leave excess luggage at the Church of Melanesia Store and Shipping Division warehouse for about 15 cents a day.

information: The Tourist Authority (Mon. to Fri. 0800-1200/1330-1600) across from the museum is very helpful and can advise you on trips to remote areas. There's even a notice board for people looking for yachts/crew. A better notice board is found in Consumer's Supermarket. The Government Information Service, in the building next to the Guadalcanal Club, has a number of informative brochures on the country. The Central Revenue Collection Office sells an official handbook and some reports on the islands. Detailed topographical maps can be bought at the Dept. of Lands and Surveys (Mon. to Fri. 0900-1130/1330-1530). The Hydrographic Office nearby sells locally produced charts ($4) and tide tables. The Public Library (Mon., Tues., Thurs., Fri. 1000-1300/1600-1800, Sat. 0900-1200, Sun. 1400-1700) also has a file of older maps. The National Library (Mon. to Fri. 0730-1200/1300-1600) is in the unmarked building directly behind the Public Library. The Bookshop has many books on the islands. There are 2 weekly newspapers: *Solomons Toktok* and *Solomon Star*. The *Star* is the more independent of the two.

Sturdy baskets of this kind are woven from the asa vine by Guadalcanal villagers. Because they were once traded at Buka in the North Solomons (P.N.G.), they are known as "Buka baskets."

TRANSPORT

by ship: Travel by ship within the Solomons is very easy. There are many services with reasonable fares—plan on doing most of your interisland travel this way. Orient yourself in Honiara by looking over the ships in the harbor; most shipping company offices are nearby. Pick the larger ships if you doubt your ability as a sailor. Cabin fares (when available) are double the OW deck fares listed below. Fares usually don't include meals. You'll make many friends on board. **Coral Seas Ltd.:** This company offers the most reliable service on the largest ships, like the *Compass Rose II* to Auki (Malaita) every Wed. and Fri. night ($12). This ship (or the *luminoa*) also leaves every Sun. for Gizo ($29). This service connects in Gizo with Western Province ships for Choiseul and the Shortlands. **others to Gizo:** The South New Georgia Development Corp. (upstairs across from the Yacht Club) runs the barge *Ulusaghe* to Gizo every Sat. evening ($22). This is a slow boat, calling at smaller ports such as Buinitusu, but you save a night's hotel bill. Less-known are the old Chinese trading boats, full of South Seas flavor, which

run between Honiara and Gizo ($20) fortnightly. Inquire in the office in the back of Joy Supermarket for details.

to Malaita and Isabel: Apart from Coral Seas Ltd., mentioned above, Adamasia Transport in the CCA Office Arcade has a ship to N. Malaita (Malu'u or Takwa) every Tues. and Sat. evening ($14). The service to Takwa is especially convenient: you can visit the Lau Lagoon area and Malu'u without having to make a RT by road from Auki. Solomon Island Navigation Services (office at the entrance to Lena Cinema) has a ship to Auki ($11) on Thurs. and Sun. evening, plus services to S. Malaita and Isabel. The Isabel Development Co. has weekly sailings, twice a month up the W coast as far as Kia, once a month up the E coast to Buolo, and twice a month to Buala ($17). **farther afield:** Mawo Ltd. (office behind the Kai Bar on Point Cruz) has monthly service to the Santa Cruz and the Reef Is., plus a monthly ship to N. Malaita. The Makira Ulawa Development Corporation runs the *Bulawa* and *Waisisi* to Makira Harbor, Kirakira, and Ulawa. There are also mission ships to many points; ask the crews along the waterfront.

An instant market forms when the supply ship Compass Rose II *calls at Patutiva near Seghe on the Marovo Lagoon.*

Marine Division: This government line offers regular service to Tulagi ($5) Tues. and Thurs. at 0830, and Sun. at 1630, returning to Honiara the following days. Once a week a government ship coasts right around Guadalcanal, traveling clockwise and counterclockwise on alternate weeks. Stop off at Marau Sound and fly back. There's a fortnightly ship to Sikaiana and Ontong Java, and a monthly trip to Rennell and Bellona. These voyages average 5 days, and with careful planning you could pick up the Ontong Java ship in Auki. The Marine Division does a monthly run to the eastern outer islands of Makira, Santa Cruz, Utupua, Duff, Vanikolo, Anuta, and Tikopia. The RT voyage takes about 25 days. The ship makes an extra circle around the Santa Cruz Is. before calling at Vanikolo for the second time, thus you could stop off for about 10 days on this remote island before reboarding the same ship to return to Honiara. Other stopovers are possible. Total transportation cost would be under $100. Add to your journey by getting off at Kira Kira (Makira) on the way back and visiting Star Harbor and Santa Ana from there. A blackboard listing departures of government ships is posted outside the Central Revenue Collection Office, where you also buy your ticket.

by canoe: To reach Savo I., ask at the market or along the beach at the Yacht Club if any canoes are going back. They charge about $6 pp. Canoes also leave for Savo and even the New Georgia Is. from Visale, near the W end of Guadalcanal. Try to do the canoe trip in the early morning, before the wind wakes the sea up. Be prepared to get soaked, even on an apparently calm day. The trip takes 4 hours from Honiara through schools of dolphins and flying fish. You can hire a canoe to go for the standard fare ($6 pp) if there are 4 of you.

by bus: Two bus companies serve Honiara and environs. Service is fairly frequent between White River and Vara (Kukum), with a bus to King George VI School at least once an hour. A standard fare of 25 cents is charged for any trip in this zone. At least 4 buses a day go on to Henderson Airport (40 cents) and as far as CDC3 ($1.20) out beyond Tetere. Schedules vary so it's best to ask at the Guadalcanal Bus Service office in Chinatown if you want to take a bus to Tetere. Buses within the town area operate until 1930 daily. Even if you don't get off, a RT ride to CDC3 is well worth taking. **by truck:** Passenger trucks depart Honiara market for Lambi Bay ($2.50) and Aola ($3), at opposite ends of the N coast highway, every afternoon except Sun. at about 1500. Other trucks make more frequent, shorter trips. Vehicles with white license plates with black lettering are public vehicles which charge fares.

rentals: Wings Rent Cars has compacts from $22 flat daily rate, $120 weekly (plus $80 deposit). Included is $500 deductible insurance, or pay $6 extra for complete collision. Inquire at the manager's office of the Shell service station across from Consumer's Supermarket.

scuba diving: Island Dive Services (Box 414, Honiara) offers snorkeling ($12 pp plus $5 for gear) and scuba ($22 with one tank, $33 with 2 tanks) trips from their base at the Mendana Hotel. Divers must bring their own buoyancy compensator, regulator, and gauges, or rent them. Certification is mandatory. They offer introductory "resort courses" for visitors. The main sites visited are several wrecked Japanese transport ships NW of Honiara (good for both snorkel and scuba), a sunken trading boat full of tame moray eels (scuba only), and Tassafaronga Reef. There's also a beach dive to a B-17 bomber 15 m down. Island Dive Services has a branch at Tambea Village Resort (Box 236, Honiara) which organizes diving on nearby reefs, caves, and perhaps Japanese submarine I-123 (if local villagers who claim to "own" the sub allow).

AROUND GUADALCANAL

At 5,302 sq km, Guadalcanal is the largest island in the Solomons. The northern coastal plain contrasts with the Weather Coast in the S, where precipitous cliffs plunge into the sea. The interior is extremely rugged, rising to Mt. Makarakomburu (2,447 m), the highest peak in the country. Most of the WW II battlefields E of Honiara can be seen on daytrips from the capital, while Lambi Bay is an overnight trip (or more). The Marau Sound area is well worth a couple of days, and the adventuresome could continue W along the S coast (but not during the rainy season). Many small hamlets in the interior, accessible only on foot, are reserved for the true explorer.

Mataniko Falls: One of the most amazing waterfalls in the South Pacific is only a 2-hour walk S of Honiara up the Mataniko River. Follow the road from Chinatown up the riverside to its end at Tuvaruhu. Galloping Horse Ridge, a major WW II battlefield, towers over Tuvaruhu to the west. Cross the river and follow a trail up over the grassy hillsides and down toward a forest. You pass a small coconut grove and Harahei village. The final descent to the falls is down a steep, slippery, forested incline. There are many large pools for cooling off after this exhausting hike, but the main sight is a gigantic swallow-infested stalagmite-covered cave which an arm of the river roars right through. The river itself pours out of a crack in a limestone cliff just above and tumbles down into the cave through a crevice totally surrounded by white water. This jungle-girdled complex of cascades alone justifies a visit, but the intrepid should swim/hike back down the Mataniko through the gorge back to Tuvaruku. You'll be floating with the current through deep water in places, so don't take anything that can't get wet. Take along an inner tube if you can. Caves on the slopes high above the river still contain the bones of Japanese soldiers who died there. You'll never forget this excursion.

Mount Austin: Walk or take a taxi up the paved highway to the summit of Mt. Austin (410 m) for a sweeping view of the N coastal plains. The river you see just below you is the Lungga, someday to be harnessed in a major hydroelectric development. Most of the historic battlefields are visible from here. In 1942 a Japanese army under Gen. Maruyama plodded around behind Mt. Austin from White River in an abortive attempt to take Henderson airstrip from the rear. At least 6 big artillery pieces and much war materiel, strewn along the Lungga River N of the mountain, are now swallowed in thick jungle. The same road you came up on ends at the Lungga, but you'll certainly need a guide to go exploring. This can be arranged at Mbarana village.

Mbarana: Halfway up the road from Honiara you pass the large white Solomon Peace Memorial Park, erected in 1981 by Japanese veterans. Above this are Forestry Dept. plots (notice the *kauri* trees). The dirt road westbound just before Forestry leads to Mbarana village. Follow a footpath (the Tuvaruhu Trail) from Mbarana back down to Honiara along grassy ridges with good views on all sides. Keep straight ahead on the path and generally L, and you'll come out at Vara near Chinatown. This is the best part of the trip.

A single gun guards Red Beach near Foxwood Timbers where the U.S. Marines landed on 7 Aug. 1942.

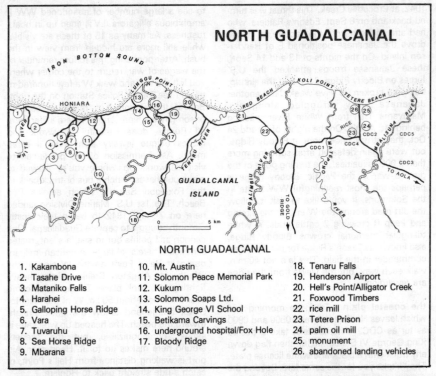

NORTH GUADALCANAL

1. Kakambona
2. Tasahe Drive
3. Mataniko Falls
4. Harahei
5. Galloping Horse Ridge
6. Vara
7. Tuvaruhu
8. Sea Horse Ridge
9. Mbarana
10. Mt. Austin
11. Solomon Peace Memorial Park
12. Kukum
13. Solomon Soaps Ltd.
14. King George VI School
15. Betikama Carvings
16. underground hospital/Fox Hole
17. Bloody Ridge
18. Tenaru Falls
19. Henderson Airport
20. Hell's Point/Alligator Creek
21. Foxwood Timbers
22. rice mill
23. Tetere Prison
24. palm oil mill
25. monument
26. abandoned landing vehicles

vicinity of Henderson airport: Catch a bus to King George VI School. The old Kukum fighter strip across the road from the school is now a 9-hole golf course. The road along the end of the course from the school toward the beach will bring you to the Solomon Soaps Ltd. factory, where famous saltwater soap is made. They'll show you around if you're interested. A km E of the school is the turnoff to Betikama Carvings, on the grounds of Adventist High School, 1.5 km off the main road. There's a good display of woodcarvings made in SDA villages in the Marovo Lagoon area, a captivating collection of WW II relics including several planes, a small war museum, and a couple of crocodiles. Open daily 0800-1200/1300-1700 except Sat., donation. Return to the main highway and cross the Lungga River bridge. Just around the bend is a small concrete bunker on the slope. This is

the original foxhole from which all other foxholes got their name—the dugout of Col. Wm. J. Fox, USMC, Commanding Officer, Henderson Field. Go over the hill behind the foxhole and past the "manager's residence" until you come to a field gun. At the foot of the hill down the road to the R of this is an underground wartime hospital. Despite the warning sign outside, it's perfectly safe to explore with a flashlight. Now proceed toward Henderson airport.

Bloody Ridge: The original control tower, a solitary steel-frame structure, still overlooks the field. Outside the modern terminal is an American War Memorial and a Japanese AA gun. Henderson Field was the center of fighting during the first part of the Solomon Islands campaign. The initial Japanese counter-attack came from the E, on 21 Aug.

1942, at Crocodile Creek. This thrust was turned back and on 8 Sept. Edson's Raiders, who had arrived fresh from the capture of Tulagi, drove the Japanese positioned E of Henderson inland. On the nights of 13 and 14 Sept., these Japanese troops attacked the U.S. forces on Bloody Ridge, 2 km S of the airstrip, but were broken up. Five weeks later another Japanese army struggled along the Maruyama Trail from White River, passing behind Mt. Austin. On the nights of 23 and 24 Oct. they struck once more at Bloody Ridge, but were again defeated after suffering more than 2,000 casualties. The turning point of the ground war in the Pacific, Bloody Ridge is perhaps the most meaningful WW II site in the Solomons. If you'd like to visit it, follow the dirt road around the W end of the airstrip and keep R crossing 2 cattle grids. A white triangular memorial crowns Bloody Ridge, also known as Edson's Ridge for the American commander in the field. This is a hot 40-min. walk each way, but the views from the ridge are rewarding.

the coastal plain: Take the morning bus which leaves Honiara between 0800 and 0900 as far as CDC2. Alternatively, take a bus to King George VI School (KG6), then flag down any truck with a black-and-white license plate. They'll take you for the same fare. Beyond the airport you'll pass Lever's copra/cacao estates, the sawmill, the rice mill, huge palm oil plantations, and finally rice paddies. Get off at the corner at CDC2 within sight of the huge palm oil mill. These fields supply the country's requirements of rice, while Solomon Islands Plantations Ltd., in conjunction with the Commonwealth Development Corporation (CDC), make the island a major exporter of palm oil. (A hectare of oil palms produces 3 times more oil than a hectare of coconuts.) Walk straight down the road which passes the palm oil mill 3 km to Tetere Beach. Follow the beach a few hundred m to the R till you see the monument to 5 Austrian explorers from the *Albatross* expedition who were murdered in 1896 to prevent them from climbing sacred Mt. Tatuba (Tatuve). Come back and follow the road along the beach to the L past a sign-bearing tree, then turn inland on an overgrown track

to see a large number of abandoned WW II amphibious alligators (LVT) lined up in hoary rustiness. As many as 15 of these are visible, while still more are hidden from view in the bush. After pondering this forlorn reminder of the wages of war, return to the corner where you left the bus and walk W a few hundred m till you see Tetere Police Station on the right. Behind the station is a minimum security prison (once a leprosarium) where a lifer named Roman does beautiful glasswork and makes unique jewelry from WW II scrap metal. Ask permission of the policemen to visit his workshop, where you're allowed to make purchases. Catch a bus or truck back to the Foxwood Sawmill which adjoins Red Beach. The 1st U.S. Marine Division landed here on 7 Aug. 1942 to begin their costly 6-month struggle to capture Guadalcanal. One cannon still points out to sea, a silent, rusted sentinel. There's a large American military dump at Hell's Point on the W side of the mouth of Alligator Creek, where heavy fighting also took place. To get there climb over the fence about 500 m W of the Alligator Creek bridge and follow the track straight toward the beach. The heaped-up wreckage is almost unrecognizable, but the scenery around here makes up for it. Henderson Airport is walking distance from Hell's Point, or catch a ride straight back to Honiara.

east of Honiara: The road E from Honiara terminates at Aola (60 km). There's an impressive 60-m waterfall on the Chea River, a 4-hour walk from St. Joseph's School, Tenaru. A truck can go most of the way. There's a good pool for swimming at the foot of the falls. It's possible to hike right across the island from CDC1 to Kuma on the S coast via Gold Ridge. This is a major undertaking requiring a local guide and 3 days of slugging. A cargo cult led by visionary Chief Moro, who called for a return to the *kabilato,* flourishes at Makaruka, a village on the Weather Coast between Avu Avu and Marau Sound. Two custom house "banks" brimming with shell money are well-guarded at Makaruka. To visit you may be subjected to a test by the locals, which you'll pass if your motives are right. A jeep track links Avu Avu to Marau Sound (50

GUADALCANAL

km), but the only vehicles on it are tractors which pass every couple of weeks. There are provincial rest houses on this coast, near the airstrips (with Solair flights) at Marau Sound, Avu Avu, and Mbambanakira. There are 2 fully-equipped cottages for rent on Tavanipupu I. at Marau Sound: $196 a week for up to 4 persons. Bring all food from Honiara; water shortages do occur. The cottages are set on an emerald lagoon flanked by fine white beaches. Giant clam shells are found in this area.

west of Honiara: Fred Kona's War Museum (admission $1-5 pp: negotiable), at Vilu village 25 km W of Honiara, includes a model custom village and picnic area for tourists, as well as a huge collection of war relics dragged in. Find outboard canoes to Savo I. in the village near Cape Esperance Lighthouse or at Visale. The Tambea Village Resort (see "resort" above) is just beyond. It was from here that many Japanese troops made their final escape from

Guadalcanal in Feb. 1943. On the shore at Paru, a couple of km W of Tambea, a Japanese submarine is almost completely swamped by sand. Look for an exposed steel pipe, or ask the villagers. The N coast highway terminates at Lambi Bay, 69 km W of Honiara. For accommodations ask for Leonid Torokava or Martine Tolule at Tavudi village near Lambi. Martine is building a small resort here—campers are welcome. A more adventuresome way to get there is to take a Marine Division boat to Tangarare ($7), then walk back to Lambi Bay in a day or more. There are 2 chest-deep rivers to cross. A good surfing spot (rights) is near the river mouth at Tangarare, and there's good diving along this beautiful coastline. A footpath travels the entire S coast from village to village. Another heads inland from Tangarare and emerges W of Honiara near Poha. Village trucks leave Lambi Bay for Honiara ($2.50) nearly every morning.

CENTRAL PROVINCE

Tulagi: Tulagi, a small island in the Florida Group about 5 km in circumference, was the island capital of the Solomons from 1895 to 1942. Burns Philp had its head station on Makambo I. nearby. The Japanese entered unopposed on 3 May 1942, after a hasty British evacuation. Tulagi was badly damaged during the American invasion 3 months later. The Americans built a seaplane base on nearby Ghavutu I., and a good concrete wharf from that time remains. Another remnant of the old days on Tulagi is the marine base, where shipbuilding and repairs are still carried out. The deep strait between Tulagi and Nggela forms a good harbor, and in 1973 the Japanese Taiyo Corporation took advantage of this by establishing a fish-freezing and canning plant. Their rubbish boat, which goes out 5 or 6 times a day to dump waste in the deep water, provides enjoyable free rides to venturesome visitors. There's a striking hand-hewn passage, like the Argyle Cut in Sydney, between the wharf and the rest house. Follow a footpath (3 hours) clockwise around the island for great views. Today Tulagi is the headquarters of Central Province, an odd collection which includes the Florida Is., Savo, the Russell Islands, Bellona, and Rennell. **amenities:** The Central Province Rest House ($7 pp) has 8 beds and cooking facilities.

a war club from Rennell

Check in at the Provincial Offices. You can get a $2-lunch or dinner at Sarah's Place. Tulagi also has a market and 2 Chinese stores. Buy frozen skipjack for home cooking at the Taiyo cold storage.

the Florida Islands: There are 2 large islands here, Nggela Sule and Nggela Pile, separated by narrow Utaha Passage. Tulagi is off the S coast of Nggela Sule. To get away for a week take a walk around Nggela Pile for its scenic views and village life. Catch a ship from Honiara to Siota, then walk a couple of days along the coast to Vuturua village, and have someone paddle you across to Peula. Then continue on the coast to Ndende and across to Dadala village on Utaha Passage. Finish your expedition with a canoe ride to Taroaniara shipyard, where you should be able to find a ship back to Honiara. An ultra-expensive Australian tourist resort has been established on Anuha, an isolated island on the N side of Nggela Sule.

Savo: Savo is an actively volcanic island on Iron Bottom Sound, named for the number of warships sunk in the vicinity during WW II. Savo last erupted in 1840, but it's still considered potentially dangerous. Near the center of the island are 2 craters, one inside the other. A trip up to the steaming crater is worth trying—if you can find a guide and you're fit. The only stream on Savo is near boiling at its source. All drinking and washing water on Savo comes from wells, and the water in them is also often warm: boil before drinking. There's a fissure just a short distance inland where the locals cook their food. Savo is also famous for its megapode bird (*Megapodius freycinet*), a small dark bush turkey which lays billiard ball-sized eggs underground, then leaves them to hatch by heat from the sun or the island's warm volcanic sands. The fledglings dig themselves out, and can run at birth. Unfortunately, the number of megapodes is declining fast due to unrestrained harvesting of the eggs. See them in the early morning

the beach at Kanggava, Rennell I. (1968)

near Panueli. There's an empty house near the clinic where visitors often stay. You'll be charged according to how affluent you look. Nathaniel Niuau of the Agriculture Division puts up visitors for a nominal fee. Although most outboards go to Visale or Honiara on Guadalcanal, it's sometimes possible to find a ship from Savo to Tulagi and vice versa.

the Russell Islands: The Russell Islands consist of 2 adjacent larger islands, Mbanika and Pavuva, plus many smaller islets. Most ships between Honiara and Gizo call at Yandina on the E side of Mbanika. Lever's Pacific Plantations Ltd. has huge copra plantations on the islands where visitors aren't welcome. Even relatives of plantation employees are

discouraged from visiting — a pretty outrageous situation. There are some big wartime guns a couple of hours walk from Yandina. The locals know where they are.

Rennell and Bellona: Two hundred km S of Guadalcanal are 2 Polynesian islands, Rennell and Bellona, about 25 km apart. Rennell, an 80-by-16-km raised atoll surrounded by 150-m sheer cliffs, is by far the larger. Lake Te Nggano on the SE side of Rennell is one of the largest in the South Pacific. The water in the lake is at sea level, but is surrounded by high cliffs. Due to the murder of 3 missionaries in 1910, Rennell was closed to Europeans until 1934. This long period of isolation has kept the Polynesian Rennellese particularly separated from other Polynesian groups. The airstrip is at Tinggoa, at the W end. A rough track leads down to the small port, Lavanggu, where the monthly ship from Honiara calls; it also stops at Tuhungganggo ($2 by canoe from Lavanggu). From Tuhungganggo you follow a steep stairway over sharp limestone cliffs to Te Nggano village, one of 4 on the shore of the lake. The Rennellese still practice *Hetakai*, traditional wrestling, at custom feasts. Among the many handicrafts are walking sticks, hardwood crocodile carvings, miniature weapons, woven bags, and mats. Ask the location of wrecked wartime aircraft in the bush.

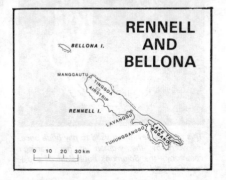

RENNELL AND BELLONA

BELLONA I.

MANGGAUTU
TINGGOA
AIRSTRIP
RENNELL I.
LAVANGGU
TUHUNGGANGGO
LAKE TE NGGANO

0 10 20 30 km

MALAITA

This hot, humid, thickly forested island is the second largest, but most populous, of the Solomons: its 75,000 inhabitants comprise almost a third of the population. Malaita is one of the country's few islands where people reside in the jungle-clad interior. The bush people live in isolated hamlets of 2 or 3 houses, and as many as 10,000 still believe in ancestral spirits (although persistent missionaries are working to change this). Many Malaitans have tried to escape their island's limited economic opportunities by emigrating to other islands; there's a large community of them in Honiara. In blackbirding times, nearly 10,000 Malaitans labored in the canefields of Queensland, Australia. Today, they work on plantations throughout the Solomons and are likely to be your fellow passengers on interisland ships. Copra production is one of the only ways most Malaitans have of making cash money, although there have been attempts to introduce cattle and cacao. Malaita has the most extensive road network in the Solomons, but most are in bad repair and can be closed by rains. The main town is Auki. There's little difficulty going inland, provided you have a guide. Malaita is wet and the forest floor is permanently damp. The walking is slow and good boots are essential. This is the world's best place to study malaria.

traditional currency: The shell money of the Langa Langa Lagoon, on the NW side of Malaita, is made by breaking shells into small pieces, boring them with a drill, and stringing them together. Patient rubbing of the shell pieces between 2 grooved stones gives them their circular shape. Thousands of minute discs go into a *tafuliae* (length of shells 2-3 m long) which bears a fixed rate of exchange to the official currency (presently $1.20 a string—each *tafuliae* has 10 strings). This auxiliary form of currency is used as far away as Bougainville for quasi-ceremonial transactions, such as buying wives (60 strings) and pigs, and as settlement or compensation for injuries, hence Malaitans go there to trade. Shells vary in value according to the color and size of the shell parts used: red is the most expensive, then orange, white, and lastly black. Generally, the smaller the size of the shell piece, the more expensive it is. Pink-lipped *spondylus* ("pink money") is made only from the lip of the shell and is the most valuable, worth 4-5 times as much as white. Dolphin teeth are also used as custom money on Malaita (1,000 teeth for a wife at 40 cents a tooth), and dolphin drives to obtain teeth are conducted at Mbita'ama Harbor (NW. Malaita), Port Adam (Maramasike I.), and Sulufou (Lau Lagoon). A sorcerer in a canoe taps magical stones together underwater to attract the dolphins, which are then led ashore by other villagers in canoes, butchered, and the meat divided. In the Western Solomons ceremonial currency is in the form of large heavy rings, 4 cm thick and 24 cm in diameter, cut out of the shell of the giant clam. Rings with a small patch of yellow on the edge are worth more than plain white ones. In Santa Cruz great rolls of feather money are used.

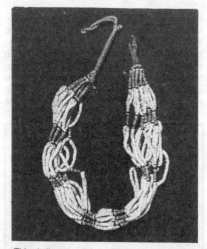

This shell money, often used to pay bride price, is worn by the woman at her marriage ceremony—the Solomons equivalent of a diamond or gold ring.

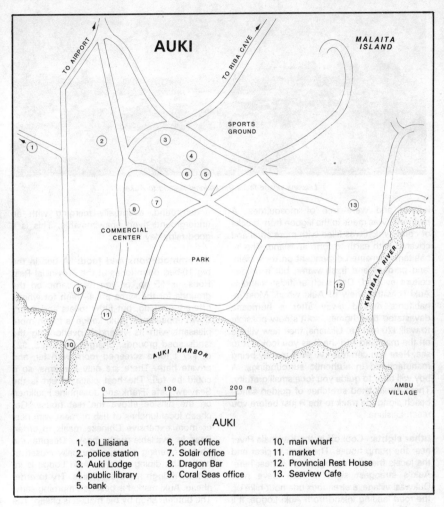

AUKI

1. to Lilisiana
2. police station
3. Auki Lodge
4. public library
5. bank
6. post office
7. Solair office
8. Dragon Bar
9. Coral Seas office
10. main wharf
11. market
12. Provincial Rest House
13. Seaview Cafe

AUKI

Auki, at the N end of the Langa Langa Lagoon, has been the administrative center since 1909. There's regular ferry service from Honiara and, for most visitors, Auki is Malaita's port of entry. The setting is picturesque and there are many interesting places to visit in the vicinity, but try to find a ship from Honiara direct to Fouia, Takwa, or

Malu'u in N. Malaita, then return to Auki by road. This way you'll avoid having to backtrack. There are sometimes ships from Auki to S. Malaita, and a trip to Kwai I. off E. Malaita is possible when the road to Atori is open.

Lilisiana: For 18 generations the saltwater people of the Langa Langa Lagoon have lived on tiny artificial reef islands which offered protection from raids by the bush people of the

Lilisiana village faces the channel leading to Auke.

interior and were free of mosquitoes. A perimeter was made in the lagoon from blocks of coral, which was filled with more coral and covered with earth to form an island. The inhabitants remained dependent on their mainland gardens and fresh water, but a unique culture evolved. One such artificial island is Auki I., within view of Auki wharf. Most inhabitants moved away after a hurricane devastated their homes, so it's now possible to walk (20 min.) to Lilisiana, their new village on the mainland—to the R as you look out to sea. Here you can observe shell money being manufactured in authentic surroundings. A boy will offer to guide you for a small gratuity. There are isolated stretches of golden sandy beach along the track to the R just before you reach Lilisiana.

other sights: Cool off in the Kwaibala River near the pump house. The water is clear and the locals friendly. Ambu village is near here. Auki's strangest sight is Riba Cave near Dukwasi village, a strenuous one-hour hike up the road leading inland from Auki Lodge. It'll cost $2 to go through (they'll start off asking $15, so bargain hard) and the cave is slippery, drippy, and muddy, so dress accordingly. Thousands of swallows inhabit the cave roof. From the entrance the cave passage leads a short distance to an impressive sinkhole. Across the sinkhole, at the entrance to the largest chamber, is a giant stalagmite in the form of a man named Louis. Once worshipped, it's been worn smooth by rubbing. The passage leads through large rooms far underground, eventually merging with an underground river, unswimmable. This is a good rainy-day trip.

accommodations and food: A bed in the big 10-bed dormitories at the Provincial Rest House is $5 pp, or you may camp on the grounds for the same price—high for what's offered: cooking, but filthy toilets and a run-down appearance. Auki Lodge is much more pleasant with its verandah overlooking the landscaped grounds. Charges are $16 s, $23 d, $27 t for a screened room with fan and private bath. There are only 8 rooms, so it could be full. The best place to eat is the Seaview Cafe (Frank and Josephine Faulkner) on the hillside above the rest house. Get cheap local lunches of fish or meat with rice, or more expensive Chinese meals to order. Beer is available with meals. Despite the posted opening hours, it's usually closed at night. The dining room at Auki Lodge is intimate, though more expensive. Try to order ahead. Auki market is best Sat. morning early. The butcher shop by the market is cheap. The Dragon Bar on the main drag is colorful but rough. **services and information:** The bank near the post office will change foreign currency and travelers cheques. There are lots of books on Melanesia at the Auki Library.

transport: Gwaunaruu airstrip (AKS) is 11 km N of Auki; the Solair minibus is $2. There are daily Solair flights to Honiara ($30), plus 2 a week to Atoifi ($13). Auki is also well-serviced by passenger ships to Honiara ($12—6 hours).

There are scheduled trips on Mon., Thurs., Fri., and Sat., plus others leaving irregularly. Coral Seas Ltd. has an office near the wharf which only seems to be open when their ship is in port. Book early as they sometimes fill up. Ask at the post office for government ships to S. Malaita weekly, often departing on Monday. There's no regular bus service on the island, so you travel by passenger truck (Malu'u $3-4, Fouia $5-6, Atori $5, Maoa $2); usually in Auki on days when ships arrive. This is the easiest time to catch rides to anywhere. On other days you may be stuck.

tours: Auki Lodge organizes outboard tours to Laulasi or Alite islands (5 hours). The $30 pp price includes custom dancing, a demonstration of shell money-making, a tour of the custom places, and lunch. Book 24 hours in advance. These trips are as artificial as the islands they visit, yet they're the only easy way to see these unusual places, and they do give the inhabitants at least one motive for preserving a version of their culture. Most other outside influences are purely culture-destructive. Auki Lodge also offers a land tour to a "custom house" N of Auki, but this turns out to be only a souvenir shop which you must still pay $1 to enter!

LANGA LANGA LAGOON

The artificial islands in the Langa Langa Lagoon are home to some of the last of the Shark Callers. Many of these people still worship their ancestors, whose spirits are embodied in sharks that the high priest summons. Skeptics say the sharks come because they hear the gongs being beaten underwater, a conditioned reflex. Yet no one knows for sure why the sharks eat the offerings but leave alone the people who swim among them. A boy stands on a submerged rock and feeds the sharks pieces of cooked pig one by one as the priest calls each by the name of its human spirit. The largest piece is given last, to the oldest shark. It's said that when the sharks have finished feeding, the priest calls the old shark to come up beside the boy, who mounts it and is taken for a ride around the lagoon and back. (Note, however, it's very unlikely you'll see shark-calling on your tour.)

Laulasi: On this small island, 13 km S of Auki, are large spirit houses with high, pitched roofs, the names of famous priests inscribed on the gables. When a priest dies, his body is taken to neighboring Alite to rot. Later the skull is retrieved and placed in the House of Skulls. Offerings are presented at shark-calling ceremonies in the gap between the 2 islands. The pigs used for these offerings are held by the shore in pens big enough for a man—the offering in times past before pigs were substituted. Women and children are forbidden to enter the custom houses, and no one dressed in red or black will be permitted to land on the island. Tourists are shown how to make shell money using manual drills; after they're gone, the diamond-headed drillbits come back out. The village on Alite is similar.

Queen Victoria's Birdwing (Ornithoptera victoriae) *is found only in the Solomon Islands. As specimens are among the most highly prized of all butterflies, their export is government-controlled.*

a clamshell ornament from Malaita incised with frigate bird designs

getting there: The road S from Auki reaches beyond Su'u Bay, but passenger trucks only go as far as Maoa ($2). There's more frequent service to Talakali (16 km—50 cents), on the mainland opposite Laulasi. There you might be able to hire a canoe across for $5 RT (less if you paddle the 2 km yourself), but you'll be charged a $10-pp "landing fee" to look around (and no dances or lunch). You pay a similar fee at Alite. Bargaining would probably lower these prices, but don't think you're dealing with innocent natives—they've seen many tourists before you. Talakali's population, incidentally, is Seventh-day Adventist, so avoid going on Saturday. You have to be a little brazen to do it this way, but it might be more adventuresome than the tours. If you can afford $30, however, take the tour this once and play your accepted role.

MALU'U

This pleasant little government station, at the island's northern tip halfway between Auki and Fouia, makes an excellent base from which to visit heavily populated N. Malaita. The villagers are very friendly and warmly welcome visitors. There's a decent rest house, and traffic from Auki is fairly frequent. There are even passenger ships between Malu'u and Honiara, but no one knows exactly when.

sights: A good short walk from the rest house is down the hill to the market, then R along the beach till you meet the main road again. There's a bathing beach here and the reef protects you from most sharks. Go snorkeling on Diula opposite the tiny offshore island. Out across the lagoon a good surf breaks at the W end of the reef. This left-hander works best at high tide in a 1.5-m swell. Where the swells come from 2 directions the shifting peaks cause havoc. There's also good diving along the inside edge of the lagoon. Visit Mana'ambu village on the main road near Malu'u for its Tofe Takwe Trail Store which offers Milo and pancakes. You can sleep in a young men's treehouse *(biu)* at Mana'ambu for $1 a night. At A'ama village on the hilltop just above, visit the *biu*. There are more *biu* at Take-Wind village off the road between Mana'ambu and Malu'u. At Manakwai village, a few km W of Malu'u on the main road, is a small cascade, a minihydro station, and a good place to swim in the river. To get to Basakana I., take a truck to the beach opposite and light a smoky fire. Someone will come across from the village to fetch you. There's a cave to visit on Basakana, plus many fine beaches.

accommodations and tours: The Malu'u Rest House, in a panoramic location overlooking the sea (great sunsets), has 6 beds costing $8 pp, and a more expensive self-contained unit. If you have a tent, you may camp at the rest house and use the facilities. Meals are provided upon request, or cook your own in the well-equipped kitchen. Buy groceries at the 3 stores down by the harbor, or from the market (Wed. and Sat., open 0800). The rest house manager, Ishmael Ilabinia, can arrange an outboard canoe to visit Sulufou for about $40 (up to 10 people). Ishmael's brother paddles surfers and snorkelers out to the reef and back in his dugout for $3-4; ask him to show you the submerged Japanese plane. Ishmael can also supply a guide for bush walks into the surrounding hills.

Matakwalao: Visit Matakwalao market (Wed. and Sat.) by truck from Malu'u (60 cents). Ask for John Risavo and hire him as a guide ($2 per day); you'll be in for a touch of real adventure. John is *nambawan* in the bush. If you don't meet him at the market, get someone to guide you to his jungle hamlet, a

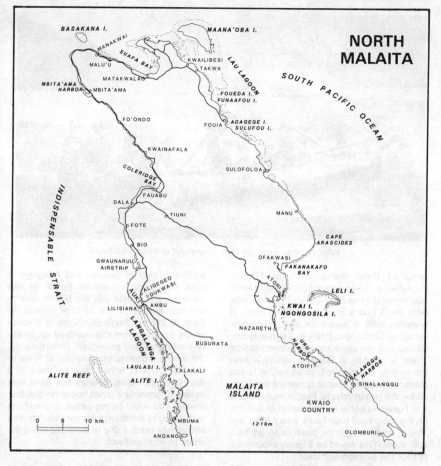

NORTH MALAITA

BASAKANA I.

MAANA'OBA I.

MANAKWAI

MALU'U

SUAFA BAY

KWAILIBESI

TAKWA

LAU LAGOON

SOUTH PACIFIC OCEAN

MATAKWALAO

MBITA'AMA HARBOR

MBITA'AMA

FO'ONDO

FOUEDA I.

FUNAAFOU I.

FOUIA

ADAGEGE I.

SULUFOU I.

KWAINAFALA

SULOFOLOA

COLERIDGE BAY

DALA

FAUABU

MANU

TIUNI

FOTE

CAPE ARASCIDES

BIO

OFAKWASI

INDISPENSABLE STRAIT

GWAUNARUU AIRSTRIP

FAKANAKAFO BAY

ALIGEGEO

DUKWASI

ATORI

LELI I.

LILISIANA

AUKI

AMBU

KWAI I.

NGONGOSILA I.

NAZARETH

BUSURATA

LANGALANGA LAGOON

URU HARBOR

ATOIFI

LAULASI I.

TALAKALI

ALITE REEF

ALITE I.

MALAITA ISLAND

SINALANGGU HARBOR

SINALANGGU

KWAIO COUNTRY

MBUMA

1219m

OLOMBURI

ANOANO

0   5   10 km

3-hour walk from Matakwalao. This will give you an idea of what you'll be in for. There may be problems in visiting the custom stones on Malaita Hill, but John knows other custom places deep in the rainforest which you can visit with less effort.

LAU LAGOON

Over 60 artificial islands are found in the Lau Lagoon on the NE side of Malaita. These are inhabited by the so-called island builders, who bring coral blocks, sand, and earth on log rafts to convert lagoon shallows into solid land. With the constant cool breezes, the air is incredibly fresh out on these man-made islands. On the mainland they grow taro, yams, potatoes, pawpaw, leafy vegetables, bananas, and sugarcane. The women travel back and forth from their island homes to the gardens, and the men fish most of the time. The large canoes for dolphin-hunting are made by sewing together long planks of wood and caulking the seams with a putty made from the nut of the *tita* tree *(Parinari glaberrima)*. People on

What could be more fun than a canoe-full of kids at Sulufou?

some of these islands such as Foueda, Funaafou, and Adagege still practice the same custom religion as the people of Laulasi/Alite. Here you'll find a *bae*, the heathen place of worship, with a sacrificial altar, cemetery, House of Skulls, etc. Entry to the *bae* is prohibited, but you can often see in from outside. There is no *bae* at Sulufou, which is now thoroughly Christianized. Shark-calling is also practiced here on special occasions announced by the pagan priests. People from Foueda and Funaafou come to the market at Sulione, on the main road near Fouia, every Mon. and Thurs., and it might be possible to go back with them. This would be a heavy experience, not for the average sightseer.

Takwa: Take the motor-vessel *Adamasia* direct from Honiara to Takwa ($4), only 15 km from the end of the road at Fouia. The *Memory* also plies this route. The final passage to Takwa wharf passes many artificial islands, a fitting introduction to the Lau Lagoon. A market near the Catholic mission at Takwa takes place every Saturday. Swim in the river at the landing where the dugout canoes of the saltwater people arrive.

Sulufou: The road from Auki ends at Fouia wharf (115 km), on the mainland opposite the artificial islands of Sulufou and Adagege. A truck from Malu'u costs $3. For $1 or less someone will paddle you the 500 m over to Sulufou, largest of the artificial islands. In front of the big Anglican church is a stone where fugitives from the mainland sat to obtain sanctuary and protection. Unfortunately, there is no organized place to stay at Fouia or Sulufou, so you either have to make it a daytrip or go native. Charles Fox Akao was talking of opening a guest house on Sulufou, so ask. You could be requested to contribute something to this church for the visit. You can sometimes catch a ship or outboard down the coast to Atori or Kwai.

SOUTHEAST MALAITA

East Malaita: Take a truck from Auki via Dala to Atori ($5), provided the road hasn't been closed by rains. It's only 3 km from Atori to Kwai I., but the outboard boys charge $15 RT, so try to hitch a ride with someone off your truck. Outboard canoe hire charges are totally unreasonable throughout this area. A road is underway from Atori to Atoifi, presently as far as Nazareth, and Solair flies Atoifi-Auki ($13) twice a week. Kwai is a beautiful island with kind, friendly people. Village houses are densely packed here and on neighboring Ngongosila Island. There's a native rest house with cooking facilities at the edge of the island where you can stay for $2 (ask for Paul Alafa or David Loke, the village baker). Wade across the sandbar from Kwai to Ngongosila at low tide to see the grave of Mr. Bell and his cadet (see below). Trips S beyond Atoifi into the Kwaio Country above Sinalanggu to see the "Hidden People" can be arranged, but be prepared for sky-high charges for transport and guides, overt suspicion by officials, and perhaps ultimate rejection by the Kwaio themselves. Somewhat easier to experience are the surfing beaches N of Atori. Fakanakafo Bay is the closest, but press on to Manu village, less than a day's hike from Atori, for the good left-handers. Cargo ships such as *Memory* call at Manu occasionally, which you could catch out if you're lucky.

the Kwaio: In 1927, British District Officer Bell, 13 native policemen, and a cadet were speared by Kwaio tribesmen at Kwaiambe, Sinalanggu District. Later British officials looked the other way when N. Malaita police murdered about 70 Kwaio prisoners, including women and children, in cold blood to avenge

their slain comrades. Two Australian destroyers were sent to carry out further retaliatory actions against the natives and they got into the spirit so well that they went on to pillage villages on Makira and Guadalcanal as well! Even today, the Kwaio Country is still largely out-of-bounds to Europeans, and Solomon Is. government officials go escorted. The pagan population lives in small, scattered hamlets on the upland plateaus. Those Kwaio who have accepted Christianity now live in larger villages along the coast. There is a possibility that you will be arrested and deported if you try to reach here without official permission. The Kwaio have a nice big metal cooking pot ready for visiting missionaries.

South Malaita: No road connects S. Malaita to Auki, so either fly to Parasi ($43 OW from Auki) or hop a ship. There's a Provincial Rest House at Maka, at the SW entrance to Maramasike Passage. Only 3.7-m deep near the center, this passage is only open to vessels of light draft. A bush road now runs from Apio, opposite Maka, to Olusu'u near the SE end of Maramasike or Small Malaita. Few tourists come here.

overmodeled ancestral skull

WESTERN PROVINCE

Western Province (8,573 sq km) is the largest in the Solomons. The New Georgia Group, which forms its core, is easily the most attractive and varied area in the country. High vegetation-shrouded volcanoes buttress the enticing lagoons of Marovo and Roviana, respectively off the eastern and southern coasts of New Georgia. These vast stretches of dazzling water are dotted with hundreds of little green islets, covered either in dense jungle or planted with coconuts. Sadly, commercial logging is gradually decimating the great rainforests of New Georgia, Kolombangara, and Choiseul. The inhabitants have the darkest skin in the Solomons. Some 20 different languages are spoken, but people in this province have had long contact with missionaries, and you'll find very eloquent, well-informed individuals in the most unlikely places. The bamboo band was invented here in the 1920s; today 15 to 24 varying lengths of bamboo are struck on their open ends with rubber thongs, to the accompaniment of guitar and ukelele. As yet little known to the world of music, bamboo rhythms will win you at once. Travel among the many islands of the New Georgia Group is almost totally by sea, which makes getting around easy, yet there are also feeder roads from the main centers, Munda, Noro, Ringgi Cove, and Gizo, which help the hiker and hitcher. There are many villages and the people are helpful and hospitable. They'll often volunteer to take you between islands in their big outboard canoes. Always offer to pay $2-3 pp, whether they ask or not. The scheduled weekly passenger ship from Honiara to Gizo offers an excellent introduction to the New Georgia Islands.

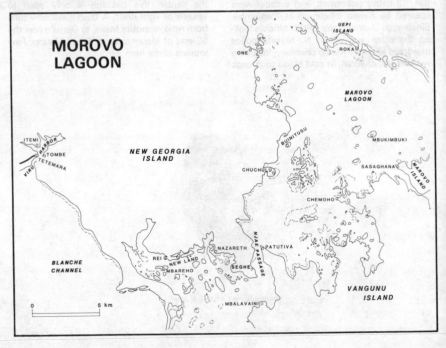

the Marovo Lagoon: On the ship from Honiara, you first travel through the huge Marovo Lagoon. A thin string of islands shelters this semicircular lagoon as it swings around Vangunu I. from Nggatokae to New Georgia. The best beaches are outside the lagoon itself, on the ocean side; mangrove swamps are more common within. A cruise through the lagoon makes for great scenic viewing, but most of the ships from Honiara pass at night. One way to see something is to get off at Patutiva and pay $10 to charter a speedboat (ask for Mr. Golden Ringi) to Buinitusu, a button-sized island with 70 inhabitants. Mr. Muven Kuve has built a few leaf houses on the mainland opposite Buinitusu for visitors who stay. The charge is reasonable (about $6 pp including tropical fruit, camping half price), and Muven has an outboard canoe which you can hire to get around the lagoon. He'll also loan you a dugout to paddle yourself. The barge *Ulusaghe* sails direct from Honiara to Buinitusu about once a week. There's another, more expensive resort by a white coral beach on Uepi Island. Village carvers around the lagoon are famous for their workmanship with kerosene wood and ebony. Unfortunately, some have begun working in a grotesque non-traditional style (the so-called "Spirit of the Solomons" series) that only tourists appreciate. Actually, you can buy Marovo carvings just as cheaply in Honiara and there'll be a better selection.

Seghe Point: Seghe, on New Georgia I. at the SW end of the lagoon, is the communications hub of Marovo. Solair has 3 flights a week from Munda ($23) and Honiara ($70) to the wartime airstrip the Americans built in only 10 days. There's a sunken plane in the water off the passage end of this airstrip. During WW II, coastwatcher Donald Kennedy held out unassisted for several months at Seghe with a small force of Solomon Islanders, supplying vital information on Japanese movements. The passenger ships all stop at Patutiva wharf on Vangunu I., just across scenic Njae Passage from Seghe. A good cheap market materializes at Patutiva whenever the Coral Seas ship arrives—jump

This Japanese gun still guards the entrance to Viru Harbor, New Georgia.

off and back on fast to buy oranges and bananas. Dugout canoes propelled by outboard, paddle, or sail carry people around the lagoon from Patutiva, and hitching a ride isn't too hard. Contribute for gas if they take you far.

Viru Harbor: The ship next enters beautiful, landlocked Viru Harbor and calls briefly at Tetemara landing. As you come in between the high coral cliffs, look up above the white triangular navigational aid on the L to see the long barrel of a Japanese gun, still pointing skyward. Five stone fortresses, 2 on the N and 3 on the S, guarded the harbor entrance in ancient times. Today Viru Harbor serves as a logging camp and is a stronghold of Seventh-day Adventist fundamentalism. the offices of Kalena Timber are at Itemi, just a short distance farther up the harbor from Tetemara. The company store sells beer only on paydays, every other Fri., and the true believers lie low. A free ferry shuttles constantly (0500-1800 daily except Sat.) between Tetemara, Itemi, and Tombe (a wood-carving village). There's a Forestry Station at Arara, 10 km from Tetemara by road. Other than the Honiara-Gizo ships, the only way to get out of Viru Harbor is by canoe to Seghe. Ask about the mail run.

Rendova: The ship also ties up at Mburuku (Ughele) on the high volcanic island of Rendova, another major WW II battlefield. You'll have about 15 min. to get off and buy food at the impromptu market on the wharf. Grab a pineapple, some bananas, and a green coconut before they're gone. The native pudding is also good. This is the best kwik-stop on the trip.

MUNDA AND VICINITY

The metropolis of New Georgia, the name "Munda" describes the whole area. Actually, it's little more than a string of villages centered on Lambete beside the Roviana Lagoon. The government wharf, administration offices, air terminal, and rest houses are all at Lambete, while the United Church maintains its Solomon Is. headquarters and a

This late-19th C. Roviana carving was probably made especially for sale to Europeans.

hospital at Kokenggolo near the commercial wharf, 2 km from Lambete. The United Church also operates Goldie College near the Diamond Narrows. A vast wartime airstrip stretching from Lambete to Kokenggolo still dominates Munda, a huge plain of crushed coral. The dark-skinned people of Roviana Lagoon were once much-feared headhunters who raided far and wide in their long canoes. Though the change from those days is striking, much remains the same around this lagoon. You might see old men netting fish, outriggers bringing in live turtles, and fish leaping through the sea.

sights: Have a swim in the spring-fed freshwater pool near the canoe house at Lambete wharf. Next, follow the coastal road E from Lambete. The Americans built the fine coral roads here by dredging up limestone, crushing it with a steamroller, then pumping saltwater over the road to harden it like cement. Just a short distance along, look for Mr. William Uluilakemba, a friendly Fijian gentleman who has a beautiful pool full of fish and sea turtles behind his house; ask permission of someone in his household to visit it. Walk a km farther to Kia village. Just behind the houses there's a large U.S. military dump with piled-up landing craft deliberately cut in half, many huge concrete platforms, and even a submerged tank just offshore. Small copra driers along the waterfront still utilize wartime 44-gallon petrol drums. Many beautiful orchids bloom in the bush beyond. Now return to Kokenggolo. The Japanese secretly built the gigantic airstrip which dominates this area. They camouflaged their work by suspending the tops of coconut trees on cables above the runway—surely one of the more remarkable accomplishments of the war. The Americans captured Munda on 5 Aug. 1943. Avid snorkelers should visit the sunken aircraft in the lagoon just off the point near Kokenggolo hospital: a single-engine fighter is near shore, while a larger 2-engine plane in good condition is farther out in about 5 m of water. There's much other sunken or dumped war materiel in the lagoon off Munda. Follow the coastal road NW from Kokenggolo to Kindu village. Women are often seen washing clothes in a large spring-fed pool at the end of

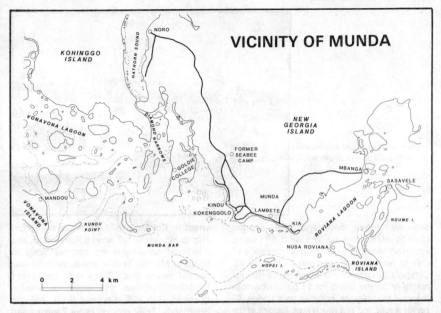

VICINITY OF MUNDA

KOHINGGO
ISLAND

NORO

HATHORN SOUND

DIAMOND NARROWS

GOLDIE COLLEGE

VONAVONA LAGOON

MANDOU

VONAVONA
ISLAND

KUNDU
POINT

MUNDA BAR

KINDU
KOKENGGOLO

LAMBETE

NEW
GEORGIA
ISLAND

FORMER
SEABEE
CAMP

MBANGA

MUNDA

KIA

SASAVELE

ROVIANA LAGOON

NDUME I.

NUSA ROVIANA

HOPEI I.

ROVIANA
ISLAND

0   2   4 km

---

the village, right beside the road. Swim here or continue one km to a clear freshwater stream. Midway between pool and stream is a road leading inland toward Noro. About a km up this road, on the L at a slight rise, is an old American well and water supply system. Continue along the road till it meets the new highway to Noro. Cross the highway and go straight ahead on a bush trail, always keeping to the right. With a little luck you'll find 2 large Japanese AA guns flanking a flagpole foundation, all that's left of the big U.S. Seabee Camp which once covered this area. Return to Munda along the highway for a circle trip.

vicinity of Munda: A new copra-exporting facility has been built near the Japanese fish freezer at Noro, 16 km NW of Munda by road. Roviana I., just SE of Munda across the lagoon, was the stronghold of the notorious headhunter Ingava, whose ferocity led to the sacking and burning of his ridgetop fortress by Commander David of the *Royalist* in 1891. The sacred "Dog Stone" is near the SE end of this broken coral fortress. There are a few other custom places near Munda, such as the

Island of Skulls near Kundu Point or the Stones of Bau deep in the interior, but access is difficult and you'll be charged excessive customary admission fees to visit. This also applies to the "Dog Stone." The local wags haven't yet claimed customary ownership of the American military junkyards, so you can still see them free.

accommodations: The Munda Rest House is just a stone's throw from the air terminal and government wharf at Lambete. Rooms in the old wing (shared bath) are $12 s, $22 d, while those in the new wing (private bath) are $15 s, $25 d. If it gets crowded, empty beds in the singles are assigned to whoever shows up. Package tours from Australia have led to declining service and spiraling prices. Agnes Kera, the proprietress, serves a 3-course dinner for $7 pp, but the food isn't highly rated. This is the only place in Munda to get a beer. At late-night sessions, locals demolish carton after carton of Fosters: "Him drink too hot." Agnes owns a lovely part-leaf cottage on nearby Hopei I., just offshore from Munda, com-

Gizo hasn't changed too much since this waterfront photo was taken in 1970.

plete with fridge, oven, and toilet—a good place to relax. Rates are $7 s, $8 d, $9 t (bring your own food). The outboard canoe ride is $7 OW or rent an outrigger and paddle for $2. Campers can pitch tents either beside the rest house or on the island for $3 pp. Just across the road from Agnes' is Wheatley's Lodge, $5 pp for a roof and not much else. Inquire at the tiny store in front of the rooms or ask Agnes for the key if her brother, the redoubtable Kitchener Wheatley, is not around. You could also stay with the villagers at Ndunde village, between Lambete and Kia. They're glad of the income. Ask Mrs. Voli Molia, the pastor's wife, if she can give you a reference.

food and entertainment: A Chinese store at Lambete, M.P. Kwan Trading, sells good hot bread. Sporadic markets happen near Lambete wharf and Kokenggolo hospital. There's custom dancing at Munda on 23 May, anniversary of the arrival of the first missionaries (in 1902), and also on 7 July (Independence Day) and Christmas. The singing and dancing show the influence of Tongan missionaries. Ask if any bamboo bands will be playing while you're there.

transport: Solair has a useful flight to Kieta, P.N.G., twice a week ($57—get your visa in Honiara beforehand). Book this flight ahead. Departure tax, $5. The Solair flight to Gizo ($16) is also convenient for island-hoppers. The Coral Seas ship to Gizo ($11) stops at the

wharf at Kokenggolo. Sometimes the return ship to Honiara is full when it leaves Gizo, and additional passengers are not permitted to board at Munda. Thus it makes sense to visit Munda *before* Gizo. Check with the United Church office near this wharf for mission boats to Gizo ($8), Choiseul ($14), and the Shortlands. They only go every 2 weeks and may take a week to get there, but they're cheaper than the other ships and full of flavor. Good roads now connect Munda to Mbanga landing (near Sasavele) and Noro. Flag down the white Dunde Transport truck to get from Kokenggolo to Lambete for 20 cents, or $1 all the way to Noro.

tours: Ask Agnes at the rest house to put you in touch with Mr. Nicely Zonga who runs canoe trips across to the former American PT boat base at Rendova Harbor ($30 RT per group). Nicely has set up a John F. Kennedy Museum (admission $2) on Lubaria I. in memory of Rendova's most famous ex-resident. On the way back Nicely will stop at Roviana I. for swimming, if you wish. Another good trip is through the Diamond Narrows to Enoghae Point where massive Japanese coastal defense guns still lurk in the bush. There's a sunken Japanese freighter in shallow water at Mbaeroko Bay nearby. Nicely is amenable, so tell him what you'd like to do. He could even drop you at Lubaria for camping, and pick you up next trip.

KOLOMBANGARA

Kolombangara is a classic cone-shaped volcano 30 km across and almost circular in plan. The native name of this island-volcano is Nduke. It soars to 1,770 m. You can climb it from Iriri village, accessible by canoe from Gizo market where the locals go to sell their products and shop. To go up and down in one day would be exhausting, so camp part way and reach the top early the next morning. By midday the summit is shrouded in clouds and you'd miss the view. But in the mist, the stunted, moss-covered forest on top will haunt you. Logging operations on Kolombangara are facilitated by a coastal road around the island's 678 sq km, with spur roads up most of the ridges. Levers Pacific Timbers, headquartered at Ringgi Cove 2 km from the wharf, loads the logs for Japan. The Iriri villagers have long struggled against Levers for adequate compensation for the use of their lands. There's a misleading sign on the wharf at Ringgi Cove (where the Coral Seas ship stops) which seems to indicate that Levers owns the island. They don't.

Ringgi Cove and vicinity: There's a small market in Ringgi Cove, but nowhere official to stay. The company people hang out at the Nduke Club up on the hill. Vilu Plantation, on Blackett Strait just S of the cove airstrip, was an important Japanese base during WW II. Rusted Japanese guns rust in the bush near the airstrip. There are Solair flights to Munda ($13) and Gizo ($14). Find outboard canoes to Noro ($2) or Munda ($3) near the canoe shed at the Ringgi Cove wharf. The Poitete Forestry Station, 42 km N of Ringgi Cove, is a government training school and an ongoing reforestation project.

GIZO

The administrative center of the Western Solomons since 1899, Gizo, on the island of the same name, is a pleasant little town, the second largest in the Solomons. It's quite a "modern" place with electric streetlights, a cinema, and many Chinese stores. It's an important shipping and shopping center for the west. A large Gilbertese community has been resettled here. There's a beautiful view across Blackett Strait to Kolombangara. After his PT boat was cut in half by a Japanese destroyer, John F. Kennedy took shelter on Kasolo or Plum Pudding Island, between Gizo and Kolombanga, from which he was rescued by a Solomon Islander. The ship from Honiara passes right beside Plum Pudding.

sights: Near the police station is a memorial stone to someone named Ferguson — "Killed by natives at Bougainville Island." For snorkeling, take the Solair boat ($2) out to the airport. Under the wharf or at the end of the runway are best. There's a sunken Japanese seaplane in 6 m of water to the L of the wharf. The Gizo Dive Center (Box 30, Gizo) offers scuba diving ($30 one tank, $50 2 tanks, including all gear); inquire at the Gizo Hotel. Gizo I. is 11 km long; climb the hill behind town for the view. Follow the road E out of town past the prison and along a beautiful beach, then return by road directly from New Manra village. A fine all-day hike begins by crossing the island, then following the beach road past the Gilbertese villages of New Manra and Titiana to Pailongge, a Melanesian village. Continue along the beach road for a few more hours to

Sagheraghi, where an overgrown lumber road along the hilltops leads back to town. Pay attention: branch tracks off the high road lead nowhere. Take food. You'll see many red-and-green coconut lorries and giant white cockatoos along the way. The snorkeling off Sagheraghi is superb with a double reef and 25-m drop-off between. Passenger trucks run to Sagheraghi twice a day ($1.20) and the Gizo Hotel arranges tours.

accommodations: Charlie Panakera, manager of the Gizo Hotel in the center of town, offers comfortable rooms with fan, hot water showers, fridge, and tea/coffee-making facilities ($28 s, $45 d). The hotel has a bar (happy hour 1730-1830) and restaurant (dinner $10 and up). When enough visitors are present, a bamboo band plays Mon. evening and there's Gilbertese dancing on Wednesdays. The hotel also has a leaf cottage on the beach at Sagheraghi for $15 pp with cooking. The Western Provincial Rest House in town charges $3 for a bunk with no mattress in 4-bed dorms. There's a 2100 curfew and no alcohol allowed. The spacious Government Rest House ($6, cooking facilities) is preferable. Visiting officials get priority here and you may be asked to evacuate if any show up. The caretaker at the Provincial Rest House looks after both facilities. But the best place to stay in Gizo is Phoebe's Rest House ($8 pp), on the hill above the town. There's a comfortably furnished lounge, cooking facilities, and a balcony with one of the most panoramic views in the South Seas. You're treated like one of the family and they'll loan you a dugout canoe if you ask. Recommended.

food and entertainment: There's a market along the waterfront Mon., Wed., and Friday. Ask someone to sign you in at the Gizo Club, just E of the main wharf. With its attractive terrace overlooking the harbor, the Club is the best place in town for a drink. Note, however, that Gizo tap water is not fit for consumption. **services and information:**   Gizo's National Bank branch changes travelers cheques and sometimes sells P.N.G. *kina*. Count your change carefully if you buy anything with a large bill in Gizo, as shortchanging happens too often to be accidental. Buy topographical maps ($3) at the Survey Department. Extensions of stay can be arranged at Police Headquarters.

transport: Solair has frequent service to Ringgi Cove ($14) and Munda ($22), plus 4 flights a week to Balalai ($48) in the Shortlands. The airstrip is on Nusatupe I., a quick boat ride ($4) from Gizo. The Coral Seas ship *Iuminao* ($11 to Munda, $29 to Honiara) has snack bar service. The barge *Ulusaghe* is slower and cheaper. Neither has an agent in Gizo — you just turn up and get on. A notice board outside the Provincial Office announces the departure times of government ships. One such vessel, the *Lanalau*, sails twice a month to Korovou in the Shortlands ($17) and on to Choiseul ($17). Inquire at the KHY Store opposite the cinema for Chinese trading boats to Honiara ($20) and Korovou ($12), leaving fortnightly. Outboard canoes leave Gizo frequently for Vella Lavella ($3) and Simbo ($4). Ask along the waterfront.

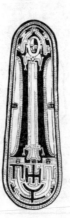

This inlaid shield shows a warrior and trophies taken on headhunting raids.

VELLA LAVELLA

This large island across the Gizo Strait is easily accessible by outboard canoe from Gizo (about $3 pp). Transport can be unreliable, however, so expect to stay a day or 2 longer than you might want. Copra boats run from

Vella Lavella direct to Noro fortnightly (passengers $2). A wartime road runs right up the SE side of the island, but all the bridges have long since been washed out, so it's now perfect for hikers. Mr. Walter Semepitu at Maravari village has erected a simply furnished leaf cottage ($5 pp, local food included). Here you'll experience typical village life with at least a little privacy. There's a clear river nearby for swimming. Aussie traders Roger and Janet run a store at Liapari, at the S tip of the island near crocodile-infested Lake Kolokolo. The Americans built an airstrip on the beach between Liapari and Maravari, and Solair flies in twice a week with flights to Choiseul Bay ($44), Balalai ($44), and Gizo ($13). These services must be booked ahead in Gizo. At Niarovai, a couple of hour's walk NE of Maravari (with several big rivers to cross), is a New Zealand War Memorial. The most unusual attraction of Vella Lavella is the thermal area, an hour's walk inland from Paraso village on the NE side of the island. There are megapode birds, hotsprings, and bubbling mud in a desert-like area near the Ngokosole River (crocs). The only access to Paraso is by chartered canoe. The owner of the Gorevaha Rural Trade Store near Maravari can supply this for $28 a day, petrol included. Ask the driver to take you around Vella Lavella rather than coming back the same way.

SIMBO

Simbo, the westernmost island of the New Georgia Group, was once a base for early 19th C. headhunting raids. Later in the 1880s, northbound sea captains called at Simbo on their way from Sydney to Canton, and it became one of the Solomon's first islands to accept Christian missionaries. Today this tiny island (12 sq km), 40 km SW of Gizo, is better known for its thermal area, one of only 4 in the Solomons (the other 3 are on Vella Lavella, Savo, and Tinakula). Note, however, it's not overly exciting to anyone who has been to Rotorua or Tanna, and visitors must pay $20 per group to customary landowners. Smoking fumaroles and a sulphur-stained hillside are clearly visible from the sea at Ove, on the SW

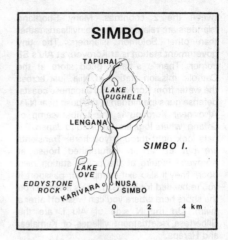

side of Simbo. Sulphur-rich seepage points drain into a brackish lake, the habitat of megapodes. The hotsprings are too hot to touch. The only access to Ove is by boat (not included in the $20 fee!) or along a roundabout trail which crosses the mountain from Karivara. Megapode rookeries at Nusa Simbo village opposite Karivara can be seen with permission of the owner, John Tione, who also sells the eggs for 10 cents each. The easiest hotsprings to enjoy are near the bridge on the trail linking Nusa Simbo to Lengana, the main village. The hot water mixes with tidal water in the lagoon and you can have a good swim. There's good anchorage for yachts at Lengana, a freshwater shower on the wharf, and several general stores nearby. For accommodations at Lengana talk to Samson Eli or sleep in a classroom at the school. Every Mon. and Fri. there's an outboard canoe from Lengana to Gizo ($4 pp). A trail leads N from Lengana to Tapurai, where the people who "own" the thermal area reside. Negotiate with them for a visit.

THE SHORTLAND ISLANDS

Alu Island: Alu, the largest of the Shortland Is., is just off the southern tip of Bougainville I., due S of Buin, Papua New Guinea. This location makes it a natural stepping stone between the 2 countries. Many Shortland Islanders are related to Bougainvilleans rather than other Solomon Islanders. The tiny government station is at Korovou, at Alu's SE corner. There's a fairly good store at the Catholic mission station of Nila, just across the water from Korovou. Big Japanese coastal defense guns are hidden in the bush near Nila. Also near Korovou is the timber camp of Lofang, where logs are exported to Japan. Expats look right through you here. Transients are put up at an unfurnished house at Korovou—inquire at the police station next door. They'll also exit-stamp your passport if you're headed for P.N.G. There's a shower on the shore here where you can wash off after a swim. On the N side of Alu I. are the Gilbertese resettlement villages of Kamaleai and Harapa.

Balalai: The airstrip serving the Shortlands is on uninhabited Balalai I., with free access to and from Korovou in the Solair canoe (30 min.). There are 2 flights a week to Kieta, P.N.G. ($39), one a week to Choiseul Bay ($11), and 4 a week to Gizo ($48). Solair passengers from Gizo or Munda to Kieta may clear Customs here. The officials confiscate all seeds or vegetables from arriving passengers. An almost perfectly preserved Japanese "Betty" bomber graces Balalai airstrip and

there are other planes and war wreckage in the bush.

to Papua New Guinea: The easiest way to go is by plane to Kieta, but it's also possible to catch a canoe ($5 pp—bargain hard if they ask much more) to Kangu Beach, just across Western Entrance on Bougainville. Your best chance of finding a canoe there is early Sat. morning when the locals go over to sell fish at the Buin market. Ask around Korovou and Nila. The trip takes roughly 1.5 hours and you may get quite wet from the spray, so watch your camera. It's a 3-hour walk from Kangu in to Buin, the main trading center for S. Bougainville, but there's a Chinese store on the beach and the friendly owner often drives into town. Also, the occasional truck costs K1.20 pp. There's no P.N.G. Immigration office at Buin, so don't hang around; proceed at once to Arawa or Kieta to complete entry formalities. You must already have a P.N.G. visa. You're almost certain to get a truck (K5) from Buin to Kieta on Sun. afternoon with miners returning to work at Panguna copper mine. This trip can also be done in reverse: just camp on Kangu Beach until you find a canoe to Korovou, probably Sat. afternoon. This route is not exactly officially encouraged for non-Solomon Islanders, so be diplomatic all the way down the line.

Massive clamshell plaques bearing dancing figures of this kind were once used on Choiseul to close the opening of a container bearing the skull of a dead chief.

CHOISEUL, ISABEL, MAKIRA

The other 3 big islands of the Solomons—Choiseul, Isabel, and Makira—are seldom visited by outsiders. A 2-month entry permit really doesn't give you enough time both to see them and visit the better-known islands described above. Communications are difficult, roads are short to non-existent, and the conveniences of modern life don't extend far beyond the narrow confines of the few small government and mission outposts. This, of course, is the very appeal of these islands, so buy a detailed map from Lands and Surveys and blaze your own trail. Be sure to let us hear what you find!

Choiseul: The name is pronounced Choysle. There's a large mission station at Choiseul Bay, at the NW end of the island, with an airstrip nearby. On the NE side near Chirovanga are the Pacho River cascades. A large Gilbertese community has been resettled on Vaghena I., off the SE end. The original Melanesian inhabitants of Vaghena were wiped out by Roviana headhunters. Vaghena's 78 sq km of uplifted coral are thought to contain significant bauxite deposits.

Isabel Province: Isabel's 200-km-long NW-SE landmass is the longest in the Solomons. The island is named after Alvaro de Mendana's wife. Headhunters from Simbo and the Roviana Lagoon depopulated much of Isabel during the early 1800s. Today most of the inhabitants live in the SE corner of the island, the point farthest away from New Georgia. One of the Pacific's rarest varieties of *tapa* originates on Isabel: stained pale blue with a leaf dye. The administrative center is at Buala on the Maringe Lagoon in SE Isabel. Solair has flights to Fera Island ($49 from Honiara), a 4-km-long offshore island from which motorized canoes cross to Buala ($2), where you can stay at the Mothers Union Rest House ($5 pp). Most villages on Isabel have a simple leaf house to accommodate visitors. An hour's walk SE of Buala is Tit'hiro Falls,

where the Sana River falls straight into the sea. Note, however, that it dries up during the dry season. Hike another hour or 2 inland from the falls up to Tirotong'na village for a sweeping view of the entire Maringe Lagoon and even Malaita. Occasionally, ships sail from Honiara to Buala, and others sail to Kia, a large village on Austria Sound at the NW end of Isabel.

MAKIRA PROVINCE

Makira: Makira (San Cristobal) has some level land in the N, but the S coast falls precipitously to the sea. Makira Harbor, on the SW coast, is the most secure anchorage in the Solomons, and Star Harbor, at the E end of the island, is also good. In 1595 the *Santa Isabel,* one of the 4 ships of Mendana's ill-fated second expedition, became separated from the others at Santa Cruz. It sailed on to

an old photo of Isabel

A century ago Makira islanders looked like this.

Makira where passengers and crew camped on a hilltop at Pamua on the N coast, W of Kirakira. Their eventual fate is unknown. Remote caves in Makira's inaccessible interior are inhabited by the Kakamora, a race of midgets a meter tall who have been called "the leprechauns of the Pacific." They go naked, have very small teeth, and their long straight hair comes down to their knees. Most are harmless, but some Kakamora have been known to attack other men. It's said that one Kakamora is as strong as 3 or 4 men. There are more pigs on Makira than people. Local craft items include carved figures, black inlaid ceremonial food bowls from Santa Ana, and talking drums.

Kirakira and vicinity: Ships between Honiara and the Eastern Outer Islands call at the administrative center of the province, Kirakira, on the middle N coast of Makira. Solair also flies to Kirakira from Honiara ($70) and Santa Cruz ($110). Two M.U.D.C. rest houses are found at Kirakira: $10 and $6 pp. The only roads on Makira run along the N coast from Kirakira, 9 km to the E and 56 km to the W (to Wango Bay). Ask about ships to Star Harbor, Santa Ana, and Santa Catalina, the most beautiful areas in the province.

the *mako mako* dance: This burlesque or mime is performed on Santa Catalina, a small island off the SE end of Makira. On the village green the males, their bodies smeared with reddish clay, don hideous make-up and high conical masks. These dancers play the "men of the trees"—primitive jungle folk. The dance is accented by the dull notes of a conch shell. Suddenly the "canoe people" arrive from across the waters, and the "men of the trees" run in panic. Then a very realistic mock-battle takes place between these 2 levels of Pacific Island civilization.

Star Harbor: About 100 skilled carvers live in the Star Harbor area. The oldest and most expert bear the title *mwane manira*, and their work is avidly sought by museums and serious collectors. Visitors buy directly from these craftspeople. Although full-sized canoes and houseposts are the most famous carvings, model canoes, decorated bowls, skull containers, human figures, and sharks are all crafted and sold. **Santa Ana:** There's an excellent, reefless beach on Santa Ana where sea turtles come ashore. Traditional Natagera village is just behind; ask to see the custom house. There are 2 freshwater lakes on Santa Ana.

THE EASTERN OUTER ISLANDS

THE SANTA CRUZ GROUP

The Santa Cruz Group, 665 km E of Honiara, is by far the most remote of the major island groupings of the Solomons. Included are 25-by-17 km Nendo, the Reef Is., the Duff Is., and the high islands of Utupua and Vanikolo. Tinakula, just N of Nendo, is a surpassingly graceful, almost symmetrical, active volcano. The Reef Is. are composed of low coral terraces and sandy cays, while the others are mostly volcanic with steep jungle slopes. The Melanesians settled on the larger islands, the Polynesians on the small, more isolated outliers. *Lapita* pottery has been found on both Nendo and the Reef Islands. The first European to arrive was the Spaniard Mendana, who attempted to establish a colony at the S end of Graciosa Bay on Nendo in 1595. Days later, when mutiny set in, Mendana went ashore and executed his camp commander. After Mendana himself died here on 18 Oct. 1595, the settlement was abandoned. The crew, sick and dying, called Nendo "a corner of hell in the claws on the devil." Of

Uninhabited, 800-m-high Tinakula I. in the Santa Cruz Group is the most active volcano in the Solomons. In 1595 one of Mendana's ships sank near Tinakula, which was erupting at the time. This photo shows the island during the brief 1971 eruption.

Mendana's 378 men, death claimed 47 within a month. The next to arrive was Carteret, on 12 Aug. 1767. As he anchored off Nendo, he observed a "wild country and black, naked, woolly-haired natives." Santa Cruz is the southern and eastern limit of betel-chewing in the Pacific, and *kava*-drinking is also popular. It's also famous for its feather money. Thousands of red feathers from the honey bird are stuck onto a coiled band as long as 10 meters. Ten belts of feather money is the traditional price of a bride.

Nendo: Nendo is by far the largest of the Santa Cruz Group. Its densely wooded hills rise to a height of about 520 meters. The island has considerable reserves of bauxite. At Venga, on the sandy W shore of Nendo, people perform custom dances unchanged since time immemorial. Dancers at Mbanua village wear traditional shell and feather ornaments as they dance and sing around a betel tree all night. At the entrance to Carlisle Bay, on the N shore of Nendo, is an overgrown memorial to Commodore Goodenough, killed here in 1875. The administrative center of Temotu Province is at Lata, at the NW corner of Nendo on the W side of Graciosa Bay. Temotu (Malo) I. partly closes this bay to the north. The airstrip (Solair from Honiara—$155) and wharf are both within minutes of Lata. John Melanoli accepts guests in his leaf house near the wharf at Lata ($1 pp with cooking). In addition, there's a Provincial Rest House (also $1) one km from the airstrip, and a Government Rest House ($10). Levers Pacific Timbers ships logs from Shaw Point, on the opposite side of Graciosa Bay, and has a sawmill there.

the Reef Islands: These low coral islands, 70 km NE of Graciosa Bay, have long golden beaches, and no malaria. The inhabitants are mostly Melanesians, excepting the Polynesians on tiny Nifiloli and Pileni, as well as Nupani I. to the northwest. Gnimbanga Temoa I. has a series of caverns containing freshwater pools. The Ngarando Island Resort on Pigeon I., Mohawk Bay, offers guest house accommodations with cooking facilities, $20 s, $30 d. There's excellent snorkeling and shell-collecting in this utterly remote location. Island trader Bressin Hepworth runs a general store near the resort with local vegetables, fresh fruit and fish, and tinned groceries. Transfers from Graciosa Bay by outboard are $20 pp, but an airstrip is due to open on adja-

cent Lomlom I., so access will become easier. Check with the Marine Division in Honiara for a government ship direct to Mohawk Bay ($30 deck). **the Duff Islands:** The Duff Is., 88 km NE of the Reef Is., consist of 9 small volcanic islands in a line 27 km long. Taumako I., the largest, is 366 m high. The inhabitants are Polynesian.

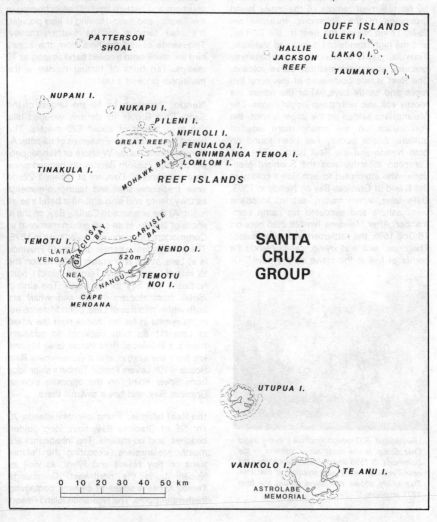

SANTA CRUZ GROUP

PATTERSON SHOAL

DUFF ISLANDS
LULEKI I.
HALLIE JACKSON REEF
LAKAO I.
TAUMAKO I.

NUPANI I.

NUKAPU I.

PILENI I.

NIFILOLI I.
GREAT REEF   FENUALOA I.
GNIMBANGA TEMOA I.
MOHAWK BAY   LOMLOM I.

TINAKULA I.

REEF ISLANDS

TEMOTU I.
LATA   GRACIOSA BAY
VENGA   CARLISLE BAY
NEA
NANGU   520 m
CAPE MENDANA

NENDO I.

TEMOTU NOI I.

UTUPUA I.

VANIKOLO I.   TE ANU I.
ASTROLABE MEMORIAL

0   10   20   30   40   50 km

feather-money: In the Santa Cruz Group scarlet feathers of the tiny honey eater bird are glued to small plaques, then bound into belts of feather money 10 m long. Over 300 birds are required to make a single belt. The great hoard of feather money depicted in this 1913 photo is the equivalent of the price of a bride.

Vanikolo: This volcanic, Melanesian island was stripped of its kauri trees by an Australian firm earlier this century. Both ships of the La Perouse expedition, the *Boussole* and the *Astrolabe*, were wrecked on the reef at Vanikolo during a terrible storm in 1788. Despite a search for La Perouse by d'Entrecasteaux 4 years later, his fate was unknown for 4 decades until an Irish sea captain happened on the remains. There's a memorial to La Perouse on the S side of Vanikolo.

THE POLYNESIAN OUTLIERS

Tikopia: This 3-by-5 km dot in the ocean, 120 km SW of the nearest other dot (Anuta), is an ancient volcano rising to 366 m, with a crater lake, Te Roto. The inhabitants of both Tikopia and Anuta are Polynesians who arrived from Wallis I. some 14 generations ago. Right up until WW II, these islanders used lime to bleach their hair blonde, which they wore, along with their beards, to maximum length.
Anuta: Anuta is less than a km across and 65 m high. Both it and Tikopia are still governed by their traditional chiefs and the influence of the Solomon Islands government is minimal. The Anutans make their point by charging everyone — police and officials included — $1 landing fee. Fatutaka I. (Mitre), 42 km SE of Anuta, is uninhabited.

Sikaiana: There's no anchorage off this tiny atoll with 4 islets in the lagoon; access is by small boat through the surf. The inhabitants migrated here from Tonga. A variety of filarial mosquito found on Sikaiana also occurs in Tonga, but nowhere else in the world.

Ontong Java: This 70-by-26-km boot-shaped atoll is comprised of 122 islands which total only 12 sq km of dry land but encloses 1,400 sq km of lagoon. Ke Avaiko Passage, just S of Liuaniua I., leads directly to the lagoon anchorage off the village. The supply ship calls at both Liuaniua and Pelau, the only permanently inhabited islands, yet the people

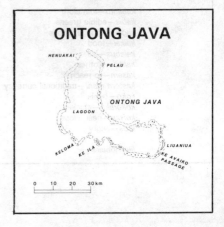

ONTONG JAVA

HENUAKAI
PELAU
ONTONG JAVA
LAGOON
KELOMA
KE ILA
LIUANIUA
KE AVAIKO PASSAGE

0   10   20   30 km

reside part-time on many others, fishing and making copra. All the islets are planted with coconuts and production is large; swamp taro is cultivated in deep pits in the interior of several islands. Ontong Java is one of the few places in the Solomons where houses are built directly on the ground (dirt floor—no stilts). The cemeteries here are striking for their large carved tombstones. These Polynesians are less extrovert than their fellows to the E: they're reticent and almost withdrawn, save for the children, of course. Ontong Java was named by Tasman on 22 March 1643. Ontong was probably derived from the Malay *untung* (luck, fortune, destiny, fate); in other words, "Java Luck." Tasman's ships had been subjected to squalls for months on end, and he was most likely congratulating himself on the improved conditions. In 179I Captain Hunter named it Lord Howe Island, but the Polynesian name is Liuaniua. If planning to stay on Ontong Java, bring your own food, as little is available from the 2 stores.

CAPSULE SOLOMON ISLANDS PIDGIN VOCABULARY

aesboks—refrigerator
araikwao—white man

bagarap—broken down
belo—noon
bia blong Solomon—betel nut
basta yu man!—damn you!
bulumakao—cattle

daedae—to be in love with

gudfala—nice

haomas?—how much?
hem i stap wea?—where is he (it)?

kabilato—loin cloth
kabis—edible greens
kago—luggage, goods
kaikai—food
kalabus—jail
kaliko—clothes
kasem—to reach
kastom mani—traditional currency
koko—penis
kokorako—chicken
kolsap—near, close
kros—angry

liu—jobless

longwe—far
luksave—to recognize

mere—woman
mifala—us

naes bola!—hey good lookin!
nambaten—the worst
nambawan—the best

pikinini—child

raosem—to clear out

samting nating—it doesn't matter
sapos—if
save—to know
save tumas—wise
smol rod—footpath
susu—milk, breast

taem before—in the old days
tanggio tumas—thank you very much

wanem—what did you say?
wantek—kinsman
waswe—why
weitim—with

yumi—we

AUSTRALIA

Australia is a vast island continent lying entirely S of the equator on the edge of Asia. It features diverse, cosmopolitan cities, the rugged grandeur of the "outback," a tropical paradise in Queensland, and a vibrant, outgoing people. To give it the attention it merits would require hundreds of pages; here we can only offer a brief summary designed to start you on your way. Since the additional airfare is minimal, few N. Americans visit the South Pacific without continuing to Australia. Try to get away from the bustle of the tourist centers and experience the adventure that has always been the essence of this young country. Your finest moments will probably be spent in places not mentioned in this book or any other.

land and climate: Australia is huge: Tasmania alone is 4 times the size of the state of Hawaii. Geologically, it's the oldest continent. It's also the flattest: a 300-m-high plateau accounts for the western two-thirds, and a chain of mountains down the E coast culminates at Mt. Kosciusko (2,228 m) be-

tween Canberra and Melbourne. Between mountains and plateau a lowland belt stretches S from the Gulf of Carpentaria to the Indian Ocean E of Adelaide. Forty percent of Australia lies in the tropics, yet Tasmania and Victoria are well within the temperate zone. December to Feb. (summer) is the rainy season in the far N as well as university summer vacation, when many traveling facilities are booked solid. July and Aug. (winter) are cold and showery in the S, so the two best times for a visit are autumn and spring (March-May/Sept.-Nov.). Summer, however, is perfect for camping in Tasmania, and Queensland is at its best in winter.

flora and fauna: Australia's eternal allure is its extraordinary plant and animal life. The many varieties of eucalyptus or gum trees are the most apparent feature, but giant ferns and lovely wildflowers also proliferate. In northern Queensland are virgin rainforests, now succumbing to chainsaws and roads. Among the mammals, pouched marsupials predominate. Best known is the kangaroo, which comes in a variety of species and sizes from tiny rat kangaroos to wallabies, from tree kangaroos to 2-m-tall red kangaroos, or "Big Reds." To supply the pet food trade, millions are shot each year in the dead of night by hunters who stun them with spotlights. Americans should know that the kangaroo is on the U.S. Threatened Species List, so souvenirs made from their bodies are prohibited entry. Other marsupials include the cuddly eucalyptus leaf-eating koalas, the clumsy-looking burrowing wombats, the possums, the cuscus, the rat-like bandicoots with long noses and rabbit ears, the tiny jerboa mouse, and the dog-like Tasmanian devil. Less common than the marsupials are the strange, egg-laying monotremes, the spiny anteater and the platypus. Australia's exotic birdlife includes multicolored parrots, cockatoos, and the various kookaburras, largest kingfishers on earth. The ostrich-like emu (3 toes) and the colorful cassowary stand tall as men. Australia is also home to the most outrageous flies on earth. They'll tour your nose, talk business on your tongue, and set up house in your ears. They're worse in summer than winter. Aussies are often seen saluting their national bird.

history: The first people reached Australia from Asia 30,000-50,000 years ago. Their bushy eyebrows, deep-set eyes, wide nostrils, protruding jaws, and slender limbs differentiate them from the Melanesians. Only in southern India and perhaps New Caledonia are similar broad-browed physical types found. These people were eventually displaced through most of Asia by the present Mongoloid inhabitants. For 50,000 years the Aboriginals lived undisturbed throughout Australia with a simple, but appropriate, technology. The most interesting question is why they never developed permanent agriculture, when in similar environment conditions across the Torres Strait (a land bridge until about 10,000 years ago) in New Guinea, there were permanent agricultural settlements. At the time of European contact the Aboriginals were still at the hunting and gathering stage, although their religious rituals were highly developed. Spaniards from the ill-fated 1606 Quiros expedition to Espiritu Santo, Vanuatu, sailed through the Torres Strait (named for their captain) on their way home. Even earlier, Portuguese from India may have seen Australia. Various Dutch explorers visited "New Holland" during the 17th C. from their base in the Dutch East Indies (Indonesia). Others followed, but none took a lasting interest until Capt. Cook charted the E coast and claimed the continent for Britain in 1770. Soon after, the British lost their American colonies, and decided that Australia would be a good substitute. On 26 Jan. 1788 the "First Fleet" of 11 ships under Capt. Arthur Phillip anchored in Sydney Harbor. Australians now celebrate 26 Jan. every year as Australia Day, and a big bicentenary is planned for 1988. Some 736 convicts were transported aboard Phillip's ships and by 1868, when the penal colony finally ended, over 100,000 convicts had been transported to Australia. Wool was the main industry during the early days and Australia is now the world leader in wool. New South Wales and Victoria saw gold rushes in 1851. The various settlements functioned as separate colonies until 1901, when the Commonwealth of Australia was proclaimed.

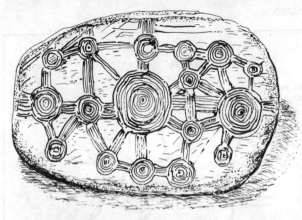

To Aboriginals, the mystic powers of totemic ancestors are captured in churinga stones. At sacred ceremonies the stones are brought out and twirling wooden "bull-roarers" recreate the voice of the spirits.

the Aboriginals: The original inhabitants of Australia will have little to celebrate in 1988. On the mainland the settlers simply pushed them deeper into the bush, but on Tasmania, where they resisted, Aboriginal-shooting was made a sport like fox hunting. In 1838 the survivors were rounded up and concentrated on Flinders Island; the last Tasmanian died in 1876. In the 1950s and early '60s, thousands of Aboriginals were affected by fallout from an inept British atmospheric nuclear testing program in central Australia. Government cover-ups have frustrated efforts to determine the full extent of that tragedy, and no medical treatment or compensation has ever been given to the victims, but now there's a major international inquiry. On the Australian mainland Aboriginals now number 159,897 (1981), about one percent of the population, roughly half as many as the Europeans found. Unluckily for them their lands contain 18 percent of the world's reserves of uranium, and the mining companies continue to push them aside with official support. The Aboriginals regard this destruction of their sacred lands as the ultimate desecration. Only in 1972 were Aboriginals first admitted to Australian universities; they're still not permitted to own land in Queensland or Western Australia. The South Africans used Queensland's "protection" laws as a model when they framed apartheid. Large numbers of Aboriginals are held in Australian prisons and most of the rest are unemployed. To date nearly all government assistance has been designed to absorb the Aboriginals into white society. No effort has been made to help them rediscover or retain their traditional way of life, except to study it for its touristic value or museums. In the Pacific, only the Hawaiians have suffered as much as the Aboriginals, although the fate of the American Indian is comparable.

GETTING AROUND

by bus: The big bus companies, Greyhound and Ansett Pioneer, offer unlimited travel bus passes: $465 for 30 days, $690 for 60 days. (A 21-day bus pass for $335 is available only outside Australia.) It's expensive, but if you travel widely it's still far less than individual tickets. The Ansett Pioneer terminals are larger and more convenient. Also, Ansett may offer free sightseeing tours to those holding their Aussiepass, making it a better deal than Greyhound's no-frills Eaglepass. Seat reservations must be made well in advance, especially at holiday time, and on many routes there's only one bus a day. Note too that major Ansett Pioneer offices in Australia sell an Ameripass for unlimited bus travel in N. America at a very substantial discount. Also check out Deluxe Coach Lines' Koala Pass.

by train: An Austrailpass is available for unlimited first-class train travel, as well as a Budget Austrailpass for second-class. These must be purchased outside Australia, are

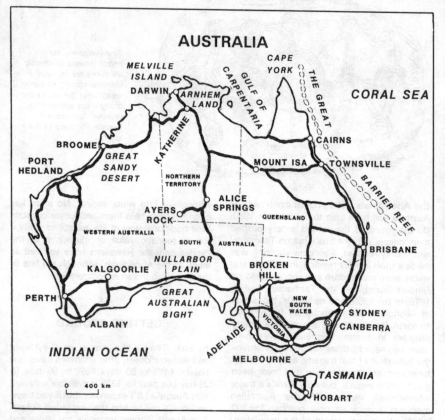

AUSTRALIA

MELVILLE ISLAND

CAPE YORK

GULF OF CARPENTARIA

THE GREAT

CORAL SEA

DARWIN

ARNHEM LAND

KATHERINE

CAIRNS

BROOME

GREAT SANDY DESERT

NORTHERN TERRITORY

MOUNT ISA

TOWNSVILLE

PORT HEDLAND

BARRIER REEF

AYERS ROCK

ALICE SPRINGS

QUEENSLAND

WESTERN AUSTRALIA

SOUTH AUSTRALIA

BRISBANE

KALGOORLIE

NULLARBOR PLAIN

BROKEN HILL

PERTH

GREAT AUSTRALIAN BIGHT

NEW SOUTH WALES

SYDNEY

CANBERRA

ALBANY

VICTORIA

ADELAIDE

INDIAN OCEAN

MELBOURNE

TASMANIA

0   400 km

HOBART

more expensive than the bus passes, and do not take you to as many places. Also, the rail passes do not include compulsory meal and sleeping berth charges—a total ripoff: between Sydney and Perth they're the equivalent of the cost of a OW bus ticket! A far better idea is to buy a regular OW train ticket between any 2 points (Brisbane and Adelaide, for example). You can take up to 2 months to make the trip and get off and on as many times as you like. **by car:** Hitching is possible, but the great distances and lack of traffic can make it a drag. Shared-expense rides are fairly easy to come by at Australian youth hostels; exactly the opposite is true in New Zealand, where they are few and far between. You might consider buying a good

used Holden ($2,000 plus), and resell it later for close to what you paid. A Canadian or U.S. driver's license is valid in Australia. **others:** Student Travel Australia offers all kinds of travel bargains to students and recent graduates. They also have the cheapest circumpacific airfares, if you're beginning your trip in Australia. Their offices are conveniently scattered right across the country: a look in the telephone book will locate the nearest.

PRACTICALITIES

accommodations: Over a hundred youth hostels are spread throughout Australia, costing $5-6 a night. You must be a member (no age limit), have a sleeping sheet, and help out with housekeeping work. The hostels close during the day. Some are better than others, but most have cooking facilities and are good meeting places. Get a copy of the *Australian Youth Hostels Handbook* ($1) which lists them all. Y.M.C.A., Y.W.C.A., and Salvation Army hostels are also usually reasonable. If you have your own tent, caravan parks are another possibility. These are rarely found in the center of large cities, but many holiday areas have them. They run about $4 pp for campers, and many have on-site caravans at $10-15 a night for up to 4 people; most have coin-operated laundry facilities. Addresses can be obtained from the state tourist information bureaus. Some of the older private hotels in the big cities offer low weekly rates for single or double rooms. These are often advertised in the classified sections of the daily papers. The atmosphere may not be as cheerful or congenial as it is in the hostels, but neither are they as bad as they look. Anything from $35-45 a week for a single room is average. There are often rooms for rent above pubs. Students can stay in university dorms during the holiday period (Dec. to Feb.). The cost of accommodations begins to rise sharply when you stop using the above.

food: Supermarkets in the big department stores (Coles and Woolworths) are the best places to shop. Lamb chops are cheap for cooking at hostels. These stores also have fast-food counters (meat pies, pasties, chips, and chiko rolls), or regular sit-down cafeterias for inexpensive meals. Local bakeries often sell excellent sultana or raisin cake, date bread, and meat pies. Ask local residents who makes the best meat pies—some are no better than factory-made. In the big cities, small sandwich bars just off the main streets are popular with office workers at lunch-time—and for good reason. Counter lunches served in the pubs are an Australian institution and the daily special is often marked on a blackboard outside. Australian wine is better and cheaper than beer. A word of warning about closing times: since employers must pay their staff double-time weekends and nights, many stores shut tight at 1700

weekdays, noon Saturday. Most do stay open till 2000 Thurs., however, and all corner stores open 12 hours a day. Ask.

visas and money: Everyone entering Australia must have a passport and visa (although New Zealanders require only the passport). Australian visas are issued promptly, free of charge. You must present one (non-machine) photo and your return or onward ticket. Be aware that they watch for people who intend to work in Australia, so don't give them any reason to suspect that. Note too that an extension of stay in Australia costs $30, so it's better to try for 6 months on arrival if you think 3 is not enough. Currency control prohibits exporting over $250 in Australian banknotes, so carry travelers cheques. American tourists have introduced tipping to luxury hotels and restaurants in the cities, but Australians themselves rarely if ever tip and are much abused when they go overseas because of it.

koala

information: Although the Australian Tourist Commission does not deal with the public and little information is available at the airports, all the Australian states and territories operate excellent tourist information offices with branches in the big cities. Make the rounds of these soon after your arrival; collecting maps and directories will prove invaluable later on. Here are the addresses of these and other information offices:

SYDNEY

New South Wales, corner Pitt and Spring Sts.
Western Australia, 92 Pitt St.
Victoria, 150 Pitt St.
Aboriginal Land Rights Support Group, 262 Pitt St.
Tasmania, 129 King St.
South Australia, 131 King St.
Northern Territory, 145 King St.
Queensland, 149 King St.
Australian Capital Territory, 9-19 Elizabeth St.
National Park Service, 1st floor, 189-193 Kent St.
Youth Hostel Assn., 355 Kent St.
Greenpeace, 785 George St. (near Central Station)
Student Travel Australia, 1A Lee St. (near Central Station)

MELBOURNE

Victoria, 230 Collins St.
Australian Capital Territory, 247 Collins St.
Tasmania, 256 Collins St.
Queensland, MLC Bldg., corner Elizabeth and Collins Sts.
South Australia, 25 Elizabeth St.
Northern Territory, 99 Queen St.
New South Wales, 345 Little Collins St.
Western Australia, Royal Arcade, 329 Bourke St.
National Park Service, 240 Victoria Parade
Youth Hostel Assn., 122 Flinders St.
Student Travel Australia, 220 Faraday St., Carlton
Friends of the Earth, 366 Smith St., Collingwood

BRISBANE

Queensland, Adelaide and Edward Sts.
New South Wales, corner Queen and Edward Sts.
Tasmania, 217 Queen St.
Victoria, 221 Queen St.
Youth Hostel Assn., 462 Queen St.
Western Australia, 2nd floor, corner Creek and Queen Sts.
Student Travel Australia, 40 Creek St.
National Park Service, MLC Center, 239 George St.
Northern Territory, 260 George St.

There is no really outstanding guidebook to Australia, although *Australia—A Travel Survival Kit* by Tony Wheeler (Lonely Planet Publications) is the best of a poor field. The Lands Map Sales Center at 23-33 Bridge St. near Circular Quay, Sydney, sells topographical maps.

AUSTRALIAN AIRPORTS

Sydney: Kingsford Smith Airport (SYD) is 6 km S of downtown. The Travellers Information Service counter on the arrivals level sells maps of Sydney and will book you a room at a higher-priced hotel. There are youth hostels at 28 Ross St. (tel. 692-0747) and 407 Marrickville Road (tel. 569-0272); the privately-owned Baden Powell Hostel, 21 Regent St., Chippendale (tel. 698-2726) near Redfern Station, is comparable. Other are found in the Kings Cross area. The Westpac Banking Corp. window on the arrivals level changes money at the usual rate. Coin lockers are $1 a day. The airport terminal closes from 2300-0600. An abusive $20 departure tax is levied on all international passengers. The yellow and blue AIRPORT EXPRESS 300 bus departs the international and domestic terminals regularly from 0600-2100 daily, costing $2 to the Central Railway Station or Circular Quay.

Melbourne: Tullamarine Airport (MEL) is 21 km NW of the city center. The youth hostel (tel. 328-2880) is at 500 Abbotsford St., N. Melbourne (on the way in from the airport). The cheapest hotels are listed in the "rooms vacant" classified section of *The Age.* There's no tourist information office at the airport, but a $20 departure tax. The Skybus Express ($4) will take you right to your hotel door, or catch the infrequent Moonee Ponds bus to Essendon Station and then a train or tram to town from there. Ask the driver.

Brisbane: Eagle Farm Airport (BNE) is 6 km NE of central Brisbane. For the youth hostel (tel. 57-1245) take bus no. 172 to stop 28. The airport extracts $20 departure tax. Skennars Coach Lines (22-34 Barry Parade, Brisbane) has a bus ($2.50) between the international terminal and downtown about every half hour, or walk 2 km to the domestic terminal where Council bus no. 160 passes regularly.

WHAT TO SEE IN AUSTRALIA

the east coast: Sydney is Australia's oldest and largest city, as well as its most diverse, with many museums, parks, historic buildings, and beaches. Its harbor is among the finest in the world, easily viewed from one of the ferries based at Circular Quay. The ferry ride to Taronga Park Zoo is a must for views (and zoos). The Blue Mountains near Katoomba to the W of the city make a good sidetrip. Brisbane, 1009 km N of Sydney, is the brash, modern capital of Queensland. South of Brisbane are the super-commercialized Gold Coast beaches of Surfers Paradise and Coolangatta. North are more beaches and the small coral islands of the Great Barrier Reef. The ferry service from Townsville to Magnetic I. is also very frequent. Cairns is a pleasant tropical town in the sugar country, terminus of the fantastic 34-km railway (built 1884-88) up to Kuranda, which has one of Australia's nicest youth hostels. Daily cruises to Green I. leave from Cairns.

the center and north: The road runs W from Townsville through Mount Isa into Outback Australia. Perhaps nowhere else in the world can such a vast, arid region be visited so easily

as here. In the middle of what's known as the "Red Center" lies the enjoyable town of Alice Springs. Best known of the many natural features in the surrounding area is Ayers Rock (called Uluru by the Aboriginals), 458 km southwest. This gigantic stone monolith has become a symbol of Australia, alongside Sydney's opera house and the kangaroo. Many Aboriginal people live in central and northern Australia. They continue to be displaced today as vast tracts of their land are seized for their uranium, bauxite, and manganese. Darwin, 1530 km N of The Alice at the "Top End," is now rebuilt after being leveled by a cyclone in 1974.

the west: The road SW from Darwin to Perth crosses 4,830 km of dry savanna and desert; only a few scattered cattle stations and small mining communities break the monotony of the now largely paved highway. The iron ore town of Port Hedland is at the halfway point. Stay in the North West Guest House. Although Perth's location 2,729 km W of Adelaide across the treeless Nullarbor Plain makes it the most isolated city in the First World, it's still a major target for Soviet missiles due to the presence of U.S. nuclear warships at nearby Cockburn Sound. The Swan River winds through Perth along freeways and parkland to the port of Freemantle. Perfect white beaches framed by high sand dunes and clear blue waters stretch N and S along the Indian Ocean.

A high point of a visit to Australia is the climb to the top of Ayers Rock.

the south and Tasmania: Most of Australia's 15 million people reside in the SE corner of the continent, largely in Adelaide, Melbourne, and Sydney, state capitals of South Australia, Victoria, and New South Wales respectively. Despite the modern encroachments, Adelaide remains a charming, planned 19th C. city with monuments, fine public buildings, and gracious squares, everything surrounded by a luxurious, continuous belt of immaculate parks and gardens unique in the world. A tramway runs from Victoria Square to the seaside at Glenelg. Australia's largest wine-growing areas are near Adelaide, the most famous of which is the picturesque Barossa Valley 65 km NE, an area first settled by Germans. A full 40 percent of Australia's 15 million people live in Melbourne and Sydney. Melbourne has been the traditional financial hub of Australia (although now overtaken by Sydney in this role); it's also an industrial and commercial center. Quaint old trams rumble continuously along the thoroughfares. The downtown area has a faded Victorian air, in contrast to the impressive new Arts Center and the many parks and gardens just across the Yarra River and to the east. The Museum and Art Gallery are by far the best in Australia. Sidetrips encompass the nightly penguin parade at Phillip Island and Ballarat's reconstructed gold-rush settlement. An overnight ferry runs S from Melbourne to Devonport on Tasmania. Launceston, Tasmania's second city (visit the cataract gorge) is on the way to the capital, Hobart. Many historical remnants of the old city may be seen and at Port Arthur, 80 km SE, are the spellbinding ruins of Australia's most famous penal colony. Two-thirds of the way to Sydney from Melbourne is the planned national capital, Canberra, actually quite an attractive and restful place with its long lake surrounded by parks and government buildings. The War Memorial Museum is surprisingly good. The Snowy Mountains, SW of the capital via Cooma, is Australia's principal winter resort, also home of the mighty Snowy Mountains Power Project.

offshore islands: Norfolk I. (35 sq km), halfway between New Zealand and New Caledonia, is a rolling, pine-clad island reaching 318 m at Mt. Bates. Uninhabited when Capt. Cook called in 1774, Norfolk was a British penal colony until 1856 when it was turned over to the Pitcairn Islanders. Forty percent of the present population are descended from the *Bounty* mutineers and their Tahitian wives. In 1913 Norfolk became an Australian territory, a status it still holds. Today it and Lord Howe I., between Norfolk and Sydney, are holiday resorts for Australians on package tours. Lord Howe (13 sq km), part of Australia's New South Wales, is a dramatic volcanic island which soars to 942 m at Mt. Gower (licensed guide mandatory for climbers). Ball's Pyramid, a 607-m-high rock pinnacle with a base diameter of 200 m, is the highest of its kind in the world. The first recorded climb of the Pyramid, 16 km from Lord Howe, took place in 1965. Connecting flights make it possible to island-hop Sydney-Lord Howe-Norfolk-Auckland at a total cost of about A$500, more than twice the direct Sydney-Auckland fare. Book well ahead.

mole cowries (Cypraea talpa)

NEW ZEALAND

INTRODUCTION

Aotearoa, the Land of the Long White Cloud, has been called a "world in miniature" for its fantastic mix of scenery, cultures, and adventure, compacted into an area the size of Colorado. The country is a paradise for lovers of geography: there are active and dormant volcanoes, geysers, glaciers, fiords, drowned craters, submerged river valleys, glacial and crater lakes, caves, swift rivers, high mountains, and lonely coastlines, all eminently accessible. This spectacular landscape offers almost unlimited opportunities for the sportsperson and explorer. Add to this a gentle, friendly people and excellent, inexpensive facilities, and you have one of the best places to visit in the entire world. Plan to stay as long as you possibly can—you'll never regret it.

the land: Throughout New Zealand's 1,600-km length, no point is over 130 km from the sea. The North Island features active volcanoes in Tongariro National Park, and a varied thermal area around Rotorua; the South

Island is far more rugged, with the Southern Alps forming a massive chain which includes 19 named peaks over 3,000 m high. This mighty range alone covers an area larger than Switzerland. There is no coastal plain on the SW side of these mountains which plummet directly into the sea. Much of the country, however, is rolling green hillside, crowded with some of New Zealand's 71 million sheep. Getting off the beaten track is easy: corners like the Coromandel Peninsula near Auckland are rarely visited by foreign tourists.

climate: The climate is similar to that of Northern California, although damper. Snow is seldom seen outside the mountain areas, but a warm coat is required in winter (June to August). December to Feb. (summer) are the best months, but New Zealanders take their holidays at this time—transportation and lodgings will be packed. Plan on camping frequently if you visit during this peak season. The best months to come, however, for good

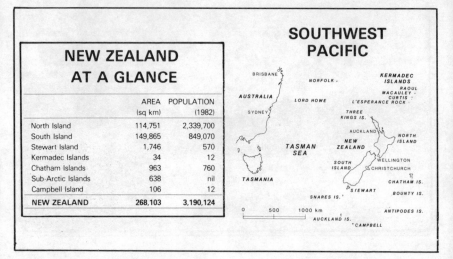

NEW ZEALAND AT A GLANCE

	AREA (sq km)	POPULATION (1982)
North Island	114,751	2,339,700
South Island	149,865	849,070
Stewart Island	1,746	570
Kermadec Islands	34	12
Chatham Islands	963	760
Sub-Arctic Islands	638	nil
Campbell Island	106	12
NEW ZEALAND	**268,103**	**3,190,124**

SOUTHWEST PACIFIC

weather, uncrowded conditions, and colorful foliage, are March, April (fall), Oct., and Nov. (spring). Rainfall is fairly evenly distributed throughout the year. The prevailing winds are from the W: as they're forced up and over the Southern Alps, they unload colossal amounts of precipitation. Milford Sound gets an average of 6,236 mm of rainfall a year, nearly 10 times as much as Christchurch (658 mm). Auckland has a variable climate: one moment it's sunny with a clear blue sky, the next it's raining.

flora and fauna: New Zealand's long isolation accounts for the almost complete absence of native mammals, the only land-based examples of which are long and short-tailed bats. There are also no snakes or mosquitoes. Apart from native frogs and snails, the only animal of note is the *tautara* (on the 5-cent coin), a reptile of ancient lineage found on islands in the Cook Strait. Birdlife is more abundant, with 275 native species. Over a hundred species of shore and seabirds breed in New Zealand. The best known are the many unusual flightless birds. The 3-m-high *moa,* largest bird that ever lived, was hunted to extinction by the Maori, but the nocturnal kiwi, with its long beak and round feathery body, is still common. Not so lucky are the flightless *kakapo,* a large green nocturnal owl parrot, and the *takahe,* together facing imminent extinction on the SW side of the South Island. Due to its ability to adapt to the human environment, the smaller *pukeho* has fared much better than the *takahe,* to which it bears a superficial resemblance. The *weka* is another flightless bird which may survive. Of the native birds with the ability to fly, the most distinctive are the *kea* (on the $10 banknote), a large, dull-green alpine parrot found on the South I., and its slightly smaller North I. cousin, the *kaka.* New Zealand's native birds have suffered considerable competition from introduced species, which now predominate in many areas. The large black-and-white birds which attack hitchhikers are magpies, introduced from Australia. Aggressive Indian mynas are now common, and many plant-destroying mammals have been introduced. There are 112 species of native trees; of the 150 species of ferns, a third are unique. Some tree ferns grow up to 15 m tall, but the tiny filmy ferns are only 2 cm high. The *kowhai* (on the 2-cent coin) is noted for its pendulant yellow flowers which bloom in spring. The slow-growing hardwoods such as *kauri, totara, rimu,* and *rata* are less ubiquitous than they once were. Giant *kauri* can grow 50 m tall and live 1,000 years. Cabbage trees are common.

HISTORY

prehistory: Before time there was Te Kore (The Void). Then came Te Po (The Dark). Papatuanuku (Mother Earth) and Ranginui (Skyfather) lived in such close embrace that their children could not grow. Finally Tanemahuta, god of the forests (son of Papa and Rangi), forced his parents apart and life began in Te Ao (World of Light). The demigod Maui fished the North Island from the sea and the Maori (pronounced MOU-ree) arrived by canoe from the legendary Hawaiki, their ancestral homeland.

the Maori: These were Polynesians who left Tahiti or Rarotonga about A.D. 850. With only tropical experience, they found a great cold land; their successful adaptation is one of the finest achievements of mankind. Over 50 generations they evolved a more vigorous, aggressive, energetic way of life. Large houses were built of timber; huge *totara* and *kauri* logs permitted the construction of great single

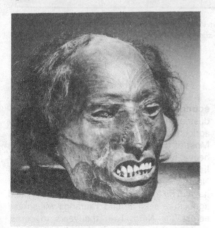

Occasionally the Maori cleaned and smoke-dried the head of a revered ancestor, so that it could be kept in the village and due respect paid to it. The typical curvilinear facial tattooing is still visible on this impressive preserved Maori head.

canoes. Some tribes became feared warriors who lived . in fortified villages *(pa)* built on easily defendable hills or ridges. Ramparts surmounted by timber stockades and deep trenches surrounded the settlements. Warfare and cannibalism were rife. Then as now, the *marae* or meeting house was the cultural center of Maori life. The people possessed their land communally as a sacred trust from the ancestors to those yet to come. Archaeologists have shown that during the Archaic Phase the Maori of the South I. hunted *moas*. As the giant birds became extinct the people became cultivators of sweet potatoes and taro, during the so-called Classic Phase. Sweet potatoes were stored in ingenious underground pits; taro has always been grown on the North I. where *moas* were scarcer. After A.D. 1500 the heartland of Maori life shifted to the N, where it remains today.

European settlement: Although the Dutch explorer Abel Tasman was the first European to sight New Zealand (in 1642), Capt. Cook made it well-known to the world. Others followed to exploit the most accessible resources: seal hunters (1790-1820) and whalers (1800-1840). The great *kauri* forests of the northern half of the North I. were cut clean, and the insatiable exploitation continued by digging into the very ground in search of *kauri* gum. As the agricultural potential became apparent, there was a rush to make N.Z. a colony; the British narrowly beat the French. On 6 Feb. 1840 British representatives signed the Treaty of Waitangi with the Maori chiefs. The treaty guaranteed the Maori inalienable rights to their lands, forests, and fisheries. The British also promised to protect the Maori from speculators seeking land, in exchange for the Crown having first option to buy Maori land. It soon became apparent that the British had no intention of honoring their treaty and were only stalling for time until their military forces arrived. The mid-19th C. saw a series of Maori uprisings to protest forced land "sales." Today the Maori hold only about 3 percent (800,000 ha) of the land. In 1861 a goldrush on the South I. attracted prospectors from Australia and California.

*New Zealand's Parliament Building at Wellington is known affectionately
as "the beehive," for reasons which should be obvious.*

More and more, however, people settled
down to raise cattle and sheep, which became
more profitable after the introduction of
refrigerated transport in 1882. Meat production became as important as wool.

politics: New Zealand has a parliamentary
system of government: the prime minister is
the leader of the largest party in Parliament.
The 2 main parties, the Labor Party and the
National Party, are both middle of the road,
with Labor slightly to the left. The New
Zealand Party and Social Credit are right-wing
groups. When Prime Minister David Lange
banned nuclear-armed warships from New
Zealand in 1984, he was subjected to considerable pressure from the bully boys in
Washington. There is a great deal of
grassroots support in N.Z. for a nuclear-free
Pacific.

ECONOMY AND PEOPLE

economy: Although New Zealand is an industrialized country, exports are mostly
agricultural: wool, mutton, dairy products.
Most of the sheep are found on the South I.;
heavy fertilization is required to keep their
fields green. When the phosphate deposits of
Nauru I. are finally exhausted, new crops will
have to be found. The trend toward diversified
agriculture seen around Tauranga will spread
across the North I. in the years to come.
Hydroelectric power is being utilized by
transnational corporations for increasing industrialization. Since Britain joined the European Economic Community in 1973, N.Z. has
suffered. Between 1980 and 1985 the N.Z.
dollar lost over half its value against American

currency while prices remained more or less stable, making the country a tremendous bargain for overseas visitors. New Zealand is something of a welfare state with social services heavily subsidized by government.

the people: In an area larger than Britain, there are only 3 million people. Over 73 percent live on the North Island. Maori comprise about 10 percent. Some 88,000 Pacific islanders also live in New Zealand, half of them Samoans, a quarter Cook Islanders. The Maori (or Aotearoans as they often call themselves) live in 2 worlds, the white man's and their own. There has never been any official discrimination against Maori; in fact governments have done much to integrate them into the European community. However, their drift to the cities, unemployment, loss of cultural values, and sense of being absorbed have led to social problems. Today you'll see the greatest concentrations of Maori in pubs of the North Island. Maori women have an incidence of lung cancer 7 times higher than white women, largely due to socializing in these bars. A disproportionately high percentage of prison inmates are Maori. Still, the Maori have fared far better than the Aboriginals of Australia or the American Indian, largely due to a greater ability to adjust. Intermarriage between *pakeha* (white) and Maori is fairly common and bears absolutely none of the lingering social stigma of a mixed marriage in N. America. There is now something of a cultural reawakening among the Maori as they rediscover the old values of their people. The often cold, businesslike ways of the white man are no longer accepted without question.

Maori arts: Maori art is outstanding for its huge, deeply-cut plank woodcarvings incorporating the same designs once used in facial tattooing. The decoration in most other Polynesian art is geometric: it's believed the Maori curvilinear style developed locally from the carvers' treatment of the mouths of their subjects. Maori artists carved mostly human forms; the only animal to appear was the lizard, a symbol of evil and death. The endless variations on a few basic forms gave Maori art its richness, unity, and strength. Nowhere else in Polynesia was woodcarving done on so monumental a scale. Maori artists also made small greenstone carvings of *tikis* with a characteristic tilted head (*manaia*). Clothing was made from woven flax (instead of *tapa* cloth), often covered with kiwi feathers. Some genuine traditional handicrafts are still made at the Maori Arts and Crafts Institute at Rotorua. It's amusing to observe that the polished items in the showcases at the Institute, which attract the tourists, are mass-produced; the rough, handmade articles on the wall behind the counter usually go unnoticed. Most of the imitiation-Maori souvenirs sold at airports and curio shops around N.Z. could just as well have been made in Hong Kong. It's well to remember that poetry, oratory, dance, and song were also important expressions of Maori art. Maori dancing features twirling *poi* balls, gentle movements from the women, and fierce, defiant war dances from the men. Shows for tourists are put on at Rotorua.

Maori greenstone pendant (hei-tiki) *with tilted face motif* (manaia): *items of this kind were worn only by women.*

windy Wellington, capital of New Zealand

events: Public holidays include Waitangi Day (6 Feb.), Anzac Day (25 April), Queen Elizabeth's Birthday (first Mon. in June), and Labor Day (4th Mon. in Oct.). On Waitangi Day there's an annual Maori protest march to Paihia, which sensitive visitors are welcome to join. The Auckland Festival coincides with Easter, while the Canterbury Agricultural Show is held in Christchurch in early November.

PRACTICALITIES

getting there: Airfares to N.Z. are outlined in the main "Introduction" to this book. Sea travel is largely history, although the MV *Fijian,* a passenger-carrying freighter, departs Auckland for Suva once every 3 weeks, about NZ$600 OW. Contact Reef Shipping, 16 Anzac Ave., Auckland (tel. 771-223).

getting around: Student Travel Services, 61 Shortland St., Auckland, can arrange a 50 percent student standby discount on all domestic flights. The big travel bargain is the railway's Travelpass, which allows unlimited travel on

trains, ferries, and railway buses (but not sightseeing tours) throughout the country. The cost is only NZ$180 for 15 days, NZ$240 for 22 days, plus NZ$15 for each additional day. The Travelpass can be purchased anytime after arriving in N.Z., but it's not available from 15 Dec. to 31 January. A High Season Travelpass valid between those dates (NZ$320 for 22 days) can only be purchased outside New Zealand. Advance seat reservations are required on all trains and buses. The NZRRS (railway buses) guarantees you a seat on any bus provided you book 72 hours in advance. Make sure you get a reservation slip (free); verbal reservations may be forgotten. Although no complete railway or bus timetable is available at newsstands, a small folder entitled "New Zealand Railways Timetables of Principal Services for Tourists and Holidaymakers" outlines the most important routes—be sure to get a copy. The Travelpass doesn't cover travel between Taupo and Napier, nor can you use it to visit Nelson or Mount Cook, but most other popular destinations are included. If you plan to do a complete circuit of the South I. and return to Auckland, the Travelpass definitely saves you money. To sidestep the 15-to-22-day rat race we recommend that you travel Auckland-Rotorua-Napier-Wanganui-Wellington on individual tickets. Begin using your Travelpass with an early morning ferry ride to Picton.

others: Mount Cook Landlines has a "Kiwi Coach Pass" valid for unlimited bus travel but, unlike the Travelpass, it must be purchased outside New Zealand (Mount Cook Lines, 9841 Airport Blvd., Los Angeles, CA 90045, USA, or GPO Box 4478, Sydney, NSW 2001, Australia). The "Kiwi Pass" costs about the same as the Travelpass and has the advantage of being valid year-round on both NZRRS and private bus routes, but not trains or ferries. Hitching is fairly easy on the North I. and down the E side of the South I.; on the W side of the South I. it can be difficult—few cars and many hitchhikers. You might have to take a bus.

tours: Venturetreks (Box 37610, Parnell, Auckland) offers outstanding 6-day seminar/tours on the natural history of Mt. Ruapehu (Tongariro National Park) from Dec. to March. During the same period they arrange 3-to-5 day guided canoe trips on the Wanganui River. Most of their clients are New Zealanders, a good recommendation. Group size is limited so book ahead. Contiki Tours (Box 3839, Auckland) specializes in packaged N.Z. bus tours for the 18-to-35 set. There are departures year-round from Auckland and Christchurch. Unfortunately, Contiki is an up-market operation aimed mostly at well-heeled young Aussies out for a bash. The following is from their brochure: "You never stay in a tent; no backpacks please, their awkward shapes take up too much room."

accommodations: The best budget accommodations are provided by the excellent network of youth hostels—you'll find them everywhere (about $6 a night). If you're not a member, go first to the YHA office at 36 Customs St. E., Auckland, for a guest membership ($19 a year). There's no age limit (although children under 5 may not be admitted). Cooking facilities are provided; members

are required to help with hostel housekeeping work. Highly recommended. There are also private hostels (which don't have memberships, rules, and chores), YMCAs, and YWCAs. Motor camps are the place to pitch a tent in summer; they also have cheap cabins, a good deal for couples. Many guest houses and small private hotels offer bed and breakfast—good value. For all the conveniences of home, watch for motel flats (not to be confused with the plastic American-style motels). From Dec. to Feb. accommodations are tight, so plan on camping unless you've booked well ahead. There are no hotel taxes or service charges. As in Australia, tipping is not the custom.

food: The best meals in New Zealand are based on lamb, beef, and dairy products. English fish and chips are available everywhere. A favorite lunch for Kiwis is sandwiches made from spaghetti or pork and beans. Don't be alarmed by the purple stuff oozing out the sides of your hamburger —"down under" no good burger is complete without beets! *Toheroa* clam soup is a local gourmet treat, though quite rare since the clams are now protected. For dessert try pavlova, made from beaten and baked egg whites. If you're a smoker, "New Zealand green" is highly rated and easily obtained.

shopping: The main stores stay open late on Thurs. or Fri. evenings (varies), but close weekends. Banks open 1000-1500 weekdays. Corner "dairies" are open daily till 1900 or later. Film is expensive in N.Z. so bring along a supply (5-roll official limit).

visas: Frankly, New Zealand's entry regulations seem to be based on skin color. For instance, white Commonwealth citizens are admitted without a visa, while dark-skinned Commonwealth passport holders must obtain advance clearance. This tendency extends to Americans: U.S. citizens get 30 days with only a passport, while U.S. nationals (American Samoans) must obtain a visa. Most amazingly of all, dark-skinned Europeans such as Italians and Spaniards require a visa while northern Europeans do not. The mentally disturbed are routinely refused entry, while Canadians get 6 months without a visa. Extensions of stay are possible, but everyone must have an onward ticket. Cruising yachts may spend a maximum of one year in N.Z. waters, after which full duty and sales tax are payable on the vessel. For such an easygoing country, Immigration officials can be strangely uptight. Don't overstay your entry permit—there have been horror stories. At one time plainclothes police were stopping suspected overstayers (mostly Samoans and Tongans) on the street, demanding identification. Fortunately, these tactics have ceased.

Customs: New Zealand has strict quarantine regulations to prevent the entry of plant and animal diseases, and insects. Airport checks of incoming passengers are strict. The need for these controls is very real, so be as patient and cooperative as you can. You can help by cleaning your shoes and boots before embarking for New Zealand. If you have a tent, wash the pegs and make sure everything's clean, as Customs will open it. Honey is prohibited entry, and dried or preserved foods are highly suspect. Fresh fruit will be kept in quarantine several days. Wooden artifacts must be free of bark. Live plants and seeds are prohibited entry (beware of artifacts made from seeds). Souvenirs incorporating animal hair, skin, bone, feathers, or wool are usually banned.

You can sometimes obtain a permit in advance to bring in such items, but it's far easier simply to avoid them.

airport: Auckland International Airport (AKL), 21 km S of downtown, gets high marks for its excellent facilities, convenient size, and friendly atmosphere. The "information" counter you see as you come out of Customs is run by the Automobile Assn.—you must show the card of an affiliated club (such as N. American associations) to get their attention. Ask about a temporary 6-month AA membership which entitles you to a thick packet of maps and booklets at their Auckland office. The "New Zealand Tourist Office" counter, just around the corner, is often unstaffed. There's a bank inside the Customs Hall itself, so change some money while you're waiting for your baggage. There are also banks in the check-in and departure areas. They open for most international flights and give the usual rate (minus $1 commission), so there's no need to try to get N.Z. dollars before you arrive. Coin lockers (50 cents) are just outside the terminal. There's also a left-luggage service ($1) at the Downtown Airline Terminal (open daily 0600-2100). The departure tax is NZ$2 ($40 for N.Z. passport holders). Even if a bus went to town after 2200 it would be hard to find a reasonable place to stay, so if you're arriving late it's better to spend the night in the terminal—the airport is open 24 hours a day. The officials are pretty understanding about this, but be as unobtrusive as possible. The Airporter bus ($4) to the Downtown Airline Terminal on the Quay operates every 30 min. from 0700-2200 daily. This same bus shuttles to the domestic terminal ($1), a 10-min. walk. A taxi to downtown would run $20.

AUCKLAND

Although there are direct flights from Australia to Christchurch and Wellington, most visitors to New Zealand arrive in Auckland, home to a quarter of the country's population. The location is scenic, but Auckland is only a gateway. Visit the War Memorial Museum (which houses one of the finest collections of Oceanic art in the world) and make a daytrip by ferry to Rangitoto I. to scale the 259-m cone, then hit the road to find out what New Zealand's really about. Below we list a few facilities to help you organize your first several days, and then a brief summary gives you an idea what the country has to offer. You'll be able to get maps and brochures at Public Relations Offices (PRO) in all the larger towns, but an independent guidebook would be advisable. For more detailed coverage than we can provide here, turn to *New Zealand Handbook* by Jane King (Moon Publications).

accommodations: There are 2 YHA youth hostels in Auckland. The one at 7 Princes St. (tel. 790-258) is close to downtown (get off the Airporter bus at the Hyatt), while the hostel at 5a Oaklands Rd., Mount Eden (tel. 603-975), is about 4 km S (bus No. 273 or 274). The Mount Eden hostel is a dollar or two cheaper. The very central Georgia Backpackers Hostel, 72 Symonds St. at Wakefield (tel. 399-560), doesn't require a YHA card (get off the Airporter bus at the Sheraton). Privately operated Ivanhoe Lodge (tel. 862-800) has both dormitory and private rooms (take a city bus to Glen Lynn Post Office, then ask directions). Ivanhoe Lodge has a branch at Rotorua complete with its own thermal pool. The YMCA on Pitt St. (tel. 32-068) has single rooms for men and women, but it's often full. Cheap weekly rooms are listed in the "board and residence" classified column of the *New Zealand Herald.*

food: The Student Union beside Albert Park is a lively place to eat, gather information, and mix at lunchtime. If you're in Auckland on Sun., don't miss the Hare Krishna festival and feast ($1 donation) at Gopals Restaurant, 291 Queen Street. This is always a good place for lunch or a cup of herbal tea. By eating vegetarian meals here you become immune to the effects of *karma*. Better still, spend a weekend at the New Varshana Spiritual Retreat, a collective farm outside Auckland. Meals, accommodations, and transport from the restaurant are free for devotees.

the Maori Court of the Auckland Museum

information: The Government Tourist Office, 99 Queen St. (weekdays 0830-1700, Sat. 0930-1200), is run on a commercial basis — you'll have to stand in line till they finish booking other people's itineraries. The PRO at 299 Queen St. is more helpful, but their information is mostly on Auckland. The Automobile Assn., 33 Wyndham St., is the most helpful, but you must be a member of an affiliated AA club or pay $12.50 for a 6-month temporary membership. In exchange you'll get a huge stack of material well worth the money. Excellent detailed maps of New Zealand are for sale at the Map Sales Room, Dept. of Lands and Surveys, 11th floor, State Insurance Bldg., Queen and Wakefield Sts. (weekdays 0800-1600). An office on the 14th floor of the same building has brochures on New Zealand's national parks. For navigational charts it's Trans Pacific Marine, 29-31 Fort Street. They also sell this *Handbook*. The YHA office, 36 Customs St. E., has a booklet ($1) listing every youth hostel in N.Z., also YHA cards (*a must*), backpacks, and money belts. Ansett Pioneer, second floor, 87 Queen St., sells Greyhound's Ameripass for unlimited bus travel in N. America considerably discounted than if you wait to buy it in Los Angeles. Greenpeace, fifth floor, Nagel House, Courthouse Lane, sells Nuclear Free Pacific T-shirts, pins, and stickers. The Corso Center, 74 Pitt St., sells posters, Third World handicrafts, and a wide selection of hard-to-find books on development issues.

THINGS TO SEE AND DO

Northland: Paihia, 241 km N of Auckland, is the center of a district full of historic and scenic interest. It was here at the Waitangi Treaty House that Maori chiefs signed the 1840 agreement bringing N.Z. under British rule. A short ferry ride across the bay from Paihia is Russell, the earliest European settlement in N.Z. and a well-preserved link to the country's past. Both towns are set on the lovely Bay of Islands which is fully accessible by daily sightseeing cruise. There's an outstanding excursion out of Paihia or Kaitaia to Cape Reinga and along Ninety Mile Beach.

Rotorua to Napier: Southeast of Auckland is the famous thermal and lake region around Rotorua. Between Auckland and Rotorua visit the Waitomo Caves where N.Z. glow worms can be observed, or see them free on the way home from the pub at Franz Josef. The smell of sulphur drifts across Rotorua, the major tourist center of the North I., where Maori culture is marketed as nowhere else. One excursion that shouldn't be missed is the full-day Waimangu Round Trip: 2 boat rides, a visit to a beautiful thermal area, views of Mt. Tarawera, and entrance to a buried Maori village. With its fine facilities, many attractions, and numerous mineral hotsprings, Rotorua is a great place to kick back for a few days. Right in the center of the island is Lake Taupo, largest in the country — outstanding trout fishing here. Just S in the mountains of Tongariro National Park is the ski resort of Chateau. On Hawke Bay to the E in wine-

Marine Parade, Napier

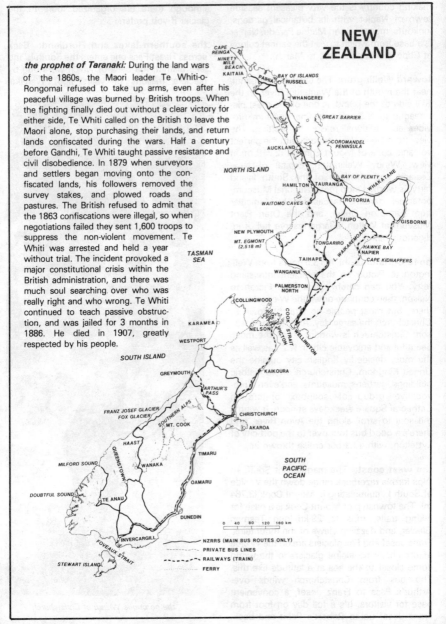

NEW ZEALAND

the prophet of Taranaki: During the land wars of the 1860s, the Maori leader Te Whiti-o-Rongomai refused to take up arms, even after his peaceful village was burned by British troops. When the fighting finally died out without a clear victory for either side, Te Whiti called on the British to leave the Maori alone, stop purchasing their lands, and return lands confiscated during the wars. Half a century before Gandhi, Te Whiti taught passive resistance and civil disobedience. In 1879 when surveyors and settlers began moving onto the confiscated lands, his followers removed the survey stakes, and plowed roads and pastures. The British refused to admit that the 1863 confiscations were illegal, so when negotiations failed they sent 1,600 troops to suppress the non-violent movement. Te Whiti was arrested and held a year without trial. The incident provoked a major constitutional crisis within the British administration, and there was much soul searching over who was really right and who wrong. Te Whiti continued to teach passive obstruction, and was jailed for 3 months in 1886. He died in 1907, greatly respected by his people.

NORTH ISLAND

CAPE REINGA
NINETY MILE BEACH
KAITAIA
PAIHIA
BAY OF ISLANDS
RUSSELL
WHANGEREI
GREAT BARRIER
COROMANDEL PENINSULA
AUCKLAND
HAMILTON
TAURANGA
BAY OF PLENTY
WHAKATANE
WAITOMO CAVES
ROTORUA
TAUPO
GISBORNE
NEW PLYMOUTH
MT. EGMONT (2,518 m)
TONGARIRO
L. WAIKAREMOANA
HAWKE BAY
NAPIER
CAPE KIDNAPPERS
TAIHAPE
WANGANUI
PALMERSTON NORTH
COLLINGWOOD
COOK STRAIT
WELLINGTON
KARAMEA
NELSON
PICTON
WESTPORT

TASMAN SEA

SOUTH ISLAND

GREYMOUTH
KAIKOURA
ARTHUR'S PASS
FRANZ JOSEF GLACIER
FOX GLACIER
SOUTHERN ALPS
MT. COOK
CHRISTCHURCH
AKAROA
HAAST
TIMARU
MILFORD SOUND
QUEENSTOWN
WANAKA
OAMARU
DOUBTFUL SOUND
TE ANAU
DUNEDIN

SOUTH PACIFIC OCEAN

0 40 80 120 160 km

INVERCARGILL
FOVEAUX STRAIT
STEWART ISLAND

——— NZRRS (MAIN BUS ROUTES ONLY)
- - - PRIVATE BUS LINES
-·-·- RAILWAYS (TRAIN)
········ FERRY

making country is the very pleasant seaside town of Napier with its botanical gardens, lookouts, museum, and Marine Parade. Napier is a base from which to visit the gannet colony at Cape Kidnappers (Oct. to March).

toward Wellington: The town of Wanganui, near the mouth of the Wanganui River on the SW side of the island, is one of the most picturesque in N.Z., and its fine museum provides an additional reason for visiting. The view from Durie Hill is superb with the perfect volcanic cone of Mount Egmont (2,518 m) in view. Windy Wellington, capital of New Zealand and terminus of the South Island ferry, is worth a stop for its National Museum, botanical gardens (accessible by funicular from Lambton Quay), and the Otari Plant Museum at Wilton, a large reserve full of indigenous plantlife.

on to Christchurch: It's 3.5 hours from Wellington to Picton on the efficient interisland ferry. You can catch a bus from Picton to Nelson, then continue down the W coast from there, but most people go straight down to Christchurch the same day. And for good reason; Christchurch is without doubt the most beautiful and enjoyable city in N.Z., as well as the most decidedly English city outside the United Kingdom. Christchurch offers historic buildings, gardens, museums, and even a provocative group of soapbox orators in Cathedral Square weekdays at noon. It warms the soul to stroll along the Avon River, and there's a good bus tour over to the port city of Lyttelton, with a harbor cruise thrown in.

the west coast: The magnificent Southern Alps form a razorback range down the W side of South I., culminating in Mount Cook (3,764 m). The township of Mount Cook is a base for hiking trails, trips to 29-km-long Tasman Glacier, and dazzling views of the mountains. Franz Josef and Fox glaciers are on the W side of the chain; no alpine glaciers in the world come closer to the sea at a latitude like this. The bus from Christchurch winds over Arthur's Pass to Franz Josef, a convenient base for visitors. It's a full day on foot from Franz Josef up to Robert's Point and back,

although there are organized tours to the glacier if you prefer.

the southern lakes and Fiordland: Back across Haast Pass one enters the South Island lake district, the beds of which were dug by glaciers millions of years ago. Wanaka,

the notorious Wizard of Christchurch

Lake Hayes near Queenstown on New Zealand's South Island

Queenstown, and Te Anau are the main centers, each with its own attractions. Wanaka is the least touristed and most quiet, a good place to relax. The eastern side of the Alps is drier and lacks the dense forests which are a feature of the W, offering sweeping vistas. Queenstown is the touroid center of the South I.; numerous activities and "attractions" separate you from your money. It's free to just walk around and enjoy the beautiful lake scenery, however. There's an excellent half-day hike to the top of Queenstown Hill, or a full-day trek to the top of Ben Lomond. Both afford a complete view of the whole vicinity. Deep fiords (also glacier-made) penetrate the mountains of the SW coast. Milford Sound is the most spectacular, and sightseeing launches connect with buses from Queenstown and Te Anau, which come in on a breathtaking road. A more expensive boat trip can be made to Doubtful Sound.

Southland to Dunedin: Invercargill, at the S end of the island, is noted mainly for its massive aluminum smelter sustained by the hydropower of Fiordland. It's also the gateway to Stewart I., accessible by ferry or small plane if you'd like to get away. Although it began as a Scottish settlement, the city of Dunedin up the E coast is now typical of New

Zealand—a mixture of old and new in rolling hill country 350 km S of Christchurch. Old churches, mansions, and museums grace the streets, while the long harbor flanks the engaging Otago Peninsula, sprinkled with a number of places well worth visiting.

OUTDOORS NEW ZEALAND

The country's rich geography and adventurous people combine to offer a range of exciting sports rarely found elsewhere in the world in such abundance: fishing, sailing, canoeing, skiing, river rafting, scuba diving, mountaineering, caving, cycling, jet boats, aerial sightseeing, float and ski planes, helicopters, and hang gliding. Excellent beach-break surfing is possible in hundreds of places, especially on the W coasts; conditions can be good anytime except mid-winter. New Zealand has a fine series of national parks, most with well-maintained trails, information centers, and other facilities. Unlike their American counterparts, many are easily accessible by public transport; during spring and autumn they are almost deserted—an outstanding refuge for naturalists. There are no dangerous wild animals to worry about and none of the parks charge admission.

tramping: New Zealanders are avid hikers, and there's even a plan underway to construct a hiking trail from one end of the country to the other. The most famous of the trails is the Milford Track, from the northern tip of Lake Te Anau to Milford Sound. Open Nov. to April, hiking it takes 4 days. You must obtain a permit from the National Park Headquarters: write Box 29, Te Anua, and give the number in your party and the exact date you wish to begin. Less crowded, easier to organize, and equally impressive is the Routeburn Track, from the top of Lake Wakatipu in the Queenstown area to the road between Te Anau and Milford Sound. Other excellent trails on the South I. are the Copland Track from Mount Cook to the West Coast Highway, and the Heaphy Track between Collingwood and Karamea. On the North I. the Ketetahi Track in Tongariro National Park and the Waikaremoana Track around the W end of the lake between Rotorua and Wairoa are among the best.

OUTER ISLAND GROUPS

the Kermadec Islands: The Kermadec Group, between New Zealand and Tonga 1,000 km N of Auckland, is uninhabited except for the staff of the weather station on Raoul Island. Raoul, largest of the Kermadecs, is a volcanic island reaching 500 m on its E end.

the Chatham Islands: The unspoiled, little-known Chatham Islands, 800 km E of Christchurch, consist of 2 rolling, swampy main islands 20 km apart (Pitt and Chatham) and 8 uninhabited islets. There are many excellent beaches; the rugged southern end of Chatham is the best hiking area. The Te

Whanga Lagoon on Chatham I. is thick with eels. Birdlife is abundant with 18 endemic species. When Lt. Broughton "discovered" the Chathams in 1791 there were 2,000 Polynesian Moriori present. In 1835 a group of Maori from the N.Z. mainland arrived on a trading ship and managed to enslave the inhabitants. Tommy Solomon, the last of the Moriori, died in 1933. His grave is outside Owenga village. Today about 750 people live in the Chathams, only 50 of them on Pitt. The economy is based on fishing and sheep raising. Safe Air Ltd. (Box 244, Blenheim, N.Z., tel. 28-416) has flights from Wellington/Christchurch about every 5 days (NZ$216 OW). A bus covers the 19 km between the airstrip and Waitangi, the port and only town. There are 2 places to stay at Waitangi: the Hotel Chatham (capacity 13 guests, NZ$39 pp including wholesome meals) and the Tuanui Motel (9 rooms, NZ$40 d, cooking facilities). The hotel bar is Waitangi's social center. Visit the museum at the Chatham Islands County Council offices to see haunting relics of the Moriori.

the subarctic islands: Under N.Z. sovereignty are a series of desolate subarctic islands between New Zealand and Antarctica. All are uninhabited except Campbell I. (106 sq km), 590 km S of Stewart I., which has a small weather station. The others are the Auckland Is. (612 sq km), the Snares Is. (2 sq km), the Antipodes Is. (22 sq km), and the Bounty Is. (2 sq km). Marine mammals and seabirds are present in great numbers. The rare New Zealand sea lion *(Phocarctos hookeri)* is now threatened by local squid fishing boats which trawl intensively around these islands during the sea lion breeding season, and net a large bycatch of pregnant sea lion mothers.

HAWAII

INTRODUCTION

The 8 mighty volcanic islands of Hawaii stretch along a 585-km axis in the Central Pacific Ocean. To the NW a string of reefs and rocky pinnacles runs 2,000 km to beyond Midway — 136 islands in all. Magnificent white beaches alternate with soaring sea cliffs; inland there's everything from arid deserts to tropical rainforests to snowcapped mountains. Waterfalls plunge into verdant valleys. Only the Society Islands come close for scenery, but Hawaii is larger and grander. There's magic in Hawaii. Captain Cook thought it his greatest discovery, while Mark Twain called them "the loveliest fleet of islands that lies anchored in any ocean." Romantics like Robert Louis Stevenson and Jack London, joined by James Michener, all extolled the legend of Old Hawaii. Today the legend is fading as congestion billows from a burgeoning military, and tourists overrun the islands. Outside events continue to shape Hawaii, which lies on the crossroads of Asia and America. Away from Honolulu, the cancer

of development eats closer and deeper into the neighbor islands. But beyond the expressways, fast food, plastic people, and almighty dollar, there's still plenty of magic. Guidebooks to Hawaii are many and this brief chapter is only a supplement to help you weather those first few days on the road to paradise. Here you'll read a few things they forgot to put in the glossy brochures and hopefully be able to find your own way through the celluloid circus from there.

the land: The "Conveyor Belt Theory" explains the origin of the Hawaiian Chain: a crack opened in the sea floor and volcanic material escaped upwards. As old volcanoes disconnected with the crack, new ones appeared to the SE, and the older islands were carried away from the cleft in the Earth's crust from which they were born. Over the past 20 million years this hot spot has moved some 3,000 km E-SE, about 15 cm a year. It's worth noting that over the same period the magnetic

HAWAII AT A GLANCE

	POPULATION (1980)	AREA (sq km)	HIGHEST POINT (m)
Niihau	226	189	390
Kauai	38,856	1,432	1,598
Oahu	762,534	1,572	1,231
Molokai	6,049	676	1,511
Lanai	2,119	362	1,027
Kahoolawe	nil	116	450
Maui	62,823	1,885	3,055
Hawaii	92,053	10,458	4,205
	964,660	16,690	

pole of the Earth has also moved about the same distance in a parallel direction. The theory of plate tectonics, or the sliding crust of the Earth, seems proven in Hawaii, which sits on the Pacific Plate. Weathering is most advanced on the low coral islets at the NW end of the Hawaiian Chain, which have eroded almost to sea level; Kauai with its spectacular canyons is the oldest of the larger islands. Island-building continues on the Big Island, and an undersea volcano to the SE will someday poke its smoky head above the waves, as the crack continues to spew forth a cubic mile of lava every century.

climate: The mountainous spines of the high islands create rain shadows as the NE tradewinds are forced up and over, painting them green to windward and brown to leeward. Ocean currents, which parallel the trades, also strike the NE coasts creating steep cliffs *(pali)*, underwater drop-offs, and ledges. The leeward coasts are gentler, with beaches sloping gradually into the sea. Because of the winds, the W sides of the islands are always much drier than the east. Mountain areas under 2,100 m are wet, and nighttime temperatures drop unexpectedly as you attain altitude. Summer is preferable if you plan to hike in the national parks. Though the seasons don't have as much meaning in Hawaii as they do elsewhere, winter is cooler. Occasional *kona* (south) winds from Oct. to April lead to stormy weather and torrential downpours. Hurricanes are rare. The peak tourist seasons are winter (Dec. to March) and summer holiday time (July and August). You'll enjoy bigger discounts and smaller crowds if you come during the other months.

flora and fauna: Of 2,500 native Hawaiian plant species, 95 percent are found nowhere else in the world. Over the 20 million-year history of Hawaii, some 600 "infections" brought by natural causes such as winds, wings of birds, or floating logs introduced new species to Hawaii, about one every 30,000 years. Since Captain Cook's time, 4,000 new species of plants have arrived, and despite the quarantine and inspection program, more than 20 new species of insects enter Hawaii each year. In the 1840s Europeans introduced mosquitoes—these disease-carrying insects wiped out many endemic bird species. Pigs and goats have been highly destructive to native plantlife, and today half of the endangered species of birds and plants in the U.S. are Hawaiian. The native plantlife survives best at the higher altitudes. None of Hawaii's native plants were capable of providing food for humans. The Polynesians brought with them coconuts, breadfruit, taro, bananas, and other useful plants. The little grey birds which jump up on your picnic table are barred doves, introduced from Malaysia in 1922. Among the underwater fauna, sharks and barracuda are not common in Hawaiian waters and should present no problem to the average swimmer or surfer. Eels, on the other hand, are found everywhere in coral holes and ledges. They rarely attack unless provoked, but this can be done unintentionally by unwary snorkelers, so be on the lookout. Fire coral is found in some protected areas and can be very irritating to the skin if touched.

HISTORY

It's believed that the Polynesians discovered Hawaii not once but at least twice. Hawaii's stone adzes have been classified into 2 groups: adzes of the earlier group resemble those of the Marquesans, while the later adzes look like those of the Society Islands (Tahiti). The Marquesans may have come between A.D. 500-700, while the Tahitians arrived between A.D. 1100-1300; the old culture of Hawaii was a blend of these 2 strains. The Hawaiians lived in balance with nature. Land was in the hands of the powerful chiefs, but nature gave abundantly.

Europeans: Captain Cook, who "discovered" Hawaii in 1778, upset this self-sufficiency by trading nails for food. He christened Hawaii the Sandwich Islands for the Earl of Sandwich, inventor of the quick lunch. A sailor in Cook's crew introduced venereal disease to the islands. Cook himself was killed in a sudden clash with the Hawaiians over a stolen rowboat on St. Valentine's Day, 1779. Europeans who followed Cook brought weapons and diseases which reduced the native population from 300,000 at the time of contact to only 56,897 by 1872.

Traders on their way to the NW coast of N. America to collect furs for the Chinese market were early visitors. They supplied firearms, with which Kamehameha, chief of the Big Island, was able to unify Hawaii under his rule by 1810. Kamehameha died in 1819; within months his successor, Kamehameha II, defied the *kapus* (taboos) and destroyed the old religion. Meanwhile, ruffian whalers were introducing alcohol and by 1820, when New England missionaries arrived on the *Thaddeus,* Hawaii was in chaos. The missionaries allied themselves with the *ali'i* (chiefs) and within 2 decades their influence was absolute. Native ties to England were stronger in the early days, and many Hawaiians hoped direct British rule would fill the void left by the fast-disintegrating indigenous culture. Kamehameha II died of measles in London while on a mission to convince the English to annex Hawaii. Although Britain rejected the proposal, the Union Jack in a corner of the present state flag recalls the time. So instead of developing into an independent nation, Hawaii was digested by American imperialism and the Hawaiians joined the peoples of the Fourth World.

the rape of Hawaii: First the islands were stripped of sandalwood, but the pretentions of the American missionaries and their mer-

the death of Capt. James Cook on St. Valentine's Day, 1779: Capt. Cook was first sent to Tahiti in 1769 by the Royal Society of London to observe the transit of Venus across the disc of the sun. Cook's murder took place on the island of Hawaii, the result of a fatal series of misunderstandings between Englishmen and Hawaiians.

betrayal underway:
American sailors and
marines from the USS
Boston land at Honolulu in
1893 to assist in the
overthrow of the Hawaiian
monarchy.

chant friends went further. The missionaries came to do good and stayed to do well. By mid-century they were strong enough to pressure King Kamehameha III into allowing the sale of his people's land. The Great Mahele of 1848 and the Kuleana Act of 1850 left the workers of the land with less than one percent. The American Civil War effectively terminated commercial whaling in Hawaii, but by this time sugar grown on large plantations by American businessmen was predominant. Since the Hawaiians were found unsuited for burdensome plantation work, large numbers of indentured Asian laborers were imported. To guarantee a market for their sugar, the planters plotted the integration of Hawaii into the United States. In 1887 King Kalakaua signed a treaty granting Pearl Harbor to the U.S. as a naval base. In 1893 American businessmen, many of them descendants of missionaries, conspired with the U.S. representative, John L. Stevens, and Captain G.C. Wiltse of the USS Boston to overthrow the legal Hawaiian monarch, Queen Lili'uokalani, who wanted to return control of the land to the Hawaiian people. Soon after, the U.S. committed an act of war against a friendly nation by landing troops from the Boston at Honolulu to "maintain order." The Queen surrendered under protest to this "superior American force." Although Presi-

dent Cleveland later repudiated the action and called on the leaders of the coup to surrender power and restore the legitimate government, he did nothing to enforce it. Queen Lili'uokalani was charged with "treason" by the provisional government and held in a stark room at Iolani Palace for 9 months. Only when she finally agreed to abdicate to avoid bloodshed was she released. Lili was a talented composer and some of her best music was written during this imprisonment. On 4 July 1894, in the presence of the American community and U.S. naval officers, Sanford B. Dole (son of the missionary, Daniel Dole) inaugurated the Republic of Hawaii in Honolulu. Hawaiians assembled at Lahaina, Maui, protested the act by burning historic Waiola Church, built by the earliest missionaries. Four years later President McKinley launched a war against Spain and snatched up the former Spanish colonies in Puerto Rico, Guam, and the Philippines. Hawaii's military value became apparent, so the U.S. government formally and finally annexed the islands in 1898. Four days later, some 1,300 U.S. Army troops arrived to establish a base on Oahu. The traitor Dole was appointed first U.S. governor of Hawaii by President McKinley. The people of Hawaii were never consulted in any of this.

to statehood: Under U.S. rule there was a massive influx of people from both E and W, which soon reduced the Hawaiians to a small minority. Territorial status with U.S.-appointed governors and judges holding veto power over the local legislature suited American business; sugar and pineapple flourished up until WW II. The story of the Japanese attack on Pearl Harbor is well-known, but less is said about serious allegations that President Roosevelt knew several days in advance of the impending attack and did nothing to prevent it or warn his men, so anxious was he to get the U.S. into the war against Nazi Germany. Bruce R. Bartlett has written a book about it (see "Booklist"). From 1941 to 1944 Hawaii was under military rule enforced by kangaroo courts. The Korean War again brought home Hawaii's strategic importance and in 1959, the same year the first jetloads of tourists arrived, Hawaii became the 50th state. Today the Commander-in-Chief Pacific (CINCPAC) directs all American military forces in Asia and the Pacific from Fort Smith in the foothills above Pearl Harbor.

ECONOMY AND PEOPLE

agriculture and land: Sugar and pineapple have declined steadily in recent years, largely due to high production costs and foreign competition. Employment in these sectors fell from 40 percent of all jobs in the early 1940s to only 3 percent in the early 1980s. Even so, over a million tons of processed sugar is still produced each year. Marijuana has become the state's number one cash crop, bringing in an estimated $750 million a year. Hawaii is also a major transshipment point for heroin arriving from Asia; organized crime in the form of the American Mafia or the Japanese Yakuza is active. Land in Hawaii is concentrated in very few hands: half of Maui, for example, is controlled by only 11 owners. A full 94 percent of all privately held land in the state is owned by 49 separate entities, 7 of which alone control a third of the total—a great imbalance of power and wealth. Perhaps nowhere else in the world will you see as many PRIVATE PROPERTY—KEEP OUT

signs. The "Big Five" corporations (Amfac, Castle and Cook, C. Brewer, Theo. H. Davies, Alexander and Baldwin) together with Dillingham Corporation have always run the economy. Until statehood they were locally owned by descendants of American missionaries and traders; today they are controlled from outside Hawaii. In 1920, the government set aside some 76,000 hectares for homesteading by native Hawaiians. Today only 10 percent of this land is being used as such. Although 23 percent of the native

Queen Lili'uokalani (1838-1917) wearing the Royal Order and Ribbon of Kalakaua. After her dethronement in 1893 she sent this message to the American people: "Do not covet the little vineyards of Naboth so far from your shores, lest the punishment of Ahab fall upon you, if not in your day, in that of your children, for 'be not deceived, God is not mocked.' The people to whom your fathers told of the living God, and taught them to call 'Father,' and whom the sons now seek to despoil and destroy, are crying to Him in their time of trouble; and He will keep His promise, and will listen to the voices of His Hawaiian children lamenting for their homes."

population are at or near the poverty line, a typical Hawaiian family must wait 15-30 years to get homestead land. Instead the military utilizes large tracts of "native land" for maneuvers and weapons storage.

military: The Pacific Command maintains 110 military installations in Hawaii; a total of 55,200 military personnel and 66,300 dependents were present in 1983. The military employs another 20,850 civilians. Military spending is increasing (currently over $2 billion a year) and is second only to tourism as a form of income for the state. The huge military reservations have caused land prices to skyrocket to the point where only 25 percent of all families in Hawaii qualify to purchase their own homes. Some 20 percent of military personnel and dependents live off-base, helping to make rents among the highest in the U.S. For those in the middle and low-income brackets, finding an affordable place to live on Oahu is close to impossible. And the tax-exempt military pays no property taxes in support of local government services used by its employees.

tourism: Tourism in Hawaii is booming, accounting for 30 percent of the economy—the largest single element. Between 1959 and 1984 tourism increased 20-fold: from 243,216 annual visitors to 4,826,600. The state economy is now so tied to tourism that a 5 percent drop in visitor expenditures can mean the loss of 7,500 jobs. Billions of dollars in public money have been used to provide in-

frastructure for the Travel Industry, while profits go mostly to corporate investors. Tourism is increasingly being redirected toward the neighbor islands. Every year new stretches of coastline are swallowed by hotels and condos for out-of-state vacationers and retirees. You have to go farther and farther from the airports, highways, and resorts to find an unspoiled scene.

the people: The masses of immigrants brought in during the 19th C. dramatically altered Hawaii's racial composition. They arrived from China (1852), Japan (1869), Portugal (1878), the Philippines (1907), Puerto Rico, Korea, and the United States. Americans continue to pour in today and, outside the Travel Industry, *aloha* is a word not often heard in the islands. In the early days, *aloha* was heard *too* often, as newcomers flocked in to stay and take the best, leaving little for the native Hawaiians. Suddenly everyone in Hawaii was equal to everyone else in the U.S. and the indigenous people, unprepared to compete in the new egalitarian, free enterprise system, were swept aside; whatever illusions they retained vanished into the dream world of tourist promoters and romantics. The continuous influx of outsiders has seriously upset human relations in Hawaii. The resident population is incredibly mixed. No single group forms a majority. The largest groups are Caucasians (26 percent), Japanese (24 percent), Filipinos (11 percent), and Chinese (5 percent). Although about 175,000 people (20 percent) are part Hawaiian, pure Polynesian

indentured Japanese plantation workers and mounted overseer

Hawaiians comprise less than one percent. Hawaii is a melting pot of races and since WW II one marriage in 3 has been interracial.

GETTING THERE

Hawaii is a convenient stepping stone between N. America, Asia, and the South Pacific, and a free stopover in Honolulu can be added to most air tickets across the Pacific. There are also flights from the U.S. W coast to Hilo and Maui. Round-trip excursion fares from mainland U.S. vary considerably, so ask at several travel agencies to see who has the cheapest. Also, watch the travel sections of Sunday newspapers for announcements of special fares.

GETTING AROUND

interisland travel: It would be nice to catch a ferry between the islands, but strict Coast Guard regulations prevent this. Strong currents, winds, and waves make the crossings rough, so you're forced to fly. Interisland airlines are numerous and departures almost continuous. Tourists generally fly the jetlines, Aloha and Hawaiian, but residents choose the smaller commuter airlines for their lower fares and more personalized service. These propeller planes also fly at lower altitudes for better views. The minutes you save flying by jet, the commuter airlines make up by delivering your baggage faster. Make the effort to phone the various airlines to see if they're running any special deals. (The numbers below are the Oahu phone numbers.) Air Molokai (tel. 536-6611), Paradise Air (tel. 833-7197), Polynesian Airways (tel. 836-3838), and Reeves Aviation (tel. 333-9555) go to Molokai, Maui, and Lanai. Princeville Airways (tel. 836-3505) flies to Princeville on the N side of Kauai. Mid Pacific Air (tel. 836-3313) serves all islands but Molokai and claims to have the lowest fares, especially on standby—you must check in an hour before flight time. Always ask about standby fares or discount round-trips. When you choose an airline, be sure to ask for specific instructions on where to go to board your flight, as there are several terminals in Honolulu. Remember too that the commuter airlines often land at smaller airports where there are fewer car rental agencies. The most convenient neighbor-island airports are Lihue (Kauai), Kahalui (Maui), and Hilo. A recommended ration of your time with 3 weeks in Hawaii is: Oahu—5 days, Kauai—4 days, Molokai—2 days, Maui—4 days, Hawaii—6 days.

road travel: Oahu has an excellent public bus service which will take you almost anywhere. Bus no. 52, for example, goes right around the island every half hour in both directions for a flat 60-cent fare. On the neighbor islands, however, it's usually a choice of hitching or renting a car. Over half a million vehicles on Hawaii's roads guarantee good hitching: you won't have to wait too long for a ride. On Oahu hitch from bus stops. On Maui, the cops have nothing better to do than hassle hitchhikers, so don't use your thumb. Just stand there facing the oncoming traffic at a good spot and drivers will know what you want.

car rentals: The car rental agencies in Hawaii are highly competitive and rival those of Florida for cheap rates. Ask your interisland airline if they can get any deals on rental cars. Sometimes they'll reserve a car for you in advance over the phone at a rate lower than you would get in person on arrival. Many agencies will refuse to rent to you if they think you're camping, so don't tell them. Have the name of a likely hotel ready. Tropical Rent-a-Car, Holiday Rent-a-Car, and Hertz are the worst offenders in this regard. Dollar Rent-a-Car, on the other hand, doesn't seem to mind campers, and most others won't push it if things are slow and they need your business. Be sure to ask about insurance rates, as they do vary, and specify that you want no insurance for personal injury, only insurance for the car. Insurance on most cars doesn't cover driving over unpaved roads, such as the

Kaena Point Road on Oahu, the Kaupo Road on Maui, and the Saddle Road on Hawaii. You drive them at your own risk, which makes it all the more exciting. Because you can go almost anywhere by car, Hawaii lacks much of the adventure of travel that the more remote Pacific islands offer.

ACCOMMODATIONS

Three charts are provided to help you find a place to stay. The first lists rooms for $20 s or less in the cheapest category in 1984. Weekly or monthly rates are often cheaper yet. There's a 4 percent hotel tax. If you don't have advance reservations, telephone the hotel before going there—they are often full. Some of the state and national parks have small, basic cabins for rent, and these are included in the chart. Accommodations are grouped under each island heading.

meet the people: There are also several active homestay programs which will find accommodations for you at a private residence. This is an excellent way to meet some local people and sidestep the packaged tourist scene. Prices average $35 d, breakfast included, and there is a 3-day minimum stay. For a comprehensive directory outlining this concept send $2 to Pacific-Hawaii Bed and Breakfast, 19 Kai Nani Place, Kailua, HI 96734 (tel. 262-6026). Doris Epp, manager of Pacific-Hawaii, speaks fluent German and Spanish. Receive a different directory for $5 guest membership from Bed and Breakfast Hawaii, Box 449, Kapaa, HI 96746 (tel. 822-7771). Bed and Breakfast Honolulu (3242 Kaohinani Dr., Honolulu, HI 97817; tel. 595-6170), operated by Unitarian Church people, arranges homestays on Oahu. Go Native...Hawaii, Ltd. has a contact in Hilo (130 Puhili St., Hilo, HI 96720; tel. 961-2080) and a reservations service in Michigan (Box 13115, Lansing, MI 48901; tel. 517-349-9598). Reservations must be made in advance by phone or mail. All of the above are highly recommended.

camping: All of the campgrounds are indicated on the maps by a code number which corresponds to the campground chart. Only official, government-operated campgrounds are listed on the chart. If you're a hiker or backpacker you'll find other places to pitch a tent. All the campgrounds on the chart (except the Seven Pools) have toilets and picnic tables, and you can drive a car up to all but those in Haleakala crater. On Oahu, all campgrounds (except 10, 11, 15, 23, and 27) can be reached easily on The Bus unless you have too much luggage—the drivers might not let you on. On each island a few conveniently located and relatively safe camping areas are recommended to help you choose from what might at first appear to be a bewildering list. For security and good company, try to set up near other campers. Parks where thefts or violence have occurred are indicated under "local hassles." Permits are required at all the campgrounds, except those in the national parks. You may camp free at national park campsites for up to a week, but permits are required to camp in Haleakala crater. The high altitudes may make the mountain parks cold at night. Permits for state and county campgrounds (except on Oahu) can be obtained in advance by mail if you know the exact day, otherwise pick them up in person on arrival. The issuing offices are only open during business hours weekdays, except on Kauai, where county camping permits are available at the Police Dept., Umi St., Lihue, evenings and weekends. You can also pay the permit inspector $5 for an on-the-spot permit at Kauai county campgrounds. On the islands of Oahu and Hawaii, there are branch offices where permits are available. On Lanai you may camp at Hulopoe Beach Park, but need a permit which costs $9 the first night ($4 for additional nights). None of the offices listed on the chart of permit-issuing offices will issue permits for islands other than their own, except in the case of Molokai where state camping permits for Palaau State Park may be obtained from the Division of State Parks in Wailuku, Maui, or in Honolulu. Note that all campgrounds tend to be heavily booked during summer vacations, holidays, and on weekends. In the interest of all, try to leave your campsite cleaner than you found it.

HAWAIIAN ACCOMMODATIONS

NAME	MAILING ADDRESS	STREET ADDRESS (IF DIFFERENT)	PHONE NUMBER	SINGLE	DOUBLE	LONG TERM RATES	NUMBER OF ROOMS	ON BEACH	POOL
Hotel Coral Reef	1516 Kuhio Highway Kapaa, Kauai, HI 96746		822-4481	$19	$19	no	40	yes	no
Motel Lani	P.O. Box 1836 Lihue, Kauai, HI 96766	4240 Rice St. Lihue, Kauai	245-2965	$18	$18	no	6	no	no
Hale Pumehana	3083 Akahi St. Lihue, Kauai, HI 96766		245-2106	$16	$16	no	23	no	no
Ahana Motel	P.O. Box 892 Lihue, Kauai, HI 96766	3115 Akahi St., Lihue, Kauai	245-2206	$16	$16	no	20	no	no
Tip Top Motel	3173 Akahi St. Lihue, Kauai, HI 96766		245-2333	$18	$24	no	35	no	no
Hale-Ka-Lani Motel	4271 Halenani St. Lihue, Kauai, HI 96766		245-6021	$15	$18	no	6	no	no
Hale Lihue Motel	P.O. Box 808 Lihue, Kauai, HI 96766	2931 Kalena St. Lihue, Kauai	245-2751	$14	$18	no	18	no	no
Ocean View Motel	3445 Wilcox Road Nawiliwili, Kauai, HI 96766		245-6345	$17	$18	week	21	near	no
Poipu YMCA	P.O. Box 1786 Lihue, Kauai, HI 96766	opposite Poipu Beach Park	742-1200	$16	$12	no	1	near	no
Kahili Mountain Park	P.O. Box 298 Koloa, Kauai, HI 96756		742-9921	$15	$15	no	24	no	no
Kalaheo Apartments	P.O. Box 54 Kalaheo, Kauai, HI 96741	behind Kalaheo Luncheonette	332-9301	$18	$23	no	20	no	no
Armed Services YMCA (men and women)	250 S. Hotel St. Honolulu, HI 96813	Downtown Honolulu	524-5600	$14	$20	no	243	no	yes
Nuuanu YMCA (men only)	1441 Pali Highway Honolulu, HI 96813	Downtown Honolulu	536-3556	$14	$19	$77 week	70	no	yes
Fernhurst YWCA (women only)	1566 Wilder Ave. Honolulu, HI 96822	University District	941-2231	$15 MAP	$30 MAP	$84 week	60	no	yes
University YMCA (men and women)	1810 University Ave. Honolulu, HI 96822	University District	946-0253	$11	$16	$67 week	40	no	no
Honolulu Youth Hostel (dorm)	2323 Seaview Ave. Honolulu, HI 96822	University District	946-0591	$ 5/ $ 7		no	30 beds	no	no
Central YMCA (men only)	401 Atkinson Dr. Honolulu, HI 96814	Beside Ala Moana Center	941-3344	$13	$22	no	112	near	yes
Big Surf Hotel	1690 Ala Moana Blvd. Honolulu, HI 96815	Waikiki	946-6525	$14	$18	no	75	near	no
Malihini Hotel	217 Saratoga Rd. Honolulu, HI 96815	Waikiki	923-9644	$20	$20	$126 week	29	near	no
Reef Lanais	225 Saratoga Rd. Honolulu, HI 96815	Waikiki	923-3881	$19	$21	no	109	near	no
Coral Seas Hotel	250 Lewers St. Honolulu, HI 96815	Waikiki	923-3881	$18	$20	no	110	near	no
Waikiki Terrace	339 Royal Hawaiian Ave. Honolulu, HI 96815	Waikiki	923-3253	$20	$20	no	24	near	no
Hale Waikiki Apt. Motel	2410 Koa Ave. Honolulu, HI 96815	Waikiki	923-9012	$18	$26	$125 week	14	near	no
Edmunds Apartments	2411 Ala Wai Blvd. Honolulu, HI 96815	Waikiki	923-8381	$16	$20	no	12	near	no

HAWAIIAN ACCOMMODATIONS

NAME	MAILING ADDRESS	STREET ADDRESS (IF DIFFERENT)	PHONE NUMBER	SINGLE	DOUBLE	LONG TERM RATES	NUMBER OF ROOMS	ON BEACH	POOL
Pau Hana Inn Longhouse	Kaunakakai, Molokai HI 96748		553-5342	$14	$17	week	10	yes	yes
Molina's Mountain View Rooms	P.O. Box 1033 Wailuku, Maui, HI 96793	corner Market and Mill Sts. Wailuku	244-4100	$12	none	week	16	no	no
The Bungalow Rooms	2044 Vineyard St. W., Wailuku, Maui, HI		244-0516	$12	$15	month	37	no	no
Pioneer Inn	658 Wharf St. Lahaina, Maui, HI 96761		661-3636	$18	$21	no	48	no	yes
Haleakala Crater Cabins	P.O. Box 369 Makawai, Maui, HI 96768	located at Haleakala crater	572-9306	$ 6	$12	no	3	no	no
Polipoli Cabin	Division of State Parks P.O. Box 1049 Wailuku, Maui, HI 96793	15 km up Waipoli Road a difficult jeep track off Highway 377	244-4354	$10	$14	no	1	no	no
Waianapanapa State Park Cabins	Division of State Parks P.O. Box 1049 Wailuku, Maui, HI 96793	3 km W of Hana	244-4354	$10	$14	no	12	yes	no
Maui YMCA Camp Keanae	P.O. Box 820 Wailuku, Maui, HI 96793	on Hana Highway W of Keanae	244-3253	$ 5	$10	no	dorm	no	no
Nalu Kai Lodge	P.O. Box 188 Paia, Maui, HI 96779	115 Hana Highway Paia, Maui	579-9035	$16	$18	month	8	no	no
Polynesian Pacific Hotel	175 Banyan Dr., Hilo, Hawaii, HI 96720		961-0426	$17	$17	week	20	no	yes
Kamaaina Hotel	110 Haili St. Hilo, Hawaii, HI 96720		935-8820	$16	$20	week	15	no	no
Hilo Hotel	142 Kinoole St. Hilo, Hawaii, HI 96720		961-3733	$18	$24	week	57	no	yes
Lanikai Hotel	100 Puueo St. Hilo, Hawaii, HI 96720		935-5556	$15	$18	week	32	no	no
Pohakuloa Cabins	Division of State Parks P.O. Box 936 Hilo, Hawaii, HI 96720	Mauna Kea State Park Saddle Road	961-7200	$ 8	$12	no	15	no	no
Kalopa State Park Cabins	Division of State Parks P.O. Box 936 Hilo, Hawaii, HI 96720	Division of State Parks 75 Aupuni St., Hilo, Hawaii	961-7200	$ 8	$12	no	4	no	no
Hotel Honokaa Club	P.O. Box 185 Honokaa, Hawaii, HI		775-0533	$13	$18	week	20	no	no
Old Hawaii Lodging	P.O. Box 521 Kapaau, Hawaii, HI 96755	opposite the Hawi Theatre	889-5577	$18	$21	no	25	no	no
Hapuna Beach A-Frame Shelters	Division of State Parks P.O. Box 936 Hilo, Hawaii, HI 96720	Division of State Parks 75 Aupuni St., Hilo, Hawaii	961-7200	$ 7	$ 7	no	6	near	no
H. Manago Hotel	P.O. Box 145 Capt. Cook, Kona Hawaii, HI 96704	in Capt. Cook	323-2642	$13	$15	no	22	no	no
Shirakawa Motel	P.O. Box 467 Naalehu, Hawaii, HI 96773	in Waiohinu	292-7462	$17	$20	no	13	no	no
Namakani Paio Cabins	Volcano House Hawaii Volcanoes Ntl.Pk. Hawaii, HI 96718	at Namahani Paio Campground	967-7321	$14	$14	no	10	no	no
Naiulani Cabin	Division of State Parks P.O. Box 936 Hilo, Hawaii, HI 96720	Kalanikoa Road, Volcano Village (1.5 km E of Kilauea Visitors Center)	961-7200	$10	$14	no	1	no	no

CAMPING PERMIT ISSUING OFFICES

TYPE OF PARK	MAILING ADDRESS	STREET ADDRESS	COST PER PERSON PER DAY	MAXIMUM STAY AT A SINGLE CAMPSITE	AVAILABLE HOW FAR IN ADVANCE?
Kauai State Parks	Division of State Parks P.O. Box 1671 Lihue, Kauai HI 96766	State Office Building Room 208 Eiwa St., Lihue	free	5 days	2 months
Kauai County Parks	Camping Permit Office 4191 Hardy St. Lihue, Kauai HI 96766		$3	4 days	1 month
Oahu State Parks	Division of State Parks P.O. Box 621 Honolulu HI 96809	State Office Building 1151 Punchbowl St. Room 310 Honolulu	free	5 days	1 month
Oahu County Parks	Dept. of Parks and Recreation 650 S. King St. Honolulu HI 96813	Honolulu Municipal Building	free	6 days	2 wks.
Molokai State Parks	Division of State Parks P.O. Box 1049 Wailuku, Maui HI 96793	on Molokai phone the Ranger, Scott Adams, at 567-6435	free	1 week	2 months
Molokai County Parks	County of Maui P.O. Box 526 Kaunakakai, Molokai HI 96748	Mitchell Pauole Center, Kaunakakai	$3	3 days	3 months
Haleakala crater campsites	Haleakala National Park Headquarters or Visitors Center		free	2 days	n/a
Maui State Parks	Division of State Parks P.O. Box 1049 Wailuku, Maui HI 96793	State Office Building High St., Wailuku	free	5 days	2 months
Maui County Parks	Dept. of Parks and Recreation County of Maui Wailuku, Maui HI 96793	War Memorial Gym 1580 Kaahumanu Ave. Wailuku	$3	3 days	1 year
Hawaii State Parks	Division of State Parks P.O. Box 936 Hilo, Hawaii HI 96720	State Office Building 75 Aupuni St. Hilo	free	5 days	2 months
Hawaii County Parks	Dept. of Parks and Recreation 25 Aupini St. Hilo, Hawaii HI 96720		$1	2 wks.	2 months

HAWAIIAN CAMPGROUNDS

CODE NUMBER	PARK NAME	NATIONAL PARK	STATE	COUNTY	DRINKING WATER	SHOWERS	SHELTER	GRILLS	ON BEACH	RECOMMENDED	LOCAL HASSLES
1	Haena Beach Park			•	•	•	•	•	•	•	
2	Anini Beach Park			•	•	•	•	•	•	•	
3	Anahola Beach Park			•	•	•			•		
4	Hanamaulu Beach Park			•	•	•	•	•	•		•
5	Niumalu Beach Park			•	•	•	•	•	•		
6	Salt Pond Beach Park			•	•	•	•	•	•		
7	Lucy Wright Beach Park			•	•	•	•	•	•		
8	Polihale State Park		•		•	•		•	•	•	
9	Kokee State Park		•		•	•		•		•	
10	Keaiwa Heiau State Recreation Area		•		•	•		•		•	
11	Sand Island State Park		•		•	•			•		
12	Makapuu Beach Park			•	•	•			•		
13	Kaiona Beach Park			•	•	•			•		
14	Waimanalo Beach Park			•	•	•	•	•	•		•
15	Bellows Field Beach Park			•	•	•			•		
16	Kaaawa Beach Park			•	•	•			•		
17	Swanzy Beach Park			•	•	•			•		
18	Kahana Bay Beach Park			•	•	•		•	•		
19	Punaluu Beach Park			•	•	•		•	•		•
20	Hauula Beach Park			•	•	•	•	•	•		
21	Malaekahana State Recreation Area		•		•	•		•	•	•	
22	Haleiwa Beach Park			•	•	•	•		•		•
23	Mokuleia Beach Park			•	•	•		•	•		
24	Kahe Point Beach Park			•	•	•	•	•			
25	Nanakuli Beach Park			•	•	•		•	•		•
26	Lualualei Beach Park			•	•			•			•
27	Keaau Beach Park			•	•	•		•	•		
28	Palaau State Park		•		•					•	
29	O Ne Alii Beach Park			•	•	•	•	•	•		
30	Hosmer Grove	•			•		•	•			
31	Holua	•			•						
32	Paliku	•			•						
33	Polipoli Springs State Recreation Area		•		•			•			
34	Seven Pools (Oheo)	•									
35	Waianapanapa State Park		•		•	•		•	•	•	
36	Kaumahina State Wayside Park		•		•			•	•		
37	H. P. Baldwin Beach Park			•	•	•	•	•	•		•

CODE NUMBER	PARK NAME	NATIONAL PARK	STATE	COUNTY	DRINKING WATER	SHOWERS	SHELTER	GRILLS	ON BEACH	RECOMMENDED	LOCAL HASSLES
38	Onekahakaha Beach Park			•	•	•	•	•		•	
39	James Kealoha Beach Park			•	•	•		•			
40	Isaac Hale Beach Park			•		•	•				
41	Mackenzie State Park		•				•				
42	Harry K. Brown Beach Park			•	•	•	•	•	•		
43	Kamoamoa Campground	•			•		•	•		•	
44	Kipuka Nene Campground	•			•		•	•			
45	Namakani Paio Campground	•			•		•	•		•	
46	Punaluu Beach Park			•	•	•		•			
47	Whittington Beach Park			•			•	•			
48	Milolii Beach Park			•				•			
49	Samuel M. Spencer Beach Park			•	•	•	•	•	•	•	
50	Mahukona Beach Park			•		•		•			
51	Kapaa Beach Park			•			•	•			
52	Keokea Beach Park			•	•	•		•			
53	Kalopa State Recreation Area		•		•	•	•	•		•	
54	Laupahoehoe Beach Park			•	•	•	•	•			
55	Kolekole Beach Park			•	•	•	•	•			

PRACTICALITIES

money and visas: As elsewhere in the U.S., changing foreign currency is difficult and unprofitable, so bring US$ travelers cheques. Beware of U.S. banknotes larger than $20, which many businesses refuse to accept. Everyone other than Canadians requires a passport and visa to enter Hawaii. Ports of entry for cruising yachts are the Ala Wai Yacht Harbor (Honolulu), Nawiliwili (Kauai), Kahului (Maui), and Hilo (Hawaii). The U.S. demonstrates its concern for human rights by refusing entry to Communists of all nationalities. miscellaneous: Hawaii is one of the only areas covered in this book where tipping (10-15 percent) is expected in restaurants. All phone numbers in Hawaii are area code 808. Phone calls within a single island are treated as local calls. The minimum drinking age is 18 years old. When leaving, remember that there's an agricultural check at the airport for all mainland-bound passengers. You may take coconuts and pineapples back with you, but avocados, bananas, and papaya require prior treatment. Sugarcane, coffee beans, and marijuana are banned.

information: An independent guidebook is essential. Ray Riegert's Hidden Hawaii (Berkeley, Ulysses Press) is recommended. The best guide for hikers is Hawaiian Hiking Trails by Craig Chisholm (Touchstone Press, Box 81, Beaverton, Oregon 97005). The Rand McNally Honolulu and Hawaii map is well worth having.

theft: Hawaii has been so inundated that a lot of anti-tourist sentiment has built up among the local people. Some show it by indifference and even unfriendliness, but the fading of the aloha spirit is also manifested in increasing crime and violence, all too often directed at visitors. Rental cars are common targets for rip-offs in Hawaii—never leave anything valuable in them overnight, not even in a supervised hotel parking lot. In the late '70s Hawaii got some bad publicity over thefts and violence directed at campers. Thankfully the situation has improved a little, though it's still best to avoid sleeping in the only tent in a campground. Don't go away and leave your tent unattended; it may be gone when you return. You might hear stories of hikers being murdered or disappearing when they stumbled innocently on marijuana patches. Most are untrue: Zane Bilgrave of Pacific Quest Inc. reports that in all his years hiking Hawaii he has never seen *pakalolo* growing beside a recognized hiking trail. This is one good reason to stay on established trails. Another is that shortcuts may lead to sudden inclines and points of no return. Even thick vegetation and exposed rock can be crumbly and unsafe. If night overtakes you on the trail, make camp until daybreak. Avoid private property as much as you can. Campfires are dangerous as the humus-rich soil can continue to smolder. Use a camping stove instead, but remember, camping fuels are prohibited on commercial aircraft. Note too that it's not possible to "live off the land," so carry enough food and water with you. Purify stream water before you drink it.

conduct: An important part of travel is knowing how to relate to people you meet. Local residents should be treated with consideration. Don't attempt to make a Hawaiian do something more quickly or efficiently than he/she wishes. Avoid being too business-like. A smile and a friendly word or two are worth more to an islander than saving a couple of minutes. Look people straight in the eye when you talk to them and put any notions of superiority aside, no matter whom you're dealing with. Learn the Hawaiian buddy wave, *shaka,* which means something between "how-zit" and "okay." Clench your 3 middle fingers and extend little finger and thumb.

AIRPORT

Honolulu International Airport (HNL) is 8 km W of downtown Honolulu. The arrivals area is downstairs, departures upstairs. There's a whole range of free tourist propaganda on racks just as you come out of Customs; grab a handful for some local color. If you want something more practical, try the newsstand upstairs, which sells excellent maps of the state and city, plus bus guides, books, etc. The Bank of Hawaii branch (Mon. to Thurs. 0830-1500, Fri. 0830-1800) is on the lower level opposite baggage claim 10, across the driveway (ask directions). The Foreign Currency Exchange counter on the upper level is open longer hours, but they give a poor rate and charge a minimum $1.50 commission on each transaction. Large lockers are available at $1 per day (limit 3 days) plus $5 key deposit. Honolulu International is the world's 17th busiest airport, with over 15 million passengers a year; nuclear-armed military aircraft also use HNL regularly. The final approach to the main runway passes within 1.5 km of 48 bunkers at the West Loch nuclear weapons storage depot. Hazardous air-traffic conditions at HNL have earned it a red-star (most dangerous) rating from the International Federation of Airline Pilots. There's a $3 departure tax on international flights, and a $10 "Customs fee" is charged all passengers arriving in the United States. Bus nos. 8 and 20 depart from the terminal's upper-level entrance, 60 cents to downtown or Waikiki, but you must carry your bags on your lap. Heavy suitcases and oversized backpacks with external frames are not allowed on TheBus. If you have much luggage, catch the Grey Line bus ($5) to Waikiki from the lowest level.

OAHU

Oahu's Honolulu, state capital and the 13th largest city in the U.S., is the stage on which the recent history of Hawaii has unfolded. Tourism, government, and the military are all headquartered in the area between Waikiki and Pearl Harbor. Over 80 percent of state residents live on Oahu, and a quarter of the island is occupied by various armed forces, making it the most heavily militarized island in the Pacific. At West Loch, on the W side of Pearl Harbor, most of the 3,100 nuclear weapons in Hawaii (about 10 percent of the U.S. stockpile) are stored. Given the proximity of this facility to the dangerously over-utilized Honolulu airport, there's a high probability of an aircraft eventually crashing into West Loch, blasting Oahu off the face of the earth. Electromagnetic radiation from military communications and tracking systems cause unperceived biological damage to residents and could unexpectedly explode one of the many nuclear devices.

the land: Two parallel mountain ranges run down the E and W sides of the island with a fertile valley in between. Dramatic high cliffs stretching inland along the bottom half of the Windward Coast are the most striking natural feature of Oahu, a stunning backdrop to many of the island's long white beaches. A view-point at Nuuanu Pali looks down from the crest of the cliffs to the sea. The North Shore of Oahu is world-renowned for great breakers which crash against the beaches to create one of the best surfing areas in the world. Nature has given a magnificent variety for so small an area. Mercifully, billboard advertising is banned in the state, so you see it in all its full unspoiled beauty.

SIGHTS

Honolulu: Many historic buildings nestle around the new State Capitol in downtown Honolulu. A few charge high admissions, but fortunately, their outside architecture is their best feature. If you're on a budget visit only the places which are free. Kawaiahao Church (1842) and nearby attractions such as the Academy of Arts, Foster Botanic Garden, and the Aloha Tower can all be enjoyed at no cost. The Academy of Arts is especially rewarding for its rich and varied collection of Asian and Pacific art. High above Honolulu is the Punchbowl, an extinct volcano where many Americans who died in the war are buried. Here, the story of the U.S. war effort in the Pacific is depicted on large ceramic maps. Another side of Honolulu is evident along

Hotel St., W from Nuuanu Ave., a sordid red light area with hostess bars and porno films frequented after dark by sailors from Pearl Harbor. **nearby:** The Bishop Museum, about 4 km NW of downtown at 1355 Kahili St., preserves many of the extant treasures of ancient Hawaii and is an outstanding research center with publications on many Pacific cultures. The $5 admission fee, however, makes it the most expensive museum of its kind in the U.S. Better value is the "Passport to Polynesia" ($7) which includes admission to the Bishop Museum and several other attractions, and doubledecker bus transportation from Waikiki. This is advertised in all the free tourist newspapers. The USS *Arizona* Memorial at Pearl Harbor (bus no. 20) commemorates the men who died in the Japanese

air strike which catapulted America into WW II. The Memorial is built over the spot where the battleship *Arizona* went down, taking over 1,000 lives. The National Park Service operates a free shuttle boat to the Memorial Tues. to Sun. 0900-1500 from the Visitors Center on the highway NW out of Honolulu. A free film on the events leading up to the war is shown and the visit is one of the most meaningful on the island.

Waikiki: Just E of Honolulu is the famous Waikiki resort area. The golden sands of the beach are always crowded with buttered bodies, fenced in by a solid line of layer-cake hotels. It's easy to use their swimming pools if you look like a guest. Waikiki is best at sunset when the surfers catch their last wave,

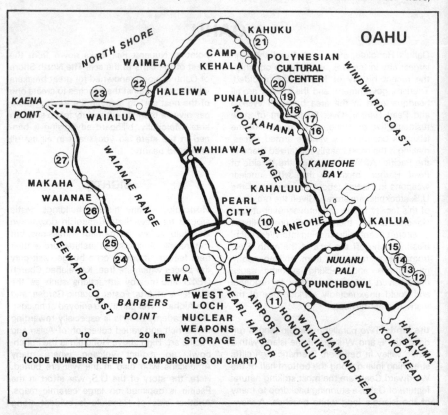

(CODE NUMBERS REFER TO CAMPGROUNDS ON CHART)

sailboats and Hawaiian canoes patrol back and forth offshore, and the sun slips slowly into the South Seas. The SE end of the beach is taken up by Kapiolani Park with a free zoo and an outstanding aquarium ($1.50). Beyond rises the bare crater of Diamond Head, a fitting backdrop to the seething humanity of Waikiki. Behind Waikiki is the University of Hawaii campus where you can observe the mixed and attractive human element.

sideshow: The Polynesian Cultural Center on the NE side of Oahu (bus no. 52) is the best known of Oahu's many commercial "attractions." Tourists arrive here by the thousands to get a taste of South Pacific culture in a Disneyland environment. Opinions about the Center vary, but it's probably worth visiting if you can afford the $14 gate fee. Actually, such places tend to lose touch with reality, especially when they're operated, as this one is, by the Church of Latter-Day Saints. However, their evening show (another $15) is one of the best of its kind anywhere. A $35 package includes admission, tours, dinner, and the show, but not transportation. None of the other commercial "attractions" on Oahu are worth the money.

offshore Oahu: Dangerous waves and currents make swimming and diving hazardous on Oahu's N and W shores during the winter months. Surfers frequent the North Shore in winter (Oct. to May), Waikiki in summer (May to Sept.), both ideal surfing locales. The Windward Coast at Kailua is excellent for windsurfing. A local company, Windsurfing Hawaii Inc. (tel. 261-3539 or 262-6676) organizes group windsurfing lessons ($20 for 2 hours, $90 for 10 hours) and rents complete sailboards ($20 half day). The best snorkeling and diving near Honolulu is at beautiful Hanauma Bay alongside Koko Head (bus no. 57). The bay is an underwater game reserve and its clear waters and coral canyons make it a favorite. A number of companies offer half-day trips there for under $10, including RT transportation from Waikiki and rental of snorkeling gear. Phone numbers are listed in most of the free tourist newspapers. Prices vary so shop around. Steve's Diving Adventures (tel.

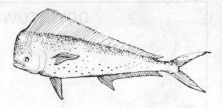

The dolphin fish (Coryphaena hippurus) *or dorado is a large, fast-moving fish with a body of luminous purple, green, and gold, which fades soon after death. Mahimahi (dolphin fish) is a favored food in Hawaii, but the fish has no relation to its namesake mammal dolphin.*

947-8900) can arrange half-day scuba diving trips (2 tanks) for about $40 to places like the Hundred Foot Hole or Fantasy Reef. American Dive Hawaii (tel. 732-2877) runs a 4-day Diver Certification Course (PADI or NAUI) for $225. The Hawaiian Sailing Academy (902 Maunakea St. near Pier 12, Honolulu, HI 96817) offers a basic course in the fundamentals of sailing. The $287 price includes three 3-hour lessons for up to 3 students. The same company handles yacht charters. Hawaii is an exciting place to acquire these skills.

PRACTICALITIES

accommodations: In addition to the accommodations listed on the chart, the Kewalo Hotel (636a Cook St., Honolulu; tel. 538-7939), rents single rooms by the week ($40) to men. Waikiki's oldest hotel, the Moana (2365 Kalakaua Ave., tel. 922-3111), is now managed by Sheraton. Rooms begin at $45 s or d, and the building (1901) manages to retain the charm of a bygone era. Rates at the Royal Hawaiian Hotel, Waikiki's other prewar landmark (1927), are almost double those of the Moana. **camping:** A rotating system operates at the county campgrounds with some closed during certain months of the year. The campgrounds are open every day during the summer (Memorial Day to Labor Day). The rest of the year, however, they close for "cleaning and maintenance" on Thurs. (Oahu county parks) or Wed. and Thurs. (Oahu state parks). The idea is to pre-

DOWNTOWN HONOLULU

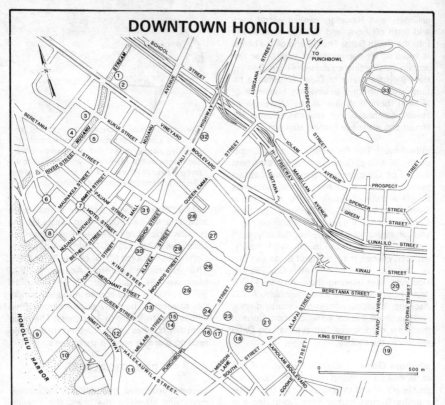

DOWNTOWN HONOLULU

1. Foster Botanic Garden
2. Kuan Yin Temple
3. Izumo Taishakyo Temple
4. Toyo Theater
5. Chinese Cultural Plaza
6. Chinatown
7. red light district
8. Tasty Broiler
9. Aloha Tower
10. Falls of Clyde
11. Federal Government Building
12. Bob's Big Boy
13. post office
14. Aliiolani Hale
15. Kamehameha I Statue
16. Lunalilo Tomb
17. Kawaiahao Church
18. Mission Houses Museum
19. Concert Hall
20. Academy of Arts
21. Municipal Building
22. State Office Building
23. City Hall
24. State Library
25. Iolani Palace
26. State Capitol Building
27. Washington Place
28. St. Andrew's Cathedral
29. Armed Services Y.M.C.A.
30. Honolulu Book Store
31. Our Lady of Peace Cathedral
32. Nuuanu Y.M.C.A.
33. Punchbowl War Cemetery

vent the homeless from living in them, but visitors who arrive those days are also out of luck. Ask about this when you apply for your permit. County camping permits are available at 10 satellite city halls around Oahu and the Honolulu office. Call 523-4525 for the nearest. Both county and state camping permits for Oahu parks must be obtained in person (not by mail). You can write ahead for camping permits for neighbor island parks. The campgrounds are less noisy and crowded weekdays than on weekends when the locals come out. There's a private campground with toilets and showers at Camp Kehala near the Polynesian Cultural Center. The charge is 50 cents pp and you can check in weekdays at the campground itself. No one may check in on weekends, but those already there are allowed to stay. Call Zion Security (tel. 293-9201) for information. If you need camping gear, the Big 88 Store, 330 Sand Island Access Road corner Nimitz Highway between downtown and the airport, has the widest range.

food: Despite the unpretentious appearance, Tasty Broiler, corner of Nimitz Highway and Smith opposite Pier 14 downtown, serves some of the biggest portions of the best seafood at the lowest prices in Hawaii. Open daily till 1930—highly recommended. For a good breakfast try Bob's Big Boy, 700 Richards St. near the waterfront in downtown Honolulu. Nearby, the Public Cafeteria (open until 1530 weekdays) in the Federal Government Building, 5th floor, is the cheapest place in Hawaii to eat. Huge bowls of Japanese *saimen* are the staple at the Kazu Coffee Shop, 1409 Kalakaua just N of King. McCully Chop Suey, at 2005 S. King St. at McCully, a few blocks E of the Kazu between Waikiki and the university, has the best Chinese food. Patti's Chinese Kitchen and Bella Italia, side by side in the Ala Moana Shopping Center, both enjoy local fame. Vim and Vigor Foods, also in the Ala Moana, is the place to pick up hiking foods. For all you can eat, Perry's Smorgy has 2 locations at Waikiki: 2335 Kalakaua Ave. in the Outrigger Hotel and 250 Lewers Street. Although the food is military-style, it's good value for such a touristy area.

entertainment: Paradoxically, there are so many freebies that Waikiki can even be cheap. Check the free tourist newspapers for leads. The movie houses downtown are much cheaper than those at Waikiki. A lively place to have a drink in Waikiki is the Rose and Crown Pub in King's Village. It's amusing to note that many of the "Hawaiian" dancers at the hotels are actually Filipinas, or anyone else with brown skin. Less amusing but worth knowing is that although it may seem easy to score dope from the rickshaw drivers at Waikiki, be aware that the cops love to bust *haoles* for *pakalolo*, even though Hawaiians leave it on their kitchen tables. A Hare Krishna Festival and Feast unfolds every Sun. at 1730 at the headquarters of the International Society for Krishna Consciousness, 51 Coelho Way, Honolulu (tel. 595-4913 or 595-3947). Take any bus northbound on Pali Highway and ask to be let off at the Philippine Consulate General. Coelho Way begins across the highway. There's music, dance, spiritual discourse, and free vegetarian cuisine. All are welcome. The Society also offers free 4-hour Sat. cruises on their teakwood ketch, the *Sri Jal.duta .II.* Reservations are required for these trips, but for the Festival and Feast you just show up.

services: Long-distance phone calls can be made through any pay phone or at Pacific Telephone, 1177 Bishop St. (Mon. to Fri. 0730-1630). For medical (or birth control) attention, call the Waikiki Health Center, 277 Ohua Ave., Waikiki (tel. 922-4787). The fee will be around $27 unless you plead poverty. If you think you have VD call 735-5302 or 922-1313. The rape crisis number is 524-7273. Need help? Call the Volunteer, Information, and Referral Service at 521-4566. For a recorded weather report call 538-7131 or 836-1952. The best photo lab is Colorprints, Inc., 324 Kamani St. (tel. 533-6131). Visiting yachts are permitted to tie up at the Hawaii Yacht Club near Waikiki: $50 for 2 weeks, plus $50 security deposit. Otherwise, anchor offshore at Keehi Lagoon near the airport, or at Kaneohe Yacht Club on the Windward Coast.

information: The Hawaii Visitors Bureau, 8th floor, 2270 Kalakaua Ave., Waikiki, has all the tourist brochures you want. The State Information Office, 7th floor, 250 S. King St., Honolulu, provides free statistical material. Maps and Miscellaneous, 404 Piikoi near the Ala Moana Center, sells topographical maps of Hawaii. Ala Wai Marine Ltd., 1651 Ala Moana Blvd., carries nautical charts. Books and maps covering the entire Pacific are available from the Hawaii Geographic Society, Box 1698, Honolulu, HI 96806 (tel. 538-3952); write for a catalog. The Honolulu Book Shop, Ala Moana Center or corner of Hotel and Bishop streets downtown, has an excellent selection of Hawaiiana. Modern Times Books, 2615 S. King St. near University Ave. (open weekdays 1200-1800, Sat. 1000-1600), specializes in political books. **ecology groups:** The Sierra Club (tel. 946-8494) welcomes visiting members on their weekend hikes. The Club also has groups on the neighbor islands—call the Honolulu office for information on all activities. For local environmental issues contact Greenpeace, 19 Niolopa Place (tel. 595-4475).

ticket offices: Several Pacific airlines have their main U.S. office in Honolulu: Air Nauru, Ste. 506, 841 Bishop St. (tel. 531-9766); Air Tungaru, Ste. 910, 3049 Ualena St. (tel. 833-2698); South Pacific Island Airways, Ste. 169, 733 Bishop St. (tel. 526-0844). Travel agencies specializing in discount airfares include: Student Travel Network, Ste. 202, 1831 S. King St. (tel. 942-7755); United Travel Agency, Room 508, 33 S. King St. (tel.

536-3616); Chartermasters (tel. 955-3777). For the cheapest airfare to California call World Airways (tel. 523-5611). If you plan to travel by bus on the U.S. mainland, save money by purchasing an Ameripass from Greyhound International in the Airport Trade Center, 550 Paiea St. (tel. 839-1909 or 836-8687).

tours: ˙ Pacific Outdoor Adventures, Box 61609, Honolulu, HI 96822 (tel. 988-3913) offers exciting ocean kayaking trips to Lanai, Fiji's Taveuni, and many other Pacific islands. Pacific Quest, Inc., Box 205, Haleiwa, HI 96712 (tel. 638-8338), has adventuresome 12-day, 4-island, hiking and camping tours from Honolulu monthly. Groups average 10 participants and 2 guides. The $965 cost includes interisland airfare, meals, and all activities. Three times a year there are 19-day outings, with an ascent of Mauna Kea and other extras are thrown in ($1,275 total price). Sea Trek Hawaii (Room 205, 46-018 Kamehameha Highway, tel. 235-6614), has a similar program (book through the Adventure Center, 5540 College Ave., Oakland, CA 94618, or WestCan Treks, 3415 W. Broadway, Vancouver, BC V6R 2B4). These packages are recommended if you have limited time, extra cash, and want to experience the best Hawaii has to offer. **others:** The Hawaiian Trail and Mountain Club, Box 2238, Honolulu, HI 96804 (tel. 488-1161, 262-2845, or 734-5515) welcomes visiting hikers to join their weekly outings. If you know how to sail, stroll around the Ala Wai Boat Harbor near Waikiki. Yachtsmen often go out for an afternoon cruise and need last-minute crew.

KAUAI AND NIIHAU

The green, fertile island of Kauai is the outermost and oldest of the large islands in the Hawaiian chain. Its age can be seen in the awesome weathering of Waimea Canyon, the deepest and most colorful of its kind in the Pacific. The road past the viewpoints over the canyon continues through Kokee State Park (with 70 km of hiking trails) to a lookout high above the Kalalau Valley on the inaccessible Na Pali Coast. Here, great ridges 1,000 m high slope down into the ocean, isolating a series of uninhabited valleys which can only be reached on foot from the end of the road at Haena. There is no safe way to hike down into Kalalau from Kokee, and many have been stranded or fallen to their deaths in the attempt. The Kalalau Trail out of Haena is one of the great adventures of Hawaii; the State Parks office in Lihue provides maps and valley camping permits for those who wish to do it. Mt. Waialeale (1,569 m) near the center of the island is the rainiest place on the planet (11,680 mm annual rainfall). The Wailua River on the E side of Kauai is the largest in Polynesia, and there are several *heiau* near its banks. Boat rides up the river are popular with tourists. The mythical Menehunes (native dwarfs) reputedly left behind a fish pond near Nawiliwili and an irrigation ditch at Waimea, but few traces remain. Lihue, the county seat, has little to offer other than a local museum ($3, closed Sunday). Condos are making inroads at Princeville in the N and Poipu in the south. The top-secret Barking Sands Missile Range, near Polihale at the W end of Kauai, is the world's most sophisticated anti-submarine

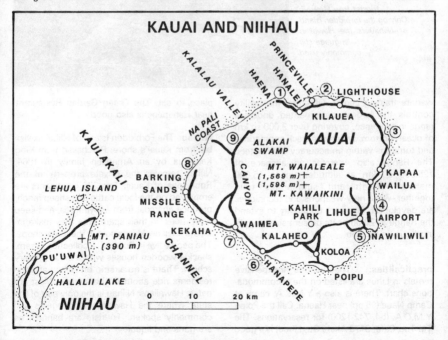

*This scenic view of
Lumahai Beach on Kauai's
N coast has been captured
on film by millions of
tourists.*

tourist-free Hawaii:
*Only on the forbidden island
of Niihau is the Hawaiian
language still
commonly used.*

warfare training center. Offshore, the facility controls the largest instrumented undersea range in existence, covering over 2,000 sq km of ocean bottom, which can track submarines and torpedos within an accuracy of 6 meters. The Range also operates an airspace of 125,000 sq km at altitudes up to 15,000 meters. Aircraft and submarines train together, while new weapons and techniques are developed. Plans are underway to extend the Range to 20 times its present size, engulfing Kauai in its web.

practicalities: The various inexpensive motels in Lihue are listed on the accommodations chart. There is also a Y.M.C.A. camp at Camp Naue ($6 pp) near Haena. Call the Poipu Y.M.C.A. (tel. 742-1200) for reservations. The Tip Top Cafe, 3173 Akahi St., Lihue, is a good

place to eat. The Green Garden Restaurant near Hanapepe is also good.

Niihau: The Forbidden Island of Niihau is visible from Kauai's shore. Purchased from King Kalakaua by an American family in 1864, Niihau remains the private property of the Robinsons of Kauai. The 226 inhabitants are employed on the local cattle and sheep ranch, produce charcoal from *kiawe* trees, and keep honeybees. In their spare time they make intricate shell necklaces sold in the Kauai shops. The people live in Pu'uwai, a collection of ramshackle wooden houses with a small primary school. There is no airstrip on Niihau and the residents ride about on horseback. Most are native Hawaiians; Niihau is the only part of the state where the Hawaiian language is still commonly spoken. Tourists are banned, as are guns and liquor.

MOLOKAI

Molokai's most distinctive feature is the incredible Pali Coastline, which runs along much of the island's N shore. The world's highest sea cliffs are here, descending 1,000 m into the sea at an average 55-degree gradient. Part of the coastline can be seen at Kalaupapa. The easternmost valley, Halawa, is reached via the S coast road. Other than that, there's only the obscure Wailau Trail which crosses private land to the N coast. The Pelekunu Valley is so isolated as to be almost inaccessible by land. These now-empty valleys once supported a fair-sized population. Some still live in the Halawa Valley, which can be easily hiked in an hour ending up at Moaula Falls. For another glimpse into this forbidden realm, there's a rough dirt road up the center of Molokai to a forest lookout over the Waikolu Valley. If you sit on the R side of the aircraft between Molokai and Maui you may be lucky enough to see the whole N coast.

Kalaupapa: Molokai is also well known for its leper colony, established by Kamehameha V in 1865. A Belgian priest, Father Damien, lived here from 1873 until his death from leprosy in 1889. The leper colony, on the Kalaupapa Peninsula, can be viewed from the lookout at Palaau State Park. If you hike down the *pali* on the mule trail, you'll be met at the bottom by a guide who will take you on a compulsory, 4-hour, $12-pp tour. Call Damien Tours (tel. 567-6171) for information. No one is allowed to wander around on his/her own or ,to photograph the patients (this is *still* a functioning leper colony). The National Park Service is working to preserve the historic buildings at Kalaupapa. **other sights:** Strung along the shallow S coast of Molokai are many old Hawaiian fishponds. There's an effete golf resort at the W end of the island. The people of Molokai are friendly—they smile and wave back when you do.

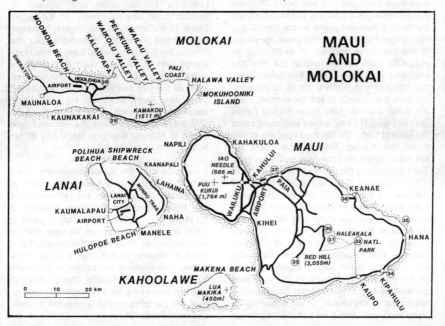

MAUI AND MOLOKAI

MAUI

The islands of Maui, Kahoolawe, Lanai, and Molokai once formed part of a single island. Maui itself was formed from 2 volcanic islands which joined as eroded material was deposited in the channel between them. After Oahu, Maui is the most visited of the Hawaiian islands: tourist hotels line the SW shore. The Lahaina/Kaanapali area is the sunny side of Maui; Hana is wetter, but far greener.

Haleakala: The mighty volcano Haleakala (House of the Sun) is traditionally the spot where Maui, the Polynesian Prometheus, caught the sun as it passed over the crater and slowed it down, so man would have longer to fish and grow his crops. Much of it is now included in Haleakala National Park, Maui's most worthwhile attraction. The park contains one of the few peaks (3,055 m) in Hawaii you can drive right up to on a good road from the coast in a few hours. Tourists see everything in a morning, but to experience the largest dormant crater in the world, you have to get out and hike. One good alternative to the car rental madness is to hitch up to Haleakala from Kahului airport the first day and camp at Hosmer Grove. Just before dawn the next morning, hitch a ride up to the summit with the tourists to see the sunrise. From the Visitors Center hike down Sliding Sands Trail to Paliku (13 km), where you could camp the second night. On the third day hike slowly down the Kaupo Trail to the coast (13 km—rest often or your legs will give out). Then hitch along the coast to the Seven Pools (Oheo) campsite. If you don't want to walk all the way to Kaupo, you can always double back from Paliku to Hosmer Grove (16 km) along the Halemuu Trail. Just W of Seven Pools, look for the grave of aviator Charles Lindbergh in the churchyard of Palapala Hoomau Congregational Church (Kipahulu). His epitaph is Psalm 138: "If I take the wings of the morning, and dwell in the innermost parts of the sea..." From Seven Pools you can hitch back to the airport, slowly exploring the Hana Highway, with a stop at Waianapanapa State Park for a night or 2 (if you obtained a camping permit by mail). A slight variation on the above is to rent a car for one day when you arrive at Kahului airport, use it to drive to Wailuku to get your camping permits and see the verdant Iao Needle, then drive around W. Maui visiting Lahaina. Turn in the car the next morning when you're ready to start hiking Haleakala. There are roads right around E. and W. Maui. The rental agencies tell you not to drive on them and there's even a misleading ROAD CLOSED sign on the Kaupo road, but they can both be easily traversed in a normal car during dry weather, provided you go slowly.

Lahaina: This old whaling town was the capital of Hawaii from 1825 to 1845. In the old days ships had to stand offshore in the open roadstead, which was protected from sudden storms by Lanai and Molokai. Nowadays Lahaina's flooded daily with masses of tourists from resorts nearby at Kaanapali. Some of the old flavor still lingers, however, and a stroll along the waterfront past the Pioneer Inn (1901) to the old banyan tree is enjoyable enough to make you forget the shiny white shoes and loud American housewives. Most of the free tourist newspapers map out the sights. Sadly, mushrooming condo/hotel developments stretch unchecked all along the SW shore of Maui, from the former hippie haven of Makena Beach to Napili Bay 60 km NW.

stay: Consult the accommodations chart. Note, however, that the cheapest rooms at the Pioneer Inn are noisy. The Hosmer Grove and Holua campsites are at an elevation of 2,134 m, while Paliku is just slightly lower at 1,920 meters. Camping can be very cold up here, especially in winter, although you feel it more at Hosmer Grove than you do in the crater. Reservations for cabins in Haleakala must be mailed in months ahead, although you can always try for a cancellation upon arrival. No camping permit is required to camp at Seven Pools (Oheo).

HAWAII

The island of Hawaii, also known as the Big Island, totals almost twice the land area of the rest of the state combined. Its highest peak is Mauna Kea, also the highest in the Central Pacific *and* in the world, if you count from its underwater base in the Hawaiian Trough, 10,204 m from sea-bed to summit. Over 4,200 m of this goliath are above sea level. Although Mauna Kea is higher, Mauna Loa (4,159 m) is much more massive—the mightiest volcano on Earth both in size and in the amount of lava discharged in recent times. Mauna Loa, home of Pele, Hawaiian goddess of fire, is active and growing, and may someday overtake Mauna Kea. The Big Island is characterized by the many vast, black lava flows which blanket much of the island's surface. The volcanic material has created the black sand beaches of Puna, while the white sands of Kona are coral-based. Macadamia nut trees do well on the NE and SW sides of the island; coffee covers the upper slopes along the Kona Coast. Taro is still grown in the Waipio Valley. Sugarcane fills the E slopes of the island's 2 mammoth mountains. The gently sloping mass of its mountains makes the Big Island easy to visualize and hard to forget. If you only have time to visit one island, Hawaii has the most to offer.

SIGHTS

Hilo: This garden city is the state's second largest, but it's small enough to enjoy in a day. Much of the rain falls on this side of the island and the city's orchid and anthurium nurseries thrive on it, as a visit to Kong's Floral Gardens near Onekahakaha Beach Park will prove.

Mauna Loa: Hawaii Volcanoes National Park, SW of Hilo, offers the best opportunity in the Pacific to observe how a volcanic island is formed. The park is on the SE side of Mauna Loa at Kilauea crater, one of the most active in the world. You can look right over the smoking rim of Halemaumau, the "Fire Pit," a crater within a crater. The park's 222 km of trails take you through unbelievably varied landscapes, from desert to thick forest, including several excellent nature trails. The most ambitious hike is up to the summit of Mauna Loa. The first 18 km up to the 2,032 m level can be done by car, then it's another 29 km on foot to the top cabin at 4,041 m. An intermediate cabin at Red Hill (3,060 m) enables you to break the climb into 2 days. The cabins are free. Anyone who wishes to do the hike may use them. Each accommodates about 8 per-

Centuries ago, the Hawaiians carved figures such as these into lava flows at Puako on the Big Island.

sons and if they're full you have to camp out. It's possible to take a different trail down the N side of the mountain to the Mauna Loa Weather Observatory (3,399 m), from which there's a road all the way down to the Saddle Road. The Observatory Trail is steeper and more difficult than the Mauna Loa Trail on the E side via Red Hill. Most people go back the way they came, after spending 3 or 4 days on the mountain. Both Mauna Loa and Mauna Kea are often snow-covered in winter, so the best months for these climbs are June to September. The Visitors Center at Kilauea has free maps of the trails, plus information on weather, water availability, how many people are using the cabins, etc. It makes good sense to sign in at the Kilauea Visitors Center before setting out.

Mauna Kea: The trip to the summit of Mauna Kea is easier, but perhaps less rewarding. You can drive a car 15 km to the 2,932-m level, then it's 5 hours (10 km) on foot along a jeep trail to the top. The first 2 km are the

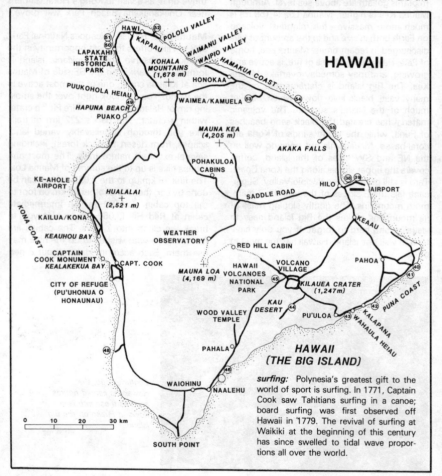

HAWAII

HAWI
KAPAAU
POLOLU VALLEY
WAIMANU VALLEY
WAIPIO VALLEY
LAPAKAHI STATE HISTORICAL PARK
KOHALA MOUNTAINS (1,678 m)
HAMAKUA COAST
HONOKAA
PUUKOHOLA HEIAU
WAIMEA/KAMUELA
HAPUNA BEACH
PUAKO
MAUNA KEA (4,205 m)
AKAKA FALLS
POHAKULOA CABINS
KE-AHOLE AIRPORT
HUALALAI (2,521 m)
HILO
AIRPORT
SADDLE ROAD
KAILUA/KONA
KEAUHOU BAY
WEATHER OBSERVATORY
RED HILL CABIN
KEAAU
CAPTAIN COOK MONUMENT
KEALAKEKUA BAY
CAPT. COOK
MAUNA LOA (4,169 m)
HAWAII VOLCANOES NATIONAL PARK
VOLCANO VILLAGE
KILAUEA CRATER (1,247 m)
PAHOA
CITY OF REFUGE (PU'UHONUA O HONAUNAU)
KAU DESERT
PU'ULOA
KALAPANA
WAHAULA HEIAU
PUNA COAST
WOOD VALLEY TEMPLE
PAHALA

HAWAII (THE BIG ISLAND)

surfing: Polynesia's greatest gift to the world of sport is surfing. In 1771, Captain Cook saw Tahitians surfing in a canoe; board surfing was first observed off Hawaii in 1779. The revival of surfing at Waikiki at the beginning of this century has since swelled to tidal wave proportions all over the world.

WAIOHINU
NAALEHU
0 10 20 30 km
SOUTH POINT

hardest. Start early, and hike up and down in a day. From Hilo, you can see the white buildings of the Mauna Kea Observatory at the summit on a clear day. Permits are no longer necessary to drive up or climb Mauna Kea.

the Kona Coast: A monument at Kealakekua Bay on the Kona Coast marks the place where Capt. Cook was slain in 1778 in a petty argument over a stolen boat. High cliffs prevent walking along the shore from Hikiau Heiau to the monument, but it's possible to hike down to the spot from a point near the junction of Highway 11 and Napoopoo Road, along a jeep track that drops sharply through the coffee plantations. Kailua/Kona was the first capital (until 1819) of the united Hawaiian Islands. The Hulikee Palace and Mokuaikaua Church (both 1837) are the most prominent relics of the early days. Unfortunately, the beaches, long hours of sunshine, and spectacular sunsets along the Kona Coast have attracted a glut of condominiums and luxury hotels, and there are almost no reasonably priced places to stay. Try to make it through to Hapuna Beach or Spencer Park in a day.

the Hamakua Coast: For good valley hiking, backpack into the Waipio Valley on the Hamakua Coast, and on into the fertile, uninhabited Waimanu Valley. This is a natural choice for those who want to get away from the highways and back to nature, but are not keen on experiencing the icy rigors of climbing the highest mountains in the Pacific. Like Kalalau on Kauai, the Waipio and Waimanu valleys are open to the adventurous, but the Kohala Corporation does not allow hikers to continue on to the Pololu Valley. The steep, 300-m bluffs cut deep valleys into the Kohala Mountains.

historic sites: Next to its volcanic wonders, the Big Island offers many well-preserved or restored archaeological sites. Best known is the City of Refuge on the Kona Coast, but Puukohola Heiau near Spencer Park and Lapakahi State Historical Park farther N are also unique. Free explanatory brochures are available at these sites; trained staff also

A fearsome feathered image of the war god, Kuka'ilimoku, once carried into battle and used to project the mana of King Kamehameha I against his foes.

answer questions. Wahaula Heiau near the Kamoamoa campground also has a well-managed Visitors Center. See petroglyphs less than a km from the road at Pu'uloa and Puako. Many other remains survive at points around the island where, perhaps better than anywhere else in Hawaii, one feels closest to the ancient Polynesians who settled these islands so long ago.

PRACTICALITIES

camping: County camping permits can be obtained during business hours at the Yano Memorial Center in Capt. Cook town, as well as at the Hilo county office (or by mail). The Namakani Paio campsite at the national park is popular, but be prepared for cool nights at 1,220 meters.

bus services: The County of Hawaii runs a limited bus service which can be used as a supplement to hitching. The most useful is the bus to Volcanoes National Park ($1.50), leaving Hilo daily except Sun. at 1430, departing the park to return to Hilo daily except Sun. at 0815. Another is the bus from Capt. Cook to Hilo ($4.25) via Honokaa, which leaves Capt. Cook daily except Sun. at 0615, and departs

Hilo for the return daily except Sun. at 1330. The other bus routes operated by the county are unlikely to be of much use to visitors. On all county buses you'll be charged $1 extra per piece of luggage. Check the times and fares by calling 935-8241.

OTHER ISLANDS

Lanai: The Castle and Cook Corporation (Dole) owns 98 percent of Lanai and maintains a large pineapple plantation. The only hotel is expensive ($42 s); to camp at Hulopoe Beach is $4 pp per day, plus a one-time $5 registration fee. Jeep rentals are also expensive. This is paradise at a price. You can fly to Lanai, or come on the catamaran *Aikane* or the 3-masted schooner *Windjammer*. These ships specialize in touristy daytrips from Lahaina, but they'll ferry you across for about $20 OW if you ask. The daytrips run $55-80 including breakfast, barbecue lunch, a minibus tour of Lanai, and transfers to the wharf.

Kahoolawe: The original name of Kahoolawe was Kohemalamalama-O-Kanaloa, "the sacred refuge of Kanaloa," Hawaiian god of the ocean. The island has great cultural and religious significance to the Hawaiians and is entered on the U.S. Register of Historic Places. There are some 544 archaeological sites on Kahoolawe. Despite this, the U.S. and Canadian navies use it for target practice. The surface is littered with unexploded shells. Blasting away the vegetation has led to serious erosion. No one lives on Kahoolawe and entry is prohibited.

the E end of the sacred island of Kahoolawe, a target for the American military

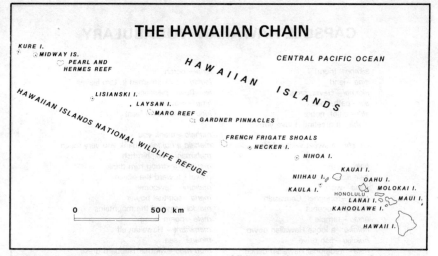

THE HAWAIIAN CHAIN

KURE I.
MIDWAY IS.
PEARL AND
HERMES REEF

CENTRAL PACIFIC OCEAN

H A W A I I A N   I S L A N D S

HAWAIIAN ISLANDS NATIONAL WILDLIFE REFUGE

LISIANSKI I.
LAYSAN I.
MARO REEF
GARDNER PINNACLES

FRENCH FRIGATE SHOALS
NECKER I.

NIHOA I.

KAUAI I.
NIIHAU I.   OAHU I.
KAULA I.   MOLOKAI I.
HONOLULU
LANAI I.   MAUI I.
KAHOOLAWE I.

HAWAII I.

0   500 km

the Northwest Islands: The State of Hawaii encompasses a string of tiny islets and reefs stretching 2,000 km NW from Niihau to Kure, but total only 8 sq km. Midway, the only inhabited island in the chain, remains under control of the U.S. Navy and is not legally part of the state. There's also a small Coast Guard post on Tern I. of French Frigate Shoals which utilizes a wartime airstrip. Some of the islands have low volcanic peaks: Nihoa (277 m), Necker (84 m), Le Perouse Pinnacle of French Frigate Shoals (37 m), and Gardner Pinnacles (58 m). Nihoa was once cultivated by the Hawaiians, and there are archeological remains on both Nihoa and Necker. Laysan I. shelters a large seabird population. Laysan, Pearl and Hermes Reef (an atoll not far from Midway), and Kure were worked for guano in the early 1900s. The Northwest Is. (also known as the Leeward Is.) are the sole habitat of the Hawaiian monk seal (*M. schauinslandi*), one of only 2 surviving species of monk seals in the world (the Caribbean monk seal was last sighted in 1952, while the Mediterranean monk seal survives in precariously small numbers in Greece). The remaining 800 Hawaiian monk seals face serious threats from the expanding shipping and fishing industries. Protective measures were first taken in 1909 and today all of the islands except Kure and

Midway are included in the Hawaiian Islands National Wildlife Refuge. Kure is a State Seabird Refuge. To protect the endangered wildlife, entry is restricted and fines go as high as $20,000 for unauthorized activities in the area. For more information write: National Marine Fisheries Service, Box 3830, Honolulu, HI 96812, USA.

a Hawaiian woman as seen by John Webber, illustrator with Capt. Cook

CAPSULE HAWAIIAN VOCABULARY

aikane — friend
aina — land
akamai — clever, smart
ala — path, road
ali'i — chief, noble
aloha — a greeting, I love you

chi chi — a sweet vodka drink

hale — house
hale lua — toilet
hana — work
haole — foreigner, Caucasian
haupia — coconut
heiau — temple
holoku — a loose Hawaiian gown
hukilau — fish drive
hula — traditional Hawaiian dance

imu — earth oven

kahili — feathered standard
kahuna — shaman, priest
kai — saltwater
kalua — baked
kama'aina — long-term resident
kanaka — human
kane — man
kapa — bark cloth
kapu — forbidden, sacred
kaukau — food
keiki — baby, child
kokua — assistance, cooperation
konane — game of Hawaiian checkers
kumu — teacher
kupuna — elder

lanai — porch
laulau — pork steamed in taro leaves
lei — flower necklace
limu — seaweed
luau — a Hawaiian feast

mahalo — thank you
mahalo a nui loa — thank you very much
mahimahi — dolphin fish
mai tai — a strong rum drink
makai — toward the ocean
malihini — newcomer
mana — spiritual power
mauka — toward the mountains
mele — poem, song
menehune — Hawaiian elf
moana — sea
muu muu — Mother Hubbard dress

ohana — extended family
okole maluna — bottoms up! cheers!
ono — delicious

pakalolo — marijuana
pali — cliff
paniolo — Hawaiian cowboy
pau — done, finished
pilikia — trouble
poi — cooked taro pounded into a paste
puka — hole
pupu — appetizer
pupule — crazy

wahine — woman
wai — freshwater
wikiwiki — hurry

BOOKLIST

DESCRIPTION AND TRAVEL

Brooks, John, ed. **South American Handbook.** Trade and Travel Publications, The 5 Princes Buildings, George St., Bath BAI 2ED, England. By far the best guide to Central and South America, plus all the islands of the Caribbean. No traveler should visit Latin America without it.

Bruce, Erroll. **Deep Sea Sailing.** London, Stanley Paul, 1953. The classic text on ocean cruising. Study it beforehand if you're thinking of working as crew on a yacht.

Ellis, William. **Polynesian Researches.** Rutland, VT, Charles E. Tuttle Co., 1969. An early missionary's detailed observations at Tahiti during the years 1817-1825.

Finney, Ben R. **Hokule'a: The Way to Tahiti.** New York, Dodd, Mead, 1979. The story of the *Hokule'a's* 1976 voyage from Hawaii to Tahiti.

Fisher, Dr. Jon. **The Last Frontiers on Earth.** Loompanics Unlimited, Box 1197, Port Townsend WA 98368. This little book and Jon Fisher's other work, **Uninhabited and Deserted Islands,** are essential reading for anyone considering moving to the South Pacific.

Gray, William R., and Gordon W. Gahan. **Voyages to Paradise: Exploring in the Wake of Captain Cook.** Washington, DC, National Geographic Society, 1981.

Heyerdahl, Thor. **Kon Tiki.** Translated by F.H. Lyon. Chicago, Rand McNally, 1950. Convinced that the mysterious origin of the Polynesians lies in the equally mysterious disappearance of the pre-Inca Indians of Peru, the author finds that only by repeating their feat of sailing some 6,500 km across the Pacific in a balsa-raft can he substantiate his theory.

Hinz, Earl R. **Landfalls of Paradise.** Western Marine Enterprises, Box Q, Ventura CA 93002. The only original cruising guide to all of Oceania; beware of **A Cruising Guide to the South Pacific** "by" Terry Harper, which is little more than a brazen reprint of the D.M.A. **Sailing Directions.**

Islands of the South Pacific. Sunset Books, Menlo Park, CA. Designed for bourgeois tourists who want Waikiki comfort while being served and entertained by smiling natives. Others in this vein include the **South Pacific Travel Digest** by Charles and Babette Jacobs, and **Fodor's South Pacific.**

Lewis, David. **We, the Navigators.** Honolulu, University of Hawaii Press, 1972. A thorough examination of the ancient art of landfinding in the Pacific.

Lucas, Allan. **Cruising the Solomons.** Australia, Horwitz Grahame Books, 1981. One of a series of yachting guides encircling the Coral Sea. A "must" if you're planning on taking your own boat.

Street, Donald. **The Ocean Sailing Yacht.** New York, Norton, 1973. A complete handbook on the operation of a cruising yacht.

Sutter, Frederic Koehler. **Amerika Samoa: An Anthrological Photo Essay.** Honolulu, University of Hawaii Press, 1984. An intimate look at American Samoa today—islands, people, and traditional culture.

Trumbull, Robert. **Tin Roofs and Palm Trees.** Seattle, University of Washington Press, 1977. A lively introduction to the Pacific by a former *New York Times* correspondent.

GEOGRAPHY

Couper, Alastair, ed. **The Times Atlas of the Oceans**. New York, Van Nostrand Reinhold, 1983. A superb study of the oceans of the world in their contemporary context—none of the difficult issues facing man and the sea today are avoided. A classic.

Derrick, R.A. **The Fiji Islands: Geographical Handbook**. Suva, Govt. Printing Office, 1965.

Fosberg, F.R., ed. **Man's Place in the Island Ecosystem**. Honolulu, Bishop Museum Press, 1963. A series of papers presented at a symposium.

Freeman, Otis W., ed. **Geography of the Pacific**. New York, John Wiley, 1951. Although somewhat dated, this book does provide a wealth of background information on the islands.

NATURAL HISTORY

DeLuca, Charles J., and Diana MacIntyre DeLuca. **Pacific Marine Life**. Rutland, VT, Charles E. Tuttle Co., 1976. An informative little pamphlet.

Dupont, John. E. **South Pacific Birds**. Greenville, Delaware, Museum of Natural History, 1975. A beautifully-illustrated field guide.

Gryimek, Dr. H.C. Bernhard, ed. **Animal Life Encyclopedia**. New York, Van Nostrand. A massive, 13-volume reference to all forms of life.

Hinton, A.G. **Shells of New Guinea and the Central Indo-Pacific**. Australia, Jacaranda Press, 1972. A photo guide to identification.

Hobson, Edmund S., and E.H. Chave. **Hawaiian Reef Animals**. Honolulu, University of Hawaii Press, 1972. A photo guide.

Mayr, Ernst. **Birds of the Southwest Pacific**. Rutland, VT, Charles E. Tuttle Co., 1978. A reprint of the 1945 edition.

Merrill, Elmer. **Plant Life of the Pacific World**. Rutland, VT, Charles E. Tuttle Co., 1981. First published in 1945, this handy volume is a useful first reference in a field very poorly covered.

Nelson, Bryan. **Seabirds: Their Biology and Ecology**. New York, A & W Publishers, 1979. A fully illustrated manual.

Shallenberger, Robert J., ed. **Hawaii's Birds**. Hawaii Audubon Society, Box 22832, Honolulu HI 96822. A compact field manual.

Tinker, Spencer Wilkie. **Fishes of Hawaii: A Handbook of the Marine Fishes of Hawaii and the Central Pacific Ocean**. Hawaiian Service, Inc., Box 2835, Honolulu HI 96803. A comprehensive, indexed reference work.

HISTORY

Allan, Helena G. **The Betrayal of Liliuokalani, Last Queen of Hawaii 1838-1917**. Glendale, CA, Arthur H. Clark Co., 1982. The biography of a remarkable woman.

Bartlett, Bruce R. **Cover-up: The Politics of Pearl Harbor, 1941-1946**. Arlington House, 1979. Bartlett believes Roosevelt was involved in covering up the attack on Pearl Harbor.

Beaglehole, J.C. **The Exploration of the Pacific**. Stanford, Stanford University Press, 1966. A history of European exploration from Magellan to Capt. Cook.

Bellwood, Peter. **Man's Conquest of the Pacific**. New York, Oxford University Press, 1979. One of the most extensive studies of the prehistory of Southeast Asia and Oceania ever published. A primary source.

Bellwood, Peter. **The Polynesians, Prehistory of an Island People**. London, Thames and Hudson, 1978. A well-written account of the archeology of Polynesian expansion.

Buck, Peter H. **Explorers of the Pacific.** Honolulu, Bishop Museum, 1953. A concise summary of the European discoveries.

Buck, Peter H. **Vikings of the Pacific.** Chicago, University of Chicago Press, 1959. A popular narrative of Polynesia migrations.

Dole, Paul W. **Seventy North to Fifty South: Captain Cook's Last Voyage.** Englewood Cliffs, NJ, Prentice-Hall, Inc., 1969. A modern annotation of Cook's final journal.

Friis, Herman R. **The Pacific Basin: A History of Its Geographical Exploration.** New York, American Geographical Society, 1967. A specialized work.

Gray, Capt. J.A.C. **Amerika Samoa: A History of American Samoa and Its United States Naval Administration.** Annapolis, United States Naval Institute, 1960. A wealth of background information on both Samoas, with special emphasis on the history of the native Samoan chiefs.

Howe, K.R. **Where the Waves Fall.** Honolulu, University of Hawaii Press, 1984. A new South Sea Islands history from first settlement to colonial rule.

Jennings, Jesse D., ed. **The Prehistory of Polynesia.** Cambridge, Harvard University Press, 1979. A new, comprehensive work on the subject.

Kent, Janet. **The Solomon Islands.** Harrisburg PA, Stackpole Books, 1973. A readable popular account of a little-known country.

Moorehead, Alan. **The Fatal Impact.** New York, Harper & Row, 1966. European impact on the South Pacific, as illustrated in the cases of Tahiti, Australia, and Antarctica.

Oliver, Douglas L. **The Pacific Islands.** Honolulu, University of Hawaii Press, 1975. The classic study of the history and economies of the entire Pacific area. Recommended reading.

Sharp, Andrew. **The Discovery of the Pacific Islands.** Oxford, Clarendon Press, 1960. A sort of dictionary of the achievements of 122 European explorers and discoverers, listing which island or island group each found.

Wawn, William T. **The South Sea Islanders and the Queensland Labour Trade.** Peter Corris, ed. Honolulu, University of Hawaii Press, 1973. A new edition of the classic account of the blackbirding period, first published in 1893.

PACIFIC ISSUES

Albertini, Jim, et al. **The Dark Side of Paradise: Hawaii in a Nuclear World.** Catholic Action of Hawaii, 1918 University Ave., Honolulu HI 96822. The whole frightening story of the military in the 50th state.

Ali, Ahmed, and Ron Crocombe, eds. **Politics in Polynesia.** Suva, University of the South Pacific, 1983. A country by country survey of political trends and developments in the area. There are companion volumes for Melanesia and Micronesia.

Crocombe, Ron, ed. **Land Tenure in the Pacific.** Melbourne, Oxford University Press, 1971. Although somewhat dated, this remains the basic study of this crucial issue.

Crocombe, Ron, and Freda Rajotte, eds. **Pacific Tourism As Islanders See It.** Suva, Institute of Pacific Studies, 1980. A collection of 24 essays and studies in which island residents give their impressions of island tourism.

Farrell, Bryan H., ed. **The Social and Economic Impact of Tourism on Pacific Communities.** Santa Cruz, Center for South Pacific Studies, 1977.

Finney, Ben R., and Karen Ann Watson, eds. **A New Kind of Sugar: Tourism in the Pacific.** Honolulu, East West Center, 1975.

Norton, Robert. **Race and Politics in Fiji.** New York, St. Martin's Press, 1977. A comprehensive analysis of how Fiji avoided racial strife.

Turner, Louis, and John Ash. **The Golden Hordes.** London, Constable, 1975. A piercing analysis of mass tourism's ravaging assault on the world, and the threat it poses to developed and developing countries alike.

Winkler, James E. **Losing Control.** Suva, Lotu Pasifika Productions, 1982. This summary of the impact of transnational corporations affords a surprising revelation of who gains most from current economic development in the Pacific.

ANTHROPOLOGY

Firth, Dr. Raymond. **We, the Tikopia.** London, Allen and Unwin, 1936. The classic study of a small, isolated Polynesian community.

Freeman, Derek. **Margaret Mead and Samoa: The Making and Unmaking of an Anthropological Myth.** Cambridge, Harvard University Press, 1983. Refutes Margaret Mead's theory of Samoan promiscuity and lack of aggression.

Heyerdahl, Thor. **Aku-aku.** New York, Rand McNally, 1958. The secret of Easter Island.

Howell, William. **The Pacific Islanders.** New York, Scribner's, 1973. An anthropological study of the origins of the Pacific peoples.

Mead, Margaret. **Letters from the Field.** ed. Ruth Nanda. New York, Harper & Row, 1977. Describes her experiences in American Samoa, Manus, the Sepik, and Bali. See also Mead's **Coming of Age in Samoa.**

Metraux, Alfred. **Easter Island.** New York, Oxford University Press, 1957. A readable cultural history.

Roth, G. Kingsley. **Fijian Way of Life.** 2nd ed. Melbourne, Oxford University Press, 1973. A standard reference on Fijian culture.

ART AND MUSIC

Brake, Brian, James McNeish, and David Simmons. **Art of the Pacific.** New York, Abrams, 1979. One of the finest, most sensitive books ever published on Oceanic art. Penetrating interviews with contemporary islanders are juxtaposed with stunning photos of the finest art objects from their past, now in the museums of New Zealand.

Buehler, Alfred, Terry Barrow, and Charles P. Mountford. **The Art of the South Sea Islands.** New York, Crown Publishers, 1962.

Danielsson, Bengt. **Gauguin in the South Seas.** New York, Doubleday, 1966. Danielsson's engaging account of Gauguin's ten years in Polynesia.

Gathercole, Peter, Adrienne L. Kaeppler, and Douglas Newton. **The Art of the Pacific Islands.** Washington, DC, National Gallery of Art, 1979. The catalog of a wide-ranging exhibition of Oceanic art. The introduction is excellent.

Gauguin, Paul. **Noa Noa.** The artist's classic account of his first visit to Tahiti.

Guiart, Jean. **The Arts of the South Pacific.** New York, Golden Press, 1963. A well-illustrated coffee table size art book with the emphasis on the French-dominated portion of Oceania. Consideration is given to the cultures which produced the works.

Linton, Ralph, and Paul S. Wingert. **Arts of the South Seas.** New York, Museum of Modern Art, 1946. Although a little dated, this book provides a starting point for the study of the art of Oceania. The section on Polynesia is especially good.

Malm, William P. **Music Culture of the Pacific, the Near East and Asia.** 2nd ed. Englewood Cliffs, NJ, Prentice Hall, 1977. A brief introduction to the music of the islands.

McBean, Angus. **Handicrafts of the South Seas.** Noumea, South Pacific Commission, 1976. An illustrated guide to what is being made today and where to buy it.

Mead, Sydney M., ed. **Exploring the Visual Art of Oceania.** Honolulu, University Press, 1979. A collection of presentations at a symposium on Oceanic art. Includes an analysis of the type of handicrafts produced today and how they are influenced by the tastes of white tourist consumers.

Parsons, Lee A., and Jack Savage. **Ritual Arts of the South Seas.** St. Louis, MO, The St. Louis Art Museum, 1975. A catalog of the Morton D. May Collection of Oceanic art.

Price, Christine. **Made in the South Pacific: Arts of the South Sea People.** London, The Bodley Head, 1979. A concise yet comprehensive examination on the handicrafts; well researched and indexed.

Waite, Deborah. **Art of the Solomon Islands.** Geneva, Musee Barbier-Muller, 1983. A valuable reference.

LITERATURE

Andersen, Johannes C. **Myths and Legends of the Polynesians.** Rutland, VT, Charles E. Tuttle Co., 1969. A massive compilation of Polynesian mythology; fully indexed.

Day, A. Grove. **Books about Hawaii: Fifty Basic Authors.** Honolulu, University of Hawaii Press, 1977. An excellent starting point for anyone interested in reading up on the 50th state.

Day, A. Grove. **Pacific Literature: One Hundred Basic Books.** Honolulu, University Press, 1971. Reviews the most outstanding books to come out of the Pacific experience over the past 400 years.

Dixon, Roland B. **The Mythology of All Races: Oceania.** Vol. 9. Boston, Marshall Jones, 1916. The collected folk tales of the Pacific.

Ellison, Joseph W. **Tusitala of the South Seas.** New York, Hastings House, 1953. The story of Robert Louis Stevenson's life in the South Pacific.

Grey, Sir George. **Polynesian Mythology.** Auckland, Whitcombe and Tombs, 1956. The myths and legends of the New Zealand Maori; first published in 1854.

Loti, Pierre. **The Marriage of Loti.** Honolulu, University of Hawaii Press, 1976. This tale of Loti's visits to Tahiti in 1872 helped create the romantic myth of Polynesia in contemporary Europe.

Melville, Herman. **Typee.** Evanston, Northwestern University Press, 1968. In 1842 Melville deserted from an American whaler at Nuku Hiva, Marquesas Islands. This book tells of his experiences during the month he spent among the Typee people. Melville also wrote a sequel, **Omoo.**

Michener, James A. **Return to Paradise.** New York, Random House, 1951. Essays and short stories. Good reading for travelers during those hours wasted in airports and on planes. Also read his **Tales of the South Pacific.**

Nordhoff, Charles Bernard, and James Norman Hall. **The Bounty Trilogy.** New York, Grosset and Dunlap, 1945. Retells in fictional form the famous mutiny, Bligh's escape to Timor, and the mutineers' fate on Pitcairn. See also **Hurricane,** by the same authors.

REFERENCE BOOKS

Area Handbook for Oceania. Washington, DC, Government Printing Office, 1971. A good source of background information.

Carter, John, ed. **Pacific Islands Yearbook.** 15th ed. Sydney, Pacific Publications, 1984. Despite the name, a new edition of this authoritative sourcebook comes out every 3 years. While the scope is similar to **South Pacific Handbook,** the approach is quite different. The information is heavily slanted toward official bureaucratic structures and overseas trade statistics. A copy belongs in every library of Pacifica. US$29.95.

Dickson, Diane, and Carol Dossor. **World Catalogue of Theses on the Pacific Islands**. Honolulu, University of Hawaii Press, 1970.

Pacific Islands. Vols. I-IV. Geographical Handbook Series. England, Naval Intelligence Division, 1945. These volumes were produced and printed for military purposes during WW II. Though much of the information is no longer relevant, it's a complete survey with thousands of pages of detail on the peoples, history, and geography, plus city and topographical maps, and wonderful illustrations.

Pacific Islands Stamp Catalogue. Seven Seas Stamp Pty. Ltd., 62 Wingewarra St., Dubbo NSW 2830, Australia. The philatelic history of the South Pacific; most issues are reproduced in full color.

Silveira de Braganza, Ronald, and Charlotte Oakes, eds. **The Hill Collection of Pacific Voyages**. San Diego, University Library, 1974. A descriptive catalog of antique books about the Pacific.

Snow, Philip A., ed. **A Bibliography of Fiji, Tonga, and Rotuma**. Coral Gables, FL, University of Miami Press, 1969.

Taylor, Clyde R. **A Pacific Bibliography: Printed Matter Relating to the Native Peoples of Polynesia, Melanesia and Micronesia**. Oxford, Clarendon Press, 1965. Extensive.

The Far East and Australasia. London, Europa Publications. A survey and directory of Asia and the Pacific. Provides abundant and factual political, social, and economic data; an excellent reference source.

PERIODICALS

Atoll Research Bulletin. A specialized journal issued by The Smithsonian Institution, Washington, DC. An inexhaustible source of fascinating information (and maps) on the most remote islands of the Pacific.

Far Eastern Economic Review. GPO Box 160, Hong Kong. Although primarily concerned with Asia, this weekly news magazine carries penetrating reports on events in the Pacific.

Islands Business. Box 5176, Raiwaqa, Suva, Fiji Islands. A monthly news magazine with the emphasis on business trends in the South Pacific.

Journal of Pacific History. Australian National University, Box 4, P.O., Canberra ACT 2600, Australia.

Journal of the Polynesian Society. Department of Anthropology, University of Auckland, Private Bag, Auckland, New Zealand. Established in 1892, this quarterly journal contains a wealth of specialized material on Polynesian culture.

Living Free. Box 29, Hiler Branch, Buffalo NY 14223. Jim Stumm's unusual bi-monthly journal of self liberation (US$7 a year). A section titled "Ocean Freedom Notes" tells you how to live free in paradise!

Mana. Box 5083, Raiwaqa, Suva, Fiji Islands. A South Pacific literary journal, with poems, short stories, and articles by island writers.

Oceania. University of Sydney, Sydney NSW 2006, Australia. An anthropological journal.

Pacific Magazine. Box 25488, Honolulu HI 96825. Published every other month, this business-oriented magazine really lets you know what's happening in the American territories in the Pacific. **Pacific's** "Air and Shipping News" keeps you up-to-date on developments in the world of Pacific aviation. Well worth the US$12 annual subscription price.

Pacific Islands Monthly. Pacific Publications, GPO Box 3408, Sydney 2001, Australia. This magazine owned by *The Melbourne Herald and Weekly Times* will keep you informed of what's happening in the South Pacific. The reports from Papeete by Marie-Therese and Bengt Danielsson are alone worth the price of the magazine. Every Pacific traveler should read at least one issue to get the feel of the region.

Pacific Perspective. Box 5083, Raiwaqa, Suva, Fiji Islands. Published twice a year, with articles on economic, social, and related fields in the South Pacific.

South Pacific Bulletin. Box A245, Sydney South NSW 2000, Australia. This quarterly magazine features articles on various development issues.

Tropical Frontiers. Bill Turner, 700 Dominik No. 1204, College Station, TX 77840-3435. A monthly newsletter of island travel. US$70 a year; write Bill a long letter about your trip and get a free 3-month subscription!

GLOSSARY

aa lava - see **pahoehoe**

ahimaa - Tahitian underground oven; see **umu**

ahu - Polynesian stone temple platform

anse (French) - cove

ANZUS Treaty - A mutual-defense pact signed in 1951 between Australia, New Zealand, and the U.S.

ariki - a Polynesian chief

atoll - a ring-shaped coral island consisting of a series of coral islets (motus) enclosing a shallow lagoon

barrier reef - a coral reef separated from the adjacent shore by a lagoon

beche de mer - trepang, sea cucumber; an edible sea slug; see also "pidgin"

blackbirder - European recruiter of island labor in the South Seas during the 19th C.

caldera - a wide crater formed through the collapse or explosion of a volcano

cargo cult - a Melanesian movement which promises the return of ancestors who will bring European-introduced goods (cargo) to their descendants

Coastwatchers - Australian intelligence agents who operated behind Japanese lines during WW II

coir - coconut husk fiber used to make rope, etc.

copra - dried coconut meat

custom owner - traditional tribal or customary owner

cyclone - A tropical storm which rotates around a center of low atmospheric pressure; it becomes a cyclone when its winds reach 64 knots. Velocities of up to 130 knots have been measured. In the Northern Hemisphere cyclones spin counterclockwise, while S of the equator they move clockwise. The winds of cyclonic storms are deflected toward a low-pressure area at the center, although the "eye" of the cyclone may be calm. Also known as a hurricane, tornado (in the U.S.), or typhoon (in the Far East).

endemic - something native to a particular area, not introduced

fa'afafine - the Samoan term for a man raised as a woman; called manu on Tahiti, fakaleiti in Tonga

fautau - the highest formal representative of the Samoan people

filaria - parasitic worms transmitted by biting insects to the blood or tissues of mammals

fissure - a narrow crack or chasm of some length and depth

gendarme - a French policeman responsible for areas outside a city; le flic is "cop"

guano - manure of sea birds, used as a fertilizer

heiau - see **marae**

kava - A Polynesian word for the drink known in the Fijian language as *yanggona*. This traditional beverage is made by squeezing a mixture of the grated root of the pepper shrub (*Macropiper methysticum*) and cold water through a strainer of hibiscus bark fiber.

kumara - sweet potato

langi - a megalithic tomb for early Tonga kings, in the form of a stepped limestone pyramid

lava tube - A conduit formed as molten rock continues to flow below a cooled surface during the growth of a lava field. When the eruption ends, a tunnel is left with a flat floor where the last lava hardened.

leeward - downwind; the shore (or side) sheltered from the wind; as opposed to windward

lei - garland, often of fresh flowers, but sometimes of paper, shells, etc., hung about the neck of a person being welcomed or feted

le truck - a truck with seats in back used for public transportation on Tahiti

mana - authority, "face," prestige, virtue, psychic power, a positive force

manioc - cassava, arrowroot, tapioca, *yuca;* a starchy root crop

marae - a Tahitian temple enclosure (*heiau* in Hawaiian); a Samoan village green *(malae);* a Maori meeting place. The Fijian word is *rara.*

masi - see *tapa*

mbalolo (Fijian) - a reef worm *(Eunice viridis),* called *palolo* in Samoa

mbuli - Fijian administrative officer in charge of a *tikina;* subordinate of the *Roko Tui*

moai - an Easter Island statue

motu - a reef islet held together by vegetation

nakamal - in the villages of Vanuatu, an open area surrounded by gigantic banyan trees where men gather nightly to drink *kava*

namba - a penis wrapper or sheath worn by the Big and Small Namba tribes of interior Malakula, Vanuatu

ndalo - see taro

pahoehoe lava - A smooth lava formation with wavy, rope-like ripples created when very hot, fluid lava continues to flow beneath a cooling surface. *Aa* lava, on the other hand, is slow-moving, thick, and turbulent, creating a rough, chunky surface.

palusami - a Samoan specialty of coconut cream wrapped in taro leaves and baked

pareu - a Tahitian sarong-like wraparound skirt; *lavalava* in Samoan, *sulu* in Fijian

pelagic - relating to the open sea, away from land

pidgin - a form of speech with a limited vocabulary and simplified grammar, used for communication between groups speaking different languages; also known as *beche-de-mer*

Ratu - a title for Fijian chiefs, prefixed to their names

Roko Tui - senior Fijian administrative officer

scuba - self-contained underwater breathing apparatus

sennit - coconut fiber twine

siapo - see *tapa*

tabu (or *tapu, kapu, tambu*) - taboo, sacred, set apart, forbidden, a negative force

tahuna (Tahitian) - a priest with supernatural powers

tamaaraa - a Tahitian feast

Tamaha - daughter of the *Tu'i Tonga Fefine* (queen of Tonga)

tamure - a very fast Tahitian dance

tanoa - a special, wide wooden bowl in which *yanggona (kava)* is mixed; used in ceremonies in Fiji, Tonga, and Samoa

ta'ovalu - a mat worn in Tonga by both sexes over a kilt or skirt

tapa - A cloth made from the pounded bark of the paper mulberry tree *(Broussenetia papryfera)*. It's soaked and beaten with a mallet to flatten and intertwine the fibers, then painted with geometric designs. Called *siapo* in Samoan, *masi* in Fijian.

taro (or *ndalo*) - starchy tuber *(Colocasia esculenta)*, a staple food of Pacific islanders; either of 2 stemless, araceous plants, *C. esculenta* or *C. antiquorum,* cultivated in tropical regions, especially the Pacific islands, for the edible root

tikina - a group of Fijian villages administered by a *mbuli*

toddy - The spathe of a coconut tree is bent to a horizontal position and tightly bound before it begins to flower. The end of the spathe is then split and the sap drips down a twig or leaf into a bottle. Fresh or fermented, toddy *(tuba)* makes an excellent drink.

tu'i (Polynesian) - king, ruler

umara - see *kumara*

umu - an underground, earthen oven. After A.D. 500 the Polynesians had lost the art of making pottery, so they were compelled to bake their food rather than boil it.

vigia - a mark on a nautical chart indicating a dangerous rock or shoal

volcanic bomb - lumps of lava blown out of a volcano, which take a bomb-like shape as they cool in the air

windward - the point or side from which the wind blows, as opposed to leeward

yanggona - see *kava*

INDEX

Italicized page numbers indicate information in captions, call-outs, charts, illustrations, or maps. (Inclusive page numbers, i.e., "147-169," may also include these types of references.)
Bold-face page numbers offer the primary reference to a given topic.

In the late '60s David Stanley learned to appreciate another culture by spending almost a year in several small Mexican towns. Later he studied at the universities of Barcelona (Spain) and Florence (Italy), before settling down to earn an honors degree (with distinction) from the University of Guelph (Canada). Since dropping out of his M.A. program in Spanish Literature at the stuffy University of Toronto in 1973, Stanley has backpacked through 121 countries, including a 3-year journey from Tokyo to Kabul. Althought Dr. Livingston proved elusive, Stanley managed to link up with "Gypsy Bill" Dalton in 1977 and together they wrote the first edition of the *South Pacific Handbook*. Since then David has mixed island hopping with computer printouts, while Bill settled into the sedentary world of publishing. (The name "Moon" originated in an early fascination with lunar poetry.) Stanley's escapist rational has turned into a feverish task as he scrambles to update guidebooks from North Pole to South. Stanley personally researches his books the way he writes them—right down to the last can of mackerel. It takes a bit of madman to pull off a project like this without fat grants or corporate backing: in *South Pacific Handbook* Stanley has found a perfect counterweight for his restless wanderlust.

about the illustrators: *South Pacific Handbook* is the fourth title in the Moon series illustrated by Chico artist Gordon Ohliger. In his drawings Gordy tried to set the theme for each chapter: the rugged majesty of Fatu Hiva's Hanavave Bay, Marquesas Is. (p. 77); the forbidding remoteness of Bounty Bay, Pitcairn I. (p. 127); Easter Island's lonely Ahu Akivi (p. 133); the marine iguanas of Galapagos (p. 139); Rarotonga's famous Betela Dance Troupe (p. 157); a tailed Nuiean boy picking passion fruit (p. 187); imposing Rainmaker Mountain, Tutuila I. (p. 229); relaxed Samoan *fale* (p. 245); haunting Lake Lalololo, Wallis I. (p. 273); men unloading supplies at Tokelau's Nukunonu (p. 281); boys playing in the Nanumea lagoon, Tuvalu (p. 287); a Fijian village (p. 293); the pine-fringed beauty of Anse de Kanumera, Isle of Pines (p. 367); Vanuatu's prover bial cattle beneath coconuts (p. 405); headhunters setting out (in times gone by) from New Georgia's Roviana Lagoon (p. 449); Sydney's striking Opera House (p. 499); magnificent Mount Cook, New Zealand's highest peak (p. 507); and Honolulu's teeming Waikiki (p. 521). When Gordy heard there mightn't be room to include his photo on this page, he decided to have the last word: that's him on page 195. Most of the other illustrations are by Louise Foote and Diana Lasich. Louise, a talented archaeologist-turned-cartographer, produced several hundred pen and ink drawings from material supplied by the author. Diana, whose artistry is taking shape in three still-unannounced Moon titles, studied woodblock printing and textile painting in Japan.

MOON TITLES OF RELATED INTEREST

HAWAII
HANDBOOK

J.D. Bisignani

Hawaii Handbook
by J.D. Bisignani
Offers a comprehensive introduction to Hawaii's geography, vibrant social history, arts, and events. The travel sections inform you of the best sights, lodging and food, entertainment, and services. J.D. Bisignani has discovered bargains on excursions, cruises, car rentals, and airfares. 12 color pages, 285 b/w photos, 170 illustrations, 74 maps, 41 charts, booklist, glossary, index. 800 pages. **Code MN34** **$14.95**

New Zealand Handbook
by Jane King
New Zealand is nature's improbable masterpiece, a world of beauty and wonder jammed into three unforgettable islands. Explore whitewater rapids, ski the slopes of a smoldering volcano, cast a flyrod in an icy stream, or have a bet on "the trots." 8 color pages, 99 b/w photos, 146 illustrations, 82 maps, index. 512 pages. **Code MN35** **$13.95**

New
Zealand
HANDBOOK

Jane King

Blueprint for Paradise

How to live on a tropic island

Ross Norgrove

Blueprint For Paradise:
How to Live on a Tropic Island
by Ross Norgrove.
Do you dream of living on a tropical island paradise? *Blueprint for Paradise* clearly and concisely explains how to make that dream a reality. Derived from his own and others' experiences, Norgrove covers: choosing an island, owning your own island, designing a house for tropical island living, transportation, getting settled, and successfully facing the natural elements. Breathtaking illustrations complete this remarkable guide. 202 pages. Available November 1987. **Code MN36** **$14.95.**

DID YOU ENJOY THIS BOOK?
Then you may want to order
other MOON PUBLICATIONS' titles.

MICRONESIA HANDBOOK by David Stanley. Apart from atomic blasts at Bikini and Enewetak in the late '40s and early '50s, the vast Pacific area between Hawaii and the Philippines has received little attention. *Micronesia Handbook's* 238 packed pages cover the seven North Pacific territories in detail. All this, plus 58 maps, 12 charts, 8 color pages, 77 photos, 68 drawings, index. 238 pages. **Code MN19**   **$8.95**

FINDING FIJI by David Stanley. Fiji, everyone's favorite South Pacific country, is now easily accessible either as a stopover or a whole Pacific experience in itself. This guide covers it all — the amazing variety of land and seascapes, customs and climates, sightseeing attractions, hikes, beaches, even how to board a copra boat to the outer islands. *Finding Fiji* is packed with practical tips, everything you need to know in one portable volume. 20 color photos, 78 illustrations, 26 maps, 3 charts, vocabulary, index. 127 pages.
Code MN17   **$6.95**

JAPAN HANDBOOK by J.D. Bisignani. Packed with practical money-saving tips on travel, food and accommodation. *Japan Handbook* is essentially a cultural and anthropological manual on every facet of Japanese life. 35 color photos, 200 b/w photos, 92 illustrations, 29 charts, 112 maps and town plans, an appendix on the Japanese language, booklist, glossary, index. 504 pages. **Code MN05**   **$12.95**

INDONESIA HANDBOOK, 4th edition by Bill Dalton. The most comprehensive and contemporary guide to Indonesia. Discover the cheapest places to eat and sleep, ancient ruins and historical sites, wildlife and nature reserves, spiritual centers, arts and crafts, folk theater and dance venues. 12 color pages, hundreds of photos, illustrations, maps, charts, booklist, vocabulary, index. 900 pages. Available in July 1988.
Code MN01   **$14.95**

MAUI HANDBOOK by J.D. Bisignani. Boasting historic Lahina, sensitively planned Kaanapali resort, power center Haleakala, and precipitous Hana Road, Hawaii's Maui is one of the most enchanting and popular islands in all of Oceania. 6 color and 50 b/w photos, 62 illustrations, 27 maps, 13 charts, booklist, glossary, index. 235 pages.
Code MN29   **$8.95**

GUIDE TO JAMAICA: Including Haiti by Harry S. Pariser. No other guide treats Jamaica with more depth, historical detail, or practical travel information than *Guide to Jamaica.* 4 color pages, 51 b/w photos, 39 illustrations, 10 charts, 18 maps, booklist, glossary, index. 165 pages.
Code MN25   **$7.95**

GUIDE TO PUERTO RICO AND THE VIRGIN ISLANDS: Including the the Dominican Republic by Harry S. Pariser. Discover for yourself the delights of America's "51st states," from the wild beauty of St. John, an island almost wholly reserved as a national park, to cosmopolitan San Juan. 4 color pages, 55 b/w photos, 53 illustrations, 29 charts, 35 maps, booklist, glossary, index. 225 pages. **Code MN21**   **$8.95**

BOOKS OF RELATED INTEREST

Exploring Tropical Isles and Seas:
An Introduction for the Traveler and Amateur Naturalist
by Frederic Martini
Learn about life on and around tropical isles—about climate, precipitation, and ocean currents—plus find handy information on the population, language, currency, and size of the islands. Discover how natural forces like volcanos and erosion are constantly creating, shaping, and destroying islands and entire island groups. *Exploring Tropical Isles and Seas* covers all this, plus detailed coverage of potential medical problems and precautions, including advice on how to treat coral cuts, stings, rashes, infections, and sunburn. Covers the Hawaiian Is., Samoa, Galapagos, Tonga, Fiji, Guam, Palau, Barbados, Martinique, Jamaica, Puerto Rico, the Bahamas, and the Virgin Islands. 8 color pages, 29 b/w photos, 44 illus., 36 maps, 5 charts, 67 tables, appendix, booklist, vocabulary, index. Size: 6 x 9. 408 pages. **PH70**   **$15.95**

The Tropical Traveller
by John Hatt
Compiled in this completely revised and updated edition are over a thousand tips, covering every aspect of tropical travel—from traveler's cheques to salt tablets, from bribery to mugging, from mosquito bite to shark attack. Whether you are a sunbather, tourist, backpacker or explorer, you'll be sure to benefit from this amusing and reassuring reference book. "Helpful, accurate and funny," writes the *International Herald Tribune*. Highly readable. 21 illus., 3 charts, appendix, booklist, index. 253 pages.
HI90   **$6.95**

Plant Life of the Pacific World
by Elmer D. Merrill
A superbly organized overview of the flora of the vast Pacific region stretching south from the Aleutians to New Caledonia, west from the Galapagos Islands to Malaysia. First published in 1945 and long out of print, *Plant Life of the Pacific World* was reprinted in 1981 so modern readers can gain a clear understanding of what the author calls "the exuberance of vegetation" on these far-flung islands. Tropical forests and jungles, the grasslands, primary and secondary forests, plants of the seashores, weeds and cultivated plants—all are discussed by this former Harvard professor, a 22-year resident of the Philippines and personally responsible for classifying and naming over 4,000 plant species. Of special interest are chapters on plant names used by local peoples as well as botanic "survival foods." 256 illus., selected botanic booklist, appendix, glossary, index. Hardcover. Size: 5½ x 8. 297 pages. **TUO5**   **$13.50**

The Last Frontiers on Earth:
Strange Places Where You Can Live Free
by Jon Fisher

This exciting book discusses living in Antarctica, on icebergs, on floating ocean platforms, in underwater habitats, living as a nomad, living in an airship, and much more. Each idea is discussed in detail as to what it would cost, availability of food and shelter, climate, and other pertinent factors. Freedom of choice always exists for those who seek it—this is a book for freedom seekers. 12 illus. Size: 5½ x 8½. 136 pages.
LO03   **$8.95**

Jon Fisher

Uninhabited and Deserted Islands
by Jon Fisher

Being alone (or almost alone) on an uninhabited island in the middle of nowhere—ah, the seduction of that vision. Should you want to activate that fantasy, take along this book as at least one of your companions. To help island fanciers evaluate their potential destinations, the author provides the exact locations for 52 groups of completely or partially unpopulated islands in the Pacific and Indian Oceans. The facts Fisher provides do deal with reality, however: sometimes there's no drinking water available; life can get pretty boring with no one around; and heavy winds might, well...blow you away. 41 maps give exact island locations. Booklist, index. Size: 5½ x 8½. 111 pages. **LO01**   **$7.95**

Uninhabited
And
Deserted Islands

Jon Fisher

Australia: A Travel Survival Kit
by Tony Wheeler

The best guide available to Australia. In this comprehensive guidebook you'll find a cheap place to stay on Magnetic Island, the best beach for an overall suntan near Cairns, the best bushwalks in the Flinders, the cheapest Turkish restaurants in Melbourne, where to rent a bicycle in Darwin. Whether you're traveling on an around-Australia airline ticket, a bus pass, driving your own car, or sticking your thumb out and hitching, you'll find the full story on the island continent in this book. 23 color pages, 3 b/w photos, 15 illus., 107 maps, index. Size: 5 x 7. 576 pages.
LP21   **$14.95**

Birds of the Southwest Pacific
by Ernst Mayr
Subtitled "A Field Guide to the Birds of the Area Between Samoa, New Caledonia, and Micronesia," this practical handbook is a popular contribution to ornithology and bird-watching. Provides easy identification of birds by name, species, habitats and locations. 3 color plates, 16 illus., fold-out map, glossary, index. Size: 4½ x 7. 316 pages. **TU18** $5.95

Best South Seas Stories
edited by A. Grove Day and Carl Stroven
A new anthology of South Sea island stories of excitement and adventure. The 15 selections are from such writers as James Michener, James Norman Hall, W. Somerset Maugham, Jack London, and Charles Warren Stoddard, with brief biographical sketches of each author. A strong, fresh, and varied collection that avoids the hackneyed, this book will make excellent reading for those leisure moments on your tropical island vacation. Size: 4½ x 7. 313 pages. **PT03** $2.95

Papua New Guinea:
A Travel Survival Kit
by Tony Wheeler
Often called "the last frontier," Papua New Guinea comprises the eastern half of New Guinea—the second largest island in the world. Just a few degrees from the equator, it is a land of snowcapped mountains, crumbling volcanos, coral reefs, white sandy beaches, isolated Neolithic tribes, and an amazing variety of art styles. Here you can search for wrecked Japanese aircraft in the jungle, scuba dive in some of the warmest and most inviting waters in the world, boat down the mighty Sepik River, or climb live volcanos, and even meet up with recently reformed headhunters. 8 color pages, 25 illus., 30 maps, index. Size: 5 x 7. 254 pages. **LP15** $8.95

MOONBELTS

A new concept in moneybelts. Made of heavy-duty Cordura nylon construction and strong water-resistant fabric, the *Moonbelt* offers maximum protection for your important papers. This pouch, designed for all-weather comfort, slips under your shirt or waistband, rendering it virtually undetectable and inaccessible to pickpockets. Many thoughtful features: 1-inch-wide nylon webbing, heavy-duty zipper, and a 1-inch high-test quick-release buckle. No more fumbling around for the strap or repeated adjustments, this handy plastic buckle opens and closes with a touch, but won't come undone until you want it to. Accommodates travelers cheques, passport, cash, photos. Size: 3½ x 8. Available in black or white.   **$8.95**

PACIFIC ISLANDS MAPS

MAP TITLE	SCALE	CODE & PRICE		COMMENTS
Australia	1:5,315,000	HD01	**$5.95**	relief
New Zealand	1:2,000,000	HD03	**$5.95**	relief
Vanuatu	1:500,000	PU07	**$13.95**	topographic
Fiji Islands	1:500,000	PU08	**$6.95**	
Tokelau	1:100,000	PU30	**$4.95**	
Niue	1:50,000	PU32	**$4.95**	topographic
Rarotonga	1:25,000	PU33	**$4.95**	topographic, relief
Aitutaki		PU40	**$4.95**	
Mitiaro		PU41	**$4.95**	
New Caledonia	1:500,000	PU37	**$5.95**	relief, city inset
Pacific Ocean	1:40,000,000	BA34	**$6.95**	relief
Galapagos Islands Tourist Map	1:1,700,000	BR40	**$7.95**	color, illus.

SAMOA

MAP TITLE	SCALE	CODE & PRICE		COMMENTS
Islands of Samoa	varied scales	UH04	**$2.95**	folded; incl. both Am. and Western Samoa
Tutuilla	1:25,000	PU19	**$3.95**	flat; incl. Pago Pago
Manua	1:25,000	PU20	**$3.95**	flat

HAWAIIAN ISLANDS

This series by University of Hawaii cartographer, James A. Bier, are four-color, detailed, shaded relief maps. The largest towns are featured in inset maps. Indexed.

MAP TITLE	SCALE	CODE & PRICE		COMMENTS
Kuaui	1:158,000	UH05	**$2.25**	folded; incl. maps of Lihue, Kapaa
Hawaii (Big Island)	1:250,000	UH06	**$2.50**	folded; incl. map of Hilo
Oahu	1:158,000	UH07	**$2.50**	folded; incl. street maps of Honolulu, Kaneohe
Maui	1:150,000	UH08	**$2.25**	folded; incl. street maps of Lahaina, Wailuku
Molokai	1:158,000	UH09	**$2.95**	folded; incl. Lanai and insets of Lanai City, Kaunakakai

THE SOCIETY ISLANDS

Bora Bora	1:40,000	PU21	**$5.95**	flat, two-color topographic map
Huahine	1:40,000	PU22	**$5.95**	flat, two-color topographic map
Moorea	1:40,000	PU23	**$5.95**	flat, two-color topographic map
Raiatea	1:40,000	PU24	**$5.95**	flat, two-color topographic map
Tahaa	1:40,000	PU25	**$5.95**	flat, two-color topographic map
Tahiti	1:100,000	PU26	**$5.95**	folded, full-color with shaded relief

note: The above featured maps are only a partial listing of all the maps we carry. For more detailed maps, nautical charts on each of the islands, detailed topographic coverage of New Zealand and Australia, plus obscure island maps of minor atolls in Tuvalu, the Cook Islands, or the Marianas, please write us for a quote.

IMPORTANT ORDERING INFORMATION

1. Codes: Please enter book and/or map codes on your order form. This will assure accurate and speedy delivery of your order.

2. Prices: Due to foreign exchange fluctuations and the changing terms of our distributors, all prices are subject to change without notice.

3. Domestic orders: We ship UPS or US Postal Service 1st class. Send $3.00 for first item and $.50 for each additional item. Please specify street or P.O. Box address, and shipping method. Deliveries are subject to availability of merchandise. We will inform you of any delay.

4. Foreign orders: All orders which originate outside the U.S.A. **must** be paid for with either an International Money Order or a check in U.S. currency drawn on a major U.S. bank based in the U.S.A. For International Surface Bookrate (8-12 weeks delivery), send U.S. $2.00 for the first book and U.S. $1.00 for each additional book.

5. Telephone orders: We accept Visa or Mastercharge payments.
MINIMUM ORDER U.S. $15.00. Call in your order: (916) 345-5413.
9:00 a.m. - 5:00 p.m. Pacific Standard Time.

6. Noncompliance: Any orders received which do not comply with any of the above conditions will result in the return of your order and/or payment intact.

ORDER FORM
(See important ordering information opposite page)

Name: _____ Date: _____

Street: _____

City: _____

State or Country: _____ Zip Code: _____

Daytime Phone: _____

Quantity	Full Book or Map Title	Code	Price

Taxable Total	
Sales Tax (6%) for California Residents	
Shipping and Handling Costs	
TOTAL	

SHIP TO: ☐ address above   ☐ other _____

_____

_____

Make checks payable to:

_____

MOON PUBLICATIONS   722 Wall St.   Chico   CA   95928   USA   tel. (916) 345-5413

WE ACCEPT VISA AND MASTERCHARGE!
To order: CALL IN YOUR VISA OR MASTERCHARGE NUMBER, or send written order
with your Visa or Mastercharge number and expiry date clearly written.

CARD NO.   ☐ VISA   ☐ MASTERCHARGE

☐☐☐☐☐☐☐☐☐☐☐☐☐☐☐☐☐☐☐

SIGNATURE_____ EXPIRATION DATE_____

MINIMUM ORDER: US$15

working together we can build a Nuclear Free Pacific

Proposed Pacific Nuclear Free ZONE

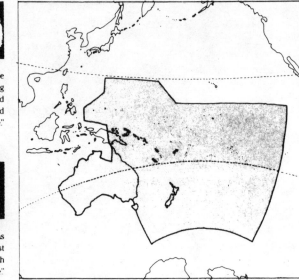

Albert Einstein
1946

"The unleashed power of the atom has changed everything save our modes of thinking and we thus drift toward unparalleled catastrophe."

President
Dwight D.
Eisenhower
1956

"The era of armaments has ended and the human race must conform its actions to this truth or die."

Today, a single nuclear submarine carries more explosive destructive force than has been used in all of recorded history. Both American and Soviet scientists tell us that if only a small percentage of existing nuclear weapons are used, all civilization will be destroyed. Even a minor nuclear accident at the French Testing Center near Tahiti could poison an entire ocean. We in this generation must respond to the greatest challenge in history. We face a clear choice: change our way of thinking or continue the spiral to extinction. The movement to build a Nuclear Free Pacific has begun. People are educating themselves and others. Working together we can change priorities, policies, and the way we think about war. If you'd like more information about the Nuclear Free Pacific movement, please call or write:

AUSTRALIA: NFIP Co-ordination Committee, Box A243, Sydney South, NSW 2000 (tel. 02-267-2030)

CANADA: South Pacific Peoples Foundation, 409-620 View St., Victoria, B.C. V8W 1J6 (tel. 604-381-4131)

EUROPE: Copenhagen Foundation Against Nucelar Tests, Solvgade 86 stet. th., 1307 Copenhagen K, Denmark

NEW ZEALAND: Greenpeace N.Z. Inc., Private Bag, Wellesley St. P.O. Auckland (tel. 31-030)

U.S.A: American Friends Service Committee, 814 NE 40th St., Seattle, WA 98105 (tel. 206-632-0500)

INTERNATIONAL: Pacific Concerns Resource Center, P.O. Box 24, Kaitia, New Zealand